Curt Simmons
Expert author and instructor in
Microsoft technologies

with James Causey

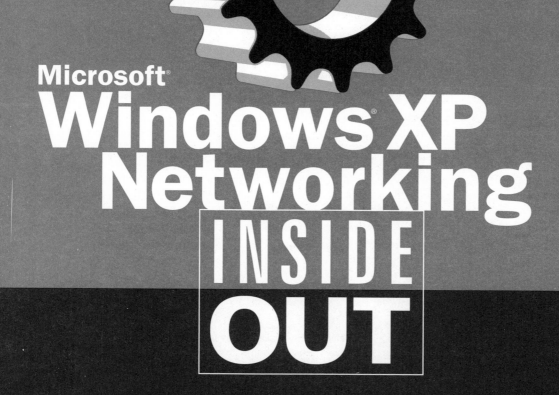

W9-CHJ-263

Microsoft®
Windows® XP
Networking

INSIDE
OUT

- **Packed with timesaving solutions—easy to find, easy to use!**
- **Get tips, tricks, and workarounds, plus the straight scoop**
- **Work smarter—and take your networking experience to the next level**

PUBLISHED BY
Microsoft Press
A Division of Microsoft Corporation
One Microsoft Way
Redmond, Washington 98052-6399

Copyright © 2003 by Curt Simmons
Portions copyright © 2003 by James Causey

All rights reserved. No part of the contents of this book may be reproduced or transmitted in any form or by any means without the written permission of the publisher.

Library of Congress Cataloging-in-Publication Data
Simmons, Curt, 1968-
    Microsoft Windows XP Networking Inside Out / Curt Simmons.
        p. cm.
    Includes index.
    ISBN 07356-1652-3
    1. Microsoft Windows (Computer file)   2. Operating systems (Computers)   3. Computer networks.   I. Title.

QA76.76.O63 S558553   2002
005.4'4769-dc21   2002075345

Printed and bound in the United States of America.

1 2 3 4 5 6 7 8 9   QWT   7 6 5 4 3 2

Distributed in Canada by H.B. Fenn and Company Ltd.

A CIP catalogue record for this book is available from the British Library.

Microsoft Press books are available through booksellers and distributors worldwide. For further information about international editions, contact your local Microsoft Corporation office or contact Microsoft Press International directly at fax (425) 936-7329. Visit our Web site at www.microsoft.com/mspress. Send comments to *mspinput@microsoft.com*.

Active Directory, ActiveX, FrontPage, Microsoft, the Microsoft Internet Explorer logo, Microsoft Press, MS-DOS, MSN, NetMeeting, the Office logo, Outlook, the Passport logo, PowerPoint, Visual Studio, WebTV, Win32, Windows, Windows Media, Windows NT, and Xbox are either registered trademarks or trademarks of Microsoft Corporation in the United States and/or other countries. Other product and company names mentioned herein may be the trademarks of their respective owners.

The example companies, organizations, products, domain names, e-mail addresses, logos, people, places, and events depicted herein are fictitious. No association with any real company, organization, product, domain name, e-mail address, logo, person, place, or event is intended or should be inferred.

Acquisitions Editor: Alex Blanton
Project Editor: Aileen Wrothwell
Technical Editor: Curtis Philips
Series Editor: Sandra Haynes

Body Part No. X08-82180

Contents at a Glance

Table of Contents

Chapter 3
Creating Network Connections   47

Part 2
Internet Networking   79

Chapter 4
Configuring Internet Connections   81

Chapter 5
Using Internet Connection Firewall 117

Chapter 6
Using Internet Explorer Advanced Features 137

Chapter 7
Using Outlook Express Advanced Features   181

Chapter 11
Understanding Domain Connectivity 311

Chapter 14
Understanding Resource Sharing and NTFS Security   397

Chapter 15
Making Files Available Offline   449

Part 5
Advanced Networking 471

Chapter 16
Remote Desktop and Remote Assistance 473

newfeature!
Exploring Remote Desktop 473
    Enabling Remote Desktop on the Host Computer 475
    Using Remote Desktop over a Dial-up Connection 477
    Using Remote Desktop over the Internet/Firewall 477
    Using Remote Desktop Through a Remote Access Server 479
    Configuring the Client Computer 480
    Logging On Automatically 486
    Generating a Remote Desktop
    Session with Microsoft Internet Explorer 487
    Choosing Remote Desktop Options 490
    Remote Desktop and Group Policy 494

newfeature!
Exploring Remote Assistance 495
    Using Remote Assistance Through Firewalls 496
    Enabling Remote Assistance 498
    Requesting Remote Assistance 499
    Using Remote Assistance 501

Chapter 17
Remote Access and Virtual Private Networking 503

Using Remote Access 504
    Configuring Remote Access Connections 504
    Configuring Remote Access Security 506
    Allowing Clients to Dial in to Your Computer 510
Understanding Virtual Private Networking 513
    Creating a Connection to a VPN Server 515
    Configuring Windows XP to Act as a VPN Server 516

Chapter 18
Interconnectivity with Other Systems 519

Connecting with Windows XP 519
    Supported Networking Protocols 520
    Supported Media Types 522
Connecting Windows XP and Novell NetWare 523
    Configuring Client Service for NetWare 525
Interconnecting Windows XP and UNIX/Linux 526

Chapter 19

Wireless Networking   531

Chapter 20

Maintaining Network Security   557

Chapter 21

Monitoring Windows XP Network Performance 597

Part 6

Appendix 611

Appendix A

Windows XP Service Pack 1 613

Glossary 617

Index to Troubleshooting Topics 629

Index 631

Acknowledgments

I would like to thank Alex Blanton for giving me the opportunity to write this book, and a big thanks also goes to Aileen Wrothwell for her guidance. A special thanks goes to David Dalan for his extra help and Jim Causey for bringing it all together. Thanks to Curtis Philips for a great technical review. Also, thanks to my agent, Margot Maley Hutchison, for her work on my behalf. Lastly and as always, thanks to my wife and children for their support.

— Curt Simmons

First and foremost, I'd like to thank Aileen Wrothwell and Curtis Philips for being such a fantastic team to work with. With a flair for both technical issues and the written word, Curt is the most amazing technical editor I've ever had the pleasure of working with. Aileen is a complete joy to work for — fun, intelligent, and supportive. I've never had so much fun while writing. Thanks also to Alex Blanton and to Danielle Bird for giving me the opportunity to work on this project.

I'd also like to make a special mention of my friend and boss, Mark Lynch. If he hadn't given me a shot all those years ago, my life and career would be nothing like they are today. Thanks for the continued support, and for everything.

Thanks also to my good friends Steve Hood, Ken Rawlings, Daniel Orrego, Ryan Hartman, Tina Golini, and especially Jennifer Dover for being there for me always, through thick and thin. Thanks to my mom, dad, and brother David for always being there too, and for everything else. My cat Miranda has also been supportive, understanding, and loving throughout this period, knowing when I needed a lap cat and when I just needed to be left to my thoughts. Meow. A final thanks to Stew, Chad, Joe (and Joe), Mary, Fitz, Brent, Kenny, P. Kevin, Matt, Art, Erica, Julie, Tom, Greg, Stacey, and everyone else who makes my life so pleasant.

— James F. Causey

The following members of the Microsoft community contributed their knowledge and expertise to reviewing the book's content:

Tom Fout, Joseph Davies, Dennis Morgan, Ethan Zoller, Igor Kostic, Kenny Richards, Anton Krantz, Rob Trace, Ricardo Stern, Matt Powell, Jason Garms, Josh Rice, Ross Carter, Greg Gille, Sanjay Anand, Stewart Tansley, Avronil Bhattacharjee, Mihai Costea, Brian Aust, Brian Dewey, Jeffrey Saathoff, and Leon Braginski.

We'd Like to Hear from You!

Our goal at Microsoft Press is to create books that help you find the information you need to get the most out of your software.

The INSIDE OUT series was created with you in mind. As part of an effort to ensure that we're creating the best, most useful books we can, we talked to our customers and asked them to tell us what they need from a Microsoft Press series. Help us continue to help you. Let us know what you like about this book and what we can do to make it better. When you write, please include the title and author of this book in your e-mail, as well as your name and contact information. We look forward to hearing from you.

How to Reach Us

E-mail: nsideout@microsoft.com
Mail: Inside Out Series Editor
       Microsoft Press
       One Microsoft Way
       Redmond, WA 98052

Note: Unfortunately, we can't provide support for any software problems you might experience. Please go to http://support.microsoft.com *for help with any software issues.*

Conventions and Features Used in This Book

This book uses special text and design conventions to make it easier for you to find the information you need.

Text Conventions

Convention	Meaning
Abbreviated menu commands	For your convenience, this book uses abbreviated menu commands. For example, "Choose Tools, Track Changes, Highlight Changes" means that you should click the Tools menu, point to Track Changes, and select the Highlight Changes command.
Boldface type	**Boldface** type is used to indicate text that you enter or type.
Initial Capital Letters	The first letters of the names of menus, dialog boxes, dialog box elements, and commands are capitalized. Example: the Save As dialog box.
Italicized type	*Italicized* type is used to indicate new terms.
Plus sign (+) in text	Keyboard shortcuts are indicated by a plus sign (+) separating two key names. For example, Ctrl+Alt+Delete means that you press the Ctrl, Alt, and Delete keys at the same time.

Design Conventions

newfeature!
This text identifies a new or significantly updated feature in this version of the software.

InsideOut

These are the book's signature tips. In these tips, you'll get the straight scoop on what's going on with the software—inside information on why a feature works the way it does. You'll also find handy workarounds to different software problems.

tip   Tips provide helpful hints, timesaving tricks, or alternative procedures related to the task being discussed.

Troubleshooting

Look for these sidebars to find solutions to common problems you might encounter. Troubleshooting sidebars appear next to related information in the chapters. You can also use the Troubleshooting Topics index at the back of the book to look up problems by topic.

Cross-references point you to other locations in the book that offer additional information on the topic being discussed.

 This icon indicates sample files or text found on the companion CD.

caution   Cautions identify potential problems that you should look out for when you're completing a task or problems that you must address before you can complete a task.

note   Notes offer additional information related to the task being discussed.

Sidebar

The sidebars sprinkled throughout these chapters provide ancillary information on the topic being discussed. Go to sidebars to learn more about the technology or a feature.

Part 1

Windows XP Networking

Chapter 1

Introduction to Windows XP Networking

Networks have been around since the early days of computing—even before the PC appeared on the scene. After all, the importance of networking—to share information and manage a computing environment—was evident even when computers used vacuum tubes and filled an entire room. The computing world has changed drastically since then, and it continues to rapidly change and evolve as networking and computing technology continues to grow.

Microsoft designed Windows XP Professional and Windows XP Home Edition with networking in mind, although Windows XP Professional is considered *the* networking platform. With the tools Windows XP Professional provides, you can use it in a small network or in a network with thousands of computers. Before getting too far ahead, let's first consider some networking background information and review all that Windows XP has to offer. If you have a limited amount of experience with networking, this chapter serves as a great primer. If you are experienced with Windows networks, this chapter serves as a review as well as a guide to Windows XP.

Windows Networking Concepts

Like any complicated process, getting your feet on solid ground from the start is always important. Networking does not have to be terribly complicated, but depending on your needs, it certainly can be. This book explores the procedures and complexities of networking. As a starting point, it is a good idea to get some solid ideas and definitions in your mind, which will make networking easier to understand as you move forward. The following sections explore different aspects and definitions of networking components and processes.

What Is a Network?

If you ask 10 people, "What is a network?" you are likely to get 10 different responses. After all, the simple concept of a network has a lot of implications. A technical guru might answer, "A network is a communication mechanism between two or more computers using a common protocol." This is true; but other people might define the term *network* much differently:

- An office worker that uses a network might answer, "A network is a way to get information and share information."

- A network administrator might answer, "A network is a way to centrally manage computers and users."

- Someone in sales or human resources might answer, "A network is a way to create and maintain connections between people."

- An Internet surfing preteen might answer, "A network is a way to play games and have fun."

Depending on your perspective, your definition of a network might vary. After all, the true purpose of a network is to meet the needs of a given group of people, whether that network is a small home network or the Internet, the world's largest network.

In this book, the definition of a network uses a mixture of concepts: "A network is a group of connected computers used to share information among people and manage resources and security."

Why Is a Network Necessary?

There are three primary reasons for networking, and any additional reasons usually lead back to these three:

- **Information sharing and resources.** Computer networks allow the sharing of information and resources. For example, suppose you have a home network with two computers. Networking those computers together allows them to share files on a hard disk drive, an Internet connection, and even hardware, such as printers and CD-ROM/DVD-ROM drives. In larger environments, the ability to share information and resources is even more critical.

- **Communications.** With the advent of e-mail and instant messaging, a lot of network traffic usually consists of communications. In corporations, thousands of internal e-mail messages are sent each day. E-mail has become a great way to manage employees, schedule meetings, and quickly communicate with people. Instant messaging is another incredibly popular form of communication, allowing both casual chatting and online collaboration.

- **Computer and user management.** In larger environments, networking functions as a means of managing users, computers, and security. Network administrators can enforce uniform standards, and with Active Directory Group Policy, they can enforce all kinds of settings and computer configurations including the automatic installation or removal of software. For more information about Active Directory, see "Understanding Active Directory Domains," page 311.

The fundamental purposes of networking are all basic, but very important. For these reasons, home and small office users find themselves at their favorite computer stores buying networking equipment, and corporate environments invest many thousands of dollars in their network infrastructure and maintenance each year.

What Is Needed for a Network?

The question of what you need for a network can be difficult to answer because a simple two-computer network needs considerably less than a network with thousands of computers. Still, there are some fundamental requirements of each network:

- **Hardware.** To create a network, you must have certain pieces of hardware. Computers must be outfitted with a network interface card (NIC), also called a network adapter. The NIC provides a way to connect the computer to the network, either with a cable or via a wireless connection. Depending on the type of network you are creating, you might also need a *hub*, which is a device to which all computers connect. You can learn more about different types of hardware in Chapter 3, "Creating Network Connections."

> **tip** Network hardware can be expensive, but there are also many prepackaged home networking kits that sell for under $100. If you want to set up a small wireless network, you might need to spend anywhere from $200 to $500. There are several options, so be sure to explore Chapter 3 if you are about to create a home or small office network to make sure you have considered all of the options available to you.

● **Software.** For one computer to communicate with the next, networking software and protocols must be configured. A *protocol* is essentially a language or a collection of rules that computers use to communicate with each other. The de facto standard protocol used in networks today, including the Internet, is Transmission Control Protocol/Internet Protocol (TCP/IP), which you can learn more about in Chapter 2, "Configuring TCP/IP and Other Protocols."

Understanding Home Networks and Workgroups

Workgroups, which are the typical configuration found in home networks and small office networks these days, consist of a small collection of computers that are connected together primarily for information and resource sharing. Workgroups generally consist of fewer than 20 computers, but this is not a strict requirement. However, Windows workgroups do have these specific characteristics:

● **There is no centralized server.** A *server* is a computer on a network dedicated to running the administrative software that controls access to the network and its resources, such as printers and disk drives. Each computer in the workgroup functions as its own unit—there is no centralized server and no centralized policies. There might be one person in charge of the workgroup (which might be you), but that person manages the workgroup on a computer-by-computer basis.

● **Each user is an administrator of sorts.** The user can share files and other data, and manage security based on his or her needs.

● **Security is localized.** Because there is no server, logon security is implemented on a computer-by-computer basis. The good news is that Windows XP provides local logon security, which makes Windows XP a better choice for workgroups than Microsoft Windows 9*x* or Microsoft Windows Me (Millennium Edition).

● **Workgroup computers are typically located in one location.** Workgroups tend to be found in one home or a small office. They are normally not distributed between offices or buildings, and there is usually no remote dial-up, although remote dial-in access can be configured in Windows XP Professional.

In the following illustration of a typical workgroup (also known as a *peer-to-peer network*), five computers are connected to each other through a central hub.

Workgroup, or Peer-to-Peer Network

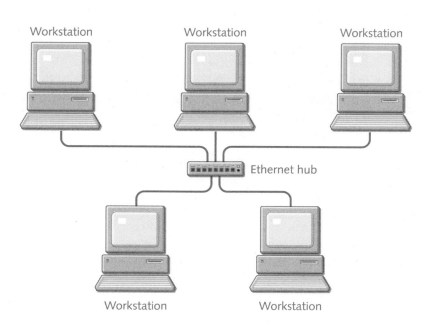

For small groups of computers and resources, workgroups are usually easier to manage and maintain than a larger domain environment, which is discussed in the next section. They can also be less expensive because servers and server software are not needed. However, businesses might soon outgrow the workgroup model and have to turn to a Windows domain environment. With a domain comes much more power, control, and yes, complexity.

Understanding Domain Environments

The workgroup design works well for home or small office environments. However, larger environments quickly outgrow the workgroup model, primarily due to administration and security requirements. When centralized administration and security are required, Windows networks move to a domain-based model. In a *domain-based network*, users' computers (sometimes called *workstations* or *client computers*) are centrally managed by one or more Windows servers. *Servers* are dedicated to running network services, and users do not sit and work at the servers. When a user wants to log on to the network, the user's user name and password are verified or *authenticated* by a *domain controller*, which is a server that maintains all the user names and passwords.

The domain controller might be running a server version of Microsoft Windows NT or Microsoft Windows 2000. These advanced versions of Windows contain the additional software programs required to centrally administer a larger network. Once authentication is successful, the user can access whatever network resources the user has been granted permission to use. If authentication is not successful, the user does not gain access to the network. As you might imagine, domain-based networking can be rather complex, and professional network administrators are usually needed to manage servers on larger networks. However, this complexity is usually balanced by the convenience that comes from managing resources and user authentication centrally rather than on a computer-by-computer basis.

A Windows domain provides a number of benefits that are not found in workgroups, especially when the client computers in the domain are running Microsoft Windows 2000 Professional or Windows XP Professional. Although Windows NT is still used in some networks, the focus of this book will be on technologies made available by *Active Directory*, the domain management system introduced with Windows 2000 Server, because it offers many newer and more powerful features. For more information on Active Directory, see Chapter 11, "Understanding Domain Connectivity."

A Windows domain provides the following specialized benefits for both users and the enterprise:

- **A domain provides security.** Using Active Directory, a number of security features can be enforced uniformly including advanced security features such as digital certificate authentication and IP Security.

- **A domain provides organization, centralized administration, and control.** A domain helps organize and manage users and resources. User accounts and resources are centrally maintained, greatly easing the burden of managing *permissions*, which enable individual users to access and manipulate local and network resources. Using an administrative tool known as *Group Policy*, network administrators can even control the way in which users' computers are used. This control ranges from what software can be installed to such details as the appearance of users' desktops.

- **A domain is highly extensible.** The concept of *extensibility* means that a domain can grow to the size you need it to as your business grows. In other words, if you need to add a thousand computers to the domain, the domain is capable of handling the growth.

- **Domains are flexible.** As the number of resources managed within a domain grows, you can delegate management tasks over particular pieces of it to others, using *organizational units*. Domains can also be grouped together in *trees* and *forests*, and managed across wide geographic areas using *sites*.

Domains and their related technologies are covered in more detail in Chapter 11, "Understanding Domain Connectivity."

Windows XP Networking Features

Windows XP contains the networking software features that you need for most any network you might want to join. However, there are important differences in the networking capabilities of Windows XP Home Edition and Windows XP Professional. Windows XP Home Edition supports workgroup networking, but does not support domain networking, meaning that a computer running Windows XP Home Edition cannot be part of or log on directly to a domain-based network. If you plan to set up a domain-based network using Active Directory, make sure all the workstations that will be part of the domain run Windows XP Professional.

> **note** Windows 2000 Professional workstations can also fully participate in an Active Directory domain; however, configuring them to do so is outside the scope of this book.

Overall, you'll see the same networking support in Windows XP Professional as you might be familiar with in Windows 2000 Professional along with some new tricks as well. The following sections provide a quick primer of the major networking features and components supported in Windows XP. You'll also find cross-references to the chapters where these features are discussed in more detail.

TCP/IP Protocol

TCP/IP is a suite of protocols (over 100) that provides computers with the vast networking capabilities you see today. All of the functions you perform on the Internet are made available by TCP/IP, or more specifically, by some protocols in the TCP/IP protocol suite. In fact, there are many protocols in the TCP/IP protocol suite that you will immediately recognize, ranging from HTTP (used for Web page transfer) to IMAP (used for e-mail access).

As the Internet has grown and become more integrated into all of our lives, TCP/IP has grown in its application as well. TCP/IP was originally designed by the United States Defense Advanced Research Projects Agency (DARPA), to support large networks with large numbers of individual segments. Today, it serves as the standard not only for Internet traffic, but for the more customized features used in major network operating systems.

As part of this shift to TCP/IP, Windows networks now use TCP/IP as the default protocol for both workgroup and domain environments. TCP/IP's power as a standard protocol used across the Internet has traditionally been counterbalanced by the difficulty involved in installing and configuring it; however, newer industry-standard systems for automatically managing client configurations greatly reduce these management burdens, as do the features for configuring and monitoring TCP/IP built into Windows XP.

Chapter 1

> The TCP/IP protocol suite itself, along with the tools provided by Windows XP to best take advantage of it, are covered in Chapter 2, "Configuring TCP/IP and Other Protocols."

NTFS File System

Windows XP supports the NTFS file system. Although a file system is a feature of a local computer, not the network service, there are many benefits in using NTFS when you are networking a computer.

All computers use a file system of some kind to organize and maintain data on a hard disk. In Windows 9*x* and Windows Me, the File Allocation Table (FAT) file system was used. However, the FAT file system does not provide several important features and functionality provided by NTFS. With Windows XP, even home users can use the NTFS file system and take advantage of its benefits, many of which are of great utility in a network environment including:

- **Compression.** NTFS drives support file compression under Windows XP. You can compress entire drives or folders and even individual files in order to save hard disk space. If you are transferring many files across your network, the compression feature can help users conserve local hard disk space.

- **Encryption.** NTFS drives support file and folder encryption in Windows XP Professional, but not in Windows XP Home Edition. You can encrypt files and folders so that other users cannot access them, and you can also encrypt files and folders so that only a certain group of users can access the data, but users outside the group cannot. The security features are obvious. When encryption is enabled, you simply use the data as you normally would (the data is automatically decrypted for you when you open a file and then encrypted again when you close the file), but other users cannot access it.

- **Security.** NTFS provides security for shared folders through user permissions. Using NTFS, you can determine which users can access a shared folder and exactly what they can do with the contents of the shared folder when it is accessed. Windows XP Home Edition only provides a few simple options, but Windows XP Professional provides all of the features of NTFS security.

> To learn more about the NTFS file system and setting file and folder permissions, see Chapter 14, "Understanding Resource Sharing and NTFS Security."

Internet Access

As with previous versions of Windows, Windows XP supports Internet connectivity and usage by providing you with a number of different tools. You can easily create Internet connections to your ISP using the New Connection Wizard. Once the connection is in place, you can share it with other computers in your workgroup using Internet Connection Sharing (ICS). You can even protect your Internet connection from external hackers by using Internet Connection Firewall (ICF). These features, all of which are designed for the workgroup, enable you to easily configure Internet access and protection as needed.

Aside from the basic Internet connection, Windows XP includes a wide range of built-in tools for accessing resources on the Internet, including Microsoft Internet Explorer 6 for Web surfing and Microsoft Outlook Express 6 for e-mail and newsgroup access. Additionally, if you want instant messaging and an easy collaborative tool, Microsoft Windows Messenger provides text messaging, voice and video transmission, a whiteboard application, and other helpful features you can use over the Internet or an intranet.

All of these applications provide enhanced features, particularly security features that help you control content and privacy settings. As the Internet has developed, more dangers have developed as well, and Windows XP goes to greater lengths than any previous version of Windows to secure your computer against malicious content and potentially dangerous downloads.

> For detailed information about Internet networking, including Internet connections, ICF, Internet Explorer 6, Outlook Express 6, and Windows Messenger, see Part 2, Internet Networking. You can also learn more about configuring ICS in Chapter 10, "Managing Workgroup Connections."

newfeature!

Remote Control and Remote Troubleshooting

Windows XP provides some new remote networking features that can make life easier, depending on what you need to do. Remote Desktop and Remote Assistance provide access to other Windows XP computers using either a corporate LAN or the Internet. These features are new, but are actually based on Terminal Services, so if you have worked in an environment that uses Terminal Services, you'll see some similarities.

Remote Desktop

Remote Desktop provides a way for you to run your computer from another computer. For example, suppose you use a Windows XP Professional computer at work. When you come home, you can use another Windows computer (including Windows XP, Windows 2000, Windows NT, Windows Me, or Windows 95/98) and a dial-up or broadband connection to your LAN to access the Windows XP Professional computer. You can then *see* the remote desktop and run applications or open files, just as if you were sitting at the remote computer.

> **note** Remote Desktop is not provided in Windows XP Home Edition. You can use Windows XP Home Edition to access and control a Windows XP Professional computer, but a Windows XP Professional computer cannot access and control a Windows XP Home Edition computer using Remote Desktop.

Remote Desktop has a number of potential applications including collaboration and console sharing, and perhaps most importantly, you can work from home or a different location and still access your office PC. Only Windows XP Professional computers can be Remote Desktop servers, but you can run the client on any Windows 95 or later computer with Remote Desktop Connection software, which you can install on any of the previously mentioned Windows versions from your Windows XP CD.

---

tip **Using Remote Desktop over the Internet**

Remote Desktop is designed for LAN connections where you access a computer on a corporate network. However, you can also access a computer over the Internet if you know the computer's IP address, and the computer is currently online. To connect, you'll need to find the computer's Internet IP address (assigned by the ISP), and if the computer uses ICF, the receiving computer will have to configure ICF to allow the Remote Desktop connection. Intrigued? Check out Chapter 5, "Using Internet Connection Firewall," to learn more about discovering a dynamically assigned IP address and configuring ICF for Remote Desktop.

Remote Assistance

The second type of remote networking feature is Remote Assistance, which is provided in both Windows XP Professional and Windows XP Home Edition. Remote Assistance is a help and support feature that enables a user to connect to another user's computer for troubleshooting purposes. The user requesting help can even give control of his or her computer to the helper who can remotely view and control the computer, hopefully being able to fix the user's problem.

Remote Assistance has a number of applications. In corporate environments, Remote Assistance can provide more flexibility and faster service from support technicians. Instead of having to blindly provide support or physically walk to a client's computer, the technician can use Remote Assistance to see the computer and fix it remotely.

In the same manner, users can get help from friends and relatives over the Internet. Let's say your cousin lives in Washington, but you live in Dallas. You want to provide some help with a computer problem, but resolving technical problems via a phone conversation can be frustrating. Using Remote Assistance, your cousin can send you a Remote Assistance invitation, and you can connect to his computer using your Windows XP computer. With the proper permission in place, you can remotely configure his computer to fix problems.

To learn more about Remote Desktop and Remote Assistance, see Chapter 16, "Remote Desktop and Remote Assistance."

Virtual Private Networks and Remote Networking

Windows XP supports *virtual private network (VPN)* connections to access corporate networks remotely. A VPN connection enables one computer to connect securely to another computer over the Internet (or an intranet). The difference, however, is that local network data is encrypted and encapsulated (known as *tunneling*) to create a secure session with another computer using a free public network, such as the Internet.

There are a number of important uses of VPNs. Suppose you run a small workgroup in one location, but you have added an office on the other side of town. Your small company cannot afford a dedicated WAN link between the two offices. You can use a VPN connection that uses the Internet's backbone for the cost of an Internet account so that the two offices can exchange data *securely* over the Internet.

You might also travel frequently with a laptop. Although you can access your LAN over a dial-up or remote broadband connection, you might want a more secure connection. In this case, you can use a VPN to create a secure tunnel. In the same manner, you can also create VPN connections over an intranet for extra security. VPN connections use either the Point-to-Point Tunneling Protocol (PPTP) or Layer 2 Tunneling Protocol (L2TP). You can learn more about setting up and using VPN connections in Chapter 17, "Remote Access and Virtual Private Networking."

The Routing and Remote Access Service (RRAS) runs on server versions of Windows 2000 and allows remote clients to dial into a private network directly (*not* using the Internet as a transit route). When you travel with your laptop, you can use the laptop modem to dial up to a designated number on the corporate LAN and use the LAN's resources, just as though you were locally connected to the LAN from your office computer. Windows XP provides all of the security protocols you need to remotely access a domain environment. You can learn more about these security protocols in Chapter 17, "Remote Access and Virtual Private Networking."

Support for Internet Information Services

Microsoft Internet Information Services (IIS) enables you to host Web services either internally over a LAN intranet or publicly over the Internet. IIS is included with Windows XP Professional (but not with Windows XP Home Edition), and it runs as a Web hosting service with limited usage features. IIS running on server versions of Windows 2000 provides the capability to host Web sites over the Internet, whereas IIS on Windows XP Professional allows for only one Web site and one FTP site and is limited to a maximum of 10 simultaneous connections. This might be enough connections to run a lightly accessed Web site, but IIS is actually included in Windows XP Professional as a way to share documents or printers on an intranet and to serve as a tool for users who develop Web content. See Chapter 9, "Using Internet Information Services," to learn more about the features and limitations of IIS in Windows XP Professional.

Wireless Networking

Windows XP provides built-in support for wireless networking. Over the past few years, the buzz about wireless networking has continued to grow. If you browse through the networking section of any computer store, you are likely to see a number of wireless network adapter cards and hubs for both home and small office use.

The purpose of wireless networking is obvious: You can set up a network without the mess, expense, and complication of running wires. Many airports, railways, hotels, and other public areas now provide network and Internet access over wireless links if your laptop is equipped for wireless communications.

Windows XP supports two types of wireless networks:

- **Wireless Personal Area Network (WPAN).** The simplest wireless network connects devices directly without an intermediary hub in what is called an *ad hoc* network. WPANs are short range, ad hoc networks using protocols such as *Bluetooth* or infrared light and are intended to be used within an extremely short distance (less than 10 meters). With Windows XP, the key method to create a WPAN is to use infrared-enabled devices over short distances with a clear line of sight between devices. Infrared devices enable fast and convenient transfer from one computer to another or between one computer and communication devices such as personal digital assistants (PDAs), digital cameras, cellular phones, and infrared-enabled printers.

- **Wireless Local Area Network (WLAN).** This wireless network can use either a hubless, ad hoc network or a central access point similar to the hubs used in wired LANs, in which each wireless computer communicates with other devices on the network through the access point. WLANs offer higher speeds and greater range, and are not limited to line of sight. Windows XP fully supports the IEEE 802.11 standard and the security features that the standard provides. This evolving standard is the primary WLAN solution.

There is a lot to learn and consider with wireless networking. Chapter 19, "Wireless Networking," is dedicated to this topic.

newfeature!
Universal Plug and Play

Windows XP provides a new feature called Universal Plug and Play (UPnP). UPnP is a feature that allows Windows XP to automatically detect, manage, and control network devices that are UPnP compliant. For example, suppose you have a UPnP printer. When you plug another device supporting UPnP into the network, such as a PDA or a laptop, the device is able to find the printer and use it automatically.

UPnP is the backbone for many advanced networking features including those provided by Windows Messenger and Remote Desktop. For more information on Universal Plug and Play, see "Connecting Through a Firewall," page 222.

Configuring TCP/IP and Other Protocols

The Transmission Control Protocol/Internet Protocol (TCP/IP) suite is a critical component of modern networking. Since its introduction, TCP/IP has proven to be flexible and robust enough for virtually any networking use, which has made it the most popular networking protocol in the world. IP is used to address the overwhelming majority of private networks, and it is the only addressing method used on the Internet.

To understand TCP/IP, it is important to start with the big picture. In this chapter, the TCP/IP protocol suite and the Open Systems Interconnection (OSI) reference model are examined. The OSI reference model closely intertwines with TCP/IP and its associated network features. Additionally, this chapter surveys other common networking protocols. Throughout this chapter, you'll learn how to implement the various protocols and features within Microsoft Windows XP.

OSI Reference Model Overview

When the first networks were developed, communication between computers was a delicate process. In most cases, a computer from a given manufacturer could only communicate with another computer from that same manufacturer. The few computers that were on networks at the time were on homogenous networks; that is, all the devices on these networks were (for the most part) from the same manufacturer. For example, a shop using IBM mainframes would only use IBM terminals so that computers could communicate with each other. If the network had the misfortune of needing equipment from multiple vendors, users would be lucky if one manufacturer's system could understand the data created on the system of another manufacturer. Even if the data formats were compatible, most of the data had to be moved via *sneaker net* (a humorous term meaning you had to put the data from one system on a disk and actually walk—presumably in your *sneakers*—to the other machine to insert the disk and copy the data onto that system) because few devices could communicate on a network at all, let alone interoperate with different makes and models of equipment.

However, a solution was on the horizon. In 1978, the International Organization for Standardization (ISO) introduced the OSI reference model. This model provided a common blueprint for all makers of networking hardware and applications. Using a *layered* approach, the model defines how networking hardware and software should function and how data should be handled and controlled. By using this blueprint, manufacturers could ensure that their equipment and software would interoperate with systems and applications from other makers. The OSI model specifies how certain parts of the network should work to support communication between applications on different computers. The actual mechanics of how the specification is implemented are entirely up to the manufacturer. In the end, manufacturers had a tool that helped them design their network standards for cross-platform compatibility and at the same time gave them flexibility in their implementation of the standard.

Using Layers in the OSI Model

A hierarchy of layers are used in the OSI model to ensure that developers focus on a single component, such as a program that converts files from one format to another, without worrying about how other components at other layers work. The OSI model also specifies how items operating at one layer of the design should interface with items at adjacent layers of the design. By using this model, equipment and software can be developed in a modular fashion.

Suppose a developer needs to specify how data is encrypted before being transmitted between hosts. Using the OSI model's layer approach, the developer does not have to worry about how the data is packaged for transmission across the network *after* encryption because that issue is dealt with by another layer. This allows the developer to focus solely on making sure that the piece he or she is working on interacts correctly with the layers above and below it in the manner specified by the OSI model.

The structure of a shipping company provides a good analogy for how a layered system works. A shipping company usually has a general management department, a sales department, distribution managers, warehouse workers, and truck drivers. Each of these groups can be thought of as a separate layer. Each one depends on the services of the departments (layers) adjacent to them, and for the most part, they are unconcerned about the needs of departments (layers) that are not directly related to them. The truck drivers need the services of the warehouse crew to locate and deliver materials. However, the truck operators are not likely to be concerned with the details of how the sales people operate. Each department (layer) might change how it accomplishes its tasks, and a department might turn over employees, but the general rules for interlayer communication do not change. The management team still needs to notify sales if there is a new customer making inquiries. Distribution must make sure it relays information to and from both the sales and warehouse layers in the appropriate form. Sales might need to know if the warehouse crew is shorthanded. The warehouse crew probably needs to know if sales are decreasing and fewer laborers will be needed. In the same manner, each layer of the OSI model has specific job duties and functions. By using this layered approach, network communication is broken down into manageable pieces.

The Seven Layers of the OSI Model

Within the OSI model, there are seven distinct layers; each defines how a specific piece of the communication process is supposed to occur. Each of these layers has unique functions, data types, and protocols. All data using the OSI model flows vertically up and down the layers, yet each layer only communicates with (or is really aware of) its corresponding (horizontal) layer on the remote computer. This communication between computers can be thought of as *logical* communication (because the layers on each computer are only concerned with communicating with one another), whereas the process of data flowing up and down the layers can be described as *physical* communication (because in reality data must be physically communicated between the layers on each computer for it to arrive at its destination). Layer 3 on the transmitting computer is only aware of layer 3 on the receiving computer; layer 2 on the transmitting computer is only aware of layer 2 on the receiving computer and so on. The seven layers of the OSI model are physical, data-link, network, transport, session, presentation, and application. The following illustration shows how the corresponding layers of the OSI model communicate when data is sent over a network.

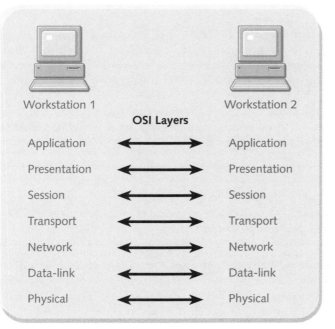

Layer 7: The Application Layer

The application layer is only concerned with determining the state of communications between two applications. The goal is to determine if the resources are available to initiate communication between two or more hosts as well as find out if participating computers are capable of successful communication. There are a large number of individual protocols and applications operating at layer 7. Even though many of these items provide services on their own, they are more often integrated to provide a feature rich environment for users. One example would be combining Telnet and File Transfer Protocol (FTP) with the intention of enabling remote management and file transfer. Telnet and FTP are described in the following list. All of the following items reside in the application layer of the OSI model.

Hypertext Transfer Protocol (HTTP)   The content rich portion of the Internet known as the World Wide Web is composed of applications such as Web page server software and protocols such as HTTP. HTTP defines how Web page information is transferred from servers to Web browser software such as Microsoft Internet Explorer. The Web browser's job is to interpret this information and display it to you.

File Transfer Protocol (FTP)   This protocol was developed to provide file transfer and management services between networked computers. It is used most often to move files from one computer to another. Although FTP is a protocol, it is also a command-line executable program in Windows XP. In addition to moving files from one place to another, FTP can be used for creating directories, deleting files and directories, and renaming the contents of directories, as well as performing other file management functions.

Trivial File Transfer Protocol (TFTP)   TFTP provides file transfer services similar to FTP, but without the bells and whistles. FTP can browse file structures and perform basic file management, whereas TFTP can only move files. The user or application calling on TFTP must know the exact location and name of the file to be moved ahead of time. In addition, TFTP does not support any higher-level functions such as creating folders or using authentication. This reduced feature set, combined with small packet size, makes TFTP-based communications faster than FTP-based communications.

> **note**   TFTP is used by a wide range of network equipment manufacturers as the preferred method for updating the firmware on their networking equipment. Because TFTP is often used as a service by user-friendly, graphical applications, the user is generally unaware of what is going on behind the scenes.

Post Office Protocol (POP) and Internet Message Access Protocol (IMAP)   POP is the most commonly used protocol for allowing graphical clients to view e-mail messages stored on remote mail servers. However, it is being supplanted by IMAP, which is more efficient and more secure than POP.

Telnet   Telnet was created years ago when terminal emulation was the only way to access another computer. It is a protocol designed to allow remote clients to connect to servers and initiate terminal emulation. *Terminal emulation* means that you create a *virtual session* between the client and a remote server, allowing the client computer to issue commands to the remote server as if the commands were being typed from a *dumb terminal* directly connected to the server. This feature proves useful when users need access to resources on other computers that are physically distant. Telnet capabilities can be combined with other programs, such as FTP, so that users can issue local commands on a remote server as well as move files between the two hosts.

Layer 6: The Presentation Layer

The purpose of the processes operating at the presentation layer is primarily to act as a translator for services operating at the application layer. Often, this takes the form of moving data from a proprietary data type to a universal type and back again. For example, data from the higher application layer is converted from the format that the application uses to a standardized format, and then back again. These conversions allow the layers below the presentation layer (layers 1 to 5) to interact with data in a standardized form. This shields processes at the application layer and the lower layers from having to be aware of data types other than their own. These processes send and receive data in the form they expect to and are unaware of this hidden conversion process. The final outcome is interoperability at the application level. A user on a Windows XP computer can create a document and save it to a server where a user on an Apple Macintosh computer can then gain access to the file. This involves more than a single process to accomplish, but much of the work is done by services at the presentation layer.

Converting data types is only the beginning of the functions specified at the presentation layer. Some other common functions such as compression/decompression and data encryption/decryption are also defined at this layer. When a user file is written to a hard disk, a process at the presentation layer might encrypt that file to protect it from unwanted eyes. The application with which the file is being written need not be aware that this decryption or encryption process is even occurring.

File sharing protocols that transfer files across the network to and from network shares function at the presentation layer.

Layer 5: The Session Layer

Ensuring that communications between two computers are properly established and maintained is the primary function of services operating at the session layer. In networked communications in general, there is a three-step process for establishing a connection between hosts. Step one is the initial establishment of the rules for the logical connection. During this portion of the process, the questions of who gets to transmit and how it is done are addressed. Communication between any two computers on a network can be in one of three modes: simplex, half-duplex, or full-duplex.

- *Simplex* communication is one-way communication from a sender to a receiver. This mode is almost entirely passive: The receiver takes no action during the communication process. On most networks, this form of communication is not widely used.

- When a *half-duplex* communications process is negotiated, each of the communication partners agrees that one host will transmit at a time. Unlike simplex communication, half-duplex is bidirectional with both hosts actively participating in the communications process. This form of communication is typically negotiated when either of the hosts is incapable of transmitting and receiving data at the same time. Half-duplex communication is still relatively common, particularly where legacy equipment and software is still in use.

- Full-duplex communication is fully bidirectional and synchronous, meaning that each participating host can send and receive data at the same time (*synchronous*), and both hosts actively participate in the communication (bidirectional). Full-duplex is the most robust form of communication. It allows both hosts to transmit and receive at will. Full-duplex communication is widely supported by current networking hardware and applications.

Once the communications rules have been established, the second step is to actually move the data from one host to another. The details of signaling and packaging data are handled by processes at other layers, so the data transfer step is fairly simple.

Once communication has occurred, the third step of the three-step process occurs, which is known as release. *Release* is an agreement between the participating hosts that communication is no longer desired. Once both hosts agree that they have done what they need to, the communications process formally ends.

The following list describes two of the more widely used session layer protocols and processes:

- **Remote Procedure Call (RPC).** RPC is widely used in client/server environments. RPC is often used to enable the processing of file requests when the requesting computer and host computer utilize different operating system platforms. RPC is also used for a wide range of interoperability functions.

- **Network File System (NFS).** NFS was developed by Sun Microsystems for UNIX computers using the TCP/IP protocol suite. NFS allows any remote resource (such as a mapped drive) to be treated as if it were a local resource.

Layer 4: The Transport Layer

The transport layer primarily serves the function of breaking apart and reassembling data (known as *segmenting* or *segmentation*) from processes and applications operating in layers 5–7. Although there are many data modifying operations occurring in the upper three layers, such as converting data formats, layer 4 is the first layer where larger pieces of data are broken into smaller components (segments) for transmission. Layer 4 protocols manage the process of sending and receiving this newly segmented data and are responsible for establishing logical connections with various communication partners. All of the physical connectivity is handled by processes operating at the lower layers (1–3) and their respective processes and protocols. The transport layer masks the underlying events from the upper-level protocols, acting as a *twilight zone* between the applications that want to communicate and the software and hardware components involved in the actual transmission of data across a network. In this role, layer 4 services conceal the existence of the physical components of the network from applications operating in the upper layers.

In addition to implementing segmentation, processes at the transport layer are responsible for implementing flow control. *Flow control* ensures that the integrity of transmitted data is maintained by regulating the flow of data so that hosts participating in data transmission can receive data as fast as their partner is sending it as well as ensuring that they do not send data faster than their partner can receive it. Transport layer protocols are often also responsible for managing connection reliability, making certain data is received by the destination partner in the same order it was transmitted, and ensuring that data that did not reach its destination is retransmitted. Protocols that offer this kind of reliability (such as TCP) are called *connection-oriented* protocols, whereas protocols that do not offer this kind of reliability, such as User Datagram Protocol (UDP), are called *connectionless* protocols.

note It is at the transport layer where TCP and UDP ports are defined. *Ports* are logical protocol assignments within the TCP and UDP protocols. For example, FTP uses TCP ports 21 and 20. TCP and UDP provide layer 4 services for the TCP/IP protocol suite. TCP and UDP are examined in more detail in "Understanding TCP/IP in Depth," page 24.

Layer 3: The Network Layer

Layer 3 protocols are tasked with determining the best way to get data from one place to another. They also logically connect network addresses (such as an IP address) with physical addresses, such as the physical address of a network interface card (NIC). Segments created in the transport layer are delivered to protocols and services in the network layer where the first bits of network addressing information are appended to the data from upper-layer applications. The segments from the transport layer that have the appropriate logical addressing information added to them are known as *packets*. It is at the network layer where devices (known as *routers*) that connect separate networks operate.

Routers collect network layer information, such as the path to networks (known as *routes*), that the router is connected to and aware of. As a result, the router builds a topology map of the network for use when deciding how to move data traffic (called

21

routing) from one network to another. This map is also known as a *routing table*. Routers come in a variety of forms and range from hardware routers such as the Cisco 2600 series to PC-based routers that use Windows Routing and Remote Access Services (RRAS).

There are many layer 3 protocols; the most important ones are IP, Address Resolution Protocol (ARP), Reverse Address Resolution Protocol (RARP), and Internet Control Message Protocol (ICMP). Each of these protocols provides address resolution services to network devices utilizing network layer services. TCP/IP networks would not be possible without the services these protocols provide.

Layer 2: The Data-link Layer

The data-link layer is responsible for making sure that data sent across the network is delivered to the proper physical device. It is at the data-link layer that physical addressing of network adapters exists. Network layer addresses such as IP are often transitory and user defined, whereas network addresses are either statically assigned by the user or dynamically assigned using Dynamic Host Configuration Protocol (DHCP). Physical addresses on the other hand are *hard-coded* onto the network interface, and they are designed to be permanent and universally unique. These physical addresses are known as Media Access Control (MAC) addresses; for example, each NIC has a MAC address that can be used to identify the source or destination of a data stream.

InsideOut

Data-link Layer Addresses vs. Network Layer Addresses

Why is the network layer needed at all if NIC devices have a hard-coded, globally unique address? The answer is that trying to manage a global map of how to reach every known MAC address would simply be impossible. No single device could maintain this mapping, and the addresses are not designed to ease routing. Network layer protocols such as IP are specifically designed to break down the task of routing data in a large internetwork into small, manageable chunks in which network segments can maintain local routing information and pass along remote data to other hosts. This process of network packet management and routing is often referred to as *packet switching*.

In the TCP/IP protocol stack, data-link layer services add the physical addressing information to packets received from network layer services. Once this new information is encoded onto the packet, the new data is known as a *frame*. Encapsulation into a frame is the last step before physical transmission occurs at layer 1.

One of the unique traits of the data-link layer is the presence of two sublayers: the Logical Link Control (LLC) upper sublayer and the Media Access Control (MAC) lower sublayer. The LLC layer acts as an intermediary between the logical upper OSI layers that are concerned with data types and logical addressing and the lower OSI layer that is only concerned with physical interfaces and signaling protocols. One of the ways the LLC bridges the layers together is by managing transmission timing and providing the working parts of flow control.

The MAC sublayer is responsible for generating the new frames that encapsulate packets from the transport layer. These frames are made up of binary values (1's and 0's). This binary format is all the physical layer (layer 1) understands. Besides making one last data change, the MAC layer performs some basic data integrity checks. The cyclical redundancy check (CRC) ensures—by means of a complex calculation—that data reconstructed out of the bits received from the physical layer is intact.

Services at the MAC sublayer control which kind of media access method is used. The media are the physical components of the network such as interfaces and cabling. These MAC sublayer methods determine how these components are controlled. The goal of these methods is to prevent hosts from communicating on top of each other, which causes data loss. Typically, one of three methods is used:

- **Contention-based media access.** This method requires that any host wanting to transmit must have control over the network segment to which it is connected. Each communicating host contends for control of the segment. It is possible for more than one host on a network to transmit at a time (under certain conditions). When this happens, the data from two transmitting computers collides, and the net result is data loss. This method is used in a common type of network called Ethernet.

- **Token passing.** This kind of media access involves the use of a special frame called a *token*. The token is passed from one computer to another in a round robin fashion. Any computer can transmit if it has possession of the token, and there is no data attached to the token. Once the host decides to transmit, the data is added to the token frame and forwarded to the next host. When the targeted recipient receives the token, it pulls the data off, and then forwards the empty token back into the ring. This method ensures that only one host transmits at a time, and data collisions are not possible.

To learn more about Ethernet and token passing networks, see Chapter 3, "Creating Network Connections."

- **Polling media access.** This method involves a central authority such as a server that polls all the devices on the network and literally asks them if they have anything to transmit. When a host replies with a positive acknowledgment, the polling computer authorizes the transmission. A computer on a polling network cannot transmit unless given permission by the central authority, and the computer must wait for its turn in the polling cycle before it can request such permission.

Chapter 2

Layer 1: The Physical Layer

The network components that exist at the physical layer have only one function: generating signals along the physical cabling and interfaces on the network. Although there are a variety of methods for generating signals on the network, both analog and digital, the goal is the same: Each method seeks to transmit binary data. The actual devices that exist at the physical layer consist of cables (or wireless connections using radio waves or infrared light), plugs connected to the cabling, and the receiver jacks along with the signaling equipment attached to network adapters (or transmitter/receiver devices for wireless communications).

Understanding TCP/IP in Depth

The majority of networks either support or depend on the TCP/IP protocol suite. Windows networks are certainly no exception, and Windows XP can use TCP/IP for any network—from large domains to small home networks.

To understand how TCP/IP really works, it is important to understand its inner workings. The TCP/IP protocol suite spans nearly the entire seven layers of the OSI model. The most important layers to understand (with respect to TCP/IP) are layers 3 (network), 4 (transport), and 7 (application).

> **note** TCP/IP was originally designed by the United States Defense Advanced Research Projects Agency (DARPA), the central R&D organization for the U.S. Department of Defense. It was designed to map directly to the *DARPA model* of networking protocols rather than the OSI reference model. However, because TCP/IP can be (and most commonly is) described in terms of the OSI model, as are most of the other protocols discussed in this chapter, OSI will be the focus.

Application Layer Protocols

Application layer protocols specify components closest to where the computer user interacts with the computer. Several TCP/IP protocols exist at layer 7, and some of them, such as FTP, HTTP, and SMTP, were discussed earlier in this chapter. There are a few other major protocols in this suite that you should get to know as well, and these are explored in the following sections.

Domain Name System (DNS)

For computers to identify resources on a TCP/IP network, each computer or server on a network must have a unique Internet Protocol (IP) address, such as 192.168.1.55. Because humans have a difficult time remembering strings of numbers like those used in IP addresses, language-based names are used. A language-based name on a TCP/IP network is known as a domain name or *fully qualified domain name (FQDN)*; for example, a user's computer located in the Atlanta marketing department of the Tailspin Toys company might be given the FQDN user09.mktg.atlanta.tailspintoys.com.

How then can a computer's FQDN be resolved to an IP address (and back again)? In the early days of the Internet, only a handful of computers were connected. At that time, all computers depended on a file known as a *host file* to turn user-friendly names such as *mailserver* into the IP addresses needed to reach the site. With relatively few computers using networks, this system worked well. However, as the Internet began to grow, it became apparent that a new, more flexible system for tracking address-to-name mappings was needed. Also, because the host file was centrally stored, every computer needed to copy the file from a common source. When the prospect of thousands of network hosts became a reality, it became clear that the system would have to include the distribution of the mapping information as well.

The solution to this problem is the *Domain Name System (DNS)*. DNS uses a lightweight (easy to process), hierarchical, distributed, and flexible database that maps FQDNs to their corresponding IP addresses. DNS is a highly expandable naming system that can accommodate the naming needs of any network (it's used to uniquely identify every Web site and resource on the Internet). DNS databases use a client/server model in which any computer trying to match a domain name to an IP address is known as a *resolver*. These servers house a portion of the DNS IP-to-name mappings and have information about where to forward requests they cannot process. Because DNS is hierarchical, no DNS server has to maintain the records for the entire Internet, and DNS is not crippled by the loss of one server.

DNS is dependable and can support private networks (networks using a range of reserved IP addresses that are unavailable to the Internet as a whole) as well as networks publicly accessible via the Internet. DNS is the standard for both Active Directory–based Windows networks and for the Internet, and computers in a pure Active Directory environment must use DNS to identify themselves.

DNS functions by using unique FQDNs. When an FQDN is requested, the name is resolved into an IP address step by step until the desired server is discovered. Let's say that a server named Server12 resides in the domain named tailspintoys.com. The server's FQDN would be server12.tailspintoys.com. If you need to contact this server from a different domain, perhaps to access a file, the process behind the scenes might follow these steps:

1 Your initial request to access the server is sent to a DNS server in your domain. If the name is held directly in the server's database, the IP address is returned and the transaction is over.

2 If the name is not stored locally on the DNS server, it sends a request to a root server. Because the server12.tailspintoys.com name is not stored locally on the root server, it sends a response containing the address of a DNS server that provides addresses for .com domains.

3 The local DNS server resends its request to resolve the name server12.tailspintoys.com to the .com server.

4 Because the requested name is not stored locally on the .com server, it sends a response containing the address of the tailspintoys.com server, which *is* stored on the .com server.

5 The DNS server sends a DNS request to resolve the name server12.tailspintoys.com to the tailspintoys.com server.

6 Because the requested name is stored locally on the tailspintoys.com server, it sends a response containing the IP address of server12.tailspintoys.com.

7 The local DNS server then sends the IP address for server12.tailspintoys.com to the requesting client computer, which can communicate with it directly.

This example is a worst-case scenario. In reality, both the network client and individual DNS servers along the way would likely maintain a temporary copy, or *cache*, of the recent DNS requests that have been made of them. This allows them to immediately service the DNS requests from local memory rather than rerunning the entire painstaking query process every time a query is made. This dramatically reduces the number of iterations made by the local DNS server on behalf of its client (or eliminates the need for the client to do a DNS lookup altogether if it has the address in its own cache).

> **note** The downside of this caching process is that it can take some time for changes to a machine's FQDN-to-IP-address mapping to propagate to DNS servers across the Internet. DNS servers do occasionally clear out the contents of their local caches to prevent a long-term breakdown in name resolution services, but until this refreshing process takes place, remote changes can make locally cached DNS data unreliable.

There are even products, such as TweakMaster from Hagel Technologies, that can be installed on Windows XP to maintain a long-term cache of commonly used IP addresses (such as for the Microsoft Internet Explorer Favorites list). If these addresses rarely change (which is most likely the case), this cache can improve the experience of using TCP/IP by eliminating the need for name resolution altogether. These programs can refresh their cache lists on a scheduled basis to keep the cache up-to-date.

Even at its worst, however, the process of resolving an FQDN to an IP address is completely transparent to the user, who simply indicates the FQDN of the server he or she wants to communicate with. DNS handles the rest in the background.

For more information on how Active Directory domains use DNS, see "Understanding Active Directory Domains," page 311.

Windows Internet Naming Service (WINS)

WINS is another method used for resolving a host name to an IP address. WINS originated to provide remote name resolution services for *Network Basic Input/Output System (NetBIOS)* computer names. NetBIOS is a protocol that was designed by Microsoft and IBM in the 1980s. It remained the standard for Microsoft networks until the introduction of Windows 2000. With NetBIOS, a computer would have a short name such as *BOBSPC*. However, pure Active Directory networks no longer rely on NetBIOS or WINS. They now use DNS, a far more commonly accepted standard for computer naming and system name resolution.

Dynamic and Static Addressing

Although computers can be assigned permanent (or *static*) IP addresses manually, the process can be complex, and mistakes can easily be made that cause network communications to fail. As machines are added or removed from the network, the network needs to be reconfigured, involving administrative overhead. When TCP/IP was first introduced, many network administrators were resistant to its adoption because it was difficult to manually assign and manage IP addresses, and to troubleshoot problems that arose when numbers were incorrectly assigned.

An alternative is to have the network itself assign and maintain the network addresses of its clients: This is known as *dynamic addressing*. DHCP is the primary mechanism for performing dynamic addressing today. DHCP servers can automatically handle the assignment of IP addresses and related addressing information to clients through a

Windows Evolution from WINS to DNS

WINS and DNS provide comparable services for name resolution, and they are both recognized, public protocols. So, what would be the reason for the move from WINS to DNS by recent Windows operating systems? Although Windows has supported DNS as a resolution protocol since its inception, WINS was the preferred method for LAN name-to-address resolution until the advent of Active Directory network services in Windows 2000. With Active Directory, DNS became the prominent name resolution method. One of the reasons for the change is the wide support for DNS as a resolution protocol. Although WINS was a public standard, it never gained the wide acceptance that DNS has enjoyed from its roots in the Internet. With the progress towards integrating local network services with Internet services and a general push towards widely distributed networks, DNS became the logical successor for WINS. WINS is still in use on many older Windows-based networks, but the shift to integrated DNS services will no doubt continue.

process called *leasing*. With DHCP leasing, a client requests IP configuration information, and the DHCP server allocates that client a particular IP address for a specified period of time, after which the client can *release* the address for other computers to use or *renew* the lease and continue to use it. In addition, DHCP servers can relate configuration data, such as preferred subnet masks and default gateways, as well as other information, such as DNS and WINS server addresses.

For users on a small business or home network, however, the benefits of DHCP might not justify the costs of a dedicated DHCP server. This is where Automatic Private IP Addressing (APIPA) comes into play. APIPA is an automatic IP addressing service that enables a Windows XP computer to auto-assign an IP address when no DHCP server is available. APIPA is active by default on all Windows XP computers. If the Windows XP computer fails to find a DHCP server to provide addressing information, the computer selects an address from a special range of IP addresses (169.254.0.1 through 169.254.255.254). This range of addresses is not used on the Internet and normally cannot be accessed over the Internet. The purpose of these addresses is to isolate a private LAN's data from the world at large. Once the address is selected, the client checks the network to determine if another host is already using the address; if so, it selects another address and tries again until an unused address is found. APIPA provides a way for Windows XP computers to handle IP addressing so that users don't have to be involved. This allows home and small office networks the functionality of dynamic IP configuration without requiring the overhead of DHCP.

Simple Network Monitoring Protocol (SNMP)

SNMP provides a standardized method of assessing information about the state of network components such as routers, switches, servers, and workstations. SNMP provides the ability to configure network attached devices as well as view information about their status. This protocol is widely used, and SNMP-enabled devices can be found on virtually every network.

Transport Layer Protocols

Transport layer protocols function at the transport layer and provide a way to move data from one computer to another. This section explores several important transport layer protocols you should become familiar with.

Transmission Control Protocol (TCP)

TCP was first developed to solve problems with the reliability of early networks. Frequently, the hardware used could not be trusted to reliably deliver data from one host to another. To solve this issue, TCP was developed to set rules for ensuring delivery of data across networks. Essentially, TCP builds in message delivery reliability by applying several techniques, most notably error detection and error correction.

Communicating by Port Numbers

Application layer protocols use port numbers (defined at the transport layer) to identify the network traffic specific to a particular application or protocol. Services using one of these protocols examine all network traffic being sent to them to determine the port number. There are default port numbers associated with all of the standardized services such as FTP, TFTP, and DNS. If the need arises, the default port numbers can be changed for security or development reasons. Some of the more common port numbers are 21 (FTP), 23 (Telnet), 25 (SMTP), 69 (TFTP), 80 (HTTP), and 161 (SNMP).

During the initial negotiation process, computers use TCP to come to agreement on several communications parameters. These parameters can include, for example, how large the segments can be and how many segments can be sent until an acknowledgment of receipt is required from the receiving station. Once these parameters are negotiated and agreed upon, the TCP controlled connection between the two computers is complete, which is called a *virtual circuit*. With the virtual circuit established, it is then possible to detect errors, correct errors if possible, and pass error messages to higher-layer protocols as required.

One of the significant features of TCP is flow control. When two computers establish a connection and begin to send data, there is a chance that the receiving computer might not be able to process the incoming data as rapidly as the sending host. To prevent a total collapse of the communications process, the receiving computer can use a halt signal to slow or alter the flow of data. For instance, if a faster computer (one with a faster network adapter or CPU, or one with a less burdened local network segment) sends data faster than a slower communications partner can process it, data will be lost because the faster computer overruns the slower one.

During flow control negotiations, the less capable participant can send a message that tells the sender to slow down and let the slower machine catch up. Either the transmission speed is reduced or the data has blank spaces (pauses) inserted into the data stream. The result is that the sending machine makes sure that the less capable computer has a chance to properly reassemble the received segments.

TCP uses a process called segmentation to better facilitate reliable data delivery. Often, applications will request or move large chunks of data from one location to another. If the entire file is sent as a single block, any interruption in the transmission would require that the entire block of data be retransmitted. To avoid this problem, TCP breaks larger pieces of data into smaller, sequentially numbered segments. The segments are then transmitted sequentially to the destination computer. Upon receipt, the receiving computer reassembles them for use by higher-layer protocols. Any segments that are not acknowledged are retransmitted until the receiving host indicates that the segments were successfully received.

What Does TCP Really Do?

TCP is a connection-oriented protocol. When one computer wants to send data to another using TCP, a connection is negotiated between the two. The negotiation involves a three-way communications process (also known as a *handshake*) that goes something like this:

1 **Computer 1:** "Hey computer 2! Are you available to communicate?"

2 **Computer 2:** "Yes, fire away!"

3 **Computer 1:** "Here comes the data!"

These three steps are officially known as the *connection request*, *connection granted*, and *acknowledgment*. But as you can see, they simply provide a way for two computers to get in touch with each other before sending data.

Features of the User Datagram Protocol

Like TCP, UDP also provides transport layer functions to higher-layer protocols and services. However, this is the only similarity they share. UDP is as featureless as a transport layer protocol can be and still be useful.

When a UDP process initiates communications, it immediately starts sending data to its communication partner. There are no negotiations, such as a handshake, or any establishment of parameters at the beginning of a transmission. There are no message acknowledgments during the communications process. This can result in lost data, but it does provide *low-latency* network communications (network communications with little delay between partners). UDP is completely unaware of the connection state of its communication partners. If a server were hosting a UDP-enabled application that had multiple clients connected at the same time, UDP would not provide a method for determining the availability of any particular client. Additionally, should the receiving computer become overwhelmed by the stream of data being transmitted, no mechanism exists in UDP to allow the receiving computer to send a stop signal. These features are left to services and protocols operating elsewhere.

note The most noteworthy benefit of UDP is that because connection negotiations do not occur with UDP, it has far less overhead than TCP. Several popular protocols and Internet services, including streaming multimedia, Internet telephony, DNS, and SNMP, are perfect matches for this service. UDP's inability to know when a packet hasn't been received and when to resend it explains the source of some of the dropped frames experienced in streaming video and sound dropouts encountered in streaming audio.

UDP has gained wide acceptance because the reliability of networking equipment that operates on the physical layer has greatly improved. This effectively minimizes the detrimental effects of UDP's inability to correct errors. Many protocols and applications that rely on UDP perform their own error detection/correction to make up for this behavior. This allows the application or protocol to take advantage of UDP's greater efficiency while minimizing its downside.

Network Layer Protocols

The network layer (layer 3) of the OSI model is primarily focused on finding the best path over the network for data transmission. There are several important TCP/IP protocols that function at this layer, and these are explored in this section.

Address Resolution Protocol (ARP)

Information passed down to IP at the network layer (layer 3) from upper-layer protocols includes the network (IP) address of the destination. For IP to send this information using a data-link layer protocol (such as Ethernet), the destination MAC address must first be resolved. Because upper-layer protocols and services are not aware of the MAC address, IP uses ARP to resolve the MAC address for a next-hop IP address. ARP is used to actively maintain a table that lists recently accessed IP addresses and their corresponding physical addresses. To build or maintain this *ARP cache*, ARP sends out a *broadcast* message to all computers on the network segment using the targeted computer's IP address and asks for the physical address (MAC address) of that computer's network adapter. This process is initiated whenever an ARP cache entry for a needed IP address is not present in the ARP cache. The targeted computer replies with its physical address, which is placed in the ARP cache and is sent back to the ARP requester. If the ARP broadcast fails to determine the MAC address of the targeted computer, an error is indicated, and the upper-layer process or application must decide whether to reattempt the communication or give up.

Internet Protocol (IP)

IP addressing is by far the most widely used method of addressing computers today. As such, it is the default addressing method used by Windows XP. Each computer in an IP network is uniquely identified with an IP address. All of the higher-level protocols in the TCP/IP suite (such as HTTP or FTP) depend on the services of IP to deliver packets to a destination computer. The IP communication process receives segments or messages from transport layer protocols such as TCP or UDP. The IP process packages these segments into packets for delivery to the data-link layer protocols.

Internet Control Message Protocol (ICMP)

ICMP is used to provide diagnostic and error reporting for IP networks. For example, the ping utility uses ICMP Echo messages to test reachability to a specified destination.

> To learn more about the ping utility and other troubleshooting tools, see "Using Command-line Tools Included in Windows XP," page 345.

Reverse Address Resolution Protocol (RARP)

A *diskless computer* (one with no hard disk drive) that is part of a network needs to have a method for obtaining its operating code from the network and thus needs to know its assigned IP address. Hardware on the computer is able to determine the MAC address of the computer's network adapter; however, to get the operating code from the network, the computer must join the network. RARP helps accomplish this task. As its name implies, it performs the opposite lookup function performed by ARP.

The diskless computer sends a RARP broadcast message indicating that it has a MAC address and that it needs to know its IP address. A RARP server responds with the IP address the computer is supposed to use. With its IP address known, the computer can then join the network and go about performing its tasks, such as downloading the code it needs to provide to a user environment.

Internet Protocol Addressing

IP addresses contain two pieces of information: the network ID and the node ID. A *node* is any device connected to an IP network. IP addresses are 32 bits long and are made up of four 8-bit *octets*. For the most part, IP addresses are displayed in the decimal equivalent of the binary data contained in each octet. For example, the user-friendly IP address of 192.168.34.9 is actually 11000000101010000010001000001001 in binary form. Each octet is capable of representing decimal values between 0 and 255, or 00000000 and 11111111 binary.

The good news is that you do not have to worry about IP address binary formats and conversions—that task is usually left to network planners and administrators of large Windows networks. Because the functionality of TCP/IP is the same whether binary or decimal equivalents are used, decimal equivalents will be used in the following discussion.

> Understanding how to use binary numbers in relation to the IP address is only essential when advanced subnetting is required. Subnetting is discussed in "Applying the Subnet Mask," opposite.

Classifying IP Addresses

To manage the distribution of IP addresses and to establish a standard for interpreting IP addresses, five IP address *classes* (A, B, C, D, and E) were originally developed. IP address Classes A, B, and C, shown in Table 2-1, were originally defined for assignment by Internet service providers (ISPs) and businesses for use on their networks. Class D addresses are reserved for multicasting, and Class E addresses are reserved for research purposes.

Table 2-1. IP Address Classes and Their Network ID Ranges

IP Address Class	IP Network ID Range
A	1.0.0.0 through 126.0.0.0
B	128.0.0.0 through 191.255.0.0
C	192.0.0.0 through 223.255.255.0

Each IP address class has a pattern for the number of octets used to represent each of the two parts of an address. The Class A network address uses one octet on the left (8 bits) for the network ID and the other three octets (24 bits) for the node ID. A Class B address uses the first two octets (16 bits) for the network ID and the last two octets for the node ID. A Class C IP address uses the first three octets (24 bits) for the network ID and the last octet (8 bits) for the node ID. The numbers of octets used for the network ID and for the node IDs are important because the number of octets reserved for nodes determines the number of devices that can be attached to a single network ID. For example, in a Class C network with one node octet, only 254 devices can be connected to a network segment (because there can only be 254 unique IP addresses in a single octet). In contrast, on a Class B network segment with two node octets, over 65,534 devices can be connected.

Along with an IP address, there are two other parameters specified for members of a TCP/IP network: the subnet mask and the default gateway.

Applying the Subnet Mask

TCP/IP networks are divided into different portions called *subnets*. Depending on the client's IP address, the client belongs to a certain IP class and a certain default subnet. The *subnet mask* helps computers know which part of the IP address refers to the network ID and which part of the address is used to refer to the clients. The subnet mask is another 32-bit, dotted-decimal number that is combined mathematically (in binary form) with the IP address. The result identifies the network ID. A subnet mask is assigned along with each IP address.

For example, if an IP address of 192.168.0.50 uses a subnet mask of 255.255.0.0, the portion of the IP address masked by 255.255, which is 192.168 in this case, identifies the network ID portion of the address. The 0.0 segment of the subnet mask represents the unmasked portion and identifies the digits of the IP address that uniquely identify each client machine on the network, in this case 0.50. In this scenario, all IP addresses of computers on the network segment must begin with 192.168., but the remaining digits can range from 0.1 to 255.254. All machines using addresses in this range will be able to communicate with each other over the network segment without requiring a router. Table 2-2 shows the default subnet masks for each IP address class.

Table 2-2. IP Address Classes and Their Default Subnet Masks

IP Address Class	Default Subnet Mask
A	255.0.0.0
B	255.255.0.0
C	255.255.255.0

note In fact, the use of IP addresses with subnet masks can be more complicated than the preceding simple example because the addresses must be translated to binary and dealt with in that format. However, for the most common subnetting schemes, simply masking in between the dotted-decimal values is sufficient.

Using Default Gateways

In addition to the IP address and subnet mask, a TCP/IP configuration might also have a default gateway. Although clients reside on a certain subnet, they sometimes need to communicate with another client on a different subnet (for example, often computers using TCP/IP are on a routed network such as the Internet). The client must know the computer (or router) to send its traffic to so the traffic can leave the local subnet and travel to another. This computer or router is known as the *default gateway*, and the IP address of the gateway is essential information for a client to send and receive data beyond the bounds of the local subnet. Depending on the network configuration, however, a default gateway might not be necessary. For example, if your network has one subnet and you do not connect to any other subnets, you have no need for a default gateway because your network clients never access other subnets. This is common primarily in small office and home network environments (although with the tremendous popularity of the Internet, even these scenarios commonly require a gateway device for the Internet connection).

Understanding Public and Private IP Addresses

Early on in IP networking, it became apparent that there was a need for specialized, *private*, address groups. These addresses would be used for internal networks, whereas connectivity to the rest of the world would be accomplished through a router that had a *public* IP address. This ensured that the finite number of IP addresses would not be consumed by (nor have to be uniquely registered and assigned to) the millions of private home and business networks operating worldwide. Because the private addresses are not reachable from the public Internet, they can be reused by all the private networks at will without those networks colliding with one another, thereby saving the vast majority of IP addresses for providing the unique public addresses needed by Internet-connected devices. The private IP address ranges are

- 10.0.0.0 through 10.255.255.255

- 172.16.0.0 through 172.31.255.255

- 192.168.0.0 through 192.168.255.255

IP routers on the Internet will not route traffic across the Internet using one of these IP addresses. If, however, someone wants to provide Internet access to hosts using a private IP network, a *network address translation (NAT)* device is used. NAT devices forward the appropriate traffic sent from the private IP addresses through a single or a few public addresses—typically the IP address of a router that securely links the private network (LAN) to the public network (Internet)—and maintain an internal table that allows response traffic to be routed to the proper initiating private host.

> NAT can be used to maintain a subnet of private network IP addresses hidden from the public Internet. This is a useful safety feature, and some home and small office networking hardware, such as residential gateways, use NAT. You can learn more about these options in Chapter 3, "Creating Network Connections."

Configuring IP Settings in Windows XP

The TCP/IP protocol suite is installed by default on all Windows XP installations. There is a wide array of configurable settings, and the options of each setting as well as the procedures for making changes to them will be explored. To access the TCP/IP properties, follow these steps:

1 Log on as a user with administrative privileges.

2 Open Network Connections. From the default Windows XP Start menu, choose Connect To, Show All Connections; from the Classic Windows XP Start menu, choose Settings, Network Connections.

Chapter 2

3 Locate the connection to the network. It will probably be labeled with the default name, Local Area Connection.

> **tip** If you do not see any connection listed under the heading LAN Or High-Speed Internet in the Network Connections window, there is probably no network adapter installed on the computer. See Chapter 3, "Creating Network Connections," to learn more about installing and configuring network adapters.

4 Right-click the Local Area Connection icon, and choose Properties from the shortcut menu.

5 On the General tab, select Internet Protocol (TCP/IP), and click Properties. The Internet Protocol (TCP/IP) Properties dialog box opens, as shown in Figure 2-1.

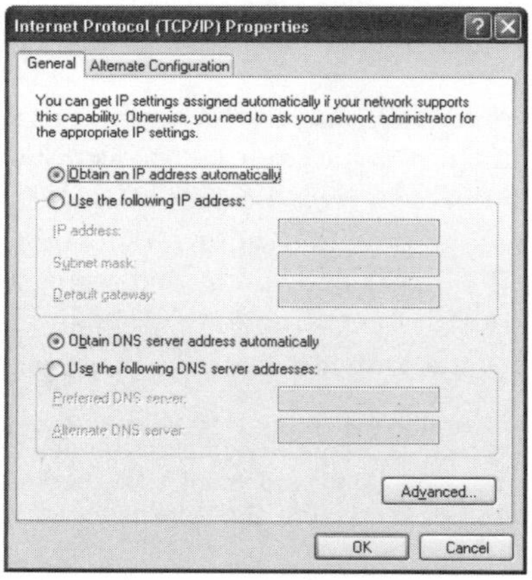

Figure 2-1. The TCP/IP configuration is accessed through the Local Area Connection Properties dialog box.

In this dialog box, the computer can be configured to use static or dynamic addressing. The default is dynamic addressing (Obtain An IP Address Automatically). If a change is not required, this setting should be left as is. It is also possible to configure the DNS settings (the address of the DNS server) from this dialog box. If both DNS and IP addressing options are set to automatic settings, the computer will use the DNS settings provided by a DHCP server. For computers not connected to a domain, the DNS servers are usually provided by your ISP. It is possible to select automatic addressing for the IP address and to manually specify a DNS server address. If no DHCP server is available to provide the IP address, APIPA will automatically configure the IP address and subnet mask. For a single subnet network that does not contain a router, APIPA should be used unless you have a specific reason to manually enter each computer's IP address.

newfeature!

If you selected automatic addressing on the General tab, you'll see the Alternate Configuration tab in the Internet Protocol (TCP/IP) Properties dialog box. This tab represents a new feature in Windows XP: Alternate IP Configuration. This feature allows an automatically assigned IP address if a DHCP server is available, and a static IP configuration when a DHCP server is not available. This enables you to connect to two different networks (for example, your home network and your employer's network) and get the appropriate address assigned. If you're not connecting to two networks, you can leave the setting as Automatic Private IP Address on this tab. If you want to configure a static IP configuration for a second network, select User Configured, as shown in Figure 2-2, and enter the appropriate settings.

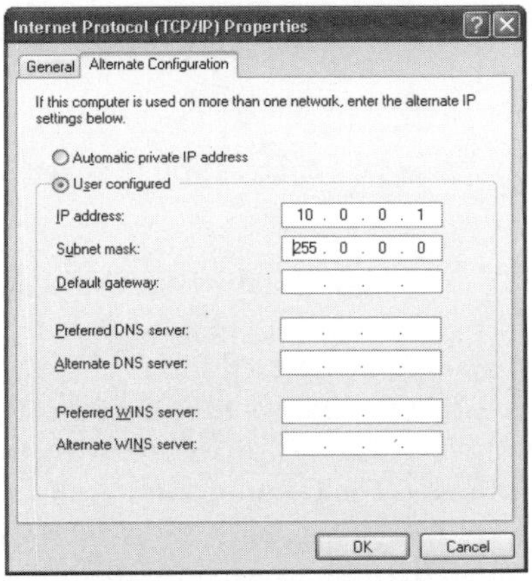

Figure 2-2. Use the Alternate Configuration tab if you want to connect to a second network.

Configuring Advanced TCP/IP Options

Under most circumstances, you do not need to manually configure TCP/IP settings. After all, in networks that use DHCP, the server leases all of the necessary TCP/IP configuration settings. In networks with no DHCP server, APIPA can handle the auto-addressing. However, Windows XP allows you to tailor the TCP/IP settings to your specific needs. It is important to always question why you are manually configuring TCP/IP and whether the manual configuration is necessary. Why would someone want to manually configure TCP/IP settings? In environments that do not use DHCP, you might want a particular IP address configuration to be used, or you might want to specify certain DNS or WINS servers. You might also want to configure some TCP/IP filtering options for added security.

To manually configure these advanced settings, return to the Internet Protocol (TCP/IP) Properties dialog box. On the General tab, click the Advanced button to open the Advanced TCP/IP Settings dialog box, as shown in Figure 2-3 on the next page. It is here that an administrator gains access to the details of the Windows XP TCP/IP configuration.

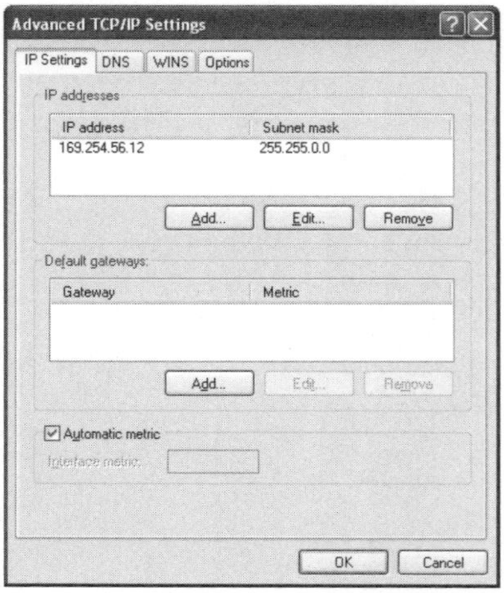

Figure 2-3. The Advanced TCP/IP Settings dialog box enables you to manually configure IP and related settings.

The IP Settings tab shows the configured IP addresses. If static IP addresses are being used, this location allows multiple IP addresses to be bound to a single network interface. This is primarily useful in the case of systems being used for tasks such as production Web servers and is not commonly needed for Windows XP Professional or Windows XP Home Edition. If you are using DHCP, this box will show the message "DHCP Enabled" instead of a list of IP addresses. The Default Gateways section of the dialog box enables you to define one or more default gateways. By assigning different interface metrics (at the bottom of the dialog box), you can specify the order in which these gateways are used. If the Automatic Metric check box is selected, the best gateway will be determined dynamically.

> **tip** The Automatic Metric setting is typically best when multiple IP gateways are available.

The DNS tab allows the specification of multiple DNS servers, as shown in Figure 2-4. The up arrow and down arrow buttons next to the text boxes allow you to configure the order in which the DNS servers are queried when name resolution is needed. The options in the lower portion of the dialog box allow you to specify which DNS suffix is appended to DNS requests for system names that are not FQDNs; for example, a user might want to substitute the shorter *mycomputer* for the full FQDN mycomputer.microsoft.com. Normally, such a substitution will result in a name resolution failure, but Windows XP will attempt to append each DNS suffix to a name resolution request and retry that request before finally returning an error to the client software. Staying with the example, if you add microsoft.com to the list of DNS suffixes, Windows XP will automatically attempt to resolve mycomputer.microsoft.com once the resolution request for *mycomputer* fails.

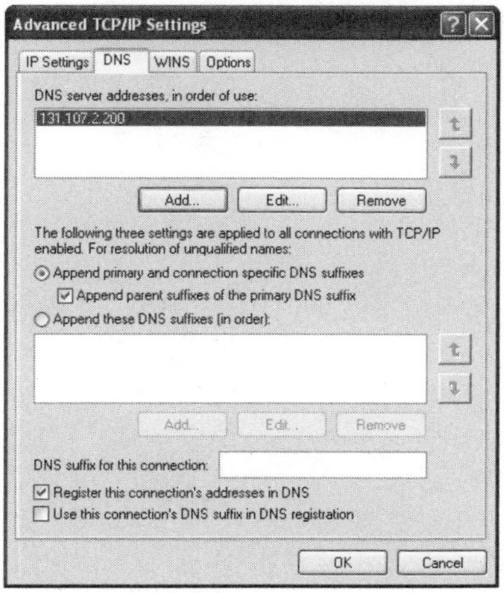

Chapter 2: Configuring TCP/IP and Other Protocols

Figure 2-4. You can configure specific DNS servers on the DNS tab.

The next tab in the Advanced TCP/IP Settings dialog box is the WINS tab, which is shown in Figure 2-5 on the next page. This tab lets you configure the servers and settings used for WINS-based name registration and resolution. Aside from specifying the address of servers and the order in which to use them, there are two other key settings. The Enable LMHOSTS Lookup option determines what the computer will do if all other attempts to resolve the NetBIOS name fail. If selected, the computer will check a local file known as the LMHOSTS file. This file is sometimes used to create custom NetBIOS computer name-to-IP mappings. If LMHOSTS files are in use on a network and there is a centralized store for the custom LMHOSTS file, clicking the Import LMHOSTS button allows you to import the file. The NetBIOS Setting section determines whether or not NetBIOS over TCP/IP (NetBT) and WINS are used. The default setting is usually best. In pure Active Directory networks, WINS is not required.

For more information on WINS, see "Windows Internet Naming Service (WINS)" on page 27.

The Options tab displays the single entry, TCP/IP Filtering. When you select this option and click Properties, the TCP/IP Filtering dialog box opens, as shown in Figure 2-6 on the next page. If you select Enable TCP/IP Filtering (All Adapters), you can then specify allowed and blocked TCP and UDP ports as well as which IP protocols are permitted for traffic destined for this computer. This is a security feature that allows you to block IP protocols and TCP or UDP ports that should not be used on the network. By filtering traffic that you don't need for communication, you also block the possibility of malicious users using those ports as access points to your computer.

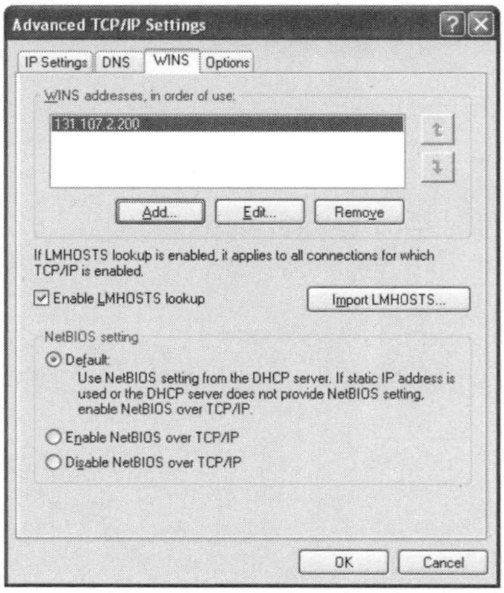

Figure 2-5. Use the WINS tab to configure WINS settings.

caution Make sure you do not block any traffic ports unless you have a specific security reason for doing so. Blocking traffic limits the functionality of TCP/IP and what you will be able to do on your network. If security is a major concern, you can block any traffic that you know will not be used, but keep in mind that greater restrictions might cause you to lose some network functionality.

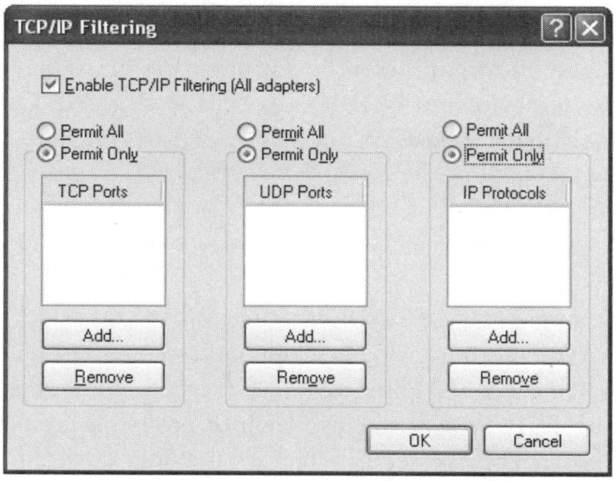

Figure 2-6. You can specify IP protocols and TCP or UDP ports that you want to allow or block using IP filtering.

For more details on using filtering to enhance security under Windows XP, see Chapter 20, "Maintaining Network Security."

Understanding Internet Protocol Version 6 (IPv6)

When TCP/IP was first developed, the Internet Protocol version 4 (IPv4) addressing scheme seemed so large that it could never run out of IP addresses. However, with the hundreds of millions of hosts on the Internet today, the limits of IPv4's address space is being felt. With IPv4, there is considerable concern about the possibility of IP address exhaustion despite attempts to work around the problem with techniques such as NAT and subnetting. In anticipation of this, the successor to IPv4 has been designed by the Internet Engineering Task Force (IETF). The new standard, IPv6, will utilize a much larger addressing space (128 bits instead of IPv4's 32 bits), allowing a multitude of new addresses. Additionally, IPv6 is designed from the ground up to provide easier configuration and better built-in security.

> **note** IPv6 provides so many potential IP addresses that every man, woman, and child on Earth could maintain their own dedicated range of IP addresses, and that range could be as large as the entire address space available for the Internet under IPv4!

Because any new IP addressing scheme will eventually affect every computer on the Internet, the details must be well established and migration paths must be clearly defined. It would not be feasible to suddenly switch addressing schemes and have millions of hosts unable to communicate with each other. IPv6 is currently undergoing testing, and some Web sites are not supporting the standard. Eventually, however, the Internet's entire IP infrastructure will migrate to IPv6.

IPv6 is provided in Windows XP mainly for software developers. You can install IPv6 and use it for testing and application development purposes. However, it should be noted that technical support for IPv6 as a production protocol is not provided, so you'll have to experiment with it at your own risk.

Using IPv6 with Windows XP

The following steps will help you install the developer preview IPv6 protocol stack on your computer. Once installed, the IPv6 protocol stack will not appear in the Properties dialog box for any network interface. Not many Web sites or networks currently support IPv6 connections, but the number is growing rapidly. To install IPv6 on Windows XP, follow these steps:

1 Log on to the computer using an account with administrative privileges.

2 From the Start menu click Run.

3 Type **cmd** in the text box that appears.

4 In the window that opens, type the command **ipv6 install** and press Enter. If the installation succeeds, you'll see the message "Succeeded."

5 To reverse the process, repeat steps 1–4 but type the command **ipv6 uninstall** instead. Uninstalling will take a few more seconds and will require that you restart the machine.

Once the IPv6 protocol stack is installed on a Windows XP computer, it is possible to attach that computer to the publicly accessible IPv6 backbone. For details about connecting to this developmental IPv6 backbone, visit *www.6bone.com*. For additional information about the use of IPv6 and Windows XP as well as the available IPv6 tools, be sure to check the Microsoft Web site link that provides IPv6 information at *www.microsoft.com/ipv6*.

Other Networking Protocols

Although the TCP/IP protocol suite is by far the most ubiquitous networking protocol suite, there are other network protocols. The remainder of this chapter examines protocols that come into play when working in a mixed operating system environment. Keep in mind that if you are on a pure Windows network, you do not need to use any other protocols besides TCP/IP. In fact, you might even be working in a mixed network that only uses TCP/IP because many other operating systems also take advantage of all that TCP/IP has to offer.

> This chapter explores the protocol side of mixed networks. However, you can learn more about Windows XP's interoperability with other networks in Chapter 18, "Interconnectivity with Other Systems."

Internetwork Packet Exchange (IPX)

The IPX protocol was developed by Novell, Inc. for its NetWare family of operating systems. At one point in the past, NetWare was the most widely distributed server platform in use. NetWare's market share has somewhat diminished since then, but it is still possible that Windows and NetWare might be required to coexist for some time. With newer versions of NetWare, the support for TCP/IP has greatly improved. Regardless, it is still very likely that if NetWare is present, support for IPX will be useful if not required.

IPX Addressing

IPX, like IP, requires that all hosts have unique addresses. IPX addresses are 80 bits in length and include a network portion and a node portion. In addition to a node and network portion, there is a component known as the *socket number*. All IPX addresses are stored in a hexadecimal format. The following is a description of the key IPX network addressing components:

- **Network number.** The first 32 bits of any IPX address is the network portion of the address and is assigned manually by an administrator. Typically, this simple number is 0001 or 1000. Because IPX does not transport over the Internet (which uses IP), there is no need for complex unique addresses. A site with six IPX segments could use (in binary form) 0001, 0002, and 0003 to 0006 to separate the six networks.

- **Host number.** The remaining 48 bits are (in most cases) the MAC address of the NIC participating in the IPX network. Some MAC addresses are programmable, so this portion of the address is also potentially manageable. But in most cases, the host number is a fixed value.

- **Socket number.** The socket number identifies a process running on an IPX node and is analogous to a TCP or UDP port. It is used to determine what application the incoming or outgoing traffic should be routed to.

- **Service Advertising Protocol (SAP).** SAP is a broadcast protocol used to advertise the set of service names and addresses across the IPX network and to resolve service names to the IPX network and node addresses. Each server advertises the services offered using a numeric type, name, and network address. IPX routers accumulate this information to use in IPX routing activities.

Implementing IPX with Windows XP

You can install the IPX protocol on Windows XP so that Windows XP can function in an IPX network. The following steps are required to install support for the IPX environment under Windows XP:

1 From the Start menu, open Network Connections.

2 Locate the connection to the network. It will probably be labeled with the default name, Local Area Connection.

3 Right-click the Local Area Connection icon, and choose Properties from the shortcut menu.

4 On the General tab, click the Install button.

5 In the Select Network Component Type dialog box, select Client, and click Add.

6 Select Client Service For NetWare, as shown in Figure 2-7 on the next page, and click OK. This will install the NetWare client components as well as Microsoft's NWLink IPX/SPX/NetBIOS protocol.

After a few moments, the client and IPX/SPX protocol stack will be installed and will appear in the Local Area Connection Properties dialog box.

Chapter 2

> **note** Some NetWare environments might require the use of Novell's own NetWare client and IPX protocol software. Contact your network administrator to determine if this is the case before attempting to use the Microsoft implementation of IPX.

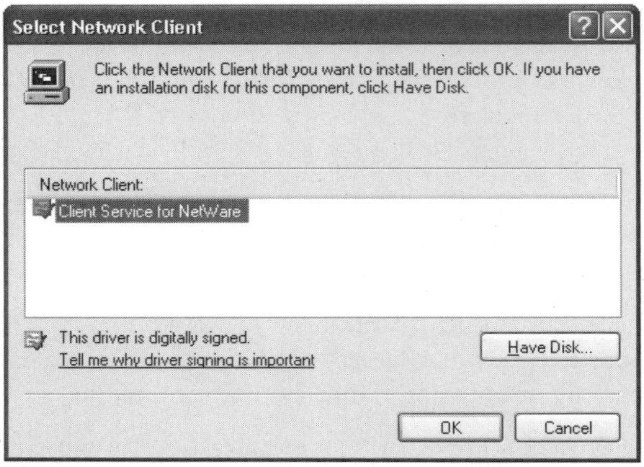

Figure 2-7. Choose the protocol you want to install.

AppleTalk

Created by Apple for Macintosh computers, AppleTalk was originally designed to support small workgroups, but was later revised to support larger, more complex networks. On an AppleTalk network, addressing is divided into four components: zones, networks, nodes, and sockets. All addresses are assigned dynamically on an AppleTalk network. When a node joins the network, it selects an address and sends out a broadcast to determine whether anyone replies at that address. If another node replies, the newly joined node chooses another address. This process repeats until the new node obtains an available network address. A brief explanation of the four components in AppleTalk addressing follows:

- **Zones.** A zone is a collection of individual nodes or networks. Zone membership is a user-configured characteristic. Nodes and networks need not be connected to the same network segment to share zone membership.

- **Networks.** A collection of nodes connected to the same switch, bridge, or router is considered a member of the same network. This is equivalent to a physical network segment. There are two types of AppleTalk networks: extended and nonextended. *Extended* networks can use what Apple refers to as a *cable range* to assign multiple network numbers to a single physical segment. This is conceptually similar to an IP virtual LAN (VLAN). *Nonextended* networks are physical segments that all share the same network number.

Managing Broadcast Protocols in Mixed OS Environments

Many network protocols make extensive use of broadcasts to maintain consistent communications across the network. Although this is rarely an issue on smaller networks, as networks begin to scale upward, broadcasting can result in out-of-control traffic that can be crippling. The biggest offenders when it comes to generating broadcast traffic include SAP and AppleTalk.

To prevent broadcast traffic from consuming an inordinate amount of the bandwidth available on the network, routing must be used. Routers can be configured to block broadcasts. This ability to segregate broadcast traffic allows a broadcast-dependent protocol such as SAP to operate on one portion of the network without negatively impacting the rest of the network.

- **Nodes.** The AppleTalk term node has the same meaning as the generic terms node, host, client, and so forth. Any device connected to the network that is capable of participating in networked communications is a node.

- **Sockets.** Sockets are the equivalent of the TCP or UDP port number. Sockets identify applications that are sending and receiving data.

Implementing AppleTalk with Windows XP

Although Windows XP can communicate with AppleTalk-enabled computers, the communication is indirect. Windows XP does not come with a user installable AppleTalk protocol suite. Earlier versions of Windows did support various forms of the AppleTalk protocol suite, but Windows XP does not. Server versions of Windows 2000, however, continue to offer support for AppleTalk clients, and Windows XP Professional users can access an AppleTalk network when a server version of Windows 2000 acts as an intermediary. Only then can you access files and printing services in the AppleTalk environment from Windows XP.

The lack of support for AppleTalk is not likely to be of significant concern for very long. Newer Apple operating systems, such as Mac OS X, include robust support for TCP/IP, so interconnectivity between those systems is much easier.

note Both NetWare and Mac OS systems have moved away from proprietary protocols and support TCP/IP as their standard protocol suite (much as Microsoft moved away from NetBIOS to use only TCP/IP in pure Active Directory environments). However, an understanding of these legacy protocols is still important because their use is still widespread.

Avoiding Spanning Tree Protocol Communication Problems

One of the more insidious problems that can occur on a mixed operating system network is incompatibilities with protocols used by networking devices. These incompatibilities often manifest themselves sporadically and can be extremely hard to track down. One very real concern with AppleTalk-enabled hosts is a known defect that causes AppleTalk communications to occasionally fail when the Spanning Tree Protocol (STP) is in use. STP is used on a wide range of network devices to provide redundancy. For example, a pair of network switches can have two links connecting each other together, so that if either link fails, communication can still occur. To prevent communication loops (which can disable the whole network), STP is used to make one of the links inactive, but kept on standby. STP is active by default on a great number of network devices. When it is active, computers using the AppleTalk protocol are likely to experience serious communications problems. The solution is to either move to another network protocol (such as IP) or to disable STP.

Creating Network Connections

To create any kind of network connection, you must have two components—hardware that allows your computer to connect to the physical network and software that allows your computer to communicate on the network. Microsoft Windows XP includes the software you need to create network connections, but you must determine what hardware you need and install it before you can set up the networking software. Your computer might have preconfigured networking hardware, but there are a number of different network solutions that you can employ, and you should understand them all before you make a final decision on which to employ.

In this chapter, network hardware, types of networks, and connections will be explored, with an emphasis on networking your local Windows XP computer.

Understanding Network Hardware Components

Network hardware enables a computer to connect to other computers, either directly or via a shared network medium. Without networking hardware, each computer lives on its own island, so to speak. Even if you are simply accessing the Internet, your computer must have either a dial-up modem or some kind of broadband hardware in order to connect. Local area connections are no different—a hardware device is required. That hardware device is called a *network adapter*. The network adapter connects to the network using wiring or a form of wireless media; depending on your network, you might also need a device that centralizes the connections, such as a hub, a switch, or an access point (depending on the type of network you're connecting to). The following sections introduce you to the primary hardware devices you'll encounter when networking.

Installing a Network Adapter

A network adapter works like any other internal or external device that you might install on Windows XP. The ways in which network adapters interface with your computer depends on the type of adapter you use. *Network interface cards (NICs)*, for instance, are typically sold as internal cards that plug into expansion slots on the computer's motherboard. Network adapters are increasingly being integrated directly onto the motherboard in desktop and laptop computers. Many laptop computers also now come with built-in wireless LAN adapters. Network adapters are also available as external devices that can connect to your computer's universal serial bus (USB) port or the PC Card slots on a laptop.

Once the network adapter is installed, your computer has the capability to physically connect to the network, and the necessary networking software can be configured in Windows XP. With most types of networks, cabling is used to connect the network adapter to other computers, either directly or via a centralized hub (see "Connecting with Hubs and Switches," opposite). Most cabled network adapters are Ethernet NICs, which you can learn more about in "Ethernet Networks," page 60.

Network adapters are readily available at all computer stores and on the Internet. Their prices vary, but most standard internal NICs will cost you around $30 and up, as will external USB network adapters. PC Cards for laptop computers are a little pricier. Wireless adapters cost even more. You have plenty of brands to choose from, but they all perform the same function. Commonly used brands include 3Com (*www.3com.com*), Intel (*www.intel.com*), and Linksys (*www.linksys.com*), but you'll find many others. Check your favorite computer store for its current offerings.

> **note** Although it can be tempting to buy the cheapest network adapter available, it never hurts to do a little research before making the purchase. Different types of network adapters provide different features, such as hardware acceleration of some tasks (reducing the demands on the system CPU for network requests) and built-in encryption. It's also important to note that some companies do a far better job of updating their adapter drivers than others, and high-quality driver software is key to system stability.

Connecting with Hubs and Switches

Most forms of wired networks utilize central concentrating devices that allow individual computers to be connected and disconnected from a network without disabling the entire network segment. The two most common forms of concentration device are hubs and switches.

A *hub* is a device that provides a central link to the computers on a network segment. All computers connected to a hub share the same network bandwidth, and in Ethernet networks, even compete with one another's traffic. A *switch,* on the other hand, is a device that actively separates each connection so that they all have a full dedicated pipeline between any other machine on the same switch and do not compete with one another's traffic for intercomputer communication (although the uplink connection to other networks, if present, is still shared). Switches provide higher-speed connections with greater security.

In either case—using hubs or switches—each computer connects to the device. In large office environments (as well as in some modern homes) where network connection jacks are mounted in walls (like phone jacks), the wiring is typically run to a *patch bay* located in a wiring closet, and each jack is patched over to a port on a hub or switch. For home and small office networks, however, external devices are almost always used.

A typical hub or switch has the requisite row of RJ-45 ports into which the RJ-45 network cables are plugged (often these are on the back of the unit along with the power cord connection, but not always). The front of the device generally has a bank of LED lights that light up or blink to show which ports are connected and to show traffic moving through the ports. On some devices, additional LEDs show other information, such as the total volume of traffic the network is handling at any given moment. Standard hubs and switches for home networks usually provide four or eight ports for connections (although some devices for large corporate networks provide up to 24 ports). Depending on the model of device you purchase, you can even link them together in a daisy chain format. You'll need to carefully read the product's documentation to determine if daisy chaining hubs and switches together is supported.

Some products on the market today also combine firewall capabilities and routing functions. Simple home hubs can cost as little as $50, whereas larger hubs and switches with additional features can cost upwards of $500. The transfer speed of the device also impacts the cost, which is discussed in "Choosing a Network Type," page 55.

note   Hubs are also used in wireless networks where they are called *access points*, but of course the access point connects to the computers wirelessly rather than with cabling. For more information about setting up a wireless network, see Chapter 19, "Wireless Networking."

Wiring the Network

By definition, all nonwireless networks use some kind of wiring that connects computers to hubs or to each other. The wiring used in today's networks is relatively standard, so you don't have to memorize many different specifications in order to network computers. When networking computers, you will typically use one of the following cable types:

- **Null modem cable.** A null modem cable is used to connect two computers using their serial ports. The computers do not use a NIC, but instead send and receive data over the ports you have connected. A null modem cable connects identical pins on both attached computer ports except it crosses over the send and receive pins so communication can take place between the two machines. Null modem cables provide good temporary solutions, but they are slow.

- **DirectParallel.** A DirectParallel cable is a lot like a null modem cable except you use the computers' parallel ports to connect two PCs rather than the serial ports that are used with a null modem cable. Like a null modem cable connection, a DirectParallel cable makes a good temporary networking solution, but the speed, although faster than a serial connection, is still slow.

- **RJ-11 cable.** RJ-11 cables are standard telephone cables. Each time you plug a phone into a wall outlet or plug a phone line into your computer's modem, you use an RJ-11 cable. RJ-11 cables can be used in a specialized network called Home Phoneline Network Alliance (HomePNA) where the phone lines inside your home are used to network computers together instead of additional cables.

- **RJ-45 cable.** RJ-45 cables are by far the most common kind of network cabling in use today. They are used primarily in Ethernet networks. Category 5 cables, consisting of eight wires in four twisted pairs with RJ-45 connectors, are currently the standard for 100 megabit per second (Mbps) network cabling. You'll find the cable in all kinds of colors and lengths at your favorite computer store, usually at an inexpensive price.

- **Crossover cable.** Crossover cables look like standard Category 5 cables, but the wires inside the cable are reversed (crossed over), so that signals can be exchanged between the two computers without using a hub or switch. This solution works great when you are only connecting two computers, but should you add a third computer, you'll need a hub. Crossover cables work well for the smallest networks as well as temporary file transfer situations because, unlike null modem cables, they provide a fast network connection.

These cabling types are discussed further in relation to the types of networks they serve in "Choosing a Network Type," page 55.

InsideOut

Networking out of the Box

Because home and small office networking has become so popular these days, your computer store will likely provide complete networking kits for Ethernet, wireless, HomePNA, and possibly even Powerline networks (see the next section). These kits usually provide a few network adapter cards, wiring (if necessary), and a hub (if necessary), along with instructions and possibly even setup software to help you. In many cases, the boxed version of a network is less expensive than buying the components individually, but of course, you'll need to be a smart shopper and compare labels to make a decision. Before you shop for networking hardware, it is a good idea to prepare a checklist of items you will need beforehand to keep you on track; otherwise, it is easy to get distracted by the many available products and options.

Adding Routers and Residential Gateways

In addition to basic hubs and switches, you'll find plenty of router or residential gateway devices on sale in the networking section of most computer stores. In the past, these devices were not needed for small networks, but with Internet connection sharing of Digital Subscriber Line (DSL) and cable Internet connections, these devices can be quite useful. Both can manage the connection between your network and other networks, such as the Internet, and some come with additional features that can enhance security.

A *router* manages traffic entering and leaving the network from the Internet or other network segments. It maintains internal tables that guide it in determining how to forward outbound traffic to remote destinations and inbound traffic to systems on the local network segment. The default gateway address configured for most TCP/IP configurations, as discussed in Chapter 2, "Configuring TCP/IP and Other Protocols," normally points to the address of a router.

A residential gateway, on the other hand, is a router with additional features that are quite useful in most home and small office networks. Residential gateways typically combine the features of a router, a hub or switch, a firewall, a network address translation device (described below), and often a Dynamic Host Configuration Protocol (DHCP) server. Some residential gateways even have built-in wireless access points.

So how does a router or residential gateway work, and do you need one? A router or residential gateway is designed to be placed between the Internet and your LAN. The following illustration shows how the router or residential gateway provides the connection from your LAN to your DSL or cable modem.

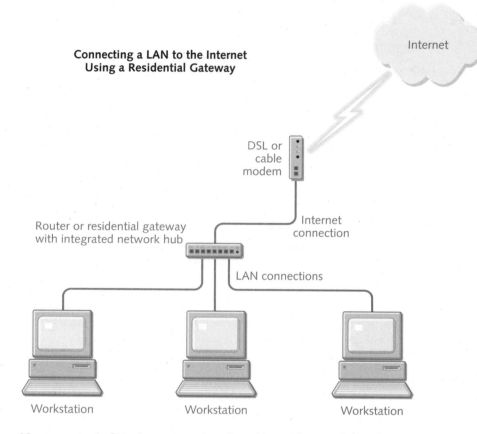

Connecting a LAN to the Internet Using a Residential Gateway

No computer is directly connected to the cable modem, and therefore no computer is directly connected to the Internet. There are two primary benefits of this kind of setup:

- No single computer acts as the gateway to the Internet. If you use Internet Connection Sharing (ICS), all Internet traffic and requests are handled by the ICS host computer (see "Using Internet Connection Sharing," page 301, to learn more). With a router or residential gateway, the device handles all Internet requests and return traffic so that an ICS host does not have to. This eliminates the performance burden placed on the computer running ICS. Additionally, if the network computer assigned to run ICS is down, no one on the LAN can access the Internet. But with a router or residential gateway running, only the client computer accessing the Internet needs to be running. The downside of course is that a router or residential gateway costs around $100 for a basic model and more like $200–$300 for one with a firewall, remote management, and switching capabilities, whereas ICS is a free software solution included with Windows XP.

- The more important benefit of a residential gateway is security. Most residential gateways provide security through a combination of firewalls and network address translation. *Firewalls* block outside networks from sending traffic to the devices they protect, limiting even response traffic to that specifically requested via outbound connections from systems behind the firewall. Many firewalls block any traffic that crosses them, other than traffic to and from specified addresses or to and from systems using virtual private network (VPN) tunnels. You can read more about firewalls in Chapter 5, "Using Internet Connection Firewall." *Network address translation (NAT)* is a feature originally designed to extend IP networks that also provides a form of security by hiding the internal IP addresses of a LAN from the Internet (or other destination of the residential gateway). NAT translates the internal IP addresses of the LAN to a different IP address range. These addresses are then used for communications on the Internet. If a hacker decides to break into your network, he or she must have the real IP address of a computer on your LAN, and with NAT, those IP addresses are not visible. Therefore, any hacker attacks using IP addressing schemes simply fall apart at the residential gateway because the IP address (of the residential gateway) that allows the hacker to access your residential gateway is not the IP address that any of the machines on your LAN are using; so, the hacker is stopped at the gateway. Of course, not all routers and residential gateways provide this service, but it is common to most of them. As an example, Linksys (*www.linksys.com*), 3Com (*www.3com.com*), and NetGear (*www.netgear.com*) provide several different kinds of residential gateways that all perform the same tasks but provide different features. You'll find these same features in other manufacturers' models as well.

> For more information on security, see Chapter 20, "Maintaining Network Security."

> **tip** Some routers and residential gateways provide DHCP services in which the router leases IP addresses to your internal network clients so that Automatic Private IP Addressing (APIPA) is not needed. This feature can provide greater client control and IP address management, especially in a growing network. For more information on DHCP, see "Dynamic and Static Addressing," page 27.

Whether you use a router or residential gateway depends on your needs, Internet usage, and cash flow. (Keep in mind that many devices currently on the market that would meet the definition of a residential gateway are sold as *routers with additional security features*). However, the sheer number of attacks launched at systems connected to the Internet makes the use of a residential gateway with built-in security features a

Chapter 3

prudent choice, particularly if you intend to connect more than one system to the network. If you decide that a residential gateway is right for you, make sure you buy one that explicitly states that it is compatible with Windows XP. Routers and residential gateways that are compatible with Windows XP will support the Universal Plug and Play (UPnP) standard, which allows Windows XP Remote Assistance and Windows Messenger to work over the Internet without complication. Without UPnP support, you're likely to have problems configuring these features to work properly without interference from any built-in firewalls.

tip   Some routers and residential gateways can also work with additional third-party security software, such as ZoneAlarm (*www.zonealarm.com*). If security is a serious issue for you, be sure to do some homework before purchasing a residential gateway so that you can find the model that supports the security and software features you need. Most manufacturers' Web sites have online documentation about their products, so you can easily study and compare products at home.

InsideOut

Getting to Know NAT

NAT is a standard previously used by server software to manage network traffic between segments as well as provide security between a private network and the Internet. You can think of NAT as a translator tool that keeps the IP addresses of one LAN separate from another. In the case of Internet access, NAT can allow the router or residential gateway to act as one computer using an IP address in a different range. For example, suppose your office network has 10 computers that use a DSL modem connection, and your internal network's IP address range is 10.0.0.1–10.0.0.10. Instead of each computer using a different IP address to access the Internet, NAT allows the router or gateway to use one IP address in a completely different class and range, such as 207.46.197.100. If an Internet hacker tries to use the 207.46.197.100 address to hack into the network, there is nothing to hack into because there is no actual computer with that IP address. Instead, the real network uses a different range and simply hides behind NAT.

In large IP networks, NAT is used to manage routing between different network segments where IP addressing between network clients and different subnets can be complicated and confusing. In many cases, NAT helps network administrators using router hardware to solve connectivity issues and problems between different network divisions. If you are interested in the technical details of NAT, you can access RFC 1631 on the Internet to learn more. A *Request for Comment (RFC)* is an official document of the Internet Engineering Task Force (IETF) that specifies the details of new Internet specifications or protocols. RFCs can be found on the Internet by using a Web search engine and entering the RFC number, in this case, **RFC 1631**.

Choosing a Network Type

Now that you are familiar with the different types of network hardware you will typically use when networking with Windows XP, this section examines the kinds of networks that are available. So, what hardware products do you need for the kind of network you want, and what performance benefits will you get from one network type to the next? These questions can be difficult to answer, but once you have identified your networking goals and budget, you can determine the kind of network that will best suit your needs. This section explores the different types of networks you can choose when creating a home or small- to medium-size office network.

> To learn more about setting up LANs, see Chapter 10, "Managing Workgroup Connections," where you'll also find a number of network scenarios and illustrations that explore different kinds of setups and configurations.

Direct Cable Connection (DCC)

Let's assume that you travel with a laptop computer to a client's site. You are not a part of the client's network, and you don't need to be a part of it on a permanent basis. However, you need to copy a number of files from a computer at the client site. The files are too large for floppy disks, and the client's computer is not equipped with a Zip or Jazz drive, or a CD burner. To easily transfer the files, you can use a DCC connection. This kind of simple network connection connects two computers using a serial cable, a DirectParallel cable, a modem, or even an Integrated Services Digital Network (ISDN) device. For computers without network adapter cards or in the case of transfers from handheld devices, such as those using the Windows CE operating system, a DCC connection is a great temporary connection you can use to transfer files. You can also use a DCC connection to connect a non-networked computer to a network on a temporary basis. When connected to a computer connected to another network, you might be able to access additional network resources, depending on permissions assigned to those resources. DCC can be a lifesaver in many situations where you need quick and easy connectivity without additional hardware. However, DCC connections tend to be slow, especially null modem cable connections using a serial port. You'll find that connection speeds are often in the modem range of approximately 24 Kbps to 50 Kbps.

DirectParallel cables that connect the parallel ports on two computers work faster, and Windows XP supports standard or basic 4-bit cables, Enhanced Capabilities Port (ECP) cables, and Universal Cable Module cables. You can purchase null modem cables at any computer store, and you can also find DirectParallel cables at *www.lpt.com*. Overall, the direct connection method is designed to be a quick networking fix, not a true networking solution.

You can establish a DCC connection between a Windows XP computer and any other Microsoft Windows computer that supports DCC (Windows 95, Windows 98, Windows Me, Windows 2000, or another Windows XP computer) using a null modem cable or a

Part 1: Windows XP Networking

DirectParallel cable. When you create a DCC network, you must first attach the two computers together using the desired cable type. When you create a DCC network, one computer acts as the *host* computer, and the other computer acts as the *guest*. The guest computer accesses information on the host computer, but the host computer cannot access information on the guest. This solution is a great way to transfer files from one computer to another, but it is not a solution for true network communications between the two computers. Once you have the cable connected between the computers, you can set up the host computer. To set up the host computer, follow these steps:

1 Log on to Windows XP with a user account that has administrative privileges. You cannot set up a DCC host unless your account has administrative privileges.

2 Open Network Connections. From the Windows XP Start menu, choose Connect To, Show All Connections; from the Classic Start menu, choose Settings, Network Connections.

3 In the task pane at the left under Network Tasks, select Create A New Connection. Click Next on the New Connection Wizard's opening page.

4 On the Network Connection Type page of the wizard, shown in Figure 3-1, select Set Up An Advanced Connection and click Next.

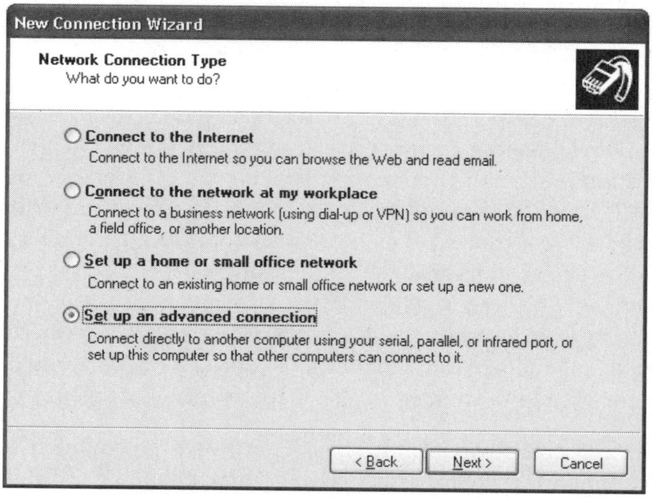

Figure 3-1. Select the Advanced Connection option to create a DCC network.

5 On the Advanced Connection Options page, select Connect Directly To Another Computer and click Next.

6 On the Host Or Guest page, shown in Figure 3-2, select the Host option and click Next.

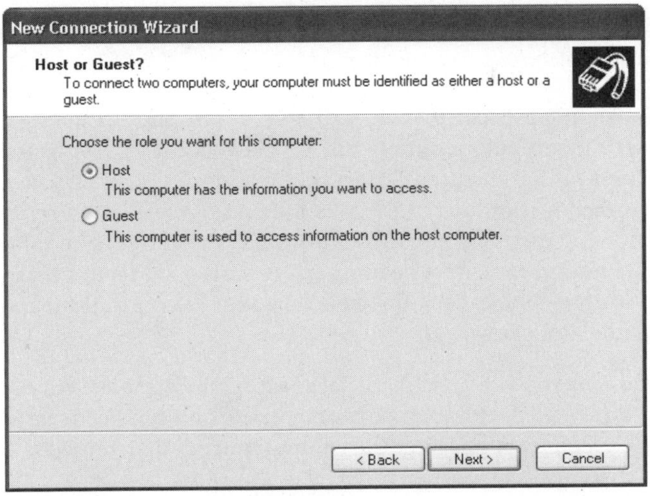

Chapter 3: Creating Network Connections

Figure 3-2. Select the Host option for the computer that will be accessed by the guest computer.

7 On the Connection Device page of the wizard, select the port that you want to use for the connection, such as Infrared Port, DirectParallel, or Communications Port, from the list. The port you select is configured for DCC. You cannot use a port that currently has another device attached to it. Click Next.

8 On the User Permissions page, select which users are allowed to access this host through the DCC connection. Notice that you can also create additional user accounts as needed directly from this window, as shown in Figure 3-3. Make your selections and click Next.

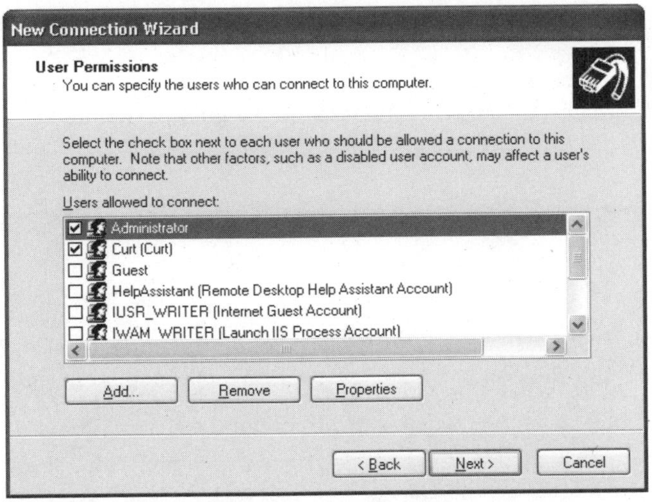

Figure 3-3. Select the users who can access the host computer over the DCC connection.

9 Click Finish. The new connection appears in the Network Connections window as Incoming Connections.

Once you have the host set up, your next task is to set up the guest computer. For Windows XP computers, simply use the New Connection Wizard again and select the Guest option instead of Host on the wizard's Host Or Guest page. If you are using another version of Windows as the guest, refer to that operating system's help files for setup instructions. In Windows XP, the connection on the guest computer appears under the Direct heading in Network Connections, as you can see in Figure 3-4. Simply double-click the icon to make the connection, and then enter a valid user name and password.

Keep in mind that you can create multiple DCC connections to connect different pairs of computers as needed, although only one connection can be active at a time. Simply create the DCC connections, enter the computer name that you want to connect to, and select the appropriate port.

Figure 3-4. The DCC connection appears on the guest computer in Network Connections under the Direct heading.

InsideOut

Managing Direct Connection Security

If you are using DCC for a device such as a palmtop computer, you can bypass the security option for the user name and password by following these easy steps:

1 On the host computer, open Network Connections.

2 Right-click the Incoming Connection item and choose Properties.

3 On the Users tab, select the check box labeled Always Allow Directly Connected Devices Such As Palmtop Computers To Connect Without Providing A Password. Click OK.

On the other hand, to increase security, you can also require that secure passwords and data encryption be used on the DCC network connection. Typically, you don't need these highly secure methods for such an ad hoc connectivity solution (if others can access your computer directly, chances are they're already bypassing much of your security), but the options are easy to configure and seamless to use. To require data encryption for the DCC connection, follow these steps:

1 On the host computer, right-click the Incoming Connections item and choose Properties. On the Users tab, select Require All Users To Secure Their Passwords And Data. Note that this setting applies to other computers that connect to the host, not devices such as palmtop computers. Click OK.

2 On the guest computer, open Network Connections, right-click the DCC item, and choose Properties. On the Security tab, shown in Figure 3-5, select Typical; then select Require Secured Password from the Validate My Identity As Follows list. Finally, select Require Data Encryption (Disconnect If None) and click OK.

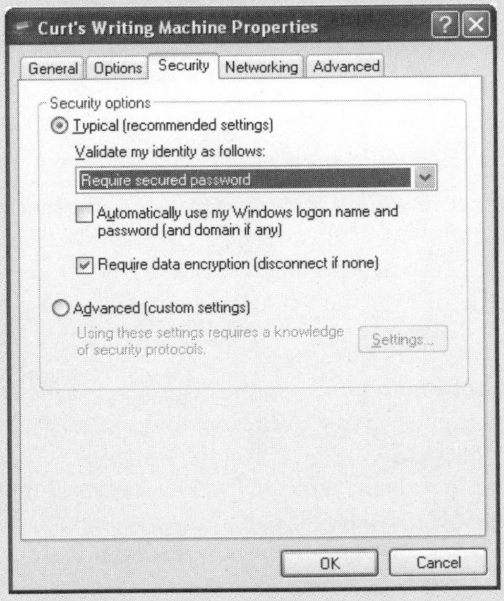

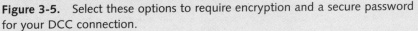

Figure 3-5. Select these options to require encryption and a secure password for your DCC connection.

Ethernet Networks

Ethernet is a networking standard that has been around since the mid 1970s when Xerox introduced the first Ethernet product. Ethernet is a network standard that is defined by the Institute of Electrical and Electronics Engineers (IEEE) 802.3 specification. It has been and continues to be overwhelmingly popular. In fact, most home and small office networks are Ethernet networks, and the vast majority of larger networks use Ethernet as well. For this reason, most NICs and networking equipment, except for more specialized networks like HomePNA and wireless, use the Ethernet standard. Even wireless networks use a form of Ethernet. When you set out to connect a group of computers using NICs, a hub, and RJ-45 cables, you are creating an Ethernet network.

So, what is Ethernet exactly? *Ethernet* is a set of specifications that define how the hardware used to create a network communicates and functions. For this reason, you can use network adapter cards created by different manufacturers and even a network hub created by yet another manufacturer, and all of the components will work together. Manufacturers adhere to the Ethernet 802.3 specification so that you can mix and match hardware without problems. If you want to read about the 802.3 specification, you can find it using a quick search on the Internet, but the rest of this section highlights the pertinent information. In fact, you'll find a few terms and concepts that you might also see listed on manufacturers' Ethernet documentation and packaging.

How Ethernet Sends Data

The 802.3 specification defines how data must be sent over an Ethernet network. Ethernet breaks data into small pieces called *frames*. Each frame contains between 46 and 1500 bytes of data. When you send data over an Ethernet network, the data is broken down into frames, sent over the wire, and then reassembled by the receiving computer.

Each frame contains header information noting the beginning of the frame, where it is coming from, and where it is going. Additionally, each frame has a component called a *cyclical redundancy check (CRC)*. The CRC allows the receiving computer to check the frame to make sure that the data in the frame has arrived intact. If it has not, the receiving computer can use the header information to request that the sending computer resend the data. This frame-sending format has been used for years and is highly reliable.

Ethernet is considered a *bus* topology, which refers to the shared physical layout of the network. More commonly, Ethernet is called a *star-bus* topology because all computers radiate from a central hub that resembles a star pattern, as shown in the following illustration.

Chapter 3: Creating Network Connections

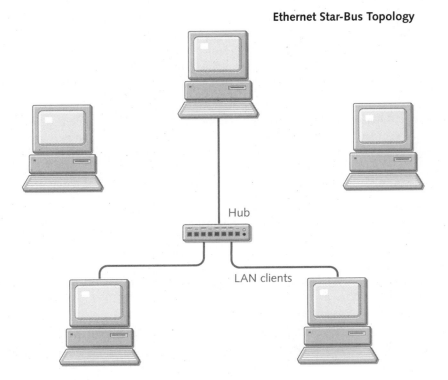

Ethernet Star-Bus Topology

Hub

LAN clients

Access Method

Ethernet networks use the Carrier Sense Multiple Access with Collision Detection (CSMA/CD) access method to send data over the network and manage transmission problems. (In fact, if you have been studying residential gateways and related products, you might have noticed that the CSMA/CD method appears on the products' specification sheets.) CSMA/CD does not need to be configured—it just tells you that the device fully supports Ethernet's mechanism for sending data.

CSMA/CD uses a method where computers *listen* to the network cable to see if any other computers are transmitting frames. If not, the computer sends the data. If there is traffic, the computer waits until the line is clear. In the event that two computers transmit data on the wire at the same time, a *collision* will occur. In this case, the data is destroyed. However, the Collision Detection feature of CSMA/CD enables the computers to detect the collision so that data can be resent.

Ethernet Speed

Ethernet devices can support three speed standards:

- **10Base-T.** 10Base-T is an Ethernet standard that simply means 10 Mbps baseband over twisted-pair wiring. *Baseband* means a single message is carried at a time (broadband carries multiple messages simultaneously). Remember that Ethernet networks typically use unshielded twisted-pair (UTP) wiring with RJ-45 connectors, which are wider versions of the standard RJ-11 telephone connectors found at the back of your phone and plugged into phone jacks. 10Base-T is an older Ethernet standard and is capable of a maximum speed of 10 Mbps.

- **100Base-T (Fast Ethernet).** 100Base-T networks use the same Ethernet standard, but are capable of up to 100 Mbps. Most hubs and network adapters sold today are considered 10/100 Ethernet. This means that they can automatically adjust for 10 Mbps communication or 100 Mbps communication, depending on what is supported by the rest of the network. Fast Ethernet requires at least Category 5 quality UTP wiring.

- **1000Base-T (Gigabit Ethernet).** Gigabit Ethernet is a new speed standard of 1000 Mbps, or 1 gigabit per second (Gbps). You'll find a number of Gigabit hubs and NICs at your local computer store. This standard is great for high-speed video transfer and related multimedia applications. To take full advantage of Gigabit Ethernet, all computers should be outfitted with a 1 Gbps NIC, and you'll also need a 1 Gbps hub. The 1000Base-T standard also requires at least Category 5 quality UTP wiring.

> **note** Other standards for Ethernet cabling exist, such as 10Base-2 (often referred to as *thinnet)* or 10Base-5 (also known as *thicknet)*. These standards use coaxial cabling in a true bus configuration. All systems must be connected in series (like links in a chain) to maintain the network's integrity, and a break anywhere in the cabling (or even an improperly disconnected workstation) can bring down an entire segment. These older standards are becoming less and less common, and are undesirable for new installations.

Is Ethernet Right for You?

Now that you know a little about Ethernet, you might wonder whether Ethernet is the kind of network you need. Table 3-1 explores the fundamental issues to consider before using Ethernet.

Table 3-1. Ethernet Networking Features

Networking Issue	Ethernet Feature or Failure
Expense and availability	Ethernet NICs, hubs, wiring, and gateways are all reasonably priced. You can also find Ethernet kits. All major networking manufacturers produce Ethernet products, and you can find Ethernet NICs for as little as $30. Hubs and switches can cost from $40 to $400 for models combining firewalls and switches for large workgroups.

Table 3-1. *(continued)*

Networking Issue	Ethernet Feature or Failure
Setup	Easy. Windows XP can automatically install NICs, and hub configuration is easy.
Speed	Up to 1 Gbps with 10/100 being the standard at this time. Ethernet is the fastest type of network for the home or small office.
Cabling	Cabling can be difficult to run in homes or existing businesses and can be an eyesore if wall outlets are not available or installed.
Reliability	Excellent.

If you decide that an Ethernet network is right for you, keep the following issues in mind:

- You need NICs, a hub with enough ports for your network (or multiple hubs), and Category 5 cabling.

- Each cable length is limited to a maximum of 328 feet, which normally isn't a problem in a home or small office network.

- Residential gateways are available that work with Ethernet if you want to use a gateway instead of ICS.

For more information about ICS, see "Using Internet Connection Sharing," page 301.

HomePNA Networks

HomePNA is a standard that was introduced a few years ago when home and small office networking started to become popular. A HomePNA network uses internal PCI NICs or external USB NICs like Ethernet, but these NICs use RJ-11 connectors, the type used by telephone connections. Not only are the plugs the same, but you plug the NIC into a nearby phone jack (one used for a telephone circuit), and the NIC uses the home or office's internal phone wiring for network data transfer. Other users who need access to the network do the same. In homes where most rooms have a phone jack, HomePNA gives you access to a network from virtually any room in the house or office—without a hub.

Whereas Ethernet uses a star-bus topology, HomePNA networks use a daisy chain topology. Computers simply plug into the existing phone line system in the home and send data over that system to the desired computer, as shown in the following illustration. The advantages are that no central hub is required, and the network lines are already installed inside the walls. All you have to do is connect. The network connections

Chapter 3

do not interfere with voice communications on the phone lines, so you can talk on the phone and use the network at the same time.

Hubless LAN Running over
Existing Telephone Wiring

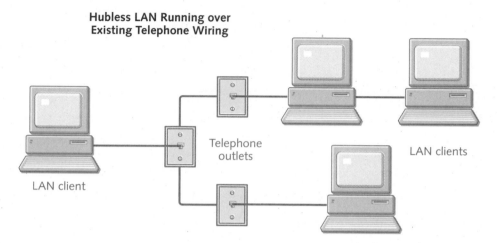

If all of this sounds too good to be true, rest assured that HomePNA is not the perfect solution. There are two primary problems with HomePNA that you should consider before adopting it. First, HomePNA networks are limited to about 10 Mbps, which is much slower than Fast Ethernet or Gigabit Ethernet. However, how much speed do you really need? This is an important question to consider, and some points to keep in mind are:

- If you use the network to share printers, files, and other peripherals, 10 Mbps is all you need.

- If you share a broadband Internet connection, 10 Mbps is fast enough because you do not receive data from the Internet any faster than 10 Mbps. Although there might be a slight slowdown using the HomePNA network, the difference is usually not noticeable.

- If you play multiuser games, 10 Mbps is fast enough as long as the games are not too graphics-intensive. If they are, you'll notice some delays.

- If you are running video applications and other multimedia, you'll experience delays with 10 Mbps.

- If you run some of the computers on your network remotely using Remote Desktop at high resolution and color depth, you'll notice hesitations in some operations such as screen redraws and moving objects about on the screen.

So, if basic networking and Internet sharing is all you need, the HomePNA network will work well and solve your cabling problems. If speed is an issue for you, Fast Ethernet or Gigabit Ethernet is the better choice.

Chapter 3: Creating Network Connections

The second problem with HomePNA concerns ICS. If you are using a DSL or cable modem, you'll need a NIC for that connection as well as the HomePNA NIC. You can set up ICS with the ICS host computer connected to the Internet, and all other computers will access data from the ICS host. However, if you do not want to use ICS, you'll need to purchase a network device called a bridge. A *bridge* connects two dissimilar networks, such as an Internet connection with the HomePNA LAN. These bridge solutions are readily available, but will certainly add to your hardware cost.

> **tip** If you need to connect dissimilar networks, there is an easy software-based solution included in Windows XP called *Network Bridge*. You can learn more about network bridges in "Bridging Network Connections," page 75.

So, is HomePNA what you need for your home or office? Consider the information in Table 3-2 as you make your decision.

Table 3-2. HomePNA Networking Features

Networking Issue	HomePNA Feature or Failure
Expense and availability	HomePNA networks require HomePNA NICs and standard phone cabling. They are often sold as kits for around $50, so they are very affordable. You'll find plenty of manufacturers of HomePNA products at your local computer store.
Setup	Easy. Windows XP can automatically install the NICs, and the manufacturer usually provides a setup CD.
Speed	Networks are limited to 10 Mbps, which is considerably slower than Fast Ethernet or Gigabit Ethernet.
Internet connections	Connecting the LAN to a shared Internet DSL or cable connection can require extra hardware.
Reliability	Excellent.

If you are still unsure about whether to use Ethernet or HomePNA, consider all the points in this section, and then revisit this simple idea—if running Ethernet cable between computers and a hub is not a problem, use Ethernet. This way, you won't have any speed problems, and you'll have more residential gateway and router options than are provided with HomePNA. If connections between computers are difficult to achieve with cabling, HomePNA might be your best bet. You can learn more about HomePNA at *www.homepna.org*. However, before choosing HomePNA, you might also want to consider a wireless network, which you can learn more about in Chapter 19, "Wireless Networking."

Powerline Networks

Powerline networking is a lot like HomePNA, but instead of using your existing telephone lines, you use your electrical lines. That's right, Powerline networking uses a NIC that plugs into a standard AC outlet. Other computers in your home plug into other outlets, and communication between computers occurs over the electrical lines without disrupting any other electrical services.

Powerline networking also provides speeds of 8–14 Mbps transfer, so the system's speed is comparable to that of HomePNA. So why use Powerline? The main reason for using Powerline networking is that AC receptacles are more readily available in homes and offices than telephone jacks, which gives you more networking flexibility.

Is Powerline a better, more flexible choice than HomePNA? Not really. You face the same speed and Internet connection challenges as HomePNA, and Powerline networking can be problematic, although sales brochures might tell you otherwise.

Powerline technologies have had a lot of problems in the past due to noise and distortion on traditional power lines within the home. For example, your home network might work fine until someone turns on a hair dryer or a toaster. Then, the static and interference could bring the network to a standstill. However, recent developments in the ways that Powerline NICs use frequencies over cabling enable the Powerline network to adjust frequencies as needed, so that network disruptions are not as problematic. Also, some providers use an encryption method for all network communications in the event that data gets transmitted from the local home or office onto the main power line.

Powerline networking is a practical and viable alternative, and one that continues to mature. In fact, you might see more and more Powerline offerings including broadband Internet over power lines in the near future, so this is certainly a technology to keep your eye on. For the home and small office network, this technology does work well, although you can expect some hiccups from time to time. If you think that Powerline networking might be right for you, be sure to purchase the required equipment from a recognized manufacturer, and review Table 3-3 for a summary of features. To learn more about Powerline networking, go to *www.homeplug.com*.

Table 3-3. Powerline Networking Features

Networking Issue	Powerline Feature or Failure
Expense and availability	Most kits cost between $50 and $100. You do not need a hub for Powerline networking.
Setup	Easy. Windows XP can automatically install the NICs, and the manufacturer usually provides a setup CD.
Speed	Network speeds run up to 8–14 Mbps, which is considerably slower than Fast Ethernet or Gigabit Ethernet. You might see more dips in speed and service than you typically do with HomePNA.

Table 3-3. *(continued)*

Networking Issue	Powerline Feature or Failure
Internet connections	Connecting your LAN to a DSL or cable Internet connection can require additional hardware. Also, network service disruption due to Powerline conditions can cause problems as well.
Reliability	Good.

Wireless Networks

Windows XP fully supports the wireless networking standard, which makes Windows XP the best Microsoft operating system to use if you want a wireless network. Typical wireless networks use radio signals between wireless NICs and access points (similar to hubs), but they are more expensive and not as fast as wired Ethernet. Chapter 19, "Wireless Networking," is devoted entirely to the subject.

Other Types of LANs

There are a few other common types of networks that are used for LANs. These types of networks are more expensive and complicated than the types of networks outlined in this chapter, so they are not used as home or small office networks. You will, however, see them in some corporate LANs, and Windows XP Professional will function on these types of networks as well.

- **Token Ring.** Token Ring networks are sometimes used in large LANs as an alternative to Ethernet. Token Ring networks use a token passing technology in which any computer sending data must have an electronic ticket, or *token*, before transmitting data over the wire. Due to the token passing scheme, Token Ring networks do not need Ethernet's CSMA/CD access method because collisions cannot occur with the token structure. IBM developed the Token Ring technology, which was later standardized in the IEEE 802.5 standard. In a Token Ring network, all computers are wired to a physical ring or loop along which the token is passed. This type of network is more complex than Ethernet, but it is a somewhat common network topology.

- **Fiber Distributed Data Interface (FDDI).** FDDI also uses a token passing technology to move data. FDDI is capable of 100 Mbps transfer speeds. FDDI is a lot like Token Ring, but it uses fiber-optic cable with a two-ring design (the secondary ring can be used for data and as a backup should the primary ring fail). FDDI is used in many environments, but it is not as popular as Ethernet or conventional Token Ring networks. Due to the expense of the fiber-optic connections, it is primarily used in providing backbones

Chapter 3

between individual LANs in a wider WAN environment. However, FDDI is rapidly being supplanted in this role by switched Ethernet networks.

- **IP over Asynchronous Transfer Mode (ATM).** IP over ATM is a collection of software components that provide IP on an ATM network. ATM is a packet-switching network technology that provides high-speed data transmission in both LAN and WAN environments. ATM networks are capable of transmission speeds of approximately 1 Gbps.

- **LAN Emulation (LANE).** LANs also work with ATM, so ATM can work with another Ethernet or Token Ring network. You can think of LANE as a type of network bridge between different components, and Windows XP Professional can be a LANE client.

> **tip** You can learn more about how Windows XP Professional supports LANE and IP over ATM as well as FDDI and Token Ring by searching Windows XP Help And Support on the Start menu.

Installing NICs

Once you have made a decision about the kind of network you will use, your immediate task is to install the NICs in the computers that will become network clients. If you have a collection of computers that are already equipped with Ethernet cards (or onboard Ethernet built into the computers' motherboards), your task is complete (assuming you've decided to use Ethernet). However, if you want to install Ethernet, HomePNA, wireless, or Powerline NICs, you'll need to carefully read the NIC manufacturer's setup instructions. The setup process can vary according to the brand of NIC you are installing and the type of connection (internal PCI slot or external USB port) you are using. Keep these points in mind:

- If you are installing an internal device, shut down the computer, and unplug it from the AC outlet. Never open a computer case and install internal components with the computer still plugged into the wall because you might get an electrical shock. Also, turn off all components connected to the computer, such as your monitor or printer, or disconnect the peripherals from the computer. It's also advisable to use a wrist grounding strap to reduce the possibility of discharging harmful static electricity inside the computer. A *wrist grounding strap*, as its name implies, attaches to your wrist and drains static electricity from your body to a grounded object in your surroundings (to which it's also attached). Alternatively, periodically touch a grounded object in your vicinity before touching the components of your computer. Although this alternative method is not guaranteed to prevent harmful static buildup, it suffices in most cases.

- For internal devices, follow the manufacturer's installation instructions. Also, check your computer's documentation—opening the computer's case might void some or all of your warranty. If you are not familiar with installing internal components, consider getting some help or even taking the computer to a service center.

- For USB NICs, follow the manufacturer's instructions. You might need to install software before attaching the NIC to the USB port.

- Once installed, Windows XP can automatically detect and install most NICs, but you should follow the manufacturer's instructions for installing the manufacturer's driver or other utilities. Check to see if the manufacturer has specific instructions for computers running Windows XP.

To learn more about hardware installation and configuration, see *Microsoft Windows XP Inside Out* by Ed Bott and Carl Siechert (Microsoft Press, 2001).

Managing Network Connections

Once you have installed the NIC, the connection appears as Local Area Connection in the Network Connections window under the LAN Or High-Speed Internet heading. If you select the connection and look at the Details section in the task pane in the Network Connections window, you will see such information as whether the connection is enabled and the brand of NIC that is used for the connection. For the icon to appear enabled, the NIC must be connected to the network or hub. If it is not, you'll see an **X** over the icon and a status message, as shown in Figure 3-6.

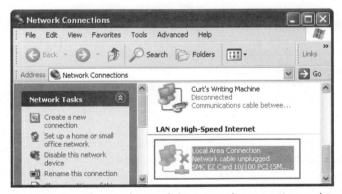

Figure 3-6. The condition of the network connection and any appropriate error messages appear in the Network Connections window.

You can manage the network connection as well as the NIC from this location. The connection should rarely need your attention, but there is valuable information you can gain from the Network Connections window that can help you troubleshoot problems should any occur.

Chapter 3

Checking the Status of the Connection

If you double-click the connection in the Network Connections window (or right-click the connection and choose Status), you'll see a simple status dialog box like the one shown in Figure 3-7. The General tab displays the current connection status, the duration of the network connection, and the current speed of the connection. Under Activity, you can see the total packets sent and received. You can also access the connection's properties and disable the connection using the buttons provided.

Figure 3-7. The General tab of the Local Area Connection Status dialog box provides you with helpful information about the status of the connection.

If you select the Support tab, shown in Figure 3-8, the fields displayed are Address Type (automatic or manual), IP Address, Subnet Mask, and Default Gateway (if any). If you click the Details button, you can see the DNS and WINS server addresses. You can also find this information at the command prompt by typing **ipconfig** and pressing Enter. If you want to see detailed IP information, type **ipconfig /all**.

To learn more about ipconfig and other helpful tools see "Using Command-line Tools Included in Windows XP," page 345.

Notice the Repair button on the Support tab as well. If your connection is not working, you can click the Repair button and Windows XP will attempt to fix the connection. The Repair option primarily works in cases where a DHCP server is used. When you click Repair, Windows XP

- Broadcasts a request for a new DHCP address lease, and if that fails, regenerates its IP address using APIPA.

- Flushes Address Resolution Protocol (ARP) entries.

70

Chapter 3

- Flushes NetBIOS and DNS local caches.

- Reregisters with WINS and DNS (if applicable).

Figure 3-8. The current IP configuration is displayed on the Support tab.

Understanding Connection Protocols and Services

If you right-click the connection in Network Connections and choose Properties, you can access the Properties dialog box for that connection. On the General tab, you'll see a list of the services and protocols that are configured for the connection. By default, a LAN connection includes the following:

- **Client for Microsoft Networks.** This service enables the computer to participate on a Microsoft network.

- **File and Printer Sharing for Microsoft Networks.** This service allows the client to share files and printers on the network.

- **QoS Packet Scheduler.** The Quality of Service packet scheduler manages network traffic and related traffic functions.

- **Internet Protocol (TCP/IP).** TCP/IP enables the client to participate on a TCP/IP network (see "Understanding TCP/IP in Depth," page 24, to learn more).

These services and protocols are all you need to participate on a standard network providing TCP/IP and Microsoft networking services. However, in network environments where other protocols and services are used (such as NetWare), you can install additional services and protocols from the General tab. See Chapter 18, "Interconnectivity with Other Systems," to learn more about Windows XP interoperability with other network operating systems.

Network Authentication

If you access the Local Area Connection Properties dialog box in Network Connections, you'll find an Authentication tab. The Authentication tab, shown in Figure 3-9, enables you to configure authenticated network access for both wired and wireless Ethernet networks if network authentication is required on your network.

The authentication option you see in the figure uses the IEEE 802.1x standard that provides network authentication of devices based on their port or connection to the network, which is why you find the 802.1x option in the connection's Properties dialog box.

Using 802.1x, you can require authentication using Extensible Authentication Protocol (EAP). *EAP* is a highly secure authentication standard for both wired and wireless Ethernet networks. Different EAP types are available for authentication including Message Digest 5 (MD5)–Challenge or a smart card or digital certificate. If you are using a smart card or digital certificate, click the Properties button to configure the option you want to use. To implement the 802.1x standard, each network client should use the authentication settings on this tab to ensure security.

You can choose to have the computer attempt to authenticate itself to the network using computer information when a user is not currently logged on. You can also choose to have the computer attempt to connect to the network as a guest when neither computer information nor a signed on user are present.

To learn more about the 802.1x standard with wireless Ethernet networks, see Chapter 19, "Wireless Networking."

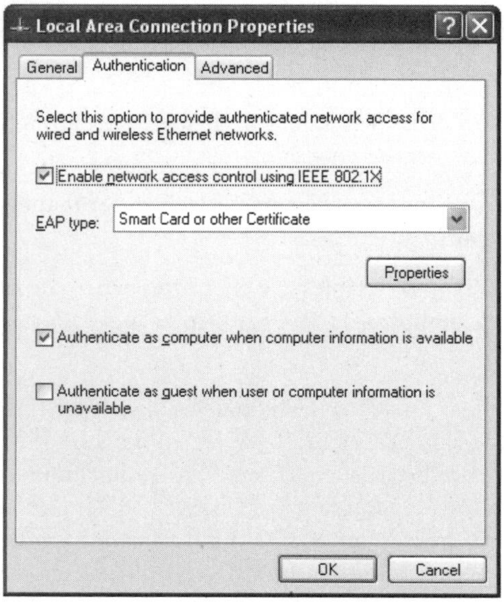

Figure 3-9. You can use 802.1x authentication by configuring the Authentication tab.

InsideOut

Getting to Know 802.1x

The 802.1x standard defines authenticated network access for wireless and wired Ethernet networks. The 802.1x standard is built on port-based network access control, which can authenticate computers and other network devices that are physically connected to a port on the LAN. It provides a highly secure method because it takes network security to a deeper level than a simple user name and password. With 802.1x, the port you are connecting from must also be authenticated, or network access will fail.

When 802.1x is in use, there is one physical LAN port that is viewed as two logical ports for authentication purposes. The first logical port is considered the *uncontrolled port* and allows data exchange between the client attempting to authenticate and the authenticating server. If the authentication succeeds, the second port, called the *controlled port*, allows data to be exchanged between the authenticated LAN client and the rest of the network. This additional security layer goes beyond the standard user name and password authentication to the IP port authentication, which is usually based on certificate credentials. The user as well as the computer must be authenticated at different security levels for network access to be available. If you are interested in the many details of 802.1x, visit the IEEE Web site at *www.ieee.org* and search for **802.1x**.

Bindings and Provider Order

If you open Network Connections and choose Advanced Settings on the Advanced menu, the Advanced Settings dialog box opens and displays advanced settings for adapters and bindings as well as provider order. These settings give you a summary of what protocols work with (are *bound to*) what connections and how different services are accessed on your network. The advanced settings are valuable because adjusting them might increase performance, especially if your computer resides in a network where several different services or protocols are used.

On the Adapters And Bindings tab of the Advanced Settings dialog box, shown in Figure 3-10 on the next page, you see a listing of connections and bindings for the LAN connection. Notice that if you select a connection or binding, you can adjust its order in the list by clicking the up arrow and down arrow buttons to the right of the list. When Windows XP participates on the network, the connections and bindings are used in the order listed. For example, if you have three connections, Windows XP attempts to use those connections for network communication in the order they appear in this list. So, for best network performance, you should move the connections and bindings you use most often to the top of the list. If you use your LAN connection more than any remote access connections, the LAN connection should be ordered first in the list, as shown in Figure 3-10. Under Bindings For Local Area Connection, if you have more than one protocol bound to a service, order the protocols by their relative importance and disconnect any protocols not needed for a given service by clearing their check boxes. Each protocol adds to the overhead of the network, so turning off those that are unused will improve performance.

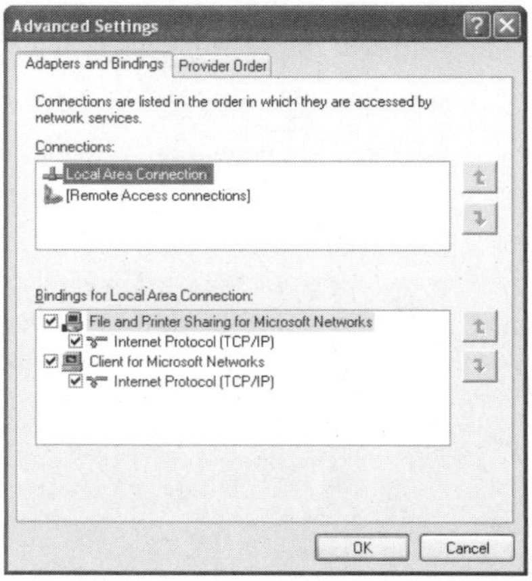

Figure 3-10. Order the adapters and bindings so that the connection or binding used most often is at the top of the list.

On the Provider Order tab, shown in Figure 3-11, the same rule applies. You see a list of network providers and the services they provide. Make sure the services used most often are at the top of each list.

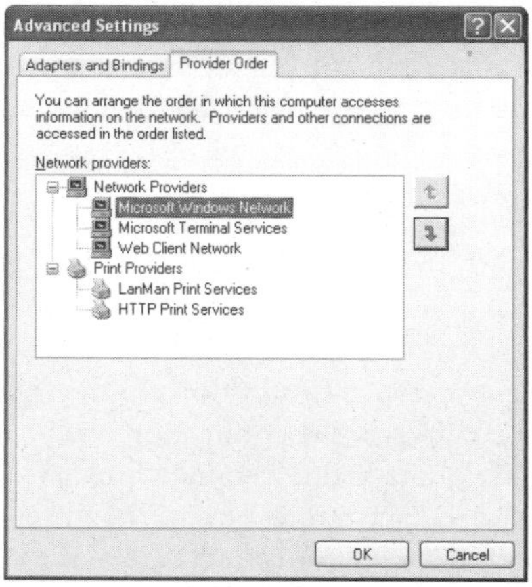

Figure 3-11. Order the network providers so that the most commonly used services are listed first.

Bridging Network Connections

As mentioned earlier in this chapter, HomePNA and Powerline networks can have some problems connecting to a shared DSL or cable connection without additional hardware. However, Windows XP comes to the rescue by using bridging software to eliminate the need for a dedicated hardware bridge. This software solution, called Network Bridge, is found in Network Connections.

Suppose that your computer resides between two different IP subnets or even two simple portions of an office network. For simplicity's sake, also assume that there are two workgroups in your office. One workgroup contains the marketing group, and the other contains the sales group. Both network segments are Ethernet segments, but your computer is outfitted with two NICs so it can communicate with each segment. One NIC communicates with the marketing group, and the other NIC communicates with the sales group.

Although this configuration might sound strange, it actually happens often, especially when small networks add additional workgroups or subnets. For this reason, Windows XP provides the capability to act as an inexpensive network bridge. This bridge provides a connection between the two segments. In the past, you needed to buy a hardware network bridge or router to accomplish the same task, but the Network Bridge feature in Windows XP gives you a simple software solution.

You can also bridge different network segments. For example, perhaps your home network consists of an Ethernet network and a HomePNA network. You can install both NICs on a Windows XP computer and let Windows XP bridge the two networks to create one IP subnet. Obviously, the network bridge provided in Windows XP is designed to be a simple and inexpensive software bridging solution, not a solution for a large IP network. Once you bridge the two segments, computers on each segment can then communicate with each other seamlessly. All data flows through the network bridge, but this process is invisible to the user.

It is important to note that a network bridge is designed to solve specific segment problems: It is not a solution that is routinely needed in a home or small office network. For example, if you have a wired Ethernet network and you want to add wireless functionality using a wireless access point, you can simply connect the wireless access point to a hub or switch port on the wired network—it serves as the network bridge.

If you do need to create a network bridge, you'll need to log on to the computer that will serve as the bridge with an administrator account. You can bridge Ethernet connections (including HomePNA and Powerline), but you cannot bridge an Ethernet connection with a VPN connection or with a dial-up connection.

> **caution** Never bridge a private network with a connection that has a public Internet address. This opens your private network to the Internet. Instead, use ICS to share the Internet connection with other users on the network. See Chapter 10, "Managing Workgroup Connections," to learn how to set up ICS.

To create a network bridge, follow these steps:

1 Log on with an administrator account and open Network Connections. You should be logging on to the computer that holds both subnets or network types because this is the machine that will need to run Network Bridge for the rest of the network.

2 For both of the connections you plan to bridge, open the Properties dialog box of the connection, and select the Advanced tab.

3 Turn off Internet Connection Sharing and Internet Connection Firewall if they are enabled for either connection. Click OK.

4 In Network Connections, select the two connections you want to bridge by holding down the Ctrl key and clicking each connection so that they are both selected.

5 Release the Ctrl key. Right-click the selected adapters and choose Bridge Connections.

Windows XP creates the network bridge. When the process is complete, the bridge appears in Network Connections along with the LAN connections that now appear under the Network Bridge heading, as shown in Figure 3-12.

> **tip** If you prefer using a wizard, the Add A Network Connection Wizard can also walk you through the bridging steps.

You can add remote connections to Network Bridge at any time by right-clicking the Network Bridge icon and choosing Properties. The Network Bridge Properties dialog box appears, as shown in Figure 3-13. You can only have one network bridge on a Windows XP computer, but the bridge can support multiple connections (up to 64).

> **note** The computer that contains the network bridge must be turned on at all times for the two network segments to be bridged. Otherwise, the segments will not be connected.

Chapter 3: Creating Network Connections

Figure 3-12. The Tiles view shows the network bridge and its two connections, and provides brief status information as well.

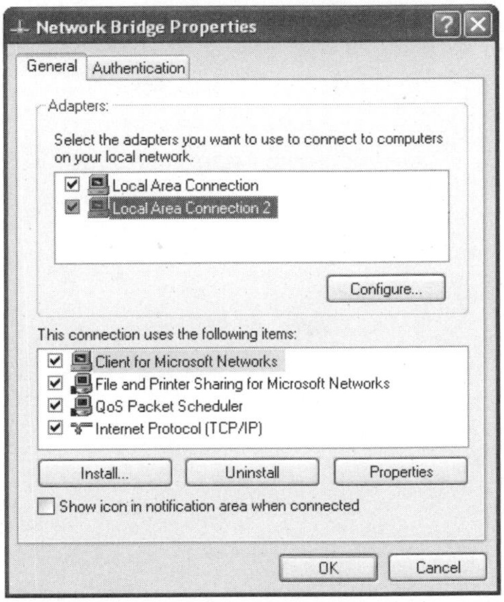

Figure 3-13. You can manage the bridged adapters from the General tab of the Network Bridge Properties dialog box.

tip You can more easily add or remove connections from Network Bridge by right-clicking the connection and choosing Remove From Bridge or Add To Bridge.

Part 2

Internet Networking

Configuring Internet Connections

To access the Internet from your Microsoft Windows XP computer, you must have some kind of Internet connection. In the recent past, workstation Internet connections were typically made via dial-up modems or over corporate local area networks (LANs). Today, more networking options and features are available and supported by Windows XP. If your Windows XP computer resides on a small office network and needs Internet access, the decision of which connection type to use can be complicated and confusing. Once that decision has been made, however, the tools and wizards provided in Windows XP greatly ease the process of configuring Internet connections.

In this chapter, you will learn about Internet connections and how to set them up. You'll discover what is available to you and how to configure and manage the connection once you have decided which type of connection is right for you.

Internet Connections 101

If you have not used Internet connections in the past or if a connection has always been provided to you via a corporate network, it is important to understand the basics of Internet connections before contemplating which type to use.

The Role of an Internet Service Provider (ISP)

You can think of an Internet connection as your access point to the Internet. One common metaphor describes the Internet as a busy freeway. Extending this metaphor a bit further, ISPs serve as the on-ramps. Just as you must locate an on-ramp to enter the freeway, you must have an Internet connection to access the Internet. Many resources available on the Internet are free, but access to those resources costs a certain amount of money per month, depending on the kind of Internet connection you choose. An ISP gives you the on-ramp so that you can request and receive information from the Internet.

> **note** In the past, there were various free Internet access options, ranging from community-sponsored dial-up servers to companies that provided free dial-up accounts in exchange for requiring their users to view advertisements. Most of these options have since disappeared. To gain access to the Internet, users who are not granted free dial-up accounts through their work or schools will most likely have to pay an ISP. Many public institutions, such as libraries, still maintain computer labs and provide free Internet access to local patrons.

To access your ISP, your computer must be equipped with the appropriate computer hardware, which you can learn more about in the next section. You must also have an account with an ISP. The account is simply a user name and password that gives you access to the ISP's network resources, and therefore the Internet. Once you are authenticated by the ISP, you are free to use the Internet's resources. As shown in the following illustration, an ISP is like the middleman between your computer and the Internet. Without an account (user name and password) on an ISP's server, your computer cannot access the ISP, which prevents anyone who is not a customer of that ISP from using their resources to connect to the Internet.

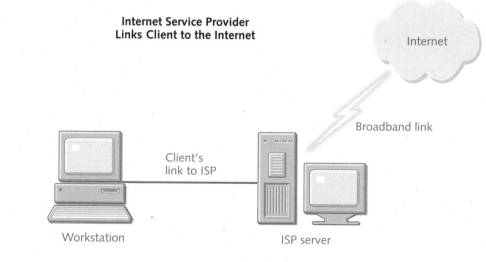

**Internet Service Provider
Links Client to the Internet**

Internet

Broadband link

Client's
link to ISP

Workstation

ISP server

InsideOut

Can You Surf Without an ISP?

ISPs provide access to the Internet, generally through backbone connections. *Backbone* connections tie directly into the Internet and are high bandwidth connections that often utilize fiber-optic technology. A backbone connection is capable of very high bandwidth transfers, which allows numerous clients to connect to the ISP for Internet access. Just as you need an ISP to connect to the Internet, so do large corporations. Although some large corporations function as an ISP to all internal network clients, the Internet access these corporations purchase costs thousands of dollars every month (and the companies who lease them this bandwidth are still technically ISPs). So, for the home or small office user who needs Internet access, be sure to find an ISP that can service your needs. Fortunately, there are many ISPs and many different plans to choose from.

What an ISP Provides

An ISP essentially provides access to the Internet. In the past, this access was often sold on a per hour basis, but in recent years, most ISPs offer a flat fee for unlimited access. No matter whether you are dialing up to the Internet using a modem or if you have an *always-on* broadband connection, the flat fee applies. You can use the Internet a few hours every month or during every waking moment for this set price.

InsideOut

Understanding Internet Domains

Internet addresses, such as http://www.microsoft.com, are built on the Domain Name System (DNS) and use Internet domains. A domain name is *resolved*, or translated, into a numerical address, or *Internet Protocol (IP) address,* that the Internet uses to route its content. In an Internet address, the elements of the domain names are separated by periods. These domain names are resolved by *DNS servers*, which are computers dedicated to maintaining millions of pairs of domain names and IP addresses.

For more information about DNS, see "Domain Name System (DNS)," page 24.

In addition to Internet access, ISPs usually offer additional services and features that you should read about before you purchase a plan from an ISP. Generally, you can expect to find features such as:

- **E-mail.** Most ISPs provide you with an e-mail address and a certain amount of storage space for your *mailbox*. Some provide you with several

Chapter 4

e-mail addresses so that different family members or office members can have their own. The e-mail address you use is most often based on the ISP's domain, such as *username@ispname*.com. For example, if you have access to the Internet through the Microsoft Network (MSN), your e-mail address will be *username*@msn.com. If you have access through another ISP, for example, EarthLink, your e-mail address will be *username*@earthlink.net. Of course, you need to replace *username* with the account name you chose or were given by the ISP when you signed up. Therefore, everyone at msn.com or earthlink.net must have a unique user name to keep everyone's mail and accounts separate.

> **tip** Some ISPs also provide a feature called *personalized domains* where you can use your own name as the domain name in your e-mail address, such as curt@curtsimmons.com. This feature, which often costs a little more, simply translates curtsimmons.com to the ISP's domain name. In other words, curtsimmons.com serves as an *alias* for the ISP's real domain. Having your own domain name can be handy because it looks nicer, is easier for people to remember, and allows you to maintain the same public e-mail address when you move from ISP to ISP.

- **Web page.** Some ISPs give you a nominal amount of Web page space on their Web servers (usually 5–10 MB). This is usually enough room to create a home page with information about you. Generally, you have to create the Web page yourself, but some ISPs provide an automated system where you can set up a home page by answering questions and uploading pictures. Of course, the automated Web pages usually look the same except for small amounts of customized content, so if you want something more interesting, you'll need to design your own page using a full-featured Web authoring tool such as Microsoft FrontPage.

> **caution** If you are planning to create a Web site with FrontPage, make sure you understand how much Web space you are getting from your ISP and make sure the ISP supports *FrontPage extensions,* a set of components available for both Windows and UNIX-based Web servers that enable many of FrontPage's advanced Web development features. If the ISP does not, you can still create Web pages, but a number of FrontPage's advanced features (such as hit counters, navigation bars, and forms, as well as the ability to seamlessly edit your Web pages from within FrontPage without separate file uploads) will not work when the page is posted on the ISP's server. Instead, you'll have to program these from scratch using Hypertext Markup Language (HTML), Common Gateway Interface (CGI), or another programming language.

- **Technical support.** Most ISPs offer technical support, and some even make that support available 24 hours a day, 7 days a week, so you can get help when you need it. With some ISPs, the technical support is good—others seem to know very little. It's a good idea to ask about the technical support personnel's training.

● **Access portal.** Some ISPs offer an access or search portal, such as MSN. These sites, although they are available to the public, also contain a number of features that are only available to members. You might want to set your Web browser's *home page* (the first Web site that appears when you open your browser) to the access portal and use it as the doorway to the Internet. Access portals are usually only provided by national ISPs and can be useful if you take advantage of all they have to offer.

● **Extended service contracts.** Some ISPs offer you the option of getting your Internet access cheaper if you sign up for a longer service contract. This means you are locked into a deal and might face early cancellation fees. If you are fairly certain that you will be comfortable with the ISP's service, you can often save money by signing up for extended service.

● **Type of Internet connection.** As with most purchases, it is important to shop around before making a decision about the type of Internet connection you want (and what you are willing to pay), as discussed in the next section.

Types of Internet Connections

A few years ago, modems running at speeds as slow as 3 kilobits per second (Kbps) were the only way to access the Internet from a single computer or a small network. Luckily, at that time, a dial-up modem connection was really all you needed. After all, the Internet primarily consisted of static, text-based pages with hyperlinks to other static, text-based pages.

In recent years, however, the Internet has become more of a multimedia resource. Web sites routinely run interactive and graphical scripts, provide audio and video downloads, and provide other interactive elements that tax today's 56 Kbps dial-up modems to the limit. This trend has led to the popularity of broadband Internet connections.

The term *broadband* refers to connections that have greater throughput than a modem connection. While *narrowband* connections use a limited number of frequencies to transfer data, broadband connections use a greater range of frequencies, which results in faster data transfer. Although a modem connection typically provides at most 48 Kbps of throughput, broadband connections often provide throughput of 400 Kbps or higher. With a broadband connection, you can easily surf the Internet, use advanced multimedia features, and download files and programs quickly. A 1 MB file download will take a few minutes with a dial-up connection, while the same file download takes only seconds with a broadband connection.

Despite the fact that most home Web users currently access the Internet via a dial-up connection, the trend toward Web sites requiring more bandwidth will continue as broadband solutions develop further and become more affordable.

So, what kind of Internet connection do you need? That depends on a few primary factors:

- **Availability.** You are limited by the type of connections available in your area. In large cities, you can purchase nearly any service, but if you live in a more rural or suburban area, you will have fewer options.

- **Money.** Broadband solutions cost more, so you should decide on an Internet access budget before you shop.

- **Network.** You need to determine if the connection will serve a single computer or a home/office network.

- **Access.** You need to determine if you require always-on access with faster access and download speeds.

So, what is available? The following sections review the types of Internet access that might be available in your area. You'll also find a quick review table at the end of each section that gives you a helpful summary of the features and issues of each connection type.

Dial-up Connections

Dial-up connections are the most commonly used Internet connection, with millions of Internet users dialing up on a daily basis. A *dial-up connection* uses a modem that connects to a phone jack in your home. When you want to access the Internet, the modem dials a phone number (preferably either a local or a toll-free phone number, so you will not incur additional telephone charges) belonging to your ISP. Your user name and password are then authenticated, and you are able to access the Internet. The following diagram shows how the dial-up connection links you to your ISP and, in turn, the Internet.

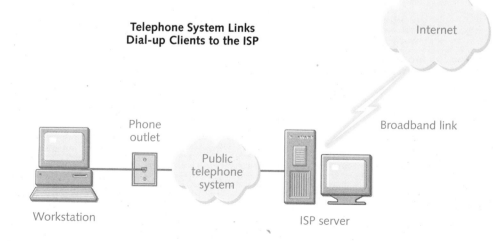

**Telephone System Links
Dial-up Clients to the ISP**

Internet

Phone
outlet

Broadband link

Public
telephone
system

Workstation

ISP server

> **tip** Dial-up connections are sometimes referred to as *narrowband* connections because the available bandwidth is limited, or narrow, resulting in slower transmission speeds.

There are a few basic advantages with a dial-up connection:

- **Availability.** Phone lines for dial-up connections are available nearly everywhere.

- **Inexpensive.** Most computers come equipped with a modem, so there is no additional hardware to buy.

- **ISPs.** There are many available ISPs that service dial-up connections, so you'll have a number of options to choose from.

- **Low monthly fee.** The dial-up connection is the least expensive Internet connection, typically costing around $20 a month for unlimited access.

There are, however, some disadvantages as well:

- **Speed.** Dial-up connections use standard 56 Kbps modems that ship preinstalled on almost every new computer. You can also purchase a stand-alone or internal modem for any computer for around $50–$70 if necessary. However, with current FCC power regulations, the best downstream bit rate you are likely to get with a 56 Kbps modem is approximately 48 Kbps. Depending on noise, line conditions, and your ISP, you might only get speeds of 34–38 Kbps. These speeds will work, but you will spend a lot of time waiting for pages to download, and you will have a difficult time using multimedia elements, such as Internet radio and video files. With a 56 Kbps modem, the upload speed is usually limited to a maximum of 33.6 Kbps, but the download speed is faster.

> **tip** Kbps represents the number of kilobits (1000 bits) that can be transferred per second. Divide this number by 8 to calculate the number of kilobytes (KB) per second. For example, a 32 Kbps connection would enable you to transfer a file at the rate of about 4 KB per second. Because files are typically measured in kilobytes, this might be a more useful measure of transfer capacity.

- **Access.** A dial-up connection is designed to give you access while you are using the Internet. It is not designed to give you an always-on connection, so you will have to dial out each time you want to use the Internet. You might also experience busy signals if your ISP is overloaded with users.

- **Connection.** Because a modem uses a phone line, your connectivity will be disrupted from time to time with line noise, particularly in older homes and rural areas. You might even get disconnected periodically, either due to line noise or timeout restrictions on the remote dial-up servers, and be forced to reconnect.

Chapter 4

● **Single use.** When you access the Internet using a modem, your phone is unavailable for voice calls. Also, if you have call waiting on your phone line, incoming calls might disrupt the modem connection. For this reason, many users add another phone line that is dedicated to Internet usage. This allows one phone to be used for voice calls and the second phone line to be used for Internet access. Of course, an additional phone line will cost you a per month charge from your phone company, which effectively increases the cost of the dial-up connection.

InsideOut

What Does a Modem Actually Do?

A *modem* is a device that MOdulates and DEModulates data. This means that it turns digital data into analog signals and vice versa. Your computer communicates with digital data, which is made of binary 1's and 0's. However, the phone line uses analog signals, which are represented by sound waves. To make these two different communication systems work, you need a device that can change the digital data that the computer sends to analog sound waves for phone line transfer and a device that can change those sound waves back into digital format at the receiving computer. Because the communication between modems uses sound waves, it is susceptible to noise and interference problems. Modems have built-in error-correction features that retransmit blocks of data that have been corrupted during a transfer. So although your transfers should ultimately be error-free, the retransmissions can further reduce the already slow speed of a dial-up connection. In addition, some noise and interference problems can actually cause modem connections to be disconnected, requiring you to redial.

Is a dial-up connection the best connection for you? Table 4-1 provides a summary of a dial-up connection's features and problems to help you make that decision.

Table 4-1. Dial-up Connection Strengths and Weaknesses

Internet Connection Issue	Dial-up Connection Feature or Failure
Expense	Dial-up connections are the least expensive connections on the market. There is usually no hardware to buy, but if you need to purchase a modem, there are many brands and styles available for around $70 or less. The monthly access fee will cost you around $20 per month for unlimited access.
Availability	Virtually all ISPs offer dial-up access, so there are plenty of ISPs to choose from in any location.
Speed	Not good, overall. The highest speed you are likely to get is around 48 Kbps, which is functional, but not fast.

Table 4-1. *(continued)*

Internet Connection Issue	Dial-up Connection Feature or Failure
Access	You must dial to establish a connection every time you want to use the Internet.
Reliability	Fair. You can expect some connection problems and failures.

Digital Subscriber Line (DSL) Connections

DSL is a broadband technology that has recently gained tremendous popularity. To use DSL, your computer must be outfitted with a *DSL modem*. Some DSL modems are external devices that connect to a computer's NIC or to a hub, switch, or router via an RJ-45 connector (or directly to a computer via a universal serial bus [USB] port). Other DSL modems are internal, plugging directly into an expansion slot on a computer's motherboard.

Similar to a dial-up modem, DSL also works over public telephone lines (but only those where the DSL service is available). DSL uses different channels to transmit high-speed digital data over the phone company's wiring. Telephone lines are made up of pairs of copper wires, and the pair that transfers analog voice data can also be used simultaneously to transfer high-speed digital data on different channels. The channels are effectively merged into one signal in the copper wire. The merging is accomplished by conversion equipment at the phone company's central office, and the signal is later separated at your home or office by a splitter or by using filters to separate the analog and digital signals. Because specialized equipment is required in the central office that serves your home or office, the phone company must have this equipment in place to support DSL in your area. In this way you can use your phone normally while also using the DSL modem on the same phone line. In other words, DSL uses your phone line's existing pair of wires—no additional lines are required, as shown in the following illustration.

ADSL Shared Telephone and Internet Connections

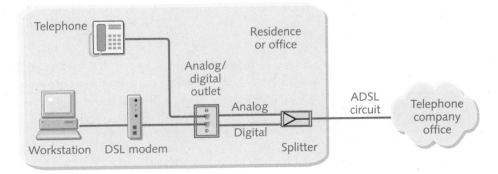

> **tip** DSL is typically 50 times faster than a standard dial-up modem.

Most DSL data services use asymmetric DSL (ADSL), which divides the phone line into three channels. One channel is used for voice, a second channel is used for data transmission from your computer (including Web page requests and files or e-mail you send), and a third channel is used to transfer data back to your computer. The throughput is slower for the channel used to request and send information, whereas the receiving channel provides greater throughput because in most situations more data is downloaded than uploaded.

Some DSL providers offer symmetric DSL (SDSL). Unlike ADSL, SDSL uses the same speed on both its uplink and downlink channels. While most DSL providers today offer ADSL because most personal users do not upload large amounts of data and simply do not need as much upstream bandwidth, if you need to transfer large files often or host an Internet server, SDSL is the better choice.

As a general rule, DSL installation is easy, works with most computers, and is very reliable. Many providers will even give you a free DSL modem if you sign up for at least a year of service. DSL service typically costs around $40–$60 a month, and it will work with Windows XP Internet Connection Sharing (ICS) or other Internet connection sharing software, such as WinProxy. Because the DSL connection works over the phone line, the connection belongs to you alone (there is no sharing with other users as with cable Internet access), and the connection is always available—there is no phone number to dial (although you might periodically have to re-establish a client PPPoE connection—for more information, see "What Is PPPoE?" on page 105). Data transfer occurs automatically over the line to the DSL provider.

Sound too good to be true? Well, for many people it is. The biggest problem with DSL is that you must have a DSL provider in your area, and you must live within a certain distance of that provider's offices. DSL traffic can only travel a certain distance before degrading, so even though your phone company provides DSL, you still might not qualify, depending on how far away you live. Additionally, although DSL connections are not shared, they are often bandwidth-limited, requiring that you pay a higher monthly cost if you want to match the maximum throughput of cable Internet connections. Table 4-2 summarizes the characteristics of DSL Internet.

If DSL is available in your area, it is an excellent broadband solution. You can find out if DSL service is available in your area by checking your local Yellow Pages or your local phone company's Web site(s), or by searching for the service online. Try *www.dslreports.com* for help locating providers in your area.

Table 4-2. DSL Connection Strengths and Weaknesses

Internet Connection Issue	DSL Connection Feature or Failure
Expense	About $50 per month for unlimited access. Many providers will give you a free DSL modem if you sign a contract for a certain time period (usually one year).
Availability	Limited to major population areas (and isn't even available in all of those). If you live in a more rural area, the service is most likely unavailable.
Speed	Good; often up to 500 Kbps for downloads.
Access	The connection is always available; there are no numbers to dial.
Reliability	Good overall. You can also use ICS with the DSL modem for access from a home or small office.

InsideOut

What Happened to ISDN?

A few years ago, Integrated Services Digital Network (ISDN) was an exciting new telephone technology for data transfer. ISDN provides guaranteed digital data transfer speeds of 64 Kbps or 128 Kbps over a dedicated line. You dial out for a connection, but you get better bandwidth than an analog dial-up connection because all data transfer is digital.

The problems with ISDN are that it is pricey, usually timed by the minute, and designed for the small office. With the introduction of DSL and cable Internet, both of which provide a higher rate of speed, easier installation, and more convenience, ISDN quickly fell out of favor among consumers. It is still available, however, and can be a viable method for faster transfer when no other type of broadband connection is available. ISDN is not subject to the distance limitations of DSL and does not require the advanced cable network installations used by cable Internet.

Satellite Connections

In 2000, the buzz about two-way satellite Internet service began appearing in online news magazines and Internet articles. By the end of 2000, Microsoft teamed with Radio Shack to provide the first high-speed, two-way satellite Internet access system. Previously,

DirecPC (part of DirecTV) offered a satellite Internet service, but this service required a standard modem connection to perform upstream data requests: Responses were then sent down to you via the much faster satellite link. MSN's satellite offering is no longer available, but Microsoft's partner company, Starband, now offers satellite Internet service. It is also available through a few other vendors, such as EarthLink's DirecWAY satellite. DirecPC is now offering a two-way satellite service of its own.

Satellite Internet is touted as a broadband alternative to DSL. Although this is somewhat true, satellite Internet is not as fast as DSL. File downloads are fast, but there are more pauses and delays during Web surfing. This delay is partly an inevitable aspect of the technology. Sending a request signal from your computer to a satellite thousands of miles in space, having that request relayed to a land-based Web server, having the requested page sent back up to the satellite, and then having it relayed back down to your satellite dish adds up to tremendous network latency, even when transmissions are made at the speed of light! Satellite Internet works with a satellite modem similar to a DSL modem. You typically attach the modem to an available USB port on your computer. The satellite modem also connects to a home satellite dish installed on your roof or a pole in your yard using coaxial cables similar to those used for cable TV. Sending and receiving transmissions are sent to a satellite, which are then sent to a hub where the transmissions are sent over the Internet, as shown in the following graphic.

Connecting to the Internet by Satellite

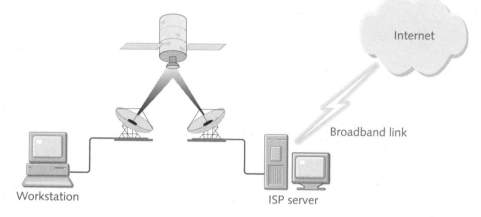

Satellite Internet in the United States relies on satellites that orbit the Earth's equator. Thus, for access from the United States, as long as you can mount the satellite dish in a location that has a clear view of the provider's satellite in the southern sky, you can likely use a satellite broadband connection. This is good news for people who live outside the coverage areas of DSL or cable Internet providers. (Satellite locations may differ in other countries that offer the service, but the need to have clear line-of-sight to the satellites remains.)

92

Satellite Internet provides an always-on connection—there is no dialing. Generally, it works well, although you might have some transmission problems during heavy rain or snowstorms. However, satellite Internet is expensive. You might have to spend around $400–$500 for the equipment, and it has to be installed by a professional in much the same way that a satellite television system must be installed. However, with increasing competition, these prices are steadily declining. Monthly unlimited service plans usually range from $50 to $80. If you are willing to spend the extra money to avoid dial-up connections, satellite Internet is certainly a viable alternative. Table 4-3 summarizes the pros and cons of satellite Internet connections.

tip See the Starband, EarthLink, and DirecPC Web sites at *www.starband.com*, *www.earthlink.net,* and *www.direcpc.com* to learn more about their satellite Internet offerings. MSN no longer offers this service. There are also other providers including America Online (AOL). Just search for **satellite Internet** on any search engine and browse the results. You'll also need to make sure that the satellite modem is compatible with Windows XP before making a decision. Consult the provider's Web site to help determine if you have a direct line-of-sight to their satellite.

If you want to network your connection with other computers in your home or office, you might have some problems, depending on the provider. However, WinProxy does offer connection sharing software for Starband users.

Table 4-3. Satellite Connection Strengths and Weaknesses

Internet Connection Issue	Satellite Connection Feature or Failure
Expense	Equipment can cost anywhere from $200 to $500 depending on the provider. Monthly access fees for unlimited access generally range from $50 to $80.
Availability	Anywhere in the continental United States as well as other countries with satellite Internet systems. You must be able to mount the satellite dish with clear lines-of-sight to the satellite (or satellites) used by your provider. The signal will not penetrate buildings, trees, or other obstructions.
Speed	Good; often 400–500 Kbps for downloads. You will notice slower speeds when browsing and sending/receiving e-mail.
Access	The connection is always available; there are no numbers to dial.
Reliability	Good overall. Some models allow ICS.

Cable Connections

Cable Internet access was introduced a few years ago and is still DSL's main competition. With cable Internet, you use a typical coaxial cable connection (the same type used for cable television programming) connected to a cable modem (a device similar to a DSL modem), which is connected to your computer. Cable Internet access is available in many locations where DSL is unavailable, but not all cable providers are equipped to provide cable Internet access.

With cable Internet access, all of your favorite television programs and your Internet connection come to you through one cable. This process works well because television programming only uses a portion of the bandwidth available, so there is plenty of room for Internet traffic. With cable access, you can expect download speeds of up to 500 Kbps, and the connection is always on and always available.

However, cable Internet access is not dedicated to your home alone. This means that the cable bandwidth is shared among others in your neighborhood, area, or town who have the same cable access. Generally, this might not be a problem, but you might experience slowdowns during certain times of the day when many users are accessing the Internet. Many cable providers are currently updating their cable systems with new high-speed fiber-optic lines that can provide ample bandwidth so that the sharing issue is less of a problem. Before you make a commitment, it is a good idea to ask your neighbors who have cable Internet access about the service. Table 4-4 summarizes the advantages and disadvantages of cable Internet service.

Table 4-4. Cable Connection Strengths and Weaknesses

Internet Connection Issue	Cable Connection Feature or Failure
Expense	Usually around $40–$60 per month for access. There might be a setup fee or modem charge, but this is often waived with an extended contract.
Availability	Your location must have cable access, and your cable provider must support Internet access. This service is still unavailable in many areas.
Speed	Good; often 500 Kbps for downloads.
Access	The connection is always available; there are no numbers to dial.
Reliability	Good overall. You can use ICS with this type of connection.

94

Corporate Connections

In corporate networks that provide Internet access to internal network users, often numbering in the thousands, Internet access becomes more complicated and certainly more expensive. Typically, in large networks, a broadband backbone connection such as a T1 line is made to an ISP. A *T1 line* is a dedicated copper or fiber-optic line that can carry data at 1.536 megabits per second (Mbps). This amount of bandwidth enables all internal network clients to use the same connection. Often, this connection is protected by a firewall or proxy server. This solution uses server computers to manage all of the Internet access over the broadband link as well as recognize and block potential threats from the Internet. Microsoft's Internet Security and Acceleration (ISA) Server, which runs on the Windows 2000 Server platform, is a good example of this kind of service.

Such broadband connections as a T1 line are expensive and are designed to service large offices. A broadband T1 or even T3 (45 Mbps) connection costs thousands of dollars per month, but it is the primary method of Internet connectivity used in corporate networks.

InsideOut

Wireless Internet

There has been a lot of excitement about wireless Internet lately, especially since cellular phones and personal digital assistants (PDAs), such as the Palm and BlackBerry, began to provide wireless access to the Internet and e-mail. How practical is it?

In many ways, wireless Internet is the best solution for portable devices. You can't see graphics or use all that the Internet has to offer over wireless connections, but you can get your mail and surf Web sites that support the Wireless Access Protocol (WAP), and there are a lot of them these days.

At this time, however, wireless Internet access direct to an ISP from a PC isn't practical due to its slow speed. Although wireless Internet works well on your text-based phone or PDA, the wireless transfer speeds are often less than 10 Kbps; therefore, a dial-up connection is still several times faster. Many phone companies allow you to connect your cellular phone to your laptop for temporary access, but the regular use of wireless and a PC is not practical because of the slow transmission speeds. As the technology continues to evolve, you can expect to see more and more wireless Internet solutions that are aimed at broadband customers.

Chapter 4

Fixed Wireless Connections

Fixed wireless is an Internet access option that is still maturing, but it is currently available in select metropolitan markets from a few providers. Fixed wireless uses a modem similar to a DSL modem that plugs into a computer's NIC or USB port, or a network hub. The modem then connects to a rooftop antenna. The rooftop antenna transmits and receives Internet content from a central antenna, which can be up to 30 or 40 miles away. Currently, download speeds can be as high as 3–5 Mbps with upload speeds of about 80–120 Kbps. This wireless connection operates at a high frequency that requires an unobstructed line-of-sight view between the rooftop and central antennas. Also, because it's a shared connection, it can suffer from impaired performance if too many people draw on the service at once, similar to the problems that can occur with cable Internet connections.

This type of Internet connection might not be readily available in your area, but it is one to keep an eye on as Internet connection technologies continue to develop. You can learn more about fixed wireless by searching for **fixed wireless** on popular computer Web sites, such as *www.cnet.com* and *www.zdnet.com*.

Configuring Modems and Broadband Hardware

To connect to the Internet, your computer must be configured with hardware that provides you with the type of Internet access you have purchased—namely, a modem or broadband hardware of some kind. Dial-up modems are standard pieces of equipment that ship in virtually all new PCs. You can even buy a specific brand of modem, internal or external, and install it separately. Regardless, modems all work the same way, and as long as the modem has a driver that is compatible with Windows XP, you shouldn't have any problems. Most of this section focuses on modem configuration, but it is important to make a few points about broadband hardware. If you purchase broadband Internet access, you will typically use some kind of modem, such as a DSL, cable, or satellite modem, that connects to a USB port or to a network interface card (NIC) in your Windows XP computer (or to a router or residential gateway). Windows XP can detect and install software drivers for most broadband hardware, but you should carefully read your provider's installation and setup guidelines so that installation occurs without any problems. You will typically use a setup CD to install the software, and then install the hardware. Thereafter, you might continue to use the software to set up the connection.

Once the broadband hardware is installed, it appears in Device Manager (open System in Control Panel, select the Hardware tab, and click Device Manager). After you create a connection for the broadband hardware, you'll see the Internet connection in the

Network Connections folder found in Control Panel. Any configuration that you might need to perform on the broadband hardware should only be done using the provider's documentation. Because not all broadband hardware functions in quite the same fashion, your ISP should provide you with specific configuration instructions as well as documentation and telephone support should you run into any problems.

If you will be using a modem to connect to the Internet, Windows XP can detect and automatically install most modems. If you have purchased an external or internal modem that you want to install, follow the manufacturer's setup instructions for Windows XP.

Once you have installed the modem, the modem appears as an installed device in Phone And Modem Options in Control Panel. On the Modems tab, as shown in Figure 4-1, any modems installed in the computer appear in the list.

Figure 4-1. The Modems tab lists any modems installed in your computer.

From this location, you can add or remove modems from your computer. You can also select a modem and click Properties to configure it. Because the configuration options often affect the modem's operation, the next few sections will point out the configuration options and issues you should take note of.

> **tip** A modem's properties dialog box can also be accessed directly from Device Manager. In Control Panel open System, select the Hardware tab, and click Device Manager. Then right-click a modem listed under Modems and click Properties.

General Tab

The General tab, shown in Figure 4-2, gives you standard information about the modem and tells you whether or not the modem is working properly. You can access the Modem Troubleshooter if you are having problems by clicking the Troubleshoot button. If you are having problems with the modem, note that you can open the Device Usage list and disable the device without removing it from your computer. This option can come in handy during the troubleshooting process.

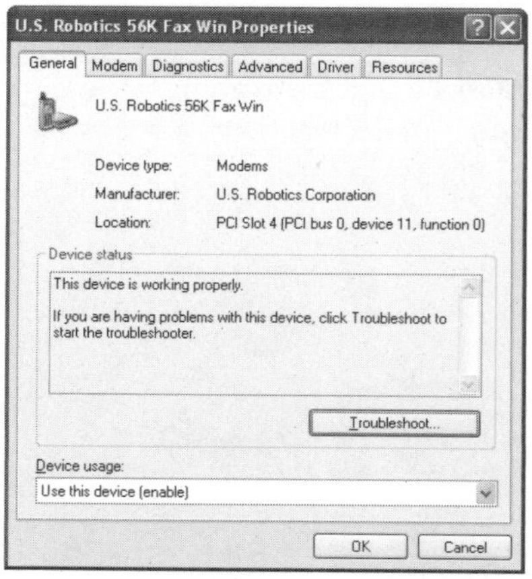

Figure 4-2. The General tab provides standard information about the modem.

Modem Tab

The Modem tab, shown in Figure 4-3, has three configuration options:

- **Speaker Volume.** You can manage the modem speaker's connection volume by adjusting the slider bar. This will let you hear (or not hear) your modem as it dials and negotiates the connection. Once the negotiation is established, the modem will be silent regardless of the volume level.

- **Maximum Port Speed.** The port speed determines how fast programs can send data to the modem, not how fast the modem sends data to another modem. In other words, this setting affects how fast the internal transfer of data from programs to the modem occurs. The default setting configured during installation is 115200, which is fast enough for most programs.

- **Dial Control.** This option simply tells the modem to wait for a dial tone before dialing occurs. This setting should remain enabled unless your modem is having problems recognizing a dial tone or if you are trying to connect in a location with dial tone problems.

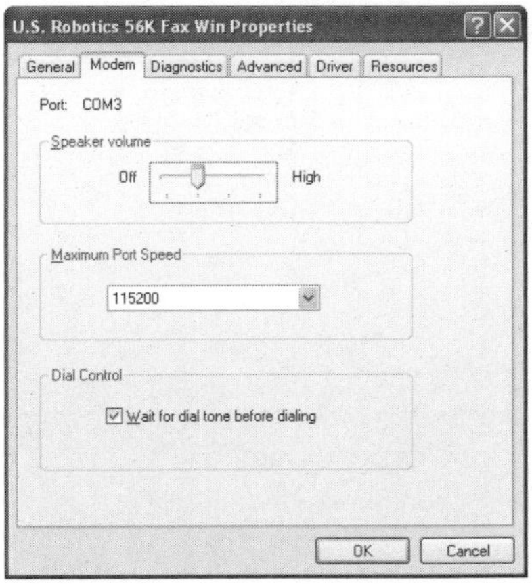

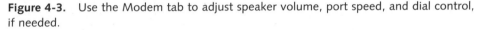

Figure 4-3. Use the Modem tab to adjust speaker volume, port speed, and dial control, if needed.

Diagnostics Tab

The Diagnostics tab provides you with a place to run a series of query commands to determine if the modem is working properly. Just click the Query Modem button, and you can view a log file that points the way to any problems the modem might have understanding common commands.

Advanced Tab

The Advanced tab provides you with a dialog box where additional initialization commands can be entered. If you refer to your modem documentation, you might find that the addition of some initialization commands can help resolve particular problems the modem is having. Again, check your documentation for details, and do not add any commands if everything is working the way that it should.

Also on this tab, you have the option of accessing Additional Port Settings or Change Default Preferences, both of which can be useful in a few circumstances. If you click the Advanced Port Settings button, you see the Advanced Settings for the modem port, as shown in Figure 4-4 on the next page. The first in, first out (FIFO) buffer is a standard used on most serial ports' universal asynchronous receiver-transmitter (UART) chipsets. FIFO buffers allow the port to buffer data traveling to and from the modem to manage data flow. Under most circumstances, both the receive and transmit buffers should be set to High, but if you are having connection problems, you can lower the settings for each buffer. Lower settings cause slower performance, but in some cases, might help to resolve connection problems.

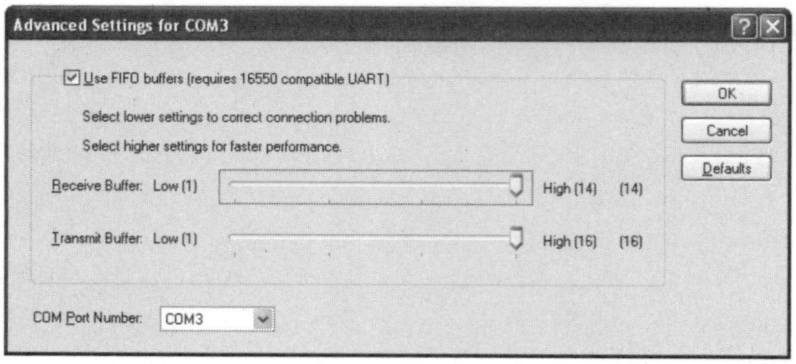

Figure 4-4. Reduce the receive and transmit buffer values if you are having connection problems, but lower settings will also mean slower performance.

If you click the Change Default Preferences button on the Advanced tab, you see a General and Advanced tab for the default preferences. The preferences you see are applied during setup, but you can change them to meet any specific needs you might have.

On the General tab, shown in Figure 4-5, are the call preferences and data connection preferences. The following list describes these options:

- **Call Preferences.** You can choose the Disconnect A Call If Idle For More Than setting if you want the modem to automatically disconnect from the Internet when there is no activity. However, many users find this setting aggravating, and it can disrupt e-mail file downloads and possibly other file downloads as well.

- **Port Speed.** This is the same Port Speed setting option you explored on the Modem tab. The standard speed is 115200.

- **Data Protocol.** The Data Protocol options are Standard EC (error correction), Forced EC, or Disabled. This setting controls how error correction is used when modems communicate with each other. Standard EC is the default and is usually all that is needed. Forced EC requires a certain error correction method called V.42 and hangs up if the standard is not used. Do not use Forced EC unless the modem you are connecting with requires it. You can also disable error correction if you are having problems connecting with your ISP, but this can make the connection unstable. Under most circumstances, the Standard EC setting should be used.

- **Compression.** You can enable or disable data compression, which is enabled by default. The data compression used by the modem, which is called hardware compression, is used to speed up the transfer process. Typically, you should leave the Compression setting enabled, but if you're having trouble making or maintaining modem connections, you can disable it to try to enhance connection reliability (at the cost of somewhat slower performance).

- **Flow Control.** Flow control refers to the flow of data between the modem and the computer. Depending on the modem, either hardware or software (Xon/Xoff) flow control can be used, and the typical Flow Control setting

Chapter 4

is Hardware. Check your modem documentation for details, but this setting normally does not need to be changed.

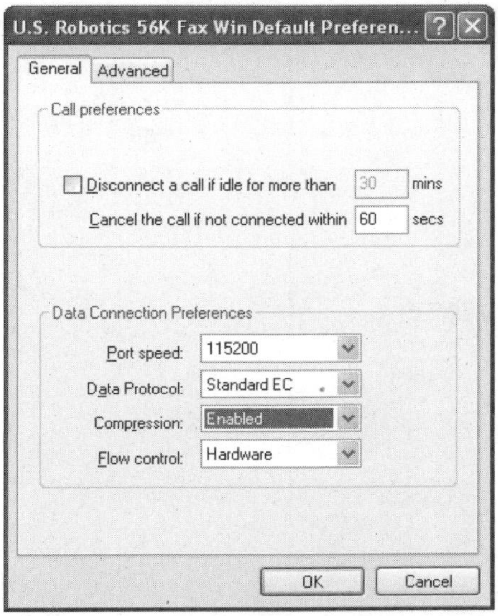

Figure 4-5. The General tab of Default Preferences enables you to make changes to call and data connection preferences.

On the Advanced tab, shown in Figure 4-6 on the next page, you can adjust additional hardware settings for the modem if necessary. Again, the standard settings are typically all you need, but the following list explains the settings in case you need to adjust them:

● **Data Bits.** Data bits refers to the number of bits that are used to transmit each character of data. The modem your modem is communicating with must have the same setting, which is typically 8 for online services. Your ISP will tell you if you need to use a different value; otherwise, this value should not be changed.

● **Parity.** Parity refers to the type of error checking. When used, a parity bit is appended to the data, which can then be checked by the receiving modem to ensure accuracy. The computer you are communicating with must have the same setting for parity to work. For online services, None is the typical setting. Again, do not change this setting unless instructed to do so by your ISP.

● **Stop Bits.** A stop bit is used to tell the computer that one byte of information has been sent. The stop bit value should be set to 1 unless you are directed to set it to a different value by your ISP.

● **Modulation.** Modulation refers to how data is changed from digital to analog and vice versa. Typically, standard modulation is used. However, if you are having problems connecting, you can also try the Nonstandard option.

Chapter 4

Depending on your modem, you might have additional options: You should only attempt to use them if specifically directed to do so by your ISP.

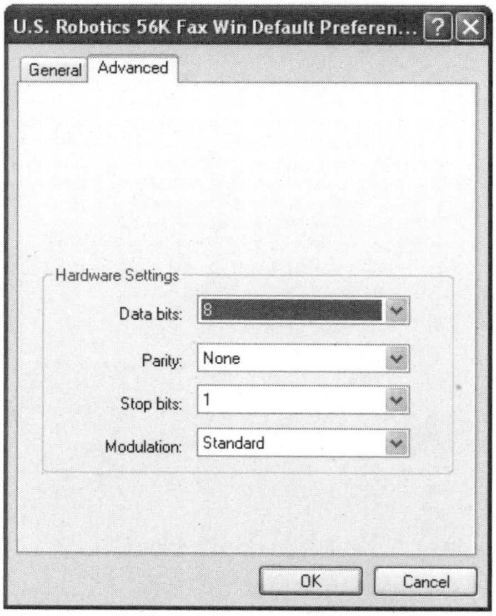

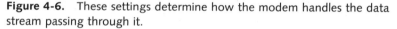

Figure 4-6. These settings determine how the modem handles the data stream passing through it.

Driver Tab

The Driver tab, shown in Figure 4-7, lets you update the current driver installed for the modem, and you can view data about the driver using the Driver Details option. If your modem shipped with an installation CD, you can use that CD to update the driver as well.

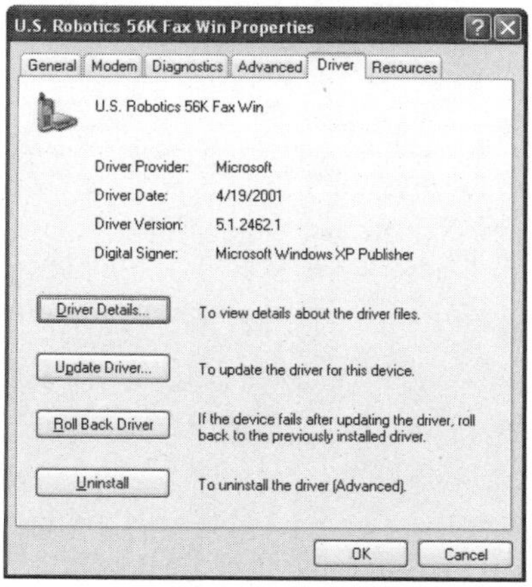

Figure 4-7. Use the Driver tab to update or change the current modem driver.

Resources Tab

Under normal circumstances, Windows XP automatically assigns system resources to hardware devices, such as interrupt request (IRQ) numbers and memory port ranges. There is nothing for you to do on the Resources tab if there are no problems with resource assignments (which there rarely are). However, if a conflict exists, you can manually assign resources to try to resolve the problem.

Creating New Internet Connections

Once your modem or broadband hardware is installed and configured correctly, your next step is to create an Internet connection. To create the new connection, you simply need to use the New Connection Wizard. Normally, you'll use your ISP's setup CD for both broadband and dial-up connections, so it is important that you read the ISP's documentation and perform the steps as required.

If you need to establish a dial-up or broadband connection for an existing account or if you want to use the manual approach, the New Connection Wizard can easily guide you through the process. See the following steps for details:

1 Open Network Connections. From the Windows XP Start menu, choose Connect To, Show All Connections. From the Classic Start menu, choose Settings, Network Connections.

2 In the task pane on the left under Network Tasks, select the Create A New Connection link.

3 The New Connection Wizard appears. Click Next.

4 On the Network Connection Type page of the wizard, shown in Figure 4-8 on the next page, you can choose the kind of connection that you want to create. Select the Connect To The Internet option and click Next.

5 On the Getting Ready page, you can select from a list of ISPs if you do not have an account. This option opens a connection to a referral service so that you can sign up with available service providers on the Internet. If you have an installation CD, you can select the Use The CD I Got From An ISP option to run setup from the CD. Or, you can select Set Up My Connection Manually, which is the option used in this procedure. Click Next to continue.

6 On the Internet Connection page, shown in Figure 4-9 on the next page, select the type of connection that you are using: dial-up, broadband that requires a user name and password, or broadband that is always on. Make your selection and click Next. Because you are most likely to use the New Connection Wizard to set up modem connections, the rest of this procedure focuses on that option.

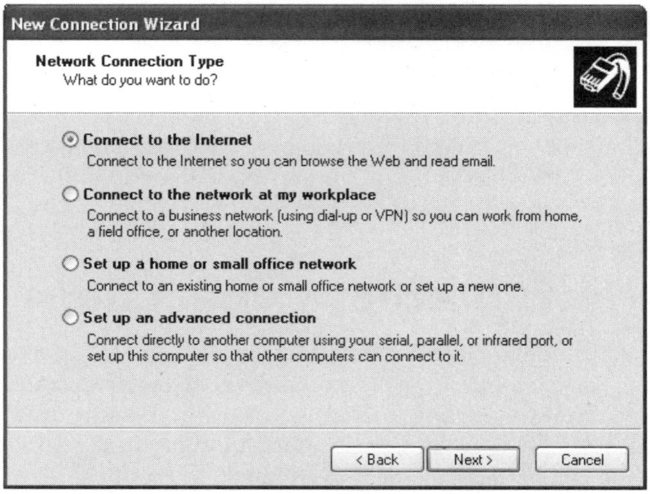

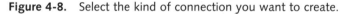

Figure 4-8. Select the kind of connection you want to create.

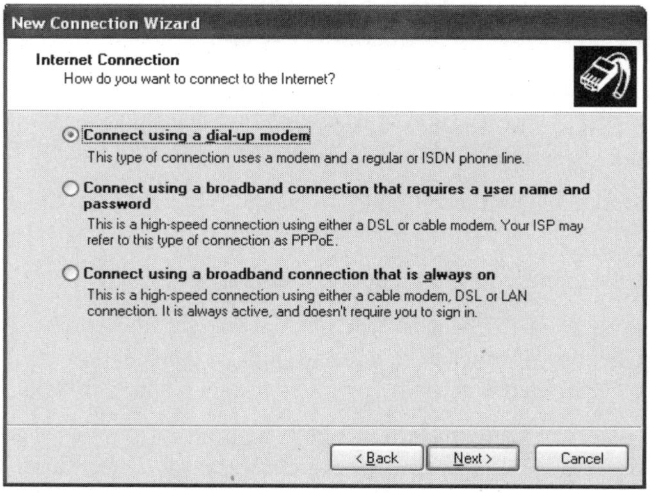

Figure 4-9. Select the type of connection you are using and click Next.

7 On the Connection Name page of the wizard, enter a name for the connection and click Next. The name should be something friendly that distinguishes the connection from other connections.

8 On the Phone Number To Dial page, enter the phone number required to dial the ISP. Include all digits necessary to dial the number from your location, such as 1 plus the area code if required. Click Next.

9 On the Internet Account Information page, shown in Figure 4-10, enter your user name and password, and then select the options you want to use. If you select the first check box, the account can be used by anyone using your computer; if you clear the check box, only you can use the connection by supplying your name and password. You can also make the connection the default connection, and you can turn on Internet Connection Firewall for the connection. See Chapter 5, "Using Internet Connection Firewall," to learn more about Internet Connection Firewall. Make your entries and selections and click Next.

Figure 4-10. Enter your account information and click Next.

10 On the final page of the wizard, you can choose to have a shortcut for the connection placed on your desktop. Click Finish. The new connection appears in the Network Connections folder as well as on your desktop, if you selected that option.

InsideOut

What Is PPPoE?

You might have noticed the reference to Point-to-Point Protocol over Ethernet (PPPoE) when you selected the type of connection that you wanted to create. *PPPoE* is a type of broadband Internet connection that is not always connected, but instead requires a user name and password to be sent each time the user wants to connect.

PPPoE is designed for users on a LAN (using standard Ethernet) who access the Internet over an Ethernet network through a broadband connection. In other words, Point-to-Point Protocol (PPP), which is used on the Internet, functions over Ethernet to provide Internet access to these users. With PPPoE, each user can have a different access configuration, even though they all reside on the same LAN.

(continued)

> **Inside Out** (continued)   One of the real-world applications of PPPoE, however, is the management of IP addresses. Instead of assigning each user a static IP address for an always-on connection, a dynamic IP address can be used. When the user does not use the Internet for a period of time, the connection becomes inactive, and the IP address is reassigned to another user. When the first user wants to access the Internet again, the user name and password are sent so that a new dynamic IP address can be assigned. This might cause a slight delay in the connection and can be a real problem for users who want to make a virtual private network (VPN) connection over the Internet to their home or small office network if that network uses PPPoE to connect to the Internet.
>
> You can learn more about PPPoE by accessing RFC 2516 on the Internet. To read more about an RFC, open your Web browser and use an Internet search engine to search for the RFC number. In this case, you would search for **RFC 2516**.

Managing Dial-up Connections

Once you have created a dial-up connection, an icon appears in the Network Connections folder for the dial-up connection. You can further configure and manage the dial-up connection by right-clicking the icon and choosing Properties. There are a number of configuration options for dial-up connections, and a few of them often cause users some difficulty and problems. This section will examine the configuration features and options that can help dial-up modem communications.

Connection Properties

Figure 4-11 shows the dialog box that appears when you double-click a dial-up connection in the Network Connections window. Although this connection window is simple, it is important to note that you can change your user name and password if necessary, and you can also make the connection private or public in terms of local user access. Figure 4-11 shows that this connection is available to all users who access this particular computer.

If you select Me Only, the connection's user name and password will be saved and made available only when the designated user is signed on to Windows XP. Other users signing on to the computer and attempting to use the connection will each have to provide a valid user name and password. If they don't know the designated user's account information and don't have their own account, they won't be able to use the connection. However, if the designated user signs on to the computer and then leaves it unattended, anyone can sit down at the computer and access the connection. Additionally, when Me Only is selected and the user either logs off the computer or uses Fast User Switching to switch to another user, the dial-up session will automatically be disconnected.

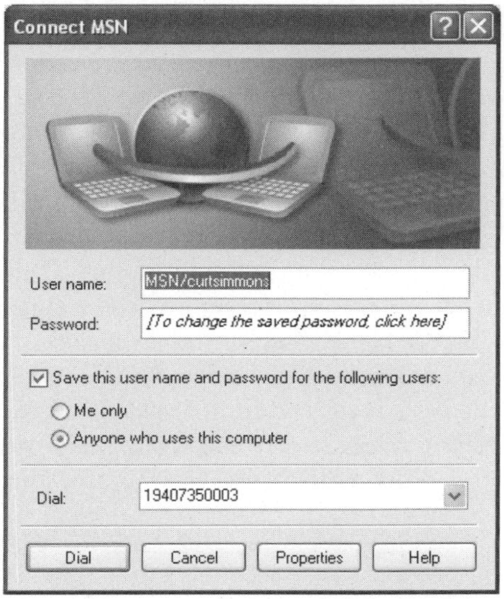

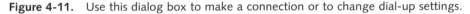

Figure 4-11. Use this dialog box to make a connection or to change dial-up settings.

If you select Anyone Who Uses This Computer, any user on the computer will be able to use that dial-up connection. If a user initiates a dial-up session and then logs off, Windows XP will prompt the user to determine if that user wants to disconnect the dial-up session or leave it running. If the first user leaves it running and another user subsequently logs on, and then does not disconnect the session manually when logging off, the session will be maintained and that user (and all subsequent users) will not be prompted. If, on the other hand, Fast User Switching is used to switch users, the connection is automatically maintained.

Another option is to clear the check box labeled Save This User Name And Password For The Following Users, which deactivates both of the suboptions. With this option, even the designated user will have to supply the user name and password each time a connection is desired. This way an unattended machine can't be used by an unauthorized person to access the Internet. As with selecting Me Only, using Fast User Switching or logging off will result in dial-up sessions being disconnected.

You can configure additional properties of a dial-up connection by right-clicking the connection in Network Connections and choosing Properties. Note that you can also delete a connection, make it the default, or connect or disconnect by right-clicking the connection.

If you access the connection's properties, you see several different tabs that you can use to further configure the Internet connection. A number of the options on the tabs are self-explanatory, but the most important configuration options are discussed next.

On the General tab, shown in Figure 4-12, you can click the Configure button to access the Modem Configuration dialog box. This takes you to the same properties options you find when accessing modem properties through Phone And Modem Options in Control Panel. Under Phone Number on the General tab, you see the number you entered when you created the connection. If you want to use alternate numbers, click the Alternates button and enter the desired numbers. Note that by default the numbers you entered in the dialog box will be dialed as-is, including the area code (if it is included). In other words, dialing rules are not used, and the computer dials the numbers exactly as you have entered them. If you want to configure dialing rules for the connection, select Use Dialing Rules on the General tab, and then click the Dialing Rules button. The Dialing Rules tab of the Phone And Modem Options dialog box appears. You can then create area code rules as needed from a specific location, and you can create multiple locations. Dialing rules are very effective when you're using a portable computer and dialing up from different locations. See "Configuring Dialing Rules" on page 111 to learn more.

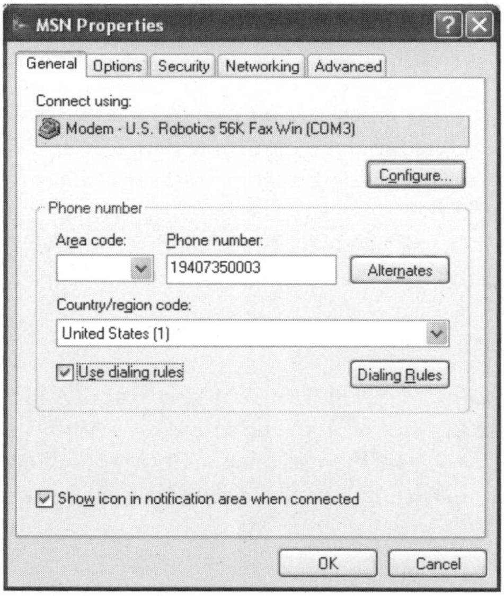

Figure 4-12. You can access the modem configuration, phone number, and dialing rules from the General tab.

On the Options tab, shown in Figure 4-13, you can configure several dialing and redialing options. These settings are mostly self-explanatory, but notice that the Idle Time Before Hanging Up value is 20 minutes by default. Even if you have the modem configured to not hang up after a set amount of idle time, the connection settings will still be invoked. Therefore, if you want to make certain that you are never automatically disconnected, select Never from the Idle Time Before Hanging Up list. Then, open

Phone And Modem Options in Control Panel. Select the Modems tab, select the modem, and click the Properties button. On the Advanced tab, click the Change Default Preferences button and clear the Disconnect A Call If Idle For More Than option.

Figure 4-13. Configure dialing and redialing options on the Options tab.

The options on the Security and Networking tabs typically apply to dial-up connections to a corporate network, such as a VPN connection, although some ISPs are now requiring secure authentication methods. You can learn more about the configuration options on the Security tab in Chapter 20, "Using Security," and the configuration options on the Networking tab in "Configuring IP Settings in Windows XP," page 35, as well as in "Other Networking Protocols," page 42.

> **caution** The default security settings for Internet connections use the Typical (Recommended Setting) on the Security tab, which uses unsecured passwords. Do not change the settings on the Security tab unless the instructions from your ISP specifically tell you to do so. Incorrect edits to the Security tab will prevent you from being authenticated by the ISP's servers.

On the Advanced tab, you can turn on Internet Connection Firewall, which you can learn more about in Chapter 5, "Using Internet Connection Firewall," and you can use ICS, which you can learn more about in "Using Internet Connection Sharing," page 301.

Troubleshooting

You need to solve common dial-up connection problems.

Users who rely on dial-up connections can suffer from a number of different problems because they have to connect to the ISP each time they wish to use the Internet, and because of possible connection problems over phone lines. The following are some common problems and solutions:

- **My dial-up connection keeps disconnecting when I am not using it.** If the connection is automatically being terminated, take a look at the Idle Time Before Hanging Up setting on the Options tab of the Dial-up Connection Properties dialog box. Also, be aware that many ISPs automatically disconnect idle users after a certain time period to conserve their resources.

- **My connection is slow.** If the Internet connection is slow over the modem, it is normally a problem with the ISP's connection to the Internet or a limitation of your phone lines. Verify the speeds you're getting over your dial-up connection by examining the connection's properties after you dial up. If they're slow, you might have noisy phone lines in your house (or between your house and the nearest fiber-optic connection). Also, contact your ISP to determine the amount of load being placed on its Internet connection.

- **My connection always tries to dial a 1 in front of the number.** Right-click the dial-up connection, choose Properties, and on the General tab, change the phone number settings. Or, if you are using dialing rules, change the dialing rule configuration so that it recognizes the phone number or area code as local. See the next section for a discussion on dialing rules.

- **I am prompted to approve the phone number every time the connection dials.** Right-click the dial-up connection, choose Properties, and select the Options tab. Clear the Prompt For Phone Number check box.

- **I have a number of connection problems on a regular basis.** If you have a number of connection problems, including dropped connections, you might need to use some additional initialization commands for the modem. See your modem's documentation for details. Also, try opening Phone And Modem Options in Control Panel, select the Advanced tab, click the Advanced Port Settings button, and adjust the FIFO buffer settings. If none of these suggestions work for you, it's possible there might be a fundamental incompatibility between your modem and the ones being used by your ISP. Contact your ISP for recommended modem brands as well as tips on how to make your modem connect properly to the ISP's modem.

Configuring Dialing Rules

Dialing rules can be very helpful when you need to dial from different locations. They can also be an annoyance if you do not have them configured correctly because they typically cause users a number of problems. If you are dialing from a laptop that is used in several different places or if you help support users who do so, it is wise to have a firm understanding of how dialing rules work.

Dialing rules work by location. This means that you configure specific locations and define how dialing should work from each location. You specify which numbers should be used for accessing the Internet from each location (a local number is preferable so you don't pay long distance or toll charges). You also specify which area codes are local to each location and which calling cards should be used for each location.

Suppose you work in a corporate office and use a laptop. From that office and your home, you use certain dialing rules to access an ISP. Several area codes are considered local, and you have several access numbers. Perhaps you frequently travel to a customer's site in another city. You use the same laptop, but you need to dial a long distance number using a corporate credit card to access your company's LAN. You simply create a new location and select that location on the Dialing Rules tab of the Phone And Modem Options dialog box whenever you are in that city. When you return to your hometown, you choose the dialing rules for that location. You might have one dialing connection that is called Local and another called Remote. By telling Windows XP where you are, it will use the dialing rules for that location to determine how to dial your ISP.

You can easily create new dialing locations and edit existing locations using the Dialing Rules tab of the Phone And Modem Options dialog box shown in Figure 4-14.

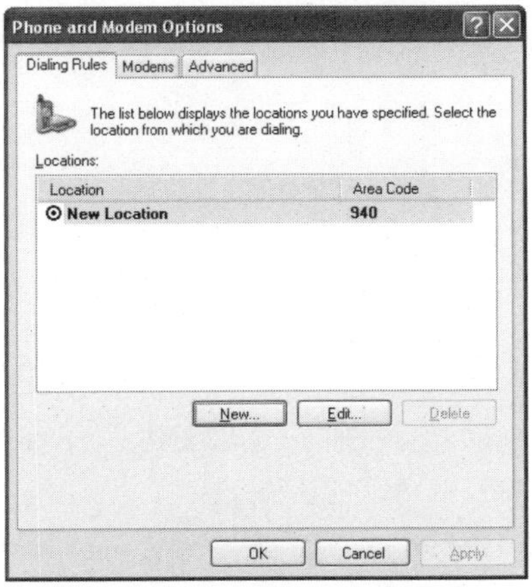

Figure 4-14. Dialing rules are based on different locations, which you can create from the Dialing Rules tab.

To create a new location, follow these steps:

1 Open Phone And Modem Options in Control Panel, and select the Dialing Rules tab. Click the New button.

2 The New Location dialog box appears. On the General tab, shown in Figure 4-15, you can configure the following important settings:

 ▪ **Location Name.** Give the location a recognizable name.

 ▪ **Country/Region** and **Area Code.** Select your country or region, and enter the area code for the location.

 ▪ **Dialing Rules.** Enter values to access outside lines for local calls or long distance calls. You can also enter carrier codes. You have several options that you can use if necessary.

 ▪ **Call Waiting.** Choose a code to disable call waiting so that your connection is not interrupted. Call waiting often disrupts dial-up connections. Select the To Disable Call Waiting option, and enter the code in the text box to the right. A typical code in the United States is *70. However, different carriers use different disable codes, so you'll have to enter the code needed for your carrier.

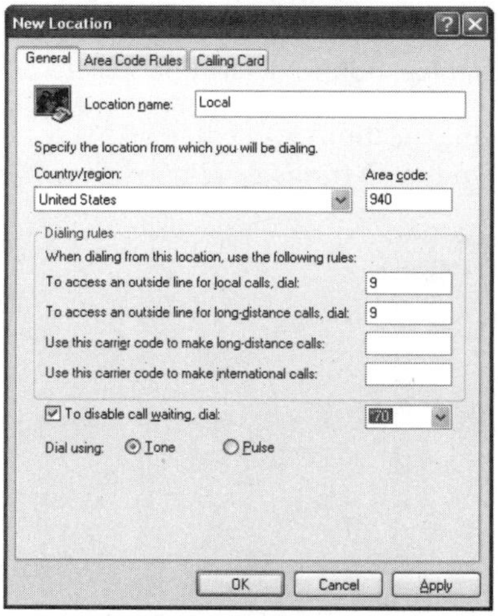

Figure 4-15. Configure basic calling options for a location on the General tab of the New Location dialog box.

3 On the Area Code Rules tab, you can create a list of area code rules that tells Windows XP how to handle certain area codes. To create a rule, click the New button.

Chapter 4

4 In the New Area Code Rule dialog box, shown in Figure 4-16, enter the area code and include any specific prefixes that should be used. Under Rules, select whether to dial 1 before the area code and whether to dial the area code. Click OK to save the rule. If an area code must be dialed for certain prefixes but not for others, define two area code rules for the area code, one rule for each group of prefixes. You can then create additional rules for other area codes by clicking the New button on the Area Code Rules tab, or you can edit an existing rule using the Edit button.

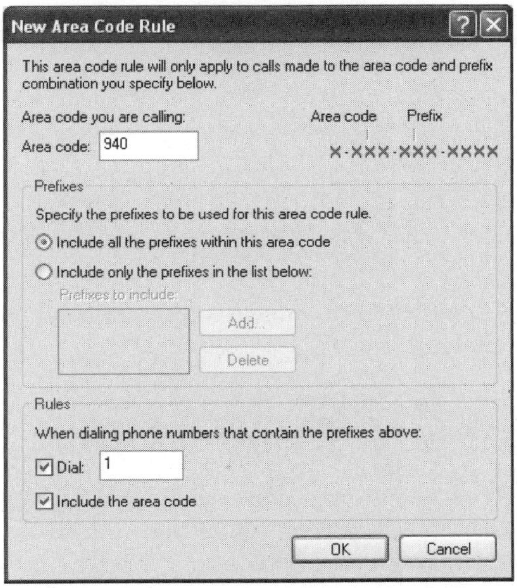

Figure 4-16. Create the area code rule by applying rules according to prefixes or entire area codes.

caution The Dial option and the Include The Area Code option at the bottom of the New Area Code Rule dialog box often cause problems. Keep in mind that a 1 will always be dialed if the Dial option is selected as will the area code if that option is selected. If you are having problems with a dialing rule concerning 1 and/or the area code, the area code rule is always the culprit.

5 On the Calling Card tab, shown in Figure 4-17 on the next page, you can select a calling card if you are using one, and enter the account and PIN numbers as needed. If your card is not provided in the default list, click the New button to enter the card name and information.

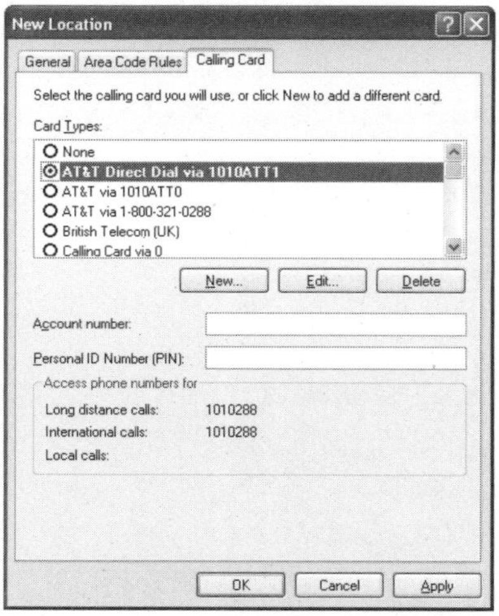

Figure 4-17. Configure a calling card for use with the dialing location if necessary.

6 When you are done, click OK. The new location appears in the Phone And Modem Options dialog box.

Managing Broadband Connections

For the most part, once a broadband connection is configured and working, there is nothing else to do, especially if the broadband connection is an always-on DSL, cable, or satellite connection. Because you do not have to connect each time you want to use the Internet, it is unlikely that you will have the problems you might expect with a dial-up connection.

Normally, broadband providers will send out a technician to install the hardware device and configure your system or allow you to use a kit to set it up yourself. The kit will provide step-by-step instructions for setting up and connecting the DSL, cable, or satellite modem, connecting it to your PC, and configuring the networking settings on your system.

Most broadband systems use either DHCP to allow your computer to automatically be configured to use the service or provide you with a PPPoE client that provides the same functionality. With PPPoE clients, however, you must manually connect each time you wish to use your broadband connection.

Other broadband ISPs will provide you with an IP address, subnet mask, default gateway, and DNS addresses, which must be manually configured, as described in "Configuring IP Settings in Windows XP" on page 35. The use of static configuration information is becoming less and less common among broadband ISPs, however.

If you intend to use a router or residential gateway on your broadband connection, you'll need to perform further configuration. Ordinarily, these devices use network address translation (NAT) to share the one IP address typically provided by the ISP with more than one computer. This functionality, combined with any firewall capabilities of the device, also helps protect your network from malicious hackers.

If you end up using a router or residential gateway, you'll need to configure it to work with your ISP. Similar to configuring a standalone computer, you will need to configure the router or residential gateway either to receive its IP address via DHCP, to use PPPoE passthrough, or to use a static configuration.

When using routers or residential gateways, you'll also need to configure your computers to request their configuration information from your router or residential gateway via DHCP (although your computers can be configured manually to private addresses if you want). See "Adding Routers and Residential Gateways," page 51, and "Getting to Know NAT," page 54, for more information on these devices as well as private IP networking. Also, consult the manual for your router or gateway device to determine how to use it with your particular ISP's configuration.

Each broadband connection and broadband provider has different configuration options and instructions; therefore, always check your documentation if you are experiencing connectivity problems or if you need to make some kind of configuration change. Also, never hesitate to use the telephone technical support provided by your ISP if you are experiencing problems.

Using Internet Connection Firewall

It seems as though hacker attacks and other malicious behavior over the Internet are quite common these days. The evening news often reports some new online threat that has appeared, and even large corporations with extensive security have fallen prey to hackers and security breaks. With security becoming more and more of an issue when accessing the Internet, attention has moved to the home and small office user as well. With always-on, always-connected broadband solutions growing in use, the potential for security problems is very real.

To help combat these problems and provide a safer way to access the Internet, Microsoft Windows XP introduces *Internet Connection Firewall (ICF)*, a tool designed for the home user, home network, or small office network that helps protect a computer or network from security threats originating from the Internet. This chapter covers the basics of activating and configuring ICF to protect your Windows XP computer from external attack.

Introducing Firewalls

Firewalls are certainly nothing new in the computing world, but you hear more about them today than ever before. With security concerns at an all time high, numerous firewall products are available on the market, with a number of third-party software products targeted to the home user or small network. With ICF's inclusion in Windows XP, you know that these security concerns are valid and should be considered by any Internet user or network user.

What Is a Firewall?

A *firewall* is a piece of hardware or software placed between two networks or computers to keep one safe from the other.

117

The most common example concerns a private local area network (LAN) and the public Internet. A firewall can be used between the two so that users on the private network can access the Internet, but Internet users cannot access the private network. In the following schematic illustration, the LAN can reach across the firewall to draw upon the Internet, but activity originating from the Internet cannot cross over the firewall and compromise the LAN's security.

Network Protected by a Firewall

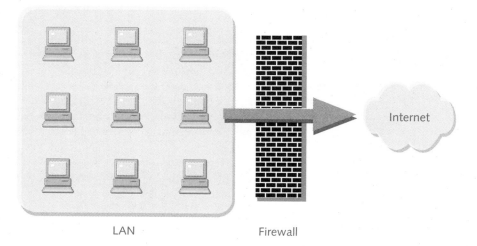

LAN   Firewall

Firewalls can also be configured to prevent LAN users from accessing the Internet or to restrict TCP/IP traffic so that only certain ports can transmit across the firewall.

Firewall solutions can be in the form of either hardware or software. Each has its own advantages and disadvantages, and staunch firewall enthusiasts might argue for one or the other. However, from a networking person's point of view, both hardware and software solutions can be very effective ways to protect your network. ICF is a software-based firewall solution.

> For more information on firewalls and their use, as well as best practices related to ICF and other firewall products, be sure to read Chapter 20, "Maintaining Network Security."

Understanding Internet Connection Firewall

ICF is readily available in Windows XP and works with any network connection. Before getting into the specifics of ICF configuration, it is important to understand how ICF works, the features it provides, and how it can be used in a home or small office network. It is important to note that ICF was specifically developed to protect modem and broadband Internet connections—it was not designed for workstations residing on large networks where other types of Internet access are used. In those networks, either firewall hardware or software on Windows 2000 servers is used to control and manage Internet access. ICF, however, was designed to support either a stand-alone computer (that is, one not providing a shared connection to other systems) or a computer that is providing a shared Internet connection to other computers on a small network.

For more information about using a Windows XP computer to share an Internet connection with multiple computers, see "Using Internet Connection Sharing," page 301.

How ICF Works

ICF works with an Internet connection to provide security from external attacks. ICF uses a method of protection known as the *table method*, in which a table or list of outbound and inbound IP addresses is maintained. Consider first how ICF works when a stand-alone computer uses ICF. You enable ICF on the Internet connection, as detailed in "Activating and Configuring ICF" on page 124. Using your Web browser, you request a Web page. ICF makes an entry in its outbound connections table noting the IP address of the site you are requesting. When the Web page is served back to the computer, ICF examines the IP packets and looks at the IP addresses. If ICF finds a match for the sending address in the list of destination addresses for outbound traffic, the assumption is that you requested the IP traffic and therefore ICF allows the traffic to enter the computer. However, if any traffic arrives at the firewall that does *not* match a destination IP address listed in the table, the IP packets are dropped and are not processed by the computer.

ICF is considered a *stateful* firewall because it examines all traffic passing in and out of the firewall and makes decisions concerning that traffic as needed. In other words, ICF considers the current state of the packets and determines whether they are allowed or not based on the ICF table, as the following diagram shows.

How ICF Works

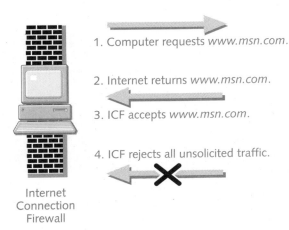

1. Computer requests *www.msn.com*.

2. Internet returns *www.msn.com*.

3. ICF accepts *www.msn.com*.

4. ICF rejects all unsolicited traffic.

Internet

Internet
Connection
Firewall

You can also protect an entire network by enabling ICF on the computer that directly accesses the Internet and by using Internet Connection Sharing (ICS) on the LAN. In the case of a network using ICS, the computer hosting the Internet over an ICF-enabled connection also serves as the ICS host for the rest of the LAN. All other computers on the network access the ICS host computer to connect to the Internet, so all network requests are recorded and managed in the ICF table, as shown in this illustration.

Software-based Firewall, ICS Network

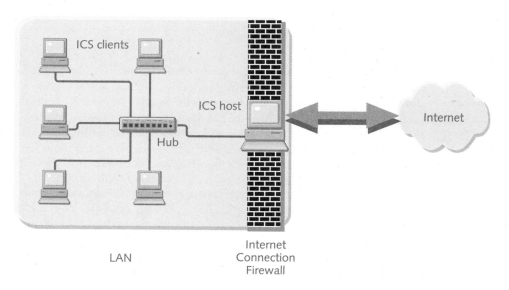

Because all inbound traffic is dropped unless it has been specifically requested from an internal network client, ICF blocks some types of traffic that can be potentially dangerous, but might also be wanted on your network. For example, all incoming ICMP traffic (such as ping requests) is blocked as well as all Remote Desktop traffic originating from outside the LAN. Because you might want to allow ICMP or Remote Desktop traffic, ICF provides a way to override the table configuration for certain services, which you can learn more about in "Enabling Services" on page 130.

InsideOut

Understanding ICF and Protocols

ICF works on a table basis, not on a protocol-by-protocol basis. Although some firewalls allow you to block certain protocols, ICF is concerned with keeping traffic that is not explicitly requested from entering the local computer or network. For this reason, ICF does not place any restrictions on protocols. If you want to download music or movies, you won't have any problems with ICF because there will be a table entry for your request and the data will be allowed to pass. However, if you want to play games over the Internet where an Internet client contacts your computer, ICF will not allow that traffic because the traffic originated from outside your LAN (as an invitation to play the game) and thus won't have a table entry in ICF. As you work with ICF, keep in mind that ICF allows any traffic that arrives from a request you made regardless of its protocol and likewise blocks all unsolicited traffic originating from outside the network despite its protocol.

How to Use ICF

ICF is easy to configure and use as long as you remember two simple rules:

- All Internet connections should be firewalled. For example, if your computer has a broadband connection to the Internet as well as a dial-up connection to the Internet, both the broadband connection and the dial-up connection should be firewalled for complete protection. Failure to turn on ICF for one of the Internet connections is considered a security breach because your computer or network will not be protected whenever that connection is used.

- Internal network connections should usually not be firewalled. Network interface cards (NICs) used to communicate on your local network must not be firewalled. If they are, computers on the network will not be able to access your computer because the ICF table will not allow any network traffic to enter the computer that is not explicitly requested by you. ICF is used on the Internet connection only, not on the internal network connections.

When You Should Use ICF

Considering the two usage rules in the previous section, a few different scenarios describing when ICF should be used and how it should be used are provided in the following sections.

Accessing the Internet from a Single Computer

If you are using a single computer, enable ICF on your Internet connection. If you have multiple Internet connections, enable ICF on each connection so that you are always protected, no matter which connection you might be using at the moment. Remember that ICF works with individual connections in Network Connections, not on your computer as a whole. When multiple Internet connections are used, you must firewall each connection for complete protection.

Accessing the Internet from a Network Using ICS

If you are using ICS (see "Using Internet Connection Sharing," page 301, to learn more about ICS), you should enable ICF on the Internet connection residing on the ICS host computer. If you have multiple Internet connections on the ICS host computer, enable ICF on each Internet connection. However, do not enable ICF on the local area connections between the ICS host and ICS clients. If you firewall other internal network connections, you will have network connectivity problems between computers.

Accessing the Internet from a Network with Multiple Internet Connections

If you are using a network in which several computers directly access the Internet through broadband or dial-up connections, you need to use ICF on each connection to the Internet, as shown in the following illustration. Again, make sure you do not firewall NICs that internally connect the LAN—only enable ICF on the external Internet connections.

ICF Enabled on Multiple Internet Connections

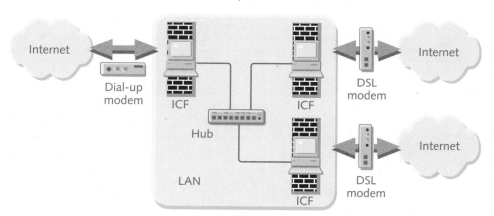

Accessing the Internet from a Large Network with Poor Security

Some large LAN and WAN environments do not have firewalls or any other kind of protective measures between them and their Internet connection. Although this situation is becoming less and less common, many colleges, universities, and other institutions continue to maintain an *open network* policy.

In such situations, workstations normally use the same connection to access both LAN/WAN and Internet resources, so it's normally wise to use some sort of firewall to protect your workstation. However, remember that although ICF will protect your Internet connection, it can cause headaches if you need to perform file and printer sharing with other Windows clients and servers within the LAN or WAN. This topic is discussed in "Enabling File and Printer Sharing with ICF," page 132.

Chapter 5

When You Should Not Use ICF

As a general rule, ICF can be used in most situations when you want to protect your computer from Internet attacks. However, you should not use ICF if

- You are using another firewall. If you are using a residential gateway or another firewall software product, do not use ICF. You should only use one firewall product, whether that product is a hardware or software solution. Multiple firewall products usually do not work together and can cause you to lose your Internet connection. So, make a choice, but do not use ICF when another firewall solution is used.

- You are using a mail client that requires remote procedure calls. Some mail programs, such as Microsoft Outlook in a Microsoft Exchange server environment, use *remote procedure calls (RPCs)*, which allow mail servers to contact the program when there is mail to be delivered. ICF will block this kind of traffic because it has not been requested internally, so in some cases, ICF will simply not allow you to receive your mail automatically. Instead, you have to manually check for mail. If you are using Microsoft Outlook as a way to connect to an ISP mail server, Outlook will work fine with ICS. See "Using ICF with E-mail Services," page 134, for more information.

- You need to share files across a virtual private network (VPN) connection, because ICF can block such sharing. However, a workaround for this problem is presented in "Enabling File and Printer Sharing with ICF," page 132.

What ICF Does Not Do

ICF is a basic firewall product that blocks traffic; however, it does not meet every possible need, and it does not protect you from every possible threat. For example:

- ICF does not protect you from viruses or worms. Downloaded viruses, e-mail viruses, and worms are not detected by ICF. You need to use antivirus software with ICF for complete protection against these dangers.

- ICF does not protect you from Trojan horse programs. Once they get into your computer (usually in e-mail you receive), *Trojan horse* programs gather information from your computer, such as addresses from an e-mail address book, and send themselves in e-mail addressed to your contacts, spreading themselves further. Because ICF is only concerned with inbound traffic, ICF does not inspect outbound traffic for these threats. To ensure that your computer is not running Trojan horse programs, you need a program that can safeguard your computer. Some third-party firewall products,

123

such as ZoneAlarm (*www.zonealarm.com*) provide this kind of protection, but you should always use a combination of firewall and antivirus software for complete protection.

- If your computer is using ICS to share its connection to the Internet with the other computers on your network, ICF does not protect your computer from *internal* attacks and threats. ICF only protects your Internet connection. If an internal user on your network decides to attack other computers inside the network or runs a Trojan horse application that attempts to do the same thing, ICF provides no protection for this kind of attack.

> Internal and external network threats, as well as countermeasures for them, are covered in Chapter 20, "Maintaining Network Security."

Activating and Configuring ICF

ICF is easy to enable and generally easy to configure, depending on your needs. There are several important actions that you need to know about, and in this section, you can explore how to best configure and use ICF.

> **note** You must be logged on with an account that has administrative privileges to enable and configure ICF.

Enabling ICF

You can enable ICF quickly and easily using a single check box. Follow these steps:

1 Open Network Connections. From the Windows XP Start menu, choose Connect To, Show All Connections; from the Classic Start menu, choose Settings, Network Connections.

2 In the Network Connections window, right-click the Internet connection on which you want to enable ICF and choose Properties.

3 In the Properties dialog box, select the Advanced tab, which is shown in Figure 5-1.

4 In the Internet Connection Firewall section, select the Protect My Computer And Network check box and click OK. The connection is now firewalled.

5 If you are using additional Internet connections, repeat steps 1–4 to enable ICF on those connections as well.

Figure 5-1. Select the check box in the Internet Connection Firewall section to enable ICF.

> **note** If your computer does not have a NIC, you'll not see the Internet Connection Sharing section that appears in Figure 5-1.

> **caution** If you open the Properties dialog box for your LAN connection, you'll also see that ICF is available on the Advanced tab. This is due to the fact that the Properties dialog boxes are the same for all network connections. However, this does *not* mean that ICF should be enabled on any NICs that are not directly connected to the Internet. If you are using ICS to share your Internet connection with an internal network, you should only enable ICF on the connections that directly connect to the Internet; all other internal connections should not be firewalled.

Using the ICF Log

When you enable ICF for an Internet connection, the firewall becomes active and immediately starts working. ICF gives you the option of logging the events that occur with ICF, but the log is not activated or configured by default. Using ICF's simple log file, you can log dropped packets as well as all successful connections.

If you choose to log dropped packets, you can view the log file and see what attempts to access your computer over the Internet have been thwarted. This gives you clues about anyone who might be trying to tamper with your network or PC. If you log successful connections, you'll see the destination IP address of every site that you have visited. But this will cause the log file to grow rapidly, especially if the Internet is used a lot on the local computer or on an ICS network. You do, however, have the ability to determine the maximum size to which individual log files can grow. To configure the security log, follow these steps:

1 Open Network Connections.

2 Right-click an Internet connection on which ICF is enabled and choose Properties.

3 In the Properties dialog box, select the Advanced tab. Click the Settings button.

4 Select the Security Logging tab shown in Figure 5-2.

5 Under Logging Options, select either or both Log Dropped Packets and Log Successful Connections.

6 By default, the log file is named pfirewall.log, and it is stored in your Windows directory. If you want to store it elsewhere, click the Browse button or type another destination in the Name box.

7 The default maximum log file size is 4096 KB. You can decrease this value if you like or increase it to a maximum size of 32,767 KB.

8 Click OK when you're done.

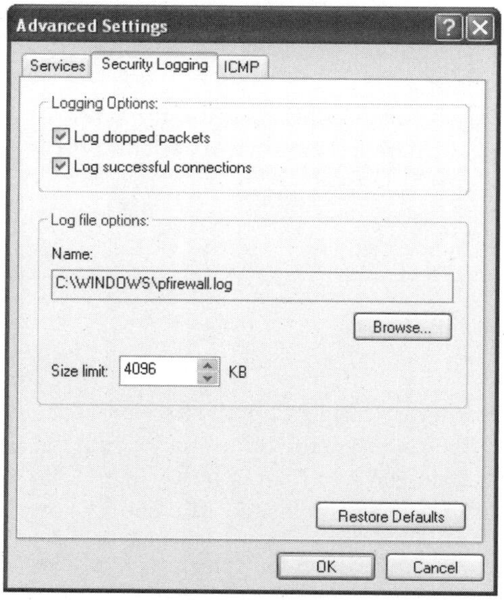

Figure 5-2. Select the logging options and configuration you want for ICF-protected connections.

Chapter 5

> **note** When the log file reaches its maximum size, as configured on the Security Logging tab, the information is written to a file named pfirewall.log.1, and the newest data is saved in pfirewall.log. Also note that log file settings are global; they apply to all firewalled connections on the computer.

Viewing the Log File

Once logging is turned on, you can view the log file at any time by opening it with Notepad, any text editor, or any word processing application. Figure 5-3 shows that the log file contains IP information about the connections that you have decided to log. In this example, both successful connections as well as dropped packets are being logged.

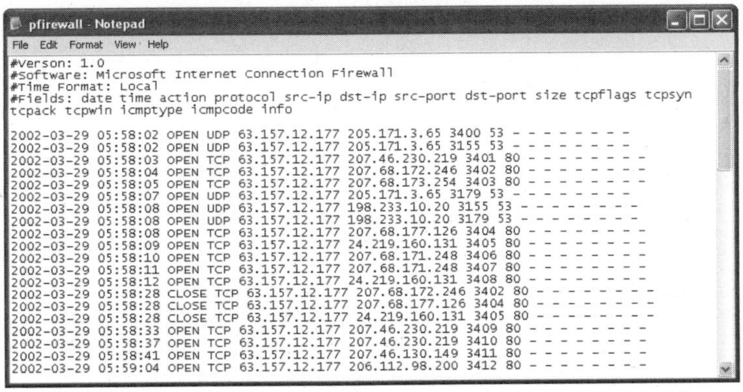

Figure 5-3.   The ICF log file contains IP addressing information for the data you chose to log.

Understanding the Log File

The ICF log file contains IP information about the connection or dropped packets. Figure 5-3 shows that the fields that are logged are listed in the order by which they are logged. The data below the field listing corresponds directly to the fields, although field data does not line up with the headers in Notepad. The ICF log is a W3C Extended File format log, which can also be opened and analyzed (or even written to a database) by third-party logging utilities. Table 5-1 on the next page describes each of the logging fields.

> For more information on how to best utilize W3C Extended File logs, see "Examining Log Files," page 582.

> **note** If an entry written to the log file has no applicable information for a field, a hyphen (-) is placed in the field instead.

Table 5-1. **Information Recorded in the ICF Log File**

ICF Log Field	Explanation
Date	Indicates the date when the action took place; listed as year, month, day.
Time	Indicates the time when the action took place; listed as hour, minute, second.
Action	Lists the action that took place, such as open, close, drop, or info-events-lost (which refers to a number of events that took place but were not recorded in the log).
Protocol	Lists the protocol that was in use for the connection, such as TCP, UDP, ICMP, and so on.
Src-IP (Source IP)	Lists the source IP address of the computer that attempted the communication. This can be your computer or a computer on the Internet.
Dst-IP (Destination IP)	Lists the destination IP address, which is the destination of the communication sent by the source. This can be a computer on the Internet or your computer.
Src-port (Source Port)	Indicates the source port that was used by the source computer. The port number can range from 1 to 65,535 and is only recorded for TCP or UDP protocols.
Dst-port (Destination Port)	Indicates the port used by the destination computer. This is also either a TCP or UDP port ranging from 1 to 65,535.
Size	Indicates the size of the packet in bytes.
TCPflags	Lists control flags in the header information of a packet. Common flags include Ack (Acknowledgment), Fin (no more data from sender), or Rst (reset). This field and the ones that follow are included for completeness, but they require a greater knowledge of TCP/IP to be useful. Search the Internet for **RFC 793** to learn more about TCP/IP headers.
TCPsyn	Notes the TCP sequence number of the packet.

Table 5-1. *(continued)*

ICF Log Field	Explanation
TCPack	Notes the TCP acknowledgment number in the packet.
TCPwin	Notes the TCP window size (in bytes) in the packet.
ICMPtype	Notes the ICMP type field number, if an ICMP message.
ICMPcode	Notes the ICMP code field number, if an ICMP message.
Info	Contains information about the type of action that occurred, if applicable.

InsideOut

Using the ICF Log as Big Brother

If several people use the Windows XP computer on which you have enabled ICF, you can use the ICF log file as a way to sample what other users are accessing on the Internet. ICF records one log file on the computer regardless of which user is accessing the Internet, so you can monitor all traffic using the single log file. Bear in mind that the ICF log is not designed as a *snooper* program, but it can be used to find out which Web sites have been accessed over the ICF-protected connection. If you are so inclined to know, follow these steps:

1. Log on with an account that has administrative privileges.

2. Ensure that the firewall log has been configured to log successful connections.

3. Open the firewall log. Locate an open connection and copy its destination IP address.

4. Open Internet Explorer or another Web browser, paste the destination IP address into the Address bar, and press Enter.

5. The browser will resolve the IP address, and the Web page will appear. Now you know which Web site was accessed.

6. For additional security, place the firewall log into an encrypted folder to make sure other users cannot access and modify it. Also, anyone else logged on with an administrator account (including anyone who uses the computer while logged on under your administrator account) can turn off the log if they know how. They can then surf and turn the log back on afterward.

Enabling Services

Because ICF blocks all incoming communication that is not explicitly requested, some services will not work with ICF unless you make further configurations. For example, if you are hosting a Web site on your computer and users try to access your Web site, the packets arriving at your computer will be dropped because they were not solicited. Or, if you want to access your computer from a remote location using Remote Desktop, ICF will not allow the communication because it is not solicited.

Because the blocking functions of ICF by default affect all protocols and ports, you might want to override the ICF behavior for certain services so that they will work with ICF. To enable a service to work with ICF, follow these steps:

1 Open Network Connections.

2 Right-click the ICF-protected connection and choose Properties.

3 Select the Advanced tab and click the Settings button.

4 On the Services tab, shown in Figure 5-4, select each service that you want to enable. Remote Desktop is enabled in this figure.

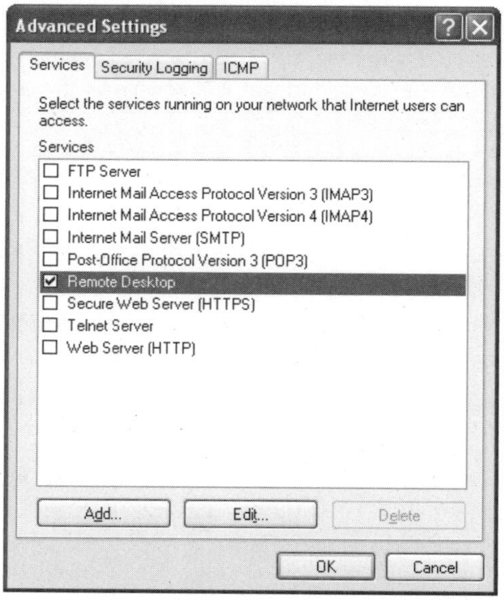

Figure 5-4. Select each service you want to run over the ICF-protected connection.

5 When you first select a service, the Service Settings dialog box appears for that service, showing its default settings—including the name of the network computer on which the service is to be enabled. If you want to enable the service on a different computer on your network, type its name or IP address in the Name Or IP Address box. Click OK. You can adjust these settings at any time by selecting the service and clicking the Edit button.

6 If you want to enable a service that is not listed, click the Add button and enter the service name, address, and port numbers.

7 Click OK to close each dialog box when you're done.

> **note** Keep in mind that you do not need to enable any of these services unless you are *providing* the services from your computer. In other words, you do not need to enable *Web Server* to access Web servers on the Internet. You only need to enable these options if you are providing those services *to* the Internet.

The predefined services listed on the Services tab are the ones most often used. But what if you are using a custom service? For example, suppose your computer hosts a custom application for your company that other users access via the Internet. Can you use the custom application with ICF? Yes, but you'll need to create a service entry and define some parameters for the service. Follow these steps:

1 Open Network Connections.

2 Right-click the ICF-protected connection and choose Properties.

3 Select the Advanced tab and click the Settings button.

4 On the Services tab, click the Add button.

5 In the Service Settings dialog box that appears, shown in Figure 5-5, enter a friendly description and the name or IP address of the computer hosting the service (such as your computer or another computer on your network), and then enter the internal and external port numbers used for the service and protocol. If the internal and external port numbers are the same, you only need to enter the external port number.

6 Click OK to add the service, and then close the remaining dialog boxes.

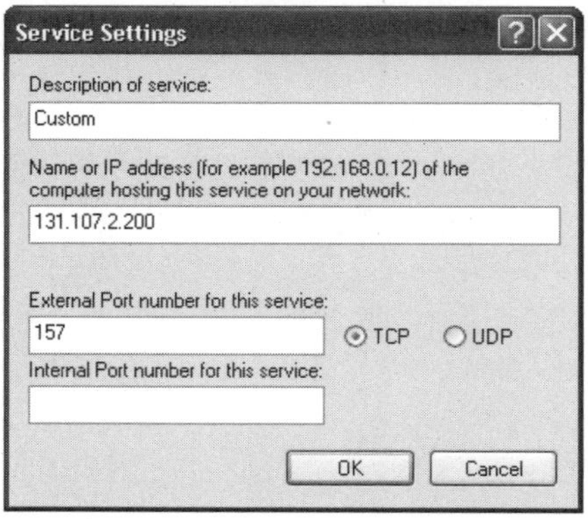

Figure 5-5. You can create a custom service entry by configuring the Service Settings dialog box.

> **note** Only user-defined entries can be deleted. You cannot delete any of the predefined entries that you see on the Services tab.

InsideOut

Enabling File and Printer Sharing with ICF

By default, ICF blocks all the ports that normally use the *Server Message Block (SMB) protocol*—the application-level protocol used for Windows file and printer sharing. This is usually not a concern for home users or on the Internet connection of a system using ICS. However, in insecure LAN/WAN environments or over VPN connections, it's often necessary to use file and printer sharing with other Windows servers and workstations. How then can you protect yourself from other kinds of traffic and still allow SMB for file and printer sharing?

The key is to open the proper ports to allow SMB traffic through. To do so, apply the previously listed steps to add a service for each of the applicable external ports in the following list.

- If your computer needs *direct-hosted* SMB traffic only (that is, you do not rely on NetBIOS for communication in a pre-Active Directory Windows domain or for communication with pre-Windows 2000 systems), you need to create two services: one each for TCP port 445 and UDP port 445.

- If, on the other hand, you need to communicate with other Windows computers using NetBIOS, you'll need to create services for each TCP port from 135 through 139 and for each UDP port from 135 through 139.

For more information on SMB, NetBIOS, and Active Directory, see Chapter 11, "Understanding Domain Connectivity."

Allowing ICMP Traffic

Internet Control Message Protocol (ICMP) is a protocol used for troubleshooting and for network diagnostics. Common IP network tools, such as ping and tracert, use ICMP. Using these tools, which you can learn more about in "Using Command-line Tools Included in Windows XP" on page 345, you can collect a great deal of helpful information about networking conditions and problems. However, by default, ICF prevents all unsolicited inbound ICMP traffic from reaching your computer because that traffic does not originate from your computer. This is usually a good thing because many types of attacks are initiated via ICMP. However, if someone wants to test your network connectivity, their diagnostic requests may fail because that traffic is unsolicited. To the remote user, it appears that your computer is not available on the network. (However, if *you* use these tools, the request will complete because the ICMP request originated from your computer.)

You can enable some or all of the ICMP information requests, depending on which features you want to make available. If you open the Advanced Settings dialog box of the ICF-protected connection's properties dialog box once again and select the ICMP tab, you'll see a list of options that enable you to specify the ICMP features you want to make available. See Figure 5-6.

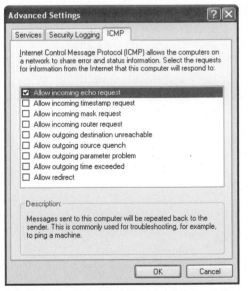

Figure 5-6. Select the ICMP traffic options you want to enable.

The following options are listed on the ICMP tab:

- **Allow Incoming Echo Request.** This option permits a ping test to complete. A message is sent to the computer and is echoed back to the sender. The ping utility is used to test for network connectivity. Enable this option if you want others on the Internet to be able to successfully ping your computer. You do not need to enable this option for you to ping a computer.

- **Allow Incoming Timestamp Request.** This option enables data sent to the computer to be acknowledged with a timestamp.

- **Allow Incoming Mask Request.** This option enables the computer to listen for and respond to requests for more information about the public network to which it is connected.

- **Allow Incoming Router Request.** This option permits the computer to respond to requests for router information.

- **Allow Outgoing Destination Unreachable.** This option causes the computer to acknowledge and send a "destination unreachable" message when data does not reach the computer due to errors or transmission problems.

- **Allow Outgoing Source Quench.** This option permits the computer to send a "slow down" message when data is arriving at the computer and the computer cannot keep up.

- **Allow Outgoing Parameter Problem.** This option permits the computer to send a "bad header" message when data is received with an incorrect or problematic header. Bad headers are dropped.

- **Allow Outgoing Time Exceeded.** This option causes the computer to send a "time expired" message to the sender when data is incomplete because it took too long to send.

- **Allow Redirect.** This option enables data that is sent from the computer to be rerouted if the default path changes.

> **caution**   Although ICMP messages are great troubleshooting tools, they can also give a hacker information about your connection. Do not enable ICMP features unless they are absolutely necessary. You can learn more about the types of attacks that can be launched via ICMP in Chapter 20, "Maintaining Network Security."

Using ICF with E-mail Services

ICF works seamlessly with most e-mail applications. This means that you usually do not need to configure the e-mail application to work with ICF. However, there is an instance in which ICF and an e-mail application can have problems, and that has to do with *notification messages*.

If you are using Web-based mail such as Hotmail, where you log on to a mail server on the Internet, ICF will not interfere with your e-mail retrieval. If you are using an e-mail client, such as Microsoft Outlook Express, which polls its mail server to see if there is new mail (and the mail is downloaded if there is), ICF will also not interfere with this kind of communication.

However, if your e-mail client waits for an RPC from a mail server that tells the e-mail client that there is mail to download, ICF will block the RPC traffic because it will appear as unsolicited traffic. Outlook, when connecting to a Microsoft Exchange server (such as in the case of a domain-based mail system), is an example of an e-mail application that uses RPCs. If you are using Outlook in stand-alone mode, you'll not have an RPC problem. If you are using Outlook and RPCs are used, you'll need to configure Outlook to poll the Exchange server for new mail instead of having the Exchange server send RPCs to you. The odds are good, however, that if you are in an environment where Exchange server is used, you'll not be using ICF anyway because the domain will probably use a proxy server or firewall server. Keep in mind that ICF is designed for the home and small office, so Outlook and the Exchange server issue usually isn't a problem.

Testing ICF

One issue that worries many ICF users is the lack of an interface that tells you what is happening at the firewall. Unless the log file tells you about dropped packets, how do you know if ICF is really protecting you? ICF is designed to do its job in Windows XP behind the scenes, but you might wonder if it is really working.

You can rest assured that ICF is working if it is enabled, but if you are the curious type, you can test ICF using the ping command. To test ICF, follow these steps:

1 On the ICF connection, open the Advanced Settings dialog box.

2 On the Security Logging tab, ensure that logging is enabled for dropped packets.

3 On the ICMP tab, make sure that no ICMP message options are selected.

4 Ensure that the ICF connection is currently connected to the Internet.

5 Open Network Connections.

6 In the Network Connections window, right-click the connected Internet connection and choose Status.

7 In the status dialog box, select the Details tab. Note the Client IP Address value, as shown in Figure 5-7.

Figure 5-7. Note the Client IP Address entry, which is 63.157.13.85 in this example. This value might change each time you connect, especially with a dial-up connection.

8 From a different computer using a different connection to the Internet, choose Start, Run. Type **cmd** and click OK.

9 At the command prompt, type **ping *ipaddress***, where *ipaddress* is the Client IP Address value you noted from your status dialog box. For this example, type **ping 63.157.13.85**. Press Enter.

10 Because ICF is blocking ICMP traffic, the request will time out, as shown in Figure 5-8.

Figure 5-8. The ping request times out because ICF is dropping the ICMP packets.

11 Return to the computer that has the ICF-enabled Internet connection, and open the firewall log (located by default at C:\Windows\Pfirewall.log). You can see in the log that the ICMP traffic was dropped.

Chapter 6

Using Internet Explorer Advanced Features

To discover and use all the Internet has to offer you, your computer needs software that can read and display Web content. As in previous versions of Microsoft Windows, Microsoft Internet Explorer is the default Web browser in Microsoft Windows XP. Internet Explorer acts as your point of interface to the Internet or an intranet. Internet Explorer is available from your Start menu and is designed to work with any kind of Internet connection including a simple dial-up connection or a local area network (LAN) connection. As Internet and intranet usage, functions, and features have changed over the past few years, Internet Explorer has also grown and expanded to meet new browsing, security, and multimedia needs. Internet Explorer 6 does more and is more complex than earlier versions. There are a number of new and helpful features in Internet Explorer 6. This chapter explores the advanced features and functions Internet Explorer has to offer you in Windows XP. You'll also learn how to resolve common problems and frustrations.

Note that Windows XP Service Pack 1 lets you change your default Web browser from Internet Explorer to another application. In fact, some newly purchased computers that have Windows XP Service Pack 1 preinstalled might not include Internet Explorer at all. For more information, see Appendix A, "Windows XP Service Pack 1."

Managing Connectivity

Internet Explorer can access the Internet or a local intranet through virtually any type of network connection including dial-up, broadband, LAN, and even wireless connections. This flexibility gives you a number of networking options so that Internet Explorer can meet your connectivity needs. To configure Internet Explorer to work with the existing connection(s) on your computer, use the Connections tab located in the Internet Options dialog box. In Internet Explorer, choose Tools, Options, and click the Connections tab, which is shown in Figure 6-1. On this tab, you can manage dial-up and virtual private network (VPN) settings as well as LAN settings. This section explores the options and features provided on the Connections tab.

Internet Explorer works with the Internet or intranet connections that you have created on your computer in Network Connections. To learn more about creating Internet and intranet connections, see Chapter 4, "Configuring Internet Connections."

Figure 6-1. The Connections tab provides a single location to configure the Internet connection(s) Internet Explorer should use.

InsideOut

Using Other Web Browsers with Windows XP

If Internet Explorer was installed as the default Web browser when you installed Windows XP, you are not required to use it. You can install another browser and use it in addition to Internet Explorer or instead of Internet Explorer. If you don't want to use Internet Explorer, you can remove the Internet Explorer icons and shortcuts by following these steps:

1 Choose Start, Control Panel, and then open Add Or Remove Programs.

2 Click the Add/Remove Windows Components button.

3 On the Windows Components page of the Windows Components Wizard, shown in Figure 6-2, clear the check box next to Internet Explorer, and then click Next.

Chapter 6

InsideOut *(continued)*

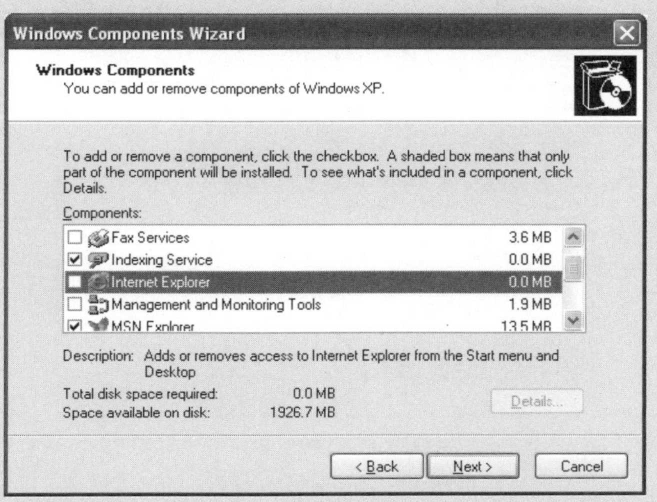

Figure 6-2. Clear the Internet Explorer check box to remove Internet Explorer icons and shortcuts.

4 Windows XP configures the change. Click Finish to close the wizard.

Note that you can also remove MSN Explorer in the same way: Just clear the MSN Explorer check box on the Windows Components page to remove it.

Dial-up and Virtual Private Network Connections

The Dial-Up And Virtual Private Network Settings section of the Connections tab provides you with dial-up and VPN settings for Internet Explorer. Keep in mind that Internet Explorer simply uses the dial-up and VPN connections you've already created in the Network Connections folder. If you have not yet created the Internet connection, you can click the Setup button on the Connections tab to open the New Connection Wizard. This is the same wizard you would use in Network Connections to set up a new Internet connection. Like all connections, the new connection you create will appear in the Network Connections folder and will be available for Internet Explorer to use.

Another way to create a new dial-up or VPN connection is to click the Add button. This button opens the New Connection Wizard and takes you to the Type Of Connection page. You can then create a new dial-up or VPN connection by following these steps:

1 On the Type Of Connection page, select the type of connection that you want to add, such as Dial-Up To Private Network or Connect To A Private Network Through The Internet, as shown in Figure 6-3 on the next page. Click Next.

139

Chapter 6

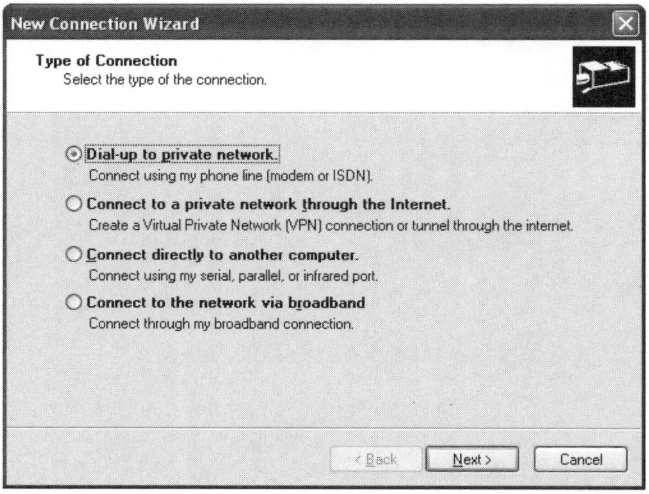

Figure 6-3. Choose the type of new connection that you want to create.

2 Depending on the type of connection you choose to create, the wizard will ask you for appropriate information, such as a phone number for a modem connection or whether to automatically dial a VPN connection. Supply the requested information and click Next. For more detailed information about completing this wizard, see "Creating New Internet Connections" on page 103, and "Creating a Connection to a VPN Server" on page 515.

3 Click Finish. If additional settings need to be configured, the appropriate Settings dialog box for the new connection will appear. Enter the settings and click OK.

As is shown in Figure 6-1 on page 138, once the dial-up or VPN connections are created, they appear in the box on the Connections tab. If you have more than one dial-up or VPN connection, you need to choose one as your default connection by selecting it and clicking Set Default. Then make one of the following three choices for the default connection:

● **Never Dial A Connection.** This option prevents Internet Explorer from automatically dialing your connection. If you select this option, you will first need to manually connect to the Internet before using Internet Explorer because Internet Explorer will not launch a dial-up session automatically.

> **tip** As a point of reference for troubleshooting, always examine this setting if Internet Explorer is unable to access the Internet. This option is sometimes the culprit.

● **Dial Whenever A Network Connection Is Not Present.** This setting, which works well for most users, automatically dials an Internet connection when you open Internet Explorer if no existing connection is available. If you are already connected when you open Internet Explorer, the existing connection will be used. Note that if Internet Explorer does dial the connection, your default Internet connection will be used.

● **Always Dial My Default Connection.** If you don't want Internet Explorer to attempt to use a network connection first, choosing this option will cause Internet Explorer to always (unlike the second option) and automatically (unlike the first option) use the default dial-up or VPN connection.

note From the Connections tab, you can also remove a dial-up or VPN connection you no longer need. To do so, select the connection in the box and click the Remove button.

There also might be instances where you need to contact a proxy server in order to access a dial-up connection. A proxy server is a computer that stands between client computers and the Internet. The proxy server works on behalf of the client computers to retrieve information from the Internet and also acts as a security boundary for the network. If you click the Settings button, you can configure access to a proxy server for the dial-up or VPN account you have selected in the window.

caution The Settings button is only used to configure proxy settings to a dial-up or VPN connection. This button is not used to configure LAN access settings, such as in the case of Digital Subscriber Line (DSL) modems, cable connections, or local area connections. See the next section for details.

The connection's settings dialog box, shown in Figure 6-4, gives you three configuration options for connecting to a proxy server.

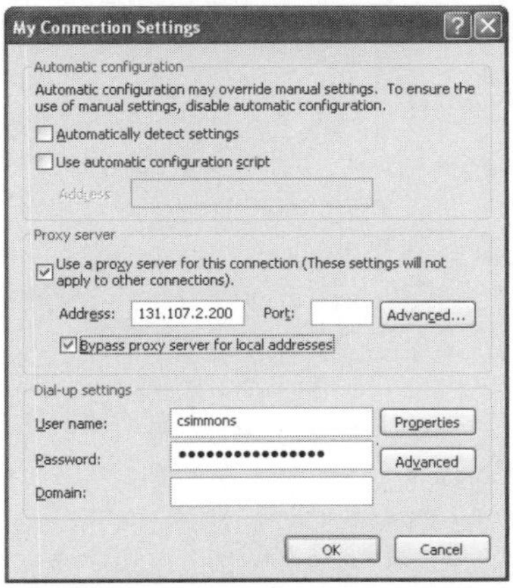

Figure 6-4. Use the connection's settings dialog box to configure proxy server access for a dial-up or VPN connection.

141

● **Automatic Configuration.** If the proxy server is set up for automatic configuration, you can select the Automatically Detect Settings option or point the way to the automatic configuration script by choosing Use Automatic Configuration Script and supplying the URL or file name containing the configurations. Automatic configuration options and scripts are set up on the proxy server, so do not use these settings unless you are sure they are supported. See the proxy server administrator for details.

● **Proxy Server.** In this section, you can provide the address to a particular proxy server. If you know that your computer should access a certain server, select the Use A Proxy Server For This Connection check box and enter the proxy server's IP address. If additional port information applies, you can add the port and click the Advanced button to specify other TCP ports that can be used. Again, you'll need to contact the proxy server administrator for details.

● **Dial-Up Settings.** In this section, you can specify the necessary user name and password to access your ISP. If you click the Advanced button, the Advanced Dial-Up options appear, which are shown in Figure 6-5. You can specify how many times Windows XP will attempt to connect, how long to wait before attempts, and how to disconnect.

> **tip** If a dial-up proxy server connection keeps disconnecting after a period of idle time, you might be able to stop that behavior by clearing both the Disconnect If Idle For and Disconnect When Connection May No Longer Be Needed options in this dialog box. However, the dial-up proxy server might be configured to automatically disconnect you after a preset amount of idle time anyway.

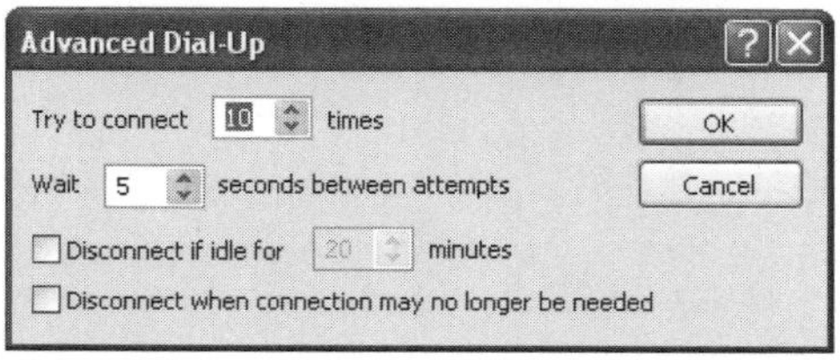

Figure 6-5. Use the Advanced Dial-Up dialog box to configure, connect, and disconnect features.

Local Area Network (LAN) Settings

The LAN Settings button at the bottom of the Connections tab is used to select broadband Internet access, such as DSL, cable, and satellite. You also use the LAN Settings option if you are using a network adapter to access a proxy server that has a network connection to the Internet or to an ISP.

In order to configure the LAN settings so that Internet Explorer can use the broadband or network connection, click the LAN Settings button and specify the correct settings in the LAN Settings dialog box shown in Figure 6-6. As you can see, you can choose from the automatic configuration options or specify the address of a proxy server. Again, check your broadband documentation for details or contact your network administrator if you are accessing the Internet through a proxy server.

> **note** In many cases, LAN Settings are configured automatically through Group Policy in Windows 2000 domains by network administrators so that no configuration is required by the user. All users have to do is open Internet Explorer and use the Internet. If your computer resides in a workgroup (home or office), you can also use local Group Policy in Windows XP Professional to apply a collection of Internet Explorer settings to all users who log on to the local computer. See "Managing Internet Explorer with Local Group Policy" on page 174 for details.

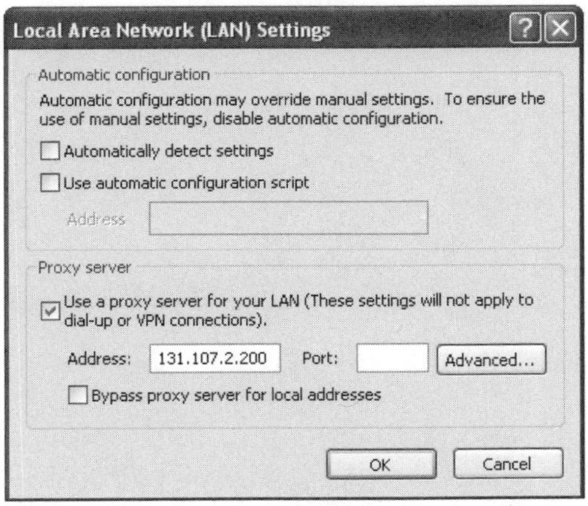

Figure 6-6. Use the LAN Settings dialog box to configure access to a broadband or network connection. This dialog box should not be used for dial-up networking or VPN connections.

Setting Internet Explorer Security Levels

As Internet usage has grown, security problems have grown as well. Virus-infected active content embedded in Java applets and ActiveX controls as well as malicious download content are all a part of using today's Internet. To face this challenge, Internet Explorer includes a number of security features that you can configure by the type of environment in which they'll operate, such as the Internet or a corporate intranet. The different security settings and features give you a way to apply a security level that is appropriate for you as well as for other Internet users who access your computer.

> To learn more about the types of security threats that you face in viewing Web content, see "Understanding Security Threats," page 560.

Security Zones

Internet Explorer provides four different security zones, which you can access by choosing Tools, Internet Options. At the top of the Security tab are the icons for Internet, Local Intranet, Trusted Sites, and Restricted Sites zones, as shown in Figure 6-7. If you select a zone, you can see the current security level of the zone in the lower portion of the window.

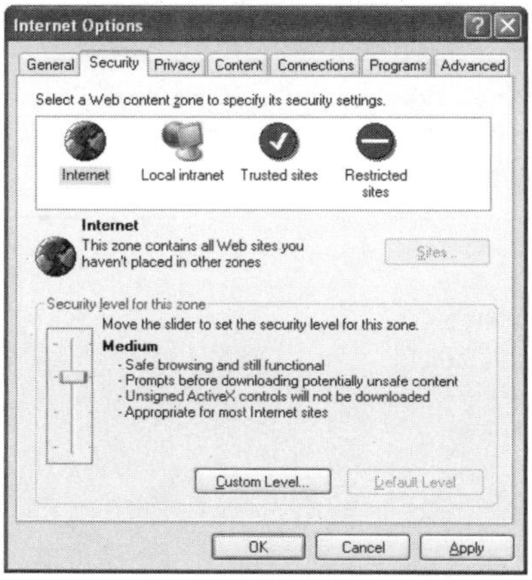

Figure 6-7. Security can be configured by zone on the Security tab of Internet Options.

There are four preconfigured levels of security that you can select for each zone by simply moving the slider:

- **High.** Using this setting, all features that are less secure are disabled. This is the safest way to use the Internet, but it provides you with the least amount of functionality. All ActiveX content is disabled along with all downloads. Additionally, there are a number of restrictions on accessing data and requesting data.

- **Medium.** The medium setting does not allow the downloading of unsigned ActiveX controls, and you see the familiar prompt before downloading potentially unsafe content. Browsing is safe yet functional under this setting, and in most cases this is the best setting to use.

- **Medium-Low.** The medium-low setting will run most content without prompts but still does not allow unsigned ActiveX controls. This setting is safe for intranet use.

- **Low.** The low setting provides basic warnings and few safeguards. All active content can run. This setting is not recommended unless the site is one you completely trust.

You can configure different settings for each zone by simply selecting the zone and moving the slider. However, you can also customize the four security levels by clicking the Custom Level button. This opens the Security Settings dialog box, as shown in Figure 6-8. You can scroll through the list of settings and choose Disable, Enable, or Prompt for each security setting. This enables you to create a custom security setting that invokes the features that you want instead of the default options.

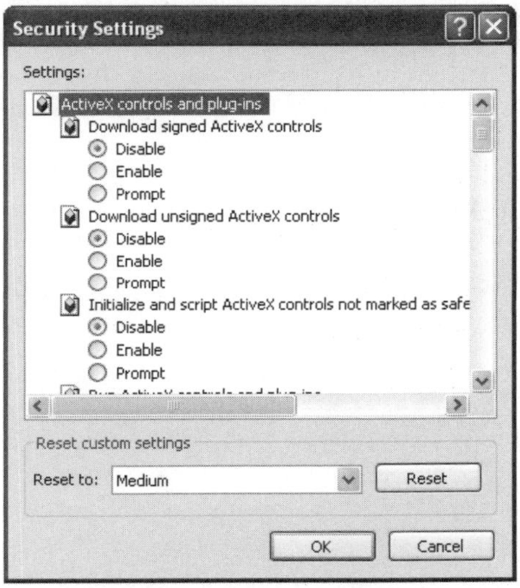

Figure 6-8. Use the Security Settings dialog box to configure a zone with a custom security configuration.

tip If you want to see the settings that are used for one of the default security levels, open the Reset To list at the bottom of the Security Settings dialog box, select a security level, and click Reset. You can view how each custom setting is applied under one of the default security options. You can then customize the settings.

So, how should you configure each zone? The following sections give you some quick and easy pointers that you should keep in mind when configuring security zones in Internet Explorer.

Internet Zone

The medium setting is the best setting for the Internet zone. You have the best browsing functionality and still have enough controls in place to keep the computer reasonably protected. You can, of course, customize the settings as needed. As you are working with the Internet zone, not only is it a good idea to keep the highest security settings in mind, but also to maintain good usage features. Even though low security settings might make browsing easier, you are just asking for trouble.

Local Intranet Zone

The default setting for the Local Intranet zone is medium-low. This setting lets you use the intranet freely, but unsigned ActiveX controls are not allowed. However, Microsoft now recommends that you set the security level for the Local Intranet zone to medium, the same setting as the Internet zone.

If you select the Local Intranet icon on the Security tab, you can also click the Sites button and set three other options that determine which Web sites are included in the Local Intranet zone security level, as shown in Figure 6-9. You can choose Include All Local (Intranet) Sites Not Listed In Other Zones, Include All Sites That Bypass The Proxy Server, and Include All Network Paths. The default setting enables all three of these options, and you should typically leave these enabled. You can also click the Advanced button and add specific, trusted public Web sites to this zone as well.

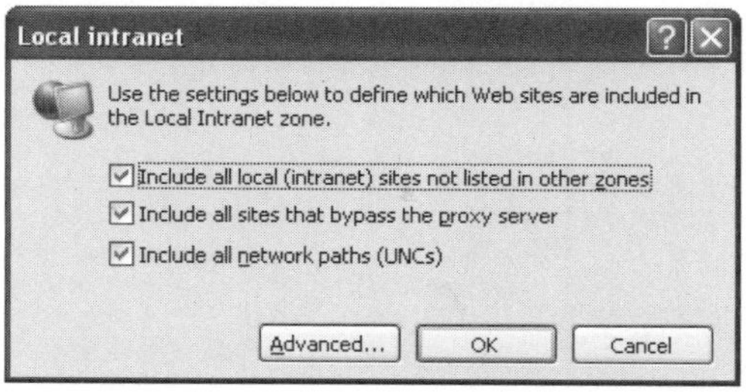

Figure 6-9. The default configuration for the Local Intranet zone accepts these three categories of sites into the zone.

Trusted Sites Zone

If you use a particular site often and you know that content from the site is safe, you can add the site to your Trusted Sites zone. The Trusted Sites zone is made up of sites that you deem trustworthy. Traditionally, when a site was added to the Trusted Sites zone, the low security setting was used, allowing you to freely use the site without any security restrictions. Recently, however, Microsoft has begun recommending that even the Trusted Sites zone be configured to use the medium level of security.

To add trusted sites to your Trusted Sites zone, follow these steps:

1 On the Security tab, click the Trusted Sites zone, and then click the Sites button.

2 In the Trusted Sites dialog box, shown in Figure 6-10, enter the URL of the trusted site and click the Add button. Repeat this process to add other sites. Note that you can remove a site at any time by selecting it in the Web Sites list and clicking the Remove button. You can also require server verification (if supported by the site) for sites in the zone. Click OK when you are done.

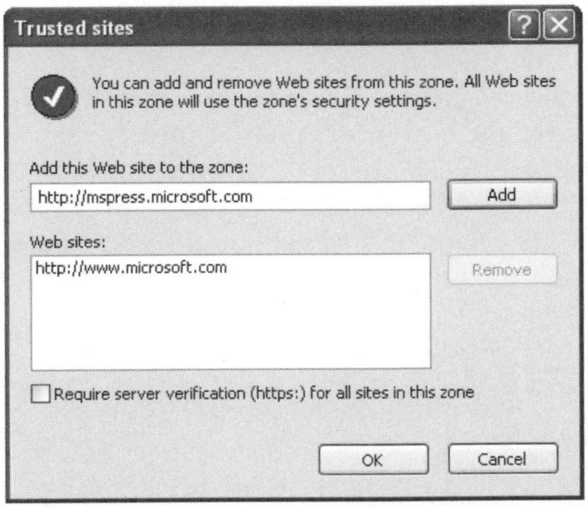

Figure 6-10. Enter trusted sites and click the Add button. You can also remove a site at any time.

Troubleshooting

You encounter problems related to your security zone settings.

Security zones are a great way to protect your computer from malicious content. However, some of the settings might prevent you from using the Internet in ways that you need to. The following list contains some common security zone aggravations and their solutions:

- **You can't enter data at Web sites.** If you cannot enter data, the Web sites are using nonencrypted forms. Some security settings prohibit this action, but you can override the settings by clicking the Custom Level button. Under Miscellaneous, set Submit Nonencrypted Form Data to Enable if you want to enter data at Web sites that don't encrypt the information you submit.

- **You are always prompted for a user name and password when you try to access sites.** The high security level requires that a user name and password be entered for authentication. You can override this requirement by clicking the Custom Level button. Under User Authentication, choose a less restrictive setting than Prompt For User Name And Password.

- **You can't download files.** The high security level does not allow file downloads. Choose a different security level, or click the Custom Level button, and under Downloads, set File Download to Enable.

147

Restricted Sites Zone

The Restricted Sites zone works like the Trusted Sites zone except in reverse. Sites listed in the Restricted Sites zone are given the high security level in order to protect the computer from harmful content. Select the Restricted Sites zone, and click the Sites button to add sites that might use harmful content. This zone's security settings also override the security settings the sites placed in this zone would otherwise receive if categorized into the Internet or Local Intranet zone.

Understanding Privacy and Content Settings

Version 6 of Internet Explorer supports new privacy settings that enable you to control how Internet Explorer responds to cookies (described next) requested by Web sites. Also, as in previous versions of Internet Explorer, content settings are available so that you can control the kind of content that is allowed on your computer.

newfeature!
Privacy Settings

A *cookie* is a text file that is exchanged between your browser and a Web site. Cookies contain personal information about you, such as your name, e-mail address, and sometimes even your surfing habits. Cookies are a great feature because they allow a Web site to recognize you, remember your browsing preferences, and in the case of online stores, remember what you have bought. The good thing about cookies is they can contain all this information…the bad thing about cookies is…well…they contain all of this information. This is personal information that could get into the wrong hands. That's where the problem comes in—cookies personally identify you, and on the Internet, that can result in different kinds of privacy invasions. Although outright identity theft is unlikely, much of the spam you probably receive in your e-mail inbox starts out from information gleaned from cookies.

Understanding Privacy

Internet Explorer 6 provides a collection of settings that can restrict and control cookies. These settings, when effectively used, can help safeguard your personal information and allow you to use sites that manage cookies in an appropriate manner. Previous versions of Internet Explorer allowed you to block all cookies or be prompted each time to accept them, but the use of these features is really impractical. You cannot even log on to some Web sites if you block all cookies, and cookies are used so much that being prompted constantly to accept this and that cookie can drive you crazy.

Internet Explorer 6 supports a standard called the Platform for Privacy Preferences (P3P), which enables Internet Explorer to inspect cookies, determine how they will be used, and then decide what to do about them. The feature is not perfect, and the standard is still evolving and being adopted by Web sites, but it is a big step forward in handling online privacy. Before taking a look at your configuration options, let's first define a few important terms and concepts:

- **Compact privacy statement.** A *compact privacy statement* describes how cookies are used on the site and the lifetime that a particular cookie is used. When you access a Web site, the compact privacy statement is contained in the HTTP header of the Web site, and Internet Explorer can read the compact privacy statement when you first access the site. The compact privacy statement works well, but it's up to individual sites to provide the statement and honestly tell you their privacy policy. Many Web sites on the Internet do not currently provide a compact privacy statement, so the real-world benefit of compact privacy statements is still limited.

- **First-party cookie.** A *first-party cookie* is a cookie that is generated and used by the site you are currently viewing. For example, if you go to *www.microsoft.com*, cookies from *www.microsoft.com* are first-party cookies. First-party cookies contain information about you and your browser, and are commonly used to tailor site content to your needs.

- **Third-party cookie.** A *third-party cookie* originates from a site other than the site you are currently accessing, such as a banner ad or an advertisement that appears on the site you're visiting. Third-party cookies can be a problem because you do not really know who is using them or what they will do with the personal information contained in the cookie.

- **Session cookie.** A *session cookie* is generated during a single session with a Web site and is deleted once the session has ended. In many cases, you cannot use a Web site unless a session cookie can be generated. Session cookies, because they're deleted when you leave the site, are generally safe and useful. They perform tasks such as keeping track of items in your shopping cart while you're shopping on a site.

- **Implicit and explicit consent.** *Implicit consent* means that you have not blocked a site from using a cookie. In other words, you have not granted permission, but you have not denied it either. On the other hand, explicit consent means that you have chosen to allow a Web site to use or gain personal information about you.

Understanding Privacy Settings

Now that you have taken a look at some basic definitions that privacy settings use, you can turn your attention to configuring privacy settings that work best for you. In Internet Explorer 6, choose Tools, Internet Options, and then select the Privacy tab, which is shown in Figure 6-11 on the next page.

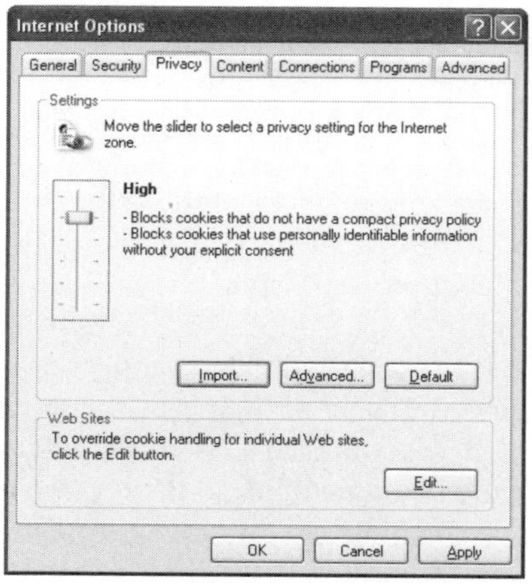

Figure 6-11.   The Privacy tab enables you to configure how cookies are handled with the Web sites you visit.

As you can see in Figure 6-11, the Privacy tab has a slider that enables you to select a desired privacy setting. The available standard privacy setting options are described in Table 6-1.

Table 6-1. Privacy Settings for Handling Cookies and What They Do

Privacy Setting	Action
Block All Cookies	All cookies are blocked. Web sites cannot generate any new cookies, and no existing cookies can be read.
High	Cookies that use personally identifiable information cannot be generated without your explicit consent. Web sites that do not have a compact privacy statement cannot generate cookies.
Medium High	First-party cookies that use personally identifiable information are blocked without your implicit consent. Cookies are blocked from third-party Web sites that do not have a compact privacy statement. Also, third-party cookies that use personally identifiable information are blocked without your explicit consent.
Medium	First-party cookies that use personally identifiable information without your implicit consent are allowed, but they are deleted when you close Internet Explorer. Third-party cookies that use personally identifiable information without your implicit consent are blocked as well as third-party cookies that do not have a compact privacy statement. The medium setting is the default Internet Explorer setting.

Chapter 6

Table 6-1. *(continued)*

Privacy Setting	Action
Low	The low setting accepts all first-party cookies. Third-party cookies are restricted from sites that do not have a compact privacy statement. Third-party cookies that use personally identifiable information are allowed without your implicit consent, but the cookies are deleted when you close Internet Explorer.
Accept All Cookies	All new cookies are allowed and Web sites can read existing cookies that they generated in the past.

To select one of the preconfigured privacy settings, move the slider to the desired position. However, you can also click the Import button to import a privacy policy from another computer, and you can configure some exceptions by clicking the Advanced button.

Configuring Advanced Privacy Options

Clicking the Advanced button on the Privacy tab of the Internet Options dialog box displays the Advanced Privacy Settings dialog box, as you can see in Figure 6-12. This dialog box allows you to override how cookies are handled for the Internet zone.

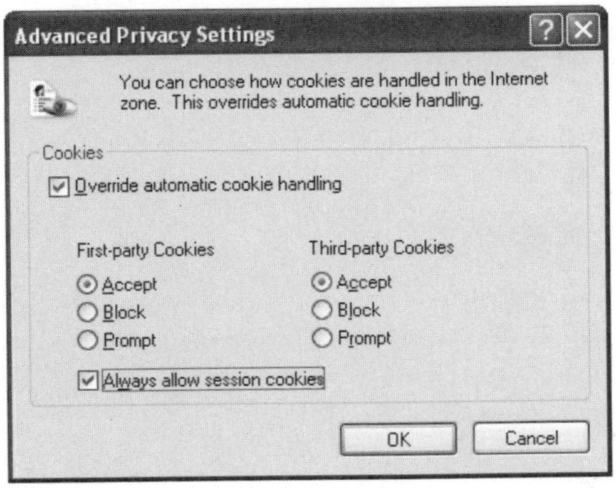

Figure 6-12. You can use the Advanced Privacy Settings dialog box to override automatic cookie handling.

Once you select Override Automatic Cookie Handling, you can choose Accept, Block, or Prompt for all first-party cookies and for all third-party cookies. You can also choose Always Allow Session Cookies (which are always deleted when you leave the site). Should you use this advanced dialog box? That all depends on your needs. For some users, the automatic cookie handling settings do not provide the desired support. In this case, you can override these settings and choose how you want to

151

Chapter 6

handle all first- and third-party cookies at all sites regardless of their compact privacy statement policies. Because these settings override the compact privacy statement and apply to all Web sites, the settings tend to be more uniform. But they also tend to be more problematic because the Block option prevents you from using cookies entirely, and the Prompt option can seriously hinder Web browsing because so many prompts appear.

In terms of the Always Allow Session Cookies option, you should typically allow session cookies to be generated so that the Web site can identify your interaction with the site while you are there. Session cookies are typically harmless, and you might find that Web surfing is hindered without them.

If you like, you can try changing these advanced settings and see how they work for you. If you want to see how often cookies are used, try the Prompt settings, and you'll find out just how many cookies are used when browsing the Internet! The Prompt action also offers a treasure trove of third-party cookies that you'll encounter on many sites due to their repetitive advertising on those sites. You can then specify these URLs individually to block just their cookies, as described in the next paragraph.

If you don't choose Override Automatic Cookie Handling, you can still override the privacy settings for specific Web sites you specify. For example, suppose there is a site you regularly visit that contains first- and third-party cookies. However, the site does not have a compact privacy policy, and suppose that your usual privacy settings prohibit first-party cookies from sites with no compact privacy policy. Rather than changing the privacy policy for all your Web surfing, you can simply create an exception for the particular Web site by following these steps:

1   On the Privacy tab, click the Edit button to open the Per Site Privacy Actions dialog box, which is shown in Figure 6-13.

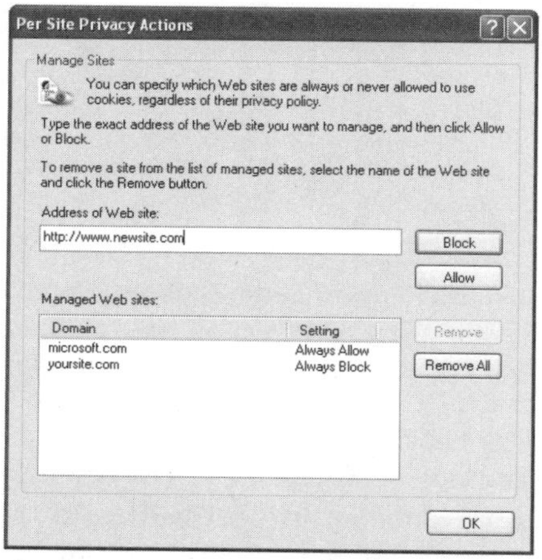

Figure 6-13.   Use the Per Site Privacy Actions dialog box to override the current privacy policy for Web sites you list here.

152

2   Enter the URL of the Web site in the Address Of Web Site box, and then click the Block or Allow button. Choosing Block always blocks the URL's cookies, and Allow always allows its cookies.

3   Web sites that you have blocked or allowed appear in the Managed Web Sites list. To remove an item on this list, select it, and click the Remove button.

Managing Cookies

There are two other actions you can perform concerning cookies. If you are curious, you can open and read the information contained in any of the cookies Internet Explorer has stored. Just follow these steps:

1   In Internet Explorer, choose Tools, Internet Options.

2   On the General tab under Temporary Internet Files, click the Settings button.

3   In the Settings dialog box, shown in Figure 6-14, click the View Files button.

Figure 6-14. To see cookies and downloaded pages and graphics, click the View Files button.

> **tip**   The View Files button shows you temporary Internet cookies, but there are also permanently stored cookies attached to your user profile. You can find them in the %UserProfile%\Cookies folder. By default the environment variable *%UserProfile%* will take you to the C:\Documents and Settings*Username* folder, where *Username* is your Windows XP account name. If you open a Command Prompt window, switch to the drive on which Windows XP is installed (usually drive C), you can go directly to the Cookies folder by typing **cd %UserProfile%\Cookies**.

4   In the Temporary Internet Files folder that opens, sort by file type by clicking the Type column.

153

Chapter 6

5 Scroll to see files of type Text Document, and then look for file names that begin with *Cookie*.

6 Double-click one of these files to open it in Notepad. Some of the information will be Web site data, but some might be personal information you are exchanging with the site.

InsideOut

Deleting Temporary Internet Files and Cookies to Improve Performance

Internet Explorer is able to store the amount of temporary Internet files and cookies that you allow it to, depending on the hard disk space configured in the Settings dialog box, as shown in Figure 6-14. However, too many cookies and temporary Internet files can make your Web surfing sluggish. If your Web surfing speed seems to have slowed down over time, try deleting all of the cookies and temporary Internet files. Internet Explorer will start storing them again, but this might help unclog your browsing experience. You can delete both temporary cookies and temporary Internet files by clicking the appropriate buttons on the General tab of Internet Options. Also, take a look at the permanent cookies stored in %UserProfile%\Cookies. You might find a number of cookies that are no longer needed. Consider deleting those as well to help speed up Internet Explorer.

You might also have noticed that Internet Explorer automatically allocated a percentage of your hard disk space to storing temporary Internet files. If you'd like to free up that space for other purposes, you can enter a smaller value in the MB field of the Settings dialog box shown in Figure 6-14, or adjust the Amount Of Disk Space To Use slider.

You can check out cookies that are blocked and also view a site's compact privacy policy if you are so inclined. When a cookie is blocked for the first time, you will see the notification dialog box, which is shown in Figure 6-15. Note that a blocked cookie icon appears on your Internet Explorer status bar. The status bar is typically visible at the bottom of the Internet Explorer window, but if you do not see it, choose View, Status Bar to display it.

Figure 6-15. This notification appears when a cookie is first blocked.

If you want to find out more about the blocked cookies, just double-click the blocked cookie icon on the Internet Explorer status bar. You'll see the Privacy Report dialog box, shown in Figure 6-16, that tells you which cookies were blocked when you visited the current site. You can then double-click a blocked listing to find out more about the site's compact privacy policy if one exists.

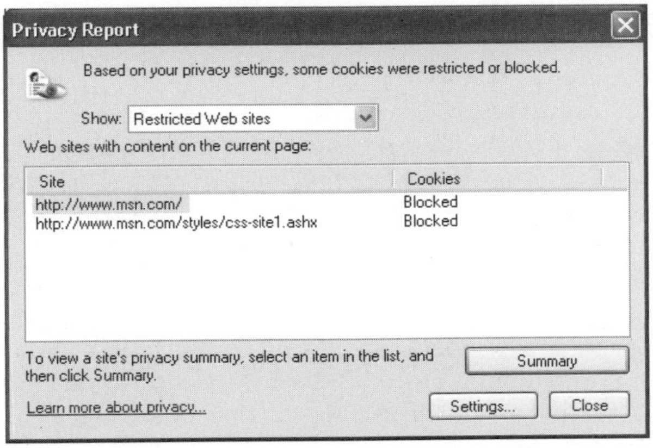

Figure 6-16. You can access this window to see which site cookies have been blocked.

In addition, if you want to review privacy policy and cookie information for a site that doesn't show you a blocked cookie icon on the status bar, go to the site and choose View, Privacy Report. In the Show box, select All Web Sites, and you'll see a list of all Web sites with content on the current page as well as whether any cookies have been accepted. (If any cookies on this site had been blocked, you would have seen the blocked cookies icon on the status bar.)

> **tip** Internet Explorer helps you control cookie usage and protect your privacy, but there are additional third-party utilities that can give you a finer level of control. Cookie Pal is a good one that works with Internet Explorer 6 and Windows XP, and you can check it out at *www.kburra.com/cpal.html*. For more information about utilities for managing potentially intrusive cookies, see "Managing EFS," page 595.

Content Settings

Internet Explorer 6 provides content settings that enable you to control the sites that can be accessed by Internet Explorer. The content settings feature can be a great way to stop pornographic, violent, racist, or hatred content from being displayed on your computer. Although content settings are a valuable feature, they depend on Web sites rating themselves in a fair and honest way, so the feature is not foolproof. If you want to configure content settings to help prevent your children from seeing offensive content, use the Content Advisor explored later in this section. But you should also investigate such third-party software products as CYBERsitter (*www.cybersitter.com*) or Net Nanny (*www.netnanny.com*). With these tools and your supervision, the Internet can be a safe place for your family members.

How Content Rating Works in Internet Explorer

Web sites can provide a rating so that Internet Explorer knows whether to allow or block a site. If a Web site wants to provide a rating, the Web site administrator completes a form at the Internet Content Rating Association (ICRA) Web site. This site then evaluates the administrator's responses and provides a label for the Web site to apply. When you or your children attempt to view the site in Internet Explorer, the site's rating label is read, and Internet Explorer takes the appropriate action, depending on how you have configured the content settings. The ICRA is an independent organization and is not a censor, so the rating of the site fully depends on how the administrator responds to questions in the application. In a nutshell, the site's rating has a lot to do with the honesty of the site administrator. However, most sites that want a rating do so in the best interest of privacy and protecting children.

> **tip**   You can learn more about the ICRA at *www.rsac.org/ratingsv01.html*.

The ICRA ratings are based on language, nudity, sexual content, and violence. You can use Internet Explorer to adjust the levels of each you want users to be able to view when using Internet Explorer. You can also assign a supervisor password to the content settings you select so that the configuration cannot be overridden by your children or others without access to the password.

Enabling and Configuring Content Advisor

To enable and configure Content Advisor, follow these steps:

1 Choose Tools, Internet Options, and then select the Content tab.

2 Click the Enable button. The Content Advisor window appears with four configuration tabs.

3 Select the Ratings tab, shown in Figure 6-17, and you will see a list of rating categories: Language, Nudity, Sex, and Violence. Select one of the categories, and then move the slider to the level of content you want to allow users to view. Note that each category starts at Level 0 at the far left, which is the least offensive, most censored setting. Adjust each of the categories as desired, and then select the Approved Sites tab.

Figure 6-17. Select a category and move the slider to the desired level of viewing.

4 On the Approved Sites tab, override the settings that you configured on the Ratings tab by entering specific Web site addresses and clicking the Always or Never button. Always will allow anyone to see the site without a supervisor password. Although the tab is named Approved Sites, by entering a URL and clicking Never, you are really *disapproving* the site because the user will always be prompted for the supervisor password to view the site, effectively blocking it. After entering any sites you want to explicitly allow or block, select the General tab.

5 On the General tab, shown in Figure 6-18 on the next page, you are provided with the following configuration options:

- **Users Can See Sites That Have No Rating.** This option should not be used if you are trying to secure the computer from harmful content. Just because a site contains inappropriate content does not mean that it has a rating. By leaving this check box cleared, if a site does not have a rating, Content Advisor will display a prompt that requires the user to enter the supervisor password before viewing the site. Entering passwords for all unrated sites can cause some surfing frustration, but it is the safest setting.

- **Supervisor Can Type A Password To Allow Users To View Restricted Content.** You should always keep this setting selected so that you can override any site prohibitions with the supervisor password if needed unless you fear that another user might guess the password (in which case you should choose a better password). If you do clear this check box and decide you want to access a prohibited page, you'll have to disable Content Advisor entirely, at least temporarily.

157

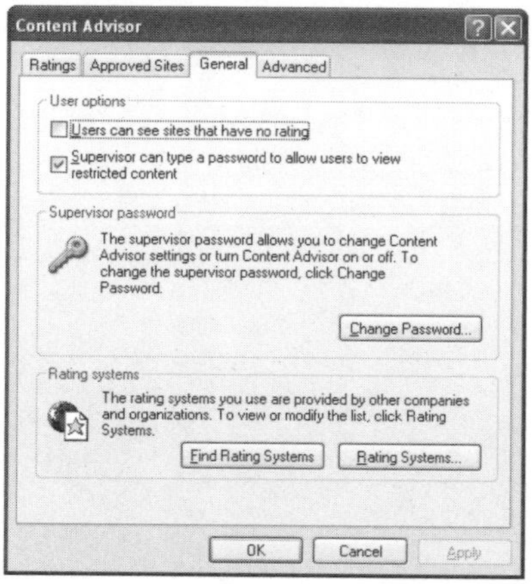

Figure 6-18. Use the General tab to configure user and supervisor access along with the supervisor password and additional ratings.

- **Supervisor Password.** In this section, you can change your supervisor password. Keep in mind that the supervisor password you assign is used to control and even turn off content management, so keep track of it. However, if you should forget your password, you can override it by editing the registry. The *registry* is a storehouse of information in Windows that contains essentially all the software and hardware configuration settings for your computer. Using Registry Editor, you can directly make changes and add or remove items (see the Troubleshooting sidebar on the next page). You'll find an entire chapter devoted to the registry in *Microsoft Windows XP Inside Out* by Ed Bott and Carl Siechert (Microsoft Press, 2001).

caution Incorrect registry edits can cause Windows XP to stop functioning, so you should only edit the registry as a last resort and only if you are sure of what you're doing.

- **Rating Systems.** In this section, you can find the available rating systems offered by other companies. Click the Find Rating Systems button to open a Web page on the Microsoft Web site that lists any additional ratings providers. The Rating Systems button can be clicked to view, add, or remove any of the rating systems installed on the computer including the default RSACi system.

6 Click the Advanced tab to see the options to locate and use a ratings bureau and to use PICSRules. A *ratings bureau* is an Internet site that can check a rating of a site if the site is not rated by the ICRA. However, using a ratings bureau can seriously slow down browsing speed. You can also import PICSRules. *PICSRules* are labels a site can contain that also help you determine if the site should be viewed or not. There are no default rules configured, but you can import them if desired.

If you decide that you no longer want to use Content Advisor after you have configured it, you can always return to the Content tab and click the Disable button. You'll need to provide your supervisor password to turn off the feature. Thereafter, you can quickly reenable the site by clicking the same button, now labeled Enable, and entering your old supervisor password again.

Troubleshooting

You forgot your supervisor password and need to remove it by editing the registry.

To remove the supervisor password for Content Advisor from the registry should the password be forgotten, follow these steps:

1 Choose Start, Run.

2 Type **regedit** in the Open box and click OK or press Enter to open Registry Editor.

3 In Registry Editor, you'll see a listing of *root keys*, which are different divisions of the registry that hold different kinds of information. The Content Advisor password is stored in the HKLM root key, which represents HKey_Local_Machine.

4 Expand the HKLM root key by clicking the plus sign to its left, and then keep expanding by clicking Software, followed by Microsoft, Windows, CurrentVersion, Policies, and Ratings.

5 Select Ratings in the left pane. In the right pane in the Name column, select Key and press the Delete key.

6 When asked to confirm the deletion, click Yes.

7 Expand Ratings in the left pane and select Default. In the right pane, double-click the Enabled item. In the dialog box that opens, type **0** (zero) in the Value Data box and press Enter.

8 Close Registry Editor.

If you are worried that your computer-savvy kids or coworkers might access the registry and delete the Content Advisor password, you can use a Group Policy setting to control access to the registry for all users of the computer who do not have administrative privileges. See "Managing Internet Explorer with Local Group Policy" on page 174 to learn more about using Group Policy with Windows XP Professional. If you are using Windows XP Home Edition, Group Policy is not available.

Setting Additional Internet Explorer Features and Settings

You can customize Internet Explorer in a number of different ways so that the browser both looks and acts in the way that you want. The settings mentioned in this section are found in the Internet Options dialog box (choose Tools, Internet Options to open it), and they can have a big impact on your Internet Explorer experience. The settings you'll learn about in the following sections are quick and easy to implement options that you might consider using on your system.

Choosing a Home Page

Internet Explorer uses a default home page when you first open the browser. This home page might be *www.msn.com*, or it might be the home page of your computer manufacturer, such as Dell, Compaq, or Gateway. No matter, you can change the home page to whatever you want, or you can remove it. In Internet Options, select the General tab, enter a new URL under Home Page in the Address box, and click the Apply button. If you're currently viewing the page you want to use as your home page, you can click Use Current instead. If you want Internet Explorer to open to a blank page (which is the fastest way to open the browser), click the Use Blank button. Should you want to return to the original home page configured by Windows XP or the manufacturer of your computer, click Use Default.

---

tip   **Getting to Your Destination Faster**

If you are using a slow Internet connection, consider selecting the Use Blank option unless you really want to go to the same page every time you start Internet Explorer. The Use Blank option loads Internet Explorer quickly and allows you to immediately enter a URL without waiting for a home page to load every time.

Customizing the Appearance of Internet Explorer

Internet Explorer uses a collection of default colors, fonts, and languages to display Web pages to you. However, those default preferences might not be suitable, depending on your likes and needs. You can easily change them, by clicking the Colors, Fonts, and Languages buttons on the General tab of Internet Options. These configuration buttons open simple dialog boxes, such as the Colors dialog box shown in Figure 6-19, so that

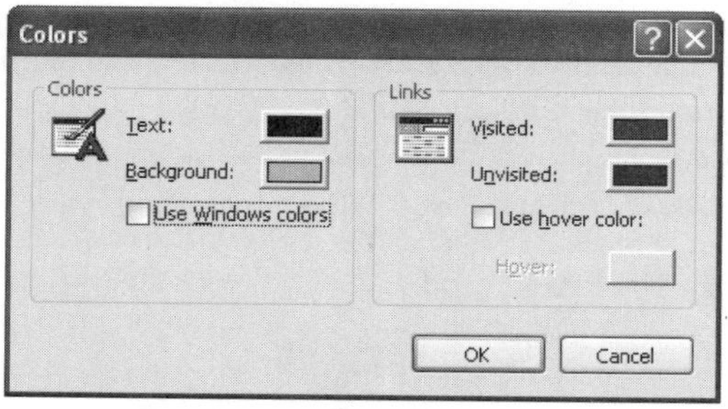

Figure 6-19.   Use the Colors dialog box to adjust the colors of the text and background of Web pages and the colors of links.

you can make Internet Explorer display Web pages in a way that is pleasing to you. Also, note that you can configure Accessibility options for Internet Explorer by clicking the Accessibility button on the General tab. This feature gives you some additional options that might make Internet Explorer easier for you to use.

Managing AutoComplete

AutoComplete is a feature that enables Internet Explorer to remember what you have typed in Internet Explorer, such as URLs of Web pages or information like your name and address in forms on Web pages. When you start to reenter that information, Internet Explorer tries to complete it for you. If the suggested completion is correct, you can select it, and press Enter instead of typing the rest of the information. Some people find this feature useful, whereas others find it annoying. You'll have to decide what works best for you. You can adjust AutoComplete's behavior by selecting the Content tab in Internet Options and clicking the AutoComplete button to open the AutoComplete Settings dialog box shown in Figure 6-20.

Figure 6-20. Use the AutoComplete Settings dialog box to adjust the way AutoComplete works.

Select or clear the appropriate check boxes in the Use AutoComplete For section to configure AutoComplete (or clear them all if you do not want to use AutoComplete).

A notable feature of AutoComplete is its ability to remember passwords. For example, you probably log on to a number of Web sites using different passwords. AutoComplete can remember your passwords and make the logon process easier. The problem, however, is that someone else using your computer can easily access those sites as well. So, depending on the sensitive nature of your Internet usage, you might consider clearing the User Names And Passwords On Forms option, and then clicking the Clear Passwords button to delete any passwords that Internet Explorer already has in memory.

Setting Default Programs

Internet Explorer maintains a list of default programs for certain Internet tasks. For example, Outlook Express is the default e-mail and newsgroup client, whereas NetMeeting is the default Internet call program. When you click one of the options on the Internet Explorer toolbar, such as the Mail button, Internet Explorer checks the settings on the Programs tab shown in Figure 6-21 to determine which program to open. However, if you have other programs installed on your computer that you want Internet Explorer to use, such as a different e-mail client, select the Programs tab and use the boxes to change the default options.

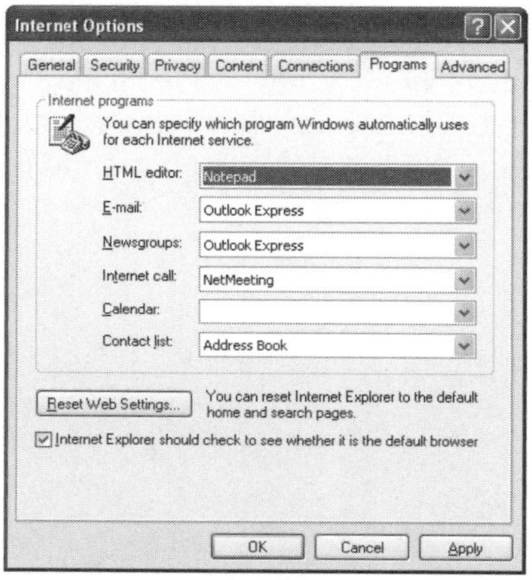

Figure 6-21. You can select alternative Internet programs for each of the six categories listed under Internet Programs.

> **tip** **Choose Your Default Internet Browser**
>
> Two obscure settings are also found on the Programs tab. If you've made a number of changes to your Internet Explorer home and search pages, you can reset them to the default settings by clicking the Reset Web Settings button at the bottom of the Programs tab. Also, are you tired of Internet Explorer always asking you if it should be your default browser? This can happen if you install another browser after installing Windows XP, and it becomes the default. The next time you open Internet Explorer, you'll be told it's not the default browser, and you'll be asked if you want to make it the default. If you want to use the other browser by default and not see this message every time you choose to start a session with Internet Explorer, clear the check box on the Programs tab labeled Internet Explorer Should Check To See Whether It Is The Default Browser. On the other hand, if you want to reestablish Internet Explorer as your default browser, click the Reset Web Settings button on the Programs tab.

Choosing Advanced Settings

The Advanced tab of Internet Options provides a number of additional settings in different categories, namely Accessibility, Browsing, HTTP, Multimedia, Printing, Searching, and Security, as you can see in Figure 6-22.

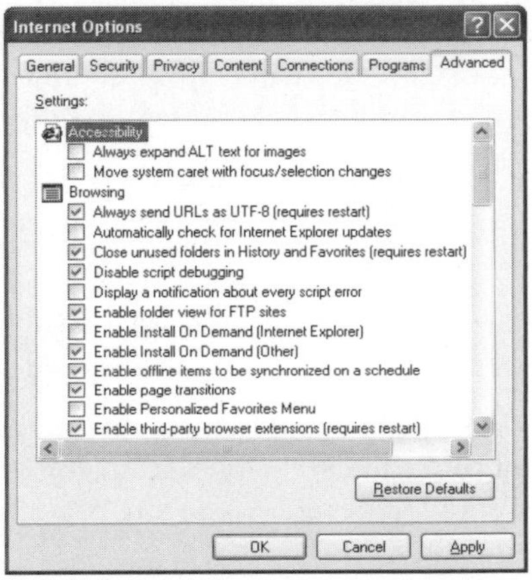

Figure 6-22. Use the Advanced tab to adjust additional settings arranged by category.

Under most circumstances, the default settings you see on this tab are all you need for the best browsing experience. However, there are several options that might be important to you. The following list points out some of the more interesting items you might consider changing:

- Under Browsing, consider enabling Automatically Check For Internet Explorer Updates if it is not currently enabled. If you have a broadband or network connection to the Internet, Internet Explorer can periodically check the Microsoft Web site for updates. With a dial-up connection, you should still check for updates periodically by selecting Tools, Windows Update.

- Under Browsing, consider disabling Enable Page Transitions if you are using a slow Internet connection. Some Web sites have page transitions configured so that one page fades into another. Although visually appealing, these transitions consume bandwidth and time, so disable this feature if your Web surfing is annoyingly slow.

- Under Browsing, consider selecting Enable Personalized Favorites Menu. If you use many favorite pages, the list can become long and hard to navigate. Selecting this option hides the links you haven't used in awhile so that the list is easier to see and use. You can still access the seldom-used links by clicking the arrow at the bottom of the Favorites menu.

163

● Under Browsing, consider clearing Notify When Downloads Complete. This removes that extra OK message box you see when a download finishes.

● Under Browsing, if you want Internet Explorer to help you complete Web addresses that you have used previously, select Use Inline AutoComplete.

● Under Multimedia, consider clearing the three options labeled Play Animations In Web Pages, Play Sounds In Web Pages, and Play Videos In Web Pages if you have a slow Internet connection. This will help speed up your browsing experience instead of waiting for multimedia content to download.

● Under Printing, Print Background Colors And Images is not selected by default. However, if you want the entire Web page to print, you can enable this option.

● Under Security, consider selecting Empty Temporary Internet Files Folder When Browser Is Closed to keep Internet Explorer clean and cookies deleted.

● Under Security, consider clearing Warn If Changing Between Secure And Not Secure Mode if you do not want to see the Security Alert dialog box that appears when moving in and out of secure and nonsecure pages.

Customizing the Internet Explorer Interface

Up to this point, the chapter has explored the configuration options provided to you through the Internet Options tabs. As you have seen, there are many customizable features and security options available to you. However, Internet Explorer can be customized in additional ways so that Internet Explorer is easy for you to use and makes your browsing experience more enjoyable. This section covers several categories of Internet Explorer settings and configuration options that aren't configured in the Internet Options dialog box. The more obvious settings are not covered to allow space for more advanced configuration features that you are likely to enjoy.

Configuring the Internet Explorer Toolbar

The purpose of the Internet Explorer toolbar is to provide you with easy access to functions and related programs, such as searching Web sites and retrieving e-mail. The Internet Explorer toolbars are easily customizable, and you can choose which toolbars you want to display by choosing View, Toolbars, and clicking the desired toolbar. You can also choose which Explorer bar appears in the left pane of Internet Explorer by choosing View, Explorer Bar, and clicking one of the five Explorer bars. You can even move the toolbars around so they are placed in different locations within the Internet Explorer window. You can separate toolbars on the top and bottom of the screen, or you can combine them into one long toolbar to save more screen space. The choice is yours—so experiment with the options to find what works best for you by dragging a toolbar by the handle at its left edge.

> **tip** If you don't see the toolbar handles and can't move your toolbars, choose View, Toolbars, and clear the Lock The Toolbars command. The toolbar handles will appear on the left side of the toolbars, and you can drag and drop them at will.

You can also customize the Internet Explorer toolbar by selecting the buttons that appear. To customize the Standard Buttons toolbar, choose View, Toolbars, Customize. In the Customize Toolbar dialog box, shown in Figure 6-23, you can see the toolbar buttons that are available to you, and you can see the current toolbar buttons.

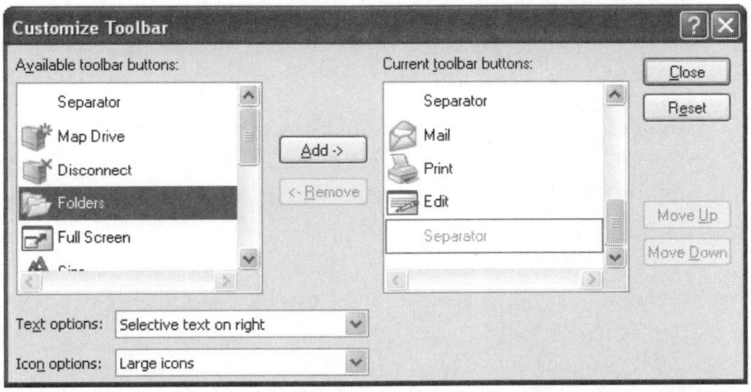

Figure 6-23. Use the Customize Toolbar dialog box to select which buttons appear on the Standard Buttons toolbar in Internet Explorer.

To customize the toolbar, follow these steps:

1 In the Available Toolbar Buttons list, select a button that you want to add to the toolbar, and click the Add button. The new button appears in the Current Toolbar Buttons list.

2 If you want to remove a button from the toolbar, select the button in the Current Toolbar Buttons list, and click the Remove button.

3 You can then configure the toolbar buttons to appear in any order that you want by selecting the buttons one at a time and clicking the Move Up or Move Down button. Buttons toward the top of the list appear on the left of the toolbar, and those near the bottom appear on the right side.

4 In the Text Options list, choose Show Text Labels, Show Selective Text On Right, or No Text Labels. If you know what each button's image means, you can save space with the No Text Labels option. The default is to show selective text, which occupies less space than the Show Text Labels option, but still labels some of the most important buttons.

5 In the Icon Options list, select Small Icons or Large Icons.

165

6 Click OK when you are done. Keep in mind that you can reconfigure the toolbar at any time to meet your current needs.

InsideOut

Using Internet Explorer to Access Your Local and Network Files

Internet Explorer is designed to be a Web browser, but remember that Internet Explorer is also integrated with the Windows XP operating system. This means that Internet Explorer can provide you with access to Web pages as well as to resources on your local computer. The idea is to integrate the Internet with your local computing experience, making both easier. As you are using Internet Explorer, keep these helpful ideas in mind:

● You can store Web page URLs in your Favorites folder, and you can store any shortcut on your computer in your Favorites list as well. Just drag the shortcut to the Favorites button on the Internet Explorer toolbar.

● Your most frequently accessed URLs, documents, files, folders, and so on can be stored on the Links toolbar for easy access. Just drag and drop them on the Links toolbar. If you don't see the Links toolbar, choose View, Toolbars, Links to display it.

● You can access Web pages as well as drives, files, and folders using the Address bar. Just enter the URL for a Web or intranet page. To access a local or network resource, specify its Universal Naming Convention (UNC) name, which takes the form *computername**drivename**foldername**filename*. For example, to open a file named News.doc located in the Data folder on a shared network drive named Datadisk on a network computer named Sales, you would type the UNC as **\\sales\datadisk\data\news.doc**.

Managing Internet Explorer History

Internet Explorer keeps track of the Web sites that you or anyone using your computer accesses. The sites are listed by URL on the History bar and are kept for 20 days by default (you can change the default setting on the General tab of Internet Options). The idea behind maintaining a history of visited sites is to enable you to find Web sites you have accessed but cannot remember their URLs, have not saved in your Favorites menu, or that are buried so deeply within a complex Web site you can't find your way back to them a second time. Also, the History bar enables you to see which sites other users are accessing when they use your computer.

You can display the History bar by clicking the History button on the toolbar, as shown in Figure 6-24. By clicking on the day and week categories to expand them, you can see the sites that have been accessed during those periods.

Figure 6-24. Use the History bar to see which Web sites have been visited.

The History bar is a simple feature, but there are a few important points to remember:

- You can click the View menu button at the top of the History bar to sort the items by date, size, most frequently visited, or by the order visited today.

- You can delete history items individually by right-clicking them and clicking Delete. You can clear the history from an entire day or week by right-clicking the category and clicking Delete. You can also delete all history items by clicking the Clear History button on the General tab of the Internet Options dialog box.

- Even though you can delete the Today category, it will reappear as you surf the Internet and will replenish itself with new sites you visit. In other words, you cannot stop the History bar from collecting a list of the sites you visit. You can, however, individually delete the items from the Today list or periodically delete the Today category as it accumulates new entries.

- If you change the Days To Keep Pages In History value to 0 on the General tab of Internet Options, the current day's history is still recorded, although it will be removed the next day and be replaced by that day's visited sites. If you don't want others to see where you've been, you'll have to remember to open Internet Options, go to the General tab, and click Clear History before closing Internet Explorer. Even then, the current page you were viewing before clearing history will become (when you return from clicking the Clear History button) the first new site recorded on the History bar under Today. If having even one remaining entry bothers you, in the Address bar, type the URL **about:blank** (which displays the same blank page you can choose as your home page on the General tab of Internet Options by clicking Use Blank), and then click the Clear History button. All history entries will be removed until you start surfing again.

InsideOut

Keeping Tabs on Users

Consider this scenario: Your computer is used in an office or home setting by multiple users, such as employees or even your children. You want to keep track of what they access when they are on the Internet. Can you do it?

The problem is that history items can be deleted by anyone logged on to your computer. You can create a local Group Policy (see "Managing Internet Explorer with Local Group Policy" on page 174) that prohibits users from making configuration changes in the History section of the General tab of Internet Options, but there is no setting to stop users from deleting entries on the History bar.

In this case, you can use a third-party program that lets you keep track of what users are viewing and doing as well as chat room transcripts. These tools can be valuable in offices that have strict usage policies or in cases where you want to keep tabs on what your kids are doing. Check out *www.computer-snooper.com* and *www.spy-patrol.com* to get started.

Managing Favorites

The Favorites bar in Internet Explorer provides you with an easy way to keep track of your favorite Web sites. Rather than remember individual URLs, you can simply add sites to your Favorites menu, give them a friendly name, and click on the link in Favorites to go to the site. It is quick and easy and allows Internet Explorer to keep track of URLs instead of you having to do so.

To add a site to your Favorites menu, just click the Favorites menu and click Add To Favorites. A small dialog box appears, as shown in Figure 6-25. You can change the name to whatever you want and click OK. To store the favorite in a particular folder on the Favorites menu, click the Create In button, and select a folder from the list that appears. You can also click the New Folder button to create a new folder at the same time you store the new link.

Figure 6-25. Enter a friendly name for the favorite link and click OK.

When you add a favorite, you can also make it available offline. This feature is helpful if you want to read information on a Web site without being connected to the Internet. To make the link available offline, select Make Available Offline in the Add Favorite dialog box, and then, if you want to customize the offline settings, click the Customize button. When the Offline Favorite Wizard appears, follow these steps to customize how the offline Web site is handled:

1 Click Next on the opening page of the Offline Favorite Wizard.

2 On the page shown in Figure 6-26, choose whether you want to make additional links from the page available offline. When you initially make a page available offline, only that page is made available to you by downloading its content to your hard disk. If you click a link on the page while you are offline, you are prompted to connect because the pages linked to the initial page were not downloaded to your computer. If you don't have the ability to connect (that's why you make a page available offline to begin with), you won't be able to retrieve the information. To avoid this problem, use this page of the wizard to also store linked pages offline. Set the Download Pages value to the number of levels of linked pages you want to store. For example, if you set this value to 2, all links on the original page will be stored offline, and all links on those pages will be stored offline, but no further levels of links will be stored. Keep in mind that the more levels of pages you choose to store, the more disk space and synchronization time Internet Explorer will require. Make your selections conservatively and click Next.

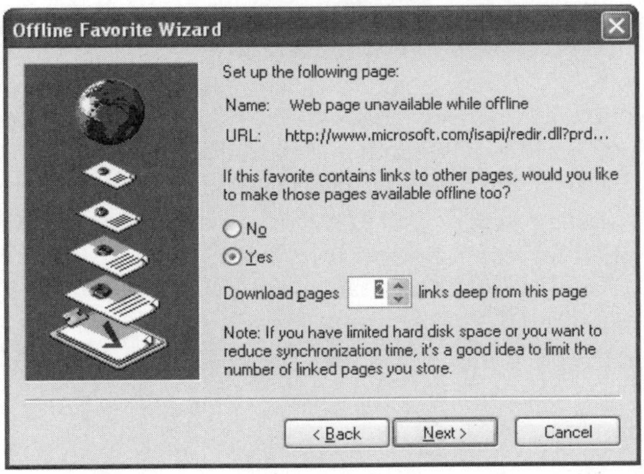

Figure 6-26. Use this wizard page to configure the link depth that you want to make available offline.

3 Choose a synchronization option. You can choose to synchronize only when you choose Tools, Synchronize, or you can create a schedule for automatic synchronization. Click Next.

4 If you chose the schedule option, the schedule page appears. Choose when you want synchronization to occur and click Next.

5 On the password page of the wizard, enter a user name and password if the site requires one for access. If not, leave the No button selected. Click Finish, and then click OK to close the Add Favorite dialog box.

> **tip** You can always make a favorite site available offline at a later time by clicking the Favorites menu, right-clicking the favorite, and choosing Make Available Offline from the shortcut menu that appears.

InsideOut

Getting an E-mail Notice When an Offline Page Changes

When offline content changes due to synchronization, you can have Internet Explorer send you an e-mail so that you know the page has been updated. Sound cool? Just click the Favorites menu, right-click the offline favorite and click Properties. Select the Download tab, and select When This Page Changes, Send E-mail To. Enter your e-mail address and the name of your e-mail server (if you don't know it, check the server specified for your outgoing mail [SMTP] in your e-mail account under Tools, Accounts in Outlook Express or the e-mail program you use). Also, note that you can make additional changes to the offline favorite in the Content To Download section, such as the link depth and hard disk space limit. You can even stop the synchronization from downloading images, sound and video, and ActiveX controls and Java Applets by clicking the Advanced button. These options help save disk space and reduce synchronization time.

To make your work with favorites easier, you can also use the Organize Favorites option. Click Favorites, Organize Favorites, and you'll see the simple organizational dialog box shown in Figure 6-27.

You can use the Organize Favorites dialog box to create folders in which you can store favorites, or you can rename items, move them, or even delete them. If you want to delete favorites, you can also right-click the link on the Favorites bar and click Delete.

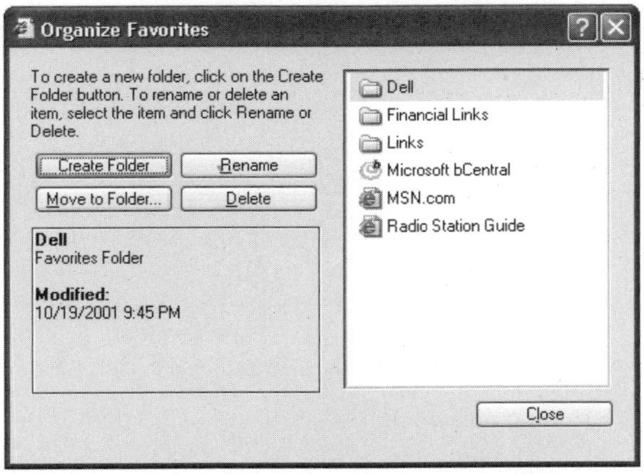

Figure 6-27. Use the Organize Favorites dialog box to manage your Favorites.

Customizing Search Options

Internet Explorer includes a search feature that queries a number of search engines for Web site content based on the information you choose to search for. To use the search feature, just click the Search button (the magnifying glass icon) on the toolbar. If you don't see the Search option, choose View, Explorer Bar, Search. The Search bar appears in the left pane of Internet Explorer, as shown in Figure 6-28. Then type a question or topic you want to search for and click the Search button.

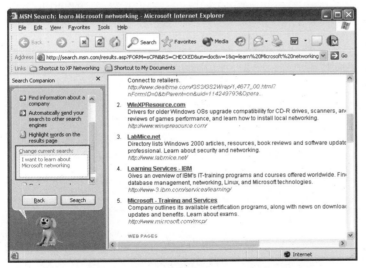

Figure 6-28. Enter words or phrases to search the Internet.

> **note** The program encourages you to enter the search in a complete sentence, but you can just type keywords if you prefer.

You can also change some search options that might make searching easier for you. For instance, you can click the Turn Off Animated Character option if you do not want to see Rover, the friendly dog. Or, you can click the Change Preferences option to display a list of basic options:

- You can choose a different animation character (if you've turned off animation, you will have to first select With An Animated Screen Character).

- You can choose With Indexing Service for very fast local searches on your computer (once the Indexing Service completes its index of your local storage).

- You can choose Change Internet Search Behavior to open the Internet Search Behavior page. The default Search Companion automatically sends your search request to additional search engines, so that setting is usually best. But if you only want results from one search engine, select With Classic Internet Search, and then select a default search engine. Click OK.

Importing and Exporting Favorites and Cookies

Internet Explorer provides you with the option to import and export certain data. For example, you can export your Favorites list so it can be used on another computer, or you can even import and export cookies. The good thing about importing and exporting is that you can import and export to a file so that you can share information with Netscape or even print your Favorites list easily. The following steps walk you through exporting your Favorites list, but you can adjust the steps for other actions:

1 To import or export an item, choose File, Import And Export.

2 Click Next on the Import/Export Wizard Welcome page.

3 On the Import/Export Selection page of the wizard, shown in Figure 6-29, choose an action. In this example, the Favorites list will be exported by choosing Export Favorites and clicking Next.

4 On the Export Favorites Source Folder page, choose to export everything by selecting Favorites or choose a subfolder. Make a selection and click Next.

5 On the Export Favorites Destination page, choose to export to another application on your computer or to a file. Make your choice and specify either the application or the name and path of the export file. Click Next, and then click Finish to start the export.

If you export your favorites, they appear in an HTML file (Bookmark.htm by default), which you can open in any browser and click the links to open the pages. If you export your cookies, they appear in a text file (named Cookies.txt by default). In the same manner, you can import favorites or cookies from another application or from a file.

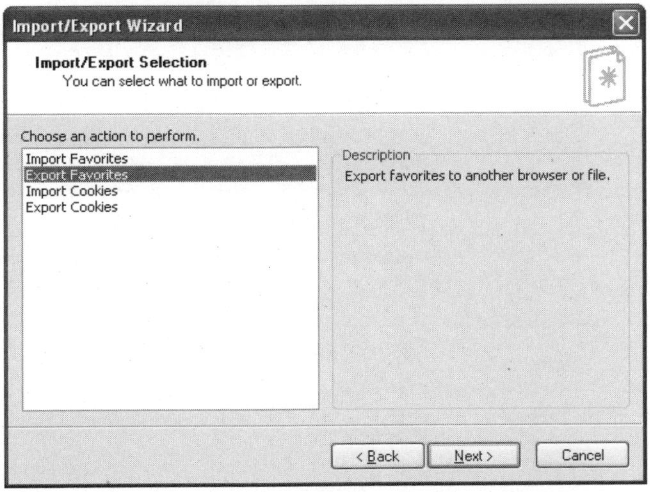

Figure 6-29. Choose an import or export action for Internet Explorer to perform.

Choosing Language Encoding Features

Internet Explorer supports viewing Web pages composed in a variety of languages so that you can view Web sites in the language and alphabets in which they were written. This process, called *encoding,* uses HTML information from the Web page to determine which language the Web page is written in. This tells Internet Explorer which character set to use to display the Web page correctly. If the Web page does not tell Internet Explorer which language is being used, Internet Explorer can usually determine the language if you have the Auto-Select feature turned on. To make sure Auto-Select is turned on, choose View, Encoding, Auto-Select.

If Auto-Select still does not display the language correctly, you can specify the language that is in use. Click View, Encoding, and choose a listed language, or click More to display the full set of available languages. In some cases, you might be prompted to install a language pack so that the Web site can be displayed correctly.

Using Keyboard Shortcuts

As with most Windows programs and features, there are a number of keyboard short-cuts that enable you to use Internet Explorer more quickly and easily. Table 6-2 lists some of the more common shortcuts for you, but you can also find a complete list in the Internet Explorer online Help.

Table 6-2. Common Internet Explorer Shortcut Keys

Keyboard Shortcut	Action
F11	Toggles between full screen view and the browser window
Alt+Home	Goes to the Home Page
F5	Refreshes the current Web page
Esc	Stops downloading a Web page
Ctrl+N	Opens a new browser window
Ctrl+E	Opens the Search window
Ctrl+I	Opens Favorites
Ctrl+H	Opens History
F4	Displays a list of addresses you have typed in the Address bar
Ctrl+Enter	Adds *http://www.* to the beginning of text entered in the Address bar and *.com* to the end
Ctrl+D	Adds the current page to your Favorites menu

Managing Internet Explorer with Local Group Policy

Group Policy is a feature that was first implemented in Microsoft Windows 2000. Local Group Policy is a feature available on Windows XP Professional computers that enables a computer administrator to configure a number of settings that are uniformly applied to all users who log on to the computer. Group Policy can be used to configure many kinds of settings including user passwords and accounts, security settings, Start menu and taskbar settings, desktop settings, and many, many more. Essentially, Group Policy can make changes to the registry and security settings, thus controlling many kinds of system parameters. Although it's beyond the scope of this book to thoroughly explore all that Group Policy has to offer you, this section will highlight the Internet Explorer group policies you might find useful in an environment where a number of users access a computer on which you want to enforce uniform settings.

> **note** You can learn more about Group Policy in Chapter 1 of this book, "Introduction to Windows XP Networking," in *Microsoft Windows XP Inside Out*, from the Help And Support Center in Windows XP Professional, and at *www.microsoft.com*.

Understanding Local Group Policy

Simply put, Group Policy enables an administrator to enforce a number of required settings for users who access the computer. These settings can vary from password issues to Internet Explorer configuration. In Windows 2000 domain-based networks, Group Policy is implemented at the site, domain, and organizational unit (OU) levels (see Chapter 1) by network administrators. Using Group Policy, the network can set uniform computing standards and even automatically roll out new software.

Windows XP Professional and Windows 2000 Professional also provide Local Group Policy. Local Group Policy applies to a single computer and to all users who log on to that computer. Settings are enforced, and administrators on the local machine can make changes to the Local Group Policy settings. Site, domain, and OU Group Policy uniformly applies policy settings across a domain-based network, whereas Local Group Policy uniformly applies policy to the users that log on to a particular computer in either a stand-alone or workgroup environment.

Before using Local Group Policy, there are a few important points to remember:

- Local Group Policy is the weakest form of Group Policy. If your computer resides in a Windows 2000 domain, any site, domain, or OU level policy will override the Local Group Policy if conflicting settings occur. You can still use Local Group Policy, but conflicting settings will be overwritten by the network policy. If the computer becomes disconnected from the domain, Local Group Policy settings will take over until the computer rejoins the domain.

- Local Group Policy only applies to the local computer. You cannot implement Local Group Policy across all computers in a workgroup from a single computer. You must configure the Local Group Policy on each computer.

- Any user who has administrative privileges can change your Local Group Policy settings and invoke new ones.

- Local Group Policy is not available on Windows XP Home Edition.

A Philosophy for Local Group Policy

If you are thinking about using Local Group Policy, rest assured that the features provided in the policy settings work well and can be very important. However, Group Policy also has a lot of power. You can unnecessarily restrict the users that log on to your computer in a number of ways—even from changing their own wallpaper.

When thinking about using Local Group Policy, it is important that you adopt a philosophy of how you will use it. Consider taking the *less is more* approach. Although you have the power to control a large number of settings, that power should be used wisely. The fewer restrictions you can place on local users, the more they can do with the computer and the fewer complaints you will likely receive. After all, you do not want to spend your time constantly trying to adjust policy settings to reverse actions that you once disallowed but now prove to be too onerous for your users. So, when the need arises, invoke a policy setting. Otherwise, leave Local Group Policy settings at the default level—you'll be happier and so will your users.

Using Local Group Policy to Invoke Internet Explorer Settings

You can start the Local Group Policy console by choosing Start, Run, and typing **gpedit.msc.** Press Enter. The Group Policy console appears, as shown in Figure 6-30. In the left pane under Local Computer Policy, there are two nodes—Computer Configuration and User Configuration. Under each of these nodes, you will find policies that you can invoke for Internet Explorer.

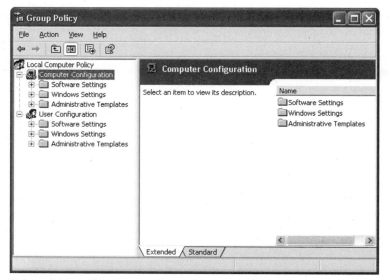

Figure 6-30. The Group Policy console can be used to configure computer and user policies.

Configuring Computer Policy for Internet Explorer

To configure the available Internet Explorer policies under the Computer Configuration node, expand Computer Configuration, Administrative Templates, and Windows Components, and then select Internet Explorer. A list of the available policies appears in the right pane of the console, as shown in Figure 6-31.

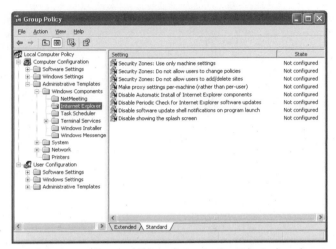

Figure 6-31. The available policies in the selected node appear in the right pane of the console.

In the Setting column in the right pane, you can read the basic description of the action the policy takes. To set a policy, double-click it. A properties dialog box, like the one shown in Figure 6-32 on the next page appears for the selected policy and provides you with the following three options:

- **Not Configured.** The policy is not configured. In other words, Local Group Policy makes no registry entry for this item—any Windows XP default setting will be in effect.

- **Enabled.** The policy is enabled, written to the registry, and applied to all users on this computer.

- **Disabled.** The policy is written to the registry, but it is disabled for all users on this computer.

These settings, although simple, can be a little confusing. Let's consider an example. As you can see in Figure 6-32, the policy setting Disable Periodic Check For Internet Explorer Software Updates has been enabled. Because this policy is worded as *Disable*, enabling this policy setting means no periodic update checks are made. If this policy is disabled, the disabling of periodic update checks is itself disabled, leaving its status the same as if it had not been configured, which means that the Windows default setting for this parameter will apply. Sound confusing? Then look at it this way: Read the policy setting, then say the words "disable" and "enable" to help you see the action that a disable or enable setting invokes on the policy. This will help you keep the items straight as you work with them.

The trick with Local Group Policy is that you always want to choose Not Configured unless there is something specific that you want to do. Keep in mind that enabled and disabled settings write settings to the registry, which must be accessed and will thus use more Windows XP overhead. So, again, less is more. Only configure a policy that you want to invoke, and simply leave the rest alone.

> **tip** If you are unsure of what a policy actually does, click the Explain tab to learn more.

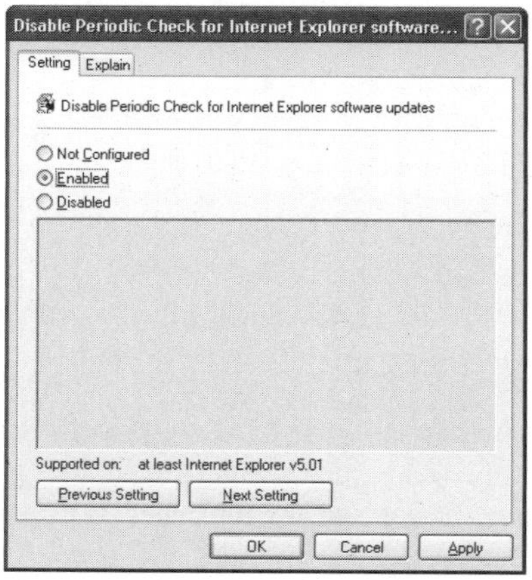

Figure 6-32. Select the Not Configured, Enabled, or Disabled option as needed.

Configure any settings that you want to use for the available policies under Computer Configuration. You can then move on and inspect the policies available under User Configuration.

Configuring User Policy for Internet Explorer

The User Configuration node contains Internet Explorer options in two different locations:

1 Expand User Configuration, Administrative Templates, Windows Components, Internet Explorer, and then select Internet Explorer.

2 In the right pane, there are a considerable number of Internet Explorer Local Group Policy settings available and even more are organized into subfolders.

These options include everything from home page settings to offline content. Browse through the setting configurations to see if there are any that need to be applied to your users. If you see a setting that needs to be applied, double-click it.

3 You'll see the same Not Configured, Enabled, and Disabled options as in the Computer Configuration node. Choose the desired setting and click OK.

In addition to these policy settings, you can also expand User Configuration, Windows Settings, and Internet Explorer Maintenance. Figure 6-33 shows the Browser User Interface subfolder selected with a few maintenance categories appearing in the right pane.

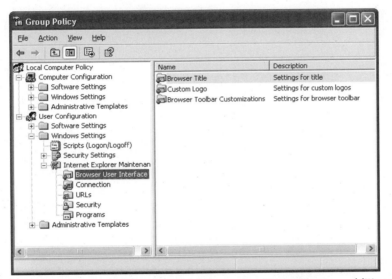

Figure 6-33. Internet Explorer Maintenance settings give you additional policy options.

Using these settings, you can configure policies for the browser interface, URLs, connections, security, and programs. Some of these settings are serious and substantial—others just provide ways to customize Internet Explorer cosmetically, such as giving Internet Explorer customized title bars and logos. Experiment with these settings and see if you want to apply any of them to your users. Remember to give your users the most freedom possible so they can get the most from their Internet experience.

Using Outlook Express Advanced Features

Like many new computing advances, e-mail was once dismissed as a passing fad that had no real value, especially during the early days when the Internet was still in its infancy. Today, many people as well as corporations are dependent on e-mail, and millions of e-mail messages are sent around the globe each day. As you need a Web browser to surf the Internet, you need e-mail software, also called an *e-mail client*, to send, receive, and manage e-mail. Microsoft Outlook Express version 6 is the default e-mail client included with Microsoft Windows XP.

Designed to work in conjunction with Microsoft Internet Explorer 6, Outlook Express provides major e-mail management functions and features that advanced users need and demand. In the past, Outlook Express was a simple e-mail client that provided a way to connect to Post Office Protocol (POP) or Internet Message Access Protocol (IMAP) e-mail servers and retrieve or send e-mail. Today, Outlook Express provides many advanced features, particularly for a free e-mail client. In this chapter, you can explore the advanced features Outlook Express has to offer. If you have not used Outlook Express in the past, you might be surprised to learn how much Outlook Express 6 has to offer, so read on!

Managing Connectivity and Accounts

Outlook Express 6 is designed to work with POP3, IMAP, and Hypertext Transfer Protocol (HTTP) servers so that you can get your e-mail from nearly any type of mail server. In fact, you can configure Outlook Express with several different accounts if you are using more than one e-mail account. Generally, Outlook Express connectivity and account management is not difficult, as long as you keep the different account information straight when configuring the e-mail accounts. The next section looks at configuring an e-mail account and resolving Outlook Express connectivity issues. Configuring multiple e-mail accounts with Outlook Express is discussed thereafter.

> You must have an Internet connection already configured before Outlook Express can connect to a mail server. See "Creating New Internet Connections," page 103, to learn more about configuring an Internet connection.

InsideOut

Using Other E-mail Clients with Windows XP

Like Internet Explorer, Outlook Express is a default program provided in Windows XP. However, you are not required to use Outlook Express as your e-mail and news client. You can easily use another e-mail program and configure Internet Explorer to default to that program. If you have used other e-mail programs in the past, you should certainly take a look at Outlook Express 6—it has a lot to offer including access to HTTP mail, such as Hotmail. If you know for sure that you do not want to use Outlook Express as your default e-mail client, see "Setting Default Programs," page 162, to learn more about configuring Internet Explorer to default to another e-mail client.

Windows XP Service Pack 1 lets you change your default mail program from Outlook Express to another application. In fact, some newly purchased computers that have Windows XP Service Pack 1 preinstalled might not include Outlook Express at all. For more information, see Appendix A, "Windows XP Service Pack 1."

Configuring Connectivity and Accounts

To use Outlook Express, you must configure at least one account. This account can be an e-mail account, but it can also be a newsgroup or a directory service. If you open Outlook Express and click Tools, Accounts, you see the Internet Accounts dialog box shown in Figure 7-1. All currently configured accounts are listed on the All tab, but you can select other tabs to configure specific types of accounts.

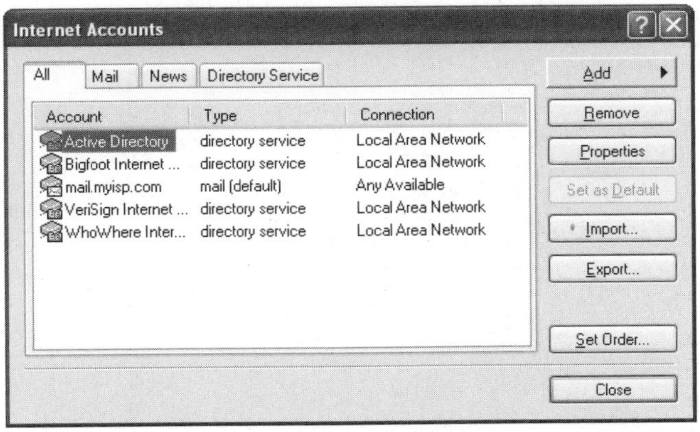

Figure 7-1. The Internet Accounts dialog box is used to configure all Internet accounts in Outlook Express.

Configuring an E-mail Account

When you initially open Outlook Express 6, the Outlook Express Internet Connection Wizard might be the first screen you see. If so, skip to step 3. Otherwise, to set up an e-mail account, follow these steps:

1 In Outlook Express, choose Tools, Accounts.

2 In the Internet Accounts dialog box, select the Mail tab, and then click Add, Mail.

3 On the Your Name page of the wizard, enter your name. This is the name that all users will be able to see when you send e-mail (it will appear in the From field of e-mail they receive from you). Click Next.

4 On the Internet E-mail Address page, enter your e-mail address and click Next.

5 On the E-mail Server Names page of the wizard, shown in Figure 7-2 on the next page, select the type of mail server your account uses from the box labeled My Incoming Mail Server Is A … Server. The most common type of mail server is POP3. If the server is a POP3 or IMAP server, you'll also need to enter the incoming mail server and outgoing mail server names. These names take such forms as pop.*ispname*.net, mail.*ispname*.net, or smtp.*ispname*.com (where *ispname* is usually the name of your Internet Service Provider (ISP), but you'll need to consult your ISP documentation for the exact name of each required server. If you are using an HTTP server (such as Hotmail), you'll need to enter the URL to the Internet server. If you select Hotmail as your HTTP provider, the URL is completed for you. Click Next when you've entered these settings.

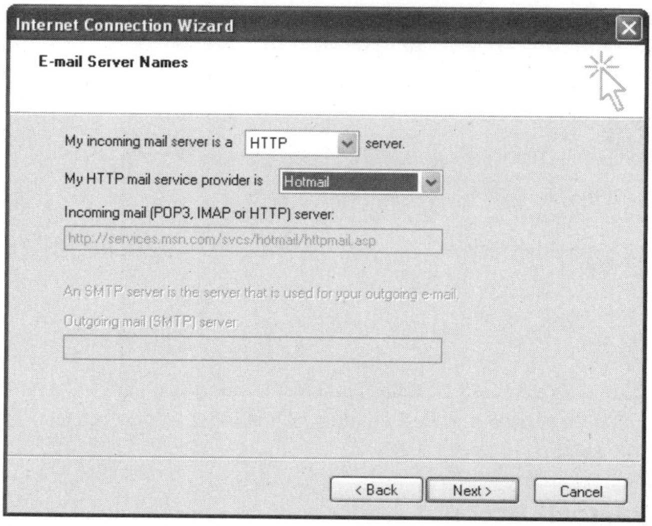

Figure 7-2. Choose the type of mail server for your account, and enter its mail server names or URL.

6 On the Internet Mail Logon page, enter your user name and password as provided by your ISP. If your ISP uses Secure Password Authentication (SPA), select the check box labeled Log On Using Secure Password Authentication (SPA). SPA is a security feature that might require you to manually log on to the mail server. You cannot use SPA unless your mail server requires it. Consult your ISP documentation for details. Click Next, and then click Finish.

The new account appears on the Mail tab of the Internet Accounts dialog box.

Once you have configured the e-mail account, you can access the account's properties by selecting the account on the Mail tab and clicking the Properties button. There are some additional settings available to you in this dialog box that are not presented when the wizard helps you set up the account, so it is a good idea to check these settings to make sure they are accurate. Also, should any of your account information change, you can return to this dialog box and adjust the settings as needed.

An account's properties dialog box includes these five tabs: General, Servers, Connection, Security, and Advanced.

On the General tab, shown in Figure 7-3, the Name, Organization, E-mail Address, and Reply Address fields appear. Note that the address you enter in Reply Address can be different than the address you enter in E-mail Address (the address that you send from). This can be useful if you send mail from two or more accounts but want to receive all your mail in one account. Enter that account in the Reply Address box.

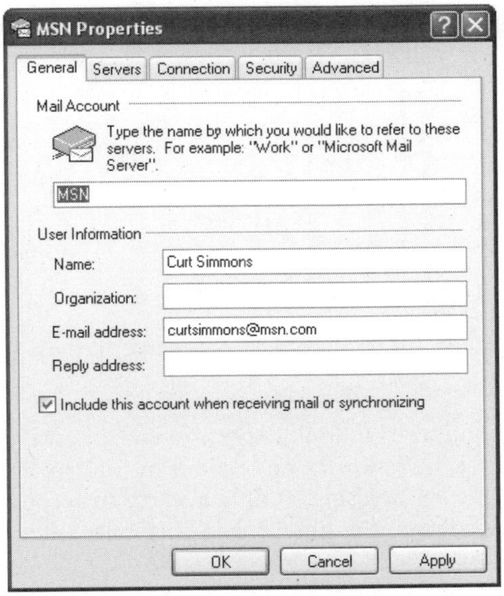

Figure 7-3. Use the General tab to configure user name and e-mail address information.

On the Servers tab, you see the server type and name or names of the mail servers. You also see your account logon name and the password field. If you want Windows XP to remember your password so that you do not have to type it each time you log on, select the Remember Password check box. Notice that the option for SPA is also included on this tab. When you provide a user name and password in the Internet Connection Wizard, the wizard assumes that information applies to both your incoming and outgoing mail. However, some people use one account to store and retrieve their mail and another account to send it. For example, if you have your own Internet domain name and Web site, you might use that as your e-mail address but send your outbound e-mail through an ISP. In this case, you'll have to specify the user name and password for the outbound account as well. To do so, select My Server Requires Authentication, and then click the Settings button.

Selecting this option opens the Outgoing Mail Server dialog box, shown in Figure 7-4 on the next page, where you can enter the logon information for your outgoing (SMTP) mail account. If your outbound mail server requires a different user name and password than your incoming mail, select Log On Using, and then supply the outgoing user name and password. Specify whether you want the password remembered so you don't have to type it each time you send mail, and select the SPA option if your outgoing mail provider requires it.

Figure 7-4. Configure security settings for the outgoing mail server if they differ from the inbound server.

On the Connection tab, you can configure Outlook Express to connect using your default Internet connection as set up in Network Connections in Control Panel, or you can select Always Connect To This Account Using, and then select an account from the list. This feature is useful if the mail account requires that a particular Internet connection be used to access it.

On the Security tab, you can configure signing and encrypting preferences if you are using a digital certificate. Use the Select buttons to choose the desired certificates. You won't have any certificates listed unless you've already installed them on your computer. Outlook Express 6 supports the use of encrypted e-mail using digital certificates. You can obtain a digital certificate from a third-party provider, such as Verisign at *www.verisign.com*.

The Advanced tab, shown in Figure 7-5, gives you additional options arranged in these groups: Server Port Numbers, Server Timeouts, Sending, and Delivery. If your mail servers require Secure Sockets Layer (SSL) connections, select the appropriate check boxes. See your ISP documentation for details.

By default, Server Timeouts is configured for one minute. This means that if the mail fails to start downloading after one minute, Outlook Express stops trying and presents a prompt to ask if you want to try again. As a general rule, the one minute setting is sufficient, but if you know your mail server is frequently slow to respond, you can increase this value.

In the Sending section of the Advanced tab, you can choose Break Apart Messages Larger Than and specify a certain value. This can be useful in cases where you need to communicate with older servers that cannot handle messages larger than 64 KB. Again, don't use this option unless you are sure you need it.

You can also choose to leave a copy of the message on the mail server for redundancy purposes, if your mail server supports this feature. This option can be useful with a POP mail server if you travel and use a laptop to access your e-mail. You can set the

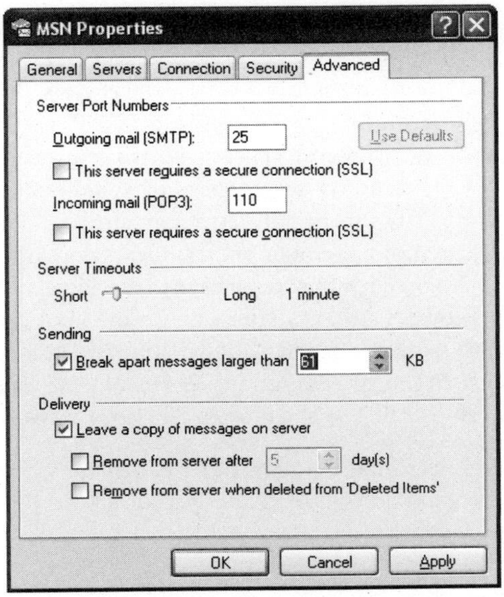

Figure 7-5. See your ISP documentation for additional details about using these advanced features.

account on your laptop to leave a copy of your messages on the mail server, so that when you return home and download your mail, all your mail is downloaded to your main computer (and removed from the mail server at that point), enabling you to maintain a complete archive of your mail on one computer. If you do select Leave A Copy Of Messages On Server, you can then specify a time interval for keeping them, to remove them when you delete them from your Deleted Items folder, or to leave them indefinitely. The final option is your best choice if you plan to retrieve these messages later from another computer. In this scenario, on your portable computer you should select only Leave A Copy Of Messages On Server, and on your main home or office computer you would clear this check box.

Configuring a News Account

Outlook Express handles newsgroups in addition to e-mail. Your ISP service probably includes access to a news server. *Newsgroups* number in the tens of thousands and are a great source of information on every topic imaginable. You can configure a news account by clicking the News tab of the Internet Accounts dialog box and clicking Add, News. This action leads you through similar steps as you used to create an e-mail account (see the previous section.) Once you've entered the news account setup, the account appears on the News tab. You can select the account and click the Properties button to make similar refinements as with an e-mail account.

Configuring a Directory Service Account

A *directory service* enables you to find information about people or services. By default, Outlook Express provides Lightweight Directory Access Protocol (LDAP) access to Active Directory (for searching on a domain-based LAN) as well as a few default Internet directory services. Active Directory is the directory service used by Windows domains starting with Windows 2000. You can learn more about Active Directory in "Finding Domain Resources," page 336. If you are not a member of a Windows domain, the Active Directory option is simply not used. If you click the arrow next to the Find button on the Outlook Express toolbar and select People, Outlook Express opens the Find People dialog box. In this dialog box, you can enter the name or other information about a person you're searching for and use the Look In box to ask Outlook Express to use either Active Directory (to find people on the local domain) or an Internet directory service.

You can add additional directory services by clicking Add, Directory Service on the Directory Service tab of Internet Accounts. Provide the desired directory service name and any necessary logon information.

> **tip** **Limiting Internet Searches**
>
> By default, Outlook Express returns up to 100 matches for your Internet search. You configure each search engine to limit itself to more or fewer matches by selecting the directory service on the Directory Service tab of Internet Accounts, clicking Properties, selecting the Advanced tab, and then specifying a maximum value in the Maximum Number Of Matches To Return box.

Outlook Express can also use the directory services listed in the Internet Accounts dialog box to match names you type in the To box of your e-mails to their corresponding e-mail addresses when those people aren't included in your address book. By default, Outlook Express only searches Active Directory (and then only if you're part of a Windows domain), but you can select one or more of the Internet directory services. Open the Properties dialog box of each Internet directory service, and select Check Names Against This Server When Sending Mail on the General tab. Then, in the Internet Accounts dialog box, click Set Order and specify in what order you want the directory services to be searched. In general, add the e-mail addresses of those you correspond with regularly to your address book because Internet searches for e-mail addresses can be time-consuming.

Once you have your accounts configured, you then need to get connected. By default, Outlook Express connects to the Internet using the preferences that you've specified in Internet Explorer. In other words, Outlook Express uses the options you have configured on the Connections tab of Internet Options, such as dialing a connection when a network connection isn't present or using various proxy settings. See "Managing Connectivity," page 137, for more information. Using Outlook Express with Internet Explorer is easy because you only have to determine the Internet connection you want

InsideOut

Importing and Exporting Account Information to Save Time

In the interest of saving time, Outlook Express provides an easy way to export and import accounts. For example, if you manage a workgroup of 10 Windows XP computers, you can configure a mail account and a news account, and specify a directory services account on one of the computers. Assuming you want to use the same accounts on each computer, open Internet Accounts on the first computer, select each account you've set up, and click Export. Each account is saved as an Internet Account File type with a .iaf file extension. You can then use the Import button in the Internet Accounts dialog boxes of the other nine computers to quickly import the accounts to those machines. Otherwise, without a domain-based network, you'll have to set up the accounts on each computer individually, and you'll waste time entering redundant information.

to use once in Internet Explorer in order for both programs to work. If you want to access the Connections tab that appears in Internet Explorer from within Outlook Express, choose Tools, Options, select the Connection tab, and then click the Change button. Although Outlook Express defaults to using the connections specified in Internet Explorer, you can override these settings on a per account basis by specifying different connection options on the Connection tab of each mail and news account's properties dialog box in Outlook Express. If you don't see the connection you need in any of these dialog boxes, you'll need to set one up. To do that, see "Creating New Internet Connections," page 103.

To connect to your provider and send and receive your mail in one step, click the Send/ Recv button on the Outlook Express toolbar. If the Dial-Up Connection dialog box appears, you can choose to connect automatically from that point on by selecting Connect Automatically (you also have to select Save Password because Outlook Express will need to know the password to make the automatic connection).

If you are having problems connecting with your ISP, check Table 7-1 for common connectivity problems and solutions.

Table 7-1. Common Connectivity Problems and Solutions

Connectivity Problem	Possible Solutions
Outlook Express will not dial the connection.	When using a modem, first make sure the modem works. Try to manually launch the connection from Network Connections. If all seems to be in order, make sure the default account is listed in the Always Connect To This Account Using box on the Connection tab of the mail account's properties dialog box.

(continued)

Table 7-1. *(continued)*

Connectivity Problem	Possible Solutions
I can connect to the Internet, but I receive error messages when I try to send or receive e-mail (or both).	If your e-mail account has never worked, there is usually a problem with the way you have configured the account. Make sure your user name and password are entered correctly and remember that passwords are often case sensitive. Also, make sure any SPA or additional logon security settings are correct. Many ISPs do not support SPA, so try disabling that option if you're in doubt. If you are sure the settings are correct, contact your ISP for help.
I always get timeout messages when trying to download mail.	If your mail server regularly takes some time to respond to your request to send or retrieve mail, you can increase the Server Timeouts value on the Advanced tab of the properties dialog box for the problematic e-mail account. This will tell Outlook Express to wait for a longer period of time before it times out the connection.
I can't access a newsgroup.	The news account might require that you log on or it might require some other setting that is not configured. Check the documentation that came with your account, and then open the properties dialog box of the news account and make sure all settings are configured as they should be.
My e-mail or newsgroup access has been working in the past, but is not working now.	If nothing has changed on your computer, the problem is usually at the other end with the mail or news server. Wait a little while and try again. If you have reconfigured your settings, double-check them against your ISP documentation to see if you've made a mistake.

Using Multiple Accounts

You can configure as many e-mail, news, and directory service accounts as you want. Simply choose Tools, Accounts to open the Internet Accounts dialog box, and select the desired tab (you can also work from the All tab if you don't find the merged list of accounts confusing). Then, use the Add button to configure the new account. Once you've established more than one account in a category (mail, news, or directory service), you can specify their priority. Most of the time, you'll be interested in managing multiple e-mail accounts. Suppose you have two e-mail accounts. Open the properties dialog box of the first account and notice the last option on the General tab, Include

This Account When Receiving Mail Or Synchronizing. Because it takes time to access each mail account when you're receiving mail, you might choose to enable this option for your most active e-mail accounts, but to leave it cleared for those that only occasionally receive mail. This way, you can click the Send/Recv button and retrieve mail from all the active accounts without wasting time looking for mail on seldom used accounts. When you do want to check mail on the less active accounts, click the arrow next to the Send/Recv button, and then click the account you want to check for mail. Also, when you have more than one mail account, you can select the main one on the Mail tab of the Internet Accounts dialog box, and then click Set Default. This account will then be the one used by default when you create a new e-mail message. The message's From field will be filled with your e-mail address from the default account; when you send the message, the message will be sent out through the Simple Mail Transfer Protocol (SMTP) server specified for this account.

Because Outlook Express 6 enables you to manage Internet mail as well as send and receive it, you can work with all of your e-mail accounts in the Folders list displayed in the left pane of Outlook Express and shown in Figure 7-6. If you don't see the Folders list, choose View, Layout, select the Folders List option, and click OK. The Folders list contains a folder structure for each e-mail or news account you have configured. If you are using HTTP mail, you can synchronize the account with the HTTP mail server by selecting the account in the Folders list and clicking the Synchronize Account button in the right pane.

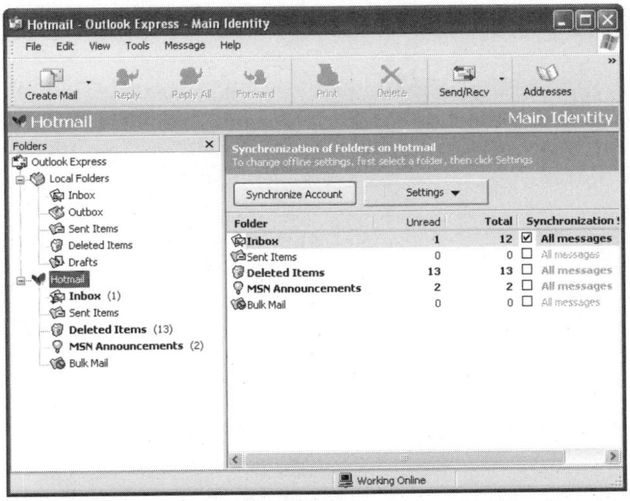

Figure 7-6. Outlook Express provides a folder structure for each e-mail account.

InsideOut

Using Mail and News While Offline

A great feature of Outlook Express, especially when working with HTTP mail accounts like Hotmail, is offline support. Typically, you must be connected to the Internet to work with HTTP mail—not so with Outlook Express. You can review your mail, delete mail you don't want to keep, prepare new e-mail messages, and compose answers to those you've already retrieved while you're offline, such as when using your laptop on an airplane. Then, when you have access to an Internet connection again, just synchronize the account with the HTTP server. Replies and new mail messages are sent out, new mail is downloaded, and messages you deleted on your laptop are deleted on the HTTP server. You can read and process the HTTP mail at any time because it is downloaded to your folders. This feature makes HTTP function like a typical POP3 e-mail account, and that is great news if you are not connected to the Internet all of the time. Newsgroups can be used in a similar fashion. You can download the headers for groups you subscribe to, and then while working offline, you can review the headers and select those you want to retrieve the messages for. When your Internet connection is available again, Outlook Express will retrieve the marked messages. If you want, you can go offline again and read them even when the Internet connection isn't available.

Using Identities in Outlook Express

Outlook Express provides a feature called identities. Suppose your Windows XP computer is used by three different people in your home. Everyone logs on using the same Windows XP account, but you want each user to have his or her own mail folders in Outlook Express. How can you do this? By using identities, several different people can use Outlook Express to access e-mail accounts while keeping their e-mail folders and address books separate. When a user logs on with a particular identity, only the e-mail folders and contacts for that user are displayed.

tip   Using Multiple Windows XP Accounts Instead of Identities

It's important to note that identities are helpful when several users log on to Windows XP under the same Windows XP account, as might be the case with a home computer that several different people use. If users log on to Windows XP with different accounts, Windows XP automatically sets up completely separate personal folders, so the use of identities is usually not necessary or useful in this case. In fact, using separate Windows XP accounts provides greater privacy that extends to all the applications users run under Windows XP. Identities can also be used by one person to, for example, keep work mail separate from personal mail.

By default, Outlook Express creates an identity called Main Identity for e-mail and for the address book. This identity cannot be deleted, but you can change its name to another name such as your own (choose File, Identities, Manage Identities; select Main Identity, click Properties, and enter a new name in the Type Your Name box), and you can add other identities and switch between them. Identities can be password protected, but this does not guarantee that someone will not be able to see your e-mail or contacts list.

If you want to ensure privacy, make sure each person uses a password to protect his or her identity folder where the e-mail is stored. Each identity has a separate subfolder with a long numerical name in this default path: C:\Documents and Settings*username*\Local Settings\Application Data\Identities, where *username* is the name of the Windows XP user account under which all identities use the computer. You can browse to this path using Windows Explorer, and then browse the numerical subfolders of Identities to actually get to your data. The data is stored in files with .dbx extensions, as shown in Figure 7-7, but it can be copied and read. The point is that password protection helps, but if you are serious about privacy, you might consider password protecting your folder or even using folder encryption to secure the data. Or, use different Windows XP user accounts instead of Outlook Express identities.

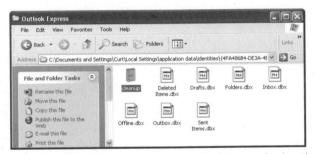

Figure 7-7. You can use Windows Explorer to display the e-mail data files contained in an identity's folder. Or, select the Maintenance tab in the Options dialog box, and click the Store Folder button to see the path to the current identity's data.

> **note** If you need to use identities and you are interested in using password protection and perhaps encrypting the user account folder, the folder must be stored on an NTFS drive. For more information about encryption and NTFS security, see Chapter 14, "Understanding Resource Sharing and NTFS Security."

To access identities, choose File, Identities, and click either Add New Identity or Manage Identities. Select Add New Identity to create a new identity. Otherwise, choose Manage Identities to open the Manage Identities dialog box shown in Figure 7-8 on the next page. If you haven't created any identities, you will only see Main Identity in the Identities list. You can also create a new identity from this dialog box by clicking the New

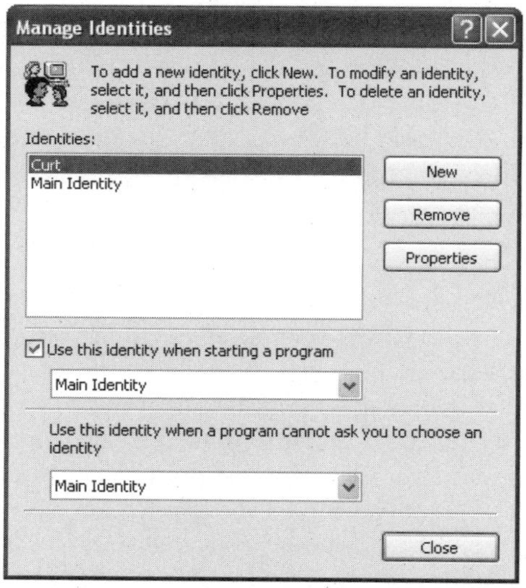

Figure 7-8. Use identities when several different people need to use Outlook Express on the same computer but want to share the same Windows XP user account.

button. This option opens the same dialog box as the Add New Identity command, in which you name the identity and optionally provide a password. Note that you should be able to use the Manage Identities dialog box to determine which identity opens as the default when starting Outlook Express. However, no matter what you select here, Outlook Express reopens to the identity it was closed in. This buggy behavior might be fixed in a future update of Outlook Express.

When you want to switch identities, click File, Switch Identity, select the new identity, and provide the password if required.

Configuring Outlook Express

Once you have your accounts configured and Outlook Express is up and running, there are many additional settings you can choose. In this section, configuration items that are easily overlooked but are very helpful and useful will be discussed. You can access all of these features by choosing Tools, Options to open the Outlook Express Options dialog box, and then setting options on its nine tabs.

General Tab

The General tab of the Options dialog box, shown in Figure 7-9, contains options to configure how e-mail messages are received. These are of special importance:

●   **Automatically Log On To Windows Messenger.** Notice that this option is selected. If you are not using Windows Messenger, clear this option to save time.

194

- **Check For New Messages Every.** If you want Outlook Express to automatically check for messages, select this option, and enter a time interval. By default, messages are checked every 30 minutes. You can also select Send And Receive Messages At Startup to check for messages as soon as you open Outlook Express. Also, select an option under If My Computer Is Not Connected At This Time so Outlook Express will know whether or not you want it to attempt to make a connection when it's time to check your mail. These settings determine whether Outlook Express automatically attempts to connect and retrieve mail on a periodic basis. This can be beneficial when you're set up at home or at your office, but can be annoying when you're using a portable laptop, and the computer repeatedly attempts to dial a connection when there is no phone line connected to the computer.

Figure 7-9. Configure message download options and features on the General tab.

Read Tab

The Read tab, shown in Figure 7-10 on the next page, provides these important options for reading mail and news messages:

- **Mark Message Read After Displaying For … Seconds.** E-mail messages that have not been read appear in a bold type. However, if you are using the Preview pane, the message is marked as read after you preview it for five seconds. This might work well for you, but if you receive a lot of e-mail, you might want the messages to not appear as read until you have actually opened them in the message window. In this case, clear the check box.

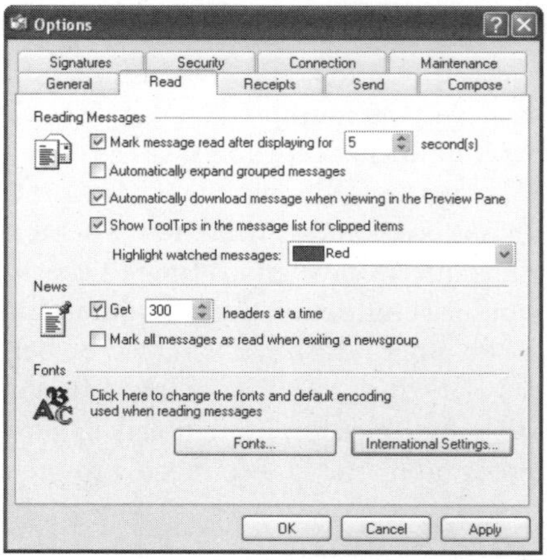

Figure 7-10. Use the Read tab to configure the way messages are read in Outlook Express.

●   **Fonts.** If you are having problems reading e-mail messages, click the Fonts button to change the font or size. In the same manner, Outlook Express supports encoding so that different languages can be displayed. If your messages are not showing up with the correct character set for your default language, set the default language encoding in the Encoding list in the Fonts dialog box. To make this setting your default, click the Set As Default button in this dialog box.

Receipts Tab

When you send a message, you can request a receipt when the message is read. To do this, select Request A Read Receipt For All Sent Messages on the Receipts tab, shown in Figure 7-11. This feature can be helpful when sending urgent messages or when you want to make sure the receiving party has received your message. This applies the receipt option to all messages that you send, which might be necessary, but think carefully before you do this because you might end up with more receipts than you want. The best option is usually to request a read receipt on a message-by-message basis.

In the same manner, users running Outlook Express or Outlook can also request a receipt from you. In the Returning Read Receipts section, you can set Outlook Express to respond to receipts requested of you by sending them automatically (Always Send A Read Receipt), by never sending them (Never Send A Read Receipt), or by prompting you each time a receipt is requested (Notify Me For Each Read Receipt Request). The default is to notify you so that you can make a decision on a case-by-case basis. Note that some junk mailers request a receipt to their spam messages. If you automatically send a read receipt, the spammer knows that a legitimate e-mail address has been reached, which might result in your address being subjected to even more spam.

Figure 7-11. Use the Receipts tab to configure the way you request receipts and respond to receipt requests.

If you are using digitally signed messages, you can also request a secure receipt. When you click the Secure Receipts button, you see the same options to request and respond to receipts for all digitally signed messages as you see for nonsecure messages on the Receipts tab.

Send Tab

The Send tab, shown in Figure 7-12, lets you select options for sending e-mail. By default, all options are selected, and these settings are appropriate for most people. However, you can review these options and clear the check boxes for any that you do not like. Notice

Figure 7-12. Use the Send tab to configure the way messages are sent to other users.

that by default all mail is sent in HTML format, and all news is sent in plain text. You can adjust these settings if you like, but HTML mail gives you more formatting options than plain text. Users who receive e-mail from you can view the HTML formatting, but if their e-mail client does not support it, it will appear as plain text anyway.

Compose Tab

The Compose tab contains three sections that concern mail composition. These options enhance your messages, but are certainly not required. Here's the skinny on these items:

- In the Compose Font section, you can choose a mail and news font, style, and color that you want to use. However, do not assume that your recipient will actually see these font and color options. That depends on his or her mail settings. If the recipient's e-mail client is able to read HTML (which it probably can), the font and colors will most likely be preserved. If not, the e-mail will appear in plain text.

- In the Stationery section, you can choose a background image or pattern to be used when you create your messages. This works like wallpaper on your desktop. Use the Select button to choose an available image or pattern, or if you want to create your own background based on a picture file, click the Create New button, which opens the Stationery Setup Wizard to guide you. Overall, stationery is pleasing, but it does increase transmission time. Also, if your recipients do not use HTML mail, the stationery will be downloaded to them as an attachment to the e-mail, not as a background design displayed in the message.

- You can also create a business card to attach to your outgoing messages. The business card contains as much or as little information about you as you like, and recipients can place the business cards in their address books. If you think the bulk of the people you communicate with will find your business card useful, create one; otherwise, disregard this feature.

Signatures Tab

The Signatures tab, shown in Figure 7-13, provides you with options to create and format a signature that you can apply to your messages. The signature is then automatically inserted into your e-mail message. Signatures typically contain information such as your name, e-mail address, Web page, and your phone number; some people also like to add a favorite quote or slogan to personalize their messages.

caution Make sure that the information you provide in your signature is information you really want to share with users you e-mail. In other words, think twice before placing your phone number or other personal information in your signature.

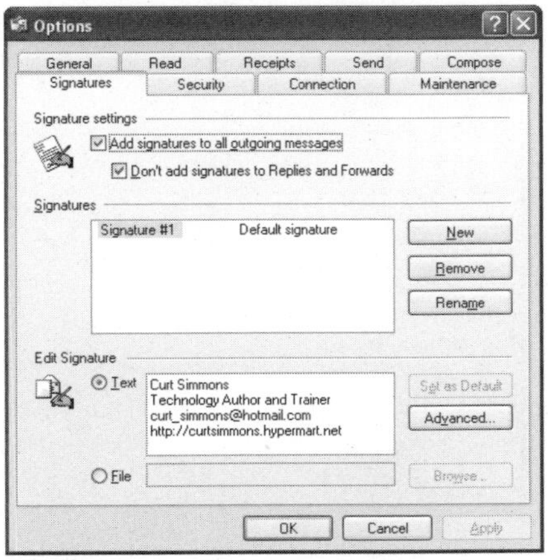

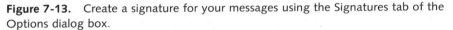

Figure 7-13. Create a signature for your messages using the Signatures tab of the Options dialog box.

To create a signature, click the New button and a default Signature #1 appears. You can click Rename to give the signature a friendlier name. Then, enter the desired signature text in the Edit Signature box. You can also select the File option to attach a signature in a text or HTML file. This is the only way to add a signature that contains a graphic or other visual image. Click the Advanced button to choose which accounts you want to use the signature with.

---

tip **Using Signatures Selectively**

If you want to use the signature on some messages but not on others, clear the Add Signatures To All Outgoing Messages check box. You can then individually apply the signature to selected messages by creating a message, and then choosing Insert, Signature from the message's menu.

Security Tab

The Security tab enables you to configure Outlook Express for minimal virus protection and for secure mail. In the Virus Protection section, shown in Figure 7-14 on the next page, you can choose an Internet Explorer security zone to apply to mail you receive, and you can have Outlook Express notify you when a message might be infected with a virus. The zone you select applies the same zone configuration found on the Security tab of Internet Explorer's Internet Options dialog box. See "Security Zones," page 144, for more information about Internet Explorer's security features.

Figure 7-14. Use the Security tab to configure low-level virus protection and to enable secure mail.

It is important to note that these extra features are in no way a replacement for antivirus software. The security features provided on this tab simply help you identify possible threats—they do not scan messages and identify viruses. For this reason, you should always run antivirus software that can scan newly downloaded e-mail for viruses.

For more information about dealing with e-mail security issues, see "Coping with E-mail Security Threats," page 591.

Be sure the Warn Me When Other Applications Try To Send Mail As Me option is selected. This option protects you from the type of virus that accesses your address book and sends a phony message from you to some or all your contacts, spreading the virus to their machines in the process. A good antivirus program will prevent you from receiving or activating such a virus. But if one should get through your defenses, this option is designed to keep it from replicating to your contacts.

If you want to use secure e-mail, you must obtain a digital certificate from a provider such as Verisign (*www.verisign.com*). If you choose Digitally Sign All Outgoing Messages, a certificate is sent with your e-mail so that other users can verify that the message has come from you and has not been altered in transit. You can also choose Encrypt Contents And Attachments For All Outgoing Messages, which will keep anyone other than the intended recipient from being able to read the message should it be intercepted. Although these security features work well, the recipient must be able to read the signature or decrypt the e-mail in order for the feature to work, which requires a bit of setup before you can start using it. The digital certificate that you acquire consists of a private portion or *key* and a public portion. To use the digital certificate, follow these steps:

1 Send the public portion of your digital certificate to e-mail recipients with whom you want to exchange encrypted e-mail.

2   The recipients must send you the public portion of *their* digital certificates so that you can read encrypted e-mail that is sent to you from those recipients.

3   The public portion of the digital certificate you send must be added to their address books and be attached to your contact information. When you receive their public keys in e-mail messages they send you, you must add those keys to your address book and attach them to their contact information. You'll find a Digital IDs tab in your contact's properties dialog box where you can add the public keys they send you.

4   Remember that both parties must first send the public keys to each other *without* encrypting the messages.

5   After both parties have added each other's public keys to their address books, activate one or both of the options in the Secure Mail section of the Security tab in the Outlook Express Options dialog box to start sending secure messages.

6   When you receive encrypted e-mail from a particular sender, the certificate for that sender is found in your address book and is used to automatically decrypt the e-mail.

---

tip   **Signing or Encrypting Your Mail Selectively**

It is unlikely that you will need to digitally sign or encrypt your mail to everyone you correspond with, so you might not want to set the options on the Security tab, which apply to all outgoing messages. Instead, you can sign and/or encrypt outgoing messages individually by clicking the Sign and/or Encrypt buttons on each message's toolbar.

Connection Tab

The Connection tab provides basic configuration for handling dial-up connections and links you to Internet Explorer's connections options, which it shares. A noteworthy item in the Dial-Up section is the Hang Up After Sending And Receiving option. If you are using a dial-up connection and you have your mail account configured to check for messages automatically, you might consider using this option so the connection will automatically hang up after mail has been checked. Of course, if you are trying to work online, this setting can get very annoying because it will automatically disconnect every time you send and receive mail.

Maintenance Tab

The Maintenance tab, shown in Figure 7-15, offers some important options for managing Outlook Express. You can review the available options concerning whether Outlook Express deletes messages from your Deleted Items folder when exiting, removes the deleted messages on an IMAP server, and compacts your message files to save space. The default handling method for news messages is also configured on this tab. The default settings are usually best, but read through these options to see if there is anything you want to change. You can choose to clean up messages in order to conserve disk space, and you might want to change the location of the store folder (where your mail and news messages are kept) so it is easier to find them and back them up. You might want to click the Store Folder button to see where your files are located, deep within the Documents And Settings folder.

Figure 7-15. Use the Maintenance tab to configure how Outlook Express handles downloaded mail and news messages.

Managing E-mail

Outlook Express provides a number of options and features for sending and receiving e-mail. Although newsgroup usage is an important feature of Outlook Express, you will probably use Outlook Express mostly for e-mail, so this section is devoted to the options and features concerning e-mail management.

Sending Mail

When you click the Write Message button in Outlook Express, a New Message window appears, as shown in Figure 7-16.

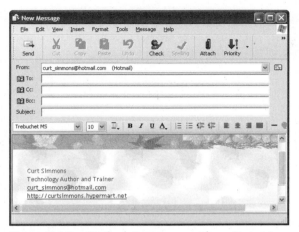

Figure 7-16. Outlook Express provides a New Message window where you can format and create a mail message.

When you create a new mail message in Outlook Express, you have several options that you can use to customize your message. You are probably familiar with many of these, but several are listed for you to review. If you discover a feature in the list that you have not tried before, you can experiment with it on your computer:

- You can use the blind carbon copy (Bcc) field to send a copy of a mail message to addressees without their names being visible to those addressed in the To and Cc fields. The blind carbon copy (Bcc) field might not be visible in your New Message window. If you do not see it, choose View, All Headers, and it will appear. You can select a message in your Inbox and choose File, Properties to learn more about it, but the Bcc field is still hidden—even when you click the Message Source button on the Details tab.

- You can designate the priority of an outgoing message as High, Normal, or Low by using the Set Priority button on the message's toolbar or by choosing Message, Set Priority. This feature can be valuable when you are trying to get someone's attention for a quick reply. But the recipient needs to be using Outlook or Outlook Express for the feature to work.

- If you have not configured stationery to apply to all messages, you can add it to individual messages by choosing Message, New Using, and then selecting the stationery you want to use.

- If you want to request a read receipt for an individual message, choose Tools, Request Read Receipt. You can also use the Tools menu to encrypt or digitally sign a message, or click the respective buttons on the toolbar.

- If you do not want to use stationery but you want to use some other HTML element, such as a picture or background color, choose Format, Background, and then make a selection.

- If you need to send a message in a different language using another encoding scheme, choose Format, Encoding, and then select from the choices or click More to reveal all the options.

- Files, business cards, signatures, pictures, and hyperlinks can all be inserted into your e-mail using the Insert menu option. You can also use toolbar buttons for several of these features.

---

tip   **Inserting Hyperlinks**

Although you can officially insert a hyperlink using the Insert, Hyperlink command, you can usually just type the URL, and Outlook Express will automatically format it as a hyperlink if you are composing your mail as HTML.

- You can also customize the New Message window's toolbar. Choose View, Toolbars, Customize to select the size and labeling of icons and to add, remove, or reorder the buttons on the toolbar.

- If you are working on a message and need to stop before sending it, click File, Save to save the message to your Drafts folder. You can then reopen the message from the Drafts folder at a later time to complete the message and send it. Unsent messages can reside in the Drafts folder as long as you like.

- You can also use the File menu to save messages to different folders, or you can use the Save As option to save a message to its own file in one of several formats: Outlook Express Mail format (.eml), Text, Unicode Text, or HTML.

- As you are working with a new mail message, you will see a formatting toolbar above the message box if you're using HTML. Use the options on the toolbar to apply fonts and styles to your message as needed. If you use plain text, this toolbar is hidden.

- For contacts in your address book, you only need to type their names in the To, Cc, or Bcc fields. Outlook Express can resolve the names to their e-mail addresses. As each name is resolved, it is underlined; if you want to force an address to be resolved, type at least a few letters of the name, and click the Check Names button on the toolbar.

- If you are sending mail to multiple recipients, simply separate the recipients with a comma when typing them in the To, Cc, or Bcc fields.

Using Mail Folders

The Outlook Express interface provides you with the Folders list in the left pane, a message list in the upper-right pane, and a Preview pane below it so that the text of a message appears when you select it in the message list. By default, Outlook Express stores messages in local folders for your account. The basic folders included are the Inbox, Outbox, Sent Items, Deleted Items, and Drafts folders. Although these basic folders do not need an explanation, there are a few important items to keep in mind about each of them:

- All e-mail received arrives in the Inbox unless you have a rule configured to move the item elsewhere. See "Creating Message Rules," page 209, for more information about sorting your mail using rules.

- All e-mail that you send goes to the Outbox. The mail resides in the Outbox until you are connected; it is then automatically sent by default. Once it is sent, it is removed from the Outbox and is moved to the Sent Items folder. If you don't want your mail sent automatically, open the Options dialog box, and on the Send tab, clear the Send Messages Automatically option. The mail will remain in your Outbox until you click the Send/Recv button.

- All e-mail that you send is stored by default in the Sent Items folder so that you can reference it later if necessary. You can, however, open this folder and delete messages. If you don't want to save copies of your sent mail, open the Options dialog box and, on the Send tab, clear the Save Copy Of Sent Messages In The 'Sent Items' Folder option.

- Deleted messages are stored in the Deleted Items folder. If you want to reclaim a message from the Deleted Items folder, open the folder, and drag the message to a different folder. If you want to permanently delete all messages in the folder each time you close Outlook Express, choose Tools, Options, select the Maintenance tab, and then select Empty Messages From The 'Deleted Items' Folder On Exit. You can also open the Deleted Items folder and individually delete items, or right-click the folder and choose Empty 'Deleted Items' Folder from the shortcut menu. Once you delete an item from the Deleted Items folder, however, it is permanently removed.

---

tip   **Use Caution When Deleting Messages**

Don't delete items from the Sent Items or Deleted Items folder unless absolutely necessary. These folders serve as a great reference and give you a safety net if you need to refer to a sent or deleted message at some point in the future. However, if you receive an abundance of spam messages, you might consider creating a different folder where deleted items are stored so that you can more easily keep spam mail separate from valid e-mail. Or, you can create a rule that sends spam to a folder you create, such as a Spam folder. See "Creating Message Rules," page 209, for more information.

InsideOut

Using the Compact Feature

Over time, mail messages can take up a lot of space on your hard disk, especially if you manage a lot of e-mail. Many users tend to keep everything in the Sent Items folder and Deleted Items folder in case the messages are needed for future reference. However, from time to time, you should consider using the compact messages feature to clean out wasted space in the message folders. To compact a message folder, select the folder in the Folders list, and choose File, Folder, Compact; or to compact all folders, choose the Compact All Folders command. Also, select the settings on the Maintenance tab of the Options dialog box to compact messages in the background based on various criteria or to use the Clean Up Now command.

Aside from the default mail folders, you can also create your own mail folders. If you right-click Local Folders in the Folders list in the left pane, you can click New Folder to create a new folder. You can also create subfolders in your Inbox, Outbox, Sent Items, or Drafts folders. Any e-mail that arrives in your Inbox can then be dragged to the desired folder, or you can create a rule to automatically place it there.

Managing Attachments

An attachment is anything sent along with an e-mail message, such as pictures, business cards, files, programs, and so on. E-mail attachments are very common and are a great way to move information from one place to another.

Overall, attachments are easy to send. When you are typing a mail message, simply click the Attach File To Message button (the paper clip icon) on the toolbar or choose Insert, File Attachment. Better yet, you can drag and drop files onto the e-mail message. Attached items appear in the Attach field when you are creating a new message (the Attach field appears beneath the Subject field once you've attached an item). Your attachments are sent with your e-mail; however, if you change your mind about including an attachment before sending, just right-click the file in the Attach field and click Remove.

tip newfeature! **Adjust the Size of Your Messages for Your Recipients**

Files consume bandwidth and might take some time to transfer, depending on the size of the file and the speed of your connection. So, if you have a fast Internet connection such as DSL, keep in mind that dial-up users might have a difficult time downloading your large attachments. Also, consider using the new Windows XP Compressed Folder feature to create a folder (actually a file using the ZIP file format) to compress items before sending them. Open Help And Support from the Start menu, and search for **Create a zipped compressed folder** for specific instructions.

When you receive an e-mail containing an attachment, you can simply double-click the attachment to open it, or you can drag the attachment to a folder on your local computer for later use. However, e-mail attachments are a major way in which computer viruses are spread, so keep these points in mind:

- Never open any file that you have not scanned with an up-to-date antivirus program. Most antivirus programs feature an e-mail scanning option that can scan your e-mail attachments as you download them. Use the feature if available. Most antivirus programs also check files as you attempt to open them and will not do so if they detect a virus.

- E-mail viruses are spread through executable files, which usually have a .exe file extension. Be wary of any *.exe files you receive. You can select the Security tab of the Options dialog box, and select the option labeled Do Not Allow Attachments To Be Saved Or Opened That Could Potentially Be A Virus. However, this might not work well, especially if some of the executable files you receive are valid and wanted. The point you'll have to remember is to use caution and common sense. If you receive an attachment from someone you do not know, delete it. If you receive an attachment from someone you do know, let your antivirus software work and proceed with caution.

> For more information about dealing with e-mail security issues, see "Coping with E-mail Security Threats," page 591.

Managing Received Messages

You can manage messages that you receive in a few different ways, depending on your needs. When you receive e-mail, it all arrives in your Inbox, usually ordered by arrival date and time. All messages appear in the Inbox whether you have read them or not until you either move them to a different folder or delete them.

However, there are some additional viewing options available to you. If you open the View menu in Outlook Express and point to Current View, you will see the options Show All Messages, Hide Read Messages, and Hide Read Or Ignored Messages. You can modify an existing view by clicking Customize Current View, or you can define your own view by choosing Define Views. When the Define Views dialog box opens, shown in Figure 7-17 on the next page, the currently applied view is selected.

To create a new view, click the New button. In the New View dialog box, select a condition for the view, select an action, and then give the new view a name. For example, in Figure 7-18 on the next page, a view is about to be created that will hide messages when the subject line contains certain words. If you scroll through the list of conditions, you see that there are several conditions that you can apply to customize your view. One view can use several conditions, linked by *and* or *or* logic.

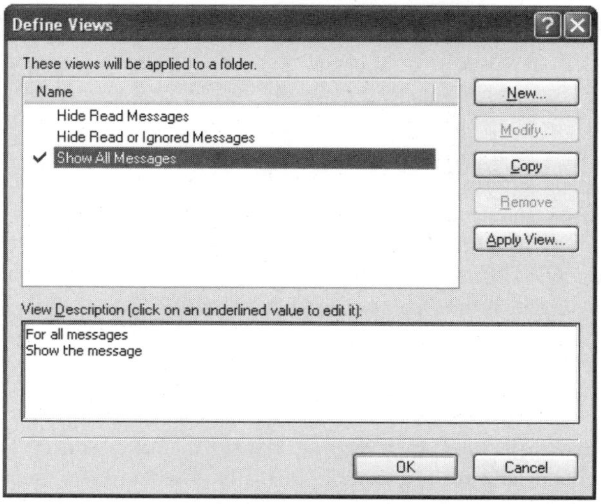

Figure 7-17. Use Define Views to create a new view.

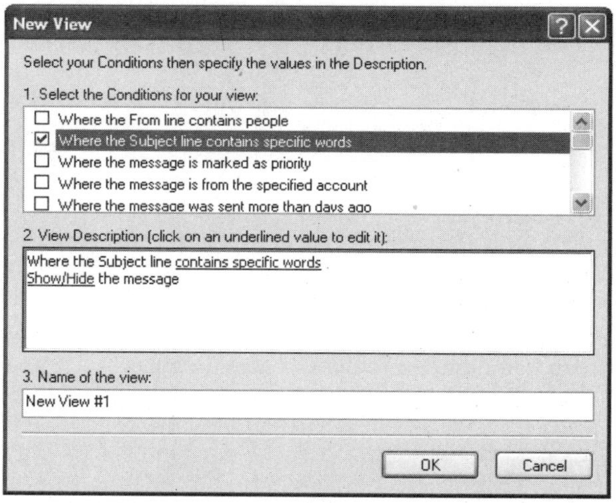

Figure 7-18. Use the New View dialog box to create a custom view.

Aside from creating or adjusting the default view, you can also sort messages using the Sort By option on the View menu. By default, messages are sorted by date in ascending order (the most recent messages appear at the bottom of the list). You can adjust this behavior so that messages are sorted differently, such as by subject, flags, attachments, and so on.

You can also flag, watch, or ignore messages. If you choose View, Columns, you see the Columns dialog box, shown in Figure 7-19, which enables you to choose the columns you want to display in the message list, such as Priority, Flag, Subject, Watch/Ignore, and so on. The list varies slightly by the type of mail account; for example, Hotmail

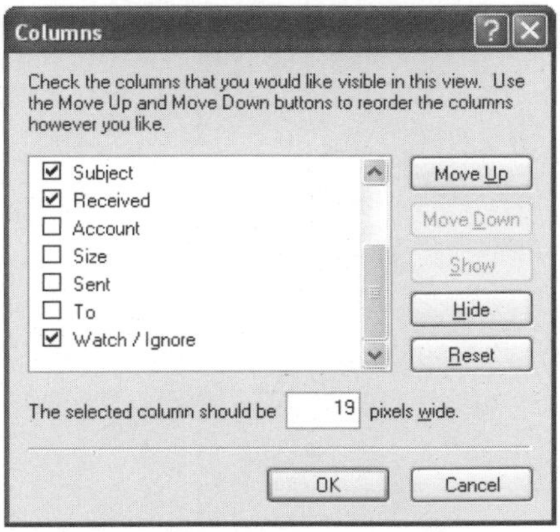

Figure 7-19. Select the columns you want to display.

accounts don't include the Flag or Priority columns. Make sure that any columns you want to view are selected. You can also use the Move Up and Move Down buttons to configure column order.

The Watch/Ignore and Flag message options give you ways to call attention to or ignore certain e-mail items. If you choose to flag a message, a small flag appears next to it so that you can remind yourself that the message is important. If you choose to watch a message, the message is displayed in red and an eyeglasses icon appears in the Watch/ Ignore column, whereas ignored messages are grayed out, and the international symbol for *No* is displayed in the Watch/Ignore column. How you use these features depends entirely on your needs, but their purpose is to help you organize messages so that you can manage and respond to them effectively.

Creating Message Rules

Message rules provide a way to handle e-mail and news messages according to such criteria as sender, subject, or date. You can use rules to have all messages from a certain person sent directly to a certain folder or to have all messages with certain subject key-words sent to a certain folder. Rules can also be used to automatically place mail in your Deleted Items folder, such as in the case of junk mail or mail from people you do not want to talk to. Separate sets of rules can be created for POP e-mail messages and for news messages, but you're most likely to use rules to process your e-mail. The fol-lowing steps take you through the process of creating a basic mail rule:

1 In Outlook Express, choose Tools, Message Rules, Mail.

The first time you choose Message Rules, you will see the New Mail Rule dialog box. After one or more rules have been created, you'll see the Mes-sage Rules dialog box shown in Figure 7-20 on the next page.

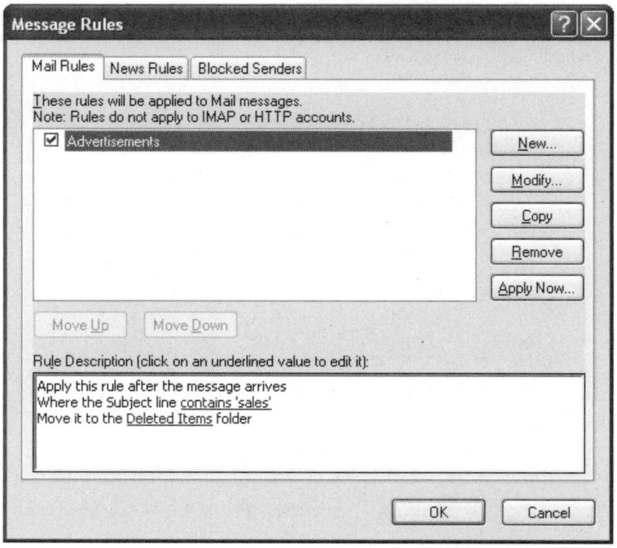

Figure 7-20. Existing rules appear on the Mail Rules or News Rules tab of the Message Rules dialog box.

2 If the New Mail Rule dialog box appears, skip to step 3. If the Message Rules dialog box appears, any existing rules appear on the Mail Rules or News Rules tab. Select the Mail Rules tab and click New.

3 Create a new rule in the New Mail Rule dialog box, as shown in Figure 7-21. Follow the numbered sections of the dialog box to first select a condition that a message must meet to be affected by the rule, then select the action to perform on the matching messages, add necessary details to the action (such as selecting a name, subject words, or a folder), and type a descriptive

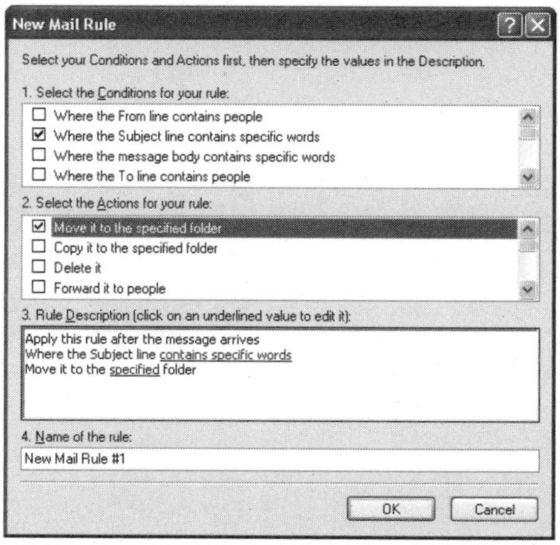

Figure 7-21. Create your rule by selecting its conditions, actions, and description.

210

name for the rule. Figure 7-21 shows that e-mail that contains specific words in the subject line should be moved to a certain folder. To complete the rule, in the Rule Description section, click the Contains Specific Words link, enter the desired words, and then click the Specified link to specify the folder you want the mail moved to. Add a friendly name for the rule, and click OK. As you receive mail that meets these conditions, the mail will automatically be moved to the designated folder. Click OK when you are done and repeat the process to create additional rules.

There are many more conditions and actions you can apply to rules than just moving specified mail to a certain folder. For example, you can:

- Mark certain messages as read, watched, or ignored
- Flag certain messages
- Automatically forward certain messages to certain users
- Reply to certain messages automatically with a standard e-mail that you create ahead of time
- Highlight certain messages and automatically delete other messages

If you scroll through the Actions list, you'll see there are many different actions that you can apply. Become familiar with the conditions and actions available to you so that you can create rules that meet your needs.

In addition to creating rules using the New Mail Rule dialog box, you can create a new rule based on a message that you receive. For example, you might want to automatically delete messages from a certain sender or with a particular subject heading. Rather than manually creating the rule, you can simply select or open the message, and choose Message, Create Rule From Message. The New Mail Rule dialog box appears with the preselected condition to select other messages with the same From line. You can adjust that condition to the Subject line or any other condition, depending on what you want the rule to do.

Remember that rules can be modified, toggled on or off, or deleted at any time. Also, remember that once you have several rules defined, your mail is filtered through the rules from top to bottom, so you'll want to use the Move Up and Move Down buttons to order the rules so they work most effectively. Like e-mail, message rules tend to be an ever changing and evolving process that need your periodic attention to manage mail and news in the manner that you want.

Managing Spam

Spam, or junk e-mail, is a problem that plagues all e-mail users to one degree or another. You can use Outlook Express rules to automatically send junk e-mail to your Deleted Items folder. However, this process is not foolproof. You have to identify the keywords that you want the rule to use to identify a piece of e-mail as junk mail, and you have to be careful that those keywords do not delete mail that you really want. To use Outlook Express mail rules to manage junk mail, follow these guidelines:

1 Create one rule that defines mail that should be trashed, such as pornography keywords and other indicators that you know belong in the Deleted Items folder. You can periodically scan the folder to make sure no good mail has accidentally fallen into the folder, and then delete the items.

2 Use a second rule with less certain keywords, such as *sale, special, limited time*, and so on. Send e-mails matching this condition to a folder called Junk, for example. Every few days, scan this folder to make sure nothing you really need has ended up there, and then delete all items in the folder.

3 The remaining mail should be allowed into your Inbox. But if you receive mail in your Inbox that turns out to be junk, use the Create Rule From Message option just described to help refine what goes in the trash. Of course, these rules do not stop 100% of the junk mail, but they do help tremendously.

In addition to using rules to manage junk mail, you can also use the Blocked Senders list. The Blocked Senders list identifies a particular e-mail address. When an e-mail is received from a person on the Blocked Senders list, the e-mail is sent directly to the Deleted Items folder. To block a sender, select or open the offending e-mail message and choose Message, Block Sender. A message appears telling you that the sender has been added to the Blocked Senders list. If you want to review or adjust the list, choose Tools, Message Rules, Blocked Senders List. You can remove a user from the Blocked Senders list by clicking Remove, or you can temporarily toggle a user's blocking on and off by selecting or clearing the check boxes next to the user's address for Mail, News, or both types of messages. If you know the address of a sender you want to block, you don't have to wait to receive the next message. Just click Add, and manually type the sender's e-mail address to add him or her to the Blocked Senders list.

Importing and Exporting Messages

You can easily import or export messages to and from Outlook Express. This feature enables you to move mail from one computer to another as needed. When you import mail, you can select from about a dozen programs that you want to import from. When you export mail, you export from Outlook Express to Microsoft Outlook or Microsoft Exchange. Perhaps you have been using Netscape Communicator for e-mail, but you now want to use Outlook Express. Using Outlook Express, you can choose File, Import, Messages, and select Netscape Communicator, as shown in Figure 7-22. If prompted, specify the location of the Communicator mail, and then complete the wizard to import the mail.

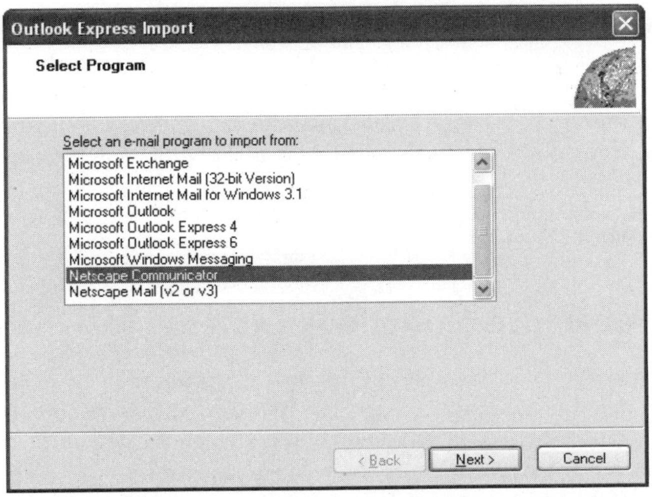

Figure 7-22. You can import messages directly from these e-mail programs.

Finding Messages

Outlook Express provides a quick and easy Find feature so you can find messages or people. If you choose Edit, Find (or click the arrow next to the Find button on the toolbar), you see an option to find a message, a message in a particular folder, or people. If you click the Message option, a Find Message dialog box appears, shown in Figure 7-23. You can search for messages based on text you enter in the To, From, Subject, and Message boxes. If you know the approximate time frame when the message was received, you can also search using the Received Before and Received After

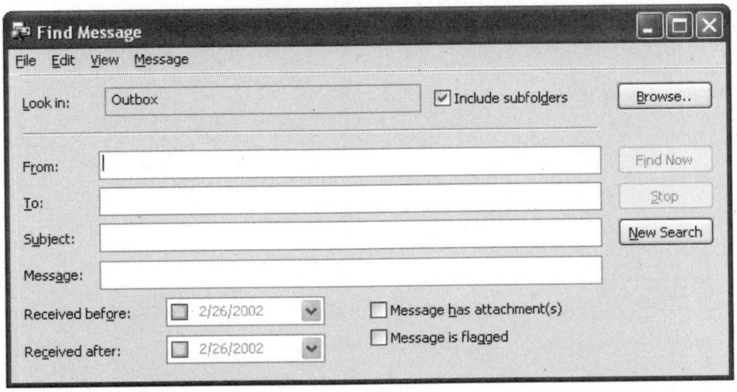

Figure 7-23. Use the Find Message dialog box to search for messages meeting certain conditions you have specified.

options, which will help narrow the search. You can further narrow the search to certain folders (click the Browse button to select folders) and to messages that are flagged and/or have attachments. If you select multiple criteria, only messages matching all the conditions will be found. If you don't receive any matches but believe the message you're looking for is in your folders somewhere, try making the search more general.

> To search for people's e-mail addresses or other information on the Internet (or in your domain's Active Directory), see "Configuring a Directory Service Account," page 188.

Managing the Appearance of Outlook Express

Outlook Express gives you considerable control over its appearance. By default, you will see your folders in the left pane's Folders list, the selected folder's contents in the message list, and a selected message's contents in the Preview pane. This is usually the easiest way to use Outlook Express, but if you want to experiment with different views, choose View, Layout. Figure 7-24 shows how you can select the elements of Outlook Express you want to display. You can experiment with the different settings and see which configuration you prefer.

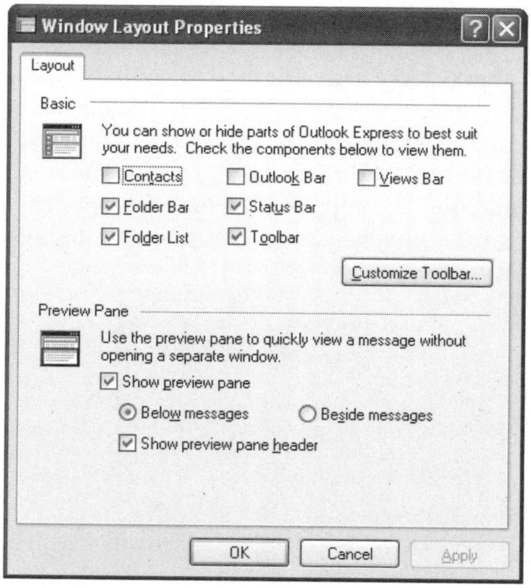

Figure 7-24. Configure the appearance of Outlook Express using the Window Layout Properties dialog box.

Using the Address Book

Windows Address Book is an application designed to work with Outlook Express as well as other Windows applications that use contact data. You can store all kinds of contact information in Address Book, and you can even access it directly by clicking the Address Book button on the Outlook Express toolbar. You can also open Address Book by choosing Start, All Programs, Accessories, Address Book or by typing **wab** from a command prompt.

Windows Address Book gives you a simple interface, shown in Figure 7-25. You can store contact information in the Shared Contacts folder or the Identity folder for your account. To create new contacts or groups (or a new folder to contain new contacts or groups), click the New button, and choose New Contact, New Group, or New Folder.

---

tip   **Organizing Contacts into Groups**

If you have a lot of contacts, consider using the New Folder command so that you can group them in subfolders. This will make browsing the contacts much easier. Also, grouping contacts gives you an easy way to send e-mail to a collection of contacts. However, some ISPs have strict restrictions on the number of users you can send an identical e-mail message to at one time. Check with your ISP for details.

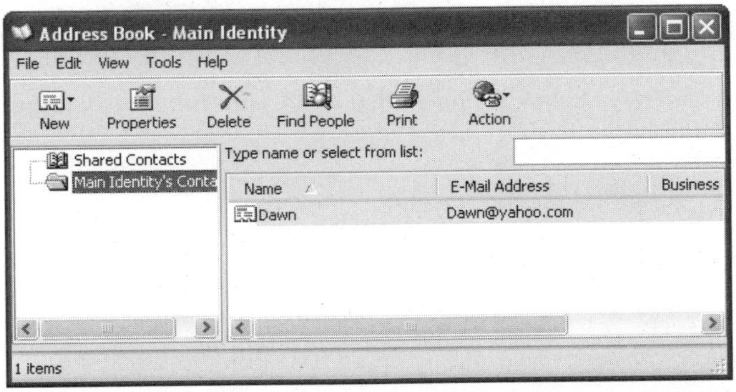

Figure 7-25. Windows Address Book provides a central location to store contact information and organize your contacts.

> **tip** **Add Senders to Your Address Book Easily**
>
> You can easily add a user to your address book directly from an e-mail message that you have received. Just right-click the message in the message list, and click Add Sender To Address Book. You can also open the Options dialog box to the Send tab, and select Automatically Put People I Reply To In My Address Book. This option assumes that if you're responding to an e-mail once, there's a good chance you might want to have that person's e-mail address handy in the future as well.

As you will see, Address Book is easy to use and very intuitive, but it should be noted that the use of identities is not a security feature; rather, it is an organizational feature. Any user can see all of the contacts by typing **wab /a** at a command prompt (include the full path to the wab.exe program or first switch to the directory that contains it, which by default is C:\Program Files\Outlook Express), so if you want to ensure that your contacts are private, you should not use identities. Instead, each user should log on with his or her own user account so that Windows XP can create and maintain a completely separate Address Book file for each user.

As with mail messages, you can also import and export your address book. If you want to import an address book other than the one created by Windows Address Book, choose File, Import, Other Address Book. The Address Book Import Tool will prompt you to select the kind of address book file you want to import, as shown in Figure 7-26. When you export from Windows Address Book by choosing File, Export, Address Book, your address book is saved as a Windows Address Book file with a .wab file extension, which you can then import into other address book programs. If you want to export your address book as a text file (comma separated values) or as a Microsoft Exchange personal address book, choose File, Export, Other Address Book.

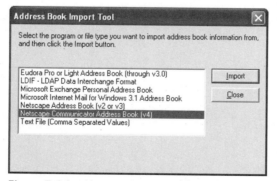

Figure 7-26. You can import address books from several different programs.

Using Keyboard Shortcuts

If you like the efficiency of using keyboard shortcuts, Outlook Express has its fair share. You can see a complete listing of keyboard shortcuts by searching Outlook Express online Help for **keyboard shortcuts.** Table 7-2 lists the more popular shortcuts.

Table 7-2. Popular Outlook Express Keyboard Shortcuts

Keyboard Shortcut	Action
Ctrl+M	Send and receive e-mail
Ctrl+P	Print the selected message
Del	Delete the selected message
Ctrl+N	Create a new message
Ctrl+R	Reply to selected message
Ctrl+Shift+R	Reply to all
Ctrl+F	Forward the selected message
Ctrl+I	Go to Inbox
Ctrl+Enter	Mark a message as read
Esc	Close a message
F3	Find text
Ctrl+Shift+F	Find message
F7	Check spelling

Using Windows Messenger

Instant messaging has become very popular during the past year or so; advertisements for products as distinct as Internet service providers (ISPs) and cellular phones bombard us with hyperbole about instant text messaging. The concept of instant messaging is certainly nothing new in Microsoft Windows XP either. Windows XP includes Windows Messenger, formerly MSN Messenger, as the default instant messaging tool. However, Windows Messenger does much more than simple text messaging. It also offers live video and live audio over the Internet; additionally, you can use Windows Messenger to collaborate on a drawing or illustration with a friend, or even have private chat conversations.

Windows Messenger is a multimedia tool designed to give you instant communications flexibility. E-mail can take too long, voice conversations are not visual (and often intrusive), and face-to-face meetings can often consume too much time. With Windows Messenger, you can have multimedia-based, real-time communications with friends, family, and colleagues using the Internet or a local intranet. It is, of course, not the answer to all of life's communication problems, but Windows Messenger does provide you with an alternative communication method that might be able to meet your specific needs.

Setting Up and Connecting with Windows Messenger

Windows Messenger is readily available on your Windows XP computer by clicking Start, All Programs. To begin using Windows Messenger, all you need is an Internet connection (see Chapter 4, "Configuring Internet Connections") and a Microsoft .NET Passport. If you want to use video or voice with your Windows Messenger calls, you'll also need a sound card, a microphone, and a Web camera.

> **tip** Your computer is probably already equipped with a sound card—see your computer's documentation for details. You can purchase a microphone and a universal serial bus (USB) Web cam inexpensively at your favorite computer store.

To set up Windows Messenger, click Start, All Programs, Windows Messenger, or you can double-click the Windows Messenger icon if one appears on your desktop in the lower right notification area. If you have not previously configured a .NET Passport, a wizard appears to help you.

Creating a .NET Passport

When you use a .NET Passport, Microsoft uses your e-mail address and a password to identify you, and notifies any services relying on Passport of your secure identity. Once you are logged on, you can take full advantage of all that Windows Messenger has to offer, and you can seamlessly log on to Web sites that use Microsoft .NET Passport. If you want to use online publishing in addition to some other features in Windows XP, you'll need a .NET Passport for those services as well. Signing up for the .NET Passport is easy and private—just follow these steps:

1 Connect to the Internet.

2 Click Start, All Programs, Windows Messenger.

3 The .NET Passport Wizard appears. If the wizard does not appear automatically, select the Click Here To Sign In link in the Windows Messenger window to start the wizard.

4 Click Next on the .NET Passport opening page.

5 The wizard connects to a .NET Passport server, and the next wizard page asks if you have an e-mail address. If you do, select Yes. If you don't, choose No, I Would Like To Open A Free MSN.com E-mail Account Now. With previous versions of Windows Messenger, you had to have an MSN or Hotmail e-mail address to obtain a passport. Now, however, any e-mail address can be linked to your passport account. Click Next.

6 On the What Is Your E-mail Address page, enter your e-mail address and click Next.

7 If you are using a Hotmail or MSN account, you'll need to provide your existing password on the next page. If not, you'll be prompted to create a

.NET Passport password to use with the account and retype it to confirm you typed it correctly the first time. Also, notice that you can select Save My .NET Passport Information In My Windows XP User Account, which is selected by default, as shown in Figure 8-1. Enter the password information and click Next.

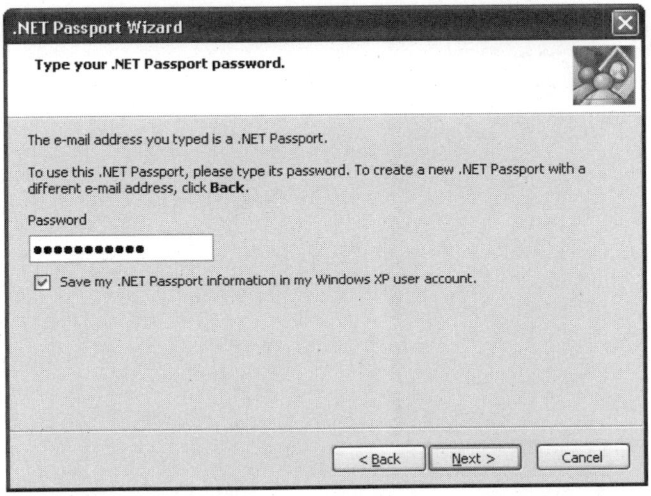

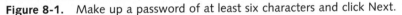

.NET Passport Wizard

Type your .NET Passport password.

The e-mail address you typed is a .NET Passport.

To use this .NET Passport, please type its password. To create a new .NET Passport with a different e-mail address, click **Back**.

Password

●●●●●●●●●●●

☑ Save my .NET Passport information in my Windows XP user account.

< Back   Next >   Cancel

Figure 8-1. Make up a password of at least six characters and click Next.

8 If you created a new password in step 7, you'll see the Choose And Answer A Secret Question page. In the Secret Question list, choose a question, and then answer the question in the Answer box. This question will be asked of you if you forget your password in the future. By answering this question, you can select a new password for your account. Click Next.

9 On the Where Do You Live page, which is also shown if you're creating a new password, you must complete the Country/Region field, the State field if you're in the United States, and then the ZIP Code field. You'll also have to provide this information in the future if you forget your password and want to choose a new one for your account. Click Next.

10 On the next page, you can read the Microsoft Passport Terms of Use. You must accept the terms to complete your Passport registration. Click Next.

11 The Share Your Information With Participating Sites page appears. You don't have to select either of the sharing options on this page; however, if you want other Web sites that use your .NET Passport to receive information such as your e-mail address and geographical information, select the appropriate check boxes. The idea is to save you from having to type in your e-mail address on those sites, as well as allow some sites to provide you with custom content tailored to your location. Click Next.

12 Click Finish. Windows Messenger automatically uses the .NET Passport you have created to sign on to Windows Messenger, as shown in Figure 8-2.

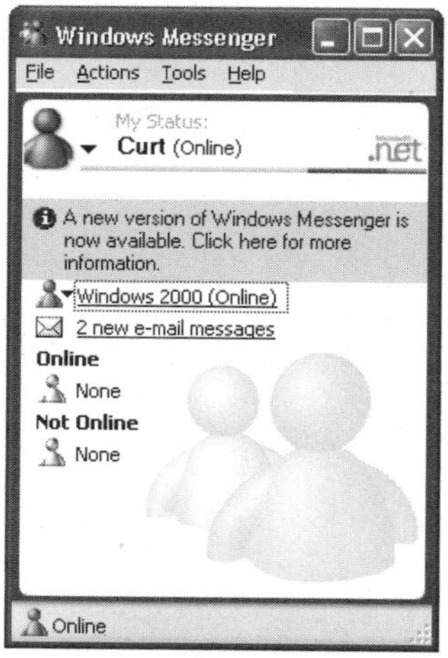

Figure 8-2. The user *Windows 2000* is online, and there's also a new version of Windows Messenger that the user can download by clicking the banner.

Connecting Through a Firewall

If you are using a firewall (or if your company uses one), that firewall might require some configuration to allow Windows Messenger to work. If you are using Internet Connection Firewall (ICF) on an Internet Connection Sharing (ICS) network with no additional router or residential gateway, there is nothing else you need to do. ICF is configured to work with Windows Messenger automatically. However, if you are using a router or residential gateway device that uses network address translation (NAT), that device must also support Universal Plug and Play (UPnP). *UPnP* is a standard supported in Windows XP that allows computers to automatically detect network devices and flexibly work with them. By using UPnP, Windows Messenger is capable of working through a NAT-enabled router or residential gateway that supports UPnP. See your router or residential gateway's documentation for details about UPnP. You can also learn more about UPnP at the UPnP Forum at *www.upnp.org*. If your firewall doesn't support the relatively new UPnP standard, you'll have to check its documentation to see if you can manually configure it to allow Windows Messenger traffic through the firewall. See the next section.

> **tip** **Upgrading Routers and Residential Gateways to Support UPnP**
>
> Many devices that do not offer UPnP support out of the box are able to provide support for it via upgrades to their onboard firmware. Check the manufacturer's Web site for their latest firmware upgrades.

Firewall Configuration

Although ICF is configured to work with Windows Messenger, there is an exception—file transfer. To use the Windows Messenger file transfer feature, you'll need to create a service entry to allow the transfer, as described in "Enabling Services" on page 130. If you are on a network that uses another firewall or in a domain environment where a firewall is used, the firewall administrator might need to statically configure TCP ports so that Windows Messenger can communicate. TCP ports are described in the following list:

- Windows Messenger uses TCP port 1863 when it is available. If port 1863 is not available, Windows Messenger uses the same port that the Web browser uses, which is typically port 80. A firewall administrator should open TCP port 1863 for best results.

- Windows Messenger uses TCP ports 6891 through 6900 for file transfers, allowing up to 10 simultaneous transfers at a time (one on each port). ICF requires a service entry to allow file transfer.

- Windows Messenger uses TCP port 1503 for application sharing and whiteboard communications (see "Whiteboard and Application Sharing," page 240).

- Windows Messenger uses dynamically assigned ports through UPnP for voice and video.

Configuring Proxy Server Settings in Windows Messenger

Windows Messenger automatically detects and uses your connection to the Internet. However, in some cases where a proxy server is used, Windows Messenger might have problems identifying the proxy server. In this case, help Windows Messenger identify the server, by following these steps:

1 Open Windows Messenger, and click Tools, Options.

2 In the Options dialog box, select the Connection tab.

3 On the Connection tab, shown in Figure 8-3 on the next page, select the I Use A Proxy Server check box, and choose the type of server in the Type box. Enter the server's IP address or name in the Server box, and any user name and password information required for the connection in the User ID and Password boxes.

223

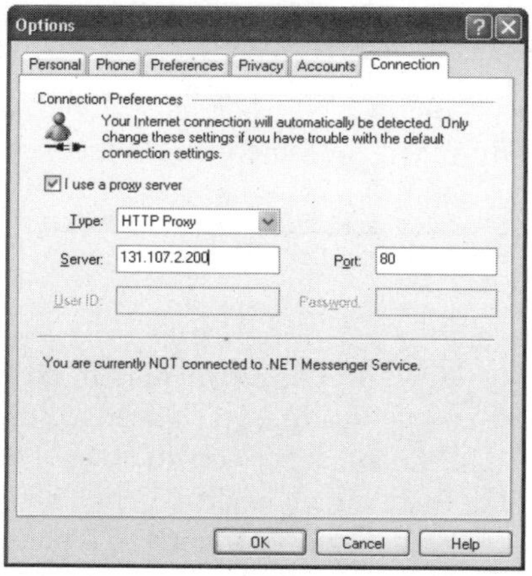

Figure 8-3. Use the Connection tab to enable Windows Messenger when you use a proxy server for your Internet connection.

Windows Messenger and Virtual Private Network (VPN) Connections

You might experience problems when using Windows Messenger and a VPN connection at the same time (see "Creating a Connection to a VPN Server," page 515, to learn more). If you are using Windows Messenger and open a VPN connection at the same time, the Windows Messenger connection might disconnect with no warnings or disconnect messages. This problem occurs because the VPN connection, while it is active, tries to use the default gateway on the remote network. This essentially stops your Windows Messenger connection from working. However, you can change the VPN connection so that the remote gateway is not used for Internet connections, which will allow you to use both a VPN connection and a Windows Messenger connection at the same time. To do that, follow these steps:

1 Open Network Connections.

2 Right-click the VPN connection and click Properties.

3 In the properties dialog box, click the Networking tab.

4 Select Internet Protocol (TCP/IP) in the list of connections, and click the Properties button.

5 In the Internet Protocol (TCP/IP) Properties dialog box, click the Advanced button.

6 On the General tab of the Advanced TCP/IP Settings dialog box, clear the Use Default Gateway On Remote Network check box, and click OK to close each dialog box.

224

Using Windows Messenger

Once Windows Messenger is set up to work with a .NET Passport account and your Internet connection, you are ready to begin using and exploring its features. The following sections explore the various aspects of using Windows Messenger and putting it to work for you.

> **note** Windows Messenger is constantly being upgraded. At the time of this writing, version 4.6 was the latest version. Depending on when you purchased Windows XP, you might have a newer or older version of Windows Messenger. Check Windows Update, or *http://messenger.microsoft.com*, to find newer versions of Windows Messenger, including any important security updates that might become available.

Managing Sign-in

Whenever you log on to Windows XP, Windows Messenger attempts to automatically sign in. Windows Messenger will not launch an Internet connection, however, so if you are not connected when Windows Messenger attempts to log on, the logon will fail. You will also see the Windows Messenger icon with an **X** over it in the notification area.

If you do not want Windows Messenger to attempt to log you on whenever you log on to Windows XP, follow these steps:

1 In Windows Messenger, choose Tools, Options.

2 On the Preferences tab of the Options dialog box, clear the Run This Program When Windows Starts option, as shown in Figure 8-4, and click OK.

Figure 8-4. The Options dialog box lets you stop Windows Messenger from automatically logging you on.

InsideOut

Your User Account and .NET Passport

When you first created your .NET Passport account, you had the option of storing the password and account information with your user account. So what happens if you change your .NET Passport at some point in the future or decide to no longer use it?

In this case, you can simply open User Accounts in Control Panel, access your account, and change the .NET Passport or remove it altogether.

tip   **Logging on to Windows Messenger**

If you are not currently signed in using Windows Messenger, you can right-click the icon in the notification area and click Sign In. However, you will have to enter your password. This option is also handy if you want to sign in under a different account than the default account for the computer, should you have more than one account or be logging on using another person's computer. To log on more quickly, either right-click the icon in the notification area and click Sign In As ... (the entry will list your sign-on e-mail address), or double-click the icon and select Click Here To Sign In in the Windows Messenger window that appears. Both options require you to have saved your password in Windows Messenger; otherwise, you'll have to try again and supply the password for the account.

Creating Contacts

Windows Messenger enables you to control who you communicate with over the Internet or intranet via its contacts feature. When you add contacts to Windows Messenger, they are stored on .NET Passport servers so that you can be contacted directly when you are online.

Contacts appear in the Windows Messenger window, as shown in Figure 8-5. Any contacts that you have added appear under Online if they are online, and any contacts that are not currently online appear under Not Online.

You can add a contact quickly and easily by following these steps:

1 Choose Tools, Add A Contact.

2 In the Add A Contact Wizard that appears, you are asked how you want to add a contact. You can choose By E-mail Address Or Sign-in Name, or you can choose Search For a Contact. The search option checks your address book or the online Hotmail directory, and frankly, is not a very useful feature. Typically, if you are adding a contact, you already know the contact's e-mail address. Click Next.

226

Figure 8-5. Online and Not Online contacts appear in Windows Messenger.

3 If you choose to enter the e-mail address, enter the address on the next wizard page, as shown in Figure 8-6. The e-mail address you are using must be an MSN, Hotmail, or Passport e-mail address. If you enter any other e-mail address (or even an MSN or Hotmail account that is not configured for .NET Passport), you can choose to e-mail that person, telling them about Windows Messenger so that they can download and use it. Of course, until the person does so and configures a .NET Passport, you can't communicate with them using Windows Messenger. Click Next.

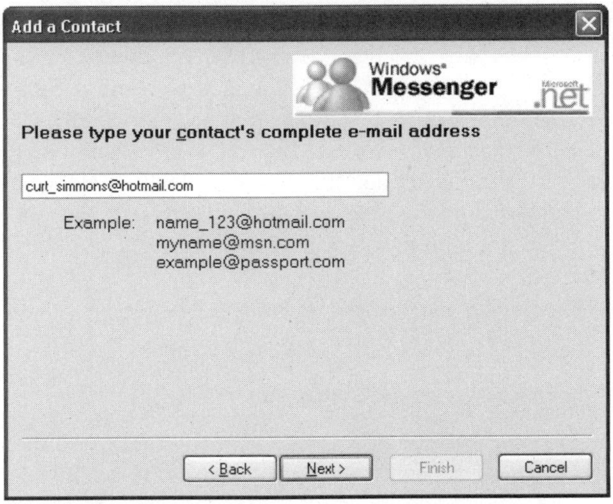

Figure 8-6. Enter the e-mail address of the contact.

Chapter 8

4 This page tells you that the name was added to your list. It also lets you click the Send E-mail button and send an e-mail to the contact that explains how he or she can add Windows Messenger if the contact is not already using it. You can even send the message in one of over two dozen languages and add a custom message at the top of the e-mail. If you know your contact already uses Windows Messenger, you can skip this step and click Finish.

---

tip **Contacting People Using a Different Instant Messaging Program**

At some point in the future, you should be able to communicate with other Internet users who use different instant messaging software. Current and emerging instant messaging standards, such as the Session Initiation Protocol (SIP) and SIP for Instant Messaging and Presence Leveraging Extensions (SIMPLE) might make the future of instant messaging applications much more flexible between different vendors.

Once you choose to add contacts to your list, the contacts are sent a message, alerting them to the fact that you have added them. At this point, the contacts can choose Allow This Person To See When You Are Online And Contact You to allow you to see them when they are online, or they can choose Block This Person From Seeing When You Are Online And Contacting You so that you won't know whether they're online and won't be able to contact them. So, contacts function as a two-way street. You can add contacts all day, but they have to allow you to see them and communicate with them while you are online.

At any time, you can also remove contacts by simply right-clicking them in the Windows Messenger window and clicking Delete Contact. If you use Outlook Express as your e-mail client, you can also directly create contacts for Windows Messenger from Outlook Express. In Outlook Express, just display the Contacts pane, right-click an existing contact, and click Set As Online Contact. You can also click New Online Contact and create a Windows Messenger contact from Outlook Express. Windows will then see if the contact has a .NET Passport. If the contact does not have a .NET Passport, you'll be told that and be invited to send an e-mail to the person inviting him to sign up for a Passport account so you can instant message with him.

InsideOut

Understanding Windows Messenger Status Messages

Note that some of your online contacts have additional status messages attached to their icon, such as busy, on the phone, be right back, and so on. These status messages allow you to be online for outgoing messaging, but to appear unavailable to others who have you listed in their Windows Messenger program. If you are online and want to use a status message, choose File, My Status, and click the status you want others to see: Online, Busy, Be Right Back, Away, On The Phone, Out To Lunch, or Appear Offline. Others see your name listed under Online with the status message appended to your name except for the Appear Offline status, which actually moves your name into the Offline list, even though you are still online. This is the same way you appear to others when you turn off your machine or sign out from Windows Messenger. As a rule of courtesy, make sure you use the My Status option when you are not available to answer instant messages, or take yourself offline so that friends, family, and colleagues are not waiting for you to respond.

Using Instant Messaging

Instant messaging is probably one of the most popular and used features of Windows Messenger. With instant messaging, you can instantly communicate with someone using a chat-like format without having to actually enter a public chat room and deal with all of the nuisances you might find there, such as congestion and lack of privacy. With instant messaging, you simply identify the contact, type the message, and send it. The contact's computer then signals that a message is incoming; the contact opens it, and then responds directly to you. It is much faster than e-mail and allows you to *talk* in real time.

To create an instant message, follow these steps:

1 In Windows Messenger, right-click the contact's name in the Windows Messenger window, and click Send An Instant Message. (If the person appears in your Offline list, you can still right-click the name and select Send E-mail to perhaps send a message that asks the person to send you an instant message when he or she is back online.)

2 In the Conversation window, shown in Figure 8-7 on the next page, enter the text of the message in the bottom text box, and click Send to send it (or just press Enter). Notice that you can also change the font of the message. Your message now appears in the upper text pane.

The message is sent to the contact. If the contact begins responding to your message, you'll see a notification in the Conversation window status bar telling you that the contact is typing a message. When the contact sends it by clicking Send or pressing Enter, the message appears in the upper pane directly beneath your message. This feature allows you to see the conversation thread and scroll it back and forth to review it as needed.

Figure 8-7. Enter the text of the instant message, and click Send to send it.

Adjusting Preferences

There are a few important preferences that you should take a look at concerning instant messaging. In Windows Messenger, click Tools, Options. On the Personal tab, shown in Figure 8-8, you can choose the screen name that you want people to see. Simply change it as desired. You can also change the font of the instant message, and you can choose to use *emoticons*, which are icons used to represent emotions. Emoticons are enabled by default, but you can choose not to use them by clearing this check box. See the next section to learn more.

Figure 8-8. The Personal tab holds your screen name and related instant messaging settings.

If you click the Phone tab, you can enter any phone numbers that you want your contacts to be able to see. Of course, you should not enter any information on this tab unless you explicitly want to share phone numbers with all of your contacts. Also, make sure you never give out passwords, credit card numbers, or any other personal information over instant messaging because the link, although private, does not encrypt data and is not considered secure.

Using Emoticons

Emoticons are icons you can include in instant messaging sessions that provide some sort of emotional denotation. Some people consider them silly, but they can be a way to express inferences and feelings quickly and easily. You can use them if you prefer, but they are certainly not required.

There are over three dozen emoticons that you can use; they range from smiley faces to smooching lips and are all available using simple keyboard shortcuts or a pop-up menu. You can learn about the available emoticons and the keyboard shortcuts for them by clicking Help, Help Topics and typing **emoticons** in the search box (next to the Go button). You'll need an Internet connection to see all of them. Table 8-1 lists the keyboard shortcuts you use to create the different emoticons.

Table 8-1. Emoticons and Their Keyboard Shortcuts

Emoticon	Keyboard Shortcut	Emoticon	Keyboard Shortcut
	(Y) or (y)		;-) or ;)
	(N) or (n)		:-(or :(
	(B) or (b)		:-S or :s
	(D) or (d)		:-l or :l
	(X) or (x)		:'(
	(Z) or (z)		:-$ or :$
	:-[or :[		(H) or (h)
	(})		:-@ or :@

(continued)

Table 8-1. *(continued)*

Emoticon	Keyboard Shortcut	Emoticon	Keyboard Shortcut
	({)		(A) or (a)
	:-) or :)		(6)
	:-D or :d		(L) or (l)
	:-O or :o		(U) or (u)
	:-P or :p		(K) or (k)
	(G) or (g)		(I) or (i)
	(F) or (f)		(S)
	(W) or (w)		(*)
	(P) or (p)		(8)
	(~)		(E) or (e)
	(T) or (t)		(^)
	(@)		(O) or (o)
	(&)		(M) or (m)
	(C) or (c)		

Inviting Other People into a Conversation

Let's say you're visiting with a colleague to discuss a project using Windows Messenger. During the conversation, you realize that an additional colleague needs to join in to offer some input. Can you have a three person instant messaging session?

Yes, you can, and you can include more people in the conversation as well. When you want to add another contact to the conversation, choose Actions, Invite Someone To This Conversation. You will then be able to invite other contacts into the conversation. When a contact accepts the invitation, he or she will see the entire conversation thread, just as though he or she had been involved in the conversation from the beginning.

Saving a Conversation

Let's say you are using Windows Messenger to conduct a business meeting between four coworkers located in different offices around the country. Once the conversation is finished, you want a hard copy of the conversation for your records. This isn't a problem. When the conversation has concluded, just click File, Save or File, Save As in the Conversation window. You can save the transcript to a text file. Text files, of course, can be a little aggravating to work with, and they might not print in an organized way, so you should consider copying and pasting the text into Word or WordPad, and then formatting it.

> **note** Emoticons are not saved as a part of the transcript.

> **tip** **Working with Alerts**
>
> Windows Messenger can produce an alert sound when one of your contacts comes online, when you receive an instant message, or when you receive mail in your Hotmail Inbox. These options are configured by default, but you can change the defaults by accessing Tools, Options. Select the Preferences tab, and in the Alerts section, choose any combination of the three display options to show a visual display when a contact in your list comes online, when you're sent an instant message, or when e-mail is received. Then select Play Sound When Contacts Sign In Or Send A Message to produce an audible alert when a contact comes online or sends you a message. Note that you can also change the sound of the alert by clicking the Sounds button and selecting a new sound for the alert.

Using File Transfer

Windows Messenger provides a handy way to send files to and receive files from your contacts. Like e-mail, you can transfer any file to a contact simply and easily, which makes work between colleagues faster and more efficient. Using Windows Messenger file transfer, you can:

● Transfer the file immediately to the contact. No mail server resides between you and your contact, so there's no time delay waiting for your mail to be delivered.

- Transfer files without file type restrictions. Due to the threat of viruses, some e-mail programs will not let you send certain kinds of files. Windows Messenger places no file restrictions on you. Of course, you should be careful of the files you accept from others.

- Ignore the file size limitations that some mail servers place on users.

The recipient will receive a message telling him how long the message is and about how long it will take to transfer the file over a 28.8 Kbps modem. If you choose to accept the file, you will see a dialog box warning you that Windows Messenger does not inspect files for viruses and advising you to check the file with an antivirus program before opening it. So, it is up to you to scan files with an antivirus program before opening them. Even though you know your contact, your computer could still get infected with a virus from a file, so beware.

> For more information on securing your computer from viruses and worms, see "Protecting Windows XP from Viruses," page 590.

note You cannot send a file if your conversation has more than one other person. If you need to send a file to a group of people, you can use e-mail, or you can start a conversation with each contact individually.

Aside from the possible virus threat, instant messaging file transfer lets you and a friend or colleague work collaboratively on a document or share documents back and forth through one window. You can be involved in a conversation and send the file from the same Conversation window. There is no need to use a different window or program, and that makes life a lot easier.

Keep in mind that Windows Messenger allows up to 10 concurrent file connections at any given time, and if you are using a firewall (even ICF), you must configure the firewall to allow the ICF file transfer traffic. See "Firewall Configuration," page 223, for configuration details.

When you want to transfer a file, simply choose the Send A File Or Photo link in the right pane of the Conversation window. A browse window appears so you can select the file that you want to send. The Conversation window in Figure 8-9 shows you the progress of the file transfer and whether the contact has accepted the file.

By default, all files are transferred to %UserProfile%\My Documents\My Received Files. The environment variable *%UserProfile%* has a default value of C:\Documents and Settings*Username*, where *Username* is your user Windows XP account name. You can open the file using the link provided in the Conversation window or by browsing the folder.

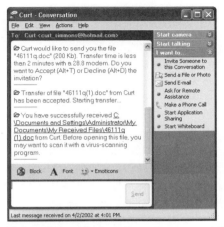

Figure 8-9. File transfers are easy and their status is reported to you in the Conversation window.

---

tip You can change the default location where received files are stored by clicking Tools, Options in the Windows Messenger window. Click the Preferences tab, and in the File Transfer section, change the path where files will be saved.

Making Voice Calls

It has been rumored over the past few years that Internet telephony would one day become so commonplace that the typical phone would become obsolete. After all, why not use your computer to make free calls over the Internet? Although that sounds like a great idea, voice calls made over the Internet have been of such poor quality in the past that they were simply too aggravating to use. Internet telephony still needs some time to develop into a robust technology.

Still, Windows Messenger includes a voice feature that allows you to use the Internet to have a voice conversation with another person. Your computer (and your contact's computer) needs a sound card, speakers or headphones, and a microphone for this feature to work. Windows Messenger actually works quite well with voice calls, and, depending on networking conditions, these voice calls can sometimes be a viable alternative to a standard telephone call.

---

tip **Improving Voice Chat Quality**

Whenever you chat over the Internet, you'll have better results if you use a headset with a built-in microphone rather than a separate mic and set of speakers. The improvement provided by a headset will be even more dramatic when compared to using the built-in microphone and speakers on a laptop computer.

235

One of the major gripes in the past has been delay—for example, you say something and then have to wait for the transmission to move your voice to the contact's speakers. Delay has been reduced to as low as 70 milliseconds (assuming ideal latency conditions), which is hardly noticeable. Windows Messenger can use different *codecs*, software that encodes and decodes audio or video messages, so that the voice quality can be adjusted as needed due to the networking conditions. Windows Messenger also uses an echo cancellation feature that helps eliminate echo often caused by typical microphone and speaker use.

Of course, not all voice calls are perfect using Windows Messenger, but when networking conditions are good, you can get surprisingly fast transmission results, even when using a modem. Before attempting to use voice calls, keep in mind that any firewall or router in the pathway must support UPnP for voice calls to work. See "Connecting Through a Firewall," page 222, for more details.

Making Voice Calls to Contacts

Before using voice calls, it is a good idea to run the Audio And Video Tuning Wizard provided with Windows Messenger. This wizard helps adjust the speakers and microphone as well as the Web camera if one is in use. The following steps guide you through this wizard:

1. In Windows Messenger, click Tools, Audio Tuning Wizard.

2. Click Next on the Welcome screen.

3. Use the Camera box to select the camera that you want to use (if you want to use one). Click Next.

4. You see a sample from the camera. Adjust the camera and the lighting conditions as necessary and click Next.

5. Position your speakers and microphone. Keep in mind that your microphone should be kept away from the speakers in order to avoid echo. Click Next.

6. Select the microphone and speakers that you want to use, as shown in Figure 8-10. If you are using headphones, make sure you select I Am Using Headphones. Click Next.

7. Adjust the speaker volume using the Test button. Click Next when you are done.

8. Speak out loud, reading the provided paragraph if you want to set the sensitivity of your microphone. Click Next when you are done.

9. Click Finish.

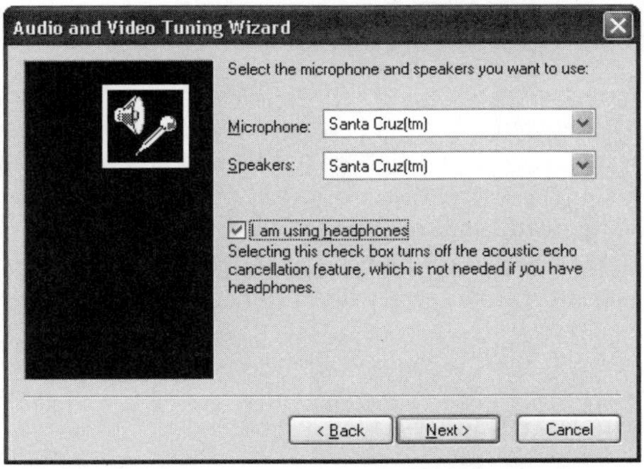

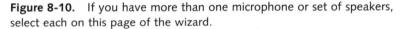

Figure 8-10. If you have more than one microphone or set of speakers, select each on this page of the wizard.

Once you have tuned your microphone and speakers, you are ready to make a voice call to a contact. In the Windows Messenger window, right-click the person you want to have a voice conversation with, and choose Start A Voice Conversation from the short-cut menu that appears. A Conversation window appears and a request for a voice conversation is sent to the contact. If the contact accepts, you can begin the voice conversation, as shown in Figure 8-11.

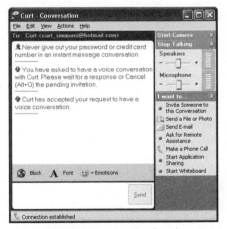

Figure 8-11. You use the familiar Conversation window to manage voice conversations.

tip When you are ready to stop talking, just click the Stop Talking link in the right pane of the Conversation window, or simply close the Conversation window to disconnect all communication.

Making Voice Calls to Phone Numbers

At the time of this writing, the latest version of Windows Messenger supports making phone calls to a regular telephone number. For example, you can use Windows Messenger to call your mother across the country, using the Internet instead of a long distance telephone service. Again, you won't have the same quality that you find with a standard phone call, but it is certainly worth experimenting with. Another big advantage is that the party you're calling doesn't need a computer or computer expertise to configure Windows Messenger—you can reach anyone who has a telephone.

To use Windows Messenger for calling telephone numbers, make sure you have the latest version. Visit *http://messenger.microsoft.com* to download and install the latest version that supports the phone call feature.

Once you have the latest version installed, choose Actions, Make A Phone Call, or click Make A Phone Call in the bottom pane of Windows Messenger. Windows Messenger opens the Phone dialog box. Check your computer to see whether you are currently subscribed to a *voice service provider*. If not, you'll see the phrase Sign Up For Voice Service Today and a Get Started Here button. Click the button to open the Select A Voice Service Provider window and compare the available calling plans. You must sign up with a voice provider to use the computer-to-telephone feature of Windows Messenger. Although there is no charge to initiate these calls from your computer beyond your standard ISP account cost, eventually your calls must be routed into the telephone system at the destination, and you must pay for this segment of the communications link. Voice service providers include Net2Phone (*www.net2phone.com*), IConnectHere (*www.iconnecthere.com*), and Callserve (*www.callserve.com*), among others. You can pay as you go or join a calling plan with a monthly rate. For example, current long distance rates within the United States can be as low as 2 cents per minute, whereas international rates vary considerably depending on the originating and destination country. Callserve offers a flat international rate of about 15 cents per minute regardless of the country of origin. These plans will certainly change rapidly as the technology evolves. If you want to try a service without making a commitment, try buying a block of minutes to see if the service works for you. Typically, you'll need to spend $10 to $25 to try out a service, and you might expect several hundred minutes of domestic calling for that price—proportionately less time for international calling.

Once you sign up with a provider, you can use the simple phone dialer interface provided in Windows Messenger, as shown in Figure 8-12, to dial the numbers that you want to call, just as you would a regular phone. Adjust the Speakers and Microphone sliders for best results. Telephone handsets or headphones with a boom microphone, both of which isolate the incoming sound from the outgoing sound, usually provide better results than using computer speakers.

238

Figure 8-12. Once you sign up with a voice provider, you can place standard telephone calls using Windows Messenger.

newfeature!
Using Video

Like voice calls, Windows Messenger also supports a Web cam feature where you can use a Web camera to communicate over the Internet with Windows Messenger. The video feature works just like the audio feature. You first need to make sure your Web camera is positioned properly and that there is ample lighting. As with voice calls, any firewalls or routers in use must support UPnP; see "Connecting Through a Firewall," page 222, for details.

The good news about video is that you'll get decent results with it. Sure, you'll still see some jerky movements and get some interference, but overall, the picture usually looks good, even over slow connections. Also, you can send video to another Windows Messenger contact, even if the contact is not using a camera. In other words, your video transmission and reception on the contact's end is not dependant on his or her use of a camera.

The bad news is that video transfer is limited to Windows XP computers. Even if other operating systems such as Windows Me and Windows 2000 have the latest version of MSN Messenger installed, you cannot initiate a video session unless the contact is using Windows XP. When you try to do so, the contact receives a message to "upgrade to Windows XP" to use the feature. So, any contacts not using Windows XP need not apply. You can't send or receive video from them.

Once your camera is set up and working, just open a Conversation window with the contact that you want to communicate with, and click the Start Camera option. Your contact must accept your invitation to receive camera transmission. Once the invitation is accepted, the contact begins seeing your video in the Conversation window, as shown in Figure 8-13 on the next page.

When you are sending video, you can click the Options button under the video window and choose Show My Video As Picture-in-Picture to see what your outgoing video

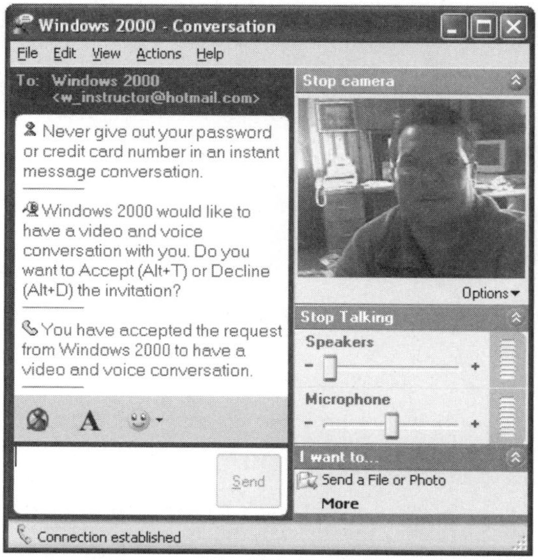

Figure 8-13. The video session appears in the Conversation window.

looks like. You can also choose to slide the microphone to the minimum position so that you are not sending voice.

When you get ready to end the conversation, click Stop Camera or Stop Talking to end the connection. You can also close the Conversation window to end the connection.

newfeature!

Whiteboard and Application Sharing

Windows Messenger now supports features that enable you to hold online meetings and share applications. These features, Whiteboard and Application Sharing, have been added to Windows Messenger from the Microsoft NetMeeting program to give you additional flexibility when communicating over the Internet. For example, suppose you are using Windows Messenger to hold a meeting, and during that meeting, you want to draw an illustration for the attendees. Whiteboard provides you with a way to draw pictures and write text that appear in the Conversation window on the receiving computer.

In the same manner, you can also share programs running on your computer. This feature enables you to collaborate on a document or file with someone else, accessing the application on one computer from both computers. The following two sections explore Whiteboard and Application Sharing.

Using Whiteboard

Whiteboard looks and behaves a lot like Microsoft Paint in Windows XP. You can create text and graphics with Whiteboard that automatically appear on the corresponding Whiteboards on the contacts' PCs. Whiteboard can be used for online meetings and training, and can be used in conjunction with voice and video. Like video, however, Whiteboard is only available in Windows Messenger running on Windows XP. MSN Messenger running on earlier versions of Windows cannot use Whiteboard.

You can start a Whiteboard session in a couple of different ways:

- Click Actions, Start Whiteboard. Select the contact(s) you want to hold a Whiteboard session with. Once the contacts accept your invitation, the Whiteboard session begins, and you see a Sharing Session dialog box, shown in Figure 8-14, which lets you know that you are connected.

Figure 8-14. The Sharing Session dialog box lets you know the status of your connection.

- If you already have a session under way, such as a text session or a video and voice session, choose Actions, Start Whiteboard, or click Start Whiteboard in the right pane of the Conversation window. Your contacts must accept the invitation for a Whiteboard session to begin.

Once the session has started, you simply use Whiteboard to create any text or graphics you desire, as shown in Figure 8-15. Whatever you create appears on the contacts' Whiteboards. Users can save the Whiteboard drawings and text and even print them

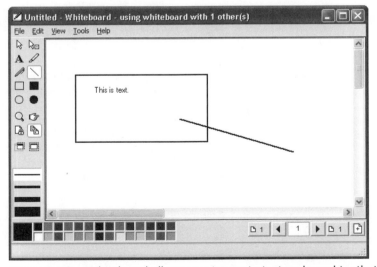

Figure 8-15. Whiteboard allows you to create text and graphics that appear automatically on your contacts' Whiteboards.

from their computers. Notice that you have a toolbar of buttons on the left side of the Whiteboard window. If you don't see the toolbar, choose View, Tool Bar. Along the bottom of the Whiteboard window is a palette for choosing colors and a set of VCR-type controls for handling multiple pages of drawings. Table 8-2 defines these tools for you.

Table 8-2. Whiteboard Buttons and Their Actions

Button	Name	Action
↖	Selector	The Selector tool allows you to select an item you have created and move it, resize it, redraw it, delete it, or manipulate it. Select the tool, and then click the object you want to select.
↖▫	Eraser	The Eraser tool deletes whatever you select with it. Select this tool, and then click the object you want removed. If you accidentally erase something, click Edit, Undelete to restore it.
A	Text	The Text tool allows you to create text on the Whiteboard. Select this tool, and then click once where you want to the text to go. A small text box appears. Use the keyboard to type the text.
✎	Highlighter	The Highlighter tool allows you to highlight text or objects. You'll need to select a color for the highlighter; yellow or pink works best.
✎	Pen	The Pen tool allows you to add freehand text and graphics. Select a line width and a color, and then hold down the primary mouse button to draw with the Pen.
＼	Line	The Line tool allows you to create a straight line. You can also select the line width by clicking the line thickness in the lower left portion of the Whiteboard window.
▢	Unfilled Rectangle	The Unfilled Rectangle tool allows you to create a hollow rectangle on the Whiteboard. Select the option, and then hold down your mouse button at the rectangle starting point to draw it.
▣	Filled Rectangle	The Filled Rectangle tool allows you to create a filled rectangle. You can select the color for the fill.
○	Unfilled Ellipse	The Unfilled Ellipse tool creates a hollow ellipse. Select the tool and hold down the primary mouse button to draw the ellipse.

242

Table 8-2. *(continued)*

Button	Name	Action
●	Filled Ellipse	The Filled Ellipse tool creates a filled ellipse.
🔍	Zoom	The Zoom tool enlarges the drawing. If you click again, the drawing will return to normal size.
☞	Remote Pointer	The Remote Pointer is a cool tool that allows a small hand to appear on the remote Whiteboards. For example, if you are trying to explain part of the drawing, you can click this option, and a pointer appears on everyone's Whiteboard. Drag the pointer to whatever you want others to focus on. Others can see your pointer but can't move it. However, they can initiate their own pointer and indicate material to you.
🔒	Lock Contents	Click this option to prevent other contacts from making changes to the Whiteboard. Click it again to unlock the Whiteboard so that others can make changes.
📑	Synchronize (Unsynchronize)	When you use different Whiteboard pages, everyone's page changes when anyone changes a page. However, if you want contacts to be able to see different pages, click this button to unsynchronize the Whiteboard.
⬚	Select Area	This feature allows you to select and paste an area from any window into your drawing. Select the option, and then hold down your mouse button to select the area you want to include. When you release the mouse button, the area appears on your Whiteboard. This is a great way to show portions of an application, picture, document, and so on.
⬚	Select Window	This option selects an entire window so that you can display it on the Whiteboard. This is a great way to show a program window or a dialog box to contacts.
🗋 1	First Page	This button displays the first page of a multipage Whiteboard.

(continued)

Table 8-2. *(continued)*

Button	Name	Action
◀	Previous Page	This button displays the previous Whiteboard page.
3	Page	Type the page you want to view and press Enter.
▶	Next Page	This button displays the next Whiteboard page.
4	Last Page	This button displays the last page of a multipage Whiteboard.
	Insert New Page	Creates a new Whiteboard page after the current page. If page 2 is showing, clicking this button creates a blank page 3. An existing page 3 becomes page 4, and so on.

tip If Whiteboard doesn't give you the creative options you need, you can create whatever you like in Paint or another application and paste it into Whiteboard!

Application Sharing

Application Sharing provides you with a great way to collaboratively work on a document or file, or even play a game (fast network games will not perform well, however). Like Whiteboard, Application Sharing is only available on Windows XP computers, not computers running MSN Messenger.

To begin an Application Sharing session, choose Actions, Start Application Sharing, and then select your contact(s). You can also just right-click the desired contact, and select Start Application Sharing. If you already have an instant messaging session in progress, choose Actions, Start Application Sharing, or click the Start Application Sharing link in the right pane of the Conversation window.

The Sharing – Programs dialog box shown in Figure 8-16 appears and allows you to select the programs that you want to share. Notice that you can click the Allow Control button to enable your contacts to control your program. If you don't click this button (or click it a second time when it is labeled Prevent Control), only you can control the program while others watch.

note Any program that you want to share must be currently open to share it.

Figure 8-16. Select the program you want to share and the level of control you want to give to contacts.

When the session initiates, the contact sees an Administrator's Programs window, shown in Figure 8-17. All changes and movements you make in the program using the open file are seen on the contact's computer.

Figure 8-17. Your contact sees the program you're sharing in a window like this.

InsideOut

Understanding Application Control and Saving Changes

If you give a contact the ability to control the application, you allow that contact to make changes to the file that is currently open. For example, let's say that you have a PowerPoint presentation you are working on. If you give a contact control, the contact can make changes to the presentation, and you'll see the changes as they are being made on your screen. When a contact wants to request changes, the contact chooses Control, Request Control in the program window. If you approve the contact's request, the contact can make changes to the file. You cannot make changes while the contact is making changes, and vice versa, so the process allows only one person to be in control at any given time. When the contact is finished, the contact clicks Control, Release Control. At this point, you can begin editing the file again.

So, where is the file the contact changed located? The program resides on your computer as well as the file. Your contact is viewing it remotely and issuing changes from a remote computer. Your contact can save the file while he or she has control, but only on your computer. If you want the contact to have a copy of the file when Application Sharing is done, simply use Windows Messenger and choose Actions, Send A File Or Photo to send a copy to the contact.

As you are working with Application Sharing, keep in mind that you can also maintain instant messaging windows as well as voice and video transmissions at the same time, which gives you a true collaborative experience!

Requesting Remote Assistance

Remote Assistance is a feature that allows a user to request help from another user over the Internet. Using Remote Assistance, a user can even allow another user to remotely control his or her computer and make configuration changes.

Remote Assistance uses Windows Messenger or Messaging Application Programming Interface (MAPI)-compliant e-mail applications (such as Microsoft Outlook or Outlook Express) to send Remote Assistance invitations. You can learn more about using the Remote Assistance feature in Chapter 16, "Remote Desktop and Remote Assistance."

Mobile Devices

Windows Messenger versions 4.6 and later have the capability to send instant messages to mobile devices. With the popularity of instant messaging, you can find a contact who is on the move with a mobile device instead of waiting until he or she is in front of a computer. To use mobile device instant messages with Windows Messenger, you need to download some add-ins and configure Windows Messenger to work with the mobile device you use, such as a cell phone or personal digital assistant (PDA). You can then send messages to other contacts who are mobile, and Windows Messenger can send instant messages to you when you are mobile. In Windows Messenger 4.6 or later, choose Tools, Add-In Web Site to download the mobile connectivity tools that you need. Follow the instructions that appear to set up this service. You'll need to open the Options dialog box from the Tools menu, select the Phone tab, and click the Mobile Settings button to set up the account. Then, enable the Allow People On My Contact List To Send Messages To My Mobile Device option. If others choose this option to enable you to contact them on their mobile devices, you'll be able to right-click their name in the contacts list and choose Send A Message To A Mobile Device.

Online Security and Privacy

As with all online services and features, privacy and security are always important, and Windows Messenger puts you in control of communications. You can choose whether to accept or decline any communication invitation. When using Windows Messenger, it is a good idea to observe these safety rules:

- Always, always use antivirus software and scan any files that you receive via Windows Messenger.

- Keep in mind that contacts can see your e-mail address. This usually isn't a big deal because you choose who you will communicate with, but if you are concerned about exposing your primary e-mail address, consider opening a Hotmail or Passport account just for Windows Messenger purposes. This keeps your Windows Messenger e-mail address separate from your primary e-mail address.

- Never give out your phone numbers unless you are absolutely certain with whom you are communicating.

- Windows Messenger sessions are not encrypted, so never give out credit card numbers or other personal identification information when using Windows Messenger. Use Outlook Express and send an encrypted e-mail for this purpose (see Chapter 7, "Using Outlook Express Advanced Features," to learn more).

Windows Messenger also gives you a few additional security options that can be found by choosing Tools, Options. Select the Privacy tab. Figure 8-18 on the next page shows how you can control which users can see whether you are online and are able to communicate with you by placing them on your My Allow List. Or you can block them by putting them on your My Block List. If you want to know which of your contacts has you in their contact lists, click the View button to find out.

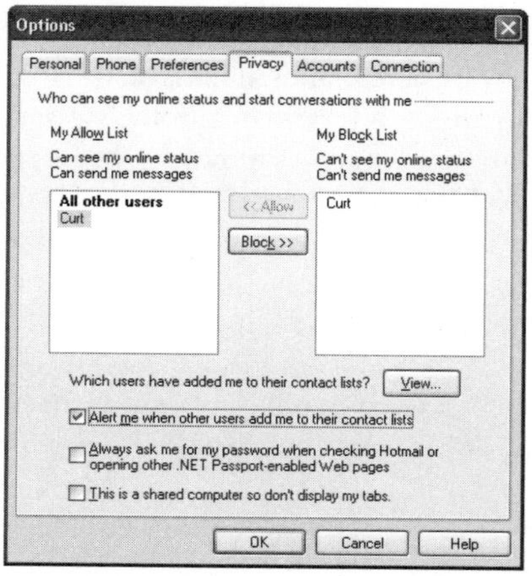

Figure 8-18. Use the Privacy tab to control who can see you when you are online and who can communicate with you.

For more information on how to best maintain the security of your Windows XP computer, see Chapter 20, "Maintaining Network Security."

tip Don't Forget NetMeeting

If you need a conferencing and application sharing tool to use on your LAN or WAN, use NetMeeting, which is available in Windows XP by choosing Start, Run and typing **conf**. NetMeeting also contains Whiteboard and Application Sharing features along with audio and video, and it will work on your LAN without requiring a separate .NET Passport for each participant. To learn more, see *www.microsoft.com/windows/ NetMeeting/Corp/reskit/default.asp* to view the entire NetMeeting Resource Kit.

Using Internet Information Services

The Internet has continued to grow at an astonishing rate. With the widespread use of the Internet, both residential and business users are seeking ways to further leverage Internet connections. Businesses often seek to reach new markets or foster collaborative enterprise with employees in distributed locations working on the same project interactively. Residential users seek new ways to stay in contact with family and friends, work from home, or just share information with others. Web servers are a tool that can be leveraged to do all of these things.

Microsoft Internet Information Services (IIS) has been the flagship Web server for the Microsoft Windows NT family of products for many years. This tradition is carried through with an IIS implementation in Windows XP Professional. IIS has been developed with the needs of many users in mind.

Microsoft is moving to an operating environment where the Internet is an integrated part of the operating system. This integration will allow a more enriching user experience and perhaps a more productive one as well. The implementation of IIS in Windows XP Professional continues along this path. In this chapter, you'll learn what you can and can't do with IIS in Windows XP Professional.

> **note**   Windows XP Home Edition does not support IIS.

Running IIS on Windows XP Professional

IIS, as included with Windows XP Professional, is designed primarily for limited use as a Web development tool or as a Web hosting system on an intranet. In Windows XP Professional, only 10 TCP connections to IIS are allowed at any given time. As a result, the maximum number of clients that can access your IIS server at any given moment is 10 (and most likely fewer, because some client requests might use additional TCP connections).

With that thought in mind, Windows XP Professional is not a practical platform on which to host an Internet Web site. However, for a small company that needs an intranet site to share HTML data, perform FTP transfers, or perform initial development of Web sites and applications that will later be deployed on Windows servers, Windows XP Professional fits the bill.

Using IIS on Windows XP Professional, you can:

- **Host one Web site.** You can use IIS to host one Web site on an intranet or even the Internet, but you are limited to 10 TCP connections at any given time across *all* IIS services.

- **Host one FTP site.** You can host one FTP site, but you are limited to 10 TCP connections at any given time. (These 10 connections constitute the total for all access to the IIS server.)

- **Use SMTP Virtual Server.** You can use IIS to host an SMTP mail service for your intranet (within the same restrictions on the total number of TCP connections to IIS). See "Configuring SMTP Services" on page 277 for more information about SMTP hosting.

- **Use IIS to test Web applications.** If you are a developer, you can easily test Web applications on Windows XP using IIS.

- **Use Internet printing.** IIS provides you with an easy way to share printers over the local intranet or even the Internet. See Chapter 14, "Understanding Resource Sharing and NTFS Security," to learn more about Internet printing.

> **note** IIS provides a way to host Web sites, not a way to design them. If you need to create a Web site, consider using Microsoft FrontPage. IIS fully supports all FrontPage features. If you need to develop advanced Web applications, you should consider using Microsoft Visual Studio .NET.

Getting to Know IIS

IIS provides a number of Web hosting features and functions in Windows XP Professional, but it is less constrained when used on a Windows server platform. IIS uses the same core engine on both XP Professional and on the server versions of Windows, allowing you to easily deploy Web sites and applications developed on XP Professional on the server editions of Windows. Those server editions of Windows provide a full suite of Web hosting, FTP, SMTP, and virtual hosting services. This chapter will take a look at what IIS has to offer. The following sections present a brief history of IIS and the services it provides, along with the technology IIS uses.

History of IIS

In one form or another, IIS has been in existence since the early 1990s. IIS 1.0 was first introduced as an add-on product for Windows NT 3.51 and included basic support for Hypertext Transfer Protocol (HTTP), static Web pages, and Common Gateway Interface (CGI) Web applications. IIS 1.0 also introduced the Internet Server Application Programming Interface (ISAPI), a method for writing Web applications and authentication systems that integrate tightly with IIS for improved performance over CGI applications.

The release of Windows NT 4.0 marked the introduction of IIS 2.0, which shipped with Windows NT 4.0. IIS 2.0 included new enhanced security features as well as enhancements to ISAPI.

The next major release, IIS 3.0, is best known for its introduction of Active Server Pages (ASP), a groundbreaking script-based Web application development system that revolutionized Windows Web site development and spawned a number of imitations for Web servers on Windows and other operating systems.

Microsoft distributed IIS 4.0, the next version, as part of the Windows NT Option Pack. IIS 4.0 included a number of refinements throughout the product. It introduced Web application process isolation and ASP transaction support via Microsoft Transaction Server, another component included in the Option Pack. (Microsoft Transaction Server was later renamed to COM+).

With the release of Windows 2000 Professional (and the suite of server editions of Windows 2000) came IIS 5.0. Numerous improvements in security, application support, and standards compliance were included in this release. Additionally, the management of IIS was made less cumbersome and less intrusive in IIS 5.0. This trend toward improved reliability and usability has continued with the release of version 5.1, which is the version included in Windows XP Professional.

Features Overview

The feature set available in the 5.*x* versions of IIS afford you a wide range of configuration options. These options let you configure your FTP server, HTTP server, and SMTP server, which are the three major components of IIS included with Windows XP Professional. Additional services are available in IIS 5.0 as part of the server versions of Windows 2000. New features are planned for IIS in version 6.0, which was in beta testing as this book went to press. For a preview of new features planned for version 6.0, see "Preview of IIS Version 6.0," page 257. For now, let's take a closer look at what IIS 5.*x* has to offer.

IIS Restart

One of the most intrusive features of IIS 4.0 was the fact that restarting IIS could be very inconvenient. In a full-featured IIS 4.0 environment, you had to manually stop the IISAdmin service (which would then stop the various services of IIS), and then track down all the worker processes used by Microsoft Transaction Server and manually stop them. Only then could you restart IISAdmin, bringing the Web server back online. Some administrators found it simpler to just restart the entire computer, thus inconveniencing all users of that system.

With the advent of IIS 5.0, it is now possible to easily restart IIS using the IISReset tool. What used to be minutes of downtime is now only a few seconds of unavailability.

Maintaining the Metabase

New to IIS 5.1 is the capability to reliably back up and restore the metabase in a couple of new ways. The *metabase* refers to the IIS configuration data for a Web site. Using the IIS backup and restore feature is now more useful than it was before. In addition to making a backup, the restore feature allows the IIS administrator to restore the backup to other computers.

Besides the new flexibility, enhancements have been added to ensure that the backup and restore process files are secure. A tool known as the Metabase Snapshot Writer (MSW) ensures that when the NT Backup tool is used (to make general system backups), the metabase portion is also backed up in a reliable manner. This tool guarantees that the current state of the metabase (a *snapshot*) is captured during a backup. It is important to note that the MSW is not related to the Configuration Backup/Restore option available in the IIS Microsoft Management Console (MMC) snap-in.

Remote Administration Features

The remote administration features of both IIS and the Windows NT family of operating systems have been around for some time. In Windows XP Professional, there are considerable improvements in the tools and the number of ways in which they can be utilized. IIS version 5.1 has a robust remote administration suite that is managed via a Web browser. This allows the administrator of the Web site to interact with the IIS

Chapter 9

server from virtually any location or computer system, as long as there is access to a standards-compliant Web browser. Also new in 5.1 is the capability to designate varying levels of administrative control, allowing some of the Web server administration tasks to be delegated to other users without providing full access to the Web server.

Remote Desktop is a new feature in Windows XP Professional (see Chapter 16, "Remote Desktop and Remote Assistance"). Actually, Remote Desktop is a new implementation of a very popular feature known as Terminal Services, which is available with the Windows 2000 family of server products. In Windows 2000, the Terminal Services server was not available in the Professional version. This has been changed in Windows XP in addition to adding new functionality. Neither of these products is part of the IIS suite, but the capability of using Remote Desktop to manage a Windows XP Professional computer running Web services is indeed significant. Remote Desktop allows a properly authorized user to create a virtual session with the IIS computer. From any computer capable of running the Remote Desktop client, the user can interact with IIS as if he or she were sitting directly in front of the computer running IIS. There are many new features in Remote Desktop that did not exist in Terminal Services, but those features relate to its configurability and multimedia support, and are covered in Chapter 16.

User Access Options

User access can now be controlled in a very granular manner with the IIS 5.1 application. Not only can general read, write, and execute access be defined (as in previous versions), but now a whole host of user rights can also be defined. The new options include the capability to define FrontPage user access at the site, directory, and file levels.

Secure Web Sessions

IIS version 5.1 makes full use of the Secure Sockets Layer (SSL) 3.0 standard as part of the Transport Layer Security (TLS) standard. This feature allows the secure transfer of information between Web servers and their hosts. Encased in this process is the capability of the IIS Web server to identify users through industry-standard public key infrastructure (PKI) certificates. When the user initiates a session, the Web server can examine the user's security certificates (issued by a certificate server) to uniquely identify the client. IIS 5.1 can then map the user certificate to a domain user account. These certificates, which use well-reviewed industry standards, allow IIS 5.1 to verify user identity in an extremely secure fashion.

Cryptography

The SSL standard is a widely used method for enabling private, secure communications as a part of Web browsing. Windows ships with an extension of the SSL package known as Server-Gated Cryptography (SGC). SGC uses specialized certificates to enable 128-bit encrypted communications with export versions of IIS (versions used outside the United States).

Kerberos Authentication

IIS makes full use of Kerberos (version 5) authentication available in Windows XP Professional. This integration allows the secure transmission of user credentials from one process or computer to another. Kerberos authentication is an open-standard–based method of securely authenticating users. Instead of sending authentication information in clear text (where it could be intercepted), Kerberos users (known as principals) use a *ticket* (an ID card of sorts) obtained from the Kerberos server. These tickets reduce network authentication traffic, are encrypted to eliminate the threat of interception, and allow servers and applications to delegate the work of authenticating a user to a centralized authentication service, such as Active Directory. (You can read more about Active Directory in "Active Directory," page 319.)

Security Certificate Storage Integration

IIS now supports the Fortezza standard. The *Fortezza* standard was outlined by the United States federal government to ensure that software systems meet the requirements of the Defense Message System architecture. This architectural specification encompasses cryptography, confidentiality, data integrity, authentication, and access control requirements. The goal of this standard is to ensure the secure access of messaging systems and the data they contain. The Fortezza support in IIS is normally used to implement smart card authentication systems.

New Security Wizards

In addition to new security features, the management of Web site security has been greatly improved. Easy-to-follow wizards now exist for several key security features. The Permissions Wizard is designed to make the assignment of user access rights on virtual directories and files easy. Of particular note is that this wizard integrates the changes with local file permissions (defined in the NTFS access list) to ensure that there are not two separate and possibly conflicting sets of access permissions. Chapter 13, "Selecting a File System," covers the various features of the NTFS file system (definitions, options, tools, and so forth) in detail.

The Web Server Certificate Wizard allows for the easy configuration of security certificates. This wizard makes it easy to create a new certificate, assign an existing certificate, or import an existing certificate from a backup.

In conjunction with the Certificate Wizard, the Certificate Trust List (CTL) Wizard contains a list of entities authorized to issue certificates for a particular location or resource. These authorized entities are known as Certificate Authorities (CA). Because the CTL is only of substantial use to IIS installations supporting multiple Web sites, this feature is unlikely to be of great value with the restricted IIS version included with Windows XP Professional.

InsideOut

Flavors of IIS

Microsoft has been moving toward a single, modular operating system platform in the last few years. The Windows 2000 family, which includes Professional, Server, Advanced Server, and Datacenter Server, exemplifies this ideology. Each of these versions is based on the same core operating system. They also share several services, including IIS.

The IIS implementation in Windows 2000 (version 5.0) varies in its feature set with the versions of Windows. The Server editions support multiple Web and FTP sites. The IIS implementation in the Professional operating system supports only a single FTP and Web site.

This difference in features is carried through in Windows XP. The IIS version included with Windows XP Professional has a reduced feature set compared to the server implementation, and Windows XP Home Edition lacks IIS altogether. Future server versions of Windows, on the other hand, will include the entire suite of IIS features.

Advanced Digest Authentication

IIS 5.1 makes use of a new feature, Advanced Digest Authentication, to enable a wide range of secure communications. *Advanced Digest Authentication* is a lightweight process that permits secure authentication of users across network security devices (such as firewalls). It does not require client-side software and does not send user credentials in a clear text format over public networks. Several other methods of authentication are available including the methods previously available with IIS 4.0 and 5.0.

Web Application Protection

IIS 5.1 offers improved protection and reliability for Web-based applications. IIS runs all of the client- and server-side applications in a common or *pooled* process that is separate from the other (sensitive) central IIS processes. In this way, the operation of the Web-based application is not tied to the operation of the components of the server itself. Therefore, disruptions in the operations of a custom-made Web application will not corrupt or interfere with the operation of the core IIS services. As an additional precaution, it is possible to run certain applications in memory locations entirely separate from the core IIS processes and the other Web-based applications in use.

Microsoft Active Directory Service Interfaces (ADSI 2.0)

The Active Directory directory service in server versions of Windows 2000 is used to store and manage comprehensive information about the domain's network resources.

By providing a centralized store for information, network management—the process of locating and managing resources—is greatly simplified. Active Directory also makes it easier for applications to access current information about the network, and it simplifies the process of developing applications that need such resources.

> You can learn more about Active Directory and Windows domains in Chapter 11, "Understanding Domain Connectivity."

To facilitate the access of information stored in Active Directory, ADSI was developed. ADSI is a directory service model that allows compliant client applications to access a wide variety of directory protocols including Active Directory and Lightweight Directory Access Protocol (LDAP) while using a standard set of interfaces. ADSI saves the developer the hassle of having to worry about interfacing with these various directory protocols. The ADSI provider has an interface that applications can connect to in order to obtain needed information.

In IIS 5.1, administrators and program developers can add custom objects, properties, and methods to the existing ADSI provider that allows access to the metabase. This flexibility gives system administrators great flexibility in configuring their sites.

HTTP 1.1

IIS 5.0 and 5.1 fully comply with the HTTP 1.1 standard. Both versions include features such as PUT and DELETE commands, HTTP error message customization, and support for custom HTTP headers. (Most of these features, however, are not new to the 5.x versions of IIS.).

Host Headers

With support for host headers, it is now possible to host multiple sites under a single IP address. For example, *www.microsoft.com* and *www.hotmail.com* can both be hosted on a single IP address that resides on a Windows 2000 server. This multihost functionality is very useful when it is impractical or not cost-effective to maintain more than a single IP address. Additionally, large Internet providers can leverage existing IP addresses to provide services to a larger number of clients. This feature is one of the components not present in IIS 5.1 as included in Windows XP Professional.

Additional Supported Features

Web Distributed Authoring and Versioning (WebDAV) is a new feature in IIS 5.x. WebDAV allows remotely located, Web page content authors to perform a wide range of content editing from anywhere on the Internet. Content builders can create, move, or delete files, modify file properties, and manage directories on a remote server over an HTTP-based connection.

To ensure a full suite of Internet-enabled functions, IIS includes an Internet mail and news server. Both of these components use Internet-standard protocols—SMTP for e-mail and Network News Transfer Protocol (NNTP) for news—to ensure maximum compatibility of the services.

FTP remains a very popular service among Internet users and content providers. It allows the transfer of files in a very efficient manner, often providing the best method for balancing the need to move large volumes of data with the need to maximize available bandwidth. One of the most useful features of FTP is the FTP restart feature. FTP restart allows a user to resume a file download in the event that the download is cancelled prematurely. Instead of having to begin the file transfer at the beginning of the file, the user can start where the interruption occurred and just download the remaining portions of the file.

HTTP compression is provided to aid in the transmission of content between the server and compression-enabled clients. This process takes the form of compressing and storing static files as well as performing compression of dynamic content on an *as-needed* basis.

---

tip   **Using IIS Without Sacrificing Security**

IIS, like most Web servers on the market, is an extremely common target for security attacks due to its ubiquity (it's been shipped with nearly every version of Windows for years) and its past reputation for having a number of security vulnerabilities.

Many of the features previously listed can increase the risk of a successful attack on your Windows XP installation. Before installing and configuring IIS, make sure you read "Securing IIS," page 577.

Preview of IIS Version 6.0

Under development at the time of this writing, IIS 6.0 promises to considerably enhance the performance of IIS 5.1. One of the primary improvements is in the scope and scale of process isolation, which is the manner in which one process (whether operating normally or failing miserably) is kept from adversely affecting other processes. Basically, this keeps something like a newly developed Web application from unexpectedly crashing the Web server service.

Another operational improvement is the worker process isolation mode. This mode essentially means that all of the individual pieces of application code are run in isolated spaces. This is done in a manner that avoids the performance impacts of isolating services presently in IIS 5.0 and 5.1. The value of this feature is obvious; it further reduces

Chapter 9

the possibilities of any kind of service disruption should one of the custom-built components, such as an ASP script, fail. Not only is systemwide disruption avoided, but should a group of custom processes have a single member that fails, the entire group can be kept in a functioning state while the defective component is restarted or replaced. Because all of the processes are running in isolated spaces, each can be given its own priority, and operating system-level features such as CPU throttling can be managed on a per application basis.

The Web Administration Service (WAS) is new in version 6.0. It plays a number of important roles in IIS 6.0, including:

- **Process health monitoring.** WAS keeps tabs on the status of client pro-cesses. By keeping in constant communication with the client processes, WAS is instantly aware of any client services that stop responding. If one of these processes fails to respond, WAS generates a duplicate process (to ensure continuity of services), and then restarts the failing service.

- **Idle timeout.** If a process is idle for a specified amount of time (configured by an administrator), the process can send a request for permission to shut down. This design element has been added to ensure that system resources are not unnecessarily used. (Administrators can also configure the system to never shut down processes, no matter how long they are idle.)

- **Rapid-fail protection.** When a client process fails, it ceases communication with the WAS process. Typically, the WAS process logs the error, and then restarts the process. New to IIS 6.0 is the capability of WAS to automati-cally disable processes that repeatedly fail.

- **Orphaning worker processes.** WAS can be configured to *orphan* a worker process if the process is deemed to be *terminally ill*. A terminally ill process fails to respond to inquiries by the WAS service for a predetermined period of time. Under normal (non-orphan) conditions, the WAS service will ter-minate nonresponsive processes, and then start a replacement service. In the orphan scenario, WAS does not terminate the failing service, but instead leaves the process running and starts a new process to replace the functionality of the failing process. The orphaned process can then be debugged to determine why it failed while the replacement process main-tains Web availability.

- **Recycling worker processes.** In IIS 6.0, worker process isolation mode can be configured to restart client processes periodically to manage faulty applica-tions. Periodic recycling can be advantageous when an application is known to leak memory, have coding errors, or suffer from other unsolved problems that cause it to fail after running for an extended period of time. No portion of the IIS server needs to be restarted; instead, the individual defective process is *recycled*. This recycling is a shutdown and restart of the process. There are a variety of configurable criteria that are used to determine when a process is recycled. Some of these criteria include daily schedules (same time each day), elapsed time since last recycle, and so forth.

Besides these features, you can expect to see additional key improvements in IIS 6.0, such as security. Because it is not possible to predict how every new security vulnerability will manifest itself, the security development component of IIS 6.0 is focused on locking out the commonly exploitable components and minimizing the impact of any new attacks. One of the major components of this new security approach is the development of the IIS Lockdown Wizard. This tool provides an easy-to-use interface for setting IIS server security to match the needs of the organization. Out-of-the-box IIS is configured to deliver static content only. To use any of the dynamic features (such as ASP and FrontPage Server Extensions), administrators will have to deliberately enable them.

Installing IIS

To use IIS on Windows XP Professional, it must first be installed.

note This is a change from earlier versions of Windows, which automatically installed IIS. This automatic installation resulted in a number of poorly maintained Web servers across the Internet, making them ripe for exploitation by hackers.

To install and run IIS, follow these steps:

1 Choose Start, Settings, Control Panel, and open Add Or Remove Programs.

2 In the Add Or Remove Programs window, click the Add/Remove Windows Components button.

3 The Windows Components Wizard appears. XP Setup appears. In the Components list, select the Internet Information Services (IIS) check box, as shown in Figure 9-1 on the next page.

4 Click the Details button. You see a list of the services that will be installed—all of which are selected by default with the exception of the File Transfer Protocol (FTP) Service and the Scripts Virtual Directory component of the World Wide Web Service component. You can clear the check boxes for specific services, such as SMTP Virtual Server, if you know you are not going to use them. Make any necessary decisions and click OK.

5 Click Next. Windows XP Setup installs IIS.

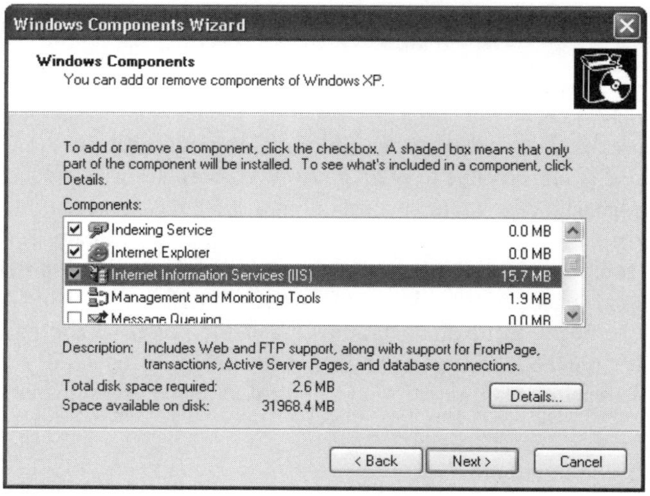

Figure 9-1. IIS is not installed by default, but you can choose to install it using the Windows Components Wizard.

Once these steps have been completed, you can begin configuring the individual IIS services, such as Web and FTP. If you decide to remove any of the components of IIS at a later date, simply repeat the preceding steps and clear the check boxes for any components you want to remove.

Configuring IIS Services

IIS provides a full suite of Web hosting, FTP, SMTP, and related services you can configure. Specifically, the IIS implementation included with Windows XP Professional provides Web server (HTTP), FTP, and SMTP services.

On a full-featured IIS installation, IIS supports the use of multiple Web sites. This allows individual applications or Web sites to be split apart, using different configuration settings, ISAPI tools, and even different server IP addresses and domain names. On Windows XP Professional, you can only use one Web site; however, IIS preserves the distinction between server-wide and site-wide configuration options to allow you to easily move your Web site or Web application to a server edition of IIS.

Configuring Global Web Site Properties

The HTTP server included with IIS is currently one of the most widely used Web server engines. An HTTP server responds to the HTTP requests made by Web browser client software, transferring Web page content to those clients using the same protocol. The IIS MMC snap-in allows the user to configure a wide range of options. To access the HTTP server global Web site properties and an explanation of each option, follow these steps:

1 Choose Start, Settings, Control Panel, and then open Administrative Tools.

2 In the list of administrative tools, locate Computer Management, and double-click to open the Computer Management Microsoft Management Console (MMC).

3 Under Computer Management in the left pane of the console, click once on the plus symbol next to Services And Applications, and then click once on the plus symbol next to Internet Information Services, as shown in Figure 9-2.

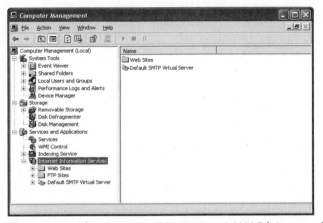

Figure 9-2. The Computer Management MMC lets you administer several important aspects of Windows XP including IIS.

4 Under Internet Information Services, right-click Web Sites, and then choose Properties on the shortcut menu that appears. The Web Sites Properties dialog box appears, as shown in Figure 9-3.

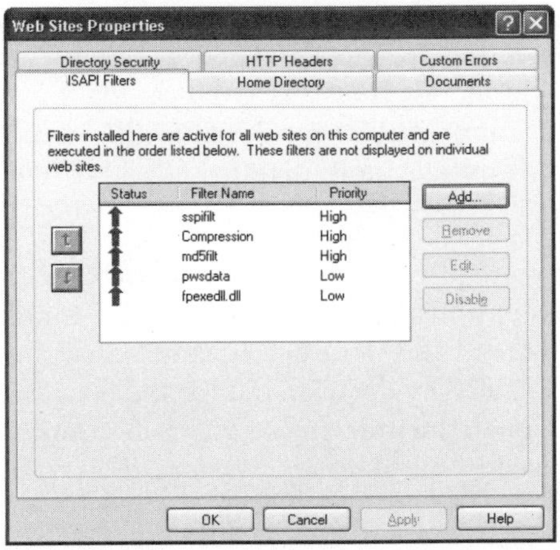

Figure 9-3. The ISAPI Filters tab of the Web Sites Properties dialog box lets you add and configure ISAPI applications.

The following sections explore the configuration options for the default Web site properties.

Configuring ISAPI Filters

The Web Site Properties dialog box opens to the ISAPI Filters tab as the default tab, as shown in Figure 9-3. An *ISAPI filter* is a program that responds to certain events that occur during the processing of an HTTP request. It can modify an incoming request, return custom results, or add completely new functionality to IIS. ISAPI filters are many in number and diverse in function. Basically, they are used to add new functionality and improve various supported features, such as user authentication.

A list of installed ISAPI filters is shown on this tab. Depending on when IIS was installed, whether it has been previously used, or whether it has been upgraded from an earlier version of IIS (as might occur when upgrading from Windows 2000 Professional to Windows XP Professional), the list of installed filters might vary slightly. Although the names of the default filters can be a challenge to decode, some of the default filters you might see are Md5filt (supports MD5 authentication) and Compression.

The Add button enables you to add additional ISAPI filters. In the event that existing filters are not needed, select the filter, and then click the Remove button. The Edit button enables you to configure the name and filter location for the selected filter. Should a new filter be added, it can be enabled (made active) by clicking the Enable button. In addition, the order in which ISAPI filters are applied to HTTP requests can be changed by selecting a given filter and clicking the up arrow or down arrow button on the left side of the ISAPI Filters tab.

Home Directory

The Home Directory tab, shown in Figure 9-4, contains several options. Note that the upper section, When Connecting To This Resource, The Content Should Come From, is disabled at the global level; this is because Web content must be placed in an actual Web site. To set the location of files for the single Web site permitted under Windows XP Professional, see "Configuring Individual (Default) Web Site Properties," page 269.

Although it is not possible to configure a global source of Web site content, it is possible to configure global access options. The check boxes in the middle of this tab control directory browsing and read and write access. Additionally, there are options to enable or disable logging (enabled by default) and for indexing the source files for the Web site. If indexing is enabled, the indexing service will create a table of the stored resources that will be used to speed up access times. This feature is also enabled by default.

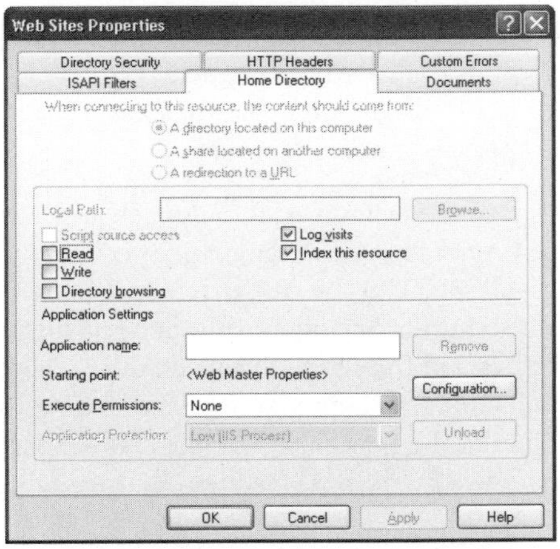

Figure 9-4. The Home Directory tab contains standard directory settings and advanced configuration options for the directory.

Other configurable options on the Home Directory tab of the Web Site Properties dialog box are in the Application Settings section. In this case, the options are accessed by clicking the Configuration button. The Application Configuration dialog box that opens has six tabs for configuring custom applications. The default Mappings tab is shown in Figure 9-5. This tab allows custom mapping of Web files according to their file extensions (.asp, .shtml, and so forth) to the applications that should execute them. This tab enables you to map new file extensions to applications and to edit or remove existing extensions. The single check box present on this tab enables or disables the caching of the ISAPI applications. By default, the caching is enabled.

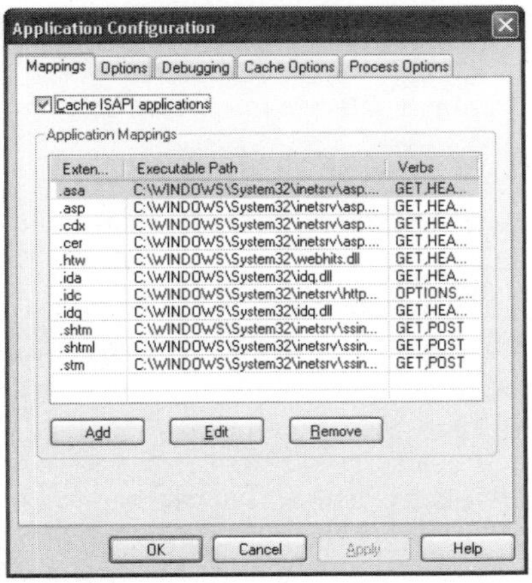

Figure 9-5. The Mappings tab determines how extensions are mapped to applications.

The Options tab, shown in Figure 9-6, lets you enable session state in ASP applications, which can help to identify a unique user as the user moves through the Web application. The Session Timeout interval ends a Web session if the user has not sent any HTTP requests to the site during the specified period.

Of the other options available on this tab, the Default ASP Language and ASP Script Timeout settings are of the most interest. Default ASP Language specifies the scripting language that the server is expecting ASP scripts to be constructed with. By default, ASP applications can be written in VBScript or JScript; additional scripting engines can be installed on the server (a topic beyond the scope of this chapter) to allow other scripting languages to be used as the default ASP language. The name entered in this text box (VBScript by default) must match the name used by the custom scripting engine exactly. (Other languages can be used within ASP scripts by specifying the language in the ASP page.)

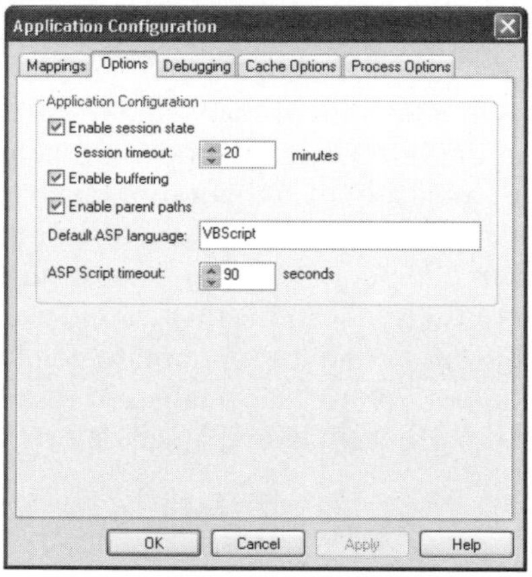

Figure 9-6. The Options tab provides the default settings for application timeouts and language options.

The Debugging tab enables you to set up client- and server-side script debugging. In the Script Error Messages section of this tab, you can choose Send Detailed ASP Error Messages To Client, which will send detailed error messages when a requested ASP page cannot be processed. Or you can choose Send Text Error Message To Client, which sends a single message for all error types. If you choose the latter option, you can type the text of the error message in the box below the option.

The Cache Options tab, shown in Figure 9-7, controls ASP file caching to both a disk cache directory and to memory. You can disable caching entirely, cache all ASP files to the directory cache, or cache a limited number of the files to the directory cache. If you choose either of the cache options, you can independently specify a maximum number of files to cache in memory.

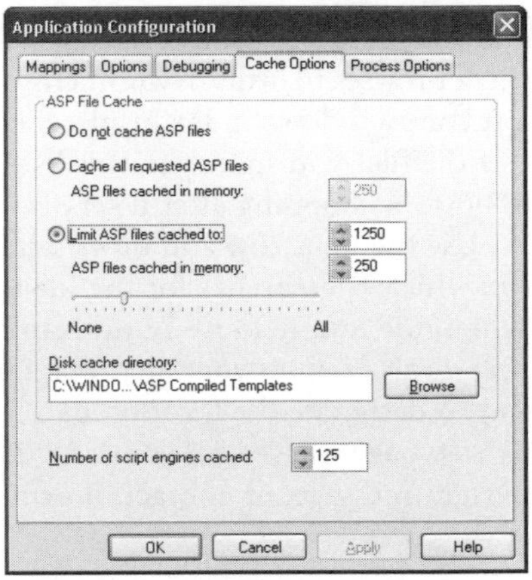

Figure 9-7. Manage the ASP file cache on the Cache Options tab.

On the Process Options tab, you can enable the logging of failed client requests. This is particularly useful if you're troubleshooting client connection problems. You can also configure the logging of debugging exceptions that occur. In addition, you can set a timeout interval for CGI scripts.

Documents

If you return to the Web Sites Properties dialog box and select the Documents tab, shown in Figure 9-8, the Enable Default Document section lets you configure the

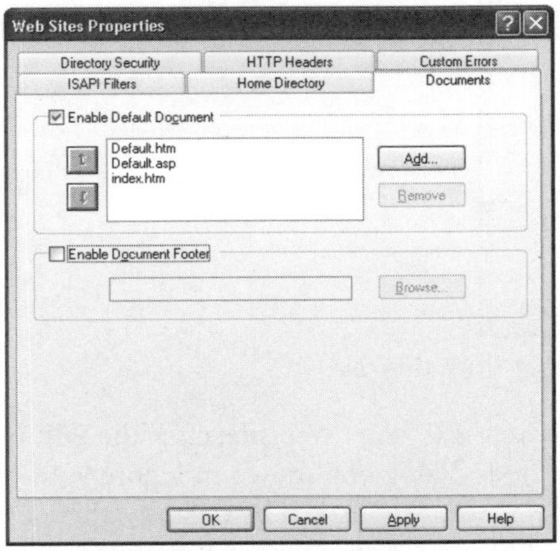

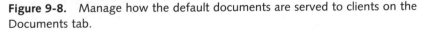

Figure 9-8. Manage how the default documents are served to clients on the Documents tab.

default documents. When a client browses to your Web site without specifying a particular page on your site (for example, if the client browses to http://www.microsoft.com/ windows/ instead of http://www.microsoft.com/windows/index.html), the *home page* that is delivered to the client will be one of the files you specify in this list. IIS serves these files in the order listed, from top to bottom, stopping after it serves the first of these files that it locates on your Web site. Use the up arrow and down arrow buttons to the left of the list to change the order in which IIS searches for the file to serve to clients visiting your site. You can also use the Add and Remove buttons to add a page with another name or to remove pages that don't exist on your site. The Enable Document Footer section, if enabled, lets you designate the location of a file that will be appended to the bottom of all the Web pages served on your site. This footer might include your company logo, a copyright message, or contact information.

Directory Security

The Directory Security tab of the Web Sites Properties dialog box, shown in Figure 9-9, only includes one section that is usable with Windows XP Professional (as a global setting, that is), the Anonymous Access And Authentication Control settings.

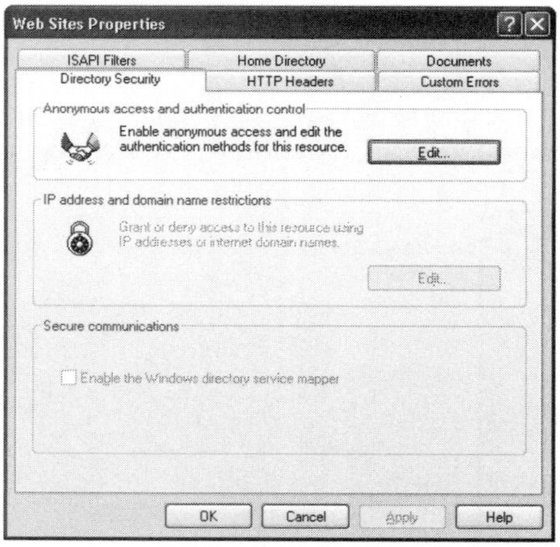

Figure 9-9. Manage directory security from this tab.

To enable and configure anonymous access to your Web site, click the Edit button, which opens the Authentication Methods dialog box shown in Figure 9-10. If the Anonymous Access section check box is selected (as it is by default), these options allow the configuration of an account to use for anonymous user access.

The Authenticated Access section contains two options for users of Windows XP Professional: Basic Authentication and Integrated Windows Authentication. The default setting is Integrated Windows Authentication, and this setting should be left as is unless compatibility issues require selecting Basic Authentication. When Basic authentication is used,

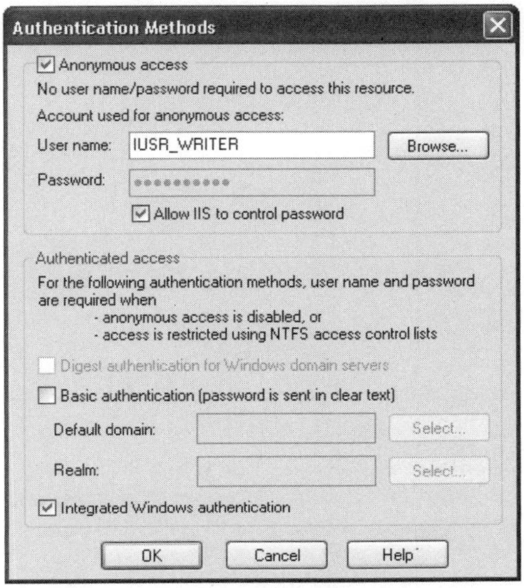

Figure 9-10. Manage the way users are authenticated with the Authentication Methods dialog box.

any authentication information (user names and passwords) are sent as clear text. An unscrupulous person could use a tool such as a packet sniffer to obtain unprotected user names and passwords that are passed using the Basic authentication method. Integrated Windows authentication does not pass unencrypted user names or passwords over the network, but it requires all clients to use Microsoft Internet Explorer to access your Web site. This effectively limits this method to an intranet on which all the clients use Internet Explorer for access.

For more information on IIS security options, see "Securing IIS," page 577.

HTTP Headers

The HTTP Headers tab, shown in Figure 9-11 on the next page, presents four sections of configurable options: Enable Content Expiration, Custom HTTP Headers, Content Rating, and MIME Map, all of which control the contents of the headers of the HTML pages sent to clients browsing your Web site.

The Enable Content Expiration section is used to keep time-sensitive information current for clients using that information. After selecting Enable Content Expiration, select Expire Immediately, Expire After (and a time interval), or Expire On (and a date and time). These options can ensure that content relating to onetime events, for example, will expire after the date they relate to passes. If the client requests a page and the expiration time has passed, the cached page is not served, but rather the server is requested for an (ostensibly) updated page.

Figure 9-11. Content expiration, custom HTTP headers, content ratings, and MIME types are all configured on the HTTP Headers tab.

The Custom HTTP Headers section adds considerable flexibility. This option is used to send a custom HTTP header from the IIS Web server in the page requested by the client. A custom header is used to send custom formatting and/or operational instructions that are not supported in the HTTP specification. Because the HTTP standards are not static, it was necessary to develop a method for implementing new features that would arise between releases of IIS as well as maintain the ability to develop new headers for use with custom applications. To create a new HTTP header, click the Add button, and enter the name and value for the custom header. Repeat this procedure for each custom header you want to add. After adding one or more custom headers, you can also edit their properties or remove them by selecting a header and clicking Edit or Remove.

Clicking Edit Ratings in the Content Rating section opens the Content Ratings dialog box. *Content ratings* are descriptive HTTP headers that are intended to identify the kind of content hosted on a Web site. Various Web browsers can use this header information to enable content filtering. The user of a compliant browser such as Internet Explorer can set the threshold for the kind of content the user wants to have blocked. This feature only works if the Web site being accessed has encoded its own ratings in its HTTP headers. You can embed your Web pages with content rating information by contacting a rating service to help you evaluate your Web content (select the Rating Service tab in the Content Ratings dialog box), and then rating your own site (select the Ratings tab, and set the ratings for your site's content).

The MIME Map section of the HTTP Headers tab contains the Multipurpose Internet Mail Extensions (MIME) configuration options. These mappings identify the types of Web content associated with the given MIME information, such as file extensions. There are a wide range of standard MIME types included with IIS, and this option allows the administrator to add to those types if needed. Configuring these MIME types allows the server to properly tell the browser which type of file is being transferred, so that the browser can then handle the file properly. By default, IIS uses the same MIME type mappings that are registered with Windows XP.

Custom Errors

The Custom Errors tab allows the user to configure customized error messages to replace the default messages provided by IIS. IIS contains many default error messages that are displayed to clients when problems occur. To create your own messages using this option, select a message you want to customize from the list, click Edit Properties, and then specify the file or URL containing your custom message.

Configuring Individual (Default) Web Site Properties

In addition to setting global Web site properties, you can also configure the properties for an individual Web site permitted by IIS running on Windows XP Professional. Some of these properties are redundant on Windows XP Professional (because only one Web site can be configured), but other options are available only on the site level and are preserved in this fashion to maintain compatibility with the server editions of IIS. To access the specific properties for a Web site hosted on Windows XP Professional, click the plus sign next to Web Sites in the left pane of the Computer Management console. Then right-click Default Web Site in the left pane, and click Properties on the shortcut menu that appears to open the Default Web Site Properties dialog box. The options available are specific to the individual Web site. You configure those options using the eight tabs of the Default Web Site Properties dialog box described in the following sections.

Web Site

The Web Site tab, shown in Figure 9-12 on the next page, allows for the configuration of several options. The Web Site Identification section lets you configure the Description (name), IP Address (individual or all unassigned), and the TCP Port to use for Web site communications. IIS will examine incoming Web requests and can use the site name to determine content delivery decisions. When you click the Advanced button, the Advanced Multiple Web Site Configuration dialog box opens. The set of options made available with this tool allows you to define multiple IP addresses and ports for the Web site's use.

This feature lingers from the HTTP 1.0 days, when the HTTP standard lacked Host Headers, and each virtual site on an IIS server had to be mapped to its own IP address. This feature is also useful if the Web server is connected to multiple networks because it will allow users on each of the attached networks to connect to the same Web site using the server IP address that is local to that network.

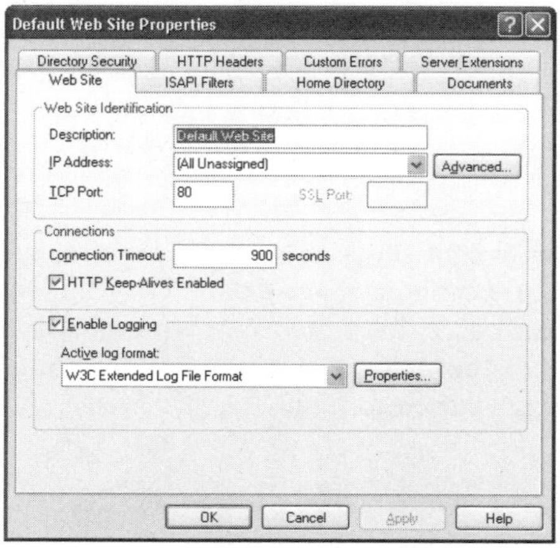

Figure 9-12. The Default Web Site Properties dialog box allows you to configure the basic properties of the default IIS Web site.

In the Connections section, selecting HTTP Keep-Alives Enabled allows clients to keep a constant connection with your Web server rather than negotiating a new connection each time additional resources or new pages are requested. This option is enabled by default and reduces the load on the server and the network. Disabling this option is not recommended. Use the Connection Timeout box to specify how many seconds of inactivity can elapse before a client is disconnected. Disconnecting inactive clients frees up connections for new clients that might otherwise not be able to access your site because of the 10 connection limit in Windows XP Professional.

The Enable Logging option, when enabled, tracks client connection information and can be used to help solve various connectivity issues. Log files can also be used to track what users access on your Web site and can aid in security audits.

> The proper use of Web site logs is critical to securing your IIS installation. For more information, see "Securing IIS," page 577, and "Examining Log Files," page 582.

ISAPI Filters

When the focus is at the individual Web site level, there are no ISAPI filters installed by default in the list on the ISAPI Filters tab. Because the ISAPI filters installed in this list will only apply to this Web site, it would seem as though there would be no particular reason to install filters at this level when working with IIS 5.1 and Windows XP Professional; however, to maintain compatibility and ease when moving applications between Windows XP Professional and Windows server editions, you can install individual site-specific ISAPI filters on the default site for development purposes.

Home Directory

At the level of the individual Web site, the location of the HTTP source files can be specified. The location of the source files can be on the computer hosting the server or in a shared directory on another network computer, or the source target can be redirected to another URL. The remaining options change according to which of these three options is selected. Most commonly, a local drive is used to host the Web site. Then, by selecting or clearing the check boxes in the middle of this tab, you can enable or disable access to script source files, directory browsing, and read and write access. Additionally, there are options to enable or disable logging and for indexing the source files for the Web site.

Unlike the global Web site settings, there are a range of application settings available at the Web site level. These options let you configure the default application behavior. This includes setting Execute Permissions to establish the level of execution privileges afforded clients. You can also set Application Protection to determine whether applications are pooled for efficiency or isolated to protect faulty applications from bringing down the Web server. You can choose High (individual processes are isolated from IIS and from one another) to run each script or application in a separate resource space, Medium to run the IIS processes in one memory space and to pool all applications in another memory space, or Low to run all applications in the same resource space as the IIS processes.

Documents

The Documents tab contains two options. Enable Default Document, if selected, specifies a list of default documents the Web server will return when a Web browser does not specify a particular document (for example, if http://www.microsoft.com/windows/ is specified instead of http://www.microsoft.com/windows/index.html). Clients requesting a default document will be served the first file in the list that is found on the Web site. Adjust the order of the documents by selecting documents and clicking the up arrow and down arrow buttons. You can also add new documents and remove unused documents.

Directory Security

The Directory Security tab contains two sections that are available to Windows XP Professional users: Anonymous Access And Authentication Control and Secure Communications. To enable and configure anonymous access, click the Edit button to open the Authentication Methods dialog box. These options are the same as those found on the Directory Security tab of the global Web Site Properties dialog box discussed earlier in this chapter.

HTTP Headers and Custom Errors

The HTTP Headers and Custom Errors tabs contain identical options to those listed in the Web Site Properties dialog box.

Server Extensions

There are three general groups of settings on the Server Extensions tab, shown in Figure 9-13. If you don't see any options and you receive a message that the server has not been configured, follow these steps:

1 Return to the Computer Management console, and right-click Default Web Site.

2 On the shortcut menu that appears, point to All Tasks, and choose Configure Server Extensions.

3 Complete the Server Extensions Configuration Wizard. You can accept most of the default values. On the Mail Server page, when asked to configure your mail server settings now, click No, and then click Finish.

4 When the wizard closes and returns you to the Computer Management console, open the Action menu and choose Refresh.

5 Right-click Default Web Site again, choose Properties, and select the Server Extensions tab, which should now appear with its options.

> If you don't see these options in your installation of IIS, you might need to apply the latest IIS updates. Maintaining a properly updated IIS installation is also critical to securing your Windows XP installation, as discussed in "Securing IIS," page 577.

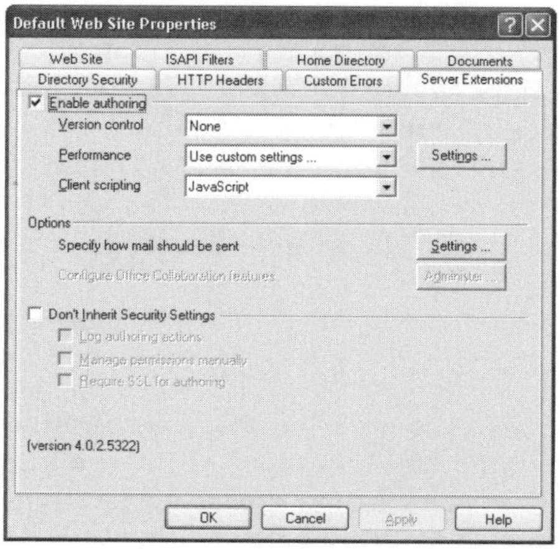

Figure 9-13. Configure Web site authoring access on the Server Extensions tab.

The Enable Authoring section allows users who possess the correct credentials to remotely edit and publish Web content. If you enable authoring, you can also specify version control, performance, and client scripting options.

The Options section lets you specify how e-mail is sent to users of your site who want to contact you or who need responses to forms they fill in on your site. Additionally, you can specify the encoding you want to use for the mail you send and the character set for your language.

The Don't Inherit Security Settings option, if enabled, lets you change security settings for this site without regard to the security settings of the global Web server.

Configuring FTP Services

FTP remains a popular online protocol for transferring files. IIS in Windows XP provides FTP services so that users can access online directories and download and upload files. If you need to set up FTP services on Windows XP Professional, the following sections review the configuration options available to you.

> If all of your users are running Windows 2000 and Internet Explorer 5 or later, you can use Web Distributed Authoring and Versioning (WebDAV) instead of FTP. See "Using WebDAV," page 276, for more details.

Configuring Global FTP Server Properties

Like Web site properties, the global FTP server properties are available by using the Computer Management console, or you can open the IIS console (or *snap-in*) found in your Administrative Tools folder.

> **note** If you do not see FTP Sites listed in the IIS snap-in or in the Computer Management console, you need to install the FTP Service. Follow the instructions for installing IIS in "Installing IIS," page 259. Click the Details button in step 4, and select File Transfer Protocol to add the service.

In the IIS snap-in or in the Computer Management console, right-click FTP Sites, and then choose Properties to open the global FTP Sites Properties dialog box. You will find three simple tabs to configure your FTP options.

On the Security Accounts tab, shown in Figure 9-14 on the next page, you can choose the account to use for anonymous access by selecting the Allow Anonymous Connections check box. Additionally, you can choose Allow Only Anonymous Connections so that users can only log on with the privileges associated with the anonymous user account, not a user name and password that might have administrative permissions.

> **caution** As discussed in "Securing IIS," page 577, allowing anonymous FTP on any system is considered an invitation to disaster by most security experts. Use this option only if you are extremely vigilant in maintaining IIS patches and examining log files or if you only intend to use it briefly.

The FTP Site Operators section of the Security Accounts tab allows the addition or removal of accounts designated as Site Operators. However, in this implementation of IIS, only members of the Administrators group are allowed this level of access.

Figure 9-14. Use the Security Accounts tab to configure FTP access permissions.

The Messages tab lets you configure a variety of messages. The text you type in the Banner Message box is the note displayed to clients when they initially connect. This often takes the form of an official notice such as "Authorized Users Only." The text you type in the Welcome box is the next message clients see. This is most often a more informational note to connected clients after they have been authenticated on the server. The text you enter in the Exit box is delivered to clients when they close their connection to the FTP server. Also available is the Maximum Connections box. In this box, you can type a message that is delivered when the maximum number of users allowed to connect to the FTP server has been reached, and the client attempting to connect must be turned away until more connections become available.

The Home Directory tab contains relatively few options. The Read, Write, and Log Visits options can be enabled or disabled to determine whether users can download or upload files to the enabled directory and whether their visits will be logged. You can also set the Directory Listing Style option to UNIX or MS-DOS. These options affect the way the list of files and folders are displayed to FTP clients. The default setting for this option is MS-DOS.

Configuring Individual (Default) FTP Site Properties

The individual FTP Sites properties are accessed by clicking the plus sign next to FTP Sites in the Computer Management console or the IIS snap-in, and then right-clicking

Default FTP Site. Click Properties to open the Default FTP Site Properties dialog box. You will see the same tabs as displayed in the global FTP Sites Properties dialog box, along with one additional tab, FTP Site.

The FTP Site tab, shown in Figure 9-15, lets you configure the FTP site's identification, connection settings, and logging information. The Identification section contains the Description box for entering a name for the site, an IP Address box if you want to route a specific IP address to the FTP server, and a TCP Port box if you want to specify a different port for the server.

The Connection section lets you set connections for the FTP Service. With IIS version 5.1 running on Windows XP Professional, the HTTP and FTP servers are limited to a maximum of 10 simultaneous connections. Any attempt to set the number of simultaneous connections to a value greater than 10 will result in a licensing warning message. However, you might want to set this to a value *lower* than 10 so that you can reserve connections for the Web service that might otherwise be consumed by those accessing the FTP Service. You can also set the Connection Timeout value so that inactive users are disconnected after the specified interval to free up connections to others who might be waiting to gain access.

The Enable Logging option, if selected, logs the activities of those accessing your FTP server. You can also choose the format of the log file and its location. (As with the HTTP server, proper use and examination of these logs is critical to server security.) Also, the Current Sessions button can be clicked to reveal the users that are currently attached to the FTP server.

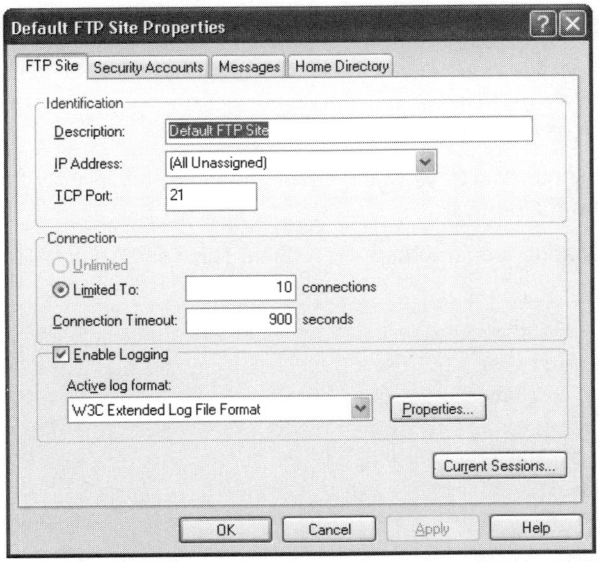

Figure 9-15. Use the FTP Site tab to configure identification, connection, and logging information.

InsideOut

Keeping Access Rights Straight

One of the most common frustrations for new IIS administrators is the looming specter of conflicting permissions. Imagine that you want to grant a remote user access to upload to an FTP folder, but after making the appropriate changes in the IIS console to allow write access, the user receives an "Access Denied" error when trying to copy files into the directory. The problem is likely the result of incorrectly configured file- or directory-level permissions, assuming you're running IIS on an NTFS volume (which you should always do for security reasons).

For more information about setting access rights, see "Configuring NTFS Permissions," page 433.

Using WebDAV

WebDAV is an HTTP 1.1 extension that allows computers running Windows 2000 and later versions (those using Internet Explorer 5 and later) to read and write files in a shared directory under IIS. Basically, users can access and manage files using a Web page just as they would using an FTP site. If all of your users are using Windows 2000 and later, you might consider using WebDAV instead of creating an FTP site—which will be less maintenance in the long run.

Setting up a WebDAV directory is easy. Follow these steps to add a directory within your default Web site for sharing files:

1 Assuming your Web site is using the default directory that IIS creates for it, the C:\Inetpub\Wwwroot directory, open Windows Explorer and create a subdirectory, such as C:\Inetpub\Wwwroot\Sharedfiles.

2 Right-click the Sharedfiles directory, and choose Sharing And Security from the shortcut menu that appears.

3 Select the Web Sharing tab, and then select Share This Folder.

note If you want to create a *virtual directory* (one located elsewhere but appearing to be a subdirectory of the default Web site), open the IIS snap-in, and right-click Default Web Site. Point to New, and click Virtual Directory to open the Virtual Directory Creation Wizard. Follow the wizard to specify an *alias* for the directory (the directory name the user will see, such as Sharedfiles), and then specify its actual physical location, such as D:\Webdav\Sharedfiles.

4 Once the directory is shared, right-click the directory in IIS or in the Computer Management console, and choose Properties. Select the Directory tab,

and then select both Read and Directory Browsing permissions for the folder.
If you want users to be able to edit files, select the Write permission as well.

Users can then access the directory through Internet Explorer and essentially work
with the WebDAV folder as they would an FTP site.

Configuring SMTP Services

SMTP Services in IIS running on Windows XP Professional can be useful for providing a
storehouse for SMTP mail on an intranet. The SMTP virtual server acts as a Web server,
and client computers can connect to the SMTP virtual server to access mail accounts.
However, you are limited to 10 concurrent connections under Windows XP Professional.

Like Web and FTP Services, you can configure the SMTP virtual server by accessing its
Properties dialog box. Open the Computer Management console or the IIS snap-in,
and right-click Default SMTP Virtual Server. Click Properties to open the Default
SMTP Virtual Server Properties dialog box. The following sections explore the options
available on the tabs of the dialog box.

note If you don't see the SMTP server entry in the left pane of IIS or Computer Management, it is probably not installed. Refer to "Installing IIS," page 259. In step 4, select
the SMTP Service check box.

General

On the General tab of the Default SMTP Virtual Server Properties dialog box, use the IP
Address box to select All Unassigned or any individual IP address that the SMTP virtual
server should respond to. Click the Advanced button to add multiple IP addresses and
custom port numbers. You can also select Limit Number Of Connections To and
specify fewer than 10 connections if you want to reserve some connections for Web or
FTP connections. Like the FTP server, this option is set to 10 simultaneous users by
default, but it is not limited to any number of users (or e-mail addresses). You can also
choose Enable Logging to maintain a log of users who utilize the mail server.

Access

On the Access tab, there are four sections of options to configure: Access Control, Secure
Communication, Connection Control, and Relay Restrictions, as shown in Figure 9-16
on the next page. The Access Control item is used to set the kinds of authentication
methods that will be allowed when accessing the SMTP server. To configure this option,
click the Authentication button. By default, all methods of authentication are enabled
(anonymous access, Basic authentication, and Integrated Windows authentication).

Chapter 9

277

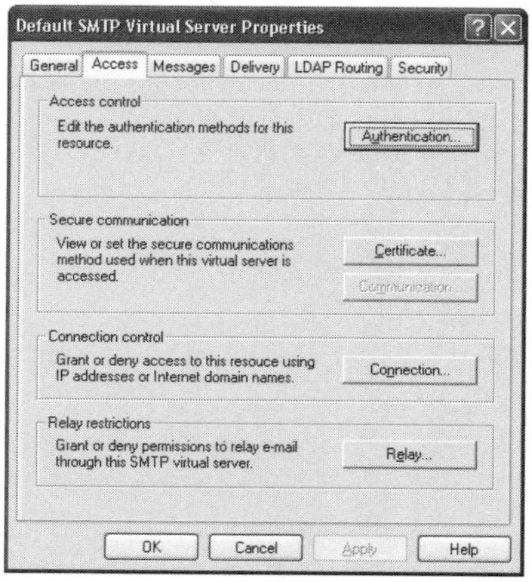

Figure 9-16. Configure access control and restrictions on the Access tab.

Click the Certificate button to launch the Web Server Certificate Wizard. This is the same wizard found in the Default Web Site Properties dialog box, and it will allow the creation of a new certificate or the installation of an existing one. Another set of security features is located by clicking the Connection button in the Connection Control section. The Connection dialog box allows the filtering of clients by their IP addresses. This can be done in one of two ways. All sites except those listed in the Computers box can be allowed access. This open, relaxed filtering method allows a few individuals to be filtered out and still ensures access to all other users who need it. The alternative option is to deny all users access *except* for those listed in the Computers box. This method is useful if there are only a few users using the service and/or security is extremely important.

To prevent inappropriate use of the SMTP server, click the Relay button in the Relay Restrictions section to control which computers can relay their mail. Anyone who has relay access will be able to use the SMTP server to relay e-mail messages from one source to another. Improperly secured SMTP sites are often exploited by spammers to anonymously relay unsolicited e-mail messages.

Messages

The Messages tab contains a number of settings affecting the types of e-mail notes that can be sent and received. This dialog box lets you limit the size of individual e-mails, limit the number or total size of e-mails transferred in a single session, and limit the number of recipients of a single e-mail. This last option keeps users from sending large numbers of spam messages through your server. Also, in the event that e-mail messages are undeliverable or they violate one of the configured restrictions, a location can be specified in the Badmail Directory box to house the offending e-mails.

Delivery

E-mail is only useful if it gets to the intended recipient. Options on the Delivery tab are intended to give you the flexibility to set delivery options for optimal results. In the event that an initial attempt to deliver an e-mail note fails, the SMTP server has a retry interval setting. As you might assume, the retry interval is the period of time between repeating attempts to deliver a failed e-mail message. You can set intervals in minutes in the Outbound section for the first, second, third, and subsequent retries. Also on this tab are the Delay Notification options for setting the amount of time required before an administrative alert concerning the undelivered e-mail is sent. The Expiration Timeout settings let you define the length of time the message will be kept if it proves to be repeatedly undeliverable.

LDAP Routing

The LDAP Routing tab is used to integrate the SMTP server with a Windows domain running Active Directory directory services. Active Directory can then be used to resolve hosts and servers, assuming that the server contains records for the requested devices. Once LDAP routing is enabled (select Enable LDAP Routing), a server name and user credentials must be entered to complete the integration.

Security

The Security tab contains an option to add or remove user groups and accounts that will have operator permissions on the SMTP server. By default, only administrators are allowed this level of access.

Part 3

Network Connectivity

Chapter 10

Managing Workgroup Connections

Workgroups and home networks have become very important in the past few years. With even the smallest of offices now using several computers as well as many homes containing more than one computer, workgroup networking has become more complex and more diverse. In fact, if you need to create a workgroup using Microsoft Windows XP or even other versions of Windows, you have more options than ever before. From a hardware point of view, you can easily create an Ethernet network, a HomePNA network, or a wireless network. You can also easily share an Internet connection, use Internet Connection Firewall (ICF) to protect the network, and use Windows XP to automatically set up your workgroup.

Workgroup refers to any network that does not use a centralized server for user authentication. Networks that rely on centralized servers for authentication, also known as domain-based networks, are discussed next in Chapter 11, "Understanding Domain Connectivity." Workgroups usually comprise fewer than 20 computers and can be created in a home or office, or just about anywhere they are needed. This chapter assumes you have read Chapter 3, "Creating Network Connections," where workgroup networking hardware is explored. This chapter also refers to Internet connections, which you can learn more about in Chapter 4, "Configuring Internet Connections," and ICF, which you can learn more about in Chapter 5, "Using Internet Connection Firewall."

Planning a Workgroup

Workgroup setups can be very simple, or they can be somewhat complex, depending on your networking needs. The good news is that there are several options available to you. It is important to consider all that Windows XP has to offer so that you can create the workgroup configuration that is right for you.

Choosing a Network Topology

The physical arrangement of computers, hubs, shared printers, and such on a network is called the topology. The *topology* is a map of where your computers will reside and how they will connect to each other. Before you create a network, it is very important that you stop and think about your needs before you start moving computers around and installing network interface cards (NICs). As you think about the physical layout of the network, consider these questions:

- Do the computers reside in one room, or are they scattered throughout an office or home?

- What is your budget?

- How can you physically arrange the network and allow room for growth, but keep the networking topology as simple as possible?

- Is mobility in the home or office important? Should you consider a wireless network?

- How will an Internet connection be used? Will all clients share the same connection?

Simplicity is your best bet. As you are developing a workgroup design, remember that the simpler the design, the easier it will be to maintain. Sure, you might need a more complex workgroup configuration, but first ask yourself, "What is the easiest and most simple design I can use that will meet my needs?" This approach will help reduce the likelihood of setup and configuration problems, and it will probably save you money as well.

Once you answer these questions and determine the possible network topology that might be right for your workgroup, you can then begin to make some decisions about that topology. You might consider creating a preliminary sketch of the workgroup topology. Consider access to power outlets, phone outlets, and Internet accessibility for all locations as you make your sketch. Think about how the network might grow or change in the near future. As you are considering these issues, study the examples and illustrations in the following sections.

Single Room Topology

The simplest type of workgroup consists of computers that reside within the same room, such as in a small office or a home office. In this situation, you can use any type of network you like, such as Ethernet or HomePNA, or even Powerline or wireless. In the following illustration, three computers are connected on an Ethernet network using a central hub. The network is contained in one room and is easy to set up.

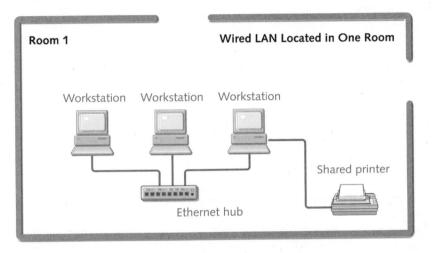

A single room topology is, of course, the easiest configuration. Setup is simple. You can choose any type of networking hardware that you want to use, and it is unlikely that you will experience any networking problems. However, there are some specific negatives to consider:

- **Wired limitations.** The network is contained in a single room; therefore, if you use a standard wired Ethernet network, you will have to run cable to another room if the network expands beyond this room. You can avoid this potential problem by using a HomePNA, Powerline, or wireless network, or you can plan ways to add such a network to your wired network if computers are later added in another location.

- **Physical constraints.** Trying to use multiple computers in one room can be a headache. Often, the space required by keeping many computers in one place becomes prohibitive (particularly if you intend to use the room for other functions) unless special furniture is purchased to organize the machines. Also, you must consider the heat, noise, and access to power outlets.

- **Fixed location.** Unless you are using a wireless network, the single room design doesn't give you a lot of flexibility. You must do all your computing from one location, which might not always be available or otherwise feasible. You'll also find it more difficult to make significant changes to the network topology.

To learn more about Ethernet, HomePNA, and Powerline networks, see Chapter 3, "Creating Network Connections." To learn about wireless networking, see Chapter 19, "Wireless Networking."

Dispersed Topology

Dispersed topology often refers to a network connected across sites that are geographically distant from one another. In this book, dispersed topology refers to computers belonging to a single workgroup that are located in different rooms or floors of the home or a small office. This type of topology has become more common in workgroup configurations. For example, suppose there are three computers in your home: one in the living room, one in a home office, and one in a bedroom. You might want to create a home network so that the computers can communicate with each other and share Internet access. The same is true for an office setting where people work in several rooms and sometimes on different levels of a building.

A dispersed topology essentially works the same as a single room topology, but you might need to be more selective about the type of network you use. For example, if you want to use an Ethernet network, you might need to hire someone to run Category 5 cabling in the attic with drops into the rooms you need; otherwise, you'll have cables running everywhere. A less expensive solution is to use a HomePNA network or a Powerline network. You might also consider using a wireless network. The following illustration shows a home network that uses HomePNA. A computer can connect to the network from any location in the office, as long as a phone jack is available.

HomePNA Network Spanning Two Rooms

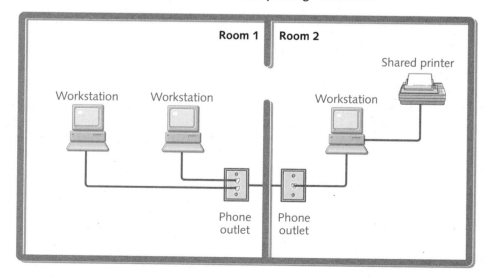

The advantage of a dispersed network is flexibility. You can add or remove computers in different rooms as needed, including carrying a portable computer from room to room and connecting to the network wherever you want to work; however, your networking won't be as fast as a wired network. Your network might also be more susceptible to interference from telephone signals with HomePNA, from power lines with Powerline, or from radio frequencies with wireless. You might incur more expenses installing a wired Ethernet network if it requires construction work, although the Ethernet NICs and hubs might be less expensive than similar wireless or HomePNA devices. These are all factors you'll need to consider in planning your network.

Multi-Segment

A *multi-segment* network consists of two different networks that are linked together using a hardware device such as a switch or bridge. In this chapter, a multi-segment network refers to two networks connected together using Windows XP and its Network Bridge feature. Network Bridge in Windows XP allows you to easily connect two dissimilar network segments together seamlessly and without additional hardware. When you use a network bridge, a network interface card (NIC) for each network is installed on a single Windows XP computer. For example, in the following illustration, you can see that the Windows XP computer has an Ethernet NIC installed as well as a wireless NIC. Using Windows XP as a bridge, clients on the Ethernet network can seamlessly communicate with clients on the wireless network using Windows XP as the network bridge. Network Bridge can connect various combinations of internal or external network devices, including PCI cards, PCMCIA cards, USB devices, or IEEE 1394 devices.

Wired LAN Bridged with Wireless LAN

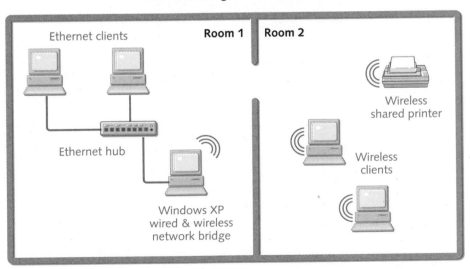

You can learn how to configure a network bridge in Chapter 3, "Creating Network Connections."

An initial question often asked concerning a multi-segment network is simply, "Why?" Why use a multi-segment network? There are a few reasons:

- A multi-segment network can solve connection problems when one networking solution does not meet all of the needs of the network.

- A multi-segment network bridged using Windows XP can join two existing networks without having to buy new hardware, thus saving money and configuration time.

- A multi-segment network can create greater flexibility.

Suppose you live in an older home with limited wiring, and it's difficult to run new wire through the walls or ceilings. Then suppose you have a home office that contains an Ethernet network consisting of five computers. Your computers are limited to residing in that single room because running Category 5 cabling up and down your hallways isn't very attractive. You could use a HomePNA network, but if some of your rooms do not have phone jacks, you still have a wiring problem. You can deal with this type of telephone problem by using remote phones that you carry from the base station room to rooms that do not have phone jacks.

In a similar way, you can extend your LAN (which might also include your Internet connection) to the rest of your house by installing a wireless network. You can then place a desktop computer in another room and plug it into a wall socket for power. The network connection is made through a wireless NIC installed in the computer. Even better, you and your family can carry a couple of laptop computers from room to room or into your backyard. Each laptop must be equipped with a wireless NIC, perhaps in the form of a PCMCIA (PC) card or a card that is integrated into the laptop. To link these wireless computers to your Ethernet network (and in turn, the Internet), you outfit one Windows XP computer on the Ethernet LAN with a wireless NIC. This Windows XP computer contains both a wired Ethernet NIC and the wireless NIC. To connect the two networks logically, you use the Network Bridge feature in Windows XP to bridge the wireless network to the Ethernet network rather than using a *wireless access point* (the name for a dedicated wireless bridge) and plugging it into the Ethernet hub. As long as the Windows XP computer serving as the network bridge is turned on, you can sit elsewhere in your house and share files with your LAN. The following illustration shows the setup of a multi-segment network using a wired LAN bridged to a wireless LAN. You have now solved your cabling problems without incurring construction costs or making holes in the walls!

Chapter 10: Managing Network Connections

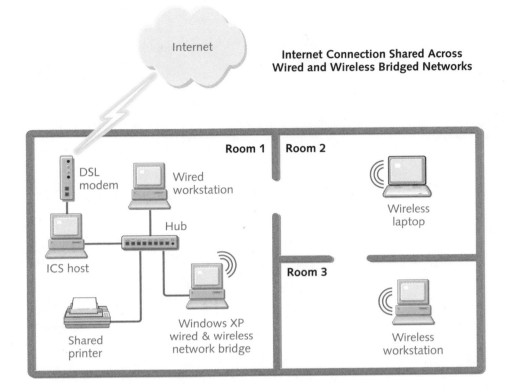

This type of configuration can give you the flexibility you need and solve difficult physical connection problems. Windows XP automatically creates a network bridge when two or more network adapters are present in a computer. You can even connect three dissimilar networks. For example, in the following illustration, a wireless network, a HomePNA network, and a wired Ethernet LAN are all connected by means of a single Windows XP computer running Network Bridge.

> **note** Networks can contain more than one bridge. A network could easily contain Ethernet, wireless, and Powerline segments in one cohesive network. In fact, Windows XP can bridge several different network connections at once—as many different types of network connections as you can install on the computer.

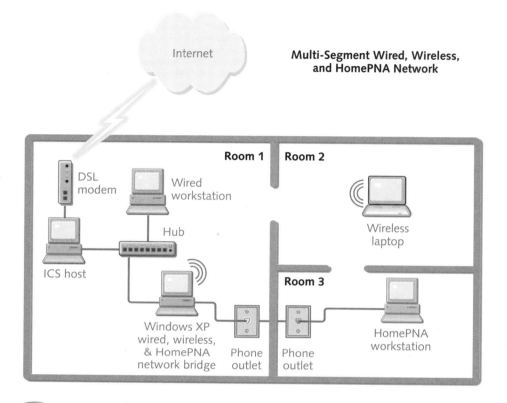

Multi-Segment Wired, Wireless, and HomePNA Network

InsideOut

What about IP Routing?

Keep in mind that you don't *have* to use the Windows XP Network Bridge feature. You can use a hardware device to bridge the networks, such as a router (a device that handles the task of routing network traffic between multiple networks) or a dedicated hardware bridge (such as an external wireless access point).

You'll first need to purchase the router or bridge that can accommodate your mixed networking needs, and you'll need to make sure the router or bridge will work well with Windows XP. Although other networking devices like NICs and hubs are relatively inexpensive, even home or small office routers and bridges can be quite expensive—often costing $200 or more. Because Windows XP can automatically provide a network bridge for you, your least expensive solution is to use one of your computers running Windows XP as your network bridge.

Gathering the Network Hardware

Once you make a decision about your network topology, create a careful sketch of the network. Include all of the computers, hubs, cabling, and any other accessories that might be necessary. Then make a list of the hardware that you need and purchase that hardware. Depending on the kind of network that you want, the hardware that you'll need will vary. Be sure to refer to Chapter 3, "Creating Network Connections," and Chapter 19, "Wireless Networking," to help you determine what you need to buy.

Planning for the Future

As you plan your workgroup, always make your plans with an eye to the future. Do you anticipate adding more computers to the network, or do you anticipate using different types of network media (wired, wireless, HomePNA, Powerline) that will require a bridge? As you think about the network, try to imagine how the network might grow and change over the next few years. This will help you make wise topology decisions as well as wise network hardware decisions. After all, you do not want to outgrow the network and quickly make your investment in networking hardware obsolete. So, think carefully and plan judiciously, and the result will be a workgroup that meets your needs well into the future.

Installing the Hardware

Once you've purchased your networking hardware, you'll need to properly install the hardware and any software support that it needs. Although the exact steps required to do this depend on your specific hardware, there are a number of guidelines that you can follow that will make the process significantly smoother.

1 Take stock of your existing setup. Determine how your computer(s) currently connects to the Internet (via dial-up, DSL, or cable modem, for instance), and make sure you have the pertinent settings for that connection handy (either by finding your ISP's documentation or writing down the settings yourself). These settings should include the details of any dial-up connections (such as phone numbers and encryption settings), any static IP configuration information that your ISP might have assigned you, and whether you have to use PPPoE to connect to your ISP.

See "Configuring Modems and Broadband Hardware," page 96, for more information on these settings.

2 While you still have a functioning Internet connection, take advantage of it. Download any instruction manuals that you might be missing for your hardware. Determine the latest driver versions for your network adapters and download those as well. Examine the *ReadMe* information for all your network hardware and download any operating system updates required to support it. If you intend to use devices such as residential gateways, hubs, switches, or routers, download the latest firmware upgrades for those devices because they often fix critical issues and security holes. Once you've downloaded all of these tools, either copy them to a removable medium (such as a CD-R/RW or a Zip disk) or keep them handy on one computer.

3 If you intend to install hardware (such as internal NICs) in any of your computers, it's a good idea to have a current backup of any irreplaceable information kept on those systems.

4 If you're using a wired network type, such as wired Ethernet, make certain that all of your Ethernet cabling has been strung (or installed in the walls) so that it can easily reach your computers. If you have access to an Ethernet cabling tester, now's a good time to use it; however, most of these devices are expensive, and Ethernet cables are rarely bad. Still, because cabling is relatively cheap, it never hurts to have some spare cables to use in case you encounter a connectivity problem that you can't resolve in any other fashion.

5 Install any internal hardware in your computers. If operating system updates are required before installing the hardware, install those updates before you shut down the computer. Follow standard precautions against static electricity buildup. Have the latest drivers for the hardware handy, and follow their installation instructions.

6 Connect any wired network media to your computers. If you're using Ethernet, it's perfectly safe to connect the cabling while the computers are powered up. For other formats, check the manufacturer's directions. For Ethernet, unless you're simply connecting two computers directly to one another with a crossover cable, you'll need to connect each computer to a hub or a switch (or a residential gateway device that includes the features of a hub or a switch). You can determine whether your media connections are successful by opening Network Connections in Control Panel, right-clicking the media connection, and choosing Status, as shown in Figure 10-1.

---

tip   **Placing Network Icons in the Notification Area**

As with Windows 2000, you can have an icon for each network connection on your computer appear in the taskbar's notification area. This icon will dynamically display outbound and inbound network traffic and warn you when network connections are broken and restored. To display this icon, open Network Connections. Right-click the media connection you're interested in monitoring, and choose Properties. In the properties dialog box, select the check box labeled Show Icon In Notification Area When Connected, as shown in Figure 10-2.

Chapter 10: Managing Network Connections

Figure 10-1. The status dialog box for a LAN connection helps you determine if it's functioning properly.

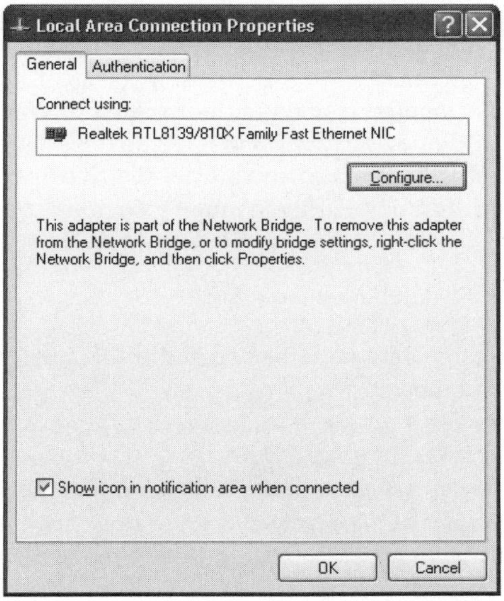

Figure 10-2. Each connection's properties dialog box lets you choose to display its status by means of an icon placed on the taskbar.

7 Now is a good time to upgrade the firmware on your hub, switch, or residential gateway device (if you're using one). *Firmware* is control code that resides in updatable read-only memory (ROM) inside a device, allowing it to be easily upgraded and replaced as necessary. To determine if any firmware upgrades are needed, visit your device manufacturer's Web site. Instructions on how to upgrade the firmware should also be available on the Web site.

8 If you're using a residential gateway connected to a broadband device, follow the manufacturer's instructions to configure that device to work with your ISP and to provide IP addresses to your network using Dynamic Host Configuration Protocol (DHCP), if that feature is available.

More information on DHCP is available in "Dynamic and Static Addressing," page 27.

Setting Up the Workgroup

After you've installed the software drivers and hardware devices, and have made your connections, you're ready to configure the workgroup. Windows XP provides the handy Network Setup Wizard to help you set up the workgroup. If you want to use the Network Setup Wizard, and you plan on using Internet Connection Sharing (ICS), you should first run the wizard on the computer that directly connects to the Internet. You can then run the wizard on the other computers on your network. If you are using a mixture of Windows XP computers and computers running earlier versions of Windows, such as Microsoft Windows 2000 or Windows 9x, Windows XP provides a way for you to create a network setup disk for those clients when you run the Network Setup Wizard. See "Configuring Computers Running Earlier Windows Versions," page 298, for more information.

To use the Network Setup Wizard, follow these steps:

1 Make sure all network computers are turned on and all NICs and media connections are functioning properly.

2 Open Network Connections.

3 Under Network Tasks in the task pane of the Network Connections window, click Set Up A Home Or Small Office Network. If you don't see the task pane, click the Folders button on the toolbar to toggle from the Folders bar to the task pane.

4 The Network Setup Wizard opens and presents the Welcome page. Click Next.

5 On the Before You Continue page, read the instructions and make sure that all network components are connected and working. If you want to use ICS to share your Internet connection but haven't set it up yet, do that at this time. Make sure the computer hosting ICS (the one directly connected to the Internet, and the one you're running the Network Setup Wizard on first) has a working Internet connection. Click Next.

Chapter 10: Managing Network Connections

6 On the Select A Connection Method page, select the first option, This Computer Connects Directly To The Internet, if the computer will function as the ICS host. See Figure 10-3. Remember, you should be running the Network Setup Wizard on the ICS host first. If there is already an ICS host computer, select the second option. If neither of these options apply to you, select Other. Click Next.

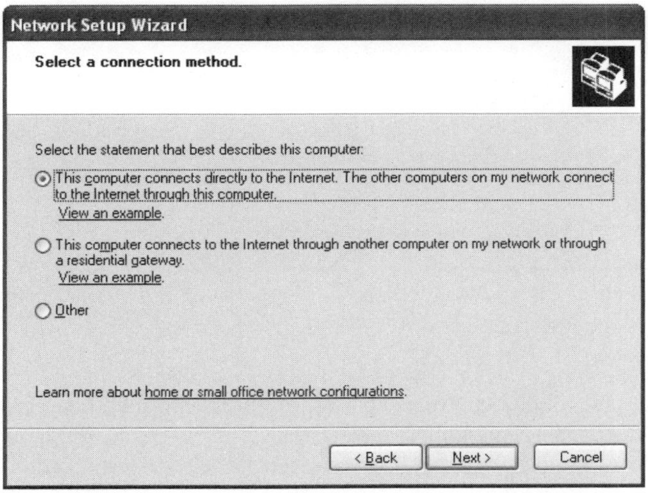

Figure 10-3. Select how the machine you're configuring connects to the Internet.

7 If you select the Other option, the page that appears allows you to select one of three alternate computer configurations:

- This Computer Connects To The Internet Directly Or Through A Network Hub. Other Computers On My Network Also Connect To The Internet Directly Or Through A Hub.

- This Computer Connects Directly To The Internet. I Do Not Have A Network Yet.

- This Computer Belongs To A Network That Does Not Have An Internet Connection.

Select the most appropriate option and click Next.

8 In step 5, if you determined that the computer should function as the ICS host, the Select Your Internet Connection page appears, which is shown in Figure 10-4 on the next page. If you selected another option, follow the steps presented by the wizard. Your choices will vary, but the ICS host scenario includes most of the same configuration steps (and more) as the other choices. Select the Internet connection that you want to share and click Next.

Chapter 10

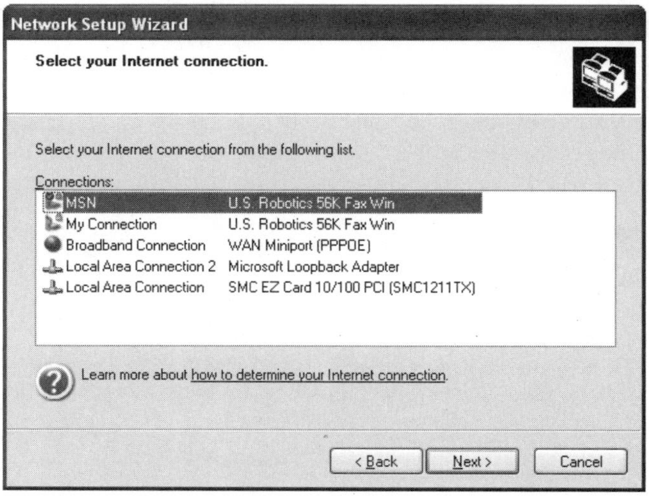

Figure 10-4. If you have more than one way of connecting to the Internet, choose the one you use most often, and if possible, choose the fastest connection.

9 If you have multiple network connections installed on your computer, the Your Computer Has Multiple Connections page appears. The wizard will ask you for the appropriate network connection. Select either Determine The Appropriate Connections For Me to allow Windows XP to automatically bridge the connections or select Let Me Choose The Connections To My Network if you want to bridge those connections. In this procedure, select the second option so you can see the bridging steps that Windows XP will attempt to perform for you automatically, and click Next.

10 The Select The Connections To Bridge page appears, shown in Figure 10-5, so that you can select the connections you want to bridge. Do not choose any Internet connections—you cannot bridge a LAN connection with an Internet connection, and doing so would introduce a serious security breach on your network! Select the check box next to each connection to your home or small office network and click Next.

11 The Give This Computer A Description And A Name page appears. You can type a short description of the computer in the Computer Description box (such as Ingrid's Laptop), and then type an easily recognizable name in the Computer Name box. The name must be unique (no two computers on the network can have the same name) and should be no fewer than three characters, and no more than 15 characters. You can use letters, numbers, and even some special characters (such as #, $, -, _, and !); however, you should avoid using any punctuation or spaces (other than the underscore character) because they can cause problems that can be difficult to diagnose. Keep it simple but descriptive, like Ingrid, Kitchen_PC, or Notebook. Click Next.

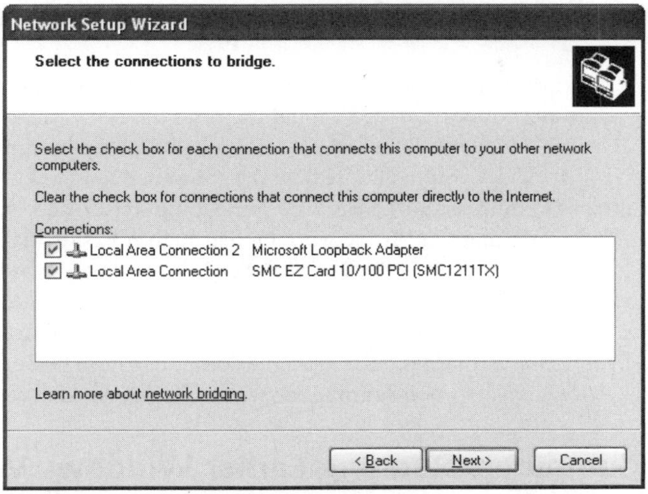

Chapter 10: Managing Network Connections

Figure 10-5. This page appears if your computer has more than one network connection.

caution If you are using a broadband connection such as a cable modem, your computer might have a required name for Internet access. In that case, do not change the name if it is required by your ISP. See your ISP documentation for additional details.

12 On the Name Your Network page, type a name for your workgroup. By default, your workgroup is named MSHOME. However, you can change it to anything you like. The name should be short and simple, and all computers on your network must use the same workgroup name to connect with each other. Click Next.

13 Review the settings you are about to apply on the Ready To Apply Network Settings page. Use the Back button to make any necessary changes. When you are sure the settings are correct, click Next.

14 As Windows XP configures the computer for networking, you'll see the Please Wait page.

15 When prompted, you can choose to create a network setup disk to apply the network settings to other computers on the network. You do not need a network setup disk if all clients on your network are Windows XP clients. If all your computers are running Windows XP, select Just Finish The Wizard; I Don't Need To Run The Wizard On Other Computers. Although you will still need to manually launch the Network Setup Wizard on your other Windows XP clients, you don't need setup disks to do so.

16 Follow any necessary instructions if you do need to create a network setup disk and then click Finish.

Configuring Other Windows XP Computers

Once the first network client is configured, which should be the ICS host on a system that shares a single Internet connection, you should then run the Network Setup Wizard on the other Windows XP network clients. If you are using ICS, keep in mind that the Network Setup Wizard will ask you to choose how the computer connects to the Internet (see step 6 in the preceding section). Select the This Computer Connects To The Internet Through Another Computer On My Network Or Through A Residential Gateway option, as shown in Figure 10-3, page 295. The Network Setup Wizard will locate the ICS host and proceed with the setup. Remember too that if you need to use a network bridge, the bridge does not have to be located on the ICS host. In fact, several of your Windows XP clients can potentially function as bridges. As long as the computers have two or more NICs installed, the option appears when running the wizard, as described in steps 9 and 10.

Configuring Computers Running Earlier Windows Versions

Computers running Microsoft Windows 95, Microsoft Windows 98, Microsoft Windows Millennium Edition (Windows Me), Microsoft Windows NT 4.0, and Windows 2000 clients can also join your Windows XP workgroup. These clients can be configured for networking manually (discussed next), or you can run the Network Setup Wizard on computers running Windows 98, Windows 98 Second Edition, or Windows Me. To use the Network Setup Wizard on these versions of Windows, you can either use the floppy disk that you created in step 15 when you configured the Windows XP clients, or you can use the Windows XP installation CD to run the Network Setup Wizard.

> **note** You can use any device that supports IP networking, including computers running variations of UNIX, Macintoshes, or even the Xbox, on your network with your Windows computers, and some of them can even share files and printers with your Windows systems! However, any computer that does not have support in the Network Setup Wizard (including older versions of Windows) will require you to manually configure their networking settings in order to properly work with your Windows XP workgroup.

To run the Network Setup Wizard from the CD, follow these steps:

1 Insert the Windows XP installation CD into the computer you want to add to the workgroup.

2 When the Welcome To Microsoft Windows XP screen appears, select Perform Additional Tasks.

3 On the Welcome To Microsoft Windows XP screen, select Set Up A Home Or Small Office Network.

4 Depending on the computer's version of Windows, the Network Setup Wizard might need to copy some additional files to your computer and restart it. Click Yes to continue.

5 At this point, the Network Setup Wizard opens. Complete the wizard as you did for the Windows XP computer. Follow the steps in "Setting Up the Workgroup," page 294, for guidance.

Configuring Network Clients Manually

If you're using an earlier version of Windows that isn't compatible with the Network Setup Wizard, you can add those computers to the workgroup manually. However, you should use the Network Setup Wizard whenever possible because it ensures that your network clients are all configured in the same way and reduces the likelihood of connectivity problems. If you need to configure your computers manually or you just want to know what goes on behind the scenes of the Network Setup Wizard, follow these steps:

1 Choose Start, Control Panel, and open Network Connections.

> **note** Earlier versions of Windows use different arrangements of dialog boxes to configure network connections. Refer to the documentation for your particular version of Windows to accomplish the tasks described in this section that apply to versions of Windows that can run the Network Setup Wizard (Windows 98, Windows Me, and Windows XP).

2 In the right pane of the Network Connections window, right-click the network connection you want to configure, such as Local Area Connection, and choose Properties.

3 If Client For Microsoft Networks and File And Printer Sharing For Microsoft Networks aren't listed on the General tab of the properties dialog box, click the Install button.

4 In the Select Network Component Type dialog box, shown in Figure 10-6, select the Client option and click Add.

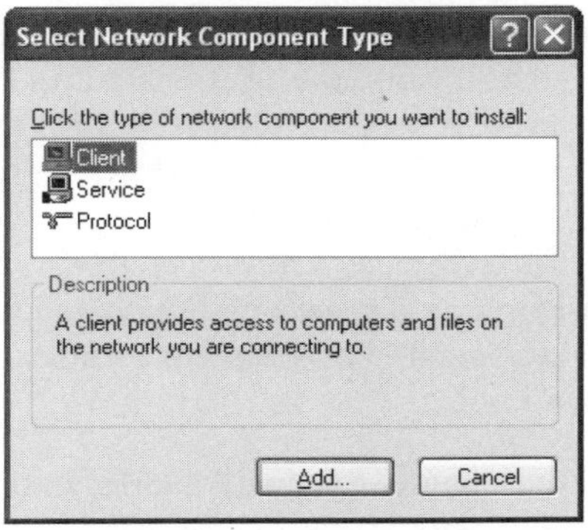

Figure 10-6. The Select Network Component Type dialog box allows you to add additional networking components.

5 In the Select Network Client dialog box that appears, select Client For Microsoft Networks, and click OK. The client software is installed for the connection.

6 On the General tab, click the Install button again. In the Select Network Component Type dialog box, select Service and click Add.

7 In the Select Network Service dialog box, select File And Printer Sharing For Microsoft Networks, and click OK. The service is installed for the connection.

8 Make sure the check boxes next to the client and service are selected, and click OK.

---

note The client and service you just installed are needed for Windows XP to participate in a workgroup. However, a properly configured IP address is also necessary. To review the IP address settings, double-click Internet Protocol (TCP/IP) on the General tab of the properties dialog box.

If you are using a residential gateway device that provides DHCP services, configure all your computers to receive their IP configuration information automatically. If DHCP is not available, Windows 2000 and Windows XP will attempt to use Automatic Private IP Addressing (APIPA) to configure these settings; however, if you are using any other operating systems on your network, APIPA will most likely fail, and you will have to manually configure these settings. See the next section for details. To learn more about configuring TCP/IP under Windows XP, see "Configuring IP Settings in Windows XP," page 35.

Changing the IP Configuration

When you run the Network Setup Wizard, if DHCP is unavailable APIPA is used to automatically avoid IP address conflicts with network clients. Computers in your workgroup are assigned an APIPA address in the 169.254.*x.x* range. Each computer receives a unique IP address, and a query method is used during setup to make sure that the IP address being assigned is not in use.

If you want to manually assign different IP addresses to the clients in your workgroup, you can easily do so by selecting Internet Protocol (TCP/IP) on the General tab of the connection's properties dialog box and clicking Properties. However, you should seriously ask yourself why before doing so. APIPA is designed to service workgroups and was specifically developed for networks where no centralized DHCP server is in use. The fact is, manual IP address configuration can be complicated and problematic, so before changing your computer's automatic IP addressing to a static addressing scheme, keep the following points in mind:

● Each client on your network must have a unique IP address in the same range with an appropriate subnet mask.

- You must manually change the IP address properties of each client on the network to the appropriate address range so they can communicate with one another.

- If you use ICS, the default gateway assigned to your network clients must be the address of the ICS host. See the next section for more information.

Using Internet Connection Sharing

As described in "Setting Up the Workgroup," page 294, the Network Setup Wizard gives you the option of using ICS when you set up a home or small office network. Using ICS, a single computer on the network becomes the ICS host, and all other computers on the network access the Internet through the ICS host's Internet connection. Of course, you are not required to use ICS, but if you plan on sharing a single Internet connection and if you want all traffic entering and leaving your network controlled by one ICF configuration, ICS is an option.

InsideOut

ICS, Residential Gateway, or a Hub?

If you want to share an Internet connection, you can do so by using ICS or a device such as a residential gateway or router. In some cases, depending on your Internet connection, you can attach the DSL or cable modem to a hub or a switch and have all other computers on the network connect to the Internet directly through the hub instead of a single host computer. A basic hub or switch, however, provides no additional security, so each client on your network must turn on ICF on the Internet connection to protect your network from being accessed by people on the Internet. Enabling ICF will protect the individual computers, but in this configuration, ICF will also protect your network computers from *each other*, so your network will not work without a great deal of custom configuration! This occurs because you're using the same IP address range for your private network and for the Internet connection. In this case, ICF can't protect you from one IP address without protecting you from all IP addresses. If you disable ICF on each computer, your network will work, but it will be wide open to attacks from the Internet. This configuration can lead to more management problems and more security holes. In other words, you should *never* run a network from a hub that has an Internet connection plugged directly into the hub and is operating in the same IP address range.

Other options include the use of residential gateways, which often use firewalls and network address translation (NAT) to protect your computer against outside threats. The difference with the residential gateway solution is that the IP address of the Internet connection (your DSL or cable modem plugs into the *in* port of the router)

(continued)

Inside Out *(continued)*   is translated into a private IP address (or range of addresses if the residential gateway has a built-in network hub) that isn't visible to the Internet. Your computers can safely network behind the residential gateway's firewall and still share a connection to the Internet that operates in a completely separate IP address range. Although residential gateways work well, their cost is approximately $100 and up, depending on certain features, such as an integrated network hub or switch. Some experts believe a hardware router is more secure because the Internet traffic never directly enters any of the computers on the network, as it must for ICF and ICS to work. Also, with ICS, the ICS host computer must be running for the other computers on your network to have Internet access, whereas only the residential gateway needs to be powered up for any computer on your network to access the Internet.

The choice, of course, is yours, but keep in mind that ICF and ICS are easy to use, they work well, and perhaps best of all, they impose no further damage to your pocketbook. However, if you can afford one, a residential gateway is the simplest solution to administer, and it provides a number of features beyond those provided by ICF and ICS.

How ICS Works

When you enable the ICS host, the ICS host computer becomes an Internet gateway for the other computers on your network. When ICS is enabled, the ICS host uses the IP address of 192.168.0.1. All other ICS clients on your network see this computer as the gateway, and no other computer on your network can use the same address. When a client computer needs to access the Internet, a request is sent to the shared connection, which causes the ICS host to connect to the Internet and retrieve the requested information. To ICS client users, it appears as though their computers are directly connected to the Internet. Clients can use the Internet and retrieve e-mail seamlessly.

When you choose an ICS host while using the Network Setup Wizard, the following items are configured on the ICS host, which gives ICS its functionality:

- The local area connection for your internal NIC is configured as 192.168.0.1 with a subnet mask of 255.255.255.0. If the ICS host has more than one NIC for your workgroup, such as in the case of a multi-segment network, you need to bridge those connections so that both network segments can use ICS.

- The DHCP Allocator service is configured on the ICS host. When additional network clients are added to the network, this service automatically assigns IP addresses to those clients. The IP addresses range from 192.168.0.2 through 192.168.0.254 with a subnet mask of 255.255.255.0. A DNS proxy is also enabled so that additional DNS servers are not required on your network. These services run automatically in the background, and they require no additional configuration.

- The ICS service is installed and runs automatically on the ICS host.

- If a modem connection is used on the ICS host, autodial is turned on by default so that the connection is automatically dialed when an ICS client makes a request to the Internet.

Troubleshooting

You want to use ICS with earlier versions of Windows.

Once you set up the ICS host, you can easily set up your workgroup computers running Windows XP and other versions of Windows. Computers running Windows 98, Windows Me, Windows 2000, and Windows NT 4.0 should be able to use ICS for Internet access. Because not all of these versions of Windows support ICS, use the appropriate steps in the following list for the operating system you're attempting to use:

- **Windows 98 and Windows Me.** Run the Network Setup Wizard from the Windows XP installation CD or from a setup disk you create. The wizard enables ICS Discovery and Control on the non-XP clients so that they can access the ICS host.

- **Windows 2000 and Windows NT 4.0 (as well as non-Windows platforms).** Configure the computers to use DHCP to automatically obtain IP configuration information; they will then contact the DHCP service running in memory on the ICS host, which will send them the appropriate configuration data. You will not be able to use ICS Discovery and Control, but you will still have access to the Internet.

When using ICF with its default settings, remember that some traffic might not be allowed to pass through the firewall from the Internet. To learn how to adjust ICF settings to allow ICF to pass through additional types of traffic, see Chapter 5, "Using Internet Connection Firewall."

Managing ICS

For the most part, ICS is easy to set up via the Network Setup Wizard and operates without any problems. However, there are a few settings you might need to change, depending on your desired Internet connection.

ICS Host Settings

You access the ICS and ICF settings for the shared Internet connection by opening Network Connections on the host computer. Right-click the shared Internet connection (the icon appears with a hand under it to indicate it is shared), and choose Properties. In the properties dialog box, click the Advanced button.

On the Advanced tab, shown in Figure 10-7, there are three options concerning ICS:

- **Allow Other Network Users To Connect Through This Computer's Internet Connection.** This option essentially enables or disables ICS. If you want to stop sharing the connection at some point in the future, clear this check box, which automatically clears the other check box options as well.

- **Establish A Dial-Up Connection Whenever A Computer On My Network Attempts To Access The Internet.** You'll only see this option if you are sharing a dial-up connection. This option allows Windows XP to automatically dial the connection when another computer in the workgroup attempts to use the Internet. If this selection is cleared, ICS clients will only be able to use the Internet when the ICS host computer is dialed up to the Internet. Under most circumstances, enabling this autodial setting is the best choice.

- **Allow Other Network Users To Control Or Disable The Shared Internet Connection.** This option, which is new in Windows XP, allows ICS clients to essentially control the connection. In a small home or office network, this setting might work well. Basically, users can manage the shared connection as though it was physically located on their computers. There are a few issues to consider though, and you can learn more about them in the next section.

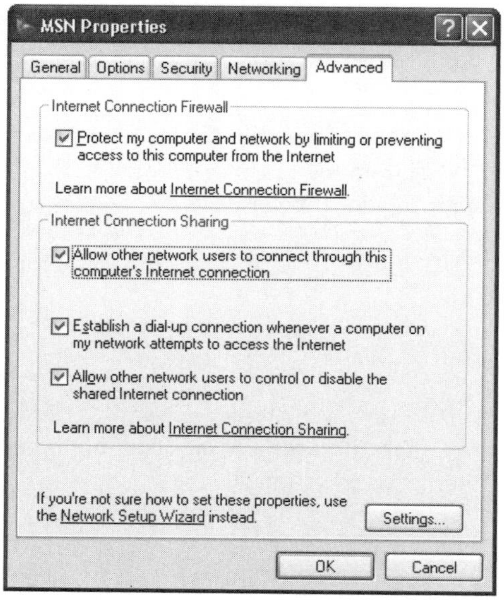

Figure 10-7. Manage ICS properties using the Advanced tab of the Internet connection's properties dialog box on the host computer.

ICS Client Connection Management

In previous versions of ICS, client management could be a problem. After all, what do you do if you do not have access to the ICS host computer, but you need to disconnect the dial-up Internet connection to free up a shared telephone line? How can you find out if the connection appears to be working? ICS in Windows XP addresses these problems by allowing users to control and disconnect the Internet connection from any ICS client computer (not just from the ICS host computer). This feature is provided by ICS Discovery and Control, which broadcasts availability of shared Internet connections from the host to client computers so they can use them. If you are using a broadband or always-on connection, these issues are not as important, but by default, client control of the Internet connection is enabled. When ICS Discovery and Control is in effect, the ICS host allows the ICS clients to *discover* the connection and manage it. Specifically, network clients can:

- View Internet connection statistics and monitor the status of the connection.

- Connect and disconnect the connection to the ISP.

- As long as the ICS host administrator does not disable ICS Discovery and Control by clearing the Allow Other Network Users To Control Or Disable The Shared Internet Connection check box on the Advanced tab of the shared connection's properties dialog box, clients can perform these actions. Once ICS is set up, ICS clients will see a category named Internet Gateway in the Network Connections folder, which contains the icon of the shared Internet connection, as shown in Figure 10-8.

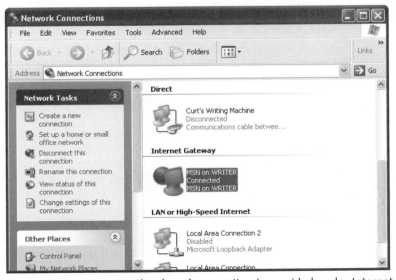

Figure 10-8.   Access to the shared connection is provided under Internet Gateway in Network Connections.

To use Internet Gateway to control the shared connection, follow these steps:

1 Right-click the connection listed under Internet Gateway and choose Status. A status dialog box appears, as shown in Figure 10-9. You can view the status, duration of the connection, its speed, and a count of packets sent and received through the gateway. Notice that you click Disconnect to close the connection. Of course, if other users are accessing the Internet at the time, they are disconnected as well.

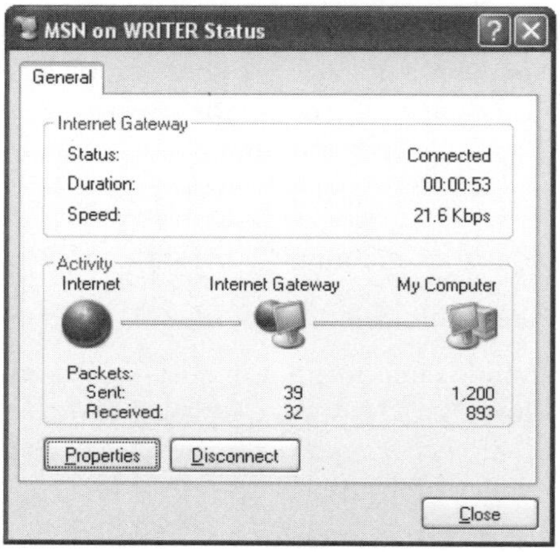

Figure 10-9. From the status dialog box, you can view the status of the Internet connection and disconnect it.

2 Click the Properties button. A simple dialog box appears telling you which connection you are using, as shown in Figure 10-10. You can select Show Icon In Notification Area When Connected at the bottom of this dialog box to give yourself quick access to this Internet connection from the Windows desktop. Click the Settings button.

3 The Services tab of the Advanced Settings dialog box appears, as shown in Figure 10-10. This dialog box lets you select which services you want ICF to allow to run on your network. By default, most of these services are disabled for security reasons, and you don't need to enable them for typical Internet activities. Do not enable any services that you don't actually need to use without knowing the security risks involved. See Chapter 5, "Using Internet Connection Firewall," to learn more about setting these ICF options.

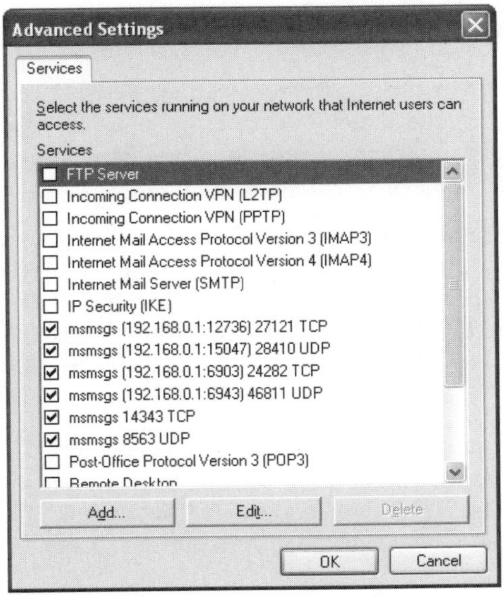

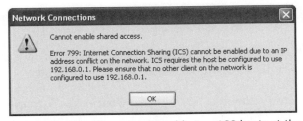

Figure 10-10. Use the Advanced Settings dialog box to configure ICF to allow or prohibit designated types of IP traffic.

Changing ICS Hosts

Networks, like life, change over time. You might add new client computers or remove existing client computers, or you might even need to change the Windows XP computer that is functioning as the ICS host. So you might wonder how you can change the ICF and ICS host computer on an established network that currently uses an ICS host, considering it is currently running the show.

Windows XP will not allow another computer on the network to become the ICS host until you remove ICS sharing on the original host. If you try to enable another computer as the ICS host, you'll receive the Network Connections error message shown in Figure 10-11.

Figure 10-11. You cannot enable two ICS hosts at the same time.

So, to change the ICS host to another computer, follow these steps:

1 Disable the ICS host computer by clearing the Allow Other Network Users To Connect Through This Computer's Internet Connection option on the Advanced tab of the Internet connection's properties dialog box. This will clear the former ICS host's IP address.

2 On the computer you want to become the new ICS host, run the Network Setup Wizard again, and select the option This Computer Connects Directly To The Internet. The Other Computers On My Network Connect To The Internet Through This Computer. When prompted, select the Internet connection directly connected to this computer that you will be sharing with the rest of the workgroup.

3 After the ICS host computer setup is complete, run the Network Setup Wizard on the client computers so that they will be configured to use the new ICS host. Select the option This Computer Connects To The Internet Through Another Computer On My Network Or Through A Residential Gateway for each client computer.

> **caution** Each time you run the Network Setup Wizard it will attempt to change the name of your workgroup to the default name, MSHOME. If this isn't the name you want, be alert and type in your own workgroup name each time. If your entire workgroup is not set to the same workgroup name, you will lose network connectivity.

Common Workgroup Problems and Solutions

You might run into problems with your network even though you've used the Network Setup Wizard. This section covers common problems you might encounter when setting up your workgroup.

Clients Cannot Connect

Client computers can only connect to each other if they have a proper IP address and subnet mask. Run the Network Setup Wizard again on the clients that are unable to connect. If you continue to have problems, make sure that the computers are physically connected to the network. See your networking hardware documentation for additional information and troubleshooting tips. Also, see Chapter 12, "Solving Connectivity Problems," to learn about additional tools and troubleshooting steps to help you.

Windows 95 Clients Cannot Connect

The Network Setup Wizard is not supported on Windows 95, Windows NT 4.0, or Windows 2000 clients. However, you can manually configure these computers to access the network. Simply configure them to use DHCP to automatically receive IP configuration information. Make sure you also install Client For Microsoft Networks and File And Printer Sharing For Microsoft Networks on each computer. See the Windows 95 help files for more information.

Manually Assigned Static IP Addresses Cause Conflicts or Access Problems

In most cases, your best solution to conflicts caused from incorrectly assigned static IP addresses is to allow Windows XP to automatically assign IP addresses using APIPA by running the Network Setup Wizard. However, if you do assign static addresses manually, you need to make sure they are all in the same IP address range and subnet. See "Understanding TCP/IP in Depth," page 24, to learn more about TCP/IP.

The ICS Host Does Not Work

If the ICS host does not seem to be working, make sure the ICS service is running by following these steps:

1 Choose Start, Control Panel, and open Administrative Tools. Then open Computer Management.

2 In the Computer Management console, expand Services And Applications in the left pane, and select Services.

3 In the right pane, locate Internet Connection Firewall (ICF)/Internet Connection Sharing (ICS) and make sure that the service is started, as shown in Figure 10-12.

4 If the service does not appear to be started, right-click the service and choose Start.

If the ICS host still doesn't work, try manually connecting to the Internet and using the Internet to ensure that your Internet connection is working. If you are using a dial-up connection, check the Advanced tab of its properties dialog box to ensure that the Establish A Dial-Up Connection Whenever A Computer On My Network Attempts To Access The Internet option is selected.

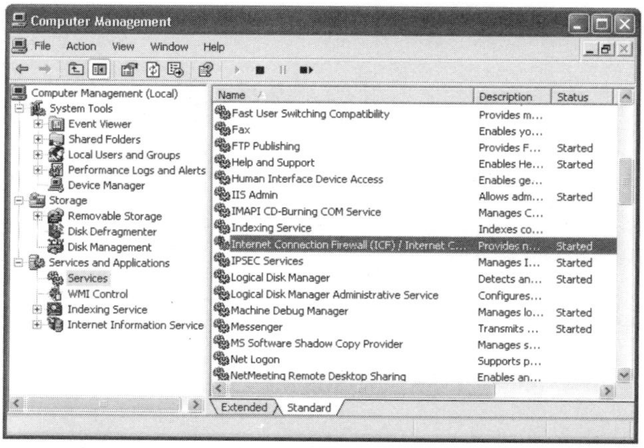

Figure 10-12. Check the Status column to ensure that the ICF/ICS service is Started.

Internet Usage with ICS Is Slow

Remember that if multiple computers are using a single Internet connection, you might experience a slowdown in browsing performance. This is particularly likely if you are using a dial-up connection or if other users are downloading multimedia files or using streaming media. You might also see a slowdown if the ICS computer is heavily burdened.

A Client Can Connect to Other Network Clients, But None Can Connect to Him

When one computer on the network can't be contacted by others on the network, most likely ICF is enabled on the LAN NIC of the computer that others can't connect to. ICF will not allow network traffic when it is enabled on the LAN's NIC. To resolve this problem, open the LAN's properties dialog box, select the Advanced tab, and clear the option in the Internet Connection Firewall dialog box.

> **caution** Be careful to disable ICF on the LAN connection, *not* on the Internet connection.

ICS Clients Cannot Autodial an AOL Connection

Some ISPs, such as AOL, do not use Windows Dial-Up Networking. In this case, you must manually establish an Internet connection from the ICS host before ICS clients can access the Internet.

> For an entire chapter dedicated to troubleshooting network problems and the tools you can use to help resolve these problems, see Chapter 12, "Solving Connectivity Problems."

Understanding Domain Connectivity

In small office and home networks, the workgroup design is often the best solution, and Microsoft Windows XP gives you all that you need to create a highly effective workgroup. However, large networks quickly outgrow the workgroup model because there is no centralized administration and security. The solution is to create a Microsoft domain-based network. Because domains can be very large and complex, and are run by network administrators, the details of administering a domain are beyond the scope of this book. This chapter discusses the components that make up a domain as well as the use of Windows XP Professional in a domain environment including information on how to join a domain, how to use the domain's resources, and how to leave the domain.

> **note** Windows XP Home Edition can access some shared resources in a domain but cannot join a Windows domain. See "Accessing Domain Resources from Windows XP Home Edition" on page 344 for more information. Windows XP Professional is the appropriate version of Windows XP to use for domain-based computing.

Understanding Active Directory Domains

Before you log on to a domain from your Windows XP Professional computer, it's important to understand the fundamental differences between a domain and a workgroup.

311

To read about computing with Windows XP in a workgroup environment, see Chapter 10, "Managing Workgroup Connections."

The Microsoft Windows 2000 line of server products introduced a new Windows domain architecture based on *Active Directory,* the underlying directory service that manages domain resources. Although some fundamentals of Active Directory domains are similar to those in Microsoft Windows NT 4.0 and earlier networks, Active Directory domains are fundamentally more powerful and flexible. This chapter focuses entirely on Active Directory domains because Windows NT 4.0–style domains have been phased out in most organizations.

For more information about the Active Directory directory service and its role in Windows domains, see "Active Directory," page 319.

Domains are centrally managed. This fact drives how domains work and how Windows XP Professional functions within a domain. Network administrators manage the domain's resources, which include the network's shared computers, printers, devices, software services, and users. The domain is run on various computers known as *servers* that are dedicated to providing network services and storage space for applications and data. Some servers *serve* applications to the network users and offer shared disk space for user files. Other servers, known as *domain controllers,* are responsible for such administrative activities of the network as authenticating users who want to sign on to the network. Servers run one of the server editions of Windows, such as Windows 2000 Server or Windows 2000 Advanced Server. The server versions of Windows enable network administrators to secure the domain and control which users can sign on and what they can do after they are connected to the domain.

Domain Servers

The domain controller mentioned in the preceding section is one type of server used to administer a domain. There are several different roles in which Windows Active Directory–based servers can be used. The following list gives you a quick overview of the more common roles:

- **Domain controller.** Domain controllers are used to manage user authentication and communication with other domains. Each domain must have at least one domain controller (although typically more than one domain controller is used to provide redundancy and to help balance network load). Active Directory domain controllers maintain the Active Directory database, which keeps track of all users, computers, and shared resources.

- **Member server.** Active Directory servers that are not domain controllers are known as *member servers.* They can function as print servers or file servers or can act in other specialized roles, such as those mentioned in this list.

- **Dynamic Host Configuration Protocol (DHCP) server.** A DHCP server assigns IP configuration data to network clients and makes sure that each client computer has a unique IP address. In a nutshell, the DHCP server handles all IP addressing automatically so that each client has network connectivity. You can learn more about TCP/IP and DHCP in Chapter 2, "Configuring TCP/IP and Other Protocols."

● **Domain Name System (DNS) server.** Active Directory networks use DNS, the same naming system widely used on the Internet, to uniquely identify network computers. DNS uses discrete names, such as www.microsoft.com, to organize all client and domain names. You can read more about DNS in "Domain Name System (DNS)" on page 24.

● **Windows Internet Naming Service (WINS) server.** WINS is used rather than DNS in pre–Active Directory networks as the default Windows naming service. In environments where older client computers, servers, and applications requiring NetBIOS name resolution are used, WINS servers can be provided for backward compatibility.

● **Terminal server.** *Terminal Services* is a program that runs on a Terminal server and allows clients to log on to the Terminal server and run applications directly from it, as though they were logged on the computer locally.

InsideOut

Managing Multiple Server Roles on One Computer

Several server roles are often combined on one server. For example, a domain controller can also be a DNS server, or a DHCP server can also be a Terminal server. Because each server role is accomplished by running a software program called a *service* on a designated computer, you can run all of these services on one server. This saves the cost and complexity of configuring multiple machines.

One problem network administrators face, however, is *load balancing*, which is the art of distributing network activity across several machines so that the network doesn't slow down due to bottlenecks on overused servers. Because of the demands placed on servers by network clients, there are often dedicated DNS or DHCP servers as well as dedicated file and print servers. This frees up the domain controllers to focus on their primary tasks instead of providing all of these additional services. Another reason to use multiple computers is to eliminate single points of failure. If one server in the domain should fail, it will not bring down multiple services. For even higher reliability, multiple computers can be used to provide *fault tolerance*, a model in which more than one server is used for each server role. If one server should fail, another can take over its functions automatically and keep the network running while repairs are made to the failed server.

As you might imagine, each server entails additional costs in terms of hardware and administrative overhead. Therefore, the decisions about the number of servers to use and how they will be managed can be difficult and complex issues for network planners.

Understanding Domain Structure

A number of components come together to provide the features and functionality of an Active Directory domain. There are three essential structural components:

- The domain
- The organizational unit (OU)
- The site

The basic unit of organization in an Active Directory network is the domain. A *domain* is a logical grouping of users and computers for administrative and security purposes. Notice that the term *logical* is used. The design of the domain is based on administration and security issues, not where the computers are physically located. In fact, a domain can hold computers located in one physical building, distributed across a corporate campus, or even spread out around the world. In the following illustration, the domain exists in a single office building. Domain controllers and other necessary servers reside at the same location and service the needs of clients. One or more administrators manage the network.

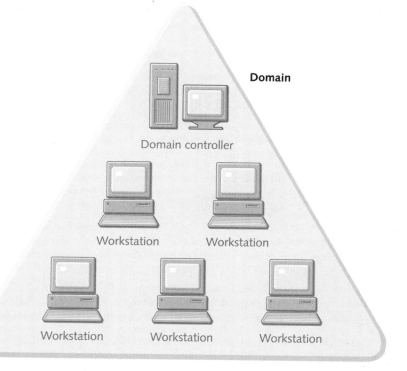

However, a domain can also encompass multiple locations and require wide area network (WAN) links, as shown in the following illustration.

Chapter 11: Understanding Domain Connectivity

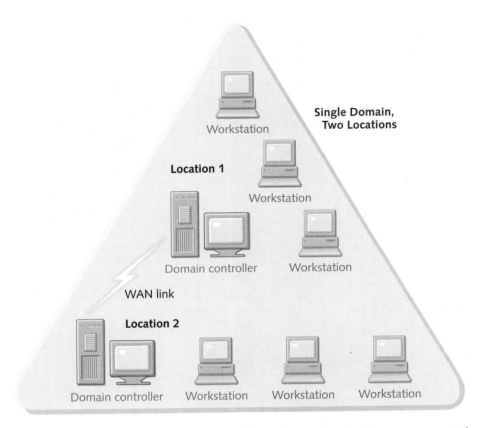

As the figure shows, there are two locations, but only one domain. Users are connected between the locations with a WAN link, but there is still only one domain. So, the domain is a logical grouping used for administrative purposes. Active Directory networks can contain thousands of users and computers in a single domain. In fact, many large networks function with a single domain.

But in some cases, different domains are necessary for the same network environment. Perhaps your company consists of a corporate headquarters and a manufacturing plant, and that security needs and user administration are completely different at the corporate headquarters and the manufacturing plant. In this case, two different domains might be preferred to implement different security standards and different administrative needs.

The problem is that domains are expensive, both in terms of computer hardware (multiple servers) and administrative personnel (more administrators). Multiple domains also can be difficult and complex in terms of communicating and accessing resources between the two domains. For this reason, network planners always prefer to use one domain whenever possible. Multiple domains are only used when portions of a network have very different security or administrative needs than other portions.

Chapter 11

However, what if you need to make some divisions within a domain without making major security or administrative changes? What if one administrator needs to control a portion of the domain and another needs to administer a different portion? In this case, network administrators create *organizational units (OUs)*. An OU is a unit of administration that is created within a domain. In the following illustration, there is one domain, but within the domain, three OUs have been established along administrative boundaries so that the Marketing, Production, and Sales groups are handled by different administrators.

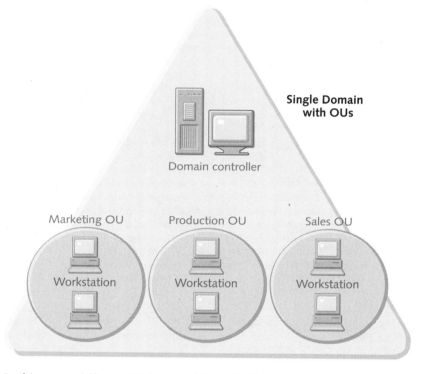

Single Domain with OUs

Domain controller

Marketing OU

Production OU

Sales OU

Workstation

Workstation

Workstation

In this case, a different OU is created for each division, and all users and shared resources for each division are stored within that division's OU. Domain administrators can delegate control of each OU to different administrators. The good news is that everything is still within the same domain and handled by the same domain controllers, but different administrators can control different portions of the domain.

OUs can be used for a variety of purposes, depending on the organizational needs of the business. Because OUs are used to *organize* data or users for management purposes, there are a number of possible applications:

● In many environments, different departments or company divisions are managed with OUs. This helps organize resources such as printers, helps to manage which users have permission to use which resources, and allows different administrators to manage different portions of the network.

- In some cases, OUs are also used to manage different classes of resources. For example, there might be a Users OU, a Shared Folder OU, a Printers OU, and so forth. Administrative responsibilities are handled based on resources—one administrator might only handle user accounts, whereas another might manage shared printers. This feature helps keep the resources organized and easy to manage.

- OUs can also be based on locations. If your domain spans Houston, Los Angeles, Seattle, and Phoenix, each physical location could function as an OU so that local administrators could manage each physical location.

There are many different applications for OUs that give networks the flexibility they need while keeping the single domain model. This structure fixed many problems that administrators often faced in Windows NT networks, where domains tended to grow out of control and were difficult to manage.

Active Directory networks also enable you to manage physical network locations by organizing them as sites. A *site* is a physical location where bandwidth between network clients is considered fast and inexpensive. For example, users located in one building might be considered a site because they all belong to a local area network (LAN). However, other users in the same domain might reside in a different site across town because a WAN link is required to link the two sites together.

So, if Active Directory uses domains and OUs to organize resources and administration, why are sites even needed? There are two primary reasons:

- **Traffic.** Sites help Active Directory determine which locations are local and which ones are not. LAN bandwidth is usually inexpensive and fast. However, if you have to use a WAN link between locations, its speed is often slower and can even be costly to the company. Sites help Active Directory know where the slower and more expensive links reside so that it can help optimize traffic from one site to the next.

- **Replication.** Active Directory domain controllers function in a peer fashion. Each contains a copy of the Active Directory database, and they all have to replicate its contents with each other to make sure that information is up-to-date and redundant in case one server goes down. For example, suppose you're an administrator. You add a user to the network using a domain controller. That domain controller then replicates the change to another domain controller, and the process continues until all the domain controllers have the same information. This replication traffic can occur frequently, which can be a big problem over a WAN link. So, sites are used to help Active Directory know how to control replication between domain controllers based on where the domain controllers physically reside.

Sites, OUs, and domains are all important to the structure, management, and functionality of an Active Directory domain-based network.

Chapter 11

Controlling Traffic by Using Sites

In networks where different sites are used, controlling traffic is very important, and this is one reason that Active Directory enables network administrators to define sites.

Consider this example: Your network consists of one domain, but you have offices in New York and Tampa. A WAN link connects the two offices so that resources can be shared, but the WAN link is expensive and often unreliable, so you want to keep traffic local as much as possible. In addition, suppose that Sally, a user in Tampa, needs to log on to her Windows XP Professional computer. Her logon request is sent to a domain controller, but without site definitions, a domain controller in the New York office might authenticate her. Rather than having what should be local traffic bounce around between New York and Tampa, sites help define the locations and make sure that user logons and resource traffic stay local. In Sally's case, because she resides in Tampa, she would never be authenticated by a domain controller in New York unless all domain controllers in Tampa were unavailable. Sites allow Active Directory to act as a traffic cop so that precious WAN bandwidth is used only when necessary.

Domain Name System

You understand that sites, domains, and OUs are used to structure the Windows network and that different servers are used to manage that structure and the available resources. However, how does each computer keep track of other computers and users as well as shared folders and other resources? In an Active Directory environment, domains are named just like Internet sites. For example, if your company is named TailSpin Toys, your network name might be tailspintoys.com. Tailspintoys.com can be an Internet Web site, but it can also be the name of your internal network. A user, Sally, can have the logon name of sally@tailspintoys.com, which functions as an e-mail address as well. DNS integration simplifies naming strategies and makes private network and Internet naming schemes the same.

InsideOut

Using Unique DNS Names for Multiple Domains

In environments where multiple domains are used, different domain names must also be used. For example, your company might have a New York domain and a London domain. The domain names can be completely different, such as tailspintoys.com and wingtiptoys.com, but this isolates the two domains from each other into two separate *forests* in Active Directory nomenclature. An alternative would be to set up two domains named newyork.tailspintoys.com and london.tailspintoys.com. Because these two domains share the same root domain name (tailspintoys.com), they are said to be in the same *tree* as well as in a single forest. Domains that share a common root name in this way automatically have a *trust* established between them, which makes the sharing of resources and the maintenance of the network much easier. In this example, london.tailspintoys.com and newyork.tailspintoys.com are considered *child domains*, and tailspintoys.com is the *parent domain*. It's possible to continue creating child domains to whatever depth is needed, although more depth adds more complexity. If a new production plant opens in New York and needs to be a separate domain, it might be called production.newyork.tailspintoys.com. Carrying the example further, if the production plant needs to again divide into another domain, it could be named division.production.newyork.tailspintoys.com. Naming structures can become long and complex, so a lot of planning has to be done by network administrators to keep the domain structure as simple as possible. Using OUs within a domain can often avoid the need to create an excess of child domains.

note Only domains are named using the DNS naming structure. OUs are logical containers and do not use DNS names.

Active Directory

Active Directory is the Windows directory service introduced with Windows 2000 Server. A *directory service* catalogs network resources and data, such as user accounts, computer accounts, OUs, shared printers, folders, and just about anything else that might be available on the network. Active Directory manages the entire network environment, and all domain controllers maintain a copy of the Active Directory database. So, where is Active Directory located? Active Directory maintains its catalog on each domain controller, and each domain controller replicates with partner domain controllers to keep the database synchronized, to provide fault tolerance, and to provide low latency.

In the past, Windows NT networks used a Primary Domain Controller (PDC) and multiple Backup Domain Controllers (BDCs) to manage the network, but all domain controllers in Active Directory domains function as peers. Instead of one PDC, each domain controller can be used to manage the network, and Active Directory data is replicated to other domain controllers.

Domain administrators manage Active Directory through three Microsoft Management Console (MMC) snap-in tools, namely Active Directory Sites And Services, Active Directory Trusts, and Active Directory Users And Computers. All user accounts, computer accounts, and even OUs are created and managed from within Active Directory. Figure 11-1 on the next page shows you the Active Directory Users And Computers tool found on a Windows 2000 domain controller.

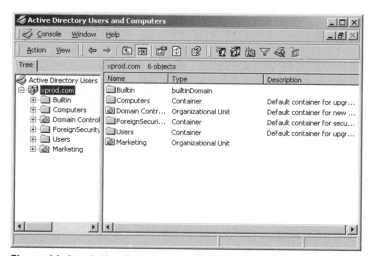

Figure 11-1. Active Directory Users And Computers is one of three Active Directory MMC tools used to administer Active Directory.

Group Policy

Group Policy was introduced with Windows 2000. *Group Policy* is a management tool that enables domain administrators to centrally control a number of settings on client computers. For example, you can configure specific security settings, applications, desktop settings, and even desktop wallpaper on each domain user's computer. Using Group Policy, network administrators can standardize all of the computers in a site, domain, or OU in any way that is desirable.

Group Policy is applied at the site, domain, and OU levels—in that order. Policies can also apply to individual computers or to user accounts, as appropriate. Computer policies are applied before user policies

For example, if a computer account resides in the Dallas site, in the tailspintoys.com domain, and in the Production OU, *computer* policies from the Dallas site are applied when a user starts the computer. The domain computer policies are applied next, and then OU computer policies are applied. When a user logs on, any *user* policies at the Dallas site are applied, then the domain user policies, and then the OU user policies. In the event that a conflict occurs between different policies, higher-level policies supersede lower-level policies (for instance, OU policies override those defined on the local computer).

Group Policy also applies to a Windows XP Professional client computer connected to a Windows 2000 domain. In fact, Windows XP Professional contains a local Group Policy console where you, as the local computer administrator, can apply certain settings to anyone who logs on to your computer. For example, you can apply certain Microsoft Internet Explorer settings and additional logon settings; these are mentioned throughout this book where applicable. However, when your Windows XP Professional stand-alone computer joins an Active Directory domain, any conflicting local policies are superseded by any site, domain, or OU policies. In other words, local Group Policy is the weakest form of Group Policy when your computer resides in a domain environment, but it becomes active again whenever the computer is disconnected from the domain and operates as a stand-alone computer.

InsideOut

Protection in a Domain Environment

Windows XP's support of Internet Connection Firewall (ICF) and the security features included in Internet Explorer 6 are designed for home networks and small offices. However, what about security in a domain-based network? In domain environments, servers handle the connections to the Internet as well as e-mail. Typically, devices such as *proxy servers* are used to function as the *proxy* or agent between internal network clients and the Internet. The proxy server's job is to retrieve information from the Internet on behalf of network clients, so as not to expose those network clients to the Internet directly. In this case, some of the local security features available in Windows XP are not needed because the proxy servers provide the necessary security. In fact, if you enable one of those features, such as ICF, in a domain environment, you might lose connectivity. You can learn more about proxy servers, firewalls, and ICF in Chapter 5, "Internet Connection Firewall."

Running Windows XP Professional in a Domain Environment

To take advantage of the previously mentioned domain services, it's important to understand the fundamental differences of how authentication is handled by domains and workgroups.

When you are a member of a workgroup, the user accounts are stored locally on the computer. For example, you might have a user account called *Diane* and a password for that account. If you want to log on to each Windows XP computer in the workgroup, each computer must be set up with the *Diane* account in User Accounts or Computer Management. You cannot move from computer to computer and log on with the *Diane* account until each computer has the account set up in its local security database. This isn't a major problem when your home network or small office has a few computers and a few users, but imagine how complex and time-consuming it would be to set up a network for a company with hundreds of employees.

In a domain environment, the domain controllers hold the local security database, and network administrators manage user and computer accounts. A network administrator assigns you a user name and password, and configures an account for you in Active Directory. When you log on to any Windows XP Professional workstation in the domain, a Windows logon dialog box appears, and you enter your assigned user name and password. The user name and password are sent to a domain controller for authentication. You are then logged on to the workstation, and your computer and user account are active on the network. Because the user accounts are not configured on each local computer, you can log on to any workstation using your user name and password.

Once you are logged on to the domain, all of the features of a domain environment, including Group Policy, are available to you on your Windows XP Professional workstation. In short, when you log on to a Windows domain, a network administrator becomes the administrator for your local computer and can invoke settings and configurations, even without your permission. The workgroup environment where you call the shots is quite different than a domain environment where network administrators are in control.

Joining a Domain

To join a Windows domain, you'll need a few essential items set up and ready before you can actually join:

- A network administrator must create a computer account for you. Contact your network administrator for assistance.

- A network administrator must create a user name and password for you. You'll need this information, along with the name of the domain, when you configure your computer to join a domain. When the network administrator creates the user account, he or she must make certain that the account has the right to add a computer to a domain. By default the Domain Admins group has this right, but in Active Directory domains the administrator can assign the right to any user or other group. Unless told otherwise by your network administrator, you should assume that only a user with administrative privileges can join the computer to the domain.

- In most cases your computer's network connection to the domain should be set to obtain its IP address automatically so that a domain server known as a DHCP server can provide an available IP address for your computer. For more information about DHCP, see "Dynamic and Static Addressing," page 27.

- Your computer must be configured with a network interface card (NIC) and be physically connected to the network. See "Installing NICs" on page 68 for details.

- You must be using Windows XP Professional. Windows XP Home Edition cannot join a Windows domain.

Joining a Domain with Wizard Help

Windows XP Professional can help you join a domain with the help of the Network Identification Wizard. You can also manually join the domain, which you can learn more about in "Joining a Domain Manually" on page 327. To join a Windows domain using a wizard, follow these steps:

1 Log on to Windows XP Professional with an administrator account.

note You cannot join a domain unless you first log on to the local computer with an account that has administrative privileges. If you don't have access to such an account, contact your network administrator to help you.

2 Choose Start, Control Panel, and open System.

3 In the System Properties dialog box, select the Computer Name tab. This tab contains the Computer Description box, the Network ID button, and the Change button, as shown in Figure 11-2.

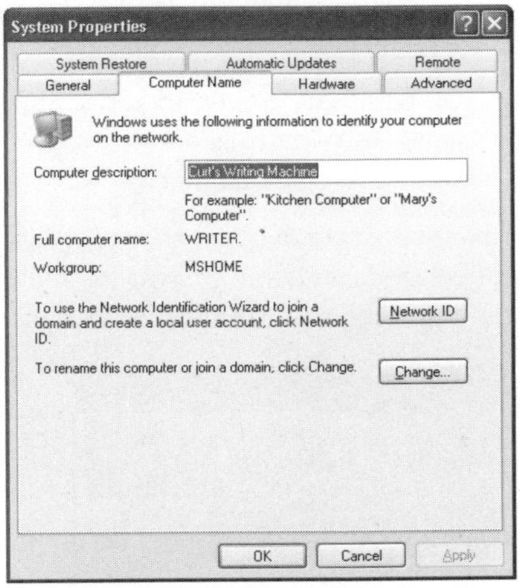

Figure 11-2. The Computer Name tab of the System Properties dialog box is the starting place for joining a domain.

4 Click the Network ID button to open the Network Identification Wizard, which will guide you through the rest of the process. Click Next on the first page that appears.

5 The Connecting To The Network page asks you if the computer will be part of a business network or if it is a home/small office computer, as shown in Figure 11-3 on the next page. To join a domain, select This Computer Is Part Of A Business Network, And I Use It To Connect To Other Computers At Work. Click Next.

Chapter 11

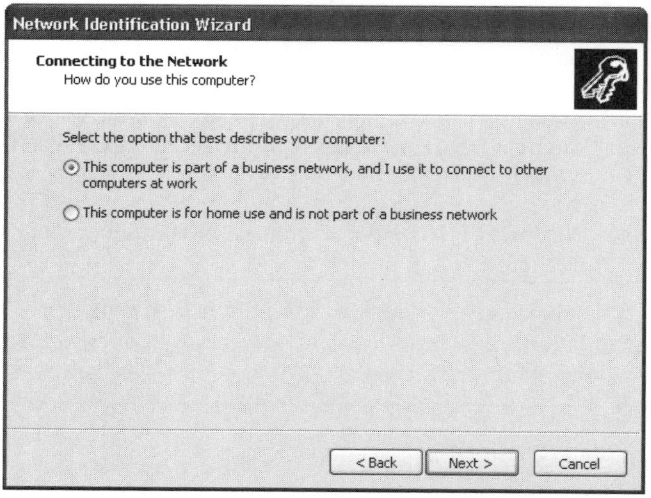

Figure 11-3.   Select the first option if you want your Windows XP Professional computer to join a domain-based network.

6 On the second Connecting To The Network page, select My Company Uses A Network With A Domain and click Next.

7 The information provided tells you what you'll need to join the domain. You'll need a user name, a password, the domain's name, and possibly some computer name information. After reading this page, click Next.

8 On the User Account And Domain Information page, shown in Figure 11-4, enter the user name, password, and domain name created for you by the network administrator. Keep in mind that the password is case sensitive. Click Next.

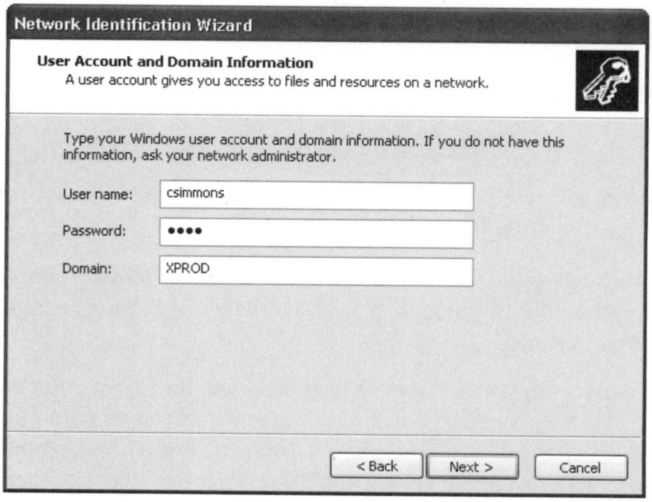

Figure 11-4.   Enter your user name, password, and the name of the domain you want to join.

Chapter 11: Understanding Domain Connectivity

9 If the Computer Domain page appears, you will also need to enter your computer's name (displayed on the Computer Name tab in the Full Computer Name field) and the computer's domain. (It is possible for a computer to belong to a different domain than the user account.) If the page appears, enter the requested information and click Next.

> **note** If you attempt to join the domain with the name and password of a user account that doesn't have administrative privileges or that hasn't been explicitly delegated permission to add the computer to the domain, you will see the Domain User Name And Password dialog box. Either you or a network administrator will have to type the user name, password, and domain of a user with administrative privileges to complete the process of joining the domain. Click OK to continue.

10 On the User Account page, shown in Figure 11-5, you can choose the account you just registered (or another user account in the domain), so that the user account can gain access to local system resources as well as the network resources. Click Next to continue.

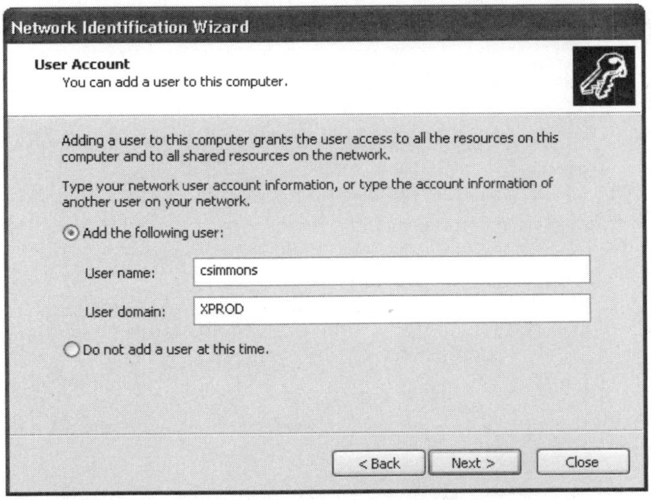

Figure 11-5. Use this page of the wizard to add a user to the local computer. Only users with a domain account can be added on this page.

11 If you choose to add a user, the Access Level page, shown in Figure 11-6 on the next page, appears. Select the level of access that you want the user to have to local computer resources: Standard User, Restricted User, or Other. This feature lets you limit what the user can do on the local machine or lets you give the user administrative privileges on the local computer (by selecting

Other and selecting Administrator from the list). Although the user's privileges on the network are centrally set in Active Directory by a network administrator, this page lets the user access the local computer with the same user name, even though the level of access on the local computer can be different than the permissions the user has on the network. Make a selection and click Next.

> **note** If the network isn't running, users can't be authenticated on the domain, but they can still log on locally because Windows XP keeps a cached copy of the domain account.

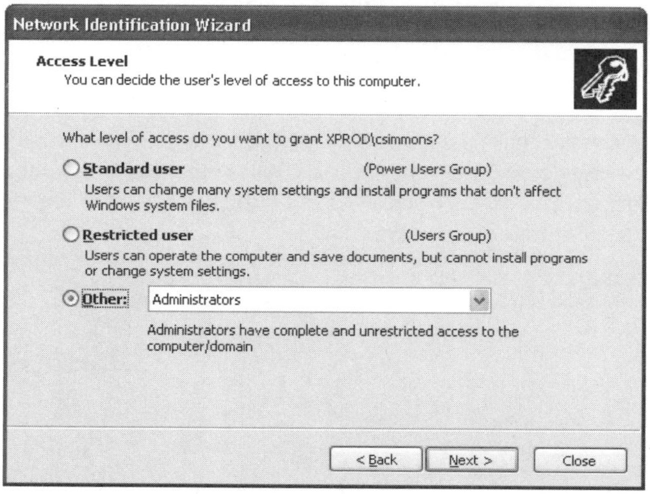

Figure 11-6. The Access Level page lets you set the level of access the user will have on the local computer.

12 Click Finish on the final page of the wizard, and restart the computer when prompted.

InsideOut

Understanding the Syntax for Signing on to the Domain

Microsoft Windows NT networks use the NetBIOS naming scheme for user accounts, which uses short names to represent computers and network objects. For example, a NetBIOS domain name might be Xprod. Users logging on to a Windows NT domain use the *domainname\username* convention, such as xprod\csimmons. However, Windows 2000 networks use the Domain Name System (DNS) naming standard, as does the Internet. For example, a company with a public URL of www.tailspintoys.com might have a corporate domain name of xprod.tailspintoys.com (unlike the URL, this domain is not visible to the public). DNS user names use the popular form of e-mail addresses, such as csimmons@xprod.tailspintoys.com. For this reason, you can type your user name in the form *username@domainname* when you are first joining a network or when logging on. If you choose to use this format for your user name when you log on, the dialog box that normally lists the domain will become grayed out because you have already specified the domain name as a part of the user name.

Joining a Domain Manually

The Network Identification Wizard helps you join a domain, but you can also join a domain by clicking the Change button on the Computer Name tab of the System Properties dialog box. This option reduces the wizard to a single dialog box, shown in Figure 11-7. Enter your computer's name in the Computer Name box and make sure Member Of is set to Domain. Type in the domain name if it isn't already listed in the box. Click OK. In the dialog box that appears, enter the user name and password of your domain account. You'll need to restart your computer once you complete the joining process.

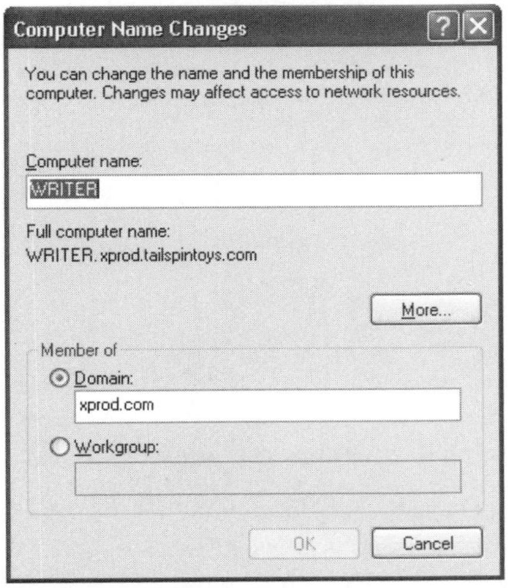

Figure 11-7. Enter the domain name and click OK to manually join the domain.

Logging On to a Windows Domain

Once you have restarted your computer, you'll notice that a few things are different. The Windows XP Welcome screen no longer appears. That's right, you can't select your local user account and log on from the Welcome screen. Rather, you see the Welcome To Windows dialog box, which instructs you to press Ctrl+Alt+Delete to start logging on. Next, you see the Log On To Windows dialog box where you enter your user name and password. If the dialog box is in its collapsed form, click the Options button to expand it. The Log On To box lets you choose to log on to the local computer or the domain. Click OK to finish logging on.

In fact, you'll find more changes than the way you log on:

● Fast User Switching is not available when you are logged on to a domain. Only one user can be logged on to a computer at a time when the computer is connected to a domain.

● The automatic logon is not supported. However, see the Inside Out tip on this page.

● There are no password hints available should you forget your password.

● When you log off or shut down the computer, you see the Log Off Windows or Shut Down Windows dialog box, which resembles the way you log off or shut down Windows 2000.

> There are other changes to the appearance of Windows XP Professional after you join a domain. To learn more, see "Surveying Windows XP Changes in a Domain Setting," page 330.

InsideOut

Bypassing the Logon Screen

Automatic logon does not work when you are set up to log on to a Windows domain, or at least it first appears that way. In fact, you can bypass the Ctrl+Alt+Delete Welcome To Windows dialog box and Log On To Windows dialog box when you log on to a domain from a Windows XP Professional computer. The question is should you?

Keep in mind that if these two dialog boxes are disabled, anyone who can physically access your computer can log on to the domain. This is because autologon stores your user name and password in the registry and uses this information to log on. If a user can simply start your computer, logon will occur automatically, which can be a very serious security breach, depending on your network. You should check with your network administrator to see if autologon is supported because many domain security tools will not allow autologon to be used.

However, if you work on a small network where security is not an issue, you can use autologon by performing the steps that follow. But note that these steps require a registry change, and great care should be taken when editing the registry because incorrect settings can keep your computer from starting:

1 Log on to the local computer with an administrator account. You cannot perform these steps while logged on to the domain.

2 Choose Start, Run.

3 In the Run dialog box, type **regedit** and press Enter.

4 When Registry Editor opens, navigate to HKLM\Software\Microsoft\ Windows NT\CurrentVersion\Winlogon.

5 Select Winlogon in the left pane, select AutoAdminLogon in the right pane, and press Enter. In the Value Data box, type **1** and press Enter. (This enables autologon.)

6 Next, select DefaultUserName in the right pane and press Enter. Type the user name of the domain account you want to use when you automatically log on.

7 Select DefaultDomainName, and make sure it is set to the name of the domain you want to automatically log on to. If it is set to the local computer name, press Enter, type the domain name, and press Enter again.

8 Open DefaultPassword in the right pane, and type the password for the user name.

If the DefaultPassword value does not exist, create a new string with this value. Choose Edit, New, String Value. Type the name of the value as **DefaultPassword** and press Enter. Press Enter again, and type the password in the Value Data field.

Notice that your password is stored in plain text in this key. Anyone who turns on your computer and logs on automatically using this method can also open the registry to this key and obtain your password.

9 Close Registry Editor. You can now log on automatically.

If you later decide to disable autologon, simply open User Accounts in Control Panel. On the Users tab, select Users Must Enter A User Name And Password To Use This Computer. Click OK. The AutoAdminLogon value in the registry will be reset to 0, which disables the feature.

Chapter 11

Ensuring That You Have Logged On to the Domain

Once you log on, you can make certain that you are in fact logged on to the domain by opening the Computer Name tab of the System Properties dialog box. Figure 11-8 indicates that the computer is logged on to the domain.

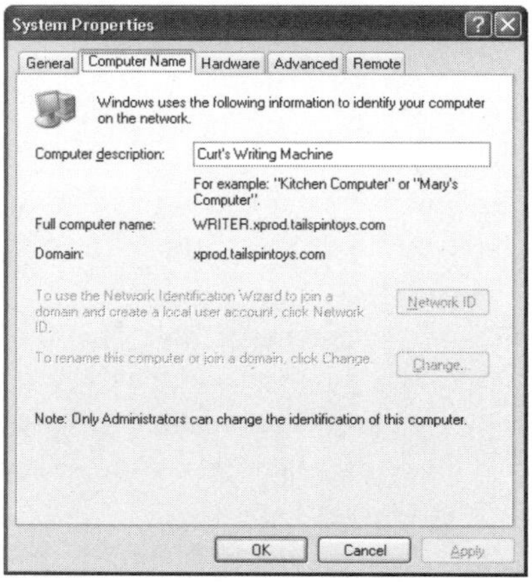

Figure 11-8. Check the Domain field of the Computer Name tab to confirm that you're logged on to the domain.

Surveying Windows XP Changes in a Domain Setting

After you have completed the logon process, you'll notice several differences in the Windows XP interface when connected to a domain. Some of these changes are major, while others are just minor differences that make Windows XP look more like Windows 2000, which most domain users will be more familiar with. These options won't radically change the way you use Windows XP, but they might stump you if you are not expecting them!

Start Menu

The Start menu looks and acts the same, as shown in Figure 11-9, but there is one minor difference: the Start menu displays your full name as stored in your domain user account instead of your user name.

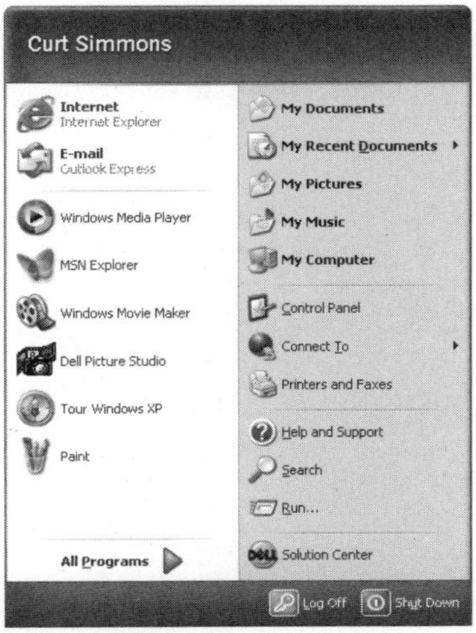

Figure 11-9. The Start menu now displays your name as stored in your domain user account.

Ctrl+Alt+Delete

When you use Windows XP on a stand-alone computer or in a workgroup, the Task Manager appears when you press Ctrl+Alt+Delete. When you configure Windows XP Professional to log on to a Windows domain, the Windows Security dialog box appears instead. In this dialog box, you can choose Lock The Computer, Log Off, Change Password, or Task Manager. Choose Task Manager to use it as you would with Windows XP in a workgroup situation. This of course is not a major change, but it is one that can cause some confusion.

User Accounts

In Windows XP, User Accounts in Control Panel is used to manage your local user accounts. When you configure Windows XP Professional to log on to a Windows domain, User Accounts still appears in Control Panel, but its interface changes, as shown in Figure 11-10 on the next page.

note If the domain user account that you used to log on to the domain does not have administrative privileges on the local machine as well, a dialog box will appear. This dialog box prompts you to enter the user name and password of a local account that does have administrative privileges, which allows you to make changes to user accounts.

Figure 11-10. The User Accounts interface changes when you are logged on to a Windows domain.

User Accounts gives you a simple way to add, remove, and manage local user accounts. You can also reset passwords. Keep in mind that these accounts only affect the local computer, not the domain. Users with a valid domain name and password can still log on to the domain at the local computer using that name and password. Any user who wants to log on to the local computer but not the domain, however, must have a valid user name and password configured in User Accounts on the local machine.

On the Advanced tab, shown in Figure 11-11, you can manage passwords. This option allows you to use different passwords to access other network resources during the

Figure 11-11. The Advanced tab contains account and password management features.

current session. You can manage passwords such as saved dial-up or virtual private network (VPN) passwords or your .NET Passport. You can also open the Local Users And Groups console (which is also available in Computer Management) where local users and groups can be managed. In addition, you can require that users press Ctrl+Alt+Delete before logging on.

InsideOut

Why Use Ctrl+Alt+Delete to Log On?

Pressing Ctrl+Alt+Delete during logon is a security measure that can help protect your computer and network security. Universally, programs running on Windows cannot intercept the Ctrl+Alt+Delete keystroke, except Winlogon.exe, the Windows service that enables logging on and logging off. Virus programs known as *Trojan horses* can present a fake logon dialog box when you start up your computer. If you were to type your user name and password into such a rogue dialog box the Trojan horse could steal your name and password. However, requiring Ctrl+Alt+Delete to be pressed when logging on ensures that the next dialog box you see is the authentic Log On To Windows dialog box. When you set Windows XP to require you to press Ctrl+Alt+Delete to log on, you can rest assured that the logon dialog box presented to you is authentic.

Aside from these changes, joining a domain also adds two global security groups to your local account database. These group additions are Domain Admins and Domain Users. The purpose of these group additions is to give users who log on to your computer certain rights. For example, users who log on to your computer as members of the Domain Admins group can log on locally to your computer and have all the rights and privileges that a local administrator has. Users that are members of the Domain Users group have the same local permissions that a limited user has in Windows XP.

So, which group do you belong to? The Domain Admins group is a powerful group that typically contains domain administrators. Your account is a member of the Domain Users group by default. You can examine the group memberships by opening the Local Users And Computers console found in Computer Management or by selecting the Advanced tab of User Accounts and clicking the Advanced button. Select Groups in the left pane, and double-click the desired group account in the right console pane to open its properties dialog box. You'll see a list of members, both locally and in the domain, as shown in Figure 11-12 on the next page.

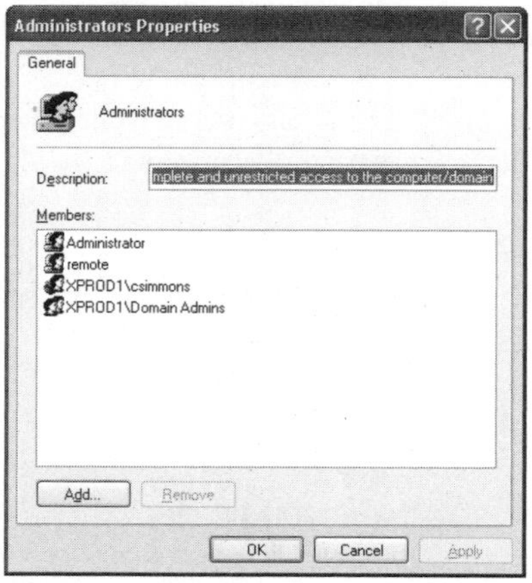

Figure 11-12. The Administrators Properties dialog box shows that the local Administrator account and the domain's Domain Admins account are members of the Administrators group.

But what if you need more permission on the local computer than the limited local control the Domain Users group affords? For example, suppose your domain account has Domain Users group membership, which gives it the same privileges as a limited account on the local computer, and you need this domain account to have administrative privileges on the local computer. Can you change it? Yes, you can use either User Accounts or the Local Users And Groups console to change the local account group permission. The following steps show you how to change the account using User Accounts, which is the easier of the two:

1 Open User Accounts in Control Panel.

2 If you are not currently logged on with an account that has administrative privileges on the local computer, a dialog box appears. Type the user name and password of an account that does have administrative privileges on the local computer. Click OK.

3 On the Users tab, select the User whose group membership you want to change and click Properties.

4 On the Group Membership tab of the properties dialog box that appears, shown in Figure 11-13, select the level of access you want applied to the user account by selecting which group the user account should belong to. If you select Other, you can then choose a group from the list. Click OK.

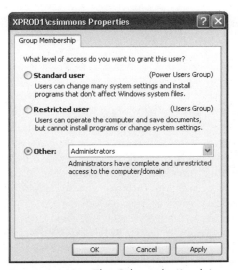

Figure 11-13. The Other selection lets you choose from a list of group memberships including the Administrators group.

Internet Time

You might have noticed that before your Windows XP Professional computer joined a domain there was an Internet Time tab in the Date And Time Properties dialog box, which is opened by double-clicking Date And Time in Control Panel. When you use Windows XP Professional on a stand-alone computer or in a workgroup setting, you can synchronize your computer's clock with an Internet time server if you are logged on under an account with administrative privileges. Once you join a domain, this Internet Time tab is removed—in fact, if you don't have administrative privileges, you won't even be able to open Date And Time. In a Windows domain, time synchronization is administered by the domain controllers because server versions of Windows 2000 use time synchronization as part of the authentication process, and improperly altering the time synchronization between the workstation and the server could cause the authentication to fail.

Simple File Sharing

Simple File Sharing is enabled by default in Windows XP. You can find this option by opening Folder Options in Control Panel, selecting the View tab, and scrolling the Advanced Settings list to find the Use Simple File Sharing (Recommended) setting. This setting provides an easy way to share files with other members of your workgroup while keeping your personal files private. However, Simple File Sharing does not apply when you are logged on to a Windows domain due to domain security features and resource management. See Chapter 14, "Understanding Resource Sharing and NTFS Security," to learn more about Simple File Sharing.

Finding Domain Resources

You can access domain resources in much the same way as you access resources in a workgroup. Locating resources is rather easy—using them might be another story, depending on your permissions. Keep in mind that many different resources, such as folders, printers, and even applications, might be shared in a domain. In fact, depending on the size of the domain, there might be thousands of shared resources. However, to use those resources, you must have permission. In other words, the administrator or user who owns the shared resource has to give you permission to access it. Without that permission, you'll receive an "Access Is Denied" message. If you want to find and use resources for which you do have permission, you'll find three common ways to do so, which are explored in the next three sections.

> **tip** Keep in mind that if you cannot access a shared resource, the reason might be due to security. If you believe that you should be able to access the resource, check with your network administrator. The denied access you encounter might simply be an error that can easily be corrected by a network administrator or the user who owns the shared resource.

InsideOut

How Domain Administrators Share Resources

Whether you are a member of a domain or a workgroup, resources, such as folders and printers, are shared in the same way (which you can learn all about in Chapter 14, "Understanding Resource Sharing and NTFS Security"). You share the resource and assign permissions to users, and users can then access the shared resource over the network.

But what about domain administrators who have thousands of users in a domain? How can access and permissions be managed in a logical and efficient manner? The answer is by using groups. Network administrators make resources available to standard groups, such as the Domain Users group. In other words, permissions are not assigned to individual users (except in rare and special cases); they are assigned to groups to which users belong. Domain administrators can create specialized groups to meet the networking environment's specific needs. For example, domain administrators might assign Print permission for an office printer to the Domain Users group so that everyone who is a member of Domain Users can print to the printer. However, there might also be a Management group that contains members of the management team. This group could be assigned the Print permission as well as the Manage Documents permission so that members of the group can have more control over the printer. Permissions and shared resources can become very complex in domain environments. For this reason, domain administrators spend a lot of time developing groups, carefully identifying group members, and carefully choosing which groups can use particular resources. As with most things in the networking world, simplicity is always best, and that same philosophy holds true for shared resources and permissions in a Windows domain.

Browsing for Resources

You can browse for resources in a Windows domain by opening My Network Places. In My Network Places, you'll see all of the computers in the domain. You can double-click a computer icon to open a list showing the shared resources available on that computer. You can then access the shared resource if your user account has the proper permission or if you belong to a group with the necessary permission.

Browsing is a good way to search for items in a domain, especially if the domain is small. But in large domains, you can spend a lot of time stumbling around looking for items if you don't already know where they're located in the domain. But if your Windows XP Professional computer is part of a Windows 2000 domain, you can search Active Directory for the resource that you want.

Searching Active Directory

Windows 2000 networks use Active Directory to store user accounts, computer accounts, OUs, and all other shared resources, such as folders and printers. This storehouse of information gives administrators an easy way to manage information and an easy way for network users to find the information they need. For example, suppose there are 15,000 computers in your domain and over 1000 shared printers, and you need to print to a color printer that can staple pages. You could browse for the printer, but an easier method is to simply query Active Directory, find the appropriate printer, and connect to it automatically to print your document.

Active Directory uses the Lightweight Directory Access Protocol (LDAP), which is a standard directory access protocol for performing queries against a directory database. By searching for particular items and *attributes*, or qualities, of those items, you can find the resources you need quickly and easily.

Searching Active Directory is easy, just follow these steps:

1 Open My Network Places.

2 Under Network Tasks in the left pane, click Search Active Directory. This option only appears if your computer is part of a domain.

Chapter 11

3 The Find Users, Contacts, And Groups window appears. In the Find box, select what you want to search for, such as Shared Folders, as shown in Figure 11-14.

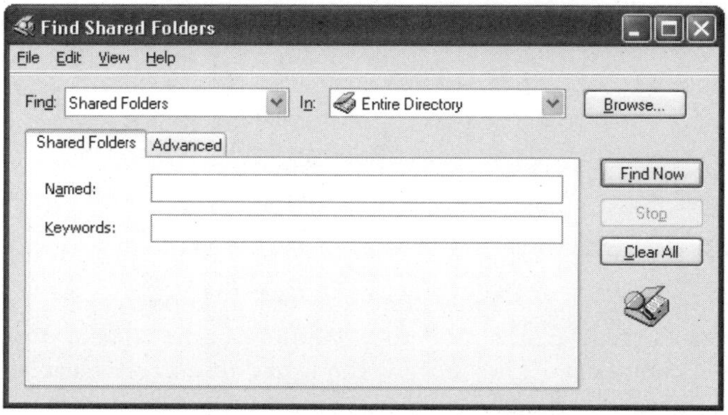

Figure 11-14. Active Directory can be searched for users, groups, folders, computers, and other network resources.

4 Complete the fields required for starting a search, which will vary depending on what you are looking for. For example, you can search for a printer by name, location, or model, as shown in Figure 11-15. You can even search for printers with certain features on the Features tab or by using more advanced fields (such as Pages Per Minute or Model) on the Advanced tab. Enter your search information and click Find Now. The results appear in a pane that unfolds at the bottom of the window. Simply double-click the shared resource that you want to access.

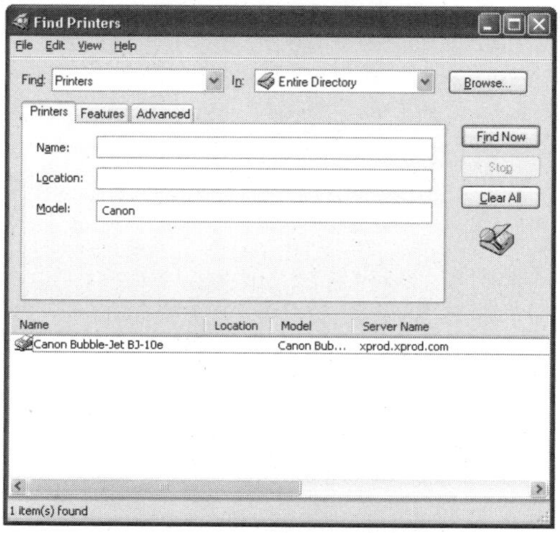

Figure 11-15. A user searches for printers of model type Canon and finds one match.

5 Depending on the resource that you are searching for, you can also search for the resource based on features or other information. For example, you can search for a shared printer based on its characteristics by clicking the Features tab, as shown in Figure 11-16. This allows you to search for color printers, printers that staple, and so on. If these options do not give you the results you want, try the Advanced tab, where you can choose fields, conditions, and values for the search. For example, you could select Pages Per Minute in the Field list and Greater Than Or Equal To in the Condition list, and then type a number in the Value list, such as **15** to obtain a list of printers that can print at least 15 pages per minute. If you select multiple criteria on the various tabs, your search will reveal printers that meet *all* the conditions you have specified.

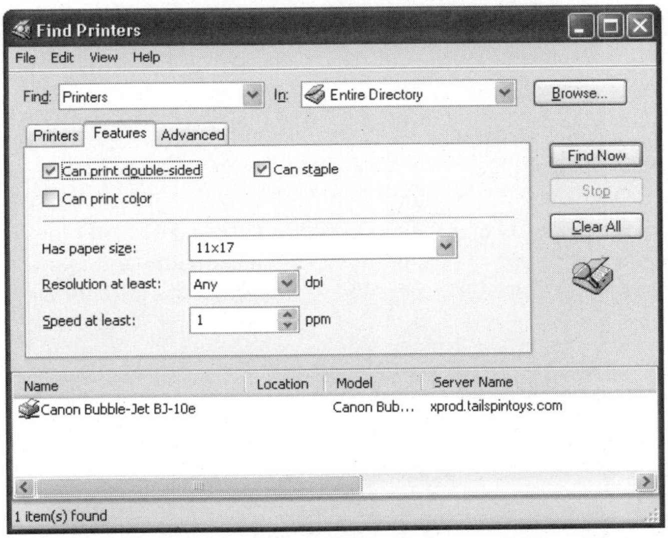

Figure 11-16. The Features tab contains the most common criteria for the type of object you're searching for. The Advanced tab offers even more selections.

Creating a Network Place or Mapping a Network Drive

Suppose you find a shared folder that contains the documents you need, and you want to make this folder easy to access directly from your desktop. You can perform this action in both a domain and a workgroup setting by adding a network place or by mapping a network drive. Both features basically give you the same result. They make the shared folder or resource appear as though it resides directly on your computer so you can easily access it any time you are connected to the network.

Creating a Network Place

A network place is a shortcut that connects you directly to a network folder or drive. If you want to create a network place, follow these steps:

1 Open My Network Places. (If you're not sure how to find My Network Places, see "Finding My Network Places," opposite.)

2 Click the Add A Network Place link under Network Tasks. This opens the Add Network Place Wizard. Click Next to move past the opening page.

3 You have the option of signing up for online storage with a storage provider. But to create a network place that points to a location in your domain or your workgroup, select Choose Another Network Location, and then click Next.

4 On the What Is The Address Of This Network Place page, type the network address, or click the Browse button to open the Browse For Folder dialog box.

5 If you opened the Browse For Folder dialog box, browse to the network resource for which you want to create a network place, as shown in Figure 11-17. You'll want to expand the Entire Network link, expand Microsoft Windows Network, and then expand your domain or workgroup name. The network computers will be listed. Expand a computer and a drive, and then select a folder. Click OK. The address appears in the Internet Or Network Address box. Click Next.

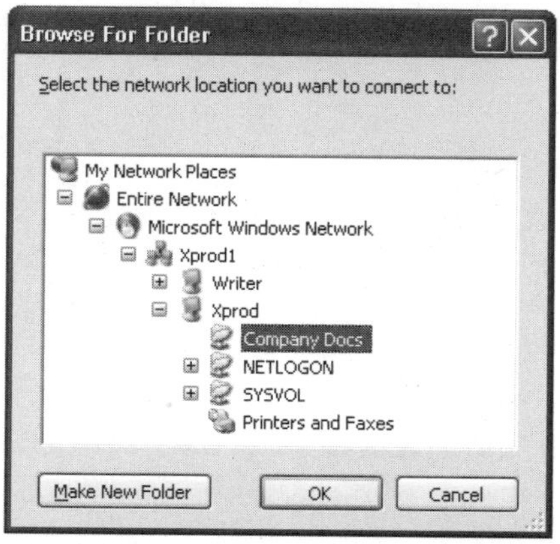

Figure 11-17. In the Browse For Folder dialog box, you select the network location for which you will create a network place.

6 On the What Do You Want To Name This Place page, type a friendly name that will identify the network place for you. Click Next, and then click Finish.

> **tip** **Finding My Network Places**
>
> If you're having trouble locating My Network Places, you can customize Windows XP in three ways to make it easy to find.
>
> First, you can display My Network Places as a shortcut on your desktop. To do so, right-click on your desktop, and choose Properties. Select the Desktop tab, and click the Customize Desktop button. On the General tab of the Desktop Items dialog box, you can activate shortcuts on the desktop to My Documents, My Computer, Internet Explorer, and My Network Places by selecting the appropriate check boxes. Click OK to close each dialog box. Now, the shortcuts you've activated will appear on your desktop.
>
> Second, you can add My Network Places to the Start menu. Right-click the Start button and choose Properties. Select the Start Menu tab and click the Customize button next to the Start Menu selection. On the Advanced tab of the Customize Start Menu dialog box, scroll through the Start Menu Items list, and select My Network Places. Click OK to close each dialog box. Now, when you open the Start menu, you'll see My Network Places in the right pane.
>
> Third, as a more drastic measure, you can revert to the Windows 2000–style Start menu, which will also place My Network Places on your desktop. Right-click Start and choose Properties. On the Start Menu tab, select Classic Start Menu, and click OK.

The network place now appears in your My Network Places folder, as shown in Figure 11-18. You can drag the icon to your desktop, another folder, or even the Start menu for easier access to the network resource.

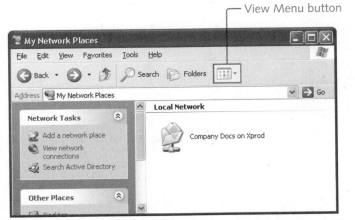

Figure 11-18. Double-click a network place in My Network Places to open it. Use the View Menu button to select the view you want to work with.

Chapter 11

Mapping a Network Drive

Besides creating a network place, you can also map a shared resource to a drive letter. For example, if your local computer has a drive C and a drive D as well as a CD-ROM drive as drive E, you can map a folder or an entire drive on another network computer to an unused drive letter on your machine, in this case, drive F, G, or so on. Mapping a drive does essentially the same thing as creating a network place in that you'll have a handy link to the shared network resource and be able to access it as if it were on your local machine. In fact, creating a mapped network drive is faster than creating a network place, so you might opt for this choice. To map a network drive, follow these steps:

1 Open My Network Places. (You can also use Microsoft Windows Explorer or My Computer.)

2 Choose Tools, Map Network Drive.

3 In the Map Network Drive dialog box, select a drive letter from the Drive list that will represent the network location. Drive letters that are already in use will not be displayed. Next, use the Folder box to enter the network path in the form *servername**sharename*, shown in Figure 11-19, or click Browse to navigate to the resource. Keep in mind that *sharename* refers to the shared folder's name, not necessarily the name of the network place. Click Finish when you're done.

Figure 11-19. After clicking Finish, drive G will access the Company Docs folder on the Xprod computer as if it were a drive on the local computer.

4 The drive now appears in My Computer under the category of Network Drives. You can create a shortcut to the drive and place the shortcut anywhere on your computer. You might also want to click the Folders button on the toolbar to toggle off the task pane and display the mapped drive in a hierarchical folder list in the left pane along with your physical drives.

> **tip**   **Removing a Mapped Drive or a Network Place**
>
> You can disconnect a network drive by right-clicking the drive and choosing Disconnect. You can also remove a network place by right-clicking the icon and choosing Delete.

Using the UNC Path or HTTP Address

You can access any network resource directly from the Run dialog box (choose Start, Run), from any window's Address box, or from within Internet Explorer by typing its Universal Naming Convention (UNC) path. The UNC path accesses network resources using the format *servername**sharename*. For example, if a shared folder called *Docs* resides on a server called *Server1*, the UNC path is \\server1\docs. Notice that you type two backslashes before the server name and one backslash before the share name. You can easily access the shared resource or the computer that holds the shared resource by typing the UNC path in the Address box in any window, as shown in Figure 11-20.

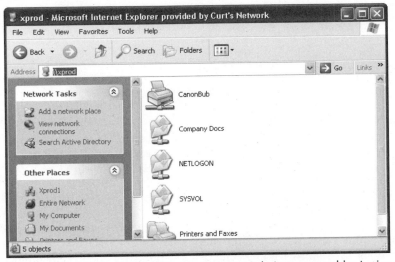

Figure 11-20. The Xprod network computer is being accessed by typing its UNC path (\\xprod) in Internet Explorer.

If a server has Internet Information Services (IIS) installed with shared virtual directories defined in IIS, you can also access the server or computer using the format http://*servername*/*sharename*. See Chapter 9, "Using Internet Information Services," to learn more about IIS.

Leaving a Domain

Should the time come when you need to leave a Windows domain so that your computer can become a member of a workgroup (or be a stand-alone computer), you can easily leave the domain by basically reversing the steps you took to join it. If you need to leave a domain, follow these steps:

1 Log on to the local computer as a user with administrative privileges.

2 Open System in Control Panel, and select the Computer Name tab.

3 Click the Change button. If the Change button is grayed out, you need to log on with a local administrator account.

4 In the Computer Name Changes dialog box, select Workgroup in Member Of, and then type the name of the workgroup. Click OK.

5 A second Computer Name Changes dialog box appears. You must provide the user name and password of a domain account that has the credentials to remove a computer from the domain. See a domain administrator for assistance if necessary.

Accessing Domain Resources from Windows XP Home Edition

Windows XP Home Edition cannot join a domain—it doesn't have the required software to join a domain and take advantage of all that a domain has to offer. But what if you have a Windows XP Home Edition computer that you want to connect to a domain? Can you make this connection and still use domain resources? The answer is yes!

If you have a valid domain user name and password, you can log on to the domain from a Windows XP Home Edition computer. You can then access shared folders and printers over the network, but keep in mind that none of the services and features of a domain, such as Group Policy, will work on Windows XP Home Edition. Therefore, Windows XP Professional is definitely your best choice for working in a domain environment.

To access a shared resource on a domain, browse for the resource using My Network Places, or you can use the UNC path to access the shared resource. You'll be prompted for a user name and password to access the resource because you are not logged on to the domain. The user name and password are kept alive for a single session, but you have to start all over each time you log on. This workaround provides some functionality for Windows XP Home Edition in a Windows domain.

Chapter 12

Solving Connectivity Problems

Difficulties connecting to the network and problems accessing resources can range from the simple to the complex, and they are often complicated enough to stump even the most experienced network users. What do you do when one computer on the network will not connect to the other network clients? What do you do when network connectivity seems to be slow? How do you solve other connectivity problems?

These issues, along with many others, fall under the collective umbrella of troubleshooting. Whether you have a small home network or you help manage a larger network, troubleshooting issues will most certainly appear from time to time. The good news is that Microsoft Windows XP has a number of built-in tools that can help you solve connectivity problems, and there are free or inexpensive utilities available on the Internet that can also help. This chapter explores the troubleshooting process and networking tools that will help you troubleshoot connectivity problems.

> To find out more about troubleshooting problems when accessing resources, see Chapter 14, "Understanding Resource Sharing and NTFS Security."

Using Command-line Tools Included in Windows XP

To troubleshoot network connections and gather information about the state of your network, you can turn to a number of troubleshooting tools. Most of these tools are command-line utilities that have been around for years, and they have proven helpful time and time again. You should become familiar with them because they can certainly help you resolve problems. Some of these tools perform tests for you, whereas others simply provide information that can help you find the source of difficulties. This section explores the tools included in Windows XP.

Using Ping

One of the most popular and common connectivity tests is the ping test. Ping uses the Internet Control Message Protocol (ICMP) to send data packets known as *echo requests* to a remote computer on a network (including the world's largest network, the Internet). The echo requests are packets that ask for a reply (an echo), which the remote computer sends back to your computer. This lets you determine whether you have basic connectivity with that computer. There are a couple of different ways that you can use the test, as detailed next.

> **note** The name for the ping test derives from sonar terminology. Sending out a brief blast of active sonar to try to locate an object is called *pinging*, which is the sound the sonar wave makes when it hits the metal hull of a ship or submarine.

Checking Your Network Interface Card (NIC)

Let's assume that your computer cannot access other computers on the network. One of the first actions you should take is to perform a ping loopback test, which tests whether your computer can talk to your own NIC—the one in your own computer. This test simply lets you determine whether your NIC is working or not. If the loopback test fails, you know something is wrong with the NIC (such as an improper driver, an IRQ conflict, or a simple failure of the NIC itself), and it must be fixed before you can gain network connectivity.

The loopback test works by pinging the reserved loopback IP address, which is 127.0.0.1. When you ping 127.0.0.1, echo request packets are sent to your own NIC. To perform a ping loopback test, follow these steps:

1 From the Start menu, choose Run.

2 In the Run dialog box, type **cmd** and press Enter.

3 In the Command Prompt window that appears, type **ping 127.0.0.1** and press Enter.

> **tip** You can also type **ping localhost** to perform a loopback test. This is the same as typing **ping 127.0.0.1**.

4 The loopback test is performed. If the loopback is successful, you'll see a series of replies, as shown in Figure 12-1. If the loopback is not successful, you'll see a series of "Request timed out" messages.

Figure 12-1. The four lines beginning with "Reply from" indicate that the loopback test is successful. The time value reveals how long it took the echo request to be received.

Testing Connectivity to a Network Computer

If the loopback test works, your next troubleshooting step is to ping a computer on your network to test for basic network connectivity. This allows you to determine whether you actually have connectivity with other hosts on your network. If it appears that you have connectivity, you should also ping your computer from another network computer to prove that other computers can successfully ping your computer.

To ping a computer, you'll need the computer's IP address. Once you have the IP address, return to the Command Prompt window and type **ping** *ipaddress* where *ipaddress* is the IP address of the remote computer. If the ping test is successful, you'll see the reply message shown in Figure 12-2.

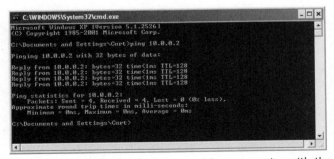

Figure 12-2. This ping test was sent to a computer with the IP address of 10.0.0.2 and was successful.

If the ping test is not successful, you might see either a "Request timed out" message or a "Destination host unreachable" message, which is shown in Figure 12-3.

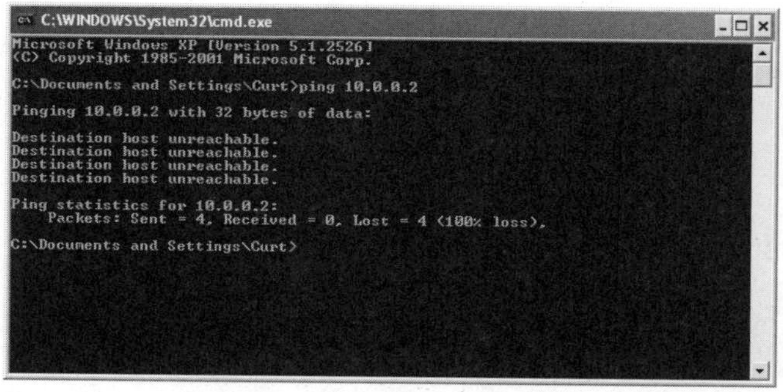

Figure 12-3. A host unreachable message is one message that can appear if the ping test is not successful.

What are the differences between the two ping error messages? A "Request timed out" message means that the ping packets appear to have been sent on the network, but the destination computer did not respond within the allotted time. This can mean a number of different things:

- The remote computer is not turned on or has crashed, its NIC is not functioning, its NIC is not connected to the network, or the remote computer has an incorrect IP address or subnet mask.

- If you cannot ping any hosts on your network, your computer probably has an incorrect IP address or subnet mask, assuming the loopback test was successful. Check the IP address and subnet mask of each computer by opening Network Connections, and then opening the LAN connection. Select the Support tab to see the current IP address and subnet mask. It's also possible that your network's hub or switch is malfunctioning, thus breaking network connectivity on all systems on your network.

- If you cannot ping any hosts beyond a router or default gateway, but you can ping hosts on the same subnet, the problem is with the router or default gateway, or your computer has an incorrect IP address for the router or default gateway.

A "Destination host unreachable" message is more specific. This message means that your computer (or an intervening router) does not know how to contact the remote address. The possible explanations include

- Your computer has been disconnected from the network.

- Your router or default gateway, or another router between you and the destination, has been disconnected from the remote network.

● Your router, or an intervening router, knows that a remote network is down, or has no way of knowing how to route traffic to that remote address. The latter reason is usually due to a misconfiguration of the router.

Testing Connectivity Using a Host Name

In addition to testing connectivity to network computers using their IP addresses, you can also use their host names. For example, if you want to contact a computer named Pentium, type **ping Pentium** at the command prompt. If you cannot ping a computer using the host name, try pinging its IP address. If you can ping the computer using its IP address but not its host name, this indicates that the connection is working, but the name resolution process in which the host name is translated to an IP address is not functioning correctly. This distinction can help you diagnose the source of the problem.

You can also use the Ping command on the Internet to test connectivity to Web sites. Simply specify the Web site's URL in the command, such as **ping www.microsoft.com**. This allows you to test your Internet connection for connectivity. However, many Web sites (and routers) block ICMP traffic as a security measure (including *www.microsoft.com*), so just because you receive a "Request timed out" message does not prove that you don't have connectivity. Make sure you ping several sites before drawing a conclusion. If you receive the error message "Ping Request Could Not Find Host *URL*," you can be pretty certain that you're not connected to the Internet. This message appears because the name you typed couldn't be resolved to an IP address, which would normally occur if your ping could reach your ISP's Domain Name System (DNS) servers. On the other hand, if you ping a URL and the first line of the ping response includes the IP address of the URL but the next four lines read "Request timed out," you should conclude that your ping reached the Internet or at least your ISP's DNS servers (because Ping was able to return the IP address), and that the Web site is just blocking ICMP traffic. In this case, if you open a browser, you should be able to retrieve a page from the URL, even though the ping appears to have failed.

> **note** If you are using Internet Connection Firewall (ICF), all ICMP packets arriving at your ICF-enabled computer are blocked by default, which means that no one can ping your computer. However, you can still ping another computer if that computer isn't blocking ICMP packets. You can use ICF but configure it to allow ICMP traffic to pass through. To learn how to enable ICMP traffic over an ICF connection, read "Allowing ICMP Traffic," page 133.

Other Ping Options

In addition to the basic ping test, there are several command-line options you can specify (also known as *switches*) to gather more information. These options are easy to use. The most commonly used options are listed in Table 12-1 on the next page, but keep in mind that they are case sensitive. To see all of the options, just type **ping** at the command prompt and press Enter.

Table 12-1. Ping Utility Options

Option	Action
–t	This switch pings the specified host until you stop the test. For example, **ping –t 10.0.0.1** pings the host until you press Ctrl+C to stop the test.
–a	This switch resolves the IP address to the host name. For example, if you type **ping –a 10.0.0.1**, the host name is returned along with the ping echoes.
–n *count*	This option pings the address for the number of echo requests specified in *count*. If you are having problems pinging a host or the ping is successful intermittently, you can use the –n *count* switch, such as **ping –n 30 10.0.0.1**, for a longer test than the default ping of four echo requests.
–l *size*	This option allows you to set the buffer size for the test. By default, an echo request is 32 bytes in size. You can try higher size numbers for longer connectivity tests and observe how the elapsed time changes with ping size. Use this option with care: Very large buffer sizes can actually crash remote computers using older, unpatched TCP/IP software.
–f	This switch keeps the ping test from fragmenting packets. Some firewalls will not allow fragmented packets, and this switch ensures that no fragmented packets are used. If, on the other hand, you're using an ICMP packet size (see the –l option) that is too large for your gateway (or an intervening gateway) to preserve without fragmentation, setting this option might cause the ping test to return an error message.
–i *TTL*	This option allows you to specify a Time to Live (TTL) value. If the route to the host crosses multiple networks, you can provide a longer TTL to give the test more time to succeed.
–r *count*	This option displays the IP address of each server your ping request passes through on its way to the host—up to a maximum of nine.
–v *TOS*	This option allows you to specify the quality of service with which the packets generated by the ping test will be delivered by routers. Most routers ignore these values, but some highly advanced networks use multiple connections (to a backbone such as the Internet, or to each other), allowing, for example, one connection to be dedicated to general traffic, one for traffic that requires a minimum amount of delay, and another for traffic that must be delivered with maximum reliability. This value is only necessary for extremely advanced TCP/IP diagnostics, and its values won't be covered in this table.

Troubleshooting

Your network connectivity appears normal, but Ping does not work.

When using Ping on the Internet or on a large Windows network, it is important to remember that ICMP requests can be considered a security threat. Hackers can use ICMP tricks to cause problems on computers and Web servers. For this reason, many firewalls do not allow ICMP traffic, including ICF, the software firewall provided in Windows XP. In fact, depending on your environment, some routers might even be configured to drop ICMP packets instead of forwarding them to the next subnet. Therefore, when you use Ping and other related tools, keep in mind that routers and even computers might block the echo requests, which will result in a failed ping test. For more information on how Ping and other ICMP tools relate to security, see Chapter 20, "Maintaining Network Security."

Using Tracert

Tracert (Trace Route) is a utility that traces the route to a host you specify. This utility can be used within a LAN to list the computers or routers from your computer to another computer. Each step or leg of the journey is called a hop. A *hop* consists of each computer or router your request must pass through to reach its destination. You can also use Tracert to trace the route to Internet URLs. Simply type **tracert** *host* at the command prompt, where *host* is an IP address or URL of a network computer or Internet site, and you'll see a listing of the resolution process to the host or Web site, as shown in Figure 12-4.

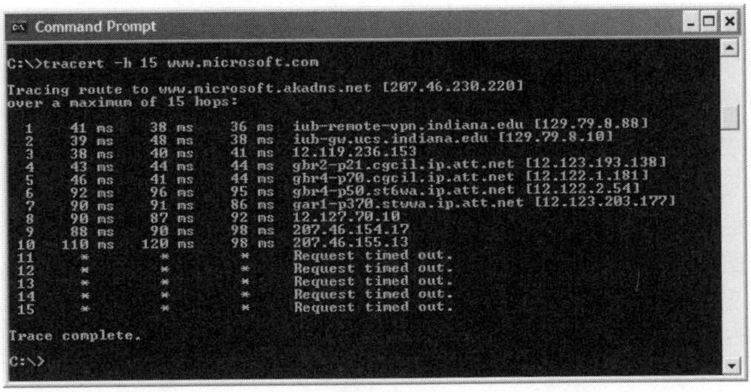

Figure 12-4. Tracert traces the path to a target host. In this case, an intervening router appears to be blocking ICMP traffic.

In terms of a LAN or WAN, Tracert can be helpful in situations where you are having problems connecting to a particular host or in a case where connectivity is intermittent. Tracert allows you to track the path to the host so that you can begin troubleshooting that path. This helps you see if the connectivity problem is at the host or at some router between the remote host and your computer.

For example, although Ping will only indicate whether or not you can communicate with a remote address, Tracert helps you to see where the breakdown in communication is taking place. If you're seeing the trace stall at a particular IP address, there might be a faulty router or broken network connection. If the trace seems to get close to the host but does not reach the host, the host computer might be down. If you don't see any hops beyond your Internet connection, your ISP might be having problems. If you see a large number of hops (or an infinite loop in the hops), your ISP's Internet connection might be misconfigured, or the ISP might not have a high-quality uplink to the Internet.

> **tip** When using Tracert, you can use the –d switch to stop the resolution of IP addresses to host names to speed up the trace. You can also use the –h *maximum_hops* switch to set a maximum hop limit.

Using PathPing

PathPing is a combination of the Ping and Tracert tools, and it contains options not found in Ping and Tracert. PathPing pings a host computer and traces the route to that host. When using PathPing, you'll see router hops, such as those you see with the Tracert tool, and you'll see the reply information. The advantage of PathPing is that it gives you an easy interface to see each hop and the response time from each. This can help you determine whether a particular router is congested or causing problems along the path. For each hop, you'll see a percentage of dropped packets; any hop with a high percentage of dropped packets is suspect. Figure 12-5 shows a sample PathPing session.

To use this tool, type **pathping** *host* at the command prompt, where *host* is the URL or IP address of an Internet site or network host. You can also specify additional options on the command line to control the information you receive and the maximum number of hops allowed. Table 12-2 shows you the important options you are likely to use. To see all of the available switches, type **pathping** at the command prompt.

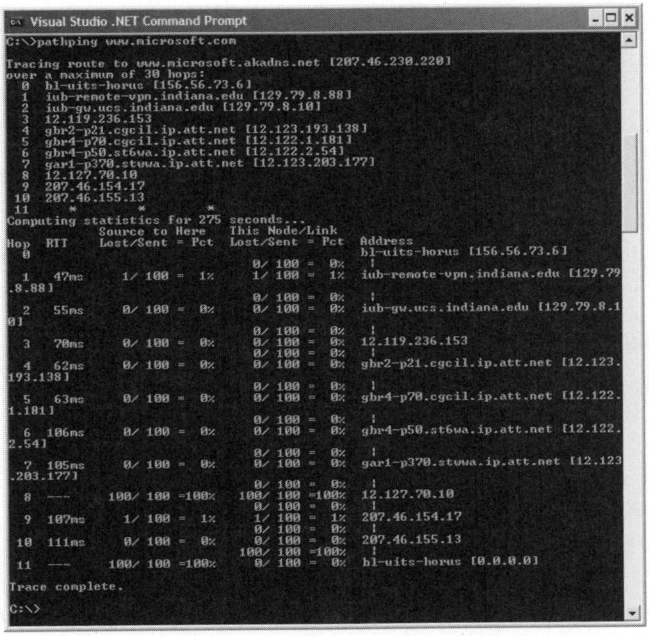

Figure 12-5. PathPing provides a much more detailed picture of the network conditions between your computer and a remote host.

Table 12-2. **PathPing Utility Options**

Option	Action
–h *maximum_hops*	This switch lets you specify the maximum number of hops to use when searching for a target host. This essentially allows you to place a limit on the search.
–n	This switch stops PathPing from resolving IP addresses to host names. Using this switch, each hop reported back to you will be listed by IP address only. This might make the test run faster, but the information you receive will certainly be less descriptive.
–6	This switch forces the use of Internet Protocol version 6 (IPv6). If you are pathpinging a host on an IPv6 backbone, consider using this switch for additional IPv6 testing purposes.

Part 3: Network Connectivity

> **tip** If you're using a residential gateway device and you find yourself unable to use PathPing across it, you might need to upgrade your device to the latest firmware revision. For more information, visit your device manufacturer's Web site.

Using Ipconfig

Ipconfig is a popular command-line tool that gives you complete TCP/IP information for the adapters configured on your computer. Use Ipconfig to identify a NIC's Media Access Control (MAC) address, IP address, subnet mask, default gateway, DNS server, Dynamic Host Configuration Protocol (DHCP) server, and so on. Ipconfig is a great tool for troubleshooting because you can quickly gain all of the TCP/IP configuration data about a computer.

> **note** The information that you'll find when using Ipconfig is the same information that is displayed in the Winipcfg graphical tool, which was included in Microsoft Windows 95, Microsoft Windows 98, and Microsoft Windows Me. Winipcfg is not included in Windows XP, but you can acquire the same information using Ipconfig or by opening Network Connections, right-clicking a network connection, and choosing Status to open the connection's status dialog box.

The most commonly used option in Ipconfig is the /all option. At the command prompt, type **ipconfig /all**. You'll see a listing of the computer's current IP address configuration, as shown in Figure 12-6.

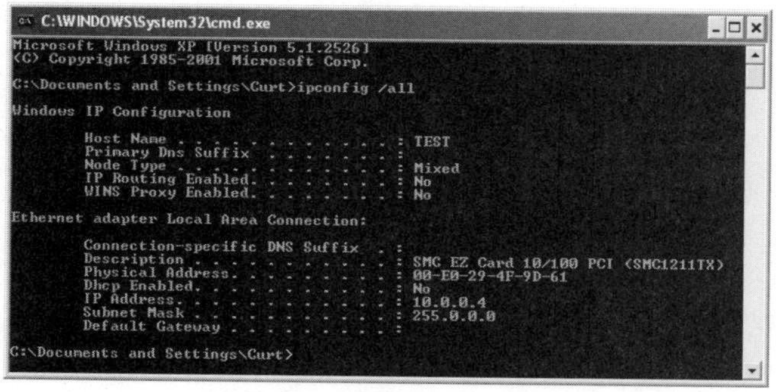

Figure 12-6. Typing **ipconfig /all** gives you complete IP addressing information.

There are additional switches that you can use with Ipconfig, but you should exercise caution because some of these switches will disrupt your computer's network connectivity. However, these options can help you solve IP addressing problems. The most commonly used options are listed in Table 12-3. To see a complete list of options, type **ipconfig /?** at the command prompt.

Chapter 12: Solving Connectivity Problems

Table 12-3. Ipconfig Command Options

Option	Action
[none]	Shows basic IP configuration information for all NICs and active IP connections on the computer.
/all	Shows the host name and detailed IP configuration information for all NICs and active IP connections on the computer.
/release	Releases an IP address lease assigned to the NIC by DHCP.
/renew	Sends a lease renewal request to a DHCP server for the NIC.
/flushdns	Purges all entries in the DNS Resolver cache.
/registerdns	Reregisters all DNS names and refreshes DHCP leases.

Using Netstat

Netstat displays all the active connections to your computer. You can also use Netstat to view the bytes sent and received from your computer as well as any dropped network packets. As shown in Figure 12-7, typing the basic form of the command, **netstat**, displays each connection's protocol, local (MAC) address, foreign (IP) address, and the current state of the connection.

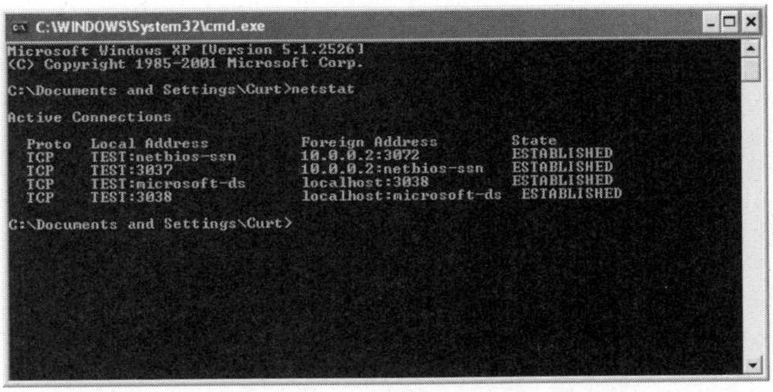

Figure 12-7. Use Netstat to see your computer's current network connections.

There are several helpful options, or switches, you can specify on the command line. Table 12-4 on the next page lists the most common, and you can view all of them by typing **netstat /?** at the command prompt.

Table 12-4. Netstat Command Options

Option	Action
–a	This switch displays all connections and listening ports.
–e	This switch displays Ethernet statistics. You can also use this switch with the –s switch.
–n	This switch displays addresses and ports in numerical form. This option can make Netstat data more difficult to read, but is useful if you need numerical data.
–o	This switch displays the numeric process ID associated with each IP connection. This allows you to determine which program is maintaining the IP connections established by (or to) your computer. For more information on this option, see "Using Netstat to Observe IP Connections," page 584.
–p *protocol*	This option allows you to specify which protocol statistics you want to see. For example, **netstat –p udp** only displays UDP connections.
–s	This switch displays connection statistics classified by protocol.

Using Nbtstat

Nbtstat (NetBIOS over TCP/IP) is a tool for troubleshooting NetBIOS names over TCP/IP. This tool is helpful when TCP/IP is having problems resolving NetBIOS names to IP addresses. Type **nbtstat** at the command prompt to see a list of command-line options for this command. For example, typing **nbtstat –c** will list the NetBIOS names of computers on your network from the NetBIOS over TCP/IP (NBt) protocol cache maintained by Windows XP along with their IP addresses. You can learn more about Nbtstat by visiting the Help And Support Center (choose Start, Help And Support).

Running Additional Network Support Tools

In addition to the built-in command-line tools included in Windows XP, you'll also find a few additional tools that can help you troubleshoot network connectivity and network connections. One tool, Network Diagnostics, is found in the Help And Support Center, and another set of tools, Windows Support Tools, must be installed from the Windows XP CD-ROM.

Running Network Diagnostics

Network Diagnostics is a Windows XP tool that is built into the Microsoft Help And Support Center. Network Diagnostics scans your computer system and gathers

Chapter 12: Solving Connectivity Problems

network-related information about your computer. The tool runs a series of tests on your computer and reports a pass or fail status for each test. When testing is complete, you can save the results to a file where you can view it at a later time and use the information for troubleshooting purposes.

To use the Network Diagnostics tool, follow these steps:

1 From the Start menu, choose Help And Support.

2 In the Help And Support Center window under Pick A Task, select Use Tools To View Your Computer Information And Diagnose Problems.

3 In the left pane under Tools, select Network Diagnostics, as shown in Figure 12-8.

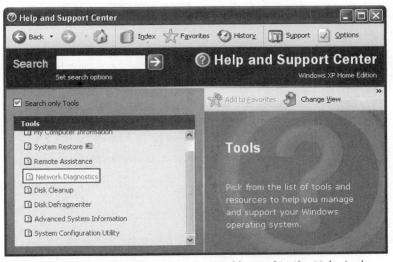

Figure 12-8. Network Diagnostics is a tool located in the Help And Support Center.

4 In the right pane, you see an option to either scan your system or set scanning options. Select Scan Your System.

5 Network Diagnostics begins a scan of your system. If you're not connected to the Internet, you'll be prompted to connect so that the diagnostic tool can check the connection as part of its network tests.

When the test is complete, a list of tested items appears, and some tests will be marked as Passed or Failed, as shown in Figure 12-9 on the next page.

6 You can expand a category by clicking the plus sign next to it. As shown in Figure 12-10 on the next page, the IPAddress test is actually a ping test.

Part 3: Network Connectivity

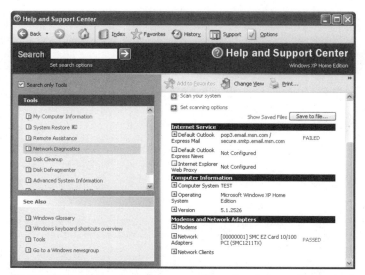

Figure 12-9. Some tests return configuration information, whereas others produce a Passed or Failed response.

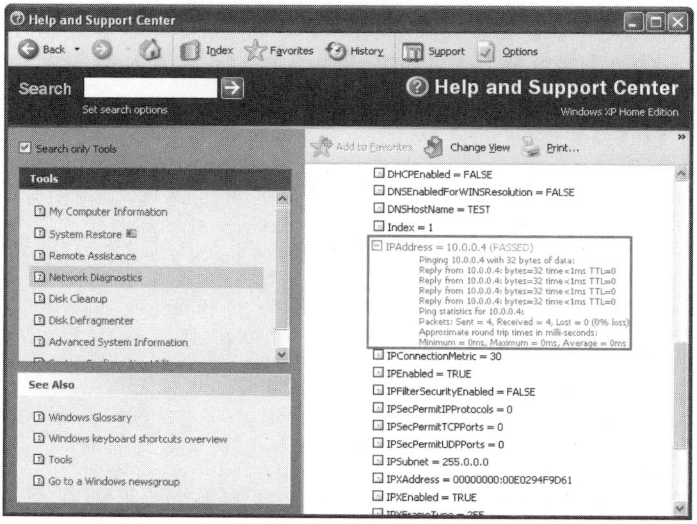

Figure 12-10. The IPAddress test pings the local computer to check for connectivity with your NIC, which is similar to typing **ping localhost**.

7 Once you have reviewed the results, you can click the Save To File button and save the file for future reference. The file is automatically saved as an HTML file.

In addition to the standard diagnostic test that is performed, you can also customize the test by selecting Set Scanning Options in step 4. The option is also available at the

Chapter 12: Solving Connectivity Problems

end of each test you run, so you can modify your selections and run the diagnostics again. The options are listed under the headings Actions and Categories. The actions the test can perform include pinging, connecting, showing, saving to the desktop, and using a verbose (detailed) mode. Categories to test include Internet connections, computer information, and network protocols, as shown in Figure 12-11. Most of the items in this figure are selected by default, but notice that DNS, DHCP, default gateways, IP address, and WINS are not selected for the test. If you want to test these items as well, select their check boxes, and then clear any items that you do not want reported to you.

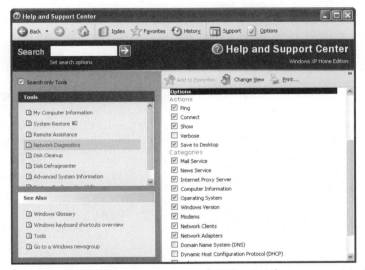

Figure 12-11. Select the actions and categories that you want to test.

Using Windows Support Tools

In addition to the tools installed by default in a Windows XP installation, Windows XP also includes another group of tools that you can install from the Windows XP installation CD. These support tools include a conglomeration of items developed for Microsoft Windows 2000 Professional and Microsoft Windows 2000 Server, so some of the tools apply more to Windows 2000 Server tasks rather than Windows XP tasks. However, there are a few networking tools in this group that you might want to use. To install the Windows Support Tools, follow these steps:

1 Insert the Windows XP installation CD into the computer's CD-ROM drive.

2 When the Welcome To Microsoft Windows XP window appears, select Perform Additional Tasks.

> **note** If the CD's installation program doesn't automatically start up, open a Command Prompt window and type *d*:\setup.exe, where *d* is the drive letter of your CD drive.

3 Select Browse This CD to display a directory of the CD.

4 Open the Support folder, and then open the Tools folder.

5 Double-click Setup.exe to open the Windows Support Tools Setup Wizard.

6 Follow the instructions in the wizard to complete the installation. Select Complete when prompted for the installation type so you won't need to run the wizard again to install additional tools.

After the tools are installed, choose Start, All Programs, and point to Windows Support Tools. Because these tools are command-line utilities, they aren't individually listed. Instead, open a Command Prompt window from the submenu that appears and read the Release Notes and Support Tools Help to learn the names and functions of the support tools. If you choose Support Tools Help and click the Alphabetical List Of Tools link, you'll see that there are nearly 50 utilities available to you. Two of these utilities are discussed in the following sections.

Network Connectivity Tester (NetDiag.exe)

The NetDiag tool is a command-line diagnostic tool that can help you locate networking problems and connectivity problems. The NetDiag tool performs a series of steps to test the functionality of the network components. It can provide a lot of information, and it is rather easy to use.

At the command prompt, type **netdiag** and press Enter. As partially shown in Figure 12-12, a long list of tests are run, data is gathered from those tests, and the results of the tests (Passed, Skipped, Failed) are reported.

> **note** If you installed the support tools but NetDiag won't run in a Command Prompt window, it's probably because the folder for the support tools isn't in the Windows XP search path. To avoid this problem, choose Start, All Programs, Windows Support Tools, Command Prompt. This will open a Command Prompt window set to the folder in which the support tools were installed, which will enable them to be located.

You can then read through the test and look for the information you're interested in. Some of the more helpful tests include the following:

- Adapter: Local Area Connections information and tests
- Default Gateway Test
- DNS tests

- Domain Membership Test

- IP Loopback Ping Test

- Modem Diagnostics Test

- IP Security Test

NetDiag also includes a few additional command-line options to control the test output. The most useful options are listed in Table 12-5. To see a complete list of switches as well as a complete list of the tests that are performed by NetDiag, type **netdiag /?** at the command prompt.

Figure 12-12. The NetDiag tool performs a number of network status and connectivity tests.

Table 12-5. NetDiag Switch Options

Option	Action
/q	This switch runs NetDiag in quiet mode. The output of the command lists only the errors.
/v	Verbose output. This option displays all the results.
/l	This option logs the NetDiag output to Netdiag.log
/debug	This switch uses debugging mode, which provides an even greater amount of output. Use this only when trying to troubleshoot specific problems because much of this output is only decipherable by network programming experts.
/fix	This switch fixes trivial problems that are found.

Chapter 12

Network Monitor Capture Utility (NetCap.exe)

NetCap is a network monitor capture utility that captures data frames, or packets, entering and leaving a computer. The data collected is then saved to a log file where you or other network support personnel can analyze it in hopes of solving problems that might be occurring.

NetCap is a rather involved tool and is most often used by network administrators to look for specific network problems. You can capture network frames by typing **netcap** at the command prompt. The frames are continually captured until you press the Spacebar to stop the capture. If you type **netcap /?**, a long list of options appears. You can define filters for the Network Monitor driver so that you can choose the type of data that you want to monitor. To learn more, read Support Tools Help by choosing Start, All Programs, Windows Support Tools.

InsideOut

What Is Found in a Data Frame?

NetCap is a program that captures network frames (also known as packets) and records the data in a log file. Because these programs are used to hunt down difficult to trace problems on a network, they are often called *packet sniffing* or *frame sniffing programs*. So, what can be found by sniffing frames? Each data frame on a network contains information that can be useful to network administrators. By analyzing the frames, you can learn more about the kind of traffic that is running on the network and determine if any problems exist. Each data frame contains:

- Control information
- Source and destination addresses
- Protocol information
- Error-checking data
- The actual data being sent

Using NetCap, you can capture this information to analyze your network. For example, if your network is running slowly, you can use NetCap to sniff frames for a period of time, and then view those frames in a log file. Suppose you find a lot of broadcast frames that are congesting the network. You can read the destination address to find out which computer is sending out broadcast packets. You can then take steps to solve the broadcast problem on that particular computer or at least investigate whether or not the broadcast traffic is necessary.

Finding Helpful Utilities on the Internet

If the many tools included in Windows XP and the Windows XP Support Tools don't keep you busy, there are also many third-party tools available for network problem solving. The selections range from commercial applications to shareware and freeware applications. Many of these programs have trial versions that you can download from the Internet to see if they fit your needs. This section highlights a few of the many Internet utilities you will find.

Ping Plotter

Ping Plotter is a trace route tool that provides you with the same standard information that Tracert does, but it presents the information to you in a graphical format and includes additional features. The cool thing about Ping Plotter is that you can see a graphic of the trace and automatically repeat the trace at intervals you specify. For example, if your network or Internet connection slows down during certain times of the day, you can set Ping Plotter to run at those intervals and record the data for analysis. This is a great way to show your ISP when problems are occurring and exactly what routers are dropping packets. ISPs can then work to fix faulty routers or route traffic around them.

Besides its basic use of tracing a route, you can also use Ping Plotter to:

- Save the graphs and charts. You can even set up automatic saving.

- Watch routes and keep track of any route changes.

- Repeatedly trace a route and examine graphs of the minimum, maximum, and average values of each router's performance.

- Configure alerts that will notify you when certain conditions occur. Alerts can even be configured to be sent to you via e-mail messages.

At the time of this writing, Ping Plotter is available as shareware or as a freeware product. The freeware product does not include all of the features that are available in the shareware product. You can download the shareware version and use it for 30 days before you have to pay for it. Be sure to try the shareware version first (the fee is only $15 to register it). It includes graphing features that provide more information than traditional text output, which makes it easier to troubleshoot the tracing process. You'll find Ping Plotter at *www.pingplotter.com*. Figure 12-13 on the next page shows a typical trace display from the tool.

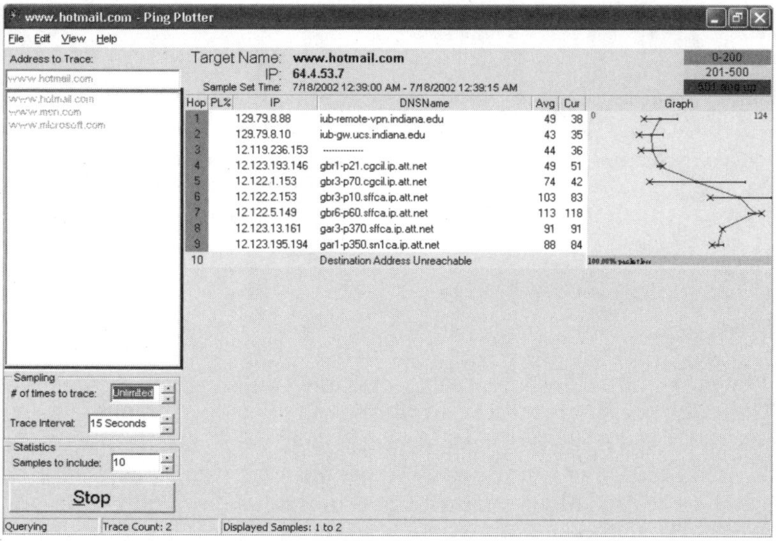

Figure 12-13. Ping Plotter performs trace route functions in a graphical format.

VisualRoute

Another utility displays geographic maps of its trace routes. VisualRoute, available in a trial version from *www.visualroute.com*, traces any URL or e-mail address (to the e-mail server) and displays the route for you on a world map. This is a fun tool, but it can also be very helpful in obtaining a graphical view of traffic patterns and access over the Internet. As shown in Figure 12-14, VisualRoute provides a simple interface where you can route Internet addresses, IP addresses, or e-mail addresses.

NetPerSec

NetPerSec is a utility that gives you the real-time speed of your Internet or network connection. You can see how many bytes of data your computer has sent and received, and you can view the data in a chart format for easy analysis. NetPerSec is a free download from *www.pcmag.com,* and it's a good tool to have around.

NetPerSec is mainly touted as a utility that keeps track of your Internet speed, but it can help you see the amount of traffic flowing in and out of your computer on the LAN. If traffic seems to be moving slowly on the network, you can use this tool to view what might be happening. If you have more than one NIC, the Options tab of the application lets you choose which NIC to monitor. You can also choose to only monitor a dial-up connection or all network activity combined. By choosing the network traffic you want to monitor, you can gain insight into how data is flowing through your computer. Figure 12-15 shows the NetPerSec interface.

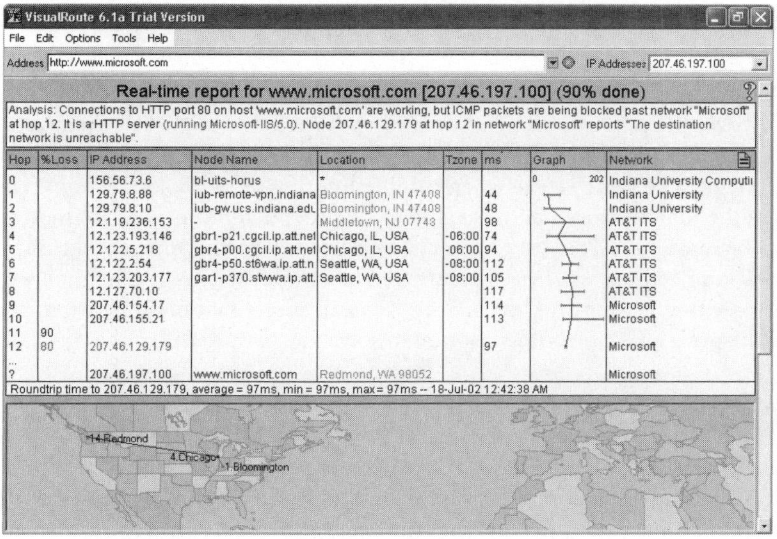

Figure 12-14. VisualRoute displays the same information as other ping utilities but adds a mapping feature that includes additional information.

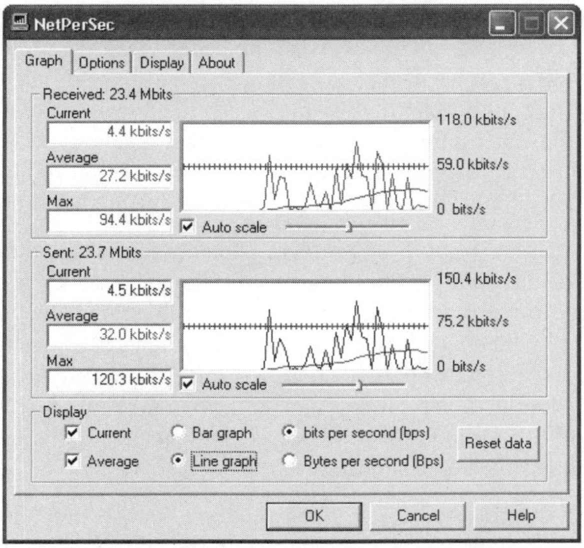

Figure 12-15. Use NetPerSec to see the speed of Internet and network connections in numerical and graphical formats—all in real time.

Troubleshooting Network Connections

Troubleshooting is a *process*—a system of eliminating possible causes of problems until you discover the actual cause. That sounds easy enough, but if you have ever tried to solve computer problems, you know that the troubleshooting process can be complicated and difficult. The same is true when troubleshooting network connections. However, if you use the tools explored in this chapter, you are much more likely to find the cause of the problem quickly. The rest of this chapter details a basic approach to troubleshooting network connections, which is then applied to a few problems you might encounter. Remember that if your problem is not specifically described in this section, you can still apply the principles of troubleshooting to solve your particular problem.

A Philosophy of Troubleshooting

Network users and administrators develop their own philosophy of troubleshooting. This philosophy often comes from years of trial and error, or it comes from books like this. Depending on your perspective, the way you troubleshoot computer problems will vary, but the following is a time-tested approach to troubleshooting you can apply to troubleshooting network connections or another problem with Windows XP.

- **Stop.** When the problem first occurs, don't do anything but stop and think. Grab a notebook and write down exactly what happened when the problem occurred. Then think about what you were doing just before the problem occurred. For intermittent problems, this approach can help you isolate the problem, which will help you find the cure for it. The act of taking notes might seem trivial, but if the problem takes several hours to solve, you'll be surprised at how convoluted your memory can become during that time!

- **Plan.** Before you attempt to solve the problem, look at your notes and think about the possible solutions to the problem. Many users who end up calling for technical support start out with a minor problem that they try to fix on their own by making random configuration changes. By the time they call for support, the minor problem has become a major one because of the additional complications caused by making changes haphazardly! Don't end up in this predicament—take a logical look at the problem and make a plan that might lead to a solution.

- **Act.** Once you have documented the problem and have sketched out a plan for solving it, try to solve the problem using the most likely tool or the most likely solution. If the problem is fixed, you are home free. If the problem is not fixed, write down what you tried to do before moving on to the next possible solution. If you cannot solve the problem and must get help, this list of actions you have documented can be very helpful to technical support personnel. Help yourself by keeping records of your troubleshooting actions!

- **Get help.** Make sure you check references that might help you, including this book and *Microsoft Windows XP Inside Out* by Ed Bott and Carl Siechert (Microsoft Press, 2001) for possible causes and solutions. A more technical but very comprehensive title is *Microsoft Windows XP Professional Resource Kit Documentation* (Microsoft Press, 2001). Don't forget to use the Internet to search for solutions. The Microsoft Web site at *www.microsoft.com* has a comprehensive Search link to search hundreds of documents about different issues. Newsgroups accessed through Microsoft Outlook Express or another newsreader provide hundreds of groups dedicated to software and hardware issues with thousands of people helping each other solve computer problems. You'll often find others with your specific problem, sometimes before the problem is documented in more official places. If you're still unable to solve the problem, open the Windows XP Help And Support Center for help from Microsoft (choose Help And Support from the Start menu). Then click the Get Support Or Find Information In Windows XP Newsgroups link. Under Support, click the Get Help From Microsoft link. The Microsoft Online Assisted Support Wizard will guide you through the support process.

Solving Common Network Connection Problems

A few of the more common network connectivity problems and their solutions are discussed in the following sections. Remember that if your problem isn't covered, the procedures described can often be applied to other problems as well.

Your Computer Cannot Connect to a Network

If your computer cannot connect to the network, follow these steps to troubleshoot the problem:

1 Check your NIC and the cable. Make sure the NIC is installed and working (use Device Manager in the System Properties dialog box in Control Panel), and make sure the cable is plugged into the NIC. If the NIC is installed, you'll see an icon for it in Network Connections. If the cable is unplugged, the icon will appear with a red X over it.

2 If the NIC is plugged in and seems to be working, use Ping to ping the loopback address and then other hosts on your network.

3 If the loopback test works but you cannot access other hosts, check your IP address and subnet mask against other hosts on the same subnet. You must use an IP address in the same range and the correct subnet mask to communicate with other computers on the network. If this information does not appear to be correct, run the Network Setup Wizard again, or manually configure the TCP/IP settings if required. You can let Windows XP try to repair the problem by right-clicking the LAN connection icon in Network Connections and choosing Repair.

Chapter 12

4 If you can ping hosts on your local network but not hosts on a remote subnet, the default gateway might be down. Check the default gateway or ask another network administrator for help. If you can ping your network but can't reach the Internet, the gateway address for the Internet connection (if any) or the DNS server addresses of your ISP might not be correct.

5 If you can ping computers but you cannot access resources on other network computers, you might not have the proper permissions to access those resources. If you're running Windows XP in a workgroup, make sure you're accessing the other computer as yourself and not as a Guest account, which has limited privileges. Even if you have a user account on the other computer, open User Accounts in Control Panel on that computer to see if the account type is listed as Limited or Computer Administrator. A Limited account will considerably restrict your activities. Of course, if the computer belongs to someone else, you'll need that person's permission to change your account type. If you're running Windows XP as a member of a domain, you'll need to ask the network administrator for permission to access the resources you want.

My Computer Can Access Other Computers on the Network, but None Can Access My Computer

When a single computer can connect to the network but other computers cannot access that computer, odds are that ICF is enabled on the LAN NIC of the computer that can't be accessed. Figure 12-16 shows the Advanced tab of the Local Area Connection

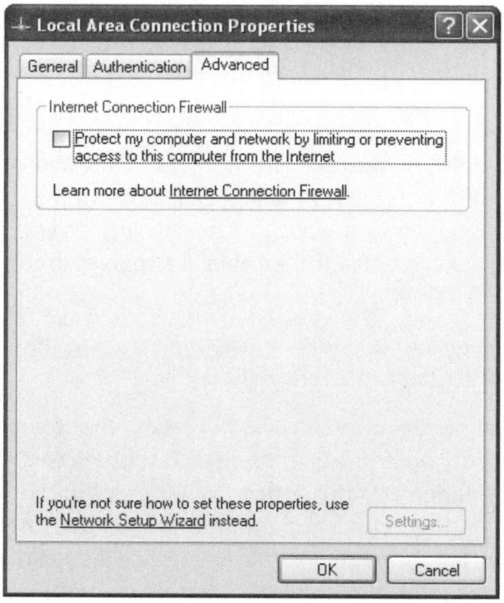

Figure 12-16. Make sure ICF is not enabled on the LAN connection, but don't turn it off on your Internet connection unless you have another firewall installed.

Properties dialog box. Open this dialog box in Network Connections and make sure the check box in the Internet Connection Firewall section is cleared.

None of the Computers on My Network Can Connect

If none of the computers can connect to each other, make sure you have tried the ping test on several different computers. Also make sure that all computers are configured for networking and are physically connected to the network cabling, hub, or whatever might be required for your type of network. Check the IP addresses and IP configuration using Ipconfig, and make sure all computers have an IP address in the same range and the same subnet mask. If these solutions do not work, run the Network Setup Wizard again on each computer.

> **note** Do not use the Network Setup Wizard if your computer is a member of a Windows domain. If your computer is a member of a Windows domain, contact your domain administrator for assistance.

Computers Cannot Connect to Other Subnets

If the computers on your subnet cannot connect to another subnet, the default gateway is either wrong or not configured on those client computers. Use Ipconfig, and type **ipconfig /all** at the command prompt to see if a gateway is configured. Repeat this step on the computers on the other side of the router to make sure they too are properly configured. If the correct gateway is configured on all systems, the gateway (router) might be down or experiencing some problems.

Part 4

Network Resources

Selecting a File System

Data files, along with printers, are perhaps the most significant resources that can be shared across a network. Network file sharing allows for collaboration between individuals, provides flexibility in allocating resources, and can save both money and time for professional and casual users.

File systems, which manage the way in which disk resources are allocated, are the basis on which all network file sharing mechanisms rely. This chapter discusses the file systems that Microsoft Windows XP offers, including their features, pros and cons, and the impact each has on network file sharing.

Understanding FAT32

Long before the development of Microsoft Windows NT (one of the predecessors to Windows XP), Microsoft released MS-DOS. MS-DOS provided a simple file system called the FAT file system, named after the mechanism it used to manage disk space. FAT used a *file allocation table* to keep track of where the individual segments of a file were stored on a disk and which parts of a disk were damaged and unusable.

Early versions of FAT were limited and designed to work primarily with the floppy disks and small hard disk drives commonly found on personal computers of the early 1980s. As both hardware capabilities and user requirements evolved, FAT had to evolve as well. Microsoft upgraded FAT in various versions of MS-DOS to support larger hard disks and partitions as well as store larger numbers of files and directories on a volume.

MS-DOS version 4 introduced FAT16, a version of the FAT file system that allowed disk partitions of up to 2 GB in size. FAT16 was the standard file system for Microsoft's basic operating systems through MS-DOS version 6.22 and the original release of Microsoft Windows 95. However, FAT16 suffered from a number of significant limitations:

- By the time Windows 95 was released, hard disks with capacities far greater than 2 GB were becoming more and more affordable, and were being installed on most new PCs.

- FAT16 inefficiently managed disk cluster sizes on large volumes. This could only be avoided by splitting a disk into multiple, smaller partitions, which made using the disk dramatically less convenient.

InsideOut

What Is a File System?

A computer's hard disk is used to store data. This data is kept on the hard disk in the form of magnetic bits oriented to represent 1's and 0's. Patterns of these binary digits, or *bits*, are the native language of computers. When a user or process creates a file, the software program creating the file sends a request to the operating system to record the information on the disk.

This operation sounds simple enough, but for it to be reliable, a couple of details must be known. First, it must be determined if there is any other data on the disk, and if so, where on the disk it is located. Second, the location of the next available space on the hard disk must be determined. It is the *file system* that keeps track of where data is located. File systems can do considerably more than track the location of data on the disk, but this is the minimum functionality needed to make writing data to a disk possible.

Of course file systems must also keep a record of where each file is stored on the disk so that the files can be accessed again. Essentially, the file system acts as a road map to the data on the disk. By accessing its system records, the file system can determine the next available location for storing information, and it can retrieve any data already stored on the disk.

Microsoft addressed the limitations of FAT16 with the release of the FAT32 file system, which initially became available with Windows 95 OSR (OEM Service Release) 2. FAT32 supports individual partition sizes of up to 2 TB (2,048 GB) in size and also

InsideOut

Understanding Cluster Size and File Systems

Any discussion concerning file systems is bound to bring up the topic of cluster size. A cluster is the smallest amount of disk space that can be used to store a file or portion of a file. The cluster size can have a significant effect on performance as well as how efficiently the disk space is used. The following example explains the relationship of cluster size to performance and storage requirements.

Suppose you have a file that is 27 KB in size. On one computer, you have formatted one disk with 4 KB clusters, another with 32 KB clusters, and a third with 64 KB clusters. On the first disk, storing the file will require seven clusters (six clusters at 4 KB each equals 24 KB, plus 3 KB more of the seventh cluster). Because there can only be one file or portion of a file in a cluster, the 1 KB of remaining space can't be used for file storage and is therefore wasted space. On the second disk, the file will fit in a single 32 KB cluster with 5 KB of space left over and therefore wasted. On the third disk, the file will also occupy a single cluster, but in this case, the 64 KB cluster will have 37 KB left over and wasted. In this case, the reduction in free disk space is more than twice the file's actual size. In general, smaller cluster sizes use disk space more efficiently.

You might think the smaller the cluster size, the better, but it's not that simple. The downside to small clusters is that it takes more effort on the part of the hard disk to read data from multiple clusters than to read data within a single cluster, especially once your files become fragmented. *Disk fragmentation* occurs when files are deleted and leave *holes* of free space on the disk. When new files are saved into those slots, they are unlikely to be the same size and fit exactly. So newly saved files are split across available free clusters all over the hard disk. When they're later retrieved, the hard disk heads (the *heads* are similar to those in a tape recorder and read and write the data to the disk surfaces, or *platters*) have to jump around the disk to read the files and open them. The smaller the clusters, the more clusters are needed for a file of a given size, and the more fragmented it can become.

However, with the continued release of faster hard disks, the performance effect of the smaller cluster size is reduced in absolute terms. There are also limits on the total number of clusters a file system can keep track of, so you can have larger volumes if you use larger cluster sizes. Choosing cluster size involves balancing the objectives of maximizing storage efficiency with hard disk performance.

allocates disk clusters far more efficiently; for example, FAT32 only reaches the wasteful 32 KB cluster size on 32 GB or larger partitions.

In addition, FAT32 maintains a backup copy of the partition's file allocation table and can switch to it should the original become corrupt. This feature, when combined with FAT32's duplication of critical data structures in the drive's master boot records, makes FAT32 significantly more robust than FAT16.

Due to these features, FAT32 has become the standard file system for Microsoft's consumer line of operating systems. Support for it has been included in Microsoft Windows 98, Microsoft Windows Me, and now Windows XP. FAT32 partitions can also be read by many other operating systems including Linux.

Understanding NTFS

In the heat of the technology boom in the early 1990s, Microsoft decided to enter the very profitable and competitive server market. At the time, UNIX and Novell NetWare, along with Microsoft and IBM's collaborative OS/2 product, were the only viable options for sophisticated server-based networks. OS/2 was not widely accepted in the marketplace, and Microsoft's successful operating system offerings at the time were MS-DOS and Windows 3.x, neither of which offered the features network administrators had come to rely on. Although they were adequate network clients, neither MS-DOS nor Windows could serve as the backbone for a secure, manageable, high-performance network.

The solution was to build a new operating system. As part of creating a new network operating system, a more full-featured file system than FAT16 (FAT32 had not yet been developed) was needed. FAT16 could not provide the performance, security, or management features that a network operating system would require. To meet those needs, Microsoft developed the NTFS file system.

Architecturally, the NTFS file system was a complete break from the FAT file system model. Rather than being based on a simple design from the early 1980s, NTFS was designed from the ground up to provide reliability, performance, and security. NTFS debuted in Windows NT in 1993. Windows NT would eventually make a huge impact on the server-based networking market.

When Microsoft introduced Microsoft Windows 2000, the more powerful update to Windows NT, NTFS was included and enhanced. Microsoft Windows XP Professional and Microsoft Windows XP Home Edition support NTFS and further enhance it in several areas, including improved performance and flexibility.

When NTFS was built, there were several key needs that had to be met. Previous iterations of the Microsoft operating system family lacked most if not all of these needed features. According to Microsoft historians, these *must-have* features included the following items:

- **Security.** One of the biggest shortcomings of the FAT file system is its lack of support for security features. Although a separate program can be used to secure files on a FAT disk, there is no inherent support in the file system itself for security. Because there are no system-level file security features, controlling access to files and folders stored on a FAT volume is nearly impossible. Of course, controlling user access to files and folders is extremely important in network environments.

- **Large and redundant disk support.** A critical feature of any shared, networked server (or high-performance, mission-critical workstation) is its ability to support large hard disks operating in a fault-tolerant file system. A *fault-tolerant* file system is a file system that has built-in features to recover from an event like a power failure without loss of data. The FAT file system lacked these features. FAT16 supported disks no larger than 2 GB and had no native support for arranging multiple disks into *redundant arrays of independent disks (RAID)* configurations. RAID allows redundancy, increased performance, and if properly implemented, fault tolerance. NTFS offers native support for RAID disk arrays. NTFS also supports disks with up to 16 terabytes (TB) of storage space—1 TB = 1000 GB or 1,000,000 MB.

- **Overall reliability.** To be useful, a server needs to be reliable. A server's operating system will have a difficult time being reliable if the file system it depends on is not inherently so. NTFS has a number of features (such as RAID support) that greatly add to the general reliability of the operating environment. NTFS is also a *journaling file system*, which means that it maintains a journal of write transactions on the hard disk as they occur. This allows NTFS to gracefully recover from abrupt system failure (such as that caused by an unexpected power failure) by simply reversing, or *rolling back,* any incomplete changes to the file system without leaving permanent damage to the disk's data integrity.

- **Efficient use of disk space.** NTFS generally uses smaller cluster sizes for data storage than even FAT32. The largest typical NTFS cluster size is 4 KB, even on 2 GB or larger disk partitions, ensuring efficient data storage.

- **Long file name support.** NTFS allows the use of long file names. File names can include up to 255 characters with the NTFS file system. In early versions of the FAT file system, all file names were restricted to the short file name format known as the 8.3 format, which consists of up to eight characters, a period, and a three-character extension.

InsideOut

Selecting an NTFS Cluster Size

By default, NTFS will automatically select an appropriate cluster size for a partition when it is formatted. However, you can override this default setting. When would you want to do so?

As discussed in "Understanding Cluster Size and File Systems," page 375, it's important to balance efficient disk space usage with performance and with the total number of files that can be stored on a volume. Limits to the total number of clusters are unlikely to be a problem with NTFS volumes because an NTFS disk using 4 KB clusters can be as large as 16 TB (that's 16,384 GB). Disks with larger cluster sizes can be much larger—up to 256 TB.

In terms of performance, Microsoft recommends NTFS cluster sizes of 4 KB, 16 KB, or 32 KB. The smaller cluster size provides the best performance when your files tend to be small and do not change size (editing a document file or adding data to a database file causes the file to grow). When your files tend to be large or increase in size over time, the larger cluster sizes provide better performance, even though they'll waste more disk space.

Before you decide to use a cluster size larger than 4 KB, keep in mind that file compression is only available on volumes formatted with 4 KB or smaller clusters. If you plan to use NTFS compression, 4 KB will have to be your upper limit.

Keep in mind that there are many parts to a file system, and the preceding list of features provides a general blueprint for the NTFS design objectives. Both Windows XP Professional and Windows XP Home Edition support NTFS, and both operating systems provide you with their best security and management features when the NTFS file system is used. This chapter explores NTFS and details how you can best use NTFS on Windows XP alone and in networking scenarios.

New NTFS Features in Windows XP

Since its inception, NTFS has undergone numerous revisions. The individual components have been retooled, and new functionality has been added. The changes that occurred to the design and implementation of NTFS typically coincide with the release of new operating system versions, such as the release of Windows 2000 after Windows NT 4.0. This is also true for the release of Windows XP. Windows XP includes enhancements to both the performance and management features of NTFS. NTFS also includes several new features designed to make installing Windows XP and converting hard disks from FAT to NTFS less time-consuming and more reliable.

Designers have taken advantage of the physical architecture of hard disks to improve the performance of NTFS. In particular, the fact that data access is faster if data is stored at certain locations on the disk is leveraged to reduce the time it takes to locate files on an NTFS partition. The overall performance gain is approximately 5–8 percent.

There are several features relating to the conversion of FAT volumes to NTFS volumes. Most of these features are intended to allow partitions that have been converted from FAT to NTFS to have the same level of functionality as a partition that was natively formatted using NTFS. One such feature is the Format command in Windows XP, which aligns FAT data clusters at the cluster size boundary. The improved alignment makes the conversion of FAT volumes to NTFS more efficient because the Convert command can now use a variable cluster size as one of its parameters. Cluster sizes for converted volumes are now supported to a maximum of 4 KB, whereas Windows 2000 only used 512-byte clusters. Another feature added to improve the functionality of converted drives is the application of default permissions in the form of access control lists (ACLs) applied to the converted volumes. Previously, ACLs were present by default only on drives natively formatted with NTFS.

> File system security in NTFS, as implemented using ACLs, is covered in detail in "Configuring NTFS Permissions," page 433.

The FAT-to-NTFS conversion process in Windows XP also uses another new feature to prevent the fragmentation of the Master File Table (MFT). By preventing the fragmentation of the MFT during the disk's conversion to NTFS, it becomes more likely that the MFT will occupy a contiguous space after converting a disk, allowing it to be accessed more rapidly. Fragmentation is prevented in a rather creative way— the MFT is temporarily stored in a placeholder file during conversion. When the conversion is complete, the contents of the file can be written to the contiguous disk space.

Preventing file fragmentation is a recurring theme in the implementation of NTFS in Windows XP. There are now two ways to initiate a defragmenting process on a Windows XP computer. The first method is to use Disk Defragmenter, a Microsoft Management Console (MMC) snap-in accessed by choosing Start, All Programs, Accessories, System Tools, Disk Defragmenter. Using Disk Defragmenter, you can analyze and (if needed) defragment drives. The new alternate method involves using the command-line tool Defrag.exe.

Exploring NTFS Features in Windows XP

NTFS supports more features than any other Windows file system (and in fact offers more features than most other operating systems in existence). These features provide a wide range of user services that enable secure, fast, and flexible disk management. The following topics describe the key features of the NTFS file system. Most of these features have corresponding MMC consoles that allow you to activate and configure them.

> You can learn how to configure many of these features by reading "Configuring NTFS Features," page 389. For more information, check out *Microsoft Windows XP Inside Out*, by Ed Bott and Carl Siechert (Microsoft Press, 2001).

Dynamic Disks

Traditionally, a hard disk is set up as a basic disk, a physical disk that has one or more basic *volumes* such as partitions and logical drives. Each of these volumes can be formatted with a file system and used to store data. Basic disks work well if there is no need to alter the storage configuration after the initial disk configuration. But in many cases, it is beneficial to have dynamically reconfigurable storage. To fulfill this need, Microsoft introduced dynamic disks with Windows 2000. Dynamic disks contain one or more dynamic volumes, which offer features that are not available with basic disks:

- Administrators can increase the size of a dynamic volume by extending the volume into unallocated or noncontiguous space available on the same physical disk; however, neither system nor boot volumes can be extended.

- Dynamic volumes can be extended across separate physical disks if they are also set up as dynamic disks. The same restrictions about system and boot volumes still apply, however.

- Each dynamic disk maintains a database that stores information about all of the attached dynamic disks and dynamic volumes. Because this database centrally stores the resource information, you have great flexibility in how you manage the volumes and even move disks between computers, and the redundant copies of the dynamic disk database ease recovery of data from corrupt volumes.

You can manage dynamic disks in Windows XP from the Computer Management console, which is available in Administrative Tools in Control Panel. Or, you can simply right-click My Computer and choose Manage. In the Computer Management console, select Disk Management to manage local hard disks, as shown in Figure 13-1.

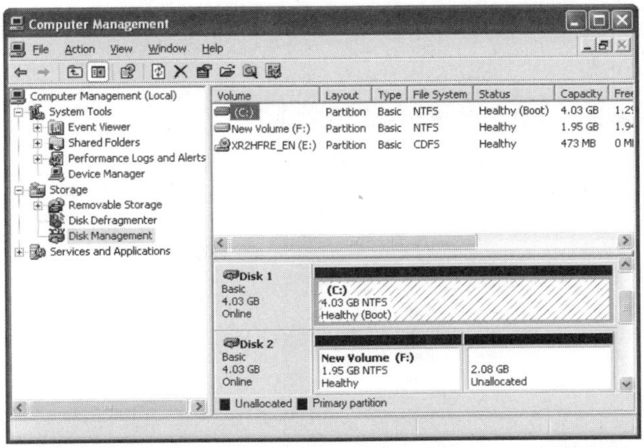

Figure 13-1. The Disk Management snap-in is available from within the Computer Management console.

InsideOut

Using MMC Snap-ins in Windows XP

MMC has been around since the early days of Microsoft Internet Information Services (IIS) in Windows NT. However, in Windows 2000, MMC and its component applications, known as *snap-ins*, took a front seat in the operating system as a way to organize the various networking tools. This same approach is true in Windows XP. Common tools are all MMC snap-ins, which means they all function within MMC. Using this approach, all of the tools in Windows XP have the same basic appearance. The Computer Management *console* is a collection of snap-ins used to enable centralized administration of many network functions. It includes such snap-ins as Event Viewer, Device Manager, Disk Defragmenter, Disk Management, and so forth.

However, you are not limited to the default consoles in Windows XP. You can easily create your own consoles that contain the mix of snap-ins that you use most often. To create your custom MMC, just follow these steps:

1 Choose Start, Run. Type **mmc** and press Enter.

2 An empty MMC appears. Choose File, Add/Remove Snap-In.

3 In the Add/Remove Snap-In dialog box, click the Add button. A list of available snap-ins appears, as shown on the next page.

4 Select the snap-in that you want to add to the console, and click the Add button. You might see a dialog box asking you which computer you want the snap-in to manage. If so, select Local Computer (or This Computer) and click Finish. This dialog box only appears with certain snap-ins.

(continued)

Inside Out *(continued)*

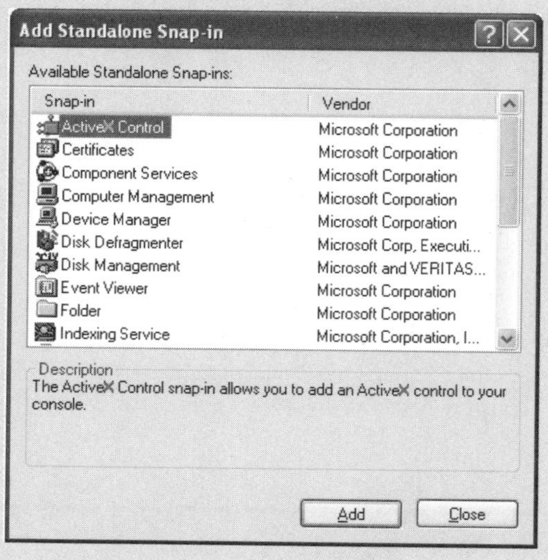

5 Repeat step 4 to add additional snap-ins. When you are done, click Close.

6 The snap-ins that you selected for this console now appear in the Add/ Remove Snap-In dialog box, shown here. Click OK.

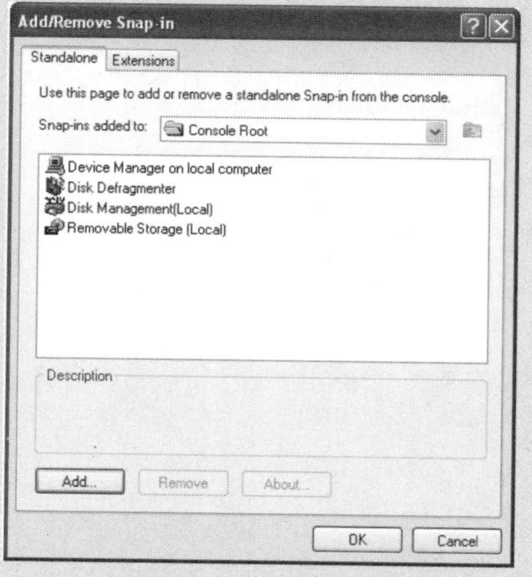

7 The snap-ins appear in the console and are ready for your use. If you plan to reuse this console, choose File, Save As and give the console a name. By default, the console is saved in your Administrative Tools folder. To open it again, type **mmc** at a command prompt, and then choose File, Open in the console window to select and open it.

> **tip** Although MMC is beyond the scope of this book, it is a powerful feature that lets you create custom consoles as well as custom views and processes. You can learn more about using MMC in Microsoft Help And Support Center (choose Start, Help And Support).

Change Journal

Another important feature of the NTFS file system is the NTFS change journal. The change journal is used to keep track of all changes made to files on an NTFS volume. For example, the journal tracks information about added, deleted, and modified files for each NTFS volume. Each of these actions triggers an update of the change journal. Because the change journal can become very large, it can be configured with a maximum allowable size. Much like other log files, when the change journal exceeds its maximum allowable size, the oldest records in the journal are removed to restore the log file to its maximum size, making room for new entries to be added.

In addition to providing robustness in the case of system failure, as discussed earlier, maintaining a change journal also allows applications that would otherwise need to scan the entire disk to detect file changes to simply check the journal for changes. This ability to reduce the overhead for applications that must track file changes (such as virus scanners, disk defragmenters, and Indexing Service) allows NTFS to perform efficiently, even on disks with large numbers of files.

NTFS Compression

With advances in disk storage technology and the dramatically lowered cost of data storage, file compression is not the burning issue it once was. But the overall amount of storage needed for computing continues to increase, even with the technological advances in storage technology. In the earlier days of computing with small and expensive hard disks using the FAT file system, compression was a hot feature and often a problematic one as well. With the FAT file system, most compression schemes resulted in a severe performance hit to any application needing to access files on a compressed volume. When compression didn't make the data inaccessible or even corrupt, it did ensure molasses-speed performance, particularly if the user compressed directories accessed by frequently used applications. NTFS builds file compression into the file system rather than requiring additional programs to be installed on top of it. Because all applications will access the compressed data through NTFS, the applications don't need to have any awareness of or support for disk compression.

In addition, add-on compression utilities required compressing entire volumes. Some of the compressed files, such·as large files that could be compressed a great deal and were infrequently accessed, improved the computing experience. But along with those files, other compressed files included binary and operating system files that compressed very little and had to be frequently (even constantly) accessed and decompressed, slowing the computing experience. By building file compression into the file system, the user can choose to compress files on a per-folder or per-file basis.

Another noteworthy performance improvement over earlier forms of compression is that a file in active use only needs the part of the file being accessed to be decompressed. The decompressed portion remains uncompressed in memory so that subsequent access to it does not suffer a performance penalty. The file is recompressed only when the data is written back to disk. A handy though not performance enhancing feature allows the user to display the names of compressed files and folders in a different color to distinguish them from regular files. This clearly indicates which files are compressed without the user having to examine the properties of the file or folder.

Of course, as everyone knows, even the best laid plans are prone to failure every now and then. So what happens if a user compresses a volume that results in the inability of Windows XP to restart normally? With Windows XP, the user can use the Compact.exe command-line tool to either uncompress the files or force the compression to finish if it was interrupted and left the computer in an unstable state. This tool can also be used to enable disk compression via a batch file. Although it's usually much simpler to compress files using the Windows XP graphical interface, command-line tools are worth their weight in gold when you need them.

> **note** Enabling compression on a server that is accessed regularly is not a good idea. Every file read and written to the compressed folder or volume will have to be decompressed and recompressed, and (if there are lots of users) this can consume a considerable amount of CPU cycles and memory. If a server is being used to archive files, compression is often appropriate. Another good candidate for compression is the end-user workstation. With NTFS file compression, you can choose to compress folders containing infrequently accessed and highly compressible content, and still leave frequently accessed application and system folders uncompressed.

File Encryption

In its latest version, NTFS also makes use of robust encryption technology. The Encrypting File System (EFS) uses a public-private key pair and a per-file encryption key to protect resources on an NTFS volume. The use of encryption ensures that only the proper individuals and recovery systems can access the protected data.

When an authorized user accesses an encrypted file, the system decrypts the file. The user can then work with the file. When the user saves the modified file back to the hard disk, the system encrypts the file again. This whole process is entirely transparent to a user who has the proper credentials to access the file. Any unauthorized user attempting to access the file will receive an "Access Denied" error message; however, unlike with NTFS file permissions, where simply being granted permission to the file will allow a user to open it, encrypted files are completely inaccessible to even users with sufficient file system rights. This allows extremely confidential data to be secured against access by individuals who have file system permissions (such as administrators) but who should not be granted the ability to view that data. Encryption also prevents individuals who manage to bypass NTFS security altogether from viewing the confidential data.

Keep in mind, however, that EFS is not available with Windows XP Home Edition.

note You cannot simultaneously encrypt and compress a folder or a volume. Folders and volumes in Windows XP Professional can be compressed or encrypted, but not both.

File and Folder Access Control List

NTFS offers the capability to configure security settings on files and folders. The security settings are stored in what is known as the *access control list (ACL)*. Every file on an NTFS volume has an ACL component. The ACL is not supported by any of the FAT file systems, and if any file with an ACL is relocated to a FAT volume, the ACL will be dropped. Most of the ACL security features are not routinely available in Windows XP Home Edition.

For a full description of security in Windows XP including ACLs and file sharing security, see Chapter 14, "Understanding Resource Sharing and NTFS Security."

Indexing Service

Simply put, Indexing Service creates and maintains an index of your files and file-related information, and enables you to search the index to quickly locate and retrieve the data you need. In the same way a book has an index revealing the location of various components, Indexing Service has information about the contents and location of certain types of files stored on your computer. The information collected by Indexing Service is used by the Windows XP Search feature, a Web browser, or a direct query of Indexing Service to locate files matching the description you provide. The individual indexes Indexing Service creates can be used in a variety of ways. For example, a Web site can be indexed (enable Indexing Service in IIS), allowing Web site clients to use the generated index to search the Web site. Indexing Service indexes a wide variety of file attributes. You can query Indexing Service based on any of these tracked parameters, such as finding all files created after a certain date that contain the text *Microsoft Windows XP*. Indexing Service also enables broad searches, such as finding all of the

Microsoft Word documents on a hard disk. Although Indexing Service supports FAT file system disks, NTFS is its file system of choice because Indexing Service was specifically designed to offer robust interoperability with NTFS. The result is that Indexing Service takes advantage of the many file system features of NTFS to yield maximum performance.

One of the most critical advantages of using Indexing Service with NTFS volumes is its awareness of the security settings of files. The Indexing Service catalog tracks file-level permissions settings along with the other file information in its catalog. The net result is that if a user does not have access to a file, that file will not appear when the user searches for the file. In addition to respecting the file permissions, Indexing Service takes special care when dealing with encrypted files. Indexing Service does not index information about encrypted files because the information itself would not be encrypted. In fact, if Indexing Service discovers that one of the files included in its index has become an encrypted file, Indexing Service will flush the file from its catalog.

Sparse File Management

Another feature of NTFS available in Windows XP and Windows 2000 is sparse files. *Sparse files* save disk space in large files that include sizable segments of null data (data composed of binary zeros). This handling method uses rather creative logic to avoid storing large quantities of null data. Basically, the null data ranges of the file are represented in nonallocated space on the disk. When the contents of the file are recalled, the data sections are pulled from allocated (normal) disk locations, and the null portions are returned from the nonallocated areas as zeros. In fact, the application programming interface (API) for the sparse file attribute does not require an application to manually recover the null data—it is simply reconstructed automatically. Indexing Service is an example of an application that uses sparse files. The use of sparse files allows Indexing Service to use roughly half the storage space on an NTFS disk as it requires on a FAT disk.

Disk Quotas

Disk quotas allow you to restrict the amount of disk space a user's files can occupy on a particular NTFS volume. This is particularly useful if disk space is in short supply. A variety of quota options exist and range from notifying you as an administrator that a user's quota is about to be exceeded to denying a user the ability to save a file once the quota has been reached.

A quota can only be configured on an NTFS volume. The quota is set administratively and tracks the files owned by each user with a quota attached to each account. The user's security identifier (SID) is used to uniquely identify the files that the user owns. Because the files are tracked by user and the quota is set per volume, the quota is bound by a folder. The quota tracks all of the files stored by a user across the entire volume.

However, disk quotas do not prevent an administrator from allocating more disk space to users than is actually available. For example, on a 20 GB volume used by 25 users where the quota is set at 1 GB each, the users can still completely fill the volume. It's up to the administrator to keep track of a volume's total free space and allocate it accordingly.

> **tip** Disk quotas can only be set up on a per-volume basis; you can't configure Windows XP to restrict the amount of space users can use via network file shares or in individual folders.

Volume Mount Points

Mounted drives or *volume mount points* are volumes that are attached as a folder to another existing volume instead of having a drive letter. Among other benefits, this allows a computer to utilize more than 26 drive letters. Because one volume can accommodate multiple mounted drives, extra capacity can be added to network access points without having to change the physical traits of the host volume. Additionally, it allows you to mount other disk volumes at directories within an already existing volume, allowing users to transparently gain additional storage without the restrictions of trying to extend dynamic volumes.

Distributed Link Tracking

Distributed link tracking ensures that shell shortcuts and OLE document links continue to work in the event that a file is moved or renamed. Every shortcut to a file that is created on an NTFS volume has a unique object identifier implanted into the target file. Information about the object ID is also stored within the referring file, which is known as the *link client*. Distributed link tracking uses this object ID to locate the link source in the event that the source file is renamed or moved to a new location on the same computer, or if the source file is moved from one shared network folder to another in the same domain. The object ID can also locate files when the host computer is renamed or in the event that the hosting volume is moved from one computer to another within the same domain.

Multiple Data Streams

A *data stream* is a sequence of bytes. Applications store data in files composed of at least one main data stream by writing data to the stream in an orderly sequence that can later be accessed by the application to read data back from the data stream. Every file system supports files that have a main, unnamed data stream. However, NTFS supports the use of additional named data streams where each data stream uses an alternate sequence of bytes. This allows applications to create multiple streams. The purpose of this feature is to allow related data to be managed as a single unit. As an example, a thumbnail image for a graphic file can be stored in the same file as the graphic image using this multiple stream capability. However, if such a file is moved to a FAT volume, the additional data streams will be lost, leaving only the main, unnamed stream.

> **note** Although Windows XP Home Edition supports NTFS volumes, it does not support all its features. For example, file encryption is not available in Windows XP Home Edition, and there is no interface for setting permissions on individual files and folders. Windows XP Home Edition uses Simple File Sharing, which only lets you make your user profiles private, which include data in users' My Documents and Desktop folders. Dynamic volumes are only available for NTFS volumes in Windows XP Professional.

Selecting a File System

Now that you've read about the features of FAT32 and NTFS, which file system should you use?

By default, NTFS is the preferred file system for fixed storage in Windows XP. Windows XP formats floppy disks using FAT12 (an older version of FAT, even older than the FAT16 used by MS-DOS 4.0) and formats DVD-RAM disks using FAT32, but you can override this behavior and use NTFS on removable devices if you prefer. Windows XP supports CD and DVD media with the Compact Disc File System (CDFS) and Universal Disk Format (UDF).

For fixed storage, on the surface, the many additional features of NTFS make it the clear winner. Its built-in enhancements over FAT make it far more flexible, powerful, reliable, and secure.

However, because of its lower overhead, FAT32 does provide better raw performance on individual disks than does NTFS. On volumes that require the highest possible performance, it might be a good idea to format them using FAT32. Additionally, very few operating systems other than Windows XP can access NTFS volumes. If you need to dual-boot your computer using Windows XP and another version of Windows or maintain volumes that are accessible via Windows or Linux boot disks, FAT32 is your best option.

Keep in mind that Microsoft now recommends that NTFS be used on any volume that can be accessed over a network as well as all volumes on a computer that is connected in any way to a network. The security and auditing features of NTFS become crucial in these situations because they add a layer of defense against hackers.

The basics of configuring NTFS permissions are covered in "Configuring NTFS Permissions," page 433; NTFS auditing is covered in "Auditing File System Access," page 594.

Configuring NTFS Features

Now that the main features of NTFS have been covered along with how to choose a file system, this section addresses using NTFS file system features in Windows XP. If Windows XP was installed on a clean system rather than as an upgrade or if your computer came to you from the computer manufacturer configured with Windows XP, the file system in use is probably NTFS. You can quickly determine the file system in use by opening My Computer. Right-click a volume and choose Properties. On the General tab, shown in Figure 13-2, you can see the file system in use.

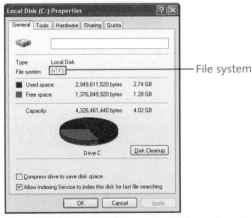— File system

Figure 13-2. The File System field on the General tab of a disk's properties dialog box indicates the disk's file system.

Converting a Disk to NTFS

What do you do if you access the General tab on the disk's properties dialog box and find that the disk is formatted with FAT, and you've decided you want to use NTFS? Windows XP includes an easy conversion utility that converts the disk to NTFS without having to back up, reformat, and restore the disk's contents. It is a simple and safe command, but bear in mind that the process is one way. Once you convert to NTFS, you cannot convert back to FAT without reformatting the entire disk (after backing up your data of course). It is also very important to back up any irreplaceable data from your system to avoid catastrophe should the system fail (due to a power failure, for instance) during the conversion. To convert a drive to NTFS, follow these steps:

1 Choose Start, Run. Type **cmd** and click OK.

2 At the command prompt, type the command **convert** *d:* **/FS:NTFS** where *d* is the letter of your drive. For example, in the following figure, drive C is being converted to NTFS.

3 Press Enter to execute the command. Conversion will take several minutes, depending on the size of the drive.

> **note** You won't be able to convert a volume that has any of its files open. Nor can you convert the boot volume of your computer (the one on which Windows XP is installed). In the first case, you're given an opportunity to force a dismount of the volume, but this can cause data loss. Answer no to this prompt, and you'll see the same message that appears when you attempt to convert the boot volume. The message gives you the option of automatically converting the volume the next time you start Windows XP. Accept this option and restart your computer.

Enabling Disk Compression

You can quickly and easily enable or disable disk compression at any time. You can compress an entire volume or just particular folders or files. To compress an entire drive, follow these steps:

1 Double-click My Computer.

2 Right-click the volume that you want to compress and choose Properties.

3 On the General tab, select Compress Drive To Save Disk Space and click OK.

> **note** If you later want to decompress the drive that you've compressed, return to this dialog box, and clear the Compress Drive To Save Disk Space check box.

4 The Confirm Attribute Changes dialog box appears and asks whether you want to compress only the volume's root folder or the drives subfolder and files as well. In most cases, you'll want to choose the second option. Click OK.

Depending on how many folders and files your volume contains, the compression process might take several minutes to complete.

If you want to compress certain folders, but not the entire drive, or if you want to compress one or more files in a folder, but not an entire folder, follow these steps:

1 Locate the file or folder that you want to modify, right-click the file or folder, and choose Properties.

2 On the General tab of the properties dialog box that appears here, click the Advanced button.

3 In the Advanced Attributes dialog box, shown in the following figure, select Compress Contents To Save Disk Space and click OK.

note If you want to remove compression from a file or folder in the future, return to this dialog box, and clear the Compress Contents To Save Disk Space check box.

Enabling Encryption

If you are using Windows XP Professional, you can encrypt any of your files or folders using EFS. You'll still be able to use that file or folder as you normally would, but no one else will be able to access the file or folder unless you choose to share the encryption with other users. Even if your machine was stolen and the hard disk files could be opened, the encrypted files would appear to be composed of meaningless characters.

To encrypt a file or folder, follow these steps:

1   On a Windows XP Professional computer, right-click the file or folder that you want to encrypt and choose Properties.

2   On the General tab, click the Advanced button.

3   In the Advanced Attributes dialog box, select Encrypt Contents To Secure Data and click OK.

> **note**   If you are using Windows XP Home Edition, the encryption option appears dimmed. Encryption is not available in Windows XP Home Edition.

4   If you are encrypting a folder, the Confirm Attribute Changes dialog box appears, as shown here. You can choose to encrypt only the selected folder or its subfolders as well. Make a selection and click OK.

new feature!
The EFS service in Windows XP Professional includes a new feature that allows you to share an encrypted file or folder so that others you specify can access it. This feature lets you encrypt the file or folder as well as make exceptions if other users on your computer need to access the file and you want to allow them to do so. To enable others to use the encrypted file, follow these steps:

1   Right-click the encrypted file and choose Properties.

2   On the General tab, click the Advanced button, and then click the Details button in the Advanced Attributes dialog box.

392

> **tip** If the Details button appears dimmed, click OK, and allow the file to encrypt. When you return to the Advanced Attributes dialog box, the Details button will be available. Also note that the Details button is available at the file level only—not on encrypted folders.

3 In the Encryption Details dialog box that appears, you see the user account that is allowed to access the file. To allow others to access the file, click the Add button.

4 In the Select User dialog box shown here, select the additional users you want to access the file, and then click OK.

> **tip** Using EFS can be perilous. If the user profile that encrypts a file is damaged or destroyed and no system recovery agent was designated when the encryption took place, the file cannot be decrypted. For more information on designating recovery agents as well as learning the safest ways to use EFS, see "Managing EFS," page 595.

Enabling Disk Quotas

Disk quotas can be enabled on a per-volume basis. The volume to be enabled must be an NTFS volume, and you must have administrative privileges to even see the Quota tab in a volume's properties dialog box. Follow these steps to enable disk quotas:

1 Double-click My Computer.

2 Right-click the volume that needs to have a quota established or adjusted and choose Properties.

3 Select the Quota tab, shown on the next page. Select Enable Quota Management to turn on quota management.

4   Select the desired quota limits and logging options available on the tab. Note that you can prevent users from storing data once they exceed their quota.

> **note**   After you've established quota limits, you can check a user's quota status by clicking the Quota Entries button.

5   Click OK when you are done.

Mounting a Volume

To mount a volume as a folder, log on to the computer as a user with administrative rights, and then follow these steps.

1   Choose Start, Run.

2   Type **diskmgmt.msc**, and click OK to open the Disk Management snap-in. (You can also find the Disk Management snap-in in the Computer Management console in the Administrative Tools folder.)

3   Right-click the volume you want to mount (attach to another volume), and choose Change Drive Letter And Paths from the shortcut menu.

4   In the dialog box that appears, click the Add button.

5   Select Mount In The Following Empty NTFS Folder, and click the Browse button.

6   Browse to an empty folder or select a location, and click the New Folder button to create and name an empty folder. (Volumes can only be mounted on an empty folder.) Click OK to close each dialog box.

Use Windows Explorer or My Computer to access the mounted volume. You should now see a *volume within a volume*, which provides more flexible and expanded storage under one drive letter. This volume can be managed separately from the volume in which it is mounted using such tools as Disk Defragmenter and Chkdsk; to do so, simply refer to it by its root path name. For example, if you've mounted a second volume in the folder C:\Dev, you should refer to it as C:\Dev in any application that manages volumes.

Understanding Resource Sharing and NTFS Security

Why bother using networks at all? This is a fundamental question to ask before embarking on any network design. The usual answer is that a network is desired for the sharing of information. Without a network, your only option to move files from computer to computer is with a removable disk, and you can't share other hardware resources such as printers.

Although this observation might appear to be obvious, sharing resources continues to be the primary reason for creating home and small office networks. In addition, the need to share an Internet connection is often reason enough to create a network. In Microsoft Windows domain-based networks, centralized control, management, and security also continue to be major reasons for networking. But to users working on small or large networks, access to resources is the most important aspect of the network.

The term *network share* refers to a resource on the network that is designated to be shared among some or all the network's users. The most common shared network object is usually a folder or hard disk, but network shares can be many types of resources, such as disks, folders, removable storage devices, and printers. This chapter examines the process of sharing network resources, which consists of creating network shares, assigning share permissions, assigning file system permissions (if the NTFS file system is used), and managing shared resources. Common sharing problems and their solutions are also discussed in this chapter.

Understanding Network Resource Access

You can share just about anything on your Microsoft Windows XP computer, so that other users can access the shared resource from the network. The act of sharing resources on the network is fast and easy, and consists of four steps:

1 Sharing the resource

2 Configuring share permissions

3 Configuring NTFS permissions (if NTFS is used)

4 Managing the shared resource as needed

Before you dive into the process of sharing resources with others on the network, it's important to understand the conceptual model used to allow access to those assets. The following real-world example of accessing shared resources is used to explain this conceptual model.

Assume that Stephanie Bourne and George Jiang are both graphic designers at Tailspin Toys. Both users are running Microsoft Windows XP Professional, and both machines are members of a Windows domain. George has done some preliminary work on a set of drawings, and he would like Stephanie to take a look at them and give him some feedback. The drawings are too large and numerous to easily send as e-mail attachments, so he decides to make them available to her by sharing them from his hard disk drive. He creates a *share* called Stephanie on his PC (which is named Gjiang_pc) and grants Stephanie's user account within the domain access to the share. Because George is using NTFS on his computer, he also grants her access to the files. After this is done, he sends Stephanie an e-mail asking for her feedback and tells her she can find the files at the share \\gjiang\stephanie.

Stephanie receives the e-mail message and attempts to access the network share. Windows first attempts to connect to the remote workstation using Stephanie's user credentials. Because she's using her domain account, George's remote computer contacts a domain controller to validate her credentials.

> **note** If George and Stephanie were not using domain user accounts, she would instead have to log on using a user account that exists locally on George's computer.

Stephanie is properly logged on to the domain, so this validation is successful. Once Stephanie's user credentials are validated, George's computer determines whether that user has been granted access to the requested resource. Because George granted Stephanie the appropriate rights to the Stephanie share, this step is also successful. If George were using FAT as the file system on his computer, the process would be complete, and Stephanie would be able to open any file in the share; however, as noted earlier, George's hard disk is formatted using NTFS. George's computer must now determine whether Stephanie has the appropriate rights to the actual files. Because George granted those rights, Stephanie can now open the files and review them at her leisure.

As shown in the illustration, the process of determining whether Stephanie can access George's files consists of multiple steps. It can be helpful to think of these steps as potential layers of security that must be passed through before being granted access to the files in question.

Security Process for Accessing a Network Resource

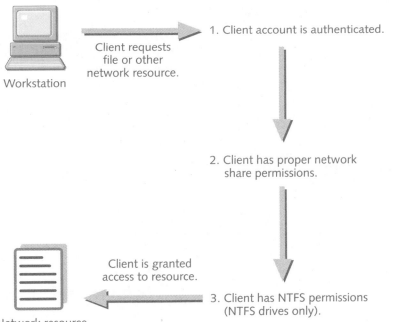

Workstation

Client requests file or other network resource.

1. Client account is authenticated.

2. Client has proper network share permissions.

Client is granted access to resource.

3. Client has NTFS permissions (NTFS drives only).

Network resource

For shared resources such as printers (or files located on FAT file systems), the third step is skipped. To summarize, once George has taken the steps to properly grant access to resources he wants to share, Windows handles all the work of user authentication to the resource whenever Stephanie (or anyone else) attempts to access them.

Now that the conceptual model for Windows resource access has been covered, the specific steps for sharing resources are discussed in the next section.

Sharing Resources

Computers running Windows XP Professional can share a tremendous array of resources including documents, music, photos, printers, Web pages, and more. However, when sharing these resources on the network, this array of resources can be sorted into three categories:

- **Printers.** Printer shares can share any type of device that uses the Windows printing interface, whether that printer is a dot-matrix, a thermal, an ink-jet, or a laser printer, or even a fax machine or document conversion system such as Adobe Acrobat Distiller.

- **File shares.** File shares encompass all types of data files, whether they are located on a hard disk, a compact disc, a removable disk, or even an offline storage system.

- **Web sharing.** Sharing files over the World Wide Web using Internet Information Services (IIS) is not covered in this chapter but rather in Chapter 9, "Using Internet Information Services."

This chapter covers the simplest forms of sharing first, working from printer sharing to file sharing and NTFS file system permissions.

Sharing Printers

Shared printers are often the driving force behind creating a home or small office network. After all, the expense of buying multiple printers, not to mention the desk space they consume, makes the concept of a single shared printer used between several home or small office computers very inviting.

To share a network printer, connect a printer directly to a Windows XP computer on your network. Then configure it as necessary so that the printer works the way you want it to from the local computer. If you are having problems installing the printer, see the printer manufacturer's help files or Web site. Once the printer is installed and working correctly on the local computer, you can then share the printer so that users on the rest of the network can access it. There are a few different ways that you can share and manage the shared printer: The following sections explore these features and options.

> Some printers have a network interface card (NIC) built into the printer that can be directly plugged into a network hub. For information about configuring a network-ready printer, see "Connecting to a Network-Ready Printer," page 418.

Sharing the Printer

To share the printer, work from the computer to which the printer is directly connected and follow these steps:

1 Choose Start and then choose Printers And Faxes (you can also open it in Control Panel).

2 Right-click the printer that you want to share and choose Sharing.

3 On the Sharing tab, shown in Figure 14-1, you have the option of sharing the printer or not. Select Share This Printer, and then enter an informative name in the Share Name box. Keep in mind that network clients will be able to see your printer and connect to it by the share name, so the share name should be simple, yet as descriptive as possible. It's a good idea to avoid using spaces in printer names.

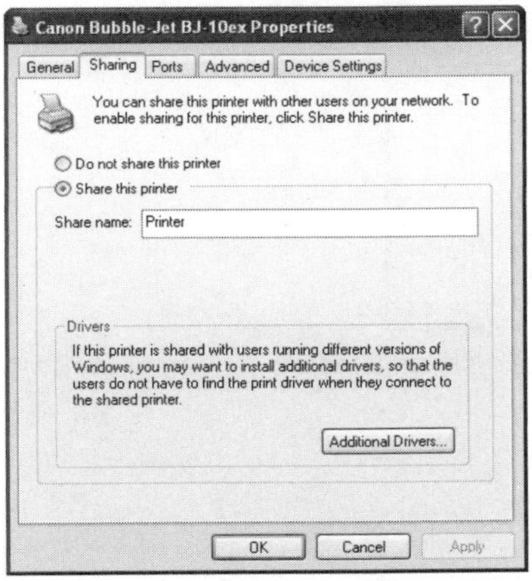

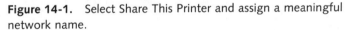

Figure 14-1. Select Share This Printer and assign a meaningful network name.

Notice that the Sharing tab has an Additional Drivers button. When a network computer wants to use the shared printer, the correct drivers must be installed on that network computer for use by its operating system. If you installed the printer on a Windows XP computer and all the other network clients are also running Windows XP, there is nothing else you need to do: Any network client that wants to print to the specified share will automatically download and install the needed driver software. However, if you have a mixture of Windows clients, such as Microsoft Windows 9*x* or Microsoft Windows NT, the driver installed for Windows XP might not work on these other computers, so Windows will instead prompt these clients to manually install the correct driver. However, Windows XP will allow you to place drivers for other versions of Windows on the computer that maintains the printer share, so that they can also be automatically downloaded and installed.

To take advantage of this feature, click the Additional Drivers button. In the Additional Drivers dialog box, shown in Figure 14-2 on the next page, select each Windows version that you want to support and click OK. When these clients attempt to connect to the shared printer, the correct drivers will be available for them. Depending on the other

Windows versions you need to support, you might need to download those drivers from the printer manufacturer's Web site. If Windows XP does not contain a compatible driver, a dialog box appears asking you to specify the location of an appropriate driver.

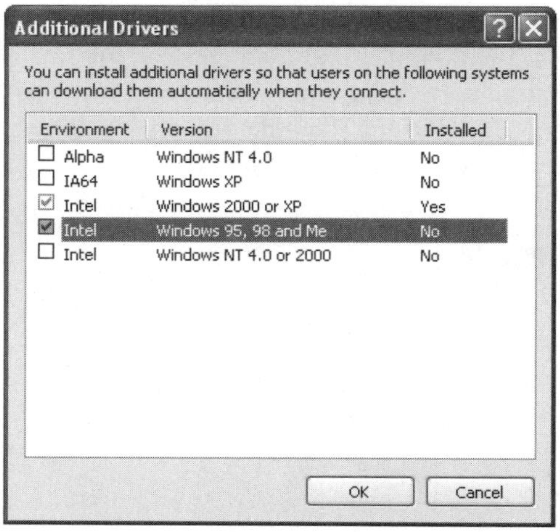

Figure 14-2. Choose the operating systems used on your network for which additional printer drivers are needed.

Assigning Printer Permissions

Printer permissions are rather simple to assign. By default, Windows XP uses a new feature called Simple File Sharing to streamline security management. When this option is activated, you are not able to directly manage printer permissions.

> See "Sharing Resources with Simple File Sharing Enabled," page 419, for more information about Simple File Sharing.

On Windows XP Professional, if Simple File Sharing is turned off, you have far more control over the ability of remote users to print to and manage printers on your system. These rights are managed using the Security tab found in the shared printer's properties dialog box. Note that Simple File Sharing must be turned off to be able to see the Security tab. There are three standard printer permissions:

- **Print.** This is the default printer permission assigned to users. This permission allows users the right to print documents and to manage their own documents in the print queue.

- **Manage Printers.** This permission, assigned to administrators by default, gives the user full control over the printer (but not the print queue). The user can change the configuration of the printer and even stop sharing it.

● **Manage Documents.** This permission, also assigned to administrators by default, grants full control of the print queue. A user with this permission can manage his or her own files in the print queue as well as everyone else's files. The user can also pause the entire printing process and delete all documents in the print queue.

> **tip** You can also set special permissions for the printer standard permissions if necessary. Click the Advanced button on the Security tab, select an account, and click Edit to access its special permissions.

By default, the Everyone group is granted the Print permission, as shown in Figure 14-3. This allows anyone on the network to print to this shared printer. On a small office or home network, the Print permission is normally sufficient, particularly if the network is either not connected to the Internet or uses a firewall to protect the network. However, your computer might be located on a more publicly accessible network, or you might want to only share the printer with certain individuals.

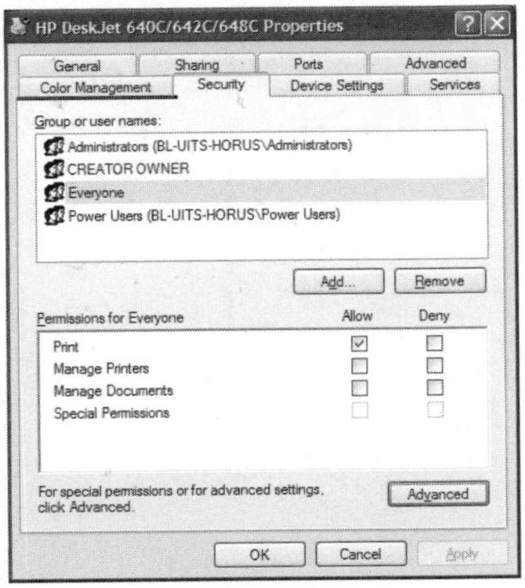

Figure 14-3. The Everyone group is granted the Print permission by default on new printer shares.

> There are other good reasons to restrict access to printer shares; you can learn more about them in "Securing Printers," page 585.

To restrict access to a printer:

1 From the Start menu, choose Printers And Faxes. Right-click the shared printer you want to configure and choose Sharing.

2 Select the Security tab, and then select Everyone in the Group Or User Names section.

3 In the Permissions For Everyone section, clear the check box under Allow for the Print permission, and then click Apply. The Everyone group should disappear from the list of groups or users that can access the printer.

Now, by default, only user accounts that belong to the Administrators or Power Users group on your computer will be able to use the printer. To grant printer access to additional users:

1 Open the properties dialog box for the printer and select the Security tab. Click the Add button to add a new user or group.

2 The Select Users Or Groups dialog box, as shown in Figure 14-4, appears. By default, this dialog box allows you to select groups or users from your computer's account database (unless your computer is a member of a Windows domain, in which case the default location for groups and users will be the Windows domain itself).

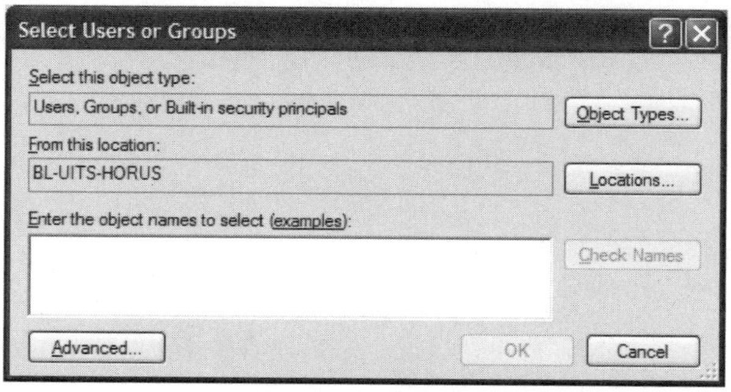

Figure 14-4. The Select Users Or Groups dialog box gives you a range of options for setting permissions on a resource.

3 If you need to find groups or users from another source (such as a Windows domain or your local account database), you can select a location by clicking the Locations button to open the Locations dialog box, as shown in Figure 14-5.

4 Once you've selected a location, you can either type in the name of the users and groups to which you want to grant printer access, or you can use the Advanced button to search for groups and users. In the dialog box shown in Figure 14-6, you can display groups and user names. If the account database you are using supports any of the attributes on the Common Queries tab, you will also be able to search on those attributes. To list all the users and groups in your account database, click the Find Now button.

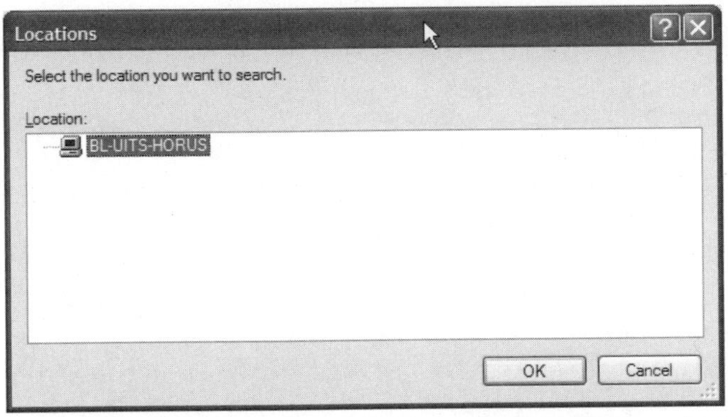

Figure 14-5. You can select an account database from which to select users and groups.

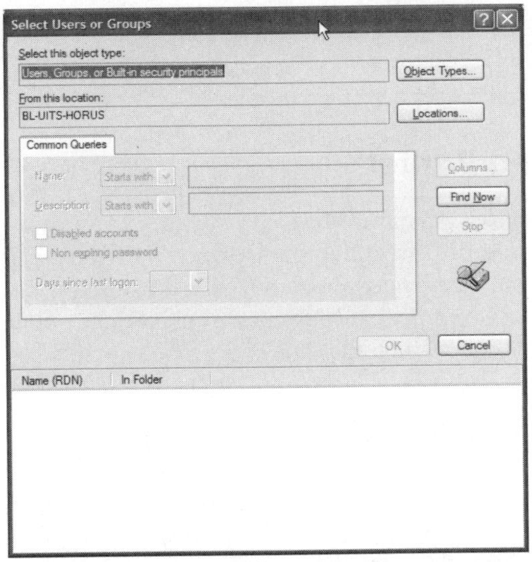

Figure 14-6. This dialog box helps you determine which users and groups are available.

5 After you've added the users and groups to which you want to grant access to the Users And Groups dialog box, click OK. You will be returned to the Security tab of the properties dialog box, where you can select each user or group and explicitly set Allow or Deny permissions.

> **caution** Be careful when assigning permissions. If you assign the Deny permissions to some groups, all members of those groups will be denied access, even if they are granted access through their user accounts or as members of other groups that have access. This occurs because Allow permissions are cumulative, but Deny permissions override all other permissions. Although denying access to entire groups might be desirable on occasion, try to establish permissions by clearing or selecting the check boxes in the Allow column and avoid using the check boxes in the Deny column.

> **note** If you are using Windows XP Professional in a domain environment, you can also advertise your local printer in the Active Directory printer list. If your computer has been placed in a domain, you'll also see a List In The Directory option on the Sharing tab. By activating this option, computers running Windows 2000 or Windows XP Professional can share printers and have them automatically published to Active Directory. Network users can then browse Active Directory and locate the printer based on its location and even by its features.

Connecting to a Shared Printer

Users can connect to a shared printer in the same way they connect to a shared folder, through My Network Places or by specifying the printer's Universal Naming Convention (UNC) path. The first time you connect to a shared printer, the appropriate drivers are downloaded to the computer, and the current print queue opens. You can browse the print queue and see which files are waiting to be printed so that you can monitor your print jobs.

By default, users on the network are given the Print permission. This means that they can print to the printer and manage their own print documents in the queue. As shown in Figure 14-7, users can access the print queue, select their files that are waiting to be printed, and use the Document menu to pause or cancel any of their print jobs. Users cannot alter the state of another user's print jobs or control the printer in any other way.

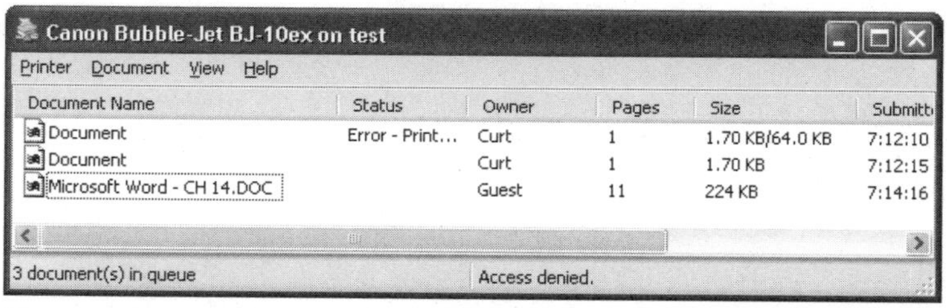

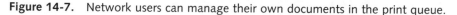

Figure 14-7. Network users can manage their own documents in the print queue.

> **tip** Users can choose the Printer menu and choose Printing Preferences to control the printing options, such as Orientation and Page Order, for their documents. Users can also choose Properties from the Printer menu and browse the printer's properties, but these options appear dimmed and are unavailable so that users don't change the printer's base configuration.

Managing the Shared Printer

Once you share a printer, it is your job to manage the printer and make sure it is available and working when network clients need it. This includes keeping the paper tray full and managing ink cartridges of course, but the tasks described in the following sections also fall within the scope of management.

Managing the Print Queue

As mentioned in the previous section, users cannot manage other users' print jobs. However, you, as the printer administrator, do have total control over the print queue. This means that you can open the print queue at any time and cancel or pause files that are in the queue. You can also use the Printer menu to cancel all documents that are waiting to be printed, or you can pause all printing. Why might you need these options or this level of control? Consider a few examples:

- In a small network of five computers, there might be a single shared printer. As the administrator, you can look in the print queue, and you might observe that five print jobs are waiting. If the second print job waiting to print is over 200 pages and the remaining three are only one page each and are needed immediately, you can select the large print job and use the Document menu to simply cancel it. You can then inform the user that larger print jobs must wait until a less busy time of the day. Or, you can pause the large print job, let the remaining jobs print, and then allow the large job to print.

- In an office network, you might observe 10 jobs in the print queue. As the administrator, you notice that the print device's ink cartridge needs to be changed. Rather than deleting all of the print jobs and disrupting users' work, you can use the Printer menu to pause printing. You can then replace the cartridge and continue printing when you are ready.

> **tip** For quicker access, right-click the printer icon in the Printers And Faxes folder and choose Pause Printing or Cancel All Documents.

- In your office, there might be several jobs in the print queue, but the printer has suddenly stopped responding. You can use the Printer menu to cancel all documents so that the printer can be repaired.

> **tip** When you cancel a user's print job, the user is not informed of the cancellation. In other words, a "printer error" message is not returned to the user. You have to inform the user that the job has been cancelled, although the user can look in the print queue and see that the job is no longer waiting in the queue.

Setting Print Schedules and Priorities

Besides managing the print queue, there are a few other management options that you should be aware of. If you right-click a shared printer's icon in the Printers And Faxes folder, you can open its properties dialog box. If you then select the Advanced tab, you see a number of printer options, as shown in Figure 14-8. In terms of networking, the important aspects of this tab are the scheduling and priority settings, described next.

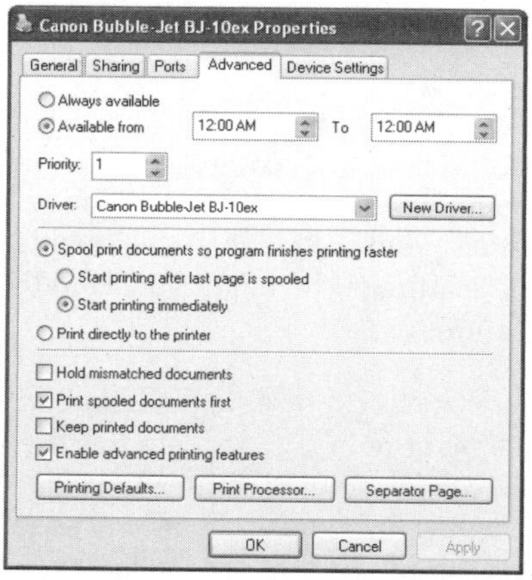

Figure 14-8. The Advanced tab of a printer's properties dialog box allows to you to configure schedules and priorities.

Establishing printer schedules   Notice at the top of the dialog box that by default the printer is always available to users. However, you might want to limit the shared printer's availability. To do so, select the Available From option, and then select the hours of operation that the printer should be available. Keep in mind that this setting affects all users including network users and users logged on locally—even you. Unless a local user has administrative privileges to modify the schedule as needed, the local or network user can only use the printer during the specified hours of operation.

The schedule option can be useful, but because it uniformly applies to all local and network users, it might not be practical. For example, you might want the printer to be available only to you from 8:00 A.M. to 10:00 A.M. each day, but you want network users to be able to use the printer after 10:00 A.M. You can do this by setting up more than one share for the same physical printing device, as described in the steps that follow. To understand how this works, you need to understand that when you install a printer, the software that Windows XP uses to run that printer is also installed. This computer and software combination is collectively called the *printer*. In contrast, the physical printing machine that sits on your desk is called a *print device*. The terms can be misleading, but the important point is that you control sharing at the level of the *printer* (the software configuration), not the *printing device*. This means you can configure multiple printers for the same physical print device, and each printer's configuration can meet different needs.

The easiest way to understand the use of multiple printers is to consider a step-by-step example. After reading these steps, you might want to implement a similar configuration on your network.

> **tip** The only way to use different schedules on the same printer is to create multiple shares, each of which prints to the same print device. You cannot assign schedules to users or groups in Windows XP Professional, but you can use different printers and alter the configurations as needed.

1 From the computer to which the printer is attached, open the printer's properties dialog box, and stop sharing the printer. To do this, select Do Not Share This Printer on the Sharing tab and click Apply.

2 Select the Advanced tab, and make sure the Always Available option is selected.

3 Create a second printer, also called a *virtual printer*, for your printing device. Choose File, Add Printer in Printers And Faxes, and follow the wizard. You can use the existing driver, and you'll be prompted for a share name for the new printer.

4 Open the virtual printer's properties dialog box. On the Sharing tab, confirm the printer's share name you entered in the wizard. Click Additional Drivers to install drivers for other versions of Windows if needed.

5 Select the Advanced tab. Select Available From, and set the hours that you want the printer to be available to network users. Click OK.

Now you have two printers installed for the same print device. The first printer is for you (and other local users) and is available all the time, but not shared on the network. The second (virtual) printer is for shared network use and is only available during the hours you have specified.

> **note** During the time period that a printer is not available to network users, users can still send print jobs to the printer queue, but they are not printed until the printer becomes available according to the schedule.

Assigning printer priorities   Consider this situation: You are the administrator of a printer connected to a Windows XP computer. The documents that you print are often very important and need to be printed quickly for clients. However, because the printer is shared, your documents often end up waiting in the print queue. You need to make your documents print faster than other users' documents. The way to accomplish this is to assign priorities.

The priority of a print job determines its order in the print queue. High-priority print jobs are serviced before low-priority print jobs, and this ensures that high-priority files are printed first. By default, each printer is configured with a priority of 1. This default value is the lowest priority, but because there is only one printer, the priority value doesn't matter. However, if you have set up two or more printers for the same print device (as described in "Establishing Printer Schedules," page 408), you can configure different priorities. This configuration is only effective on Windows XP Professional computers where you can assign different users and groups to different printers, thus creating the desired priority structure. In Windows XP Home Edition (or if Simple File Sharing is being used), you cannot differentiate between permissions for network users and groups, so the priority feature isn't beneficial.

When you create multiple printers, the printer with the lower priority number has the least amount of priority. Consider this example: In a certain network environment, a Windows XP Professional computer has three shared printers (for the same *printing device*). One share is configured for the Administrators group with a priority of 75. The second share is for a marketing team and has a priority of 50. The third printer share is for all general users and has a priority of 1. The administrators' print jobs will be moved ahead in the print queue over marketing and general users, and marketing print jobs will be moved ahead of the general users.

Managing the Print Spooler

The *print spooler* is a program that holds print jobs in a location on your computer's hard disk until they are printed. If you select the Advanced tab on a printer's properties dialog box, you'll see the default spool settings. These options enable you to use the spooler or not and to start printing immediately or wait until the last page is spooled. Usually, you should use the print spooler, and you should *always* use it in a networking situation. If you disable spooling, users' print jobs must remain on their computers until the printer is ready for them, which causes applications to pause during the printing process until the printer is ready to print their documents. On a heavily used printer, this delay can become unacceptable. For the fastest printing results, select the Start Printing Immediately option so that printing starts as quickly as possible.

On occasion, the print spooler might hang or lock up due to a faulty print request or a bug in the printer driver. When this happens, the printer will become unresponsive to network printing requests, even though the printing device might be functioning perfectly. It's normally sufficient to simply restart the Print Spooler service by following these steps:

1 From the Start menu, choose Administrative Tools, Services.

2 Scroll through the list of services until you find Print Spooler.

3 Right-click Print Spooler, and choose Restart. This will cause the document that was being processed when the print spooler hung to be lost, but all other documents in the queue will continue to print normally.

> **note** The print spooler folder is located in %SystemRoot%\System32\Spool\Printers. (The environment variable %SystemRoot% resolves to the Windows XP installation folder, which by default would be C:\Windows.)

Managing Print Server Properties

When you share a network printer, you can also configure a few other options that might be helpful to you by accessing the Print Server Properties dialog box. In the Printers And Faxes folder, choose File, Server Properties. The following list explains the options the Print Server Properties dialog box provides:

● **Forms.** On the Forms tab, shown in Figure 14-9, you can configure the forms and paper sizes for the printer to use. You can also create new custom forms and specify their size. This setting is helpful in situations where users need to print on custom business forms.

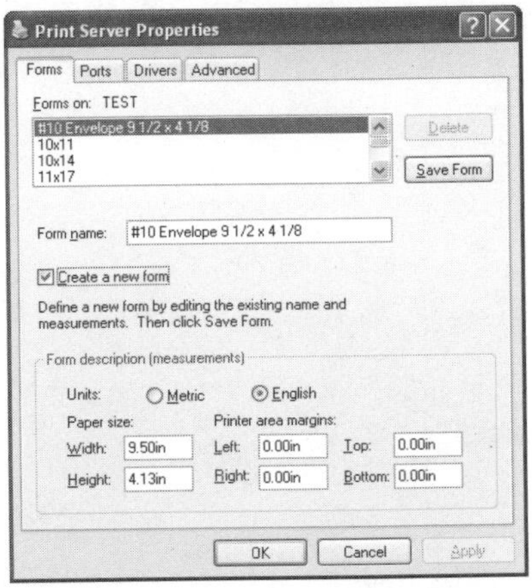

Figure 14-9. The Forms tab allows you to specify custom forms that can be used.

411

● **Ports.** The Ports tab lists all available ports on the computer. You can add, delete, and configure ports on this tab.

● **Drivers.** The current printer drivers installed on the computer are listed on the Drivers tab, shown in Figure 14-10. You can easily add, remove, and replace drivers from this tab, and check their properties.

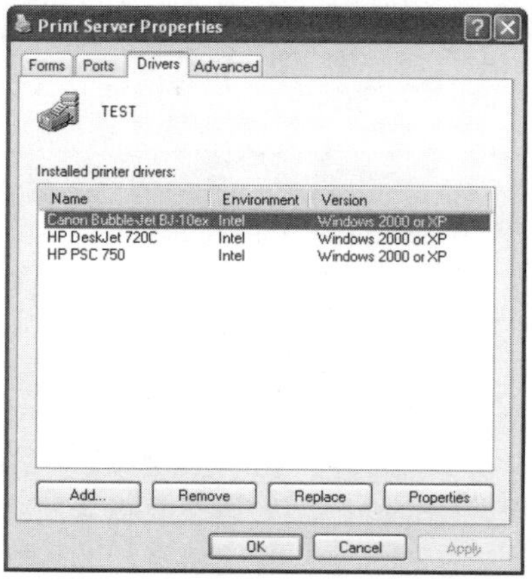

Figure 14-10. The Drivers tab lists the currently installed drivers.

● **Advanced.** The Advanced tab, shown in Figure 14-11, contains information about the print spooler folder and some additional settings. You can choose to log print spooler errors and warnings. You can also choose to send informational notifications, which are pop-up messages that appear in the notification area, for local and network printers. In addition, you can set notification options to use for *downlevel* clients—those running earlier versions of Windows.

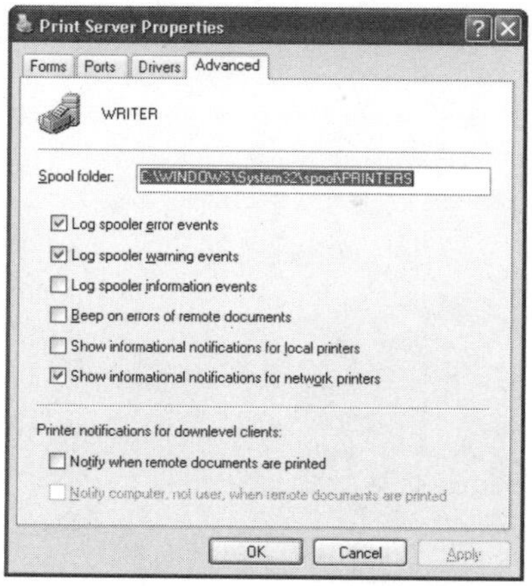

Figure 14-11. Print spooler settings and informational notifications are managed on the Advanced tab.

412

Using a Separator Page

You might want to use separator pages with a shared network printer. The *separator page* prints between each print job so that users can more easily distinguish their print jobs from those of other users. Open the printer's properties dialog box, select the Advanced tab, and click the Separator Page button. In the Separator Page dialog box that appears, click Browse. Windows XP opens to the location of the four default separator pages included in Windows XP:

- **Pcl.sep.** This separator page switches the printer to Printer Control Language (PCL) and prints a separator page that includes the account name, job number, date, and time.

- **Sysprint.sep.** This separator page switches the printer to PostScript, and then prints a separator page that includes the account name, job number, date, and time.

- **Pscript.sep.** This separator page switches the printer to PostScript, but does not actually print a separator page.

- **Sysprtj.sep.** This separator page is the same as Sysprint.sep, but it uses Japanese fonts if they are available.

The separator pages are text files that you can open with any text editor. They consist of printer language code that tells the separator page how to print, as shown in Figure 14-12. You can modify any of these pages to meet your needs, or you can create your own separator pages if you know the printer language. See *Microsoft Windows XP Inside Out* by Ed Bott and Carl Siechert (Microsoft Press, 2001) for more information about customizing separator pages.

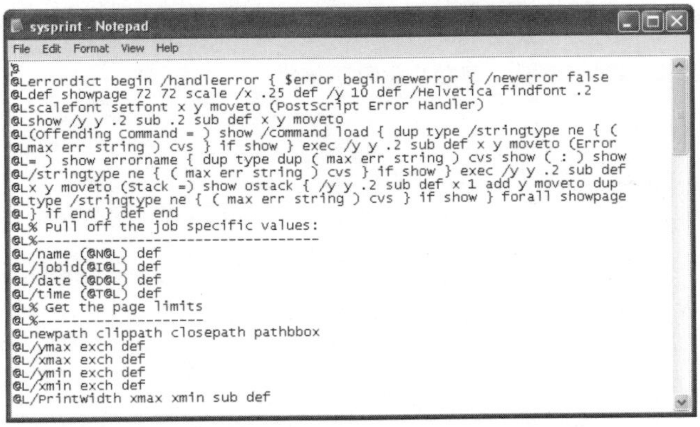

Figure 14-12. This separator page uses PostScript code to insert an informational page between print jobs.

Creating an Internet Printer

Windows XP supports the Internet Printing Protocol (IPP), which allows Windows XP to share a printer over the Internet or an intranet, or connect to an Internet or intranet printer. To share an Internet or intranet printer on Windows XP, the computer to which the printing device is attached must be running IIS, which is only supported in Windows XP Professional. Therefore, if you are using Windows XP Home Edition, you can connect to an Internet or an intranet printer, but you cannot share a printing device connected to your computer.

If you want to share an Internet printer, you must first install and set up IIS. See Chapter 9, "Using Internet Information Services," to learn more about setting up IIS. Once IIS is set up and configured, the printers that you share on the Windows XP Professional computer automatically become available through IPP as long as IIS is running. Essentially, this means that users can use Microsoft Internet Explorer to connect to your computer and access any shared printers by typing **http://*hostname*/printers**, where *hostname* is the name of the Windows XP Professional computer running IIS and sharing the printer or printers. For example, users on a LAN can access shared printers on a Windows XP Professional computer named Writer by typing **http://writer/printers**. Figure 14-13 shows the Web page listing the name and status of the shared printer on the Writer computer.

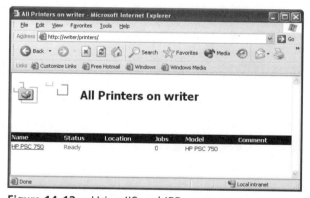

Figure 14-13. Using IIS and IPP, users can access a printer through a Web browser.

A user can click the printer link and view the printer queue in a Web browser format, as shown in Figure 14-14. Similar to using a typical print queue, users have the right to see the print queue and cancel or pause their own print jobs, but not the print jobs of others. Those with an administrator account on the local machine can manage the entire print queue.

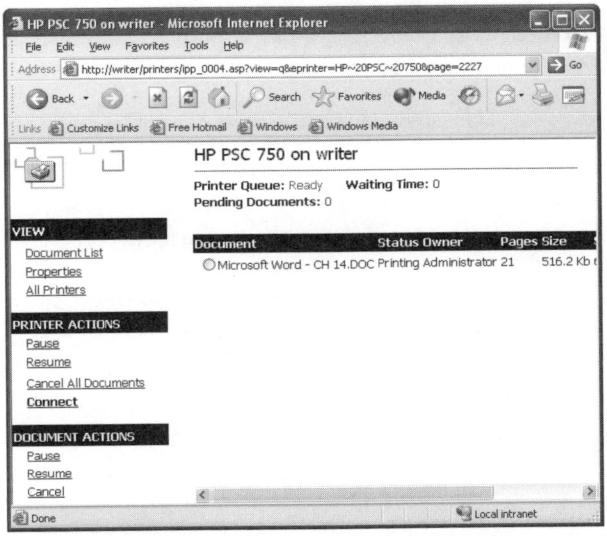

Figure 14-14. Users can view and manage their print documents using an HTML print queue.

Users can also click the Properties link under View in the left pane to obtain more information about the printer, such as its speed, color capability, and resolution, as shown in Figure 14-15.

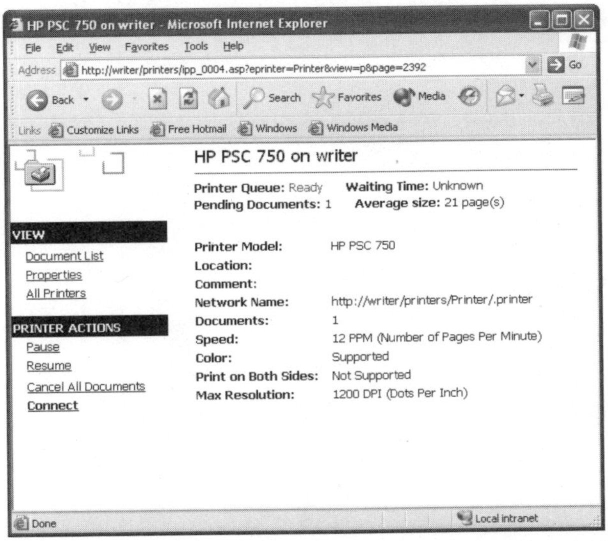

Figure 14-15. Users can view a shared printer's properties through the HTML interface.

> **tip** You can view the entire list of available printers on a computer by typing **http://** **hostname/printers**. But if you know the name of the printer you want to use, you can access it directly by typing **http://*hostname*/printers/*printername*/.printer**, where *printername* is the shared name of the printer.

Although you can access an Internet printer using Internet Explorer, you can also add the Internet printer to your Printers And Faxes folder so that it becomes an option you can print to from any Windows application. To install an Internet printer in either Windows XP Professional or Windows XP Home Edition, follow these steps:

1 Open Printers And Faxes from the Start menu or from Control Panel.

2 Click Add A Printer under Printer Tasks in the left pane, or choose File, Add Printer.

3 When the Add Printer Wizard appears, click Next.

4 On the Local Or Network Printer page, select the option labeled A Network Printer, Or A Printer Attached To Another Computer, and click Next.

5 On the Specify A Printer page, select Connect To A Printer On The Internet Or On A Home Or Office Network. Enter the URL in the format shown here.

6 You might be prompted to choose an account or enter a specified account if the printer's folder is password protected. Enter any necessary information on the Configure Internet Port page of the wizard, shown on the next page, and click Next.

7 Complete the wizard. You might also be prompted to select a driver for the printer if you are using an earlier version of Windows.

Whenever you print a document from a Windows application after the printer is installed, the Internet printer will be listed along with any local printers or network printers.

InsideOut

Internet Printing in the Corporate Environment

On a home or small office network, Internet printing might not seem like a very valuable feature. However, imagine that your computer is part of a corporate network of thousands of computers where an intranet is used. Instead of the usual network methods of accessing printers, Internet printing gives users an easier way to access the printer through the intranet using a simple HTML interface.

Or, consider another use: Suppose your network consists of one Windows domain with offices in three geographically distant locations. You travel frequently between these locations, and you produce a number of documents that must be disseminated often. Sure, you can e-mail the document to a colleague, but you can also simply send the document directly to an Internet printer available through IIS. If you are in Tampa and the printer is in Seattle, you can access the printer server and print directly over the Internet, making your work directly available to people who are thousands of miles away. Internet printing is a powerful feature that can meet your networking needs in many ways.

Connecting to a Network-Ready Printer

Most printers connect directly to a single computer on a network through a computer's parallel, USB, IEEE (FireWire), or infrared port, especially in home and small office networks. You then share that printer with other network clients who access the printer through your computer on the network.

However, you might have a printer that is outfitted with a NIC and connects directly to your network hub (particularly in a larger office). In this case, the printer is not installed on a computer, but instead acts as a stand-alone network device that connects to the network just like any computer. Every computer on the network can then access the printer directly and print to it.

In the case of a network-enabled printer, you can connect to the printer through its IP address. To do so, you have to define a TCP/IP port. Follow these steps:

1 Connect the printer to the network and turn it on.

2 Open Printers And Faxes from the Start menu or Control Panel, and click the Add A Printer link under Printer Tasks in the left pane. (You can also choose File, Add Printer.)

3 When the Add Printer Wizard appears, click Next.

4 On the Local Or Network Printer page, select Local Printer Attached To This Computer. Clear the option beneath it, Automatically Detect And Install My Plug And Play Printer, and then click Next.

5 On the Select A Printer Port page, shown here, select Create A New Port, and then select Standard TCP/IP Port in the Type Of Port box. Click Next.

6 The Add Standard TCP/IP Printer Port Wizard appears. Click Next.

7 On the Add Port page, enter the IP address of the printer. You can get this information by having the printer print a configuration page. See the printer's documentation for details. The Port Name field will be filled in automatically, but you can change the name if necessary. Click Next.

8 The computer connects to the Internet printer and displays a connection page. Click Finish.

The network-ready printer will now be available in Printers And Faxes along with any printers shared through a network computer connection or the Internet, or connected directly to the local computer. Although any computer on the network can print directly to the printer using this technique, it often simplifies the management of printers to have one computer (normally a server) connect to the printer directly, and then share that printer to other clients. This provides all the advantages of print queuing, allowing the computer to manage documents with its ample hard disk space instead of relying on the printer and its limited amount of onboard RAM. Using a print queue also adds reliability, allowing documents to be held on the server in case the printer goes offline.

It's also wise to manage networked printers through print queues on Windows computers for security reasons. See "Securiting Printers," page 585, for more information.

Sharing Files

Shared files are another important network resource that people come to depend on, particularly in large corporate environments. They can also be handy in home and small office networks. You can do such things as maintain central stores for commonly used files and collaborate on larger documents.

By default, Windows XP computers that are not members of a domain use a new feature called Simple File Sharing, which was designed to streamline the process of managing file shares (and NTFS permissions, when NTFS is used instead of FAT32 as the underlying file system).

Sharing Resources with Simple File Sharing Enabled

Simple File Sharing is a computer-wide setting in Windows XP that provides you with a measure of security and makes NTFS permissions easy for users to manage. When you share a resource such as a file on the network with Simple File Sharing enabled, other users can read (but not change) the resource. Depending on your preferences, you can also give full control to users so they can make changes as well. Simple File Sharing enables you to make your personal files private and to quickly share resources over your network.

> **note** Windows XP computers that are participating in a domain cannot use Simple File Sharing.

Sharing Folders

One of the most common network shares is shared folders. After all, you can put just about any kind of document, picture, or file in a folder and share it. Network users can then browse the network, locate the folder you have shared, and access the information inside the folder, depending on the permissions you have assigned.

To share a folder with Simple File Sharing enabled, you first need to ensure that the folder does not currently reside in a private folder. If it does, you'll need to either remove the private setting from the parent folder or move the folder to another location. To share the folder, follow these steps:

1 Right-click the folder you want to share and choose Sharing And Security.

2 On the Sharing tab, shown here, select Share This Folder On The Network, and then enter a name for the folder in the Share Name box.

The name of the share is the name network users will see. It can be completely different from the actual folder name.

3 After you select Share This Folder On The Network, the option beneath it becomes available—Allow Network Users To Change My Files. If this option is selected, users will have full control to edit and even delete files. If you only want users to be able to read your files, clear this check box. Click OK.

The folder is now shared. An open hand appears as part of the folder's icon, signifying that the object is shared on the network.

Limitations on Network Security with Simple File Sharing

Simple File Sharing doesn't give you many security options. When you share a network folder, users can either read the contents, or they can have full control. This lack of flexibility in determining who can view or modify data on your computer makes Simple File Sharing unsuitable on any computer that is accessible over the Internet because it makes your computer extremely vulnerable to hackers and to software worms. For this reason, it is strongly recommended that you not use Simple File Sharing unless its use is absolutely necessary (or if your computer is not connected in any way to the Internet). If you are using Windows XP Professional, you can disable Simple File Sharing and assign NTFS permissions manually, which you can learn more about in "Managing Permissions with Simple File Sharing Disabled," page 426.

If you are using Windows XP Home Edition, however, Simple File Sharing is your only option. This makes Windows XP Home Edition somewhat unsuitable for sharing files over the network, particularly if you need to write or create files from a remote location. If you are using Windows XP Home Edition, and you must share files with others, be certain that your computer is firewalled from the Internet (either via Internet Connection Firewall [ICF] or a hardware device), and that you aggressively use antivirus software to protect your computer from threats that can be propagated via other computers on your network. For more information about the security limitations of Simple File Sharing, see "Evaluating Simple File Sharing," page 585.

tip   **Using Friendly Share Names**

Remember that users access shared folders by the *share name*, which doesn't need to match the *folder* name. To make network users' lives easier, use share names that are readily understandable. If you keep company documents on your hard disk in a folder named CMPYDCS, rather than accepting the folder name as the default share name, give the share a meaningful name, such as Company Docs. Many users on your network might not have the skills and networking knowledge that you do, so make network share names simple and descriptive.

Before you share network folders, consider the implications of sharing carefully—even on a home network. After all, do you really want your kids accidentally deleting your files and folders? In an office setting, do you really want other network users to have access to all the shared folder's files? You should think through these issues carefully as you decide whether to share files with other users. Because of the security and management issues involved, consider adopting these practices:

- Only share files that need to be shared. That sounds obvious, but make sure you are not sharing folders that contain some files that need to be shared as well as other files that don't. Sharing folders that contain more than the files you really need to share tends to make management more difficult for you.

● Create folders that are used just for network sharing. Give the folders network-friendly names, and make sure subfolder names are easily understandable. This will help you manage the files that are shared more easily.

Sharing Drives

Similar to sharing folders, to share a drive, simply right-click the drive, and then choose Sharing And Security. The difference is that the Sharing tab will warn you that sharing an entire drive is not recommended. To continue you'll have to click the link that reads If You Understand The Risk But Still Want To Share The Root Of The Drive, Click Here. You'll then see the familiar Sharing tab, where you select Share This Folder On The Network and give the drive a share name. But the advice to not share an entire drive should be taken seriously. If you decide to share your boot and system volume, other users on the network will have complete access to your drive and could render your machine inoperable by deleting important system files.

But there might be times when sharing an entire drive makes sense. For example, suppose you have a home network with three computers, and only one computer has a Zip drive. If you want to store data on the Zip drive from all three computers, you could create a network share on the computer with the drive where users can store data, and then you could copy that data to the Zip drive. However, why not just share the Zip drive? If you keep a disk inside the Zip drive for storing data, you can access the drive from any computer and copy data to the drive. The same concept is true with a writable (CD-R) or rewritable (CD-RW) drive. There are even times when you might want to share a fixed disk volume. Suppose you've used Microsoft Windows Media Player to create a digital library of your entire CD collection. If you place that library on its own volume and share it, the entire music collection is available from any computer. This can save you from having to buy extra hard disk capacity for each machine because the music remains stored on only one computer.

Always stop and think carefully before you share an entire hard disk drive. Under no circumstances should you give access to the Everyone group (as is done by Simple File Sharing), unless your computers are not connected to the Internet in any way, as doing so would leave the volume extremely vulnerable to Trojan horse programs and Internet worms. Even in home networks, files are accidentally deleted and problems arise. So when you share a drive, consider that you are giving everyone complete access to the drive. If you are not comfortable doing this, look for an alternative way to reach your network share goals.

Sharing Applications

Some applications can be shared so that they can be accessed over the network by network users. However, before you begin sharing applications, there are some important items to consider:

- Some programs will not work in a shared environment. Because of the way the programs install on the local machine, they cannot be run remotely on the network.

- The licensing agreement accompanying some programs might not permit you to share the program over the network or at least not without paying additional licensing fees. Check the licensing agreement carefully.

- Sharing applications over a network can consume a lot of network bandwidth and create excessive network traffic. Carefully consider your available bandwidth and the need for application sharing before doing so.

---

tip   **Using Remote Desktop as an Alternative to Sharing Applications**

You can run nearly any application remotely by running the computer on which it resides remotely, using Remote Desktop. Applications accessed by remotely running the computer on which they're installed will avoid the first two issues in the previous list—incompatibility because of the way programs are installed on the remote computer and licensing restrictions. The third issue, network bandwidth, can still be an issue. Also, running software remotely in this fashion is not really a replacement for application sharing among multiples users, because a computer that is providing remote services can't be used by another user at the same time. See "Exploring Remote Desktop," page 473, for more information about Remote Desktop.

If you decide to share an application, locate the application's folder (typically a folder within %SystemRoot%\Program Files) and share the entire application folder. You might have to assign users the Full Control permission to the application's folder for them to be able to launch the application and use it. If you don't want to grant users the Full Control permission, you can experiment with more restrictive permissions to find the minimum level of permissions that allows the application to run correctly.

Making Folders Private

In a home or small office network, a sense of trust is usually established among users, and for this reason, Simple File Sharing gives you an easy way to make shares available to network users. However, what about users that log on to the same computer? By default, when a new user account is created in Windows XP, the account is set up with a profile and a series of folders. The user has full control of these folders. But users with an administrator account (or the operating system's built-in System account) also have full control of these folders. In fact, there might be several users accessing your local computer who have administrator accounts, and if you are working with sensitive data that you don't want others to see, you can choose to make any or all of your user profile folders private. If you are using NTFS, when you make a folder private, the Administrators group and the built-in System account are removed from the resource's access control list (ACL), leaving only the user in control of the folder and able to view and alter its contents. ACLs are discussed in more detail in "Configuring NTFS Permissions," page 433.

To make one of your user profile folders private, right-click the folder, and then choose Sharing And Security. On the Sharing tab, shown in Figure 14-16, select Make This Folder Private. Once you make a folder private, all its subfolders are made private as well.

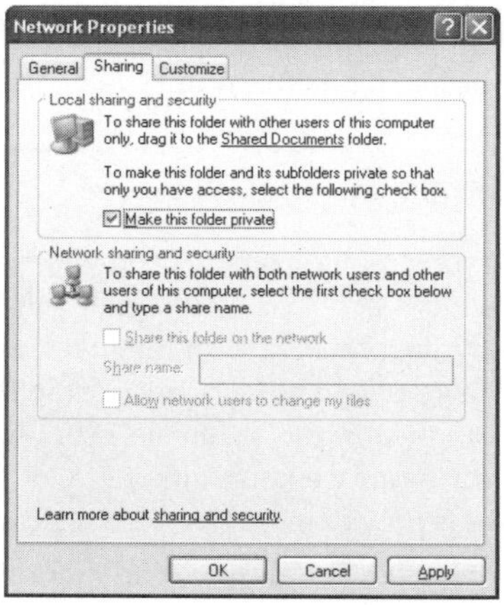

Figure 14-16. Selecting Make This Folder Private removes the Administrators group and the built-in System account from the ACL of the folder and its subfolders.

> **note** If your Sharing tab is different from the one shown in Figure 14-16 and you also see a Security tab, Simple File Sharing is turned off on your Microsoft Windows XP Professional computer. If you want to turn it on and you're not a member of a Windows domain, you can open Folder Options in Control Panel and select the View tab. In the Advanced Settings list, select Use Simple File Sharing (Recommended). In Windows XP Home Edition, Simple File Sharing is always in effect and cannot be disabled.

If the Make This Folder Private check box is already selected but the option appears dimmed, the folder is a subfolder of another folder that has been made private. To change this subfolder from being private, you either have to remove the private setting from the parent folder (you might have to navigate up several levels to find the top level at which the folders were shared), or you have to drag the folder to the Shared Documents folder. If the Make This Folder Private option appears dimmed but is not selected, it means you can't make the folder private. The folder might not be in your user profile, it might belong to another user or one of the All Users (shared) folders, or it might not be a user profile folder at all. Only NTFS drives are able to use the security features of Simple File Sharing to restrict how local users access files, and Simple File Sharing only makes your own user folders private.

caution As discussed in Chapter 13, "Selecting a File System," FAT drives do not maintain any security-related data about files; thus, although shares can prevent remote users from accessing files on your computer, any user who is logged on to your system locally can access any file on a FAT partition. To prevent this, format or convert your drives to NTFS.

Using the Shared Documents Folder

Windows XP maintains a Shared Documents folder (and subfolders) that is available to anyone who has an account on the computer. Users that have administrative privileges have full control over the Shared Documents folder and its subfolders (which include Shared Music and Shared Pictures). Users with Limited accounts (as well as remote users who use the Guest account when Simple File Sharing is enabled) can browse the folders and read the data, but they cannot create new folders or files, and they cannot move or copy existing files and folders to this location. The purpose of the Shared Documents folder is to provide a way for administrators to make common documents and files available to all users on the computer. The Shared Documents folder is a subfolder of the All Users folder located in the Documents And Settings folder. You can also find the Shared Documents folder listed in My Computer.

InsideOut

The Truth About Private Folders

Private folders give users an easy way to keep folders private from anyone else on the computer, including computer administrators. However, they also have serious limitations.

- You can make folders private only in your own user profile. If the folder is on a different NTFS volume or in another folder that is not within your user profile hierarchy of folders, you cannot make the folder private. A good example is application data, which is often saved in a specific application folder. Because the folder is not within your user profile, you cannot make it private. Therefore, you are somewhat limited as to what you can make private.

- Private folders are private without exception. You cannot override the private settings and give another user access when Simple File Sharing is enabled. Once you make the folder private, only you can access the folder.

- All files and subfolders in the private folder are also made private. You cannot apply different settings to individual subfolders or individual files.

- Private folders cannot be shared on the network.

(continued)

> **Inside Out** *(continued)* It is important to keep in mind that private folders are applied to the local computer and users who log on locally. Network users do not have access to local folders unless they are specifically shared, so it is important to understand the difference between shared folders and private folders. Private folders are beneficial when multiple people log on to the same computer, and you want to make sure that no one with administrative privileges is able to read or access data in a particular folder.

> **caution** If you are a Windows XP Professional user, don't assume that you can simply encrypt the folder that you want to make private instead of using the Make This Folder Private option. Keep in mind that system recovery agents (discussed in "Managing EFS," page 595) might be able to decrypt the files!

Managing Permissions with Simple File Sharing Disabled

The concept of permissions often causes considerable trepidation even on the part of experienced computer users, and rightly so. Permissions can be complicated and confusing. For this reason, when Windows XP was released, Microsoft recommended using Simple File Sharing and enabled it by default in Windows XP. Using Simple File Sharing, users have basic Read access to network shares, or you can assign them Full Control access to the shares, depending on your needs. However, this simplistic network security model is not sufficient in these days of constant security threats and Internet worms. When using Windows XP Professional, it's normally a better idea to turn off Simple File Sharing. This section explores the possibilities that turning off Simple File Sharing provides to users of Windows XP Professional.

Removing Simple File Sharing

If you're running Windows XP Professional, you can disable Simple File Sharing by changing a single setting. If you choose to do this, the full range of NTFS permissions and security features become available to you. Of course, make sure that you really want to administer NTFS permissions manually before disabling Simple File Sharing because Simple File Sharing is your easiest choice.

To remove Simple File Sharing from Windows XP Professional, follow these steps:

1 Choose Start, Control Panel, and open Folder Options. You can also access Folder Options from Windows Explorer or most folder windows by choosing Tools, Folder Options.

2 In the Folder Options dialog box, select the View tab. Scroll to the bottom of the Advanced Settings list and clear the Use Simple File Sharing (Recommended) option, as shown next. Click OK.

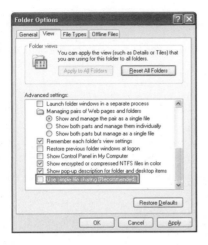

Assigning Share and NTFS Permissions

Once Simple File Sharing is disabled, you'll find several significant changes when you access the properties dialog box for a folder, drive, or application that you want to share. The Sharing tab changes its appearance so that the Simple File Sharing components and the Make This Folder Private feature are no longer displayed. Instead, you see a Sharing tab that resembles the one found in Windows 2000, where you can share the object, limit the number of concurrent connections to it, and set permissions, as shown in Figure 14-17. In addition, there's an entirely new tab, the Security tab, which is used to assign NTFS permissions. (The Security tab won't be present on a FAT volume.)

Figure 14-17. The Sharing tab changes to a Windows 2000 style once Simple File Sharing is turned off.

427

Setting Permissions for Network Shares

Notice that the Sharing tab now includes a Permissions button. If you click the Permissions button, you can set the permissions for the shared folder, as shown in Figure 14-18.

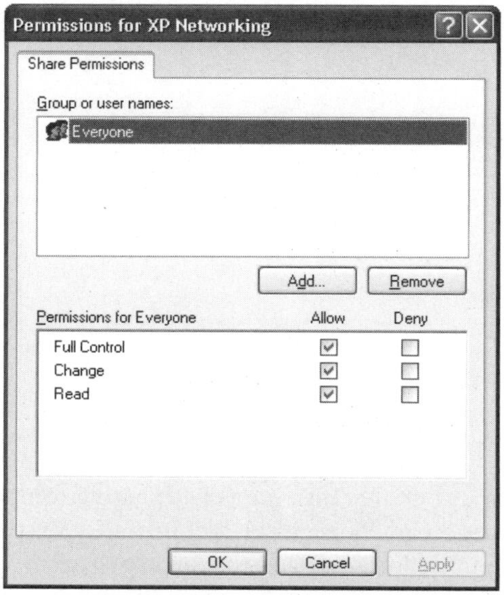

Figure 14-18. Permissions are configured by accessing the Share Permissions tab.

Permissions for file shares are controlled very much like permissions for printer shares. See "Assigning Printer Permissions," page 402, for more information on setting individual permissions on a share.

> **caution** By default, on a file share, the Everyone group has the Full Control permission. *This permission should always be removed!* If the underlying NTFS permissions are not correctly maintained (or if you're using the FAT file system), allowing the Everyone group Full Control to a share makes your share accessible to anyone who can reach your computer over the network and allows for the propagation of Internet worms and Trojan horse programs. It also allows people to stash data in that share without your knowledge. If you want everyone in your home or company to be able to write to a volume, create a group that specifically lists those people and grant rights to that group. See "Configuring Network Shares," page 585, for more information.

Before proceeding, it is important to keep in mind how network share permissions interact with NTFS permissions. When network share permissions and NTFS permissions are both active (which is the case whenever a folder or file is shared on an NTFS drive), the most restrictive permission applies. For example, if a user has the Full Control permission for the network share but his NTFS permission is set to Read, the user can only read the resource. If a user has the Full Control permission for a network share but his NTFS permission is Modify, the user can only modify the resource. If a user has no NTFS permission whatsoever on the file, the user cannot access the file. The *effective* (or resultant) permissions between network share and NTFS permissions can be confusing. Keep the following points in mind as you work with network shares on NTFS volumes:

- Network share permissions only apply to users accessing a folder or file over the network, not to a user directly logged on to the computer that contains the resource. Network share permissions are assigned from the Sharing tab of a resource's properties dialog box.

- NTFS permissions apply equally to both network users and local users of the computer, and they are assigned from the Security tab of the resource's properties dialog box.

Managing Shares with Network Tools

Once you have set up the network shares that you want to make available and have configured any necessary NTFS permissions (if you are not using Simple File Sharing), your management tasks for the shares are rather minimal. When the network share is available, the only tasks you need to perform are as follows:

- **Adjust network share contents.** In the case of a shared folder, you might need to change items that are available in the share from time to time by adding and removing files and folders. However, you can perform this addition and removal of files and folders as needed without any additional configuration to the network share. Because the share is created at the folder level, you don't have to worry about setting permissions on individual files that you add to the folder. Simply move them in and out of the folder as needed.

- **Adjust network share permissions.** Over time, the content of a shared resource can change, and the permissions that you apply to that shared content might need to change as well. Also, as new users who should have access to the network share are created, the users must be added to groups that have access to the shared resource.

- **Monitor the network share.** Depending on the share, you might want to monitor the share from time to time. You can easily monitor all of your shared folders through the Computer Management console, which is found in the Administrative Tools folder in Control Panel. This monitoring tool allows you to see the shared folders, current connections, and current open shares, as shown in Figure 14-19 on the next page. You can right-click a share or user connected to a share and stop sharing the resource or disconnect the user. You can also access the share's properties and change permissions. This console provides a great way to keep track of which users are accessing different shares and for what amount of time.

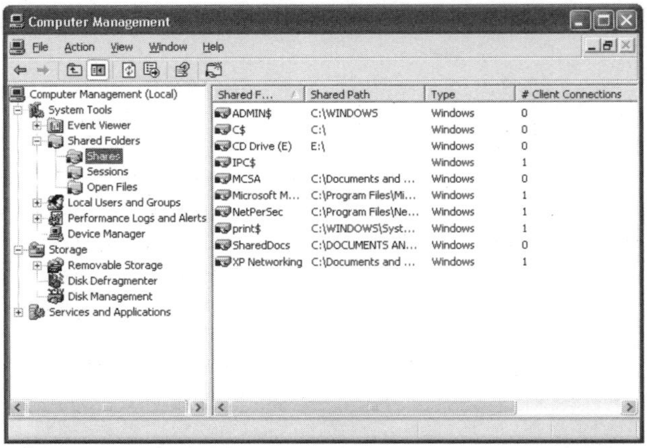

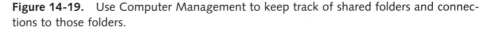

Figure 14-19. Use Computer Management to keep track of shared folders and connections to those folders.

---

tip You can also open the Shared Folders snap-in more quickly without opening Computer Management by typing **fsmgmt.msc** at any command prompt. Also, note that this console is not available if sharing has not been enabled on the computer or if Simple File Sharing is in use.

InsideOut

What Are the Admin$, C$, IPC$, Print$, and Fax$ Shared Folders?

If you open the Shared Folders snap-in in Computer Management, you'll see the Admin$, C$, IPC$, and Print$ shared folders. These shares are administrative shares that are automatically configured by Windows XP and are hidden from the network (all share names ending with a dollar sign are hidden shares). When the dollar sign is used to make these shares invisible, users do not see them when they browse your computer for shared resources over the network. However, if a user on the network knows the names of these shares, he or she can connect to them by name. These shares are necessary. In fact, you cannot permanently delete them. If you delete one, it will reappear the next time the Server service is started or when you restart your computer. The hidden administrative shares and a brief description of each follows:

- **C$ (or D$, E$, and so on).** These shares give members of the Administrators and Backup Operators groups access to the root folder of a hard disk. These shares are used for backup purposes and also allow administrators to remotely access a system's disks even if no shares have been created.

- **Admin$.** This share is used for remote administration, and it maps to the %SystemRoot% folder on the particular computer, which is usually C:\Windows.

- **IPC$.** This share is used when remote computers are viewing resources on your computer. The share provides the named pipes that programs use to communicate with each other.
- **Print$.** This share is established when you share a printer, and it is used for remote administration of printers.
- **Fax$.** If you have a fax server attached to your computer, this share is used by clients to send faxes and access cover pages that are stored on the server.

You can also manage shares using the Net command. This command gives you fast and easy information about your network and other Windows services, and you can even manage network shares with it. The following sections review several uses of the Net command.

Net Use

You use the Net Use command to connect to a shared resource on another computer or to view the resources to which you are currently connected. At the command prompt, type **net use** to see the current network connections, as shown in Figure 14-20.

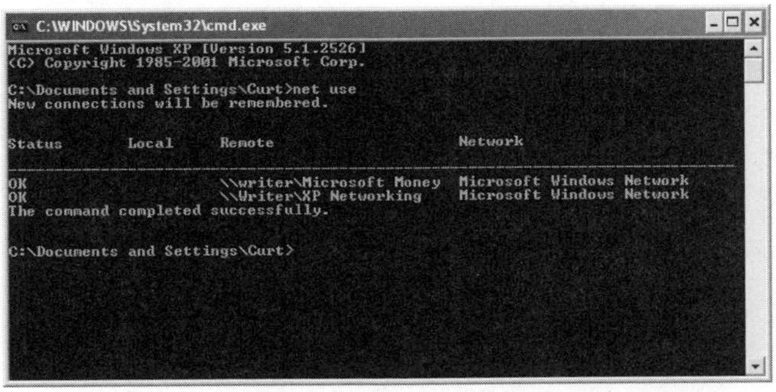

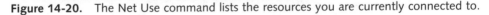

Figure 14-20. The Net Use command lists the resources you are currently connected to.

To connect to shared resources, type **net use ***computername******sharename*. Using Net Use, you can also map a network drive to a share by choosing a drive letter and typing **net use** *driveletter***: ***computername******sharename*. If you simply want to use any available drive letter, use an asterisk (*) instead of specifying the drive letter, and an available drive letter will be assigned starting from the end of the alphabet (Z) and moving backward. For a listing of additional switches you can use with Net Use, type **net use /?** at the command prompt.

Net Share

The Net Share command works like the Shared Folders console in that you can view, create, modify, and delete shared resources on your computer. If you type **net share** at a command prompt, you'll see a listing of the computer's shared resources, as shown in Figure 14-21.

Figure 14-21. The Net Share command provides a command line interface where you can manage shares.

If you type the Net Share command followed by the name of the shared resource, such as **net share SharedDocs**, you'll see basic information listing the full path of the network share, the users connected to the share, the type of caching for the share, and the maximum number of users permitted to access the share at one time. You can add, modify, and delete network shares by using the appropriate switches at the command line. To learn more about these switches, type **net help share** at the command prompt.

Net Session

You can quickly view a list of the current sessions on your computer by typing **net session** at the command prompt, shown in Figure 14-22.

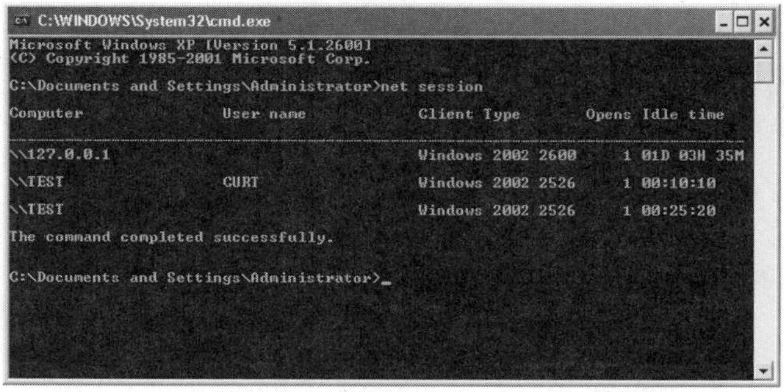

Figure 14-22. The Net Session command lists the users connected to any of your computer's network shares as well as their number of connections and their computers' operating systems.

You can disconnect all sessions by typing **net session /delete**, or you can disconnect a specific computer by typing **net session *computername* /delete**, where *computername* is the IP address of the connecting computer.

Net File

The Net File command lets you view the files that are open in network shares and close the files as needed. Type **net file** to see the current open files. An ID number is displayed next to each open file. To close a file, type **net file** *IDnumber* **/close**.

Solving Common Problems with Network Shares

Under most circumstances, shared folders will not give you much trouble in terms of connection or access problems, but there are three main issues you are likely to run into as you work with shared folders.

- Incorrectly set permissions are the most common source of problems you are likely to encounter. Users might complain about not being able to access shares or not having the needed level of permission.

- Remember that you can't set individual NTFS permissions on a resource when Simple File Sharing is in use. There is no workaround for this condition, so don't waste your time trying to find workarounds with Simple File Sharing enabled. You must disable Simple File Sharing in Windows XP Professional to control NTFS permissions. Simple File Sharing cannot be disabled in Windows XP Home Edition. You can use the Cacls.exe command-line utility to set NTFS permissions in Windows XP Home Edition (and Windows XP Professional), but it's not as easy as working in a graphical environment. If you want to administer NTFS permissions on your network, Windows XP Professional is your best choice.

- If you are using NTFS permissions and users report intermittent access to the share, check the User Limit settings on the Sharing tab of the resource's properties dialog box. The network share might have a limited number of concurrent connections that is periodically being exceeded. You can select Maximum Allowed to provide the maximum number of concurrent connections permitted, which is five concurrent connections for Windows XP Home Edition and 10 concurrent connections for Windows XP Professional Edition. If you need to provide more network connections than the maximum number allowed, you must purchase a server version of Windows along with the correct number of needed client access licenses.

Configuring NTFS Permissions

Every file and folder on an NTFS volume contains an object called a *security descriptor*. This object maintains information about which users create files, own them, and have the ability to access them. The security descriptor contains two ACLs: the discretionary access control list and the system access control list.

The *system access control list* (SACL) determines which types of file system access will be tracked by the operating system. For more information on how SACLs are used, see "Auditing File System Access," page 594.

The *discretionary access control list* (DACL) maintains the list of user accounts that can access a particular file or folder and which types of access they have been granted (or explicitly denied).

For each file and folder housed on an NTFS volume, there are six basic security rights that can be assigned to any user or group. In addition to these six basic access rights, there are a number of additional access rights that fall under the category of special permissions. NTFS permissions should not be confused with share permissions, which apply to folders or other resources shared over the network. When you right-click a file or folder on an NTFS volume and choose either Properties or Sharing And Security, the properties dialog box that appears shows both a Sharing and a Security tab. The Sharing tab is used for creating network shares, whereas the Security tab is used to configure NTFS permissions, as shown in Figure 14-23.

> **note** If you don't see a Security tab, make sure the volume is an NTFS volume, not a FAT volume. If it is an NTFS volume, you probably have Simple File Sharing enabled. Turn off Simple File Sharing by opening Folder Options in Control Panel. Select the View tab, and scroll through the Advanced Settings list until you find Use Simple File Sharing (Recommended). Clear the check box and click OK.

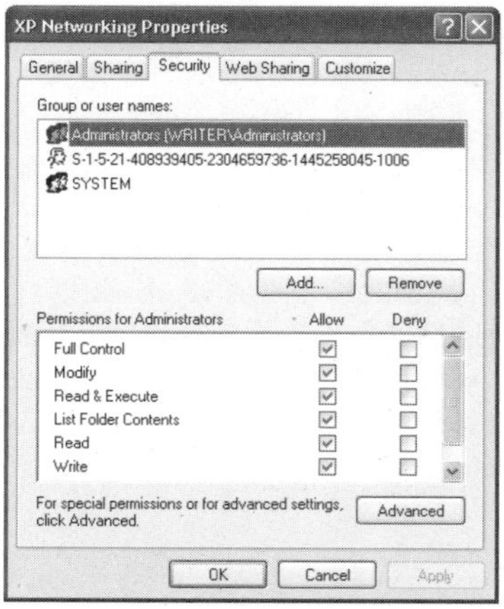

Figure 14-23. NTFS permissions are configured on the Security tab of the properties dialog box of a file or folder.

> **note** NTFS permissions exist in Windows XP Home Edition and Windows XP Professional. However, with Windows XP Home Edition, you cannot directly access the NTFS permissions. The rest of this section assumes that Windows XP Professional is being used.

434

To assign permissions to additional different users and groups for a folder or file, follow these steps:

1 Right-click the folder or file (or a group of files) and choose Properties.

2 Select the Security tab and click the Add button.

3 In the Select Users Or Groups dialog box, shown here, click the Advanced button.

4 A larger Select Users Or Groups dialog box appears. Click the Find Now button, and a list of all users and groups defined on the local computer appears in the dialog box, as shown here.

5 Select the user or group for which you want to configure permissions. If you want to add more than one group or user account at a time, press the Ctrl key, and click each account you want to configure. Click OK in each dialog box to return to the Security tab.

6 The selected user or group now appears on the Security tab. Select the user or group in the upper list, and then set its permissions in the lower list, as shown here. You can also modify permissions for the existing default groups, such as Administrators or Users, in the same way.

As you are planning and working with NTFS permissions, it is important to keep a few concepts in mind that will make your work easier and your users' access to network resources less complicated:

- Always try to assign permissions on a shared resource to a group, such as Users, rather than to an individual user account, such as Curt. This allows you to set one standard permission for all users who belong to the configured group and a different setting to members of the Administrators group or other special groups. Permissions applied to individual users are certainly fine when necessary, but this approach should only be used when you can't achieve the same results using group permissions. This will make managing permissions for the resource easier to implement and much easier to manage on a continuing basis.

- Remember that NTFS permissions are cumulative. If a user is a member of two different groups and one group has Read permission and the other group has Write permission, the user has both Read and Write permission. The exception to this cumulative rule is if you assign the Deny permission, which overrides all matching Allow permissions. For example, if a user has the Write permission in one group (the Allow check box next to Write is selected), and in another group the user has the Write permission denied (the Deny check box next to Write is selected), the user's Write permission will be denied, even though it was granted in the first group. As you are planning and assigning permissions, make sure you consider how permissions work across multiple groups and that some users might be members of several groups. Because the Deny permission breaks the cumulative rule in evaluating effective permissions, avoid its use as much as possible to make the effective permissions of your users easier to understand.

Setting Advanced NTFS Permissions

You can also set advanced NTFS permissions on folders and files. The more important consideration, however, is whether you should. To make NTFS permissions as robust as possible, you can manipulate the special permissions that make up the standard NTFS permissions. Although this capability gives you a very fine level of control over users and the permissions they have on network resources, those special permissions often become complex, and you might not achieve your desired outcome. If you think that you need to alter special permissions, stop and consider your real reasons. Can the apparent need for different permissions be managed by selecting different groups of users and configuring their standard permissions?

If you do determine that you need to configure special permissions, you should apply those permissions to a test user account (one not accessible to anyone on the network but you), and then test the account's effective permissions to see if the special permissions have the effect you intended. To set special permissions, follow these steps:

1 Right-click the folder or file you want to manage and choose Properties.

2 Select the Security tab and click the Advanced button.

3 In the Advanced Security Settings dialog box shown here, select the user or group in the Permission Entries list for whom you want to configure special permissions, and then click the Edit button.

4   In the Permission Entry dialog box shown here, select Allow or Deny for the special permissions you need to modify. Wherever possible, refrain from using the Deny permissions and depend on selectively enabling the Allow permissions to achieve your objectives. Click OK when you're done.

When the Advanced Security Settings dialog box reappears, notice that in the Permission column for the modified user or group, the previous standard permission has been replaced with the label Special. You won't know what the characteristics of the special permissions are from this dialog box. You'll have to select the Edit button again to examine which permissions the account has.

newfeature!
Checking an Account's Effective Permissions

To help you understand the ramifications of special configurations you've made, especially for an account that is a member of more than one group, check the effective, or net, permissions of the account you've modified by taking these steps:

1   Open the resource's properties dialog box by right-clicking the folder or file and choosing Properties.

2   Click the Advanced button, and then select the Effective Permissions tab. Notice that the Group Or User Name box is blank and that you can't type into the box directly.

3   Click the Select button, click the Advanced button in the second dialog box, and then click the Find Now button in the third dialog box.

4   All the computer's user and group accounts will be displayed at the bottom of the Select User Or Group dialog box. Select the account you've modified and click OK.

5 Click OK again to close the remaining Select User Or Group dialog box.

6 The Effective Permissions tab reappears with the account you selected displayed in the Group Or User Name box, and its effective NTFS permissions are displayed in the Effective Permissions list, as shown in Figure 14-24.

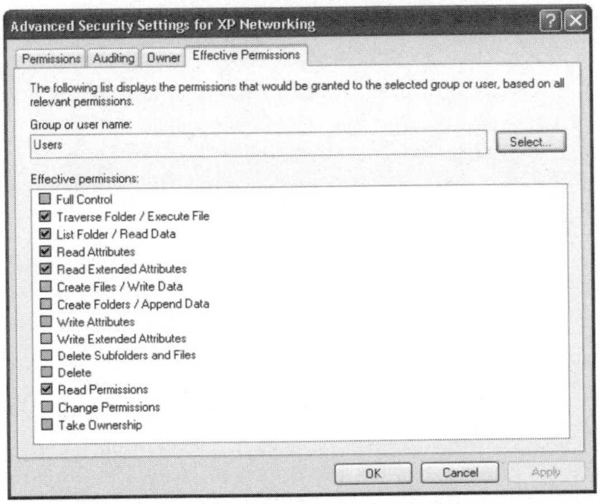

Figure 14-24. The Effective Permissions tab can help you understand the actions a selected user or group can take with a particular NTFS resource.

A list and brief explanations of the six basic access permissions available on an NTFS volume follows:

- **Full Control.** Users with the Full Control right assigned can view, create, modify, and delete files or folders. This right also allows a user to change the ACLs for the object in question. That means a user with Full Control permission can also change the object's access permissions as well as the object itself.

- **Modify.** Essentially, the Modify permission allows a user to make changes to the file or the files inside a folder but does not allow the user to change the access level to those resources or to take ownership of a file. This is the same as selecting both the Read & Execute and Write permissions.

- **Read & Execute.** A user assigned the Read & Execute permission has the right to read the contents of a file or folder, and execute programs and batch files that have the Read & Execute permission. Selecting this permission also selects the List Folder Contents and Read permissions.

- **List Folder Contents.** This permission allows the user to view the individual objects contained within the folder. It is similar to the Read & Execute permission but only acts on folders and is passed down to subfolders but not to the files in those subfolders.

- **Read.** The user can read the file or folder. This is the most basic permission of all the permissions.

- **Write.** The user can create files and modify new or existing files and folders.

An additional entry in the Permissions section of the Security tab of an object's properties dialog box is called Special Permissions. To access these special attributes, perform the following steps:

1 Right-click a file or folder, and choose Properties from the shortcut menu that appears.

2 Select the Security tab.

3 Click the Advanced button.

4 Select a user name or group, and click the Edit button. The Permission Entry For dialog box displays a listing of special permissions in the Permissions list, as shown in Figure 14-25.

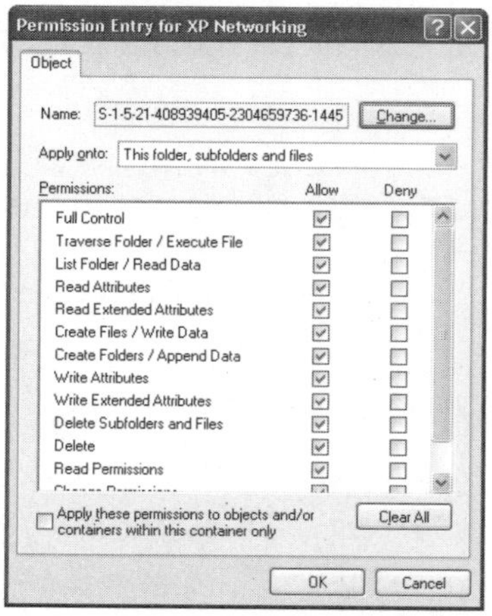

Figure 14-25. Special permissions enable you to set up complex and highly specific permissions for a user or group.

> **caution**   Adjust the permissions in this dialog box only if you're sure of the effects of your actions. Although most of these settings are self-explanatory, they are best left alone unless you are trying to address a specific security issue that the standard rights will not accommodate.

440

For example, suppose there is a user who needs to have most of the rights that make up the Full Control permission, but you don't want the user to have the ability to change permissions (ACLs) or take ownership (taking ownership of a file or folder restores a user's ability to change permissions). To make these special settings, you could set two permissions in the Permissions list, Change Permissions and Take Ownership, by clearing their Allow check boxes or by selecting their Deny check boxes. Check the results by selecting the Effective Permissions tab of the Advanced Security Settings dialog box and entering the user or group name in the Group Or User Name box (you'll have to click the Select button to enter the name—it can't be typed directly). Notice that the check boxes are cleared in the Effective Permissions list for Take Ownership and several permissions relating to managing attributes. The Full Control check box is also cleared because the user no longer has the full set of permissions that make up the Full Control permission.

InsideOut

Using the Create Shared Folder Wizard

If you want help sharing a folder, you can use the Create Shared Folder Wizard. You can access it from Computer Management (in the Administrative Tools folder). In Computer Management, open System Tools, Shared Folders, right-click Shares, and then choose New File Share from the shortcut menu. You can also run the wizard directly by typing **shrpubw** at any command prompt. Using the wizard, you can share a folder and configure NTFS permissions by choosing from three preconfigured basic share permissions or by selecting the Custom option to make the full slate of NTFS permissions available. However, even though you can use the wizard on a Windows XP Home Edition computer to specify different permissions for different users and groups, the permissions will not work because all network users are authenticated as Guests in Windows XP Home Edition and therefore have the permissions of the Everyone group. However, for Windows XP Professional, you might prefer using the friendly interface of a wizard when creating a network share.

Exploring Scenarios to Troubleshoot NTFS Permissions

Understanding NTFS permissions and the steps to configure them is beneficial and useful. However, the cumulative effect of group and user rights, and the *least common denominator* effect of NTFS level and network share permissions makes it important to understand how to identify and correct permissions conflicts and confusions relating to disk formats. This section presents several scenarios or case studies that point out some common problems and solutions when using NTFS.

Scenario #1: Implementing Permissions

Melanie is the new systems administrator for the Tailspin Toys Company. Melanie's first task is to configure a new Windows XP Professional computer as a workstation for a member of the Power Users group (Power Users is a predefined group in Windows XP that grants many but not all privileges of the Administrators group). This workstation will be used to support a small portion of the company's intranet, store user files for the marketing department, and also act as the primary workstation for the marketing director. The computer, named Marketdept, has two disks installed. One disk is a 10 GB disk used for the operating system and boot files, and the other disk is a 60 GB disk used for the intranet files and the marketing director's personal data.

Melanie formats the 10 GB boot and system disk with the FAT32 file system. This volume will contain the files needed to boot the computer and the Windows directory. FAT32 is required because the company has standardized on a disk imaging software package that does not support NTFS volumes. This imaging software is used to make a master image for every computer that provides multiple user services and that does not have a backup device attached locally. The Marketdept computer does not have a backup device attached, so the boot disk has to be FAT32. The 60 GB disk will be formatted with the NTFS file system, and the drive will be partitioned into three volumes of approximately 20 GB each.

After all the required applications are installed and the user storage file structures are created, Melanie configures the NTFS file permissions to only allow members of the Domain Admins group (this is a group present only on computers joined to a domain, as discussed in Chapter 11, "Understanding Domain Connectivity"), not local Administrators, to access the folder. The marketing director is added to the local Administrators group so that she can configure the IIS services when changes are needed and perform general management tasks.

After configuring the computer, Melanie takes ill and is out of work for a week. Upon her return, there is a small but serious list of issues with the Marketdept computer. The following issues have been reported to the marketing director who is frustrated that her new workstation is already failing:

1 The marketing director is now sharing the new computer with the vice president of Finance for reasons unknown. The marketing director is worried that the Finance VP will start tinkering with system files, and she has made attempts to secure them. She is unable to configure security permissions for the system files. She has managed to share the Windows directory and assign permissions there, but she is concerned that this is not an adequate solution. She wants to know how to completely secure the drive.

2 Users have complained that the marketing director is accessing their files, modifying them, and occasionally deleting them. Collectively, they want the files secured from the tinkering of the marketing director. How is the market-

442

ing director gaining access to their files? What change(s) can be made to correct this problem?

3 Some users report that they have never been able to access their folders on the Marketdept computer. Melanie double-checks the permissions for the directories and notices that the share permissions allowing access are correct for all the users reporting access trouble. What has Melanie overlooked?

4 Access to the intranet only works for the marketing director. Melanie attempts to connect and finds out that she can connect as well. Melanie checks the IIS configuration and finds nothing out of order. Where might Melanie look to find the source of the intranet troubles?

The solutions to these problems follow:

1 The boot drive, which contains the system files that the marketing director wants to protect, has to be converted to NTFS. The current file system (FAT32) does not support ACLs.

2 The marketing director is a member of the local Administrators group and can add herself to any ACL on the local computer. Melanie should place the marketing director in a different group that has the functionality needed but does not have permission to change the ACLs of computer objects.

3 Melanie has not checked the NTFS permissions. If they are more restrictive than the share permissions, they will limit the access of the users who can't access their folders on the Marketdept computer.

4 Melanie should check the NTFS permissions on the root folder of the intranet site. It is probable that only members of the Administrators group have access to the intranet files.

Scenario #2: A Permissions Nightmare

Melanie has moved on to a new job at Wingtip Toys as a network technician. Users are complaining about access problems and demand that these problems be fixed as quickly as possible. Melanie begins to correct the access issues. While doing so, she also encounters additional issues:

1 The previous network administration staff left the NTFS file level permissions wide open. The previous staff decided to use the network share permissions to control access. Unfortunately, the members of the staff did not configure the share permissions correctly. Melanie starts configuring the NTFS permissions to the correct settings but neglects to first modify the share permissions. This results in a serious mess of access rights. What can Melanie do to quickly clean up this mess?

2 To help a user gain some much needed disk space, Melanie enabled disk compression on the user's boot drive, which had about 10 percent free

443

space. During the compression routine, the computer crashed and now will not start Windows. What steps can Melanie take to complete the compression process and hopefully regain access to Windows XP?

3 Another user is complaining about the amount of free disk space available on his computer. Melanie does not want to tamper with compressing another volume, and the user doesn't have any files on the computer that can be deleted to free up more disk space. What other options does Melanie have?

Melanie could implement the following solutions:

1 Melanie needs to reset the NTFS permissions for the folders in question. She needs to remove all the existing (and incorrect) user and group permissions and replace them with the correct permissions. These changes then need to be applied to all subfolders and files. The share permissions should be modified to allow the desired level of access by users, while removing the Everyone group's Full Control over the computer. The following are the steps for clearing the existing permissions and restoring the correct ACL configuration:

- Locate the problematic files or folders using Microsoft Windows Explorer.

- Right-click the file or folder, and choose Sharing And Security or Properties.

- Select the Security tab, and then click the Advanced button.

- Clear the check box labeled Inherit From Parent The Permission Entries That Apply To Child Objects. Include These With Entries Explicitly Defined Here.

- When prompted, select either Copy or Remove. Either choice breaks the inherited permissions from the parent folder. Copy lets you start over with the current inherited permissions, whereas Remove lets you start over with a clean slate.

- If you select Remove, the Permission Entries list will be empty. Click the Add button to add users and groups, and specify their permissions. If you select Copy, use the Remove, Add, and Edit buttons to remove unwanted permission entries, edit those you want to change, and add new entries as needed to reconfigure the ACL properly.

- Select the check box labeled Replace Permission Entries On All Child Objects With Entries Shown Here That Apply To Child Objects. This will propagate the corrected ACL entries downward to subfolders and their files.

- Click Apply. In the Security message box that appears, click OK.

- When the process of applying permissions has been completed, click OK in each dialog box.

> **note** For a large number of computers, Melanie could use the Cacls.exe command-line tool. This tool would allow Melanie to build a logon script that changes the ACL automatically for all of the user folders in question when the users log on. If constructed correctly, this file will save Melanie a lot of time.

2 Melanie needs to reboot the computer and press F8 during startup to access the boot options. From the boot menu, she should select Safe Mode With Command Prompt and press Enter. At the prompt, Melanie needs to log on and run the Compact.exe utility to force the compression of the drive to complete. Presuming it is drive C that is not starting up correctly, Melanie would switch to the root of the problem drive, type **compact /C /I /F /S:C:**, and then press Enter. The /C parameter compresses the specified files; the /I parameter continues the operation, even if errors occur; the /F parameter forces the compression of all specified files, even if they are already compressed; and the /S:C:\ parameter includes all subfolders starting from the root folder. If the previous compression resulted in some files being incompletely compressed, the /F parameter might enable the compression to complete successfully. Once the compression is complete, Melanie should reboot the computer. If all goes well, the compressed drive will again be accessible.

3 Melanie can mount another volume onto the full drive to provide more disk space. If the drives cannot be converted to dynamic disks (perhaps the full drive is also the system or boot volume), she can create a volume mount point within the full drive to provide additional space. Melanie can also move the user's data to another location on the network and reformat the drive using a smaller cluster size. The smaller cluster sizes will help free up additional disk capacity.

Scenario #3: Managing Sensitive Data

Stephanie was recently hired as the new network services manager at Wide World Importers. Although the previous manager's departure was apparently on good terms, management is concerned about the level of access general users have, in particular, whether they have access to sensitive managerial information. Also of concern is that users who have left the company might be able to access sensitive corporate data after their departure. These are more of their concerns:

1 The primary data server, World1, had three new drives installed immediately prior to the departure of the previous manager. Network users are becoming quite vocal about obtaining additional space to store files and increase the space for the company's sales database. All network users access the storage space on World1 through a shared folder called Data Access. What is the most streamlined way in which Stephanie can make the new disk space available to current network users?

2 It is company policy to restrict the amount of data stored in users' personal directories. Currently, there is no system in place to enforce this policy. What steps can Stephanie perform to implement disk quotas?

3 Operations management is unsure of who has access to which files on the network. Management has requested that Stephanie ensure that the permissions for the Human Resources folders on the file server do not allow anyone outside that department to access them. How can Stephanie determine which user rights are currently configured? How can she make changes if they are needed?

4 Stephanie has to make sure that the previous manager does not have access to any internal files through hidden accounts. How can she ensure that these secret accounts do not have access to sensitive information?

Stephanie could implement the following solutions:

1 The new volumes should be added by Stephanie as mounted volumes to the existing volume. By mounting the new space inside the existing share point, users will be able to immediately access the new space.

2 Stephanie needs to access the Disk Quota tab in the volume's properties dialog box and configure disk quotas that are in compliance with company rules and policies.

3 Stephanie should reset the permissions on the sensitive folders so that only authorized users have access. To do this, she needs to access the security settings for the folders in question, make changes, and then propagate those changes to all the subfolders and files within the parent folders.

4 This solution is essentially the same as the previous solution. Barring the ability to identify and disable rogue accounts, the next step is for Stephanie to identify the users who should have access and remove everyone else from the ACLs. The individual members of groups with sensitive access must also be scrutinized so that the ex-manager can't gain access through a group account.

Scenario #4: Restricting User File System Access

Trey Research is in the middle of a major company-wide systems overhaul. It has come to the attention of the executives that there is a need for expanded storage on client computers.

Each of the 2000 user computers worldwide will have additional hard disks installed, and the operating systems will be upgraded to Windows XP. The new drives will be formatted using the NTFS file system, and the existing disks, which are currently FAT volumes, will be converted to NTFS. Additionally, the company has decided to crack down on users installing personal software on their work computers. Along with removing individual user accounts from the local Administrators group, the NTFS permissions will be configured to restrict access to the newly installed drives.

Disk quotas will also be implemented on the new volumes. A portion of each new volume will be used to store administrative files. The disk quotas will be used to prevent users from filling up the new drives with nonwork-related files such as digital music files and other personal material. The network staff has collected a list of current issues that must be addressed before and during the upgrades:

1 All the administrative data needs to be protected as much as possible. What options are present in the NTFS file system that will allow the data in question to be protected?

2 The company's summer intern left for college yesterday. His last task was to configure the NTFS and share permissions on the personal folders of 23 new hires. Of the 23 new hires starting today, 15 have access to their shared folders. What is the likely reason that 8 of the new hires can't access their shared folders?

3 One of the network administrators is able to create and add files to his departmental share, but he cannot delete any of the files in the share. The share permissions are set to allow Full Control to the Everyone group. What might be the cause of his inability to delete files?

4 Users need to be able to read the administrative files stored on their computers. But they should not be able to modify, remove, or create files within the administrative data folder. What is the most convenient method of controlling access to the administrative files?

The solutions follow:

1 NTFS supports both DACL permissions and file encryption. With the two features combined, the net result is a robust security scheme.

2 Most likely, one of two things is happening. First, the DACLs for the individual folders might not all have been configured to allow access to their intended users. Second, there might be a conflict between the NTFS permissions and the network share permissions.

3 This user had the Delete permission specifically denied in the DACL for the folder in question. By checking the Advanced Security properties and clearing the Deny option for the Delete permission, the problem is easily solved.

4 By configuring NTFS permissions to only allow the Read permission in the administrative folders, users will be able to access the administrative data without the danger of compromising the information stored on the disk.

Making Files Available Offline

What's the big deal about making files available offline? Suppose you've been working on an important document for the past week. The document is stored on a network server and from time to time other users access the document and make reference to it as well. You need to travel to another city, and it would be great if you could take that document along on your laptop computer, continue working on it, and synchronize with the original document when you return. Can you? Yes, in Microsoft Windows XP Professional, you can use network documents offline using the Offline Files feature, which was originally introduced with Microsoft Windows 2000.

Offline Files allows you to keep copies of network files on your local computer. When you are not connected to the network, you can use the cached copy and continue working. When you reconnect to the network, the offline file is synchronized with the online copy. If only the offline document has been changed, the offline version is copied to the network version. If the network version has changed but the offline version has not, the network version is copied over your offline version. If both versions have changed, a dialog box gives you the option of selecting which one to keep or keeping both files under different names. In all cases, the final result is that both sets of files or folders are synchronized (identical) on the two computers. Because Offline Files works on a synchronization basis, this feature works well for:

- **Users working with network documents.** You can edit online or offline, and your changes will be synchronized.

- **Mobile users.** Offline Files is particularly helpful to mobile users who are not connected to the network for long periods of time, but who need access to files. Offline Files enables the files to be stored locally so they are always available to the user, whether he or she is connected to the network or not. Any type of document or resource material can be made available this way. Additionally, when synchronization is invoked (either manually or by the Synchronization Manager, which is covered in "Setting Synchronization Options" on page 459), if a change has been made to the document in one location or the other, you'll be notified and be given the chance to synchronize them. Not only are your documents always available, but you also don't need to worry about whether you have an old version of a file, which makes file management much easier and more accurate.

● **Users with an unreliable connection.** Users whose network connection is not stable can use Offline Files to copy needed network files to their local computer and minimize their dependency on a troublesome network connection.

This chapter explores the Offline Files feature. You'll learn how to enable and configure Offline Files and how to use the files while offline. You'll also learn how to make files available offline to other users when the files reside on your computer. Briefcase, an earlier offline file feature that has been superseded by the more enhanced features of Offline Files, will be briefly examined as well in "Using Briefcase" on page 467.

> **note** Offline Files is not available with Microsoft Windows XP Home Edition. If you frequently travel or otherwise work offline from your network, you should consider using Windows XP Professional as your platform.

Enabling the Offline Files Feature

You can easily turn on the Offline Files feature to begin using offline files on your network. However, before enabling Offline Files in Windows XP Professional, you need to turn off another feature if it's enabled, Fast User Switching.

Offline Files is not compatible with Fast User Switching, the new Windows XP feature that lets one or more additional users log on to the local computer without the other user or users logging off. You'll recognize this feature by the Switch User button that's available when Fast User Switching is enabled. This feature makes it quick and easy for a family or group of users who share a single computer to take turns using the computer without having to close down their applications between sessions. To disable Fast User Switching, follow these steps:

1 Choose Start, Control Panel, and open User Accounts.

2 Select the Change The Way Users Log On Or Log Off option.

3 Clear the Use Fast User Switching check box, as shown in the figure, and click Apply Options.

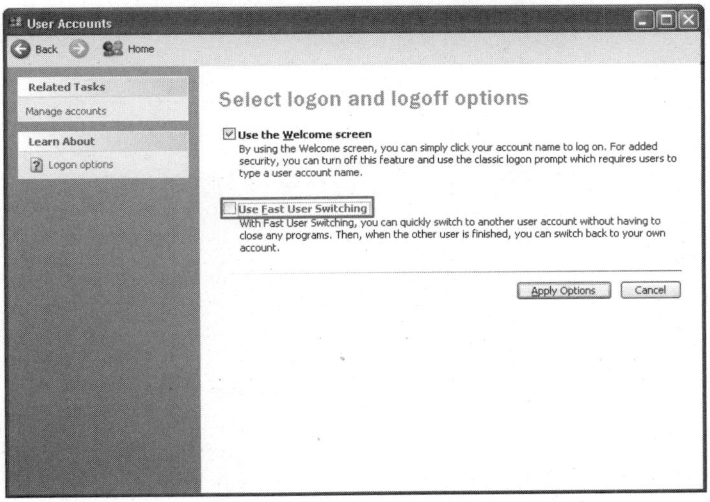

> **note** Keep in mind that computers that participate in domains already have Fast User Switching disabled.

After Fast User Switching is turned off, you can turn on Offline Files. To enable Offline Files, follow these steps:

1 Choose Start, Control Panel, and open Folder Options.

2 Select the Offline Files tab.

3 On the Offline Files tab, shown here, select the Enable Offline Files option. Click OK.

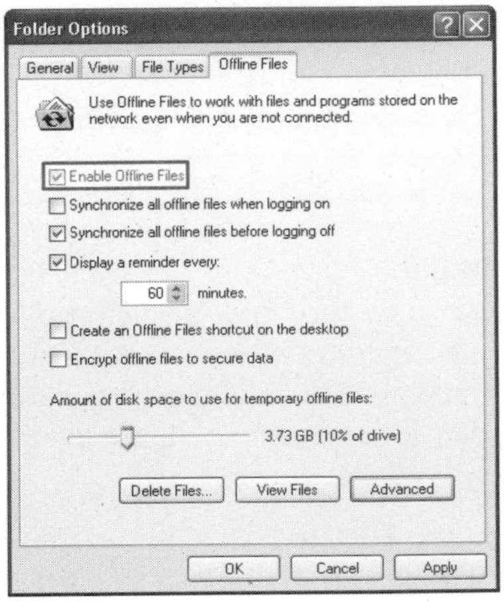

451

> **tip**   Any file or folder that you can access via network sharing can be configured for offline use.

Configuring Offline Files Options

Once you enable Offline Files, several additional options become available on the Offline Files tab. These options determine how Offline Files works in terms of synchronization and general file management. The following options can be set:

● **Synchronize All Offline Files When Logging On.** This option, which is not selected by default, synchronizes all offline files when you first log on to the computer. If you want to make sure your files are synchronized as soon as you log on to the network, choose this option. However, many users become frustrated with having to wait for the synchronization process while they log on, so you might consider not using this option and simply synchronizing at your leisure after you have logged on and are working.

● **Synchronize All Offline Files Before Logging Off.** The option to synchronize all files before logging off is enabled by default. When this option is selected, a full synchronization occurs before you log off (or shut down). This action ensures that your offline files are completely up-to-date with the server copy so that you have the most current version of the offline files before you log off the network. For most users, this setting is best. However, if you are the only person using the network file, or you are using a reference file that rarely changes, you can clear this option to log off quickly. If this option is cleared, a partial synchronization occurs. In a partial synchronization, you end up with complete copies of the files you've marked to be available offline, but you might not have the most current copy of each file.

> **caution**   The act of logging off or shutting down prompts Windows to synchronize with the server. If you simply unplug from the network, the offline file might not be current because Windows XP has not had an opportunity to synchronize.

● **Display A Reminder Every *x* Minutes.** This option causes balloon reminders to appear in the notification area on the desktop when you work offline. By default, this message appears every hour. So every hour you are working offline, you'll see a balloon reminder, which might become annoying. If you want a less frequent reminder, adjust the interval rate to another value, such as every four hours.

● **Create An Offline Files Shortcut On The Desktop.** This option places a shortcut to the Offline Files folder on your desktop so you can easily access any offline files. You might consider initially selecting this option, after which you can move the shortcut to the Start menu or elsewhere.

- **Encrypt Offline Files To Secure Data.** This option encrypts offline files on your local hard disk to protect them from prying eyes or theft while the files reside on your computer. The encryption feature works just like the encryption of any other file or folder on your computer. Only you (or a user signed on with your user name and password) can view the offline files. Because all encryption and decryption is handled transparently by Windows XP, you continue to use the file as you normally would. If your offline files are not stored on an NTFS volume, this option will be unavailable.

tip When you open an encrypted document, many applications create temporary files, and these files are not encrypted. For maximum security, you should encrypt the entire folder the application uses to store temporary files.

- **Amount Of Disk Space To Use For Temporary Offline Files.** When you choose specific files and folders to use offline, Windows XP Professional reserves as much space as those files require, which is only limited by the amount of storage space on your computer. However, if you access network files that are automatically cached (copied) to your local computer when you open them, this setting lets you control the amount of disk space that is reserved for these *temporary offline files*. By default, Windows allocates 10 percent of your computer's hard disk space for temporary offline file storage. See "Managing Caching Options on the Server," page 463, for more information about different types of file caching.

Making a File or Folder Available Offline

Once you have enabled Offline Files, you can begin making files and folders available offline. Offline Files is a client-side application, which means that the software needed to use Offline Files resides on your Windows XP Professional computer. Therefore, the operating system running on the network or *server* computer (the computer that is providing the files and folders to your local computer) doesn't matter, as long as the server computer supports *Server Message Block (SMB)*, a protocol used for file sharing. Microsoft Windows 95, Windows 98, Windows Millennium Edition (Windows Me), Windows NT 4, Windows 2000, and Windows XP all support SMB (as well as many UNIX-based operating systems running the Samba tools). Therefore, you can make files available offline from any of these operating systems, even though some of the earlier versions of Windows are completely unaware of the Offline Files feature.

tip If you are working in a mixed environment that includes Novell NetWare servers and clients, NetWare does not support SMB, so you can't make files that are stored on NetWare computers available offline. Additionally, Offline Files are not available from a Windows 2000 computer running Terminal Services in any mode other than single-user mode.

To make a file or folder available offline, you must have Read and/or Write permission to the file or folder. However, any network share you can access online means that you have at least Read permission, which means you can make any network folder or file you can access available offline. To make the file or folder available offline, follow these steps:

1 Using My Network Places, browse to the desired file or folder on the network server that you want to make available offline.

> **note** Remember that you're making files on *other* network computers available on your *local* computer. Because Offline Files runs as a client service, you need to work from your local computer and select the files on each network computer that you want to make available on *your* computer.

2 Right-click the network file or folder, and choose Make Available Offline.

The first time you use the Make Available Offline feature, the Offline Files Wizard appears. Subsequently, the folders or files you choose will be cached without the wizard appearing.

3 Read the wizard's welcome message and then click Next.

4 On the second page of the wizard, shown here, you'll see a single setting that combines the separate log on and log off settings available in Folder Options. You can set different synchronization settings for each network share using Synchronization Manager at any time. Make a choice here or accept the default setting, and then click Next.

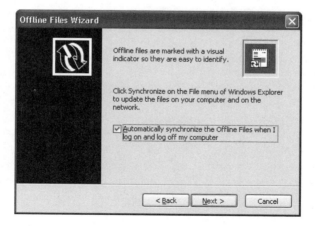

5 On the third page of the wizard, shown next, make a choice or accept the default settings. Click Finish.

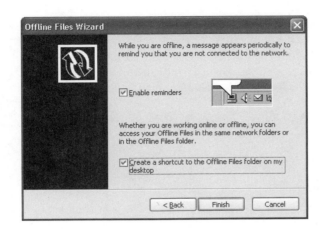

6 If you choose to make an entire folder available offline and that folder contains subfolders, you'll see the Confirm Offline Subfolders dialog box, which asks whether you want to make only the folder you selected available offline or all its subfolders as well. Make your choice and click OK.

The Synchronizing window appears, and the files or folders you selected are synchronized for the first time, which means they'll be copied from the network computer to your local computer and then appear in your Offline Files folder.

InsideOut

Understanding SMB

SMB is a presentation layer protocol used in file and printer sharing on Microsoft computers. SMB is used to share files, printers, serial ports, and other communication layers, such as named pipes. Using SMB, clients request service from a server, and the server responds to those requests. With SMB, you can cache network files and then write to those files on the server. This process occurs through the use of messages that the client and server pass back and forth. These messages allow the two systems to communicate over the network and to know how to manage a file or other resource between them.

Using Offline Files and Folders

After making a file or folder available offline, you can begin working with it whether you are online or not. The following sections describe how to use offline files and folders.

Once a file or folder is made available offline, you can access it through My Network Places, Windows Explorer, My Computer, or a network drive, just as you would access any other shared resource (including those that are only available when you're online).

You can also view and remove cached resources in the Offline Files folder. When you are not connected, only the files or folders that you have made available offline appear. Figure 15-1 shows that the Employees document is available offline. Notice that the document icon appears with a pair of blue arrows, signifying that the file or folder has been *pinned*. Automatically cached files may be available offline, although they do not display this icon.

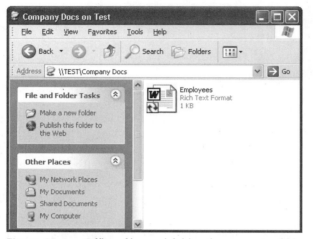

Figure 15-1. Offline files and folders have a pair of blue arrows displayed on their icons.

> **note** You can view all offline files and folders by opening the Offline Files folder or by clicking the View Files button on the Offline Files tab found in Folder Options.

While you are offline, you can work with the file as you normally would. You can make any desired changes to it and save those changes. Like a local file, any changes you save are saved to the local, cached copy.

While you are working offline, the icon shown here appears in the notification area. If you select the Display A Reminder option on the Offline Files tab of Folder Options, balloon messages will appear periodically reminding you that you are working offline.

Offline Files Icon

If you double-click the Offline Files icon in the notification area, you'll see the message shown in Figure 15-2. The Offline Files Status dialog box contains the Work Online Without Synchronizing Changes option. You might want to select this option if you're about to connect to the network but don't want to take the time to synchronize files before you can access the online network shares. This is useful when your local computer has a slow link to the network, when you want to conserve battery power, or when you want to connect to the network just long enough to retrieve the latest copy of a document.

Chapter 15

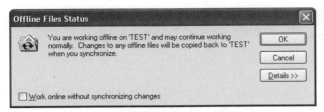

Figure 15-2. The Offline Files Status dialog box informs you that you're working offline and lets you choose whether to synchronize when you reconnect to the network.

---

tip   **Using the Offline Files Folder**

You can find additional information about an offline file and folder, such as its location on the network, its synchronization state, the resource's permissions, and the status of the server on which the share is located by opening the Offline Files folder. Choose View, Details to see this information. You can also right-click the Offline Files icon in the notification area to access a shortcut menu with commands to open the Offline Files folder, synchronize files, and adjust the Offline Files settings.

Synchronizing Offline Files and Folders

Synchronization of offline files occurs when you log on or log off the network, depending on the settings you've chosen on the Offline Files tab of the Folder Options dialog box. If you've turned off both automatic synchronization options, you can manually synchronize a file or folder at any time by right-clicking the file or folder and then choosing Synchronize. When you synchronize offline files to the network computer, there are four basic actions that can occur.

- If you have not made any changes to the file since it was cached on your system, Windows will check the server copy for updates. If there are updates on the server, those updates are copied to your computer. If the network version hasn't changed, nothing happens.

- If you have made changes to the offline file, the file needs to be synchronized with the network copy. If no changes were made to the network version, your changes are written to the network copy so that the network has the latest version. If you connect to the network and access an online file before offline files have been synchronized, you'll see a yellow warning icon (on the files and on the Offline Files tray icon), which indicates that you are working on the file's associated network share without having synchronized changes from the local cache. If you click the Offline Files tray icon, you'll see the Offline Files Status dialog box shown in Figure 15-3 on the next page, which informs you that files need to be synchronized. If you set synchronization to occur automatically when you log on, you won't see this message once the systems have been synchronized.

Chapter 15

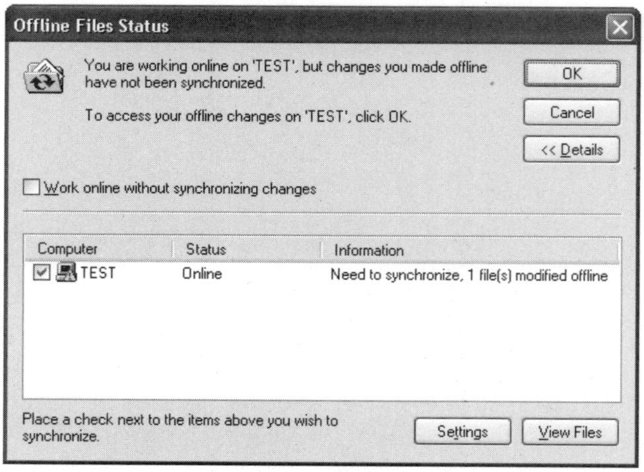

Figure 15-3. This dialog box appears when you have files and folders that need to be synchronized.

- If you have made changes to the offline file and someone else has made changes to the network file, you'll see the Resolve File Conflicts dialog box, which is shown in Figure 15-4. You have the choice of saving both copies (under different names of course), replacing the network version with your version, or replacing your version with the network version. Also notice that you can make your decision the default by selecting the Do This For All Conflicts check box if you don't need to examine conflicts on a case-by-case basis.

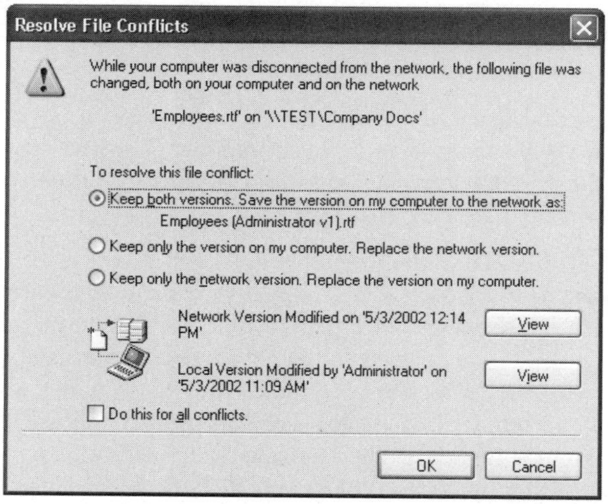

Figure 15-4. The Resolve File Conflicts dialog box provides you with three ways to resolve file synchronization conflicts.

● If either the offline or network copy of a file is deleted, the file on the other computer is deleted as well, if no changes have been made to the remaining file. If changes have been made to one of the files and the other one has been deleted, you'll be given the option of deleting the remaining file or saving the changed file to both locations.

Setting Synchronization Options

In addition to manually synchronizing when logging on and when logging off, you can specify other synchronization options using the Synchronization Manager, which you can open by choosing Start, All Programs, Accessories, Synchronize. In the Items To Synchronize dialog box, you can configure synchronization when the computer is idle, according to a schedule, or immediately. The following steps show you how to select these options.

1 Choose Start, All Programs, Accessories, Synchronize.

2 The Items To Synchronize dialog box appears as shown here. If you want to manually synchronize immediately, click the Synchronize button. If you want to configure how synchronization occurs, click the Setup button.

note Remember that the synchronization tool can only be used to synchronize items you have already made available offline. You cannot use this tool to make items available offline.

3 Clicking the Setup button opens the Synchronization Settings dialog box. On the Logon/Logoff tab, shown next, you can choose the files or folders that you want synchronized when you log on or log off. Notice that you can select Ask Me Before Synchronizing The Items if you want to receive a prompt before synchronization actions occur—doing so lets you override the settings you select on this tab. If you have more than one network connection, you can set different synchronization settings for each connection by selecting the connection in the When I Am Using This Network Connection list. For example, you might want to synchronize a partial list of your offline folders and files when you're using a slow dial-up connection and all your files when you're using a network or broadband connection.

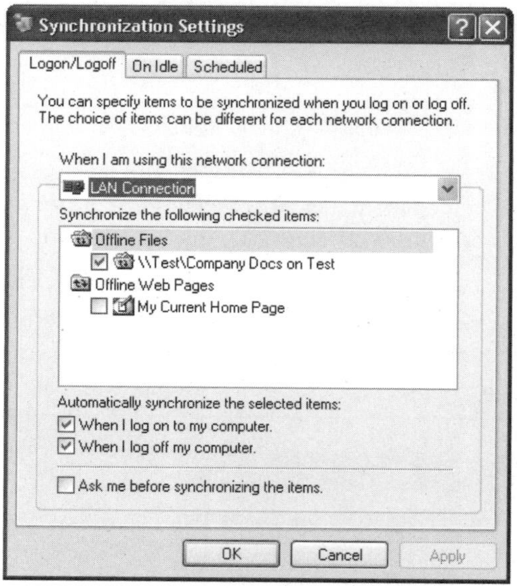

4 The On Idle tab, shown next, allows you to select items to be synchronized when the computer is idle. This feature allows you to synchronize the items more often but without interfering with your work. But if your computer never goes idle, this option will not be terribly useful. Your computer might never go idle if it's running a CPU-intensive application in the background, such as screen saver utilities that use your idle CPU cycles to iterate massive numerical calculations. SETI@home is one such fascinating *cycle-scavenging* program that uses your CPU's idle time to exhaustively analyze astronomical data for signs of intelligent life from deep space (*http://setiathome.ssl.berkeley.edu*).

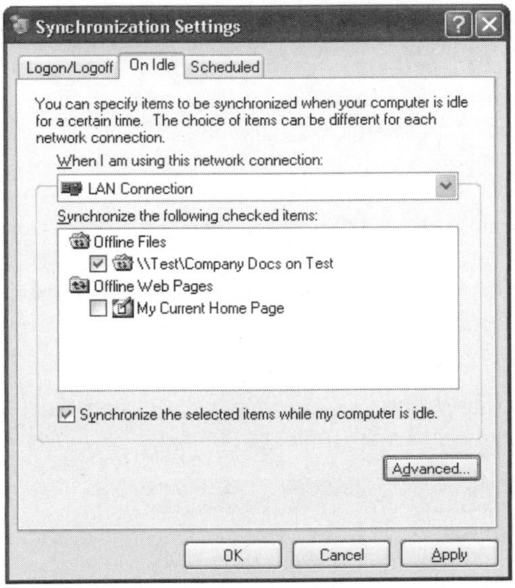

5   If you click the Advanced button on the On Idle tab, you see the Idle Set-
    tings dialog box shown here. You can specify how long the computer must
    remain idle before synchronization will begin (15 minutes is the default) and
    how often synchronization should be repeated while the computer remains
    idle (60 minutes by default). You can also choose to prevent idle-time syn-
    chronization when the computer is running on battery power.

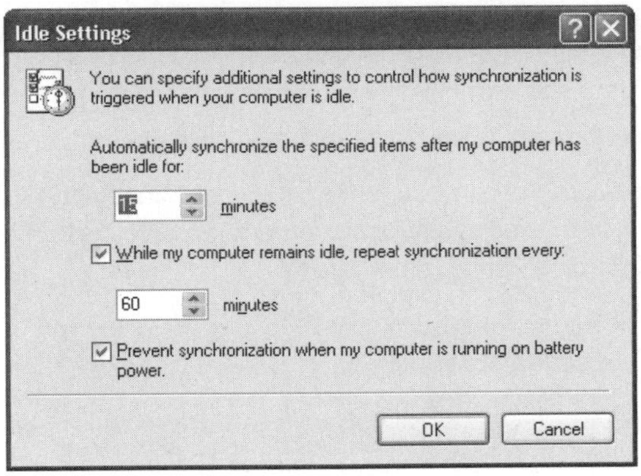

6   If you select the Scheduled tab in the Synchronization Settings dialog box,
    you will see a list of scheduled synchronizations, and you can schedule a

synchronization by clicking Add. Scheduling is useful if you want to synchronize files at specific times, perhaps when the computer is on but not being used or if you have certain files that need to be synchronized at particular times or intervals. Click Add to create a schedule.

7 The Scheduled Synchronization Wizard appears. Click Next.

8 Select a network connection and the offline files and folders that you want to schedule. You can also select the option at the bottom of the page if you want Windows XP to automatically connect to the network when the scheduled synchronization occurs, if it's not already connected at that time. Click Next.

9 On the wizard page shown here, select the start time, start date, and the interval for the synchronization schedule. Click Next.

10 Give the schedule a name. Click Next, and then click Finish.

The scheduled synchronization now appears on the Scheduled tab. You can select the desired scheduled synchronization and remove it at any time or adjust the schedule by clicking Edit.

---

tip **Using Multiple Synchronization Schedules**

You can run the wizard as often as you like to carry out these tasks:

- Schedule other files and folders for synchronization.
- Create schedules using other dates, times, or intervals; or schedule synchronizations using alternate connections.

Stop Using an Offline File or Folder

There might come a time when you want to stop using a particular offline file or folder. In this case, all you need to do is right-click the offline file or folder and choose Make Available Offline so that the option is no longer selected. If you want to stop using Offline Files altogether, clear the Enable Offline Files option on the Offline Files tab of Folder Options.

Managing Caching Options on the Server

If the files you are sharing reside on a Windows 2000 or Windows XP computer, you can adjust their caching settings. Although offline folders and files are selected by users working from their local computers, caching options are set as part of the sharing process on the serving computers. The following caching options can be applied to network shares:

- **Manual Caching Of Documents.** By default, all shared files and folders start out with manual caching. *Manual caching* means that the user has to select the files and folders for them to be made available offline. A characteristic of manual caching is that the selected files and folders are always available offline because they are downloaded to the local computer when the resource is first marked for offline use. On the other hand, only the files and folders that the user *manually* chooses (by selecting Make Available Offline) are cached. Manual caching is most appropriate for users who spend a lot of time working off the network, such as those using portable computers they take home from their office network or use while traveling.

- **Automatic Caching Of Documents.** Both types of automatic caching copy files to the user's local computer as they are requested, that is, as they are opened. The server automatically caches the file or folder on your computer. When you open your locally cached copy, the server also opens its copy to prevent multiple users from writing to the file at the same time. Automatic caching is useful on networks that have occasional disconnections, so users can continue working during outages. However, there is no guarantee that the needed files will be available offline because as the user's cache space fills up, older files are deleted from the cache. This method of caching generally isn't a good solution for users of portable computers because they have to open the file while they're connected to the network before the file will be copied to their portable computer. On the plus side, the user doesn't have to wait for large numbers of folders to be entirely downloaded and synchronized on the local computer: Files are only downloaded as they are needed. Automatic caching of documents is especially useful for document folders or files that the user must be able to update.

● **Automatic Caching Of Programs And Documents.** This automatic caching option is useful for folders and files that are used for read-only access, such as applications and reference documents. By caching these types of files, the user can access them more quickly because the network doesn't need to be repeatedly accessed as the program or document is used.

To set the caching options for a network share, follow these steps:

1 Right-click the shared folder or file and choose Properties.

2 On the Sharing tab, click the Caching button.

3 In the Caching Settings dialog box, shown in Figure 15-5, select one of the three cache options from the Settings list.

note If you are using Windows XP Home Edition, this option is not available because Simple File Sharing is always in use and doesn't permit setting caching options. If you're using Windows XP Professional, you'll need to make sure Simple File Sharing is turned off to see the version of the Sharing tab that contains the Caching button. See Chapter 14, "Understanding Resource Sharing and NTFS Security," for more information about Simple File Sharing.

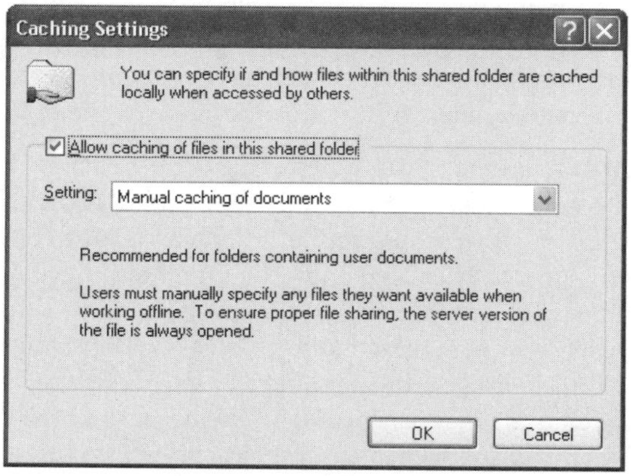

Figure 15-5. When you first share a folder, caching is set to manual caching, but you can change that setting in this dialog box.

Handling Network Disconnections

One issue that can come up with Offline Files concerns how Windows should respond when a network connection is lost. In other words, if you are working on a cached file, can you continue to work on the file when the connection to the other computer is abruptly lost? The choice is up to you. By default, when a network connection is lost, a message appears in the notification area informing you that you are disconnected from the network and that you can continue working offline with any folders and files you previously made available offline or that were automatically cached on your local computer. This is the usual behavior you'll want, but there are other choices available as well.

To alter how your computer responds to going offline, open Folder Options in Control Panel, select the Offline Files tab, and click the Advanced button to open the Offline Files—Advanced Settings dialog box, shown in Figure 15-6.

Figure 15-6. Use the Offline Files—Advanced Settings dialog box to control access to offline files when a network connection is lost.

You have two options that govern how your computer behaves when a network connection is lost:

- **Notify Me And Begin Working Offline.** When you use this default setting, network files you made available offline will continue to be available to you. You can work offline when the network connection is lost, and you'll see a message informing you that you are working offline.

- **Never Allow My Computer To Go Offline.** If you select this setting and then lose your network connection, you'll be notified that you are offline, but you will not be permitted to use the offline files cached on your local computer. Ordinarily, this defeats the purpose of offline files, so you usually wouldn't apply this option globally. However, this feature is useful when it's applied to specific serving computers whose content you might never want to make available offline.

Chapter 15

Rather than choose one of these settings for all your offline files, you can assign a mix of these settings to different network computers by using the Exception List section of this dialog box. For example, suppose that the default setting is Notify Me And Begin Working Offline. There might be a particular network computer whose shares you only want to use when you are online. In this case, you can leave your default setting configured and create an exception to the rule for that server only. To do this, click the Add button, type the network computer's name in the Add Custom Action dialog box that appears, and tag that computer with one of the two preceding options listed. When you click OK, the computer's name along with the behavior of your offline access to its network shares will be listed in the Exception List section. You can repeat this process to add more network computers.

Troubleshooting Offline Files

Once configured, offline files are generally easy to use and problem free, but there are some difficulties that you might encounter:

- **Offline Files and Fast User Switching.** Offline Files and Fast User Switching are not compatible with each other. In Windows XP Professional, you can use one or the other, but not both features at the same time. (Offline Files is not available in Windows XP Home Edition.)

- **Network disconnects.** If you lose access to an online file when the network is disconnected, make sure you have actually configured the file for offline use. If you have, check the Offline Files—Advanced Settings dialog box and make sure you have selected Notify Me And Begin Working Offline, as discussed in the preceding section.

- **Certain files are not synchronized, or you receive an error message.** If Windows cannot synchronize certain files, or you receive an error message, there are two possible explanations. First, the server that holds the file is offline. If this is the case, Windows cannot connect to the server and therefore cannot synchronize your files. The second possibility is that someone else has the file open over the network. In this case, Windows will not be able to synchronize the file because it is already open. You'll simply have to wait until a later time to synchronize the file.

> **note** Files with .mdb, .ldb, .mdw, .mde, and .db extensions are not synchronized by default. This is to prevent potential corruption of these file formats that can occur via synchronization. Also, network Group Policy can prohibit the use of offline files. If your computer is a member of a Windows domain and you cannot use Offline Files, most likely there is a policy configured that prohibits it.

- **No offline file availability.** If you cannot make a file or folder available offline, you probably have Fast User Switching enabled. Disable Fast User Switching to make Offline Files available.

- **Slow synchronization.** Synchronization can require a lot of network bandwidth, especially if several users are trying to synchronize at the same time. One solution is to configure synchronization for nonpeak network usage times. If you have more than one type of network connection, try to synchronize when you are using the faster connection.

Using Briefcase

Briefcase is a tool that appeared in several previous versions of Windows and is also included in Windows XP. Briefcase allows you to copy files for offline use, and then synchronize the files when you are reconnected.

Briefcase is not as easy to use as Offline Files and requires more manual synchronization work on your part; however, it does support synchronization of files using removable media (such as floppy disks or Zip disks) or Direct Cable Connection, whereas Offline Files requires file sharing via SMB, which limits you to files and folders you can reach over a standard network connection, such as Ethernet. This makes Briefcase the tool to use if you do not have a local area connection. It's also your only option when using Windows XP Home Edition.

Briefcases act as containers, holding files that you want to synchronize with other systems, either across the network or on removable media. You can maintain as many briefcases as you need on your system, allowing you to synchronize different content from different locations.

Creating a Briefcase

Creating a new briefcase is easy:

1 In Windows Explorer or My Computer, navigate to a folder for which you want to create a briefcase (or simply use the desktop).

2 Right-click in the folder (or on the desktop) and choose New, Briefcase.

Once you've created a briefcase, you need to insert files you'd like to synchronize. To do so, simply drag the files into the briefcase. Then, when you're ready to use those files in another location, copy the briefcase to the remote computer (when using a network or Direct Cable Connection) or to a removable disk.

Chapter 15

You can view the contents of a briefcase just like any other folder by double-clicking it. The first time you open a briefcase, you'll see a brief description of how Briefcase works, as shown in Figure 15-7.

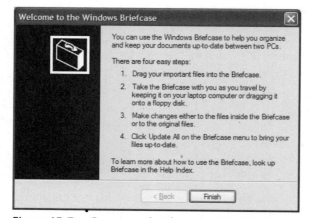

Figure 15-7. Opening a briefcase for the first time triggers an introductory dialog box.

You can open the briefcase on the remote computer, edit the files, and save your changes. These changes will be tracked by Briefcase.

If you right-click a file within a briefcase and choose Properties, you'll see a new tab, Update Status, as shown in Figure 15-8.

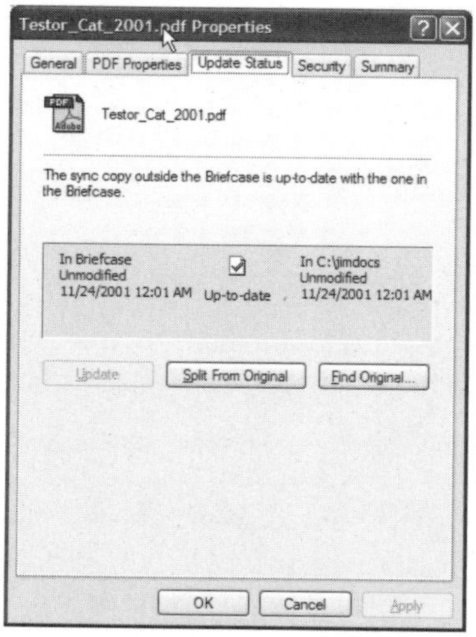

Figure 15-8. Files within a briefcase display an additional tab called Update Status in their properties dialog boxes.

Selecting this tab displays the synchronization status of the file, which shows the time it was last changed both in its original format and in the briefcase itself. If you're using this dialog box on the machine that contains the original file, you can click Find Original to open the folder containing the original file. You can also click Split From Original if you do not want changes that have been made to the briefcase file to be synchronized. This creates an *orphan file* that you'll have to manually copy out of the briefcase to a new location if you want to keep its changes.

Synchronizing Files with Briefcase

Once you've made changes to the files within a briefcase on a remote system, synchronizing them with your main computer is quite simple.

1 If your briefcase was on a removable disk, place that disk back in your main computer. If you used a network connection or Direct Cable Connection, reestablish the connection.

2 Open the remote briefcase, either on the removable disk or on the remote computer, by double-clicking it.

3 To update all the files in the briefcase, choose Briefcase, Update All. If you only want to update a subset of the files, you can select them, right-click them, and then choose Update.

> **note** Any orphaned files will not update changes to their original documents on your main computer. If you want to copy or move the orphaned files back to your computer, you will have to do so manually.

Choosing Between Briefcase and Offline Files

When should you use Offline Files for file synchronization, and when should you use Briefcase?

● If you are using Windows XP Home Edition, you must use Briefcase because Offline Files is not available in Windows XP Home Edition.

● If you are using a LAN or a dial-up network connection that supports File And Printer Sharing For Microsoft Networks via SMB, use Offline Files to take advantage of its greater power, speed, and flexibility.

● If you need to use a Direct Cable Connection or removable media to transfer the files, you must use Briefcase.

Part 5

Advanced Networking

Chapter 16

Remote Desktop and Remote Assistance

As computer use has become more mobile, the ability to connect to remote resources and even get help from remote resources has become more and more important. Microsoft Windows XP provides some flexible features for remote networking, including two new features called Remote Desktop and Remote Assistance.

Remote Desktop lets you control another computer located at a remote location. For example, if you have an office computer on a LAN and a Windows XP Professional computer at home, you can connect to your office computer from home and access files and run applications as though you were at work sitting in front of the office computer. In a similar manner, if a coworker or relative in another city needs help configuring her Windows XP computer, Remote Assistance lets you provide help (and receive help) over the Internet. Using Remote Assistance, you can see a remote user's desktop and even configure the system remotely.

Exploring Remote Desktop

Remote Desktop, available with Windows XP Professional, provides features previously available only on server versions of the Microsoft operating system family, such as Microsoft Windows 2000 Server. The remote access solution available with the server versions of Windows 2000 and Microsoft Windows NT 4.0 is known as Terminal Services. Remote Desktop permits an authorized user running Remote Desktop Connection to connect to a remote computer running Windows XP Professional, Windows 2000 Server (running Terminal Services), or

Microsoft Windows NT 4.0 Terminal Server Edition (TSE) and interact with it, as if that user were sitting in front of the remote computer.

When the connection is initiated, a window appears that shows the desktop of the remote computer. A Remote Desktop client can launch programs, open files, make system changes, and so forth in the same manner as a local user would. For example, a user who is working at home for an extended period of time could connect to his computer at the office and run applications, check e-mail, and access remote resources from his home computer. If a user connects to the office computer (or any computer supporting Remote Desktop) she can start an application such as Disk Defragmenter, and then disconnect from the remote computer. The process or application will continue to run without the user being connected.

> **note** Windows XP Home Edition cannot act as a host for Remote Desktop. In other words, you cannot access a computer running Windows XP Home Edition remotely. Remote desktop sessions can only be *hosted* by Windows XP Professional, Windows 2000 Server (running Terminal Services), and Windows NT 4.0 TSE. However, you can connect to one of these three remote hosts from a computer running either Windows XP Professional *or* Windows XP Home Edition. Furthermore, by installing Remote Desktop Connection software, computers running the following versions of Microsoft Windows can also access Remote Desktop hosts: Windows 2000, Windows NT 4, Windows Millennium Edition (Windows Me), Windows 98, and Windows 95. For more information, see "Installing Remote Desktop Connection on non–Windows XP Computers," page 480.

Before you start using Remote Desktop, there are three important points to remember:

- When a remote user connects to the workstation serving the Remote Desktop session, the local desktop is locked. This is done to prevent other users from interacting with the user's workstation directly. In other words, if you are accessing your office computer from home, no one in the office can use your computer interactively while you are remotely connected; in fact, even when you're done, a user will have to unlock the desktop with a valid user name and password in order to use the computer interactively. While you're connected, however, the computer's network services, such as file and print sharing and Microsoft Internet Information Services (IIS), continue to function normally.

- Remote Desktop allows multiple users to connect to the same computer (although not at the same time). This allows each user to run individual groups of applications, just as when those individual users log on to the same computer locally.

- Each user accessing the Remote Desktop must have a direct connection to the computer hosting the session. To meet this requirement, the user must either be on the same LAN/WAN as the remote computer or use a virtual private network (VPN) connection to the LAN, or the remote computer must have an Internet-accessible (public) IP address. The last scenario should be implemented using a firewall to redirect traffic on the Remote Desktop port to the hosting machine. It is unwise to leave a computer connected directly to the Internet without some kind of firewall protection. You can learn more about this issue in "Using Remote Desktop over the Internet/Firewall," page 477.

Enabling Remote Desktop on the Host Computer

You must first enable Remote Desktop on the Windows XP Professional computer that you want to reach remotely via Remote Desktop. Remember that only Windows XP Professional, server versions of Windows 2000, and Windows NT 4.0 TSE computers can host a remote connection, but other Windows computers can run the *client* software required to connect to the remote hosts. For example, if you use Windows XP Professional at your office, you can enable Remote Desktop on your office computer, and you can access that computer from your home computer running Windows XP Home Edition. (However, you won't be able to access this home computer from the office.) In this example, the office computer is the Remote Desktop *host*, and the home computer is the Remote Desktop *client*. The client computer accesses, or connects to, the host computer and controls the host computer remotely.

To turn on Remote Desktop on a Windows XP Professional computer, follow these steps:

1 Log on to the Windows XP Professional computer as a member of the Administrators group. You cannot enable Remote Desktop without an administrator account.

2 From the Start menu, choose Control Panel, System. In the System Properties dialog box, select the Remote tab, shown here.

3 Select the Allow Users To Connect Remotely To This Computer check box to enable Remote Desktop. Once enabled, the current user and any member of the Administrators or Remote Desktop Users group can access the computer using Remote Desktop. However, you might want to change the default settings to allow or prevent specific users to access Remote Desktop. To manage the users that can access the remote desktop, click the Select Remote Users button.

---

caution Any user who wants to use Remote Desktop must have a password. Remote Desktop connections do not allow blank passwords.

---

4 In the Remote Desktop Users dialog box, shown next, click the Add button to add users to the Remote Desktop Users group, or use the Remove button to remove users from that group. Remember that all users with administrative privileges automatically have access; however, you can also grant non-administrative users the right to connect to the computer.

Remote Desktop Users

The users listed below can connect to this computer, and any members of the Administrators group can connect even if they are not listed.

remote

Administrator already has access.

[Add...] [Remove]

To create new user accounts or add users to other groups, go to Control Panel and open User Accounts.

[OK] [Cancel]

5 When you are done, click OK.

InsideOut

Using Administrative Privileges Selectively

It's extremely common for people to log onto their Windows XP computers using either the local Administrator account or another user account with administrative privileges. This is normally done for convenience, as many configuration changes (and even some software installers) require administrative privileges.

It's wise, however, to avoid logging on to your Windows XP computer(s) using accounts with administrative privileges more often than is absolutely necessary. If you are logged on as an administrative user, it is more likely that an accidental change (such as a file deletion) will impact the system's performance and stability. Additionally, if a Trojan horse or Internet worm is launched using your user credentials, having administrative privileges will give the malicious code the ability to do far more damage to your system or even to your network. See "Using Administrative Privileges," page 593, for more information.

Using Remote Desktop over a Dial-up Connection

You can access a Remote Desktop connection through a dial-up connection as long as that connection has been configured to allow TCP/IP connections. If you're dialing into a traditional ISP or to a Windows computer configured to provide remote access connections, you need only establish that dial-up connection as usual (as described in "Creating New Internet Connections," page 103.

If you want to dial directly into a remote computer running Windows XP Professional and use Remote Desktop, you can set it up to provide remote access connections, as described in "Using Remote Desktop Through a Remote Access Server," page 479.

Using Remote Desktop over the Internet/Firewall

You can access a Remote Desktop computer over the Internet or through a firewall, but the process can be a bit tricky. The only way you can access a remote computer is via a DNS name or IP address. On a LAN, this isn't much of a problem. Normally, you're either assigned a static IP address, or you are in a Windows domain that maintains a dynamic DNS server, so your computer's DNS name is static even if your IP address changes.

However, if you need to access a computer connected to an ISP, the DNS name and IP address on the public network are frequently *dynamic*. In other words, in a typical ISP arrangement, your external IP address is assigned by the ISP and will change each time you connect the computer to the Internet. If you are always connected, such as in the case of a DSL or satellite connection, you might have a static IP address, but this depends on how your service provider handles IP addresses.

> **tip** **Using a Dynamic DNS Service**
>
> If you need to regularly connect to a computer that has both a dynamic DNS name and a dynamic IP address, you might want to look into a service that maps your dynamic IP address to a fixed DNS name. Such services typically run client software on your computer that registers your IP address with them, and they use dynamic DNS to update a fixed DNS name to point to the IP address. Two vendors that provide this service are CanWeb Internet Services (*www.dynip.com*) and Tzolkin (*www.tzo.com*).

The point, however, is that you must know the DNS name or IP address of the Remote Desktop host computer in order to connect to it. To find the current IP address of the host computer's Internet connection, work at the remote computer and double-click the Internet connection icon in Network Places. Select the Support tab; you'll see a listing for the client IP address. On the computer from which you are launching the Remote Desktop client, you can specify this IP address as the remote host address. If the remote computer is using a dial-up connection, you must connect the remote computer to the Internet, determine the IP address for that session, and then remain connected so that the computer can be accessed remotely. If the remote computer is protected by a firewall (which it should be), the firewall administrator needs to configure the firewall to allow Remote Desktop traffic in these ways:

- If you are using Internet Connection Firewall (ICF), you'll need to open the connection's properties dialog box, select Advanced, click Settings, and on the Services tab, enable the Remote Desktop service. See "Enabling Services," page 141, to learn more.

- If you are using a different firewall product or the computer resides on a network with a server firewall product, the network administrator needs to configure the firewall to allow incoming access to TCP port 3389. As shown in the following illustration, the client computer accesses the remote desktop across the Internet, but the remote desktop traffic is allowed over the firewall because TCP port 3389 is open.

Client Computer Reaching Remote Computer Through Port 3389

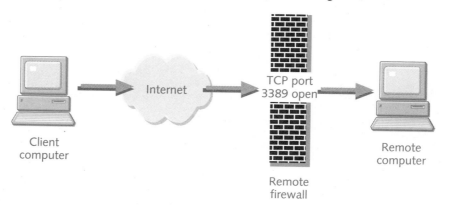

Client computer

Internet

TCP port 3389 open

Remote firewall

Remote computer

---

tip   **Remote Desktop and Bandwidth**

If you are accessing a remote computer over a LAN connection or a broadband Internet connection, you will see fast performance with Remote Desktop. However, if you are using a dial-up connection to access a remote desktop (or the remote desktop has a dial-up connection), you might find that Remote Desktop operates very slowly. Because Remote Desktop must display the remote computer's desktop for you, the connection has to carry a lot of graphics data, which can make screen updates painfully slow. However, there are some ways you can reduce this problem when using Remote Desktop over a dial-up connection. See "Optimizing Remote Desktop Performance," page 490, for more information.

Using Remote Desktop Through a Remote Access Server

If you access a corporate LAN by dialing into a remote access server, the Remote Desktop connection works in a similar fashion to other remote desktop connections. Dial into the remote access server. Once authenticated, you begin the Remote Desktop session. However, if a firewall is in use between your remote access server and the Remote Desktop computer, the firewall must support Remote Desktop traffic on TCP port 3389.

---

tip   **Dialing into Your Own Workstation**

You can configure your own Windows XP Professional computer to provide remote access dial-up connectivity so that you can dial directly into it to access the network and/or to use the Remote Desktop service. To learn more about this process, see "Allowing Clients to Dial in to Your Computer," page 510.

If you need to connect to a LAN using a VPN connection, you can still connect to a remote desktop on that LAN. To do so, establish a VPN connection with the network. Then, start Remote Desktop and specify the IP address or machine name of the remote computer you want to access. Whether you are using a VPN or simply dialing up to a remote access server, you must first connect to the private network before you try to access the remote computer because the remote computer's IP address is private and is not exposed to the Internet. As shown in the following illustration, the client connects to the VPN server, and then connects to the remote computer inside the network. To learn more about remote access servers and VPN, see Chapter 17, "Remote Access and Virtual Private Networking."

Client Computer Reaching Remote Computer Through VPN Server

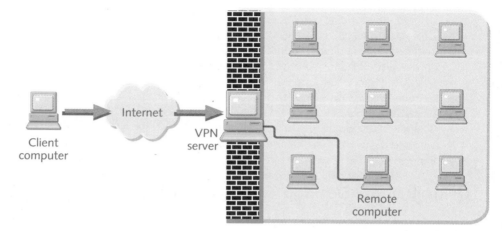

Configuring the Client Computer

Once you have enabled Remote Desktop on a Windows XP Professional computer and have examined your connectivity options, you can configure your client computer—the computer from which you will access the remote computer. If you're using Windows XP Professional or Windows XP Home Edition as your client computer, there is nothing you need to install. The Remote Desktop Connection software is already installed on your system. See "Opening a Remote Desktop Connection in Windows XP," opposite.

Installing Remote Desktop Connection on non–Windows XP Computers

Before Remote Desktop, a program known as a *terminal services client* was used to create sessions with the hosts running Terminal Services. With Windows XP, a new client known as Remote Desktop Connection is used. This tool is backward compatible with the older Terminal Services software included with Windows 2000, Windows 2000 Server, and Windows NT 4.0 TSE, and it is the preferred method for connecting to a remote computer. If you want to use another version of Windows as a Remote Desktop client, the client software is available on both the Windows XP Professional and Windows XP Home Edition installation CDs, or it can be downloaded from Microsoft at *www.microsoft.com/windowsxp/pro/downloads/rdclientdl.asp*.

To install the Remote Desktop Connection client software from one of the Windows XP installation CDs, insert the CD and choose Perform Additional Tasks when the Welcome To Microsoft Windows XP menu appears. Then, choose Set Up Remote Desktop Connection. Follow the simple installation instructions that appear. If you are installing the Remote Desktop Connection software from the download, just run the executable file to set up the software.

> **tip** **Installing Remote Desktop Connection on Several Computers**
>
> If you need to install the Remote Desktop client software on several computers that are not running Windows XP, you might want to put the installation package onto a CD or Zip disk so you can carry the required software with you as you move about and configure each machine. (The download is 3.4 MB in size, so it is too large for a floppy disk.)

Opening a Remote Desktop Connection in Windows XP

To start a Remote Desktop session from a Windows XP computer, ensure that you have installed the software. Choose Start, All Programs, Accessories, Communications, Remote Desktop Connection. The Remote Desktop Connection dialog box appears, as shown in Figure 16-1. Enter the name of the remote computer or IP address, depending on how you intend to connect. If the computer's name can be resolved via DNS, you can enter the computer name; otherwise, you might need to use the IP address. This dialog box also contains an Options button that lets you adjust various settings for your remote session. These settings are discussed in "Choosing Remote Desktop Options," page 490. Click the Connect button to begin the Remote Desktop session.

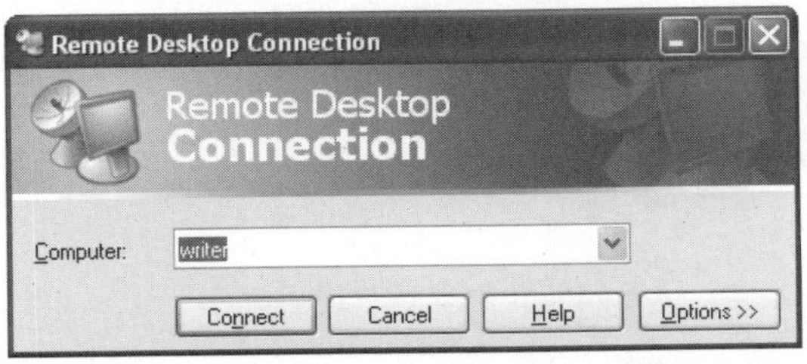

Figure 16-1. Enter the name or IP address of the remote computer.

Once the initial connection is established, the Log On To Windows dialog box appears, as shown in Figure 16-2 on the next page. Enter the user name and password of an account that is a member of the Remote Desktop Users group or one that has administrative privileges on the remote computer. Click OK to complete the connection.

Once the connection is complete, the remote desktop appears, as shown in Figure 16-3 on the next page. By default, the window is maximized so that it appears as though you are actually working on the remote computer. You can now open applications, create and save files, make system configuration changes (if you are logged on with an administrator account), and do anything else you would do if you were logged on locally.

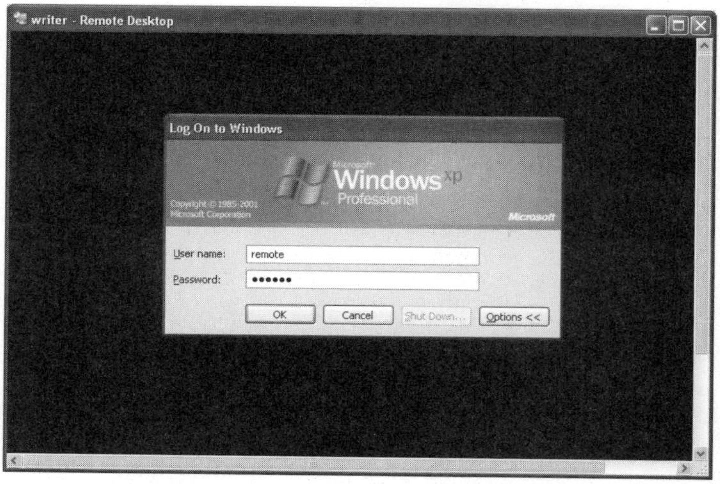

Figure 16-2. Log on to the remote computer using an account with administrative privileges or one that's a member of the Remote Desktop Users group.

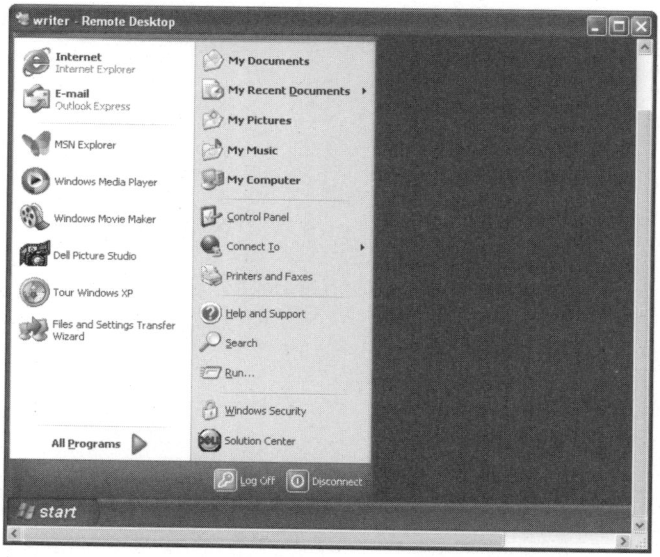

Figure 16-3. You can now use the Remote Desktop session as if you were actually sitting in front of the remote computer.

InsideOut

Saving Files in a Remote Desktop Connection

When you are using the Remote Desktop connection, you can create and save files as though you are actually working at that the remote computer. You have the ability to create and save files to the remote hard disk drive as well as to any network share for which your user account has permissions.

However, keep in mind that during a Remote Desktop session, you are actually working on the remote computer. What you see at your end of the connection is only a terminal display of what is happening at the remote end. For this reason, although you can create and save files on the remote computer, you cannot drag and drop them to your computer without taking advantage of Remote Desktop's ability to map your system's drives to the Remote Desktop session. For more information on this process, see "Configuring Local Resources," page 492.

Connecting to a Remote Computer When Another User Is Logged On

When you make a Remote Desktop connection, you are quickly and easily connected if no one else is using the remote computer. If, however, another user is logged on to the computer, one of two things will happen:

- If Fast User Switching is enabled on the remote computer, you'll see the message shown in Figure 16-4 on the next page, and the remote user will see the message shown in Figure 16-5. The remote user has the opportunity to reject your message. If no one is actually sitting at the remote computer to answer your message, the remote user account is switched off after a few seconds of inaction. The remote user's session actually remains logged on because Fast User Switching allows more than one person to be logged on, and no unsaved files or documents will be lost because the user has technically not logged off. However, the user at the remote computer won't be able to actually use the computer until you log off or until the user decides to take control. The remote computer displays the Windows Welcome screen (if it's enabled on the remote machine) while the client is using the remote computer. In other words, no one at the remote computer can see what you are doing, although from the Welcome menu they can see that you are signed on. But if a user with an account on the remote computer wants to use it, he can click his icon on the Welcome screen, sign on, and terminate the client's Remote Desktop session.

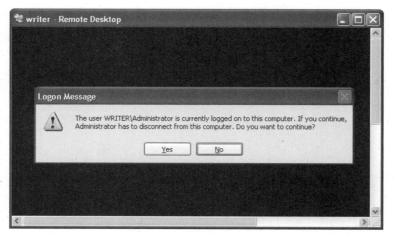

Figure 16-4. When you attempt to log on, you see a message telling you that another user is logged on. Click Yes to continue.

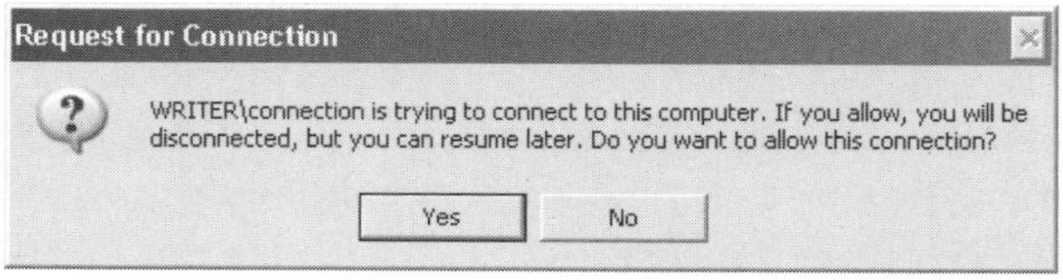

Figure 16-5. A user logged on at the remote computer sees this message, which lets that person decide whether you can log on.

- If Fast User Switching is not enabled on the remote computer, things do not work as nicely. Figure 16-6 shows that you have the option of forcefully ending the user's session without even giving the user an opportunity to save any open files.

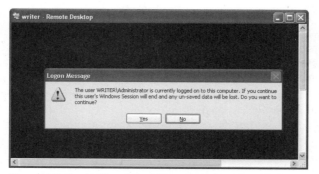

Figure 16-6. Without Fast User Switching enabled, another user's session can be forcefully ended.

caution To ensure that users do not lose any data, it is a good idea to use Fast User Switching with Remote Desktop; however, if the Remote Desktop host is a member of a domain, using Fast User Switching is not an option. This is usually not a problem because machines that participate in domains usually only have one regular user, and you're not likely to kick anyone off your office computer.

If the remote computer is using Fast User Switching and a user is signed on at the remote computer, the user has time to save his or her data before the Remote Desktop session begins, or if the user does not save the data, it is not lost because the user is not actually logged off. In fact, the user at the remote computer can even deny permission for the Remote Desktop session. Of course, if you are the only one who uses your computer, this issue is of no consequence.

Note that any user with administrative privileges can disrupt a remote session by simply logging on at the remote computer. Also, if more than one person uses the same account, logging on locally with the same account that is being used remotely disconnects the remote user. In fact, whatever the client was working on remotely appears on screen at the remote machine where that user has signed on. This allows the user at the remote computer to save the work that was interrupted in the Remote Desktop session or to simply discard it. Of course, if you want to maintain privacy, you should never share user accounts in the first place.

Troubleshooting

You cannot connect to a Remote Desktop host.

If you attempt to make a Remote Desktop connection and you see the message displayed in Figure 16-7, your Remote Desktop connection has been rejected. Most frequently this occurs when Remote Desktop has not been enabled on the remote machine.

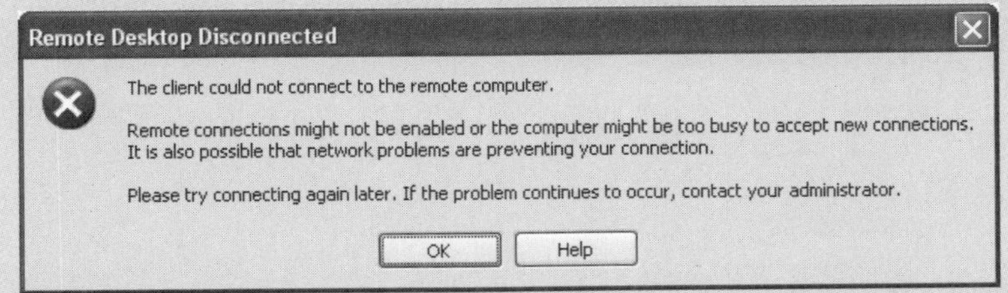

Remote Desktop Disconnected

The client could not connect to the remote computer.

Remote connections might not be enabled or the computer might be too busy to accept new connections. It is also possible that network problems are preventing your connection.

Please try connecting again later. If the problem continues to occur, contact your administrator.

[OK]   [Help]

Figure 16-7. This message often indicates that permission to run Remote Desktop is not enabled on the remote computer.

(continued)

> **Troubleshooting** *(continued)*   To remedy this situation, make sure that Remote Desktop has been enabled on the remote computer, and then check that the user account that couldn't complete the remote connection has an administrator account on the computer or has been added to the Remote Desktop Users group. Next, from the client computer, if you're using a computer name to access the remote computer, make sure that the computer name can be resolved by DNS. If you're using an IP address, make sure you can reach that IP address from the client computer, and that no firewalls are blocking Remote Desktop between the client computer and the Remote Desktop host.

Logging On Automatically

If you routinely use Remote Desktop to connect to a remote computer, you can save yourself a bit of effort in the logon process by configuring Remote Desktop to log you on automatically. For example, you might want to do this if you typically use your home computer in the evening to log on to your office computer and check e-mail. To configure the automatic logon option, follow these steps:

1 Choose Start, All Programs, Accessories, Communications, Remote Desktop Connection.

2 In the Remote Desktop Connection dialog box, click the Options button.

3 On the General tab that appears, enter the computer you want to connect to, the user name, password, and domain (if necessary.) Select the Save My Password check box, shown here.

4 Click the Save As button. By default the file is saved as Default.rdp in the My Documents folder using the Remote Desktop Files format (with a .rdp file extension). If you want the settings you entered to be your default settings, click Save. If not, type a different name.

5 Click Connect to make the connection. From now on, you'll not be asked to provide the user name and password when you make the Remote Desktop connection.

---

tip   If you are logging on to different remote computers, you can double-click the appropriate .rdp file, and the connection will be launched automatically.

Generating a Remote Desktop Session with Microsoft Internet Explorer

If you don't have access to the full version of Remote Desktop from the computer you have available (for example, you might be logging on from a public computer in an airport terminal or library), you can open a Remote Desktop session using Internet Explorer 4 or later if the Windows XP Professional remote computer is configured to allow you to do so. However, this process requires the use of IIS, and because Web servers are the most commonly attacked networking software, it's important to recognize the responsibility you'll have for configuring and securing IIS once it's running. For more information, see "Securing IIS," page 577.

Configuring Windows XP Professional for Web Access

If you want to access Windows XP Professional Remote Desktop connections using Internet Explorer, you have to configure IIS to allow the connection. If you do not have IIS currently installed or you need to learn more about IIS, see Chapter 9, "Using Internet Information Services." To configure IIS to allow Remote Desktop, you must run the Remote Desktop Web Connection software. Follow these steps:

1 Open Add Or Remove Programs in Control Panel.

2 Select Add/Remove Windows Components.

3 When the Windows Components Wizard appears, select Internet Information Services (IIS), and click the Details button.

4 In the Internet Information Services (IIS) dialog box, select World Wide Web Service and click Details.

5 In the World Wide Web Service dialog box shown on the next page, select Remote Desktop Web Connection and click OK. Click OK, click Next, and then click Finish to complete the wizard.

World Wide Web Service

To add or remove a component, click the check box. A shaded box means that only part of the component will be installed. To see what's included in a component, click Details.

Subcomponents of World Wide Web Service:

☑ 📁 Printers virtual directory	0.0 MB
☑ 📁 Remote Desktop Web Connection	0.3 MB
☐ 📁 Scripts virtual directory	0.0 MB
☑ 🌐 World Wide Web Service	1.9 MB

Description: ActiveX control and sample pages for hosting Terminal Services client connections over the Web

Total disk space required: 2.6 MB

Space available on disk: 31466.9 MB

[Details...]

[OK] [Cancel]

tip If you are worried about anonymous access to your remote session, don't be. Anonymous access only allows Web browsing access. Remote Desktop will still require a valid user name and password to operate the computer remotely.

Configuring the Remote Client for Web Access

Once the remote computer is configured to allow Web access to Remote Desktop, you can use your client computer to connect. Keep these important points in mind:

- You might not be able to trust all the clients you want to connect from. If you go to an Internet café, an unscrupulous owner might have installed software that monitors your keystrokes and could capture your remote computer's name and your user name and password.

- You must be using Internet Explorer 4 or later.

- If you are connecting over the Internet to the remote computer, use the computer's public DNS name or IP address to connect. See "Using Remote Desktop over the Internet/Firewall," page 477, for more information.

- If you are connecting through a remote access or VPN server, first make the network connection, and then use the name or IP address of the remote computer to complete the connection.

Chapter 16: Remote Desktop and Remote Assistance

To connect to the remote computer using Internet Explorer, open Internet Explorer and type the default address, which is http://*server*/tsweb. Again, if you are connecting over the Internet, use the public DNS name or IP address to connect, as in http://*ipaddress*/tsweb. If you're able to access both port 80 (HTTP) and port 3389 (RDP) from your remote location, you'll see a Remote Desktop Web Connection screen, as shown in Figure 16-8.

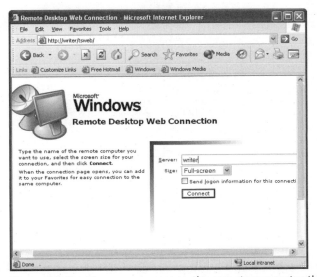

Figure 16-8. You can connect to the remote computer through IIS.

To connect, enter the remote computer's name and choose between full screen and a variety of resolutions. Keep in mind that lower resolutions reduce the amount of bandwidth consumed and will help speed up the connection. Also, full screen will take up the entire computer screen. Other options give you a resizable window. When you first connect, you'll probably see a Security Warning (depending on your Internet Explorer configuration). Remote Desktop installs an ActiveX control on your computer, so just click Yes in response to the Security Warning (if you do not, Remote Desktop will not work). You'll see the standard Remote Desktop logon dialog box. Enter your user name and password and click OK. The Remote Desktop session opens in Internet Explorer, as shown in Figure 16-9 on the next page, or in full screen mode, depending on your selection.

Figure 16-9. The Remote Desktop session works exactly the same in Internet Explorer as it does when using the Remote Desktop Connection software.

Choosing Remote Desktop Options

Remote Desktop can be used for many purposes and can connect very different computers over networks of varying bandwidth. To address these multiple variables, Remote Desktop offers a rich selection of customization options, which are discussed next.

Optimizing Remote Desktop Performance

If you are accessing a remote computer over a LAN or intranet, the performance of Remote Desktop will be quite responsive. However, if you are running Remote Desktop over a heavily used network connection or via a dial-up connection, you might find its performance to be somewhat slow. There are a few actions you can take to help reduce the amount of bandwidth consumed by Remote Desktop, thereby increasing its performance. Follow these steps:

1 On the client computer, open Remote Desktop Connection.

2 In the Remote Desktop Connection dialog box, click the Options button, and then select the Experience tab.

3 In the Choose Your Connection Speed To Optimize Performance box, select the connection type you're about to use to contact the remote computer. As shown in Figure 16-10, when Modem is selected as the connection type, only the Themes and Bitmap Caching features are transmitted over the remote connection. These default settings typically provide the best

performance for modem users. However, the default settings provided to you are just suggestions. You can change any of these settings by selecting or clearing the check boxes as desired. You might need to experiment with these settings to find the ones that work best for you. You should usually leave Bitmap Caching enabled because it helps speed up your connection by saving images in your local cache so that they can be reused during the session instead of having to be downloaded repeatedly. But if you're using a very fast connection and want to watch video over the Remote Desktop connection, you should clear this option.

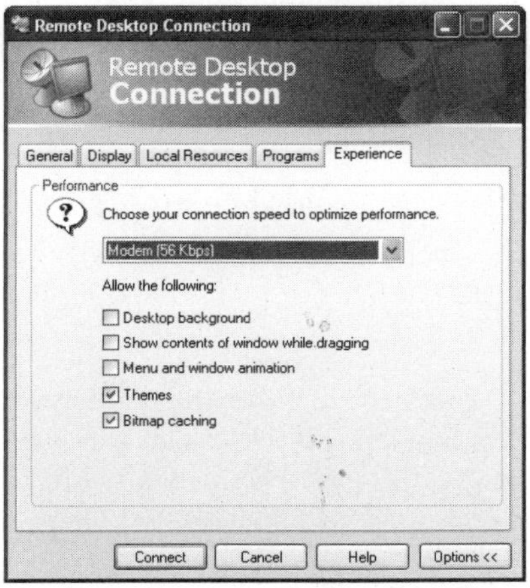

Figure 16-10. You can speed up the performance of Remote Desktop by adjusting the options on the Experience tab.

note The remote computer might also have policy settings that enforce certain Experience settings. See "Remote Desktop and Group Policy," page 494, to learn more.

Managing the Remote Desktop Display

The Display tab, shown in Figure 16-11 on the next page, allows you to modify the display options for the window containing the remote session. The supported resolutions range from 640×480 to Full Screen. You can also specify the color depth to use for the connection as well as decide whether or not to display the connection bar when in full screen mode. The connection bar is displayed at the top of your display. It displays the name or address of the computer hosting the remote session and lets you minimize the remote desktop, maximize it to full screen, place it in a window that you can size on your local computer, or close it entirely (which terminates the session).

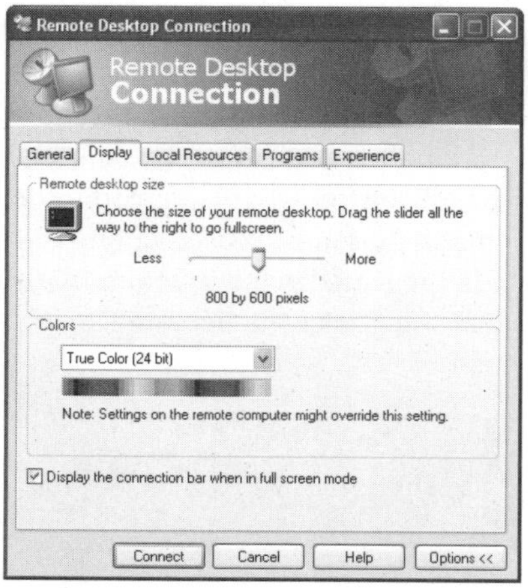

Figure 16-11. Use the Display tab to adjust the desktop size and color depth of the remote session.

Configuring Local Resources

The Local Resources tab, shown in Figure 16-12, allows the configuration of some of the newer features available with Remote Desktop. Three categories of options exist: Sound, Keyboard, and Local Devices. The Sound option allows you to specify how sounds emanating from the remote computer will be handled. There are three options:

- **Leave At Remote Computer.** With this setting enabled, any sounds from the remote computer play at the location of the remote computer. (This can be useful when controlling media jukeboxes remotely.)

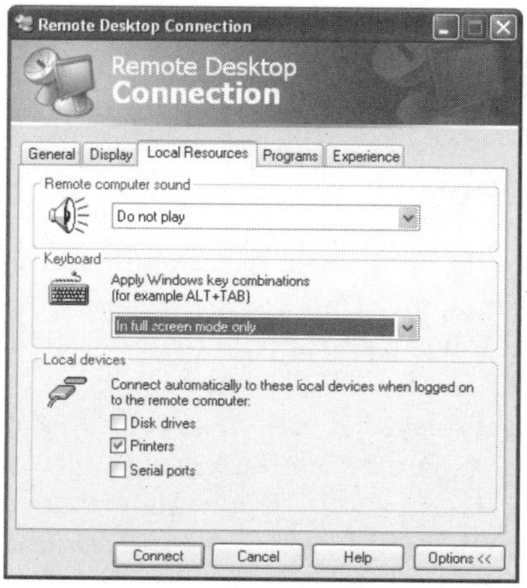

Figure 16-12. Choose the Local Resources tab to configure sounds, keyboard commands, and devices.

- **Do Not Play.** This option silences sound at the remote computer as well as on your local computer. After all, if no one is at the remote computer (or maybe more importantly if someone *is* in the vicinity), there is usually no reason to play sounds generated by your remote session.

- **Bring To This Computer.** This option plays the sounds you generate at the remote computer on your local computer, so you have the full experience of running the remote computer. For example, you could use this option to play music or other media stored on the remote computer at your client location. Keep in mind, however, that transmitting sound also consumes more bandwidth.

The Keyboard section lets you decide which computer will respond to certain Windows keys that you press on the client computer. These Windows key combinations include Alt+Tab, the Windows key, and Ctrl+Alt+Del. You can choose to have these keys control the remote computer instead of your local machine when the Remote Desktop window has the focus, or you can have the keys always control your local computer. You can also choose to have the Windows key combinations control the remote computer only if the remote session is running in full screen mode. If you choose not to apply the Windows key combinations to the remote session, Remote Desktop assigns the following alternate set of special keys to control the remote computer:

- **Alt+Page Up.** Switches between currently running applications (equivalent to Alt+Tab on the client computer).

- **Alt+Page Down.** Switches between applications in the reverse order (equivalent to Alt+Shift+Tab).

- **Alt+Insert.** Switches between applications in the order they were started (equivalent to Alt+Esc).

- **Alt+Home.** Displays the Start menu (equivalent to Ctrl+Esc).

- **Ctrl+Alt+Break.** Switches the Remote Desktop client between running as a window and running in full screen mode.

- **Ctrl+Alt+End.** Displays the Windows Security dialog box (equivalent to Ctrl+Alt+Del).

- **Alt+Del.** Displays the current application's Windows menu.

- **Ctrl+Alt+Keypad Minus.** Places a snapshot of the active window within the client on the remote clipboard (just as if you'd pressed Alt+PrintScrn on the remote computer).

- **Ctrl+Alt+Keypad Plus.** Places a snapshot of the entire remote window on the remote clipboard (just as if you'd pressed Shift+PrintScrn on the remote computer).

The Local Devices section lets you map the client computer's disk drives, printers, serial ports, and smart card devices to the Remote Desktop host. For example, if you're connected to your work computer from your home computer and need to print a document located on your work computer at your home, you can select the Printers option, and the document will print on your home printer. You might also want to access information stored on disk drives in your local computer while in the Remote Desktop session. Selecting Disk Drives makes your local disk drives appear in the My Computer window of the remote computer so that you can access them.

Remote Desktop and Group Policy

There are many ways to use Remote Desktop, and Group Policy can be a useful tool in controlling that usage. Imagine that you own a small company with a network of 10 Windows XP Professional computers. One of the computers stores company documents. Because several of your users also have laptop computers, you decide to use Remote Desktop to enable the laptop users to connect to the Windows XP Professional computer so that company files and documents can be edited, read, created, and used in any way necessary. The problem, however, is that you want to control bandwidth, and you want user sessions to be disconnected after they are idle for a certain period of time. You can't do this directly within Remote Desktop, but you can if you use Local Group Policy.

Local Group Policy gives you a way to enforce certain settings on users who log on to the local computer. This includes everything from desktop settings to Internet Explorer settings. You can also use Local Group Policy to set Remote Desktop policies as well. This collection of settings includes such items as performance settings, user management settings, and even folder redirection.

To use Local Group Policy to manage Remote Desktop sessions, follow these steps:

1 Log on to the host computer locally using an account with administrative privileges.

2 From the Start menu, choose Run and type **gpedit.msc.** Click OK.

3 When the Group Policy console appears, expand Computer Configuration, Administrative Templates, Windows Components, and click Terminal Services. The Remote Desktop (Terminal Services) policies you can administer appear in the right pane, as shown in Figure 16-13.

To configure a policy, simply double-click it and choose to enable (or disable) it. Enter any additional information as required by the policy.

If the computer resides in a domain, the policy can be applied at a domain level, to individual organizational units (OUs), or to individual computers, allowing you to control either all computers or subsets of them. If the computer is running in a workgroup, however, Local Group Policy must be configured on each computer.

Chapter 16: Remote Desktop and Remote Assistance

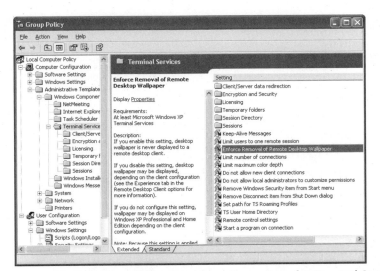

Figure 16-13. Group Policy provides policy options for Terminal Services.

InsideOut

Making the Most of Remote Desktop

The availability of Remote Desktop with Windows XP Professional facilitates a class of remote working and management options that have not been easy to implement before. By using Windows XP Professional at home and at the office, users can access resources from both the home and business networks. This is a boon to telecommuters because Remote Desktop allows the client computer to access the remote resources. Because the drives and resources of the local computer can be mapped to the remote computer, the client user can access the resources of both computers and move data across the two machines as needed. Applications can be run remotely on more powerful work computers, and the results can be viewed and printed at the same physical location as the client computer. This flexibility opens a new world of easy remote networking and access.

newfeature!
Exploring Remote Assistance

Remote Assistance is a new feature in Windows XP Professional and Windows XP Home Edition that enables users to help each other over the Internet. With this tool, one user who is termed the *expert* can view the desktop of another user known as the *novice*. When properly authorized by the novice, the expert user can engage in remote troubleshooting of the novice user's system. For a Remote Assistance session to succeed, both users must be connected to the same network (typically, the Internet or a corporate network) and be using Windows XP. Remote Assistance is easy to use and configure, and can be helpful in many situations including the following:

- It can be used on a company network where help desk personnel connect to remote computers and provide assistance.
- It can be used by individuals who need help from other individuals.
- It can be used as a tool for collaboration.

> **note** Remote Assistance is only available in Windows XP Professional and Windows XP Home Edition, whether you are in the role of expert or novice.

Remote Assistance works by sending Remote Assistance invitations. The novice computer uses Microsoft Windows Messenger or e-mail (or a file that can be saved to removable media, copied via file sharing, or attached to an e-mail message) to send a Remote Assistance invitation to another user. Once the expert user accepts the invitation, a window opens showing the desktop of the novice. The expert can see the novice's desktop and exchange messages with the novice. If the novice wants the expert to actually fix the computer, the novice can give the expert control of the computer. From this point, the expert can manage the novice's computer remotely. The invitations that are sent use an *RA ticket*, which is a text file containing Extensible Markup Language (XML) fields. The RA ticket establishes a terminal session with the novice user's computer so that the expert can view it. This is established through TCP/IP addresses when the two computers are connected to the Internet. Using the established IP addresses, the two computers communicate with each other directly using TCP port 3389. These details are hidden from the users because Remote Assistance is designed to be an easy to use help application.

Using Remote Assistance Through Firewalls

Firewalls are likely to be the single biggest impediment to making a successful Remote Assistance connection. The firewall packaged with Windows XP, ICF, is designed to allow Remote Assistance connections if either the requestor (novice) or respondent (expert) is using ICF. When a request is made, ICF automatically opens port 3389 to allow the Remote Assistance traffic. Firewalls from other vendors, either hardware- or software-based, must be configured to allow incoming and or outgoing connections on port 3389 if Remote Assistance requests are to be sent or accepted.

Universal Plug and Play (UPnP)–Compliant Network Address Translation (NAT) Devices

Remote Assistance is designed to work with all UPnP NAT capable devices. UPnP NAT allows a Windows XP client behind the device using UPnP NAT to request that a Remote Assistance client be allowed an incoming connection on port 3389. Although the use of

Chapter 16: Remote Desktop and Remote Assistance

UPnP NAT is not yet widespread, it is particularly useful in that neither user needs to make any manual configuration changes to use Remote Assistance with a NAT firewall.

> **tip** If you use Windows XP's Internet Connection Sharing (ICS) feature to provide NAT functionality, it won't interfere with Remote Assistance because ICS acts as a UPnP-compliant NAT. You might still have to cope with firewalls along the route, however.

Network Address Translation

Network address translation, a common method for connecting private networks to the Internet, presents a potential roadblock to Remote Assistance. All users accessing the Internet through a NAT device use the single, publicly accessible IP address on the external side of the NAT device. Any Internet host replying to a request from the private network or any user or process attempting entry to the private network must come through this gateway address. Remote Assistance is not the only example of incoming services that have to contend with NAT. Incoming VPN, File Transfer Protocol (FTP), and Web (HTTP) server requests must also come in through the NAT device's external IP address. Any external viewer sees all outgoing traffic from the NAT device as originating from the external IP address of the NAT device. No information about the internal hosts that are actually initiating the requests is revealed. It is this masking process that has the potential to interfere with Remote Assistance requests.

If only one of the participants in a Remote Assistance session is behind a NAT device, then there is not a problem. However, if both users are situated behind their own NAT devices on different private networks, the Remote Assistance session will not be established. It is this impasse that is overcome by the UPnP NAT devices mentioned earlier.

Proxy Servers

Proxy servers are used for a variety of reasons. They can be used to cache commonly accessed Internet content so that when a user on a private LAN requests a resource, the proxy server can provide the requested materials from its cache of stored materials rather than actually going to the Internet to retrieve the resource. This allows a proxy server to make the most out of limited Internet connections that might otherwise be over utilized and ineffective. Proxy servers can also be used as a security and policy enforcement tool. Proxy servers can be used to track the Internet activity of the users required to use them as gateways to other networks. Because many proxy servers log incoming and outgoing activity, potential security breaches can be analyzed when they are detected.

If a proxy server is in use between the novice and the expert in a Remote Assistance session, and if the expert is behind a proxy server, such as Microsoft Proxy Server 2.0, the expert must have the proxy server client installed. This client allows the expert to pass through the proxy as the client would when Web browsing. If, however, the novice system lies behind the proxy server, packet filtering will have to be configured on the proxy server to allow inbound connections on port 3389 to the novice system.

497

Enabling Remote Assistance

Before your computer can use Remote Assistance, you must make sure the feature is enabled. (It's enabled by default in both Windows XP Professional and XP Home Edition.) Follow these steps:

1 Open Control Panel and double-click System.

2 On the Remote tab, select Allow Remote Assistance Invitations To Be Sent From This Computer, as shown here.

3 Click the Advanced button. You can use the dialog box shown in the following illustration to allow the expert to control your machine when connected via a Remote Assistance session. Note that if you do not enable remote control, the expert will be able to see your computer, but will not be able to make any configuration changes. You can also specify the maximum period of time that an invitation can remain active. By default, an invitation is good for one hour, but you can change this value if necessary when you create each invitation.

Chapter 16

> **note** You only need to enable Remote Assistance if you plan on asking for assistance. You can accept remote assistance invitations without enabling Remote Assistance on your computer.

Requesting Remote Assistance

Requesting remote assistance can take several forms, from using messaging software such as Windows Messenger to saving an invitation file to a floppy disk and hand delivering it to the expert. The easiest place for the novice to start is the Window XP Help And Support Center. Follow these steps:

1. From the Start menu, choose Help And Support.

2. Under the Ask For Assistance section, click the link labeled Invite A Friend To Connect To Your Computer With Remote Assistance.

3. On the Remote Assistance page that appears, click the Invite Someone To Help You link, as shown here.

4. You can request assistance of an expert in three different ways:

   ■ **Use Windows Messenger.** Sign in to Windows Messenger if you're not already online, choose an expert from the Online list, and click Invite This Person. The expert receives the request in Windows Messenger and can accept your invitation.

> **tip** Note that you can also bypass the Windows Help And Support Center and use Windows Messenger directly to start a Remote Assistance session. In Windows Messenger, choose Actions, Ask For Remote Assistance.

■ **E-mail.** You can send the invitation via e-mail by entering the e-mail address in the Type An E-mail Address box and then clicking the Invite This Person link below it. In the window that appears, enter your name and a message and click Continue. In the next window, specify a time duration for the invitation and enter a password the user must enter to access your computer. Click Send Invitation. The message is entered in your default mail client (such as Outlook Express). As shown in Figure 16-14, the e-mail contains instructions and a file called rcBuddy.MsRcIncident. When the user receives the file, he can double-click the attachment to start the Remote Assistance session.

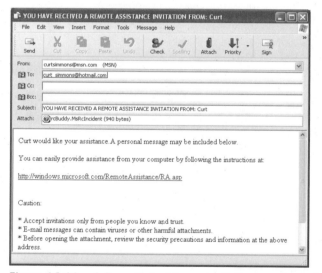

Figure 16-14. A Remote Assistance invitation can be sent as an e-mail attachment.

> **tip** For security purposes, it's always wise to avoid sending the password needed to access your computer via the same method the invitation was sent.

■ **Invitation file.** If you cannot e-mail the invitation or use Windows Messenger, you can save the invitation as a file, which can then be given to the expert. Using this option, you can also enter a duration for the invitation and a password. The file is saved as RAInvitation.MsRcIncident. You can then transfer the file by hand, in an e-mail, or via a network share.

> **note** In the event that the novice needs to cancel the invitation, the novice can click the View Invitation Status link in Remote Assistance. The novice can then select and delete any pending invitations.

Troubleshooting

You want to use Remote Assistance with a dynamic IP address.

If you are using a dial-up account to the Internet, you'll need to connect to the Internet before generating and sending the invitation so that the correct public IP address will be used in the invitation. Because ISPs use dynamic IP addressing, your computer usually has a different IP address each time you connect to the Internet. To make Remote Assistance work, you need to connect and stay connected until the expert assists you and the remote session is over. If you are disconnected at any time, you might need to cancel the invitation and start over with a new invitation that will convey your new dynamic IP address.

Using Remote Assistance

Once the expert accepts the invitation, the novice's computer validates the password supplied by the expert and confirms that the invitation is still valid. If all of the components are in order, the novice's computer notifies the novice that the expert wants to connect to his computer. The novice must complete the process by accepting the Remote Assistance session.

Once the session begins, the Remote Assistance window appears on the novice's and expert's computers, and a console window opens on the expert's computer showing the novice's desktop, as shown in Figure 16-15 on the next page. The desktop view is updated in real time, and the responsiveness of the remote session depends on the bandwidth of the network connection.

The expert can take control of the novice's computer by choosing Take Control on the Remote Assistance menu. The novice is then prompted on whether to permit the expert to share control of the computer. If the novice clicks Yes, the expert will be able to take control of the novice computer. At this point, the novice and the expert are essentially sharing the same computer. Should the novice decide to take back control and end the session, the novice can press the Esc key or click the Stop Control button in the Remote Assistance window.

Part 5: Advanced Networking

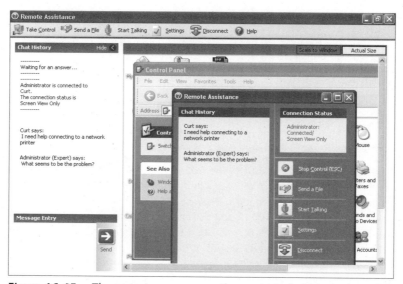

Figure 16-15. The expert user can see the novice's desktop and control it if the novice accepts the Remote Assistance session.

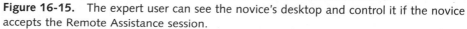

caution The expert has only as much control over the novice's system as the novice has. For example, if the novice only has a limited account, the expert will only have limited permissions. Remote Assistance does not override existing Windows permissions. If solving a novice's problems necessitates making changes that require the permissions of an administrator account, and the novice has only a limited account, the expert won't be able to fix the problem.

Chapter 17

Remote Access and Virtual Private Networking

Modern computing, more often than not, involves the sharing of information between one or more systems. This information sharing requires a network, most often a local area network (LAN). However, what if the network you need to connect to is not local? For example, your company might have an office in Paris and one in New York. You work at the New York office, but you need to connect to the private network in Paris. Or perhaps you're attending a conference in Dallas, but you need to connect to the New York office. How can you make these connections?

LAN networking and its various components were examined in earlier chapters. This chapter focuses on the methods for connecting a Microsoft Windows XP computer to a remote network. For the purposes of this chapter, a *remote network* can be considered any network that is physically distinct and separate from the network that you are currently connected to. The concept of a remote network applies to any separate network, whether it's in a different building across the street or thousands of miles away.

In this chapter, remote access services available with Windows XP will be examined in two categories. The first part of the chapter covers providing remote access dial-up services using Windows XP. Remote access connections are commonly used to connect computers to the Internet or to connect telecommuters to their work-based servers. The second part of the chapter discusses virtual private network (VPN) connections, including the concepts behind using them, providing VPN connections to others, and troubleshooting VPN connections.

Using Remote Access

A wide area network (WAN) refers to any network that includes links provided by telecommunications providers. In terms of remote access and remote networking, connectivity typically involves the use of WAN technologies such as modems, an Integrated Services Digital Network (ISDN), a Digital Subscriber Line (DSL), and broadband cable. For example, if a user makes a connection to the Internet using a dial-up modem, the user is using a remote access connection. Because the Internet does not reside on the user's LAN, the modem makes a connection to a remote server, which then provides access to the remote network (the Internet). The same concept is true when accessing remote networks that are private.

Access to private networks from remote locations is accomplished through remote access. The term *remote access* typically implies that a dial-on-demand technology, such as dial-up modem or ISDN, is used to connect to a private network. Remote access also includes the use of VPN connections and broadband Internet connections.

You can learn more about the types of connections that can be used with remote access in "Types of Internet Connections," page 85.

Remote access can be used to establish connections with both dial-up services that use Point-to-Point Protocol (PPP), a standard protocol for encapsulating network protocols such as TCP/IP over dialup, as well as Windows remote access servers, which also leverage PPP. "Creating New Internet Connections," page 103, covers using remote access services to dial up to a standard ISP using PPP. This chapter focuses on using remote access services to connect to remote Windows networks running remote access servers.

Configuring Remote Access Connections

This section examines how to configure some of Windows XP's remote access services. Windows XP does not distinguish between remote access connections to the Internet and to a private network; after all, the connection is much the same. For an Internet connection, you connect to an ISP's dial-up server. For a remote access connection to a private network, you connect to a private remote access server.

note Windows servers include the Routing and Remote Access Service (RRAS), so it is not unusual for a server to function solely as a remote access server to support remote network clients.

You use a modem (or possibly an ISDN connection) to connect to the remote access server, which then authenticates you so that you can gain access to the network. Typically, you use the same user name and password as you would use when you are connected to the domain.

Chapter 17: Remote Access and Virtual Private Networking

Once the hardware is installed for either a modem or an ISDN connection, the next step is to create a connection profile that can be used to initiate a connection to the remote network. To create a remote access connection, you use the New Connection Wizard. The following steps walk you through the process.

1 Choose Start, Connect To, Show All Connections.

2 In the Network Connections window, click the Create A New Connection link under Network Tasks.

3 The New Connection Wizard appears. Click Next.

4 Four options appear. Select the option to Connect To The Network At My Workplace, shown here. Click Next.

5 Choose the Dial-Up Connection option, as shown here, and click Next.

6 Type a name for the connection and click Next.

7 Type a phone number to dial. Remember to use a 1 and the area code if necessary. Click Next.

8 If Fast User Switching is disabled (or if your computer participates in a domain), you'll be asked whether you want the connection to be available for anyone using this computer or just for your use. Select the option you prefer, and click Next.

9 Click Finish.

10 The connection dialog box appears, shown next. Type the user name and password required to create the connection to the remote network.

Configuring Remote Access Security

Each remote access connection has a set of properties that can be configured. The properties dialog box you'll find by right-clicking the connection's icon and choosing Properties is identical to the properties dialog box you see for any modem connection.

See "Configuring Modems and Broadband Hardware," page 96, to learn more about modem configuration and troubleshooting.

Besides the basic modem configuration options, there are a number of potential security configurations that might be required to connect to a remote access server. The security configuration used depends on your network, so you'll need information from the remote access server administrator to make sure you choose the correct security settings.

To access the security settings for the connection, select the Security tab in the connection's properties dialog box, as shown in Figure 17-1.

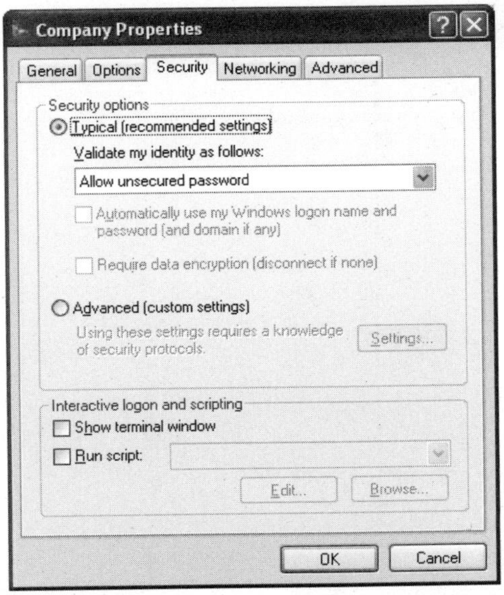

Figure 17-1. Remote access connection security settings are configured on the Security tab.

The default setting is Typical (Recommended Settings), which is used for Internet connections. However, in many cases, network security requires stronger security settings. If this is the case, all security settings can be configured on this tab. The window is divided into two general sections, Security Options and Interactive Logon And Scripting.

In many situations, the Typical setting is selected, but a secured password is also required. In Figure 17-2 on the next page, the Require Secured Password option is selected, and the options to use your Windows logon name and password as well as data encryption are selected. These settings are appropriate for dialing into a private network. You can also select Use Smart Card instead of Require Secured Password if *smart cards*, a form of hardware-based secure authentication, are used in your environment.

caution Keep in mind that your settings must match those of the server you are dialing into. If they do not, the connection will fail.

In some networks, custom security settings are used, and in this case, Windows XP allows you to specify the authentication protocol that should be used. Select the Advanced (Custom Settings) option on the Security tab, and then click the Settings button. As shown in Figure 17-3 on the next page, you can choose a data encryption method and the desired logon security. These are all different authentication protocols that can be used by the remote access server.

Chapter 17

Part 5: Advanced Networking

Figure 17-2. Additional security settings can be chosen with the Typical setting to increase security.

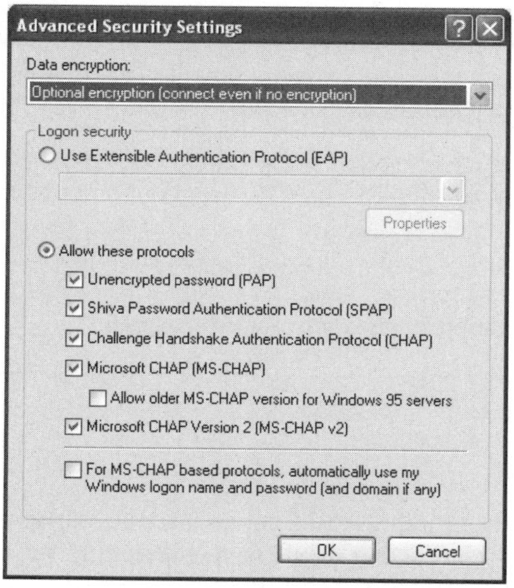

Figure 17-3. The Advanced Security Settings dialog box provides encryption and protocol settings.

The following list defines each protocol.

- **Extensible Authentication Protocol (EAP).** EAP provides security extensions, such as authentication based on token cards, that administrators can use in addition to the security technologies built into Windows servers.

- **Password Authentication Protocol (PAP).** PAP is a clear-text authentication scheme. The hosting server asks for the user name and password, and the PAP process returns the user response in an unencrypted or *clear-text* format. This authentication method is not robust, and it is certainly not secure. Malicious users can use a packet sniffer or similar tool to obtain the user name and password passed with PAP because they are unencrypted. Note that this authentication scheme does not work if the option Require Encryption (Disconnect If Server Declines) is selected in the Data Encryption field.

- **Shiva Password Authentication Protocol (SPAP).** This protocol is used with Shiva (now Intel) remote access servers, but does not work with the Require Encryption (Disconnect If Server Declines) setting.

- **Challenge Handshake Authentication Protocol (CHAP).** CHAP is an encrypted authentication mechanism that does not transmit the password across the connection. The remote access server sends a request known as a challenge to the potential remote access client. This information includes a session ID and an arbitrary challenge string. The remote access client responds with its user name and a Message Digest 5 (MD5) hash of the password, the challenge string, and the session ID. In this way, proof of knowledge of the user's password is sent without actually sending the password. To calculate the MD5 hash, passwords must be stored on the server in a reversibly encrypted form. A malicious user using a network sniffer to capture the CHAP traffic will only find a user name followed by the MD5 hash.

- **Microsoft CHAP (MS-CHAP).** The MS-CHAP protocol makes use of an encrypted authentication process that is in many ways similar to CHAP. Two key differences exist between CHAP and MS-CHAP. Passwords are encrypted using both the MD4 hash algorithm and the Data Encryption Standard (DES) algorithm. MS-CHAP also makes use of encrypted server/client messaging that allows the client to securely change its password from a remote location.

- **Microsoft CHAP version 2 (MS-CHAP v2).** Version 2 of the MS-CHAP protocol utilizes a more complex authentication system that provides two-way authentication. Not only does the server verify that the client is using the correct password for the provided user name, but the client also verifies that the server has knowledge of the user name and password as well. One application of this protocol is to prevent malicious users from impersonating a server. For a higher level of protection, MS-CHAP v2 establishes independent encryption keys for incoming and outgoing data transmissions.

Allowing Clients to Dial in to Your Computer

Suppose you have a small home network and carry a laptop computer with you when you travel. If you often need files and data from the computers in your home network while you are traveling, a computer running Windows XP can act like a miniature remote access server for dial-in capabilities on home and small office networks. This feature allows you to access shared files and even printers from a remote location.

Using the client computer, you configure a dial-up connection just as you would any other dial-up connection. From the home or small office computer that will act as the remote access server, connect the modem to the desired phone line, and then follow these steps:

1 Choose Start, Connect To, Show All Connections.

2 In the Network Connections window, click the Create A New Connection link under Network Tasks.

3 Click Next on the New Connection Wizard's opening page.

4 On the Network Connection Type page shown here, select Set Up An Advanced Connection and click Next.

5 On the Advanced Connection Options page shown next, select Accept Incoming Connections and click Next.

Chapter 17: Remote Access and Virtual Private Networking

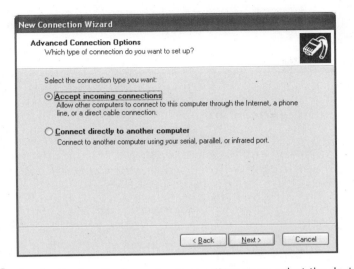

6 On the Devices For Incoming Connections page, select the device that will be used to accept the incoming connection, such as a modem. Click Next.

7 On this page, you can choose whether to accept VPN connections. Choose Do Not Allow Virtual Private Connections and click Next.

8 On the User Permissions page, shown here, select the local user accounts that are allowed to use the connection. If a user account on the local computer does not exist for the user who will be dialing in, click Add to create it. Click Next.

New Connection Wizard

User Permissions
You can specify the users who can connect to this computer.

Select the check box next to each user who should be allowed a connection to this computer. Note that other factors, such as a disabled user account, may affect a user's ability to connect.

Users allowed to connect:

- ☑ Curt
- ☐ Guest
- ☐ HelpAssistant (Remote Desktop Help Assistant Account)
- ☐ Mattie Simmons (Mattie Simmons)
- ☐ SUPPORT_388945a0 (CN=Microsoft Corporation,L=Redmond,S=Washingt
- ☐ Test (Test)

[Add...]   [Remove]   [Properties]

[< Back]   [Next >]   [Cancel]

9 On the Networking Software page, you can choose to install additional networking software if needed. To gain full access to network resources, you need to select File And Printer Sharing For Microsoft Networks (if it is not enabled by default). Click Next and then click Finish.

The Incoming Connections entry now appears in Network Connections in the Incoming section.

InsideOut

Making the Incoming Connection Secure

Even with a simple incoming connection, you can still require users to submit an encrypted password, which gives you a stronger level of security and helps ensure that someone doesn't dial your modem's number and try to break into your computer or private network. To configure this option, perform these steps:

1 In Network Connections, right-click Incoming Connections and choose Properties.

2 Select the Users tab, shown next. Select Require All Users To Secure Their Passwords And Data and click OK.

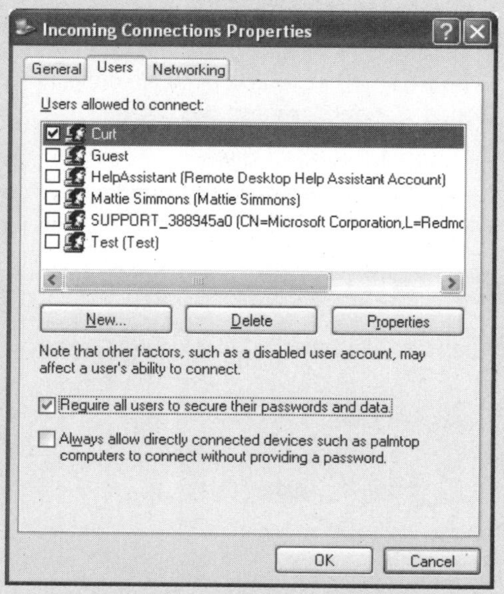

3 On the users' computers, open the properties dialog boxes for the dial-up connection that dials in to your computer.

4 On the Security tab, select Requires Secured Password in the Validate My Identity As Follows box, and then select the Require Data Encryption (Disconnect If None) option. Click OK. Computers that do not have this configuration will not be able to connect because Windows XP requires that a suitable authentication protocol be used and data be encrypted.

For more information on the best ways to secure remote access connections, see "Securing Remote Access Connections," page 586.

Understanding Virtual Private Networking

A *VPN* is an extension of a private network that encompasses links across shared or public networks such as the Internet. This virtual network allows the connected users to interact as if they were all on the same private network. To compare VPN connections to other network types, think of a VPN connection as a WAN link that exists by tunneling traffic through the Internet. The individual VPN connection behaves in the same manner as a direct point-to-point link, such as a leased line or a Frame Relay link.

To emulate a point-to-point link, data is encapsulated in a manner that allows it to traverse the Internet and reach the other VPN host. To ensure that the data on this private network remains private, encryption is used. If a malicious user intercepts the packets traveling between a VPN client and server, the data will be meaningless because it requires an encryption key to decrypt.

VPN connections are extremely useful because a computer can use virtually any Internet connection to reach the private network. Whether using a residential high-speed Internet connection or using a dial-up modem from a hotel room, the process is the same (of course the speed of the connection will vary). The user can connect to the protected network as needed. This is not only useful to telecommuters and traveling employees, but VPN connections can also allow a company to leverage cheaper, high-speed access methods (cable and DSL for example) to connect remote offices instead of using expensive leased lines or building its own Frame Relay network.

When building a remote network infrastructure, most companies and individuals will want to preserve the security requirements that they have for the existing LAN or WAN. A proper VPN implementation will allow the connection of remote users without compromising internal security. In fact, VPN connections are often more secure because of their encryption than normal LAN or WAN traffic. The following features make VPN traffic secure:

- **Authentication.** A VPN server will verify the VPN client's identity and prevent access from being assigned to unknown or unauthorized users. Most VPN servers have the capability to log all users who have connected. As an example, Microsoft Windows 2000 Server VPN services can log the user name, the IP address the user is connecting from, the IP address assigned to the VPN tunnel, the connection time, the connection duration, and other features of each VPN connection session.

- **Address management.** VPN servers, using Windows 2000 as an example, assign the network addresses to VPN clients (such as IP addresses).

● **Encryption.** Because the information transmitted using a VPN connection must cross a public medium, it is important to protect the data. Encryption of the transmitted data is used to secure it from prying eyes.

● **Key management.** Dynamic encryption keys are generated as part of the authentication process.

A VPN connection makes use of tunneling to transport data securely. *Tunneling* is the act of moving data destined for one network over the infrastructure of another network. The following is an example. Traffic from a computer on network #1 is delivered to another computer on network #1 using the components of network #2. Most virtual private networking solutions make use of one of two tunneling protocols. The protocols most widely used are Point-to-Point Tunneling Protocol (PPTP) and Layer Two Tunneling Protocol (L2TP) with Internet Protocol Security (IPSec) because they are flexible and widely supported. The VPN client encapsulates packets that are destined to be routed between the two tunnel endpoints. The information that is added during the encapsulation process allows the VPN packets to traverse the intermediate network to the VPN server.

InsideOut

Understanding VPN Protocols

What are the differences between the two VPN protocols supported by Windows XP, and when should you use each?

PPTP was developed by Microsoft and was originally delivered with Windows NT 4.0. It builds upon the foundations of standard PPP to both encapsulate and encrypt IP traffic (as well as other protocols). When configured to use MS-CHAP v2, PPTP is quite secure. Few non-Microsoft platforms can use PPTP tunneling without buying commercial VPN client software.

L2TP/IPSec uses a newer, Internet standard-based protocol for establishing remote VPN connections. L2TP/IPSec provides an extremely secure environment because it encrypts and authenticates each password transmitted across the network. In addition, it is supported by multiple platforms including UNIX-based and Macintosh systems. It does, however, require an infrastructure for allocating computer encryption certificates. Only Windows 2000, Windows XP, and later Windows operating systems support L2TP/IPSec.

Not sure which protocol to use? If you must support older Windows VPN clients, or you cannot maintain a certificate distribution system, PPTP is your best choice. However, if you want to support multiple platforms and are only using very recent Windows clients, and your network administrators are willing to maintain a certificate system, L2TP/IPSec might be the way to go.

Creating a Connection to a VPN Server

Now that you understand what a VPN is, it is time to configure Windows XP to use a VPN connection. Think of a VPN connection as similar to a dial-up connection. They both allow access to remote resources. In the case of the VPN, an existing connection to the Internet is utilized rather than making a direct connection to a modem at the remote location. To make a VPN connection, the steps are almost the same as those used to create a dial-up connection.

1 In Network Connections, click the Create A New Connection link to start the New Connection Wizard.

2 Click Next on the Welcome screen, and then select the Connect To The Network At My Workplace option. Click Next.

3 Choose Virtual Private Network Connection and click Next.

4 Enter a name for the connection and click Next.

5 On the Public Network page, you can choose to have Windows automatically dial the connection so that the VPN connection can be established, or you can manually dial the connection as needed. If you are using a broadband connection that is always connected, select Do Not Dial The Initial Connection. If you select Automatically Dial This Initial Connection, you should choose the connection that will be used. Make your selection and click Next.

6 On the VPN Server Selection page, enter the fully qualified domain name (FQDN) or IP address of the VPN server that you will connect to. Click Next and then click Finish.

note Keep in mind that the VPN connection works *on top of* the Internet connection. To use the VPN connection, you must first be connected to the Internet.

Troubleshooting

Using a VPN might interrupt your Internet connection.

If you are using a VPN connection and other Internet applications such as Microsoft Internet Explorer stop working, your VPN connection is configured to use the default gateway on the remote network as your Internet connection, but the remote network is not routing traffic to the Internet. To stop attempting to use the remote default gateway for Internet access, open the VPN connection's properties dialog box and select the Networking tab. Select Internet Protocol (TCP/IP) from the list and click Properties. Click the Advanced button and on the General tab of the Advanced TCP/IP Settings dialog box, clear the Use Default Gateway On Remote Network check box.

Chapter 17

(continued)

> **Troubleshooting** *(continued)*   Once this is done, standard Internet traffic will be routed out using the local network's default gateway, and the VPN connection will still be used for traffic to and from the private network.

Configuring Windows XP to Act as a VPN Server

Just as you can allow incoming connections on your Windows XP computer, you can also configure Windows XP to accept VPN connections from VPN clients. Basically, this process works the same as allowing incoming connections. Follow these steps:

1   Open Network Connections and start the New Connection Wizard by clicking the Create A New Connection link.

2   Click Next on the New Connection Wizard's opening page.

3   On the Network Connection Type page, select Set Up An Advanced Connection and click Next.

4   On the Advanced Connection Options page, select Accept Incoming Connections and click Next.

5   On the Devices For Incoming Connections page, select the modem or broadband device you want to use to allow incoming connections. Click Next.

6   Select Allow Virtual Private Connections and click Next.

7   On the User Permissions page, select the local user accounts that are allowed to connect to the computer via a VPN connection. If a user account on the local computer does not exist for the client, click Add to create one. Click Next.

8   On the Networking Software page, you can install and select, or clear or uninstall, the mix of networking software that can be used over the incoming VPN connection. Click Next and then click Finish.

> ## Troubleshooting
>
> **Your VPN connection is blocked by a firewall.**
>
> For the most part, utilizing VPN connectivity when one endpoint is behind a firewall is not an issue. Most firewalls allow liberal privileges when it comes to outgoing connections. Incoming connections are another story. For a VPN server that sits behind a firewall to accept incoming connections, the firewall needs to be configured to allow PPTP and/or L2TP/IPSec traffic.
>
> A number of different techniques for setting up a VPN server allow you to connect to a network that is placed behind a firewall device that you manage. One technique is to

configure the firewall device to allow inbound traffic from a series of IP addresses that you specify. Unless you have a static IP address (or set of static addresses) from which you want to guarantee inbound connectivity, this solution is less than ideal because it's normally impossible to determine which IP addresses you'll be given by a Dynamic Host Configuration Protocol (DHCP) server, particularly if you travel with a laptop or use a number of remote networks. Even if you do have one or more static IP addresses that you want to grant access to, this solution is of limited value unless you can guarantee that only machines that you manage will use those addresses. You must also guarantee that those machines will always be well patched and not run any malicious Internet worms or Trojan horse applications. Additionally, a clever hacker could determine the range of IP addresses that are commonly connecting to your network and configure his system to *spoof*, or appear to be connecting from, one of those addresses to penetrate your firewall.

Another option is to configure your firewall device to be managed remotely (via the Internet or a WAN connection). Then, whenever you want to connect remotely, you simply determine your local client's IP address and reconfigure the firewall to allow inbound traffic from that address. Again, this solution is less than ideal because it requires a number of steps, it leaves your firewall vulnerable to hackers who might attempt to gain control of it remotely, and it requires you to remember to disable those addresses when you're done.

Yet another option is to place the computer that provides the VPN connection in the firewall's *demilitarized zone (DMZ)*. Computers that have been configured to use the firewall's DMZ are completely exposed to the outside network (and if the firewall is also providing network address translation [NAT], a computer in the DMZ is exposed using the firewall's external IP address). This computer should be locked down tightly using a software firewall and should be configured to provide only VPN server services. This will allow external computers to establish a VPN connection safely into the network.

If the firewall is also providing NAT, the firewall could instead be configured to forward VPN traffic to the VPN server behind the firewall. External hosts cannot directly request access to hosts on a private LAN, so the firewall is left to play matchmaker and ensure that the incoming requests are forwarded to the correct internal server and nowhere else. Most software firewalls offer relatively simple interfaces for configuring the incoming ports, whereas many hardware firewalls (especially business class equipment) can require moderate expertise to configure them correctly.

You might also want to consider purchasing a firewall/gateway/switch device that includes a built-in VPN server. These devices are becoming increasingly common and allow for the greatest ease of setup when you want to provide secure VPN services to a small-to-medium size network.

For more information on configuring firewalls to work with a VPN, see the white paper "Virtual Private Networking with Windows 2000: Deploying Remote Access VPNs," available at *www.microsoft.com/windows2000/techinfo/planning/incremental/vpndeploy.asp*.

Chapter 18

Interconnectivity with Other Systems

Early in the history of personal computers, it was known that interoperability among computers is critical for truly effective computing. Coping with incompatibilities between various operating systems and applications has always proven to be a significant challenge to running a smooth network.

The interoperability problem is still an issue today; however, many operating system vendors now include services that enable interoperability with other platforms. Most large organizations today operate heterogeneous networks containing a variety of workstation and server computers running operating systems such as Microsoft Windows, Apple's Mac OS, various versions of UNIX-based operating systems such as Linux, or Novell's NetWare. However, to enable the sharing of resources and information across these different platforms, there must be common communication mechanisms that enable interoperability across the network.

Microsoft Windows XP Professional includes services that help you solve common interoperability and interconnectivity problems. This chapter explores the Windows XP Professional features that provide these interoperability services.

Connecting with Windows XP

If you are planning on integrating Windows XP into a heterogeneous network, it is important to understand where Windows XP and the other systems match up in terms of supported technology. The next two sections examine the networking protocols and media types that Windows XP supports.

Supported Networking Protocols

Successfully managing a heterogeneous computing environment depends to a large degree on which networking protocols the environment supports. Some protocols, such as TCP/IP, are supported by all modern operating systems. On the other hand, older protocols, such as IBM's Systems Network Architecture (SNA) mainframe communication protocol, require specialized third-party software to interconnect non-IBM clients, such as Microsoft Host Integration Server 2000. The following sections discuss the operational features and developmental issues of several common networking protocols.

TCP/IP

Without a doubt, TCP/IP is the most widely used protocol in the world. In addition to the fact that the Internet depends on Internet Protocol (IP), a wide range of systems make use of the protocol as well. Devices such as mainframes, personal computers, handheld computers, and computer-augmented appliances (like WebTV) all use (or can use) IP to deliver a variety of data. Not only is IP needed to access the Internet, but IP is also very scalable and extremely fast and efficient when properly configured.

Nearly all modern operating systems come with support for the TCP/IP protocol suite. The following list contains the more common operating systems that support this protocol suite.

- **Microsoft Windows 9x.** All versions.
- **Microsoft Windows NT.** All versions.
- **Microsoft Windows 2000.** All versions.
- **Windows XP.** All versions.
- **Novell NetWare 6.x and 5.x.**
- **Apple Mac OS 8.x and later.** Earlier versions had partial support for TCP/IP applications.
- **Apple Mac OS X.**
- **UNIX/Linux.** This is a very diverse grouping, but TCP/IP support is widespread.
- **Nearly all mainframe operating systems.**

Internetwork Packet Exchange/Server Packet Exchange (IPX/SPX)

IPX resides at the Layer 3 location of the Open Systems Interconnection (OSI) reference model and is a component of the native protocol stack used with the Novell NetWare network operating system. IPX is not as widely supported as TCP/IP. The following operating systems can utilize the IPX protocol for network communications.

- **Windows 9x.** All versions.

- **Windows NT.** All versions.

- **Windows 2000.** All versions.

- **Windows XP.** All versions.

- **Novell NetWare.** All versions.

- **UNIX/Linux.** IPX/SPX protocol stacks are available for many versions.

Systems Network Architecture

In the early 1970s, IBM developed a suite of network protocols known as the Systems Network Architecture (SNA). This proprietary networking architecture has several components that enable communication on a network that supports mainframe servers and terminals. The SNA architecture mimics the OSI reference model discussed in Chapter 2, "Configuring TCP/IP and Other Protocols." SNA has a layer model as a design guide and has seven individual layers.

The following operating systems can use the SNA networking protocols:

- **Microsoft Windows NT Server.** Using the SNA Server product if Data Link Control (DLC) is installed. (*DLC* is a key protocol in the SNA suite that provides error correction.)

- **Windows 2000.** Using Host Integration Server, if DLC is installed.

- **Novell NetWare.** All versions.

- **UNIX/Linux.** There are SNA add-ons for a variety of versions.

AppleTalk

AppleTalk is the native networking protocol of the operating systems produced by Apple Computer. AppleTalk was originally introduced as a complete set of proprietary network protocols; however, recent versions of Mac OS support a new protocol named *AppleShare IP*, which relies on the standard TCP/IP protocol as the basis for its file sharing.

The following operating systems can use AppleTalk and AppleShare IP:

- **Windows NT.** Can serve printers and files to AppleTalk clients using Services for Macintosh; no AppleShare IP support.

- **Windows 2000.** Supports both AppleTalk and AppleShare IP.

- **Novell NetWare.** Supports AppleTalk; no AppleShare IP support.

- UNIX/Linux. Supports both AppleTalk and AppleShare IP.
- Apple Mac OS and Mac OS X.

Supported Media Types

In addition to logical networking protocols, interoperating systems will need to support the same physical media if they are to interconnect. Because networking devices exist that can be used specifically to bridge differing physical network media, each of these media types will be mentioned briefly. Also, because the bridging of these technologies is possible, it can be assumed that all network-capable operating systems can work with any of the technologies discussed in the following sections.

Token Ring/Fast Token Ring

Token Ring was originally developed by IBM as a critical component of its networking products. Token Ring networks pass a special data package from one host on the network to another. This package is known as a *token*. The only time a client on the network can transmit is when it is in possession of this token. This communications method ensures that token networks can support large numbers of users and yield a high percentage of successful communications attempts. Token Ring can move data at 4 or 16 Mbps. Fast Token Ring uses new signaling methods to transport data at 100 Mbps.

Ethernet

The Ethernet protocol specifies a physical connection and signaling process. Instead of using the token passing method of Token Ring, Ethernet uses the Carrier Sense Multiple Access with Collision Detection (CSMA/CD) algorithm. This algorithm specifies that a host that wants to communicate must listen on the network for other communicating computers. If no other computers on the network are communicating, the host can begin transmission. Ethernet uses half-duplex communication, meaning that each computer can transmit or receive at any given time, but cannot send and receive simultaneously. Ethernet can transport data at 10 Mbps.

The only practical differences between Ethernet and Fast Ethernet are the signaling used and the presence of full-duplex communication. Higher speeds of 100 Mbps are achieved through the new signaling methods used in Fast Ethernet. The use of full-duplex allows nodes that support this feature to transmit and receive data at the same time.

Gigabit Ethernet uses a third-generation signaling method that increases the speed of Ethernet to 1 Gbps (1000 Mbps). The trade-off is that under many conditions, the distance that a Gigabit Ethernet network can reach is far less than slower Ethernet networks.

InsideOut

Using Windows XP to Bridge Media

Windows XP supports a wide range of networking technologies. One of its most useful innovations is the Network Bridge feature. Many networks, especially home and small business LANs, use a variety of connection media. This use of differentiated network adapters is a problem unless a method exists for interconnecting them.

In many networks, a specialized device must be purchased and maintained to bridge different types of media. Typically, this is accomplished with some kind of hardware bridge or a router. Fortunately, any computer using Windows XP can be used to provide the same functionality. If the computer has a network adapter for each media type in use, say a Token Ring adapter and an Ethernet adapter, and if the computer is running Windows XP, the Network Bridge feature in Windows XP can connect the networks via software, negating the need to buy sometimes expensive hardware bridging devices. To learn how to configure a network bridge using the Windows XP Network Bridge feature, see "Bridging Network Connections," page 75.

Connecting Windows XP and Novell NetWare

To make use of the NetWare services included with Windows XP, NWLink (Microsoft's implementation of IPX/SPX) must be installed along with Client Service for NetWare. Client Service for NetWare provides access to the file and printing services provided by NetWare servers. It allows access to any NetWare server that is using Novell Directory Services (NDS) or Bindery security and using IPX/SPX. This service even allows Windows XP to run NetWare management tools (if installed) and NetWare-aware applications.

The following steps guide you through the installation of both the required components:

1. Choose Start, Connect To, Show All Connections to open Network Connections.

2. Right-click the Local Area Connection icon and choose Properties.

3. Click the Install button.

4. The Select Network Component Type dialog box appears, as shown on the next page. Select the Client entry and click Add.

5 In the Select Network Client dialog box that appears, shown next, select Client Service For NetWare and click OK.

6 Client Service for NetWare along with NWLink NetBIOS and NWLink IPX/ SPX Compatible Transport Protocol will be installed and listed on the General tab of the Local Area Connection Properties dialog box. When the installation is complete, you will need to restart the computer for the changes to take effect.

note NWLink NetBIOS is not required for NetWare access; instead, it allows you to use NetBIOS over IPX/SPX to connect to Windows NT 4.0–style domains using that particular network architecture, which is somewhat rare. Unless you're in such an environment, it's best to disable all bindings for this protocol.

> **caution** The 64-bit version of Windows XP does not support Client Service for NetWare (or IPX for that matter). Also, Client Service for NetWare cannot be used to connect to a NetWare 5.x server that is operating in native IP mode. A third-party tool, such as Novell's Client for NetWare, which can be downloaded from *http://support.novell.com*, is required to connect Windows XP to a Novell network under either of these conditions.

Configuring Client Service for NetWare

There are three configuration options within Client Service for NetWare that bear examining. Within the CSNW utility, you can specify the preferred server, the default tree and context, and the printing options.

If you are connecting to a NetWare Bindery–based resource, such as a NetWare 3.x or earlier server (or a newer NetWare server running Bindery emulation), you'll need to configure the preferred server as follows:

1 Open Control Panel and double-click the CSNW icon.

2 In the Client Service For NetWare dialog box, in the Select Preferred Server text box, type the name of your preferred NetWare server, as shown in Figure 18-1.

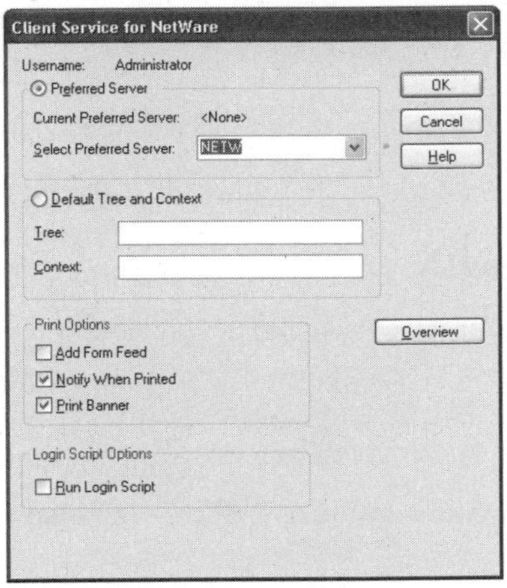

Figure 18-1. Enter the preferred NetWare server.

If, however, you're using an NDS tree, you'll need to enter the default tree and context. Open the CSNW utility, select Default Tree And Context, and enter the NetWare tree and context that will be used for accessing the NetWare network.

Once the client options are properly configured, the Windows XP computer will be able to map local drive letters to volumes shared from the NetWare server. Drive mappings can be made to NetWare volumes just as they can be made to shares on remote Windows network resources, by opening Windows Explorer and choosing Tools, Map Network Drive.

Interconnecting Windows XP and UNIX/Linux

UNIX has been a staple component of computing since the earliest days of computing. Although UNIX and its derivatives have been used for a dizzying array of functions, it was the rise of a recent variation that brought UNIX to the attention of most computer users. The Linux operating system has garnered a great deal of attention from the media and from IT managers. Although the future of this relatively new operating system is still unclear, it has already become common in many network environments. Fortunately, there are a couple of services available with Windows XP to help integrate the Windows and UNIX operating systems.

Making UNIX/Linux servers provide friendly services to Windows XP clients is generally done by installing and configuring a Server Message Block (SMB) service on the UNIX/Linux server, such as the Samba application. However, the process for installing this application is beyond the scope of this text.

The following sections describe how to configure the services that Windows XP provides for UNIX/Linux integration.

Installing Print Services for UNIX

Print Services for UNIX is the only obvious service that can be added (or removed) from a Windows XP computer. To install UNIX printing services, complete these steps:

1 Choose Start, Control Panel, Add/Remove Programs.

2 When the Add Or Remove Programs window, click the Add/Remove Windows Components button.

3 When the Windows Components Wizard appears, select Other Network File And Print Services (but don't select its check box), and then click the Details button.

4 Select Print Services For Unix in the Other Network File And Print Services dialog box, as shown in Figure 18-2. Click OK, and then click Next to install the service. You might be prompted to insert your Windows XP installation CD to complete the installation.

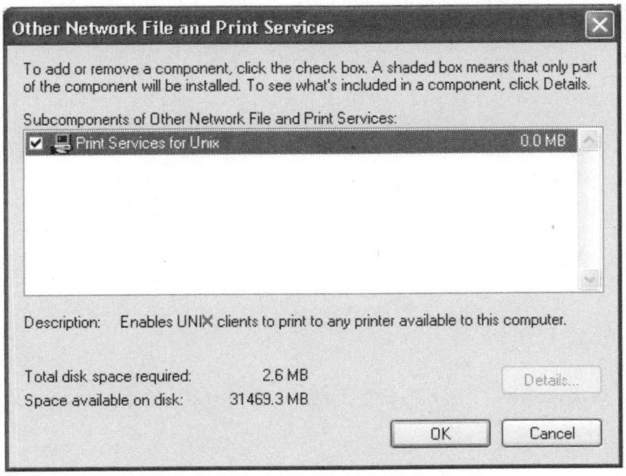

Figure 18-2. Choose Print Services For Unix and click OK.

Microsoft Windows Services for UNIX

Print Services for UNIX is designed to let a UNIX computer print to a Windows XP computer and any printers it is sharing. In the event that the Windows XP computer is dependant on the services of the UNIX computers, a more robust solution is needed. Microsoft offers a stand-alone product called Windows Services for UNIX (SFU) that provides a wealth of connectivity and cross-platform development and application support tools. SFU version 3.0 provides a large array of cross-platform services that support the integration of new Windows XP and Windows 2000 computers into the existing (UNIX-based) network environment. SFU 3.0 is relatively new and includes some additional significant functionality to the set of components offered by SFU version 2.0.

One of the key differences between SFU versions 2.0 and 3.0 is the availability of the Interix subsystem with the 3.0 installation. The Interix subsystem technology provides an environment where both UNIX and Windows applications can be run from a single operating system platform. This increases the flexibility of a Windows-based computer that is in use in a primarily UNIX-based network environment. In particular, a user who is familiar with the Windows environment will not have to learn the somewhat cryptic commands often present in a pure UNIX environment.

The Interix subsystem creates an environment that is layered on top of the Windows kernel. This behavior enables UNIX applications and scripts to be easily ported with a recompilation to run on a Windows computer. SFU 3.0 also includes approximately 300 UNIX utilities and tools that will be familiar to veteran UNIX users. These

Chapter 18

527

components behave in a similar manner as they would if used from a UNIX-based computer. Also included is the Interix Software Development Kit (SDK), which supports over 1900 UNIX application programming interfaces (APIs).

---

tip For more information about Microsoft Services for UNIX and Windows XP, check out the Microsoft Windows Services for UNIX Web site at *www.microsoft.com/windows/sfu/default.asp*.

Requirements for SFU 3.0

To install SFU 3.0, your computer must meet the following minimum requirements:

- 16 MB of RAM.
- 19 MB of available hard disk space. 184 MB is required for a complete installation.
- CD-ROM drive.
- Microsoft Internet Explorer version 5.5 or later.
- Network adapter.

In addition to the minimum requirements, there are several Microsoft recommendations for any computer running SFU. There are also some limitations associated with SFU 3.0. The following list outlines recommendations that should be met to ensure maximum performance as well as limitations to keep in mind:

- If Windows 2000 is used to host SFU 3.0, Service Pack 2 should be installed, although it is not required.
- Gateway for NFS requires a server edition of Windows.
- SFU 3.0 cannot be used with Windows NT 4.0 Terminal Services Edition.
- Client for Network File Systems (NFS) and Gateway for NFS cannot be simultaneously installed on the same computer.
- Server for NIS must be installed on a Windows 2000 domain controller.

Installing Services for UNIX

To install SFU, you need the SFU installation CD and a computer running Windows XP, Windows 2000, or Windows NT 4.0. After the install process is completed, your SFU installation will be ready for use.

InsideOut

Using UWIN 3.0 to Run UNIX in Windows XP

A number of companies have developed tools for porting and running UNIX tools on Windows. One of the more interesting is UWIN, which was developed by AT&T Labs.

The UWIN 3.0 software package provides an environment for developing and using UNIX applications from within Windows XP and other Windows environments. There are three parts to the UWIN support package. UWIN includes the libraries needed to provide a UNIX operating environment. These libraries provide support for the UNIX APIs. A group of UNIX tools, such as cc, yacc, lex, and Make, are also provided so that Windows users can compile their programs in the same manner as they would from a UNIX workstation. In addition to the compiler tools, there are approximately 250 other UNIX programs and commands available.

For additional information about UWIN 3.0, check out the research and development Web site for the public domain version at *www.research.att.com/sw/tools/uwin*. Also available is a commercial version of UWIN 3.0 developed by Wipro Technologies; for more information, visit *www.wipro.com/uwin*.

Connecting Windows XP to Apple Macintosh Systems

Connecting Windows operating systems with Apple operating systems typically requires a third party to act as a gateway between the two systems. In most cases, that third-party device is a Windows 2000 server running Services for Macintosh. However, Windows clients can connect to a share located on a Mac OS X system if the Samba SMB tool is installed.

Connecting Windows and Mac OS X Using Samba

Because Mac OS X is based on a distribution of UNIX, it offers some of the interoperability features possible with other UNIX systems. If a Mac OS X system running Samba is present on the network, you can connect to the server using its Universal Naming Convention (UNC) path, such as *macosx_server**sharename*, where *macosx_server* is the NetBIOS name used by Samba on the Macintosh, and *sharename* is the name of the SMB resource being shared. In addition, Samba allows the Mac OS X systems to connect with SMB resources shared by Windows (or other Samba) systems.

Although this configuration depends on the availability of a Mac OS X server, there are few other options for connecting Windows and older Macintosh systems. Commercial tools are available that provide SMB functionality for Macintosh clients, allowing them to serve data to Windows systems and in turn access Windows network resources via SMB. The other more common method is through the use of Services for Macintosh or Windows 2000 Server.

Macintosh File Services for Windows 2000 Server

The Services for Macintosh (SFM) service that comes with Windows 2000 Server makes it possible for computers running Windows and Mac OS (both Mac OS X and previous versions) to share files and printers. A Windows 2000 server that has SFM installed can provide file, remote access, and printer services to any Macintosh computers in use on the network.

The SFM service enables the network administrator to designate a directory as a Macintosh-accessible volume. It also ensures that Macintosh file names are valid NTFS file names and manages access permissions. The following list describes other features available with SFM.

- Apple File Protocol (AFP) traffic can be transported over TCP/IP links. With this functionality, Macintosh clients can access shared resources via the faster TCP/IP protocol.

- The AFP 2.2 specification is supported. The AFP 2.2 implementation allows Macintosh clients to view partitions larger than 4 GB. Prior to the introduction of AFP 2.2, Macintosh clients could access a larger volume, but the volume's size was reported incorrectly.

- Print Server for Macintosh lets Macintosh users print in the background. They no longer have to wait for a print job to complete before moving on to other tasks. Also, users who have the appropriate access can now manage Macintosh print jobs spooled to a Windows 2000 server.

Wireless Networking

The buzz about wireless networking has been around for years, but only recently has wireless networking begun to become a reality for corporate networks and for home and small office networks. In fact, if you browse your local computer store, you are likely to find many different brands of wireless access points as well as wireless network adapters for desktop computers and laptops.

What does all this mean for you? Wireless networking has finally arrived; it works well, it offers different levels of security, and it's cost effective, although sometimes more expensive than traditional wired networking. If you are currently planning a home or small office network, a wireless network is certainly a viable alternative. In an existing corporate network, adding wireless functionality to the network might solve a number of problems and give mobile network users added flexibility.

In this chapter, you'll learn about wireless networking. You'll learn how it works, your security options, the network designs you can use, and whether wireless networking is right for you.

Getting to Know Wireless Networking

Microsoft Windows XP helps make configuring a wireless network simple. Before trekking off to the computer store to buy the components needed, however, you should read this section to gain an understanding of wireless networking, the kinds of wireless networks supported by Windows XP, and whether you can benefit from wireless networking.

Part 5: Advanced Networking

Why Wireless Networks Are Important

Wireless networks provide freedom—that is the basis for their appeal. In a world of mobile employees, networking needs to be just as mobile, and that mobility goal has evolved into the wireless technologies available today. Here are just a few examples of some common uses for wireless networking.

- In a home network, you can use a laptop computer with a wireless network adapter and travel from room to room, retaining network connectivity. Combined with Internet Connection Sharing (ICS), you can have your desktop computer provide an Internet link, and your wireless computer can access the Internet through the ICS host computer. This not only allows you to access shared information available on the desktop computer (such as folders and printers), but also allows you to browse the Internet from any room in your house or even in your yard—anywhere within the usable range of your wireless equipment! The coverage area for your wireless network depends on many factors, such as the locations of your wireless equipment, how well the signal can travel through various obstructions, and any interference on the frequencies used by the wireless equipment.

- In a home network, wireless networking can help reduce computer costs and give you more flexibility. For example, your family room might have two computers networked together. One computer provides Internet access to your home network. Your children use the Internet for homework as well as game playing on a regular basis, and using the computer in the family room is sometimes inconvenient for you. You could add a wireless adapter to a laptop computer and do your computing in the quiet and privacy of another room while your children do their homework or play games in the family room.

- You could have a home network that is completely wireless, or you could have a residential gateway with an integrated wireless hub, known as a *wireless access point,* connected to a DSL connection for Internet access. Each computer in your house can be outfitted with a wireless NIC, and the network will work just like a wired network, but you'll have the added freedom of placing each computer in any location you want without worrying about running cables. Additionally, should you need to rearrange your network at some point in the future, the computers can be easily moved with no network disruption.

- In a small office environment, wireless networking provides many of the same features that a home network user would find attractive; however, in an office setting, the key benefit provided by wireless networking is its flexibility. For example, you might work in a small office building and your job duties might include attending meetings in various rooms throughout the building, taking notes at each meeting using your laptop. Traditionally, you might use a laptop for such purposes, but you would have to disconnect from the network each time you moved and reconnect with a cable to a jack in the wall. The cabling can be clumsy and aggravating, if such jacks are available at all. Plus, you must disconnect and log back on to the network each time. Using a wireless network, you can move about as needed without concern for the locations of network jacks and even keep continuously connected if you like.

- In corporate networks, wireless networks are often used as a workaround for particular access problems. For example, they might be used in a portion of an office building where cables cannot be placed. Wireless connections can easily solve these problems and provide the required network connectivity.

- If your company or site hosts network or Internet access for outside visitors, you can even configure wireless networking to provide network access to visiting clients or business partners (with appropriate security of course). By equipping a laptop with a wireless network adapter, Windows XP can automatically configure its wireless adapter for access to the wireless network where available, giving your clients and partners instant access to the Internet when they arrive at your site.

- Many public areas, including airports, conference centers, and hotels, now provide wireless Internet access on open networks. These areas, called *hot spots*, give mobile users access to the Internet on the users' own computers. Because Windows XP can automatically configure access to the wireless network, you can essentially step off an airplane, turn on your laptop, and access the Internet. After you arrive and check in to your hotel, you can resume your Internet connection and continue to access it while attending a conference. If you have a VPN or other remote access connection via the Internet to your private network, you can access your personal documents as well.

Types of Wireless Networking

There are several different types of wireless networking technologies. Some are available now, and others are under development. These technologies can be sorted into the following groups:

- **Infrared.** Infrared wireless networking uses beams of infrared light to transmit data from one device to the next. Infrared networking is good for short distance, line-of-sight networking. For example, wireless keyboards, mice, printers, and game devices can broadcast to an infrared port on your computer. Additionally, laptops and PDAs can connect to a desktop computer for data transfer. Infrared is a great solution for device-to-PC connectivity, but in terms of a LAN solution, infrared is not the preferred method. In many cases, however, infrared can provide solutions to unique problems. In addition to not being practical for a LAN, infrared is restricted to computers and devices in one physical area, such as a single room.

- **Wireless Personal Area Networks (WPANs).** A WPAN is a personal area network, which means it resides in one generalized space, such as a room. Quite literally, a *personal area* is the area surrounding a person. WPANs are useful for wireless network computing in one location or wireless networking between PDAs, cellular phones, laptop computers, and so on. WPANs can use infrared connections for objects that are very close (for example, objects sitting on the same table), or they can use radio frequency technologies such as Bluetooth, which can communicate up to 30 feet. The IEEE (its full name is the Institute of Electrical and Electronics Engineers) has established a working group (IEEE 802.15) for the development of WPAN standards. The 802.15 standard seeks ease of interoperability, simple designs, and compatibility with other wireless networks. You can learn more about the standard at *www.standards.ieee.org*.

InsideOut

Keeping the Standards Straight

As you investigate different wireless technologies and standards, it's easy to become confused by the many standards and numbers. Keep in mind that the IEEE's job is to create standardization for different kinds of networks that use the same technology. The end result is that different devices can work together on the same network. Using the 802.15 standards, devices such as laptops, PDAs, cellular phones, and other portable devices can implement the Bluetooth specification, and they can all communicate and work together on the same WPAN. You'll see different IEEE standards apply to different kinds of wireless networks (as well as wired networks), and each time you read about an IEEE standard, you'll know that standards for communication are in place or being developed that will make the technology a viable means of networking for you.

- **Wireless Local Area Networks (WLANs).** A WLAN is a wireless network located in a home, office building, school, or other such structure. A WLAN can also exist as a separate network in addition to a wired LAN if desired. The WLAN uses radio frequencies to enable all computers within the

WLAN to communicate with each other. The IEEE 802.11 standard for WLANs defines speeds of 1 and 2 Mbps. Clearly, the 802.11 standard is rather slow. However, the new IEEE standard for WLAN networking is 802.11b, which defines transfer rates of up to 11 Mbps using the 2.4 GHz Industrial, Scientific, and Medical (ISM) frequency band. The 802.11b standard is currently the most popular standard, giving you speeds comparable to a typical Ethernet network. IEEE 802.11a, a newer standard that provides bit rates of up to 54 Mbps using the 5 GHz frequency band, is now available as well.

- **Wireless Metropolitan Area Networks (WMANs).** WMANs allow wireless communications within a single metropolitan area. For example, a WMAN in New York City could let a company connect wirelessly to its three offices located around the city. The IEEE 802.16 standard, which defines the technologies that can be used in WMANs, is still under development. WMANs can use radio waves, infrared light, or even laser connections to transfer data between locations.

- **Wireless Wide Area Networks (WWANs).** A WWAN connects WLANs that are separated over wide geographic areas. For example, if your company has offices in New York, Seattle, and Dallas, a WWAN could be used to wirelessly connect the different WAN network segments. WWAN technologies involve the use of satellite communications maintained by service providers and also use the same technologies as cellular phones and wireless PDAs. Common technologies include Global System for Mobile Communications (GSM), Cellular Digital Packet Data (CDPD), and Code Division Multiple Access (CDMA).

Wireless Networks Supported by Windows XP

Microsoft Windows XP Professional and Microsoft Windows XP Home Edition both support wireless networking. If you are planning on using a wireless network, Windows XP is the easiest operating system to configure and use on a wireless network.

Windows XP supports infrared networking as well as the 802.11b (or Wi-Fi) and 802.11a (which might soon also be included under the Wi-Fi umbrella) standards. IEEE 802.11b is the accepted standard among most hardware manufacturers today. With speeds up to 11 Mbps, it has a range of up to 300 feet from point to point and offers wireless security standards as well. There are currently several thousand 802.11b public access points available in the United States.

The rest of this chapter focuses on infrared and 802.11b/802.11a technologies because they're the most popular standards and the ones best supported in Windows XP.

How Infrared and Wi-Fi Work

Windows XP is optimized for two kinds of wireless networking—infrared and Wi-Fi. Each network type has its own advantages and challenges, and is typically used for different purposes. The following sections examine how infrared and Wi-Fi networking work in Windows XP.

How Infrared Works

Infrared technology uses an infrared beam of light to transfer data from one computer to another. Infrared technologies use a *line-of-sight* transmission method, which requires the two infrared ports to be aligned with no obstructions. Once the two infrared ports are aligned, and infrared communication is configured, the two computers can begin exchanging information with each other over the beam of light.

Infrared wireless is a great way to transfer data from one computer to another or from a PDA to a computer. You can also use a cellular phone that has an infrared port to create a cellular Internet connection. You can learn more about these features and how to configure infrared connections in the section "Using the Infrared Connection," page 548.

How Wi-Fi Works

Wi-Fi provides two different modes, or topologies, of wireless networks: infrastructure mode and ad hoc mode.

Infrastructure mode   In *infrastructure mode*, wireless access points are used to build a network that can be accessed by wireless devices. This wireless network can be completely independent, or it can extend an existing wired LAN. The wireless access point connects to the wired network, and all computers on the wired network can then communicate with the wireless computers through the access point. In other words, the access point acts as a bridge between the wireless and wired LANs.

The wireless access point is able to receive and transmit data over an area defined both by the technology (including the allowable power used in the wireless radio transmitters and the types of antennas used) as well as by more fundamental physical restrictions (including interference on the radio bands used by Wi-Fi and physical obstructions between wireless devices). In large environments, multiple access points can be used. For example, if you carry your wireless laptop computer from one floor of a building to another floor, your connection might shift from an access point located on one floor to another located on the next floor. Network administrators place the access points so that they just overlap each other's coverage, thus providing uninterrupted service to the client. From a user's point of view, the coverage is continuous. In the following illustration, an access point connected to a wired network acts as a bridge to connect the two dissimilar networks.

Wired and Wireless LANs Bridged Using a Wireless Access Point

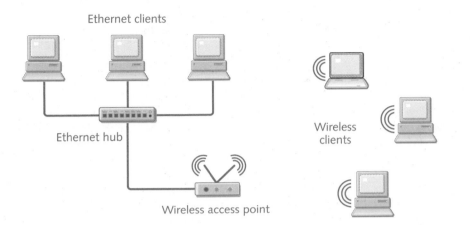

When infrastructure mode is used, the access point sends out beacon management frames that let wireless devices know the access point is available as well as the name of the wireless network. If the wireless network name is recognized by the wireless client, an association process occurs that creates a logical connection between the wireless client and the wireless access point. After the association process is complete, the wireless client authenticates itself to the wireless access point. If the authentication process is successful, the wireless client is recognized on the network and can begin sending data frames to the wireless access point and access network resources. All communication, whether bound for another wireless client or the wired network, is passed through the wireless access point. To avoid collisions on the wireless network, the Carrier Sense Multiple Access/Collision Avoidance (CSMA/CD) protocol is used. Before transmitting data, clients must listen for other data transmissions for a period of time before transmitting. This helps the clients know that the radio frequencies used for communication are clear and can be used to exchange data.

InsideOut

Mobility Challenges in Large Networks

Large networks use multiple access points so that users can roam from location to location and still stay connected to the network. However, planning the wireless infrastructure takes time and preparation. For example, if a user in Building A walks to Building B for a meeting, and the wired network in Building A is on a different subnet than the network in Building B, the user's TCP/IP stack must be able to use new IP configuration data. Also, if a user is moving from domain to domain, you might expect similar logon

(continued)

Inside Out *(continued)*   headaches and access problems. The point is that wireless networking is rather easy in single subnet networks, especially those that are small and located in one place. In larger networks, access can certainly become a more complex issue, depending on how the user needs to move about and how the user intends on accessing the wireless network.

The good news, however, is that Windows XP is able to detect changes in the access point used and automatically reconfigure itself. Each time that a computer running Windows XP associates with a new wireless access point, it uses DHCP either to renew its current IP configuration (its *lease*) or to obtain a new lease that is valid for the new subnet. Additionally, Windows XP can even redetect proxy server settings for Microsoft Internet Explorer so that Internet connectivity is not disrupted when a move is made to a different access point. As a general rule, these automatic configuration tactics work well and are invisible to the user. Because an association with an access point has to be formed, that information can be passed from access point to access point as the user moves. This association passing is performed through *Inter-Access Point Protocol (IAPP)* so that an association only has to be made one time instead of each time the user moves from one access point to another. IAPP is supported by most access point vendors so that different access points from different manufacturers can be used, providing seamless operation.

Ad hoc mode   *Ad hoc mode* allows wireless client computers to connect directly without the use of an access point. For example, a collection of clients in a conference room can use ad hoc mode to create a network, as shown in the following illustration. However, if you want to access a wired LAN, you'll need some sort of bridge, such as a wireless access point or a Windows XP computer acting as a network bridge. Otherwise, the wireless network clients can only communicate with each other.

Wireless Clients Networking in Ad Hoc Mode

Wireless
clients

InsideOut

Using Both Infrastructure Mode and Ad Hoc Mode

Windows XP can operate in both wireless modes. Perhaps you use a wireless laptop at work in an office that uses infrastructure mode. Your laptop uses the office network during the day through a wireless access point. However, at night, you might bring your laptop home and want to connect your laptop to your home network for Internet access by connecting to a wireless-equipped desktop computer. Windows includes a service called *Wireless Zero Configuration,* which initiates a sequential process for determining the appropriate wireless network mode to use. Windows XP first searches for a wireless access point. If one is found, Windows XP switches the wireless adapter to infrastructure mode. If no access point is available, Windows XP looks for other computers operating in ad hoc mode. This process lets you move from infrastructure to ad hoc mode as needed without making any changes to the configuration of the wireless adapter. This feature requires that the software drivers for the wireless adapters support the Wireless Zero Configuration service.

Wireless Networking Hardware

To create a wireless network, you need wireless NICs for the computers that will participate on the wireless network as well as a wireless access point if you plan on configuring your wireless network to use infrastructure mode.

- **Wireless NICs.** Wireless NICs are readily available as PC Cards for laptop computers. PCI adapters are also available and allow you to plug a PC Card wireless NIC into a desktop computer. Some laptops also include built-in wireless NICs. Each wireless NIC has a miniature antenna for transmitting and receiving wireless data. Major networking companies like NetGear, Linksys, and SMC produce wireless networking devices in addition to their more traditional wired networking devices. Wireless NICs typically range in cost from $60 to $100; thus, they're a little more expensive than Ethernet NICs, but the price difference should not deter you from building a wireless network. Make sure that any wireless NIC you buy is compatible with the standard you intend to use, either 802.11b or 802.11a.

- **Wireless Access Point.** Wireless access points can either be stand-alone devices or can be built into other devices such as residential gateways. Some have built-in wireless NICs and antennas, whereas others provide a PCMCIA slot in which to insert a PC Card wireless network adapter. They also often include ports for adding more flexible external antennas.

If you want to extend a wired LAN with the wireless network connection, you simply connect the wireless access point to the Ethernet network with an RJ-45 cable. Wireless clients can then communicate with one another through the wireless access point, and if the access point is also connected to a wired network hub, the clients can communicate with the wired network as well. Wireless access points tend to be more expensive than simple wired hubs, and as with hubs, there are many options to choose from.

Selecting a Wireless Network Topology

Topology refers to the physical layout of your network. Before purchasing any wireless networking equipment, you need to take a look at your needs and make a firm decision about how the wireless network will benefit you. How many computers will have wireless network adapters? Do you need an access point? Will you combine an existing network with wireless access, or do you want an entirely wireless network? These are important questions to consider, and the following sections point out some topology options for you. Note that the following sections describe wireless networking in a home or small office setting because that is what you will most likely be configuring. In a large network environment, wireless networking takes more advanced planning and administrative planning, which is beyond the scope of this book.

Completely Wireless Network, Ad Hoc Mode

In a completely wireless network, each computer can be outfitted with a wireless network adapter and configured in ad hoc mode. You do not need a wireless access point unless you are bridging two dissimilar networks, such as a wired Ethernet network and a wireless network.

Ad hoc wireless networks are useful if you want to minimize the initial costs of bringing up a wireless network, if you don't need to connect to any outside networks, or if one of the ad hoc wireless hosts will also serve as an ICS host. In this latter configuration, the computer connected to the Internet acts as the ICS host, and the wireless clients access the Internet by connecting to the ICS host over the wireless network. With this configuration, ICS works the same way as it does in a wired network, as shown in the following illustration. You can learn more about setting up ICS in "Using Internet Connection Sharing," page 301.

Although ad hoc networks reduce the initial hardware cost of a wireless network, the limited range of each wireless card means that it's easy to disrupt network communications by moving computers too far apart from one another. This drastically limits the utility of ad hoc wireless networking in medium-to-large size network installations.

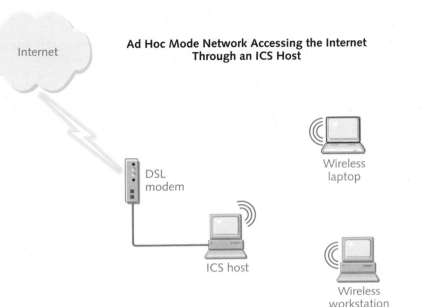

Ad Hoc Mode Network Accessing the Internet
Through an ICS Host

Completely Wireless Network with a
Wireless Access Point as a Residential Gateway

If you are using a wireless access point as a residential gateway to the Internet rather than using ICS, you will use infrastructure mode, and all computers will connect to the network through the wireless access point. The advantage to this configuration over an ad hoc network is that you do not need a computer that acts as an Internet gateway— all of your computers can be mobile. Also, an ICS computer must always be on for any of the other network computers to reach the Internet. With a wireless access point, only the wireless access point must be powered up. Furthermore, the wireless network will not be disrupted if one or more network clients move out of range of one another. Individual computers will drop off the network as they move out of range of the wireless access point, but the others will continue to function normally. However, you'll have to buy a somewhat expensive wireless access point ($200 and up) that includes residential gateway or router functions, whereas ICS is included with Windows. If you decide you want an infrastructure mode network, configure each computer with a wireless network adapter and connect your Internet connection's DSL or cable modem connection to the wireless access point, as shown in the following illustration. Follow the manufacturer's instructions for configuring the access point for Internet and wireless connectivity.

Part 5: Advanced Networking

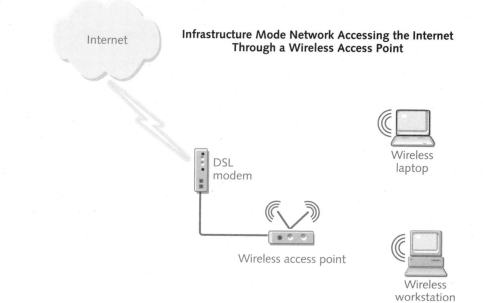

Internet

Infrastructure Mode Network Accessing the Internet Through a Wireless Access Point

DSL modem

Wireless laptop

Wireless access point

Wireless workstation

Wireless Access Point as a Bridge

If you have an existing home or small office network, such as an Ethernet network, you can add wireless clients to the network, but you'll need to bridge the two networks together. A wireless access point can serve this function. When you use a wireless access point, it connects to the wired network, typically by being plugged into an Ethernet hub. All traffic from the wireless computers flows through the access point so that wireless clients can communicate with the wired clients and reach the Internet as well.

Windows XP as a Bridge

If you want to bridge wireless and wired networks without purchasing additional hardware, you can do so using the Network Bridge feature built into Windows XP. To use this feature, you'll need to install both a wireless and wired NIC in one of your Windows XP systems. That computer then serves as the network bridge device. You will have to leave this computer running for the two networks to have connectivity. To set up Network Bridge, follow the instructions listed in "Bridging Network Connections," page 75.

Understanding Wireless Security

Network security is always a concern regardless of the kind of network that you choose to implement. However, with a wireless network, where data flows freely in the air as radio waves instead of being confined to a cable, security becomes more of a challenge.

For example, how can you stop a corporate spy from accessing your wireless network from outside your building? In a home network, what's to keep a neighbor from using your wireless network to gain access to your network resources and your personal data or to tap into your Internet connection? In the past, these problems had few solutions. Fortunately, new security standards for wireless communications can set your mind at ease.

Wired Equivalent Privacy (WEP) is an encryption algorithm system that's included as part of the IEEE 802.11 standard. It's commonly used and supported by wireless networking hardware devices. The WEP encryption algorithm sends data through the air in encrypted form. WEP can utilize either 40- or 104-bit shared encryption keys, along with a standard 24-bit *initialization vector*, which augments the shared keys to produce a different encryption key for each data packet. The combination of the encryption key and the initialization vector produces WEP keys with a total length of 64 or 128 bits.

The WEP encryption standard prevents unauthorized access to the network as well as to the data that's being transmitted over the wireless network. WEP, however, does not define a key management protocol. A single WEP key can be configured on all the wireless clients and the wireless access point of a home network, but there is no way to manage or distribute WEP keys on a large organization's network; instead, they must be manually distributed and configured on each system. To provide a stronger authentication mechanism and a method to automatically distribute WEP encryption keys, the IEEE 802.1x standard was developed, and 802.11b uses this standard.

> **caution** Unfortunately, WEP encryption suffers from a number of well-understood flaws that make it far less secure than the length of its encryption keys would imply. These flaws, along with best practices for securing your wireless network, are covered in "Securing Network Protocols" on page 588.

IEEE 802.1x is a standard for port-based network access control. This control method is used to provide authentication for access to Ethernet networks. The standard, which enforces authentication before LAN ports can be used, is an Ethernet standard that has been adapted to 802.11b. When 802.1x is used on networks, the wireless access point authenticates wireless clients in conjunction with a Remote Authentication Dial-in User Service (RADIUS) server. The RADIUS server provides authentication and authorization of wireless connections for the wireless access point. In large wireless networks, the use of 802.1x, RADIUS, and digital certificates provides a high level of authentication security and a method to determine strong per-session WEP encryption keys. Windows XP supports 802.1x authentication for all types of LAN adapters including wireless. For a large network, ensure that your wireless access points support WEP and IEEE 802.1x.

Setting Up Your Wireless Network

After you've carefully thought through the design possibilities of your wireless network and have decided how the network can best suit your needs, you're ready to purchase the wireless networking equipment that you need to begin setting up your wireless network. The following sections explore the setup and configuration of infrared and Wi-Fi networks.

Setting Up an Infrared Wireless Network

Most laptop computers ship with an infrared port. If your desktop system does not have an infrared port (many do not), you can purchase an external infrared device that connects to either a serial or USB port on your PC. In addition, some desktop motherboards have a built-in specialized connector to which you can connect an infrared device. If you need to buy an infrared port, check the Windows Hardware Compatibility List at *www.microsoft.com/hcl* to make sure the device is compatible with Windows XP. After the port is installed, it appears in Control Panel as Wireless Link, as shown in Figure 19-1.

Figure 19-1. The infrared wireless link is found in Control Panel.

To make the best use of your infrared port, Windows XP uses several protocols under the IrDA specification that give you the infrared flexibility you need:

- **Wireless Link File Transfer.** This protocol gives you the ability to transfer files over the wireless port.

- **Infrared Printing (IrLPT).** This protocol gives you the ability to print to wireless printers using infrared.

- **Infrared Image Transfer Protocol (IrTran-P).** This protocol is used to transfer photos from a digital camera to your computer.

- **Infrared Networking (IrNET and IrComm).** These protocols give your computer the capability of communicating with other computers using infrared. IrNET is a point-to-point protocol between two computers, whereas IrComm uses a central infrared hub when several computers need to connect.

InsideOut

How Fast Is Infrared Networking?

Infrared networking, despite its distance limitations, remains a viable networking alternative because of its speed and ease of use. Infrared provides a quick and easy way to transfer information from one computer to another or synchronize with a PDA. There are two flavors of infrared devices, and the speed depends on which you use. *Serial IrDA* uses existing serial port hardware without the additional expense of other hardware. Serial IrDA is the most common type of infrared networking, and you can expect transfer speeds of up to 115 Kbps. Serial IrDA obviously is not as fast as an Ethernet or HomePNA connection, but it is much faster than using a null modem cable. On the other hand, *Fast IrDA (FIR)* can transfer data up to 4 Mbps and *Very Fast IrDA (VFIR)* can provide speeds of up to 16 Mbps. These solutions require additional hardware, however.

Configuring the Infrared Connection

After the infrared device is installed on your computer, you can double-click the Wireless Link icon in Control Panel and configure a few important options concerning the infrared port.

On the Infrared tab of the Wireless Link dialog box, shown in Figure 19-2 on the next page, you can set the following options:

- **Display An Icon On The Taskbar Indicating Infrared Activity.** This option allows you to see when you are connected to an infrared link and when another computer or device is within your infrared range.

- **Play Sound When Infrared Device Is Near By.** This option sounds a tone when an infrared device first comes within range of your infrared port.

- **Allow Others To Send Files To Your Computer Using Infrared Communications.** If you want to let other devices send files to your computer over the infrared link, make sure this item is selected. Otherwise, users will receive an error message stating "Access is denied."

- **Notify Me When Receiving Files.** If this item is selected, a transfer status dialog box appears when files are being received.

- **Default Location For Received Files.** If you choose to receive files, you can specify a default location where those files are stored. Click the Browse button to help select the location.

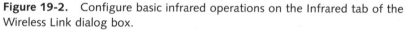

Figure 19-2. Configure basic infrared operations on the Infrared tab of the Wireless Link dialog box.

On the Image Transfer tab of the Wireless Link dialog box, shown in Figure 19-3, you can choose to use the wireless link to transfer images from a digital camera to your computer. Simply enable the first option, and then choose a default storage location for the picture files. Also notice the option Explore Location After Receiving Pictures. If you select this option, the folder in which the pictures are stored will automatically open after you have received the files.

The Hardware tab of the Wireless Link dialog box lists the infrared device that is installed. It displays basic information about the device, such as the manufacturer, COM port location, and the current device status. If you select the device and click the Properties button, a properties dialog box opens—the same dialog box you see from within Device Manager. You'll see the standard General and Driver tabs, but depending on your hardware, there might also be an IrDA Settings or Advanced tab that will let you further configure your port. Figure 19-4 shows the IrDA Settings tab for a serial infrared device and the Advanced tab for a FIR device. On these tabs, you can set the maximum connection rate and, for the serial device, select the COM port. The highest possible speeds are selected by default for both devices. Notice that the serial device tops out at 115.2 Kbps, whereas the FIR device can reach 4,000 Kbps (4 Mbps).

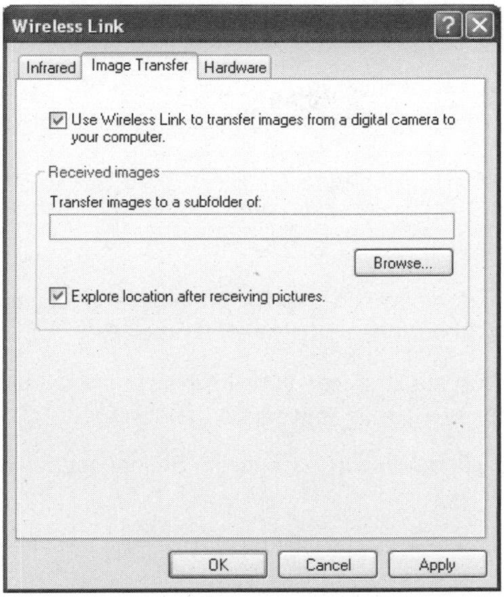

Chapter 19: Wireless Networking

Figure 19-3. You can choose to receive digital photos on the Image Transfer tab and specify where to store them.

> **tip** If you find you're having problems communicating with a certain IrDA device, try lowering the maximum values.

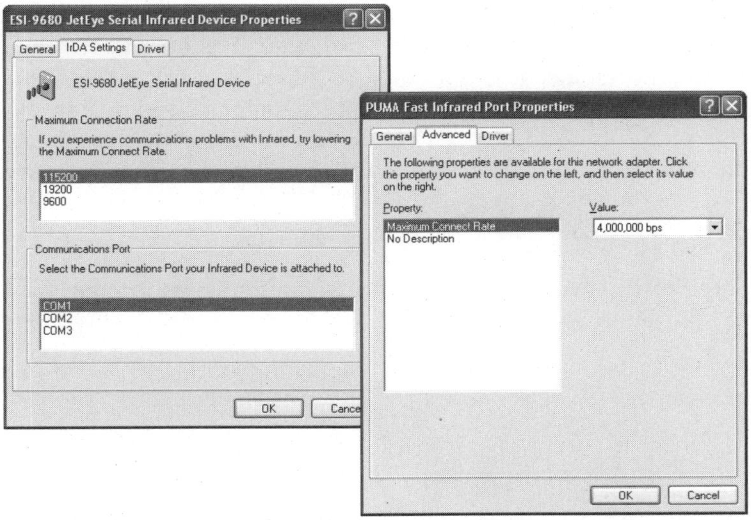

Figure 19-4. Use the IrDA Settings or Advanced tab to set properties such as the port's connection speed.

Using the Infrared Connection

You can use an infrared link to link two devices directly, or you can link up to a network. The following sections describe how to use the different connections.

Establishing an infrared link   An infrared link allows one computer or device to transmit information to another infrared device or computer. To establish an infrared link, follow these steps:

1   Move the infrared computers or devices so that the infrared receivers are facing each other and are within about one meter of each other.

When the infrared device is detected, an icon appears in the notification area of the taskbar, and the Wireless Link icon appears on the desktop.

2   Right-click the Wireless Link icon and choose Connect. The connection is made and data can be transferred.

> **tip**   You can receive files from a Windows XP computer, a Microsoft Windows 2000 computer, or a Microsoft Windows 98 computer. You can also receive files and data from other IrDA devices such as PDAs and digital cameras.

Establishing an infrared network connection   An infrared link allows you to transfer files and data to another computer. An infrared network connection provides a direct connection between two infrared computers where the two computers can communicate with each other over the network connection. One computer acts as the host, and one computer acts as the guest. The guest computer primarily accesses shared resources on the host computer. The guest computer must have a user account configured on the host computer, just as if this were a direct network connection. The guest provides the user name and password to the host computer, and then the host computer authenticates and lets the guest access shared information from the host computer. The authenticated guest can connect to shared resources on the host computer, just like with a typical wired network connection. To set up an infrared network connection between two computers, follow these steps:

1   On the host computer, create a user account for the guest computer if necessary.

2   Align the two computers so that the infrared transceivers are within about one meter of each other and are pointing at each other.

The infrared icon appears in the taskbar's notification area, and the Wireless Link icon appears on the desktop.

3   To establish the network connection, open Network Connections on the host computer, and click Create A New Connection.

Chapter 19: Wireless Networking

4 Click Next on the New Connection Wizard Welcome page. On the Network Connection Type page, shown here, select Set Up An Advanced Connection. Click Next.

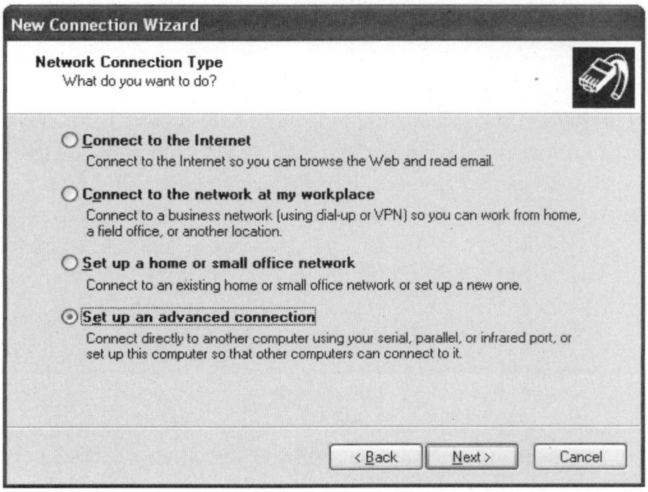

5 On the Advanced Connection Options page, select Connect Directly To Another Computer and click Next.

6 Choose the role of the computer, which is Host in this procedure. Click Next.

7 On the Connection Device page, select the infrared port as the connection device, as shown here. Click Next.

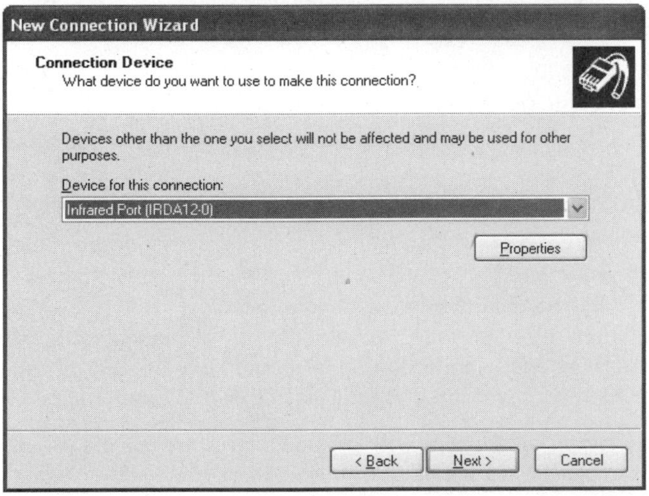

8 On the User Permissions page, select the accounts that can connect over the infrared port. Click Add if you need to add additional accounts. Click Next.

9 Click Finish. The connection now appears in Network Connections as Incoming Connections.

10 Repeat these steps on the guest computer, but select the Guest option in step 6. You'll also be prompted for the name of the host computer you'll be connecting to. When the wizard is completed on the guest computer, the network connection appears in Network Connections with the name of the host computer, and a Connect dialog box automatically opens. The guest can sign on to the host by entering a valid user name and password and clicking the Connect button. At any time in the future, the connection can be reestablished from the guest computer by right-clicking the connection in Network Connections and choosing Connect from the shortcut menu that appears.

InsideOut

Linking Your Laptop to the Internet via an Infrared-Capable Cellular Phone

If you travel frequently with your laptop computer, you might want to check your e-mail at times when a phone jack is not available for establishing a dial-up connection from your laptop. If you also carry an infrared-enabled cellular phone, you can establish a dial-up link through the cellular phone wherever you have cellular phone coverage, such as in an airport or a car. With current cellular phone technology, this kind of Internet link will not give you very good speed, but it might be your only option when a broadband or wired dial-up connection is unavailable. To create the connection, you'll need to check your cellular phone's manual to make sure that such connections are supported. If they are, follow these steps:

1 Align your cellular phone and laptop so that the infrared transceivers are facing each other and are within one meter.

2 Once the link is established, use the New Connection Wizard in Network Connections to create a new dial-up connection. Configure the connection and choose the infrared port as the dial-up hardware.

3 After configuring the dial-up connection, use the connection to launch the dial-up sequence. The infrared port will send the data to the cellular phone, which will then dial the number to your ISP. Once connected, you can use the Internet as you normally would, but you will be limited to the speed of the cellular phone's connection to the phone network (which will typically be slower than your laptop's infrared link to the cellular phone).

Note that some cellular phone service providers do not allow the use of a cellular phone as a dial-up connection device. Again, check your cellular phone's documentation for details and restrictions.

Troubleshooting

You encounter problems with infrared connections.

Infrared connections are generally easy and problem free, but there are some common snags that people sometimes experience. Keep these points in mind as you work with infrared connections:

- Make sure the infrared transceivers are aligned and close enough to each other for transmission to occur. Watch the icon in the notification area. If it fades in and out, the devices need to be closer together or better aligned.

- If you want your digital camera or another computer to send files to your computer, make sure you have enabled the option on the Image Transfer tab of the Wireless Link dialog box.

- If the connection seems to work intermittently, open the infrared device's properties dialog box in Device Manager. On the IrDA Settings or Advanced tab, try reducing the maximum connection speed.

Setting Up a Wi-Fi Network

Infrared connections work great for temporary network connections where you need to exchange files and such. But if you want a true wireless network, Wi-Fi is the way to go. As mentioned earlier in the chapter, Windows XP is fully Wi-Fi compatible and compliant. However, be sure to purchase wireless networking hardware that

- Is completely 802.11 compliant (most wireless devices on the market are)

- Is compatible with Windows XP

- Includes a driver that supports the Windows XP Wireless Zero Configuration service

The following sections explore the setup and configuration of a Wi-Fi network.

Installing the Wireless Equipment

Once you have made a topology decision and have purchased the required hardware, you can set up your Wi-Fi network. Follow the manufacturer's installation instructions for the hardware. Your hardware devices might also include setup CDs to install drivers or software.

By default, the Windows XP Wireless Zero Configuration service automatically tries to associate with an infrastructure mode wireless network. If one is not found, an association with an ad hoc network is tried. As the wireless network adapter looks for a network to connect to, you'll see a Connect To Wireless Network dialog box, as shown in Figure 19-5. If there is more than one network, select the network you want to connect to. If WEP is required, enter the WEP key in the Network Key box.

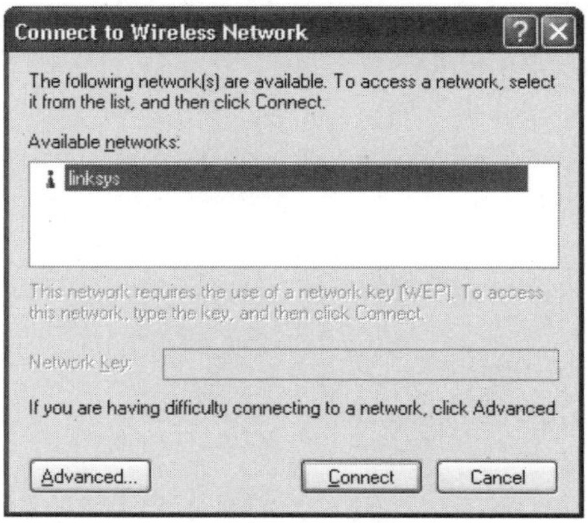

Figure 19-5. The wireless network adapter presents you with a choice of available networks.

---

tip **Manage Your Wireless Connection from the Notification Area**

If the Connect To Wireless Network dialog box does not appear, or you need to connect to a different wireless network at a later time, just right-click the wireless icon in the notification area and choose View Available Wireless Networks. The Connect To Wireless Network dialog box will appear. If you are having problems connecting, you can click the Advanced button in the dialog box. This opens the Wireless Networks tab of the wireless connection's properties dialog box, which is examined in the next section.

Configuring Wireless Settings

Windows XP, using the 802.11 standard and the Wireless Zero Configuration service, does a good job of locating wireless networks for you and gives you the option to connect to those networks. However, the wireless connection's properties dialog box also provides a Wireless Networks tab where you can manually configure some settings if they are required. The following steps show you the options and how to configure them.

Chapter 19: Wireless Networking

1 Open Network Connections and right-click the wireless connection. Choose Properties.

2 On the Wireless Networks tab, shown here, notice that by default Windows configures the wireless network settings for you. You see the available networks and the preferred networks. If you need to configure an available network that you want to connect to, select the network in the Available Networks list and click Configure.

caution Remember that Windows XP usually does a good job of managing your wireless network settings. If you have connectivity and everything seems to be working well, do not change any of the settings on the Wireless Networks tab!

3 The Wireless Network Properties dialog box appears, shown next. By default, data encryption and network authentication are enabled. If you need to enter the network key manually, do so in this dialog box and configure any necessary options. Check the network adapter's documentation for details. For home or small office networks (where IEEE 802.1x is not used), clear The Key Is Provided For Me Automatically and type the key in the Network Key box. If you are use using ad hoc mode, you can disable the settings on this tab by selecting This Is A Computer-To-Computer Network. Click OK.

Part 5: Advanced Networking

4 In the Preferred Networks list on the Wireless Networks tab, you can reorganize the list if you have more than one network by clicking the Move Up or Move Down button. Place the network that you use most often at the top of the list to speed up your initial access to that network.

5 If you only want to connect in infrastructure mode, or you only want to connect in ad hoc mode, click the Advanced button at the bottom of the Wireless Networks tab. The Advanced dialog box opens, shown here. By default, Any Available Network (Access Point Preferred) is selected. If you want to restrict the connection, select either Access Point (Infrastructure) Networks Only or Computer-To-Computer (Ad Hoc) Networks Only.

Troubleshooting

You encounter problems with your Wi-Fi connections.

If you are having problems connecting to a wireless network, check the following items:

- If you are connecting in infrastructure mode, make sure the wireless access point is available and within range.

- If you are connecting in ad hoc mode, make sure other ad hoc clients are available and within range.

- Make sure your wireless adapter is functioning properly. Open Network Connections and double-click the wireless connection. Check the speed and signal strength on the General tab, as shown in Figure 19-6.

- If you are having problems connecting to a specific access point, check the access point's settings and manually configure your NIC on the Wireless Networks tab to connect to that access point. Provide any security keys needed.

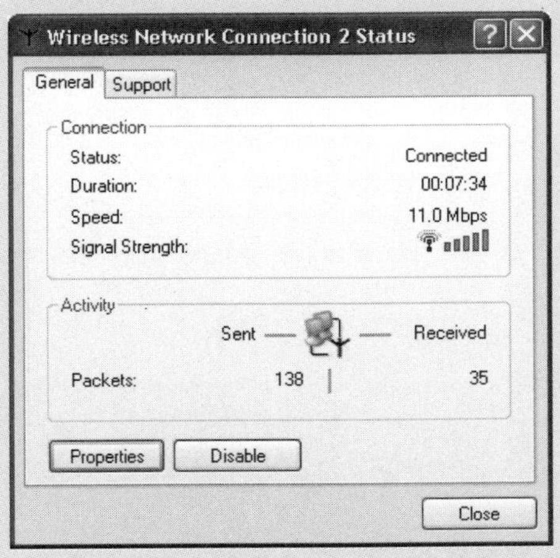

Figure 19-6. Check the wireless connection's General tab for possible connection problems.

Maintaining Network Security

Understanding potential security issues has always been an advanced topic, particularly in the Windows world. For many years, Windows clients were used in isolated LANs or as limited Internet clients. In either case, Windows systems were expected to have little or no interaction with the outside world, and serious security concerns were left to be dealt with by system administrators of other operating systems.

However, two major changes in the Windows networking arena have shattered this utopia forever. Ever since the introduction of Microsoft Windows NT, the Windows family of operating systems has gradually grown more powerful and functional in WAN environments and has become more and more Internet-aware. In addition, the continued popularity of Windows on the desktop, as well as the expanding popularity of Windows in Internet server environments, has created a massive number of potential security targets for hackers to exploit.

Out of the box, Microsoft Windows XP is the most secure operating system ever produced by Microsoft, and most remaining potential security liabilities can be addressed using the tools included with Windows XP along with the right know-how. In this chapter, you'll learn about the most common threats to running a secure Windows XP installation and the countermeasures you can take to make your computing safe and secure.

Examining Windows Security History

Microsoft Windows was originally developed as a stand-alone desktop computing environment based on MS-DOS. As such, Windows was not originally intended to function in a modern network environment; in fact, when Windows first began to gain market share, the Internet itself was barely known outside academic circles.

As Windows evolved, it eventually became able to participate in LANs, via third-party components as well as later Microsoft enhancements. Later, the Internet became more and more commonplace in both home and corporate networks, and Windows' ability to connect to the Internet improved with every release of both the consumer and business-oriented versions of Windows.

Because the inclusion of, and later focus on, network and Internet functionality was a gradual process, Windows' security features grew gradually as well.

In addition, Microsoft's focus has always been on developing products that provide the maximum number of features for users. Part of this focus has traditionally resulted in Windows (and other notable Microsoft products, including Office) being installed with nearly every enhancement and feature enabled and disabling options that would increase security but decrease ease of use or limit functionality.

As Windows clients have become more and more prevalent across the Internet, this policy has become more controversial. The existence of these features, along with Windows' traditional focus as a stand-alone operating system, has led to numerous security vulnerabilities, many of which have been exploited on large numbers of computers.

Originally, Microsoft's policy was to continue to provide as much easy-to-use functionality as possible and to suggest that individuals running in networked environments simply disable what they didn't need. Unfortunately, many Windows users either didn't understand that everything was enabled in a default product installation or didn't pay enough attention to the security vulnerabilities of some of those features; thus, they continued to be left vulnerable to many types of security exploits. To compound this problem, as security holes were discovered in Microsoft's products, its recommendations for configuring or patching the computer to block the threats were commonly unnoticed or ignored by many users and system administrators.

With Microsoft Windows 98, Microsoft introduced Windows Update, a Web-based tool that makes it even easier for Windows users to update their operating system. At first, remembering to regularly visit this site required vigilance on the part of the user, but Microsoft eventually released components that allowed users to automatically receive notifications when critical patches became available and even to have these patches downloaded and installed automatically.

For more information about using Windows Update to patch Windows XP installations, see "Keeping Software Up to Date," page 573.

Unfortunately, the fact remained that many installations of Windows operating systems connected to the Internet remained highly insecure. In addition, the fundamental design of many Microsoft products, as well as that of many features included with Windows, led to a large number of security flaws.

In 2002, Microsoft attempted to address these issues at every level of the company with their Trustworthy Computing Initiative. Triggered by a memo sent to all company employees by Microsoft Chairman and Chief Security Architect Bill Gates, Microsoft's Trustworthy Computing Initiative is an attempt to improve both the security and reliability of the company's products as well as Microsoft's public image. The Trustworthy Computing Initiative includes a number of extremely important steps:

- Sending all Microsoft programmers to security training classes to help eliminate the introduction of low-level security vulnerabilities during the development process.

- Freezing all new product feature development until top-down security reviews, designed to discover and document security vulnerabilities, are completed and software patches for those vulnerabilities released.

- A focus on security as a critical feature of all new product development.

- An end to the practice of automatically enabling features that could potentially expose users to security risks. Those features would have to be explicitly enabled by the end user.

The first major product release to benefit from Microsoft's Trustworthy Computing Initiative was Windows XP. Windows XP was in the latter stages of testing when the Trustworthy Computing Initiative began; however, Microsoft had already committed to making Windows XP the most secure operating system the company has ever released.

This determination shows in a number of areas. For example, Windows XP Professional includes Internet Information Services (IIS), but for the first time, IIS is not enabled by default during installation of the operating system. Additionally, Windows XP includes built-in support for automating Windows Update as well as the ability to automatically report application and system errors to Microsoft for analysis. Windows XP also includes Internet Connection Firewall (ICF), and security has been improved in both Microsoft Outlook Express and Microsoft Internet Explorer.

No operating system, however, can remain completely secure without vigilant attention from users and system administrators, and adherence to secure practices. You'll learn all about these practices in this chapter. The next section analyzes the types of security threats that Windows XP users face.

Understanding Security Threats

There are two major categories of security threats that Windows XP users need to protect themselves from:

- Network-initiated threats in which remote hackers attempt to take advantage of security flaws in software installed on network systems across WANs such as the Internet

- Local threats initiated by software running on local client computers

The line between these types of threats is often blurred; for instance, some Internet worms are triggered by being executed on a local e-mail application such as Microsoft Outlook Express, but can also attempt to exploit remote computers over a computer's network connection. Another example is remote Web content that takes advantage of flaws in Microsoft Internet Explorer to attack a user's computer. However, these two categories are still useful when trying to understand the types of threats Windows XP users need to address.

Understanding Network-initiated Threats

The public image of security attacks centers on those initiated across remote networks, such as dial-up connections or the Internet. Although these attacks are far less melodramatic than those depicted in movies such as *War Games* (MGM, 1983), they remain a significant risk to any computer connected to a large network.

Individual hackers can launch attacks across a network with a number of different goals in mind. They might want to gain control of a remote system to access sensitive information, to deface or damage data located on the system, or simply to use the system as a staging ground for other attacks. They might also want to disable the computer or the network to which it's connected.

Denial of Service Attacks

Attacks that disable a computer or the network to which it's connected are referred to as *denial-of-service (DoS)* attacks. DoS attacks are designed to prevent normal network functionality on a computer or a group of computers. Individuals can launch DoS attacks in several ways, for example:

- Attackers can transmit specially crafted network packets to a target system. These packets, which do not meet the required standards of the network or application protocol running on the destination system, cause applications or services (or even the entire operating system) on the target machine to close or crash. Perhaps the most famous example of this type of attack is the *Ping of Death*, where an Internet Control Message Protocol (ICMP) ping packet is sent with a gigantic packet size. Many IP stacks on several operating systems share a bug that causes the computer to crash when this packet is received.

- Attackers can flood a computer with so much traffic that it has no CPU time left for normal tasks, effectively making it unable to perform any other tasks. Some systems or services can even crash due to this overload. If properly executed, a traffic overload can flood the target computer's entire network.

- Attackers can transmit the packets required to initiate a connection to a protocol or application without completing the connection. This consumes a limited resource on the target system, and if repeated enough times, can slow the computer to a halt.

DoS attacks launched against individual computers were once a popular form of network attack. However, many of the flaws in the IP protocol (as well as in other application protocols) that left computers vulnerable to simple DoS attacks (such as those launched by one originator against one target) have been fixed. Additionally, network administrators are familiar with normal DoS attack signatures and can easily block traffic from individual computers or networks launching an attack.

Today, DoS attacks are more commonly launched by multiple computers located across the Internet in what is called a *distributed denial-of-service (DDoS)* attack. To maximize the effect of such an attack, hackers take over computers across the Internet (using techniques that will be discussed later in this chapter), and then use all of these hacked computers to launch DoS attacks on a target computer or network. Because the traffic comes from multiple sources, it can quickly overload a network's routers and computers; for the same reason, blocking the attack can be extremely difficult.

Exploiting Insecure Resources

Disrupting target computers and networks is not the only potential goal of a hacker, however. A hacker might want to gain control of a target computer for other purposes. This section discusses how a hacker can gain control of a computer by exploiting vulnerabilities in services on target systems.

These exploits typically begin with a hacker probing a system to determine its vulnerabilities. This probing usually takes the form of a *port scan* in which the hacker's computer attempts to connect to ports on the target computer to build a list of IP ports that are listening for connections. This can either be done by sweeping all numerical IP ports or through a more targeted scan of certain well-known IP ports used by applications known to be vulnerable to attack.

Once the port scan is complete, the hacker can use the list of available ports on the target computer to determine which attacks to launch. Often, simply knowing which ports are listening (such as port 80, the common HTTP port used by Web servers) tells the hacker something about what programs are running on the target computer. These ports can also be probed in more detail by connecting to them manually to see what responses are returned from the target computer. These responses can be used to identify the services and the operating system more specifically. For instance, in the case of a Web server, a manual connection to the HTTP port normally returns the name and version number of the Web server as well as the underlying operating system. With this information, the hacker can then refine his or her attack on the system and perhaps attempt to take advantage of known vulnerabilities in the specific Web server or search for other commonly used services on the target operating system.

What, then, are the vulnerabilities that can be exploited? There are many different kinds in many different types of software; however, most fall into one of the following categories.

- **Buffer overruns.** Most operating systems (as well as network services that run on them) are written in some derivative of the C or C++ programming language, or even assembly language. These languages are used because of their high levels of performance, which is critical for both operating systems and network services that are intended to handle heavy loads. However, these languages can require programmers to manually manage buffers of memory for many tasks including the input and output of data. Many (if not most) programmers using these languages simply place input data directly into these buffers without performing more than perfunctory checks for the validity of the data including its length and contents. This practice leaves these applications extremely vulnerable to being hijacked by a malicious user. For instance, if input gathered by an IP application is not checked for length, a hacker can perform a *buffer overrun* attack, in which a large amount of data is transmitted to a vulnerable IP application, thus *overrunning* (exceeding the size of) its input buffer. If the buffer is sufficiently overrun with machine instructions of the hacker's choosing, the target computer can be induced to run those instructions, thereby hijacking the system's normal processing. These machine instructions can perform any task on the target system that the target application has rights to perform. For applications such as IIS, which runs by default with System-level permissions, such an attack can be truly disastrous. The hacker can gain complete control over the target computer.

- **Unsecured network services.** Many network services were developed with little or no concern for security. A number of these services predate the modern Internet environment with its constant security threats, whereas others were intended to rely on other security features (such as firewalls) provided by the network administrator. When installed and configured by default, these protocols provide no security whatsoever or have security settings turned down or disabled completely. One example of such a protocol is Simple Network Management Protocol (SNMP). SNMP provides the capability to both query and manage a vast array of configuration settings on network devices such as computers and routers, and it does not provide a facility for logon authorization. It simply specifies *community names*, so any computer in a specified community can perform SNMP tasks on other systems in that community. SNMP traffic can be blocked by host name or IP, but this feature is also disabled by default. Also, many devices and applications, such as residential gateways, network-enabled printers, and even Microsoft SQL Server 2000, provide default administrator accounts with standard or blank passwords that provide full control over those devices or programs.

- **Insecure network protocols.** Many common Internet applications in their default configurations transmit all data across the network as *clear text*, meaning that no encryption is used to protect the data from being intercepted and read by an unauthorized third party. One example of such a protocol is Telnet. When making a Telnet connection, all data, including your user name and password, is transmitted in the clear. HTTP, the communications protocol used by Web browsers and Web servers, also transmits all information in the clear by default, although an encrypted version of the protocol, *Secure Hypertext Transfer Protocol (HTTPS)* is available. Clear-text information can be intercepted in a number of ways. Because most modern networks use a shared broadcast medium for communication, a hacker normally only needs to take over some kind of device on that network, install an application known as a *packet sniffer* to listen to all traffic on the network, and then scavenge for user name and password pairs. In fact, in a worst-case scenario, that same hacker might be able to scavenge even more critical information, such as credit card numbers, personal identification data, or proprietary company data.

- **Brute-force attacks.** Brute-force attacks use the automation power of computers to attack secure systems, either by trying all possible combinations of a logon password or by attempting to perform cryptographic analysis on protected network traffic. These techniques require extreme computational power and are unlikely to work on properly encrypted data and secure systems. For example, decrypting a data packet that has been protected with 128-bit encryption could take a standard desktop PC literally millions of years of constant computation. However, flaws in encryption mechanisms or system logon routines can be relatively easily exposed using these brute-force techniques.

> **caution** Even well-crafted encryption mechanisms are not sufficient to protect network traffic from interception and eavesdropping. If the communication channel between two systems is not properly authenticated, an attacker could perform a *man-in-the-middle* attack, in which the attacker poses as the remote communication partner for an encrypted data exchange to both the client and server. This enables the attacker to negotiate encryption channels with both partners and watch all the traffic being exchanged between them. For this reason, secure protocols such as HTTPS rely on *signed certificates* that are verified by a trusted third party (such as Thawte or VeriSign) to represent the identity of the remote communication partner.

These are only samples of the types of network attacks that can be initiated by a remote attacker. It should be clear that protecting a computer against these attacks is critical. However, only protecting against network-initiated attacks is not enough to truly ensure the security of your Windows XP computer.

Understanding Local Security Threats

Using the term *local* to refer to the threats categorized in this section can be misleading. For the most part, these threats do not have their *true* origin on the local computer. Computer viruses normally arrive on the local computer via an infected disk or file, and most often, the file is downloaded over the Internet. However, because these threats primarily do their damage by running software on the end user's computer, the designation of local remains apt.

Local security threats also tend to rely on design flaws and vulnerabilities in operating system software and applications, but they equally tend to rely on how people use their computers. This section examines the different types of local threats that Windows XP users face.

Viruses

Perhaps the most commonly known form of malicious software is the computer virus. *Computer viruses* are named after their biological equivalent because, like the viruses that make humans and animals sick, they take advantage of their hosts to propagate from target to target and cause damage.

Computer viruses are transmitted from system to system via mechanisms built into the operating systems or applications that they infect. Although many viruses are harmless, developed as exercises in software development by their authors, many others carry destructive *payloads* designed to alter or destroy user data or operating system installations (or in some rare cases, computer hardware).

There are several types of viruses, for example:

- **Executable viruses.** Executable viruses alter an application's executable files with their own machine instructions, causing their payload to be loaded into memory the next time the user launches the program.

- **Boot sector viruses.** Boot sector viruses install instructions onto the boot sector of a floppy disk or hard disk. These instructions can then load the virus's payload into memory when the system next starts up.

- **Macro viruses.** Macro viruses take advantage of the macro scripting facilities built into popular productivity applications such as Microsoft Office. In earlier versions of these applications, macros were automatically triggered when the files were loaded into the applications, causing the payload contained within the macro scripts to be executed. More recent versions, such as Microsoft Office XP, require explicit user permission to enable macros, but if the user chooses to enable the macros and the macros contain viruses, the viruses will still be executed and do their damage.

In each case, once the payload is executed, it can have its desired effect. Some viruses simply patch copies of themselves onto other applications or files (or disks, in the case of boot sector viruses). Others alter or delete files, damage the target operating system, or alter a hardware device's firmware to render it unusable.

Because of the expansion of scripting facilities into e-mail applications such as Microsoft Outlook and Outlook Express, macro viruses have expanded beyond the initial annoyance of a periodic infected Microsoft Word document. Infected e-mail messages can automatically send copies of themselves from the infected user's computer to the user's address book contacts, thus propagating across the Internet like wildfire. Viruses that propagate from computer to computer without any form of user intervention are more properly referred to as *worms* because of their ability to *crawl* across the network from computer to computer.

Trojan Horses

Unlike a virus, which patches itself onto an innocent program to spread its payload, a *Trojan horse* is an application that claims to provide a set of features, but instead contains a payload that performs more insidious tasks behind the user's back, much like the mythical gift to the defenders of Troy that contained warriors who took over the city from within its walls. Trojan horse applications can perform a number of different tasks, from using the target computer to illicitly store files to acting as *spyware*, software that quietly gathers data about how the target computer is configured, what software is installed, and even what Web sites the target user visits on the Internet. Even worse, many Trojan horse applications install *back doors* that allow hackers to easily take control of the target computer to use it for such purposes as DDoS attacks (see "Denial of Service Attacks," page 560).

Active Web Content

Web browsers, like Internet Explorer, include a number of features, such as JavaScript, Java run-time environments, and ActiveX, that allow Web sites to include executable scripts and code to enhance Web-based applications. Unfortunately, many of these features have security vulnerabilities that allow hackers to develop Web sites that can take control of, damage, or install spyware on computers that visit them.

Web sites can also use cookies as spyware. Cookies can be installed by remote Web sites, and then later detected by other Web sites, allowing any Web site to track which sites a user has visited.

Of course, applications downloaded from a Web site can also be a threat because they can be Trojan horse programs or be infected with viruses.

Protecting Windows XP from Security Threats

With all these potential risks to the security and privacy of computer users, it's clear that a multilayered approach is required to protect the computer and the data stored on it from both local and network threats. The following sections begin by explaining how to protect the computer at its Internet connection, and then work back progressively to explain how to protect the computer itself.

Using a Firewall for Protection from Network-initiated Threats

In "Introducing Firewalls," page 117, the importance of firewalls was discussed as well as some of the options available via software and hardware to provide firewall protection at the Internet connection.

In these days of almost constant remote scanning for vulnerable Internet hosts, protecting your network with either a software or hardware firewall solution is crucial. Firewalls provide this protection using a number of methods including one or more of those discussed in the following sections.

Port Management

Firewalls commonly use a number of different schemes to manage IP ports. The firewall either works with the local computer accessing the Internet, or in the case of a large network, the firewall might function on a server that sits between the Internet and clients. In both situations, port management features all focus on the same issue—ports that are open enable hackers to access applications or services over the port and possibly gain entry to the computer. For this reason, firewalls often use an *open/close* policy with TCP and UDP ports. All ports are closed at all times. When a user requests information from the Internet, the firewall opens the necessary port to receive that information (such as TCP port 80 to receive a Web page). Once the information is received, the port is closed. Because ports do not remain open for long periods of time, a hacker has a difficult time finding an IP port on the computer that he or she can access.

Network Address Translation (NAT)

NAT is often used in firewall solutions, especially in hardware-based residential gateways. NAT translates the local network's entire range of internal client IP addresses into a single external IP address in a different subnet, which is then used for Internet access. Any attacks launched against the external IP address will simply be ignored by the residential gateway's network router, which cannot be affected by many types of attacks that can affect computers, and the attacks will not be able to pass through the residential gateway and reach the computers, where it *could* do damage.

Tables

Some firewalls, known as *stateful firewalls*, use tables to track outbound data requests against inbound data transmissions that arrive at the firewall. For example, if a user makes a request for the URL *www.microsoft.com*, the firewall table records the request. When data arrives back from *www.microsoft.com* at the firewall, the firewall checks its table to see if data was requested from that URL. When an entry is found in the table, the data is allowed in and forwarded to the specific computer or network that initiated the request. On the other hand, any outside data that has not been explicitly requested by an internal computer is not allowed to pass through the firewall.

Rules

A number of firewall products use a rules-based approach. Rules can get complicated and confusing, but they are effective. Microsoft ISA Server and a number of third-party software products use rules that administrators create. The rules determine the kinds of TCP/IP traffic that are allowed into the network by defining which Web sites and IP addresses are allowed or not allowed. Rules enable you to create a configuration that works best for your environment and allow you to override default rules settings for particular users. For example, trusted sites can be granted extra access privileges, and troublesome sites (or unknown sites) can be shut out entirely.

Intrusion Detection

Some higher-end software applications, including ISA Server, and some dedicated intrusion-detection hardware devices can detect an attack from the Internet by watching inbound connections for the common signatures of IP-based network attacks. When an attack is detected, the intrusion-detection system can either close the port through which the attack is being initiated, stop all Internet traffic, notify an administrator, or perform some combination of these actions. In practice, because attempted attacks are so common and the range of appropriate responses so limited, intrusion-detection systems are of little use; in fact, they are often extremely difficult to configure, and they issue many false alarms.

Authentication

Firewall software can also require authentication from both internal and external requests. Although authentication schemes are very secure, they can interfere with the operation of the network and restrict the data that can be accessed from the Internet. However, for networks requiring a high level of security, authentication requirements can provide it.

Given the benefits provided by these firewall features, it's clear that installing and configuring a firewall on any network that is connected to another network (especially the Internet) is an essential security step. Obviously, if a remote attacker cannot detect or reach target computers over the network, that attacker cannot launch attacks directly against them, even if the computers are otherwise vulnerable to those attacks.

---

tip **Securing Your Firewall from Attack**

Many firewalls, including residential gateways, have features that allow them to be administered and/or updated remotely via the external IP address. It's almost never a good idea to enable these features. If some unknown security vulnerability exists in your firewall device, enabling these features can leave your network open to attack. In fact, even if vulnerabilities do not exist, enabling these features can cause your firewall to respond to a port scan, giving remote attackers validation that your network exists, which is all the encouragement they need to begin probing your defenses further.

Inbound vs. Outbound Firewalls

Most firewall software and devices act as *inbound firewalls*; that is, they protect a network or a computer from inbound traffic initiated outside the protected computer or network. However, for the highest level of protection, it's wise to stop undesired outbound traffic initiated from computers behind the firewall as well. This will prevent Trojan horse applications, spyware, and other unwanted and undetected applications present on your computer from being able to send data out across the Internet.

Most large, dedicated firewall devices for medium-to-large sized networks can be configured to provide both inbound and outbound protection. However, residential gateways, smaller dedicated firewalls, and software solutions such as Windows XP's Internet Connection Firewall (ICF) are not designed to prevent unwanted outbound traffic.

For a strictly locked-down corporate environment, using a firewall device with a strict policy of blocking all Internet traffic might suffice; however, if you want to maintain Internet functionality and still protect against inbound threats and unwanted outbound transmissions, a more flexible solution is needed.

One popular solution is ZoneAlarm, a software product from Zone Labs. ZoneAlarm automatically detects inbound and outbound connection attempts, allowing the user to quickly and easily build rules to define which applications should be allowed to establish outbound connections or provide Internet services from your computer. You can learn more about ZoneAlarm at the company's Web site, *www.zonealarm.com*.

TCP/IP Filtering

In addition to using a firewall, you might want to simply use TCP/IP filtering to protect your Windows XP computer. TCP/IP filtering gives you the ability to allow specific TCP and UDP ports or IP protocol numbers to connect to your computer.

To configure TCP/IP filtering for a network connection, follow these steps:

1 Right-click the network connection's icon in the system tray, and choose Open Network Connections. You can also open Network Connections from Control Panel or the Start menu.

2 Right-click your network icon in Network Connections, and choose Properties from the shortcut menu to open the dialog box shown here.

3 On the General tab, select Internet Protocol (TCP/IP), and click Properties to open the Internet Protocol (TCP/IP) Properties dialog box shown in the following illustration.

4 Click the Advanced button and then select the Options tab, shown next, in the Advanced TCP/IP Settings dialog box.

5 Select TCP/IP Filtering in the Optional Settings box, and then click Properties to open the TCP/IP Filtering dialog box shown in the following illustration.

Chapter 20: Maintaining Network Security

6 Select Enable TCP/IP Filtering (All Adapters).

7 For each of the sections, TCP Ports, UDP Ports, and IP Protocols, select either Permit All or Permit Only. If you select Permit Only, click the Add button to add only the ports or protocols that will be accepted. If you change your mind at any time, select the port or protocol and click Remove.

> For more information on deciding which ports and protocols to specify, see "Enabling Services," page 130.

InsideOut

TCP/IP Filtering or Internet Connection Firewall?

Because ICF and TCP/IP filtering provide similar services, how can you tell which to use?

ICF is somewhat simpler to configure, and its configuration (and activation) options are easier to find in Windows XP's configuration options than are the settings for TCP/IP filtering.

TCP/IP filtering runs in kernel mode on Windows XP, whereas ICF is a user-mode application. Running in kernel mode enhances system performance because inbound filtered packets are examined and dropped immediately within the context of Windows XP's kernel-mode TCP/IP drivers without forwarding the packets all the way up the protocol stack to be examined in user mode.

(continued)

> **Inside Out** *(continued)*   Additionally, by default, ICF blocks all inbound traffic unless configured otherwise; on the contrary, TCP/IP filtering can allow all inbound traffic for particular protocols with minimum configuration while excluding ports for other protocols.
>
> Also, TCP/IP filtering acts on all network adapters on the computer, whereas ICF must be enabled on each adapter you want to protect.
>
> Both TCP/IP filtering and ICF work only on inbound network connections. To filter outbound traffic, another solution, such as ZoneAlarm, is needed.

Detecting Windows XP Security Issues

Microsoft has developed a powerful tool for scanning Windows computers to detect potential security risks. This tool, the Microsoft Baseline Security Analyzer (MBSA), is available from Microsoft at *www.microsoft.com/security*.

MBSA scans your computer and compares its configuration to security standards maintained by Microsoft. These standards are downloaded in an XML file each time a scan is run to ensure that the latest patches and security issues are included. MBSA can scan for missing service packs and hotfixes for the operating system, IIS, Microsoft SQL Server, Internet Explorer, and the Office applications, as well as scan to check that the local computer is configured to meet recommended security standards.

To scan a computer using MBSA, download the tool, and then launch it by double-clicking its icon. Click the Scan A Computer button to display the following screen.

On the Pick A Computer To Scan screen, you can scan either the local computer or a remote computer, which can be specified by computer name or IP address in the Computer Name or IP Address box. You can also select which types of vulnerabilities to scan for in the Options section. Click Start Scan to begin scanning the specified computer.

Once the scan is complete, a report is displayed, similar to the one below, showing a summary along with detailed results for each portion of the scan. Each result contains links showing exactly what was scanned, what was detected, and instructions on correcting the vulnerability. This is an extremely powerful tool for securing Windows XP from the most up-to-date list of threats.

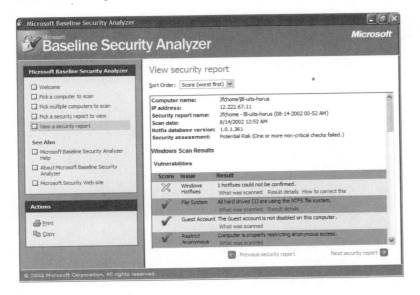

Keeping Software Up to Date

Part of Microsoft's Trustworthy Computing Initiative involves the aggressive development of patches whenever security vulnerabilities are discovered in Windows XP or in other Microsoft applications, such as Internet Explorer, Outlook Express, or Office. Taking advantage of these patches is critical to maintaining system security.

Windows Update is a service that can download and install the latest critical updates (as well as feature enhancements) to Microsoft products. It can be launched manually by choosing Start, Windows Update. It can also be automatically run by the Automatic Updates service.

To configure Automatic Updates, follow these steps:

1 Open Control Panel and then open System. Select the Automatic Updates tab, as shown on the next page.

Chapter 20

2 Select the check box labeled Keep My Computer Up To Date to enable Automatic Updates.

3 In the Settings section, you can choose to be notified before anything is downloaded and installed, choose to have updates automatically downloaded but to be notified before they're installed, or choose to have updates downloaded and installed automatically. If you select the last option, you can even schedule the updates by specifying a day (or Every Day) and the time of day.

note The Declined Updates button enables Windows to renotify you about any updates that you previously chose not to install.

Automatic Updates displays an icon in the taskbar's notification area to notify you when updates are ready to be downloaded or installed if it is not configured to install them automatically. You can click this icon and select whether or not to download and install the update. Once installation begins, you will be notified if a system restart is required.

Removing Unneeded Services

Another effective method for preventing attacks on network services is to disable those services entirely. It's normally wise to disable *all* network services that aren't specifically needed. Before doing so, however, it's important to understand what those services provide and what functionality will be lost if they are disabled.

To view the services currently installed on your computer, follow these steps:

1 Launch the Services MMC snap-in by choosing Start, Administrative Tools, Services, as shown next.

Chapter 20: Maintaining Network Security

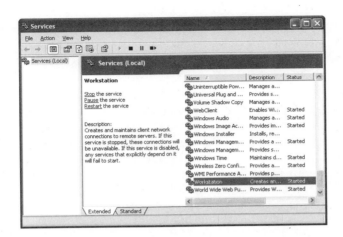

2 Select the Extended tab to see all currently installed services with a short description to the left of each service you click.

3 To disable a service, double-click the service, and select Disabled in the Startup Type box, shown here.

Although many services in Windows XP rely upon, or take advantage of, network connections, there are several that are commonly disabled in order to *lock down* (protect) a Windows XP installation.

● **FTP Publishing.** This service, which can be installed as part of IIS, allows for the uploading and downloading of files via the File Transfer Protocol (FTP). If the computer does not need to act as an FTP server, this service should be disabled (or uninstalled completely).

- **Infrared Monitor.** This service supports IrDA infrared communications devices and detects other IrDA devices within range. Unless you specifically intend to perform infrared communications between devices, this service should be disabled.

- **Remote Registry.** This service allows remote users who have the appropriate rights to connect to a Windows XP computer over the network and view and modify the system registry. Intuitively, it would make sense to disable this service unless remote registry access is absolutely necessary. However, because remote registry access is key to being able to remotely scan a computer for proper security configuration and updates, disabling it causes those scans to fail. In fact, the scans return (strangely enough) error messages claiming the target of the scan is insecure! Therefore, if you intend to scan a computer remotely for security purposes, leave this service enabled; in addition, if you wish to centrally manage your computers (a process that normally requires at least some registry access), and they are placed behind a firewall, this service can also be left enabled. Otherwise, it should be disabled.

- **Server.** The Server service allows Windows XP to serve file and printer shares across the network via Server Message Block (SMB). If this functionality is not needed (for instance, you do not intend to share files or printers with others on any network), this service should be disabled. Keep in mind, however, that if you disable the Workstation and Server services, you will not be able to share files or printers with other Windows users.

- **Simple Mail Transfer Protocol (SMTP).** The SMTP service, which is installed as part of IIS, serves as a delivery and routing agent for electronic mail. SMTP is notorious for its security flaws and should be disabled unless absolutely needed.

> **note** Keep in mind that you do not need to run an SMTP service in order to send and receive personal e-mail messages; using an SMTP service is only required in order to use your computer as an e-mail server or relay.

- **SNMP Service.** The Simple Network Management Protocol (SNMP) allows for the examination and administration of remote computers and network devices; however, its security mechanisms are limited, and by default, SNMP is totally insecure. Unless needed for network administration, SNMP should be disabled.

- **SNMP Trap Service.** The SNMP Trap Service allows the computer to receive *trap* messages, or alerts, sent by local or remote SNMP agents. Unless needed for network administration, the SNMP Trap Service should be disabled.

- **TCP/IP NetBIOS Helper.** This service allows the use of the NetBIOS Over TCP/IP (NetBT) protocol. The service provides compatibility with Microsoft Windows NT 4.0–style networks. If the computer does not need to perform file and printer sharing with those networks, this service should be disabled.

- **Telnet.** This service allows remote users running the Internet-standard Telnet client to connect to your Windows XP computer and administer it as though they were connected locally, if they have an account with sufficient privileges on your computer. Telnet passes all data in clear text, including logon user names and passwords; for this reason, this service should be disabled.

- **Workstation.** The Workstation service allows Windows XP to access file and printer shares across the network via SMB. If this functionality is not needed (for instance, you have no intention of connecting to another computer to access its file and printer shares), this service can be disabled. Keep in mind, however, that if you disable the Workstation and Server services, you will not be able to share files or printers with other Windows users.

- **World Wide Web Publishing.** This service, which is installed as part of IIS, acts as its HTTP server. Unless you specifically need to serve (host) Web content to others, this service should be disabled.

Securing IIS

Microsoft has included IIS in one version or another of every Windows release since Windows NT 4.0. Its relative ease of configuration and use has made it a popular option for serving Internet and intranet content.

However, IIS also has a reputation for being insecure due to a rash of security vulnerabilities discovered over time in various releases of the product. Some of these vulnerabilities led to the propagation of major Internet worms such as the infamous Code Red. Although these worms did not bring the Internet to its knees, as many doomsayers predicted, they proved to be a major source of frustration and expense for Internet users and system administrators everywhere. These same vulnerabilities can be used to take control of the attacked computer, allowing a hacker to deface Web site content, download or destroy valuable data, or use the computer as part of a DDoS attack (see "Denial of Service Attacks," page 560).

These security issues were not, however, due to fundamental, irreparable security flaws in IIS. In fact, the vast majority of famous IIS security exploits had been publicized, along with patches to correct them, by Microsoft for weeks, months, or even years before widespread attacks were launched to take advantage of them. However, due to its default installation in previous versions of Windows, many Windows users had no idea IIS was even installed on their computers (or they had forgotten), leaving them wide open to attack. Additionally, in the past, it was difficult for Windows users to learn of new security updates to Microsoft products.

Microsoft has addressed these issues in a number of ways, including increasing the visibility of security updates and releasing tools for securing IIS installations. Perhaps the single most important improvement to IIS security comes with Windows XP, where IIS is *not* installed by default. On Windows XP, the user must deliberately choose to install IIS if its services are needed.

The previous section discussed disabling or removing various components of IIS to increase system security. However, if you actually need to serve Internet content from Windows XP, these recommendations are not practical. Instead, if you choose to enable IIS, follow these guidelines to secure your IIS installation.

Prepare for security before installing IIS   A default installation of IIS contains a number of vulnerabilities that can be remotely exploited, and computers across the Internet are actively scanning IP addresses around the world looking for vulnerable computers. Make sure that you have the latest service pack for Windows XP and the latest security hotfixes for IIS downloaded and available (either on your local hard disk or removable media) before installing IIS. Although Windows Update will download and install these patches once it has been run, an unpatched and exposed IIS system can easily be exploited during the few minutes between product installation and updating. It's also a good idea to have the IIS Lockdown Tool (see "Run the IIS Lockdown Tool," page 580) and the MBSA handy before you install IIS.

> You can learn more about MBSA in "Detecting Windows XP Security Issues," page 572. You can download these and other tools, and program patches, and subscribe to security notification e-mail lists at *www.microsoft.com/security*.

Install IIS while disconnected from the network   This prevents a remote attacker from detecting and exploiting an unpatched copy of IIS immediately after its installation. Alternatively, effectively firewalling the computer from the Internet (and from other IIS installations, which could be infected with a worm such as Code Red) provides sufficient protection from such an exploit.

Install only those IIS features that are absolutely necessary   For example, if the Windows XP computer doesn't need to act as an e-mail server, do not install SMTP. If it isn't intended to act as an FTP server, do not install FTP. And, if the computer will not be used to host content developed and posted via Microsoft FrontPage, do not install the FrontPage Server Extensions. Also, it's wise to avoid installing any of the default applications or virtual directories that come with IIS, such as the Printers and Scripts virtual directories and the Remote Desktop Web Connection. To remove unneeded services, take these actions:

1 Open Add Or Remove Programs in Control Panel.

2 Click Add/Remove Windows Components.

3 Scroll through the Windows Components Wizard list of components to Internet Information Services. Select Internet Information Services (IIS), and click the Details button.

Chapter 20: Maintaining Network Security

4 Clear the check boxes of subcomponents of IIS you don't need, as shown here.

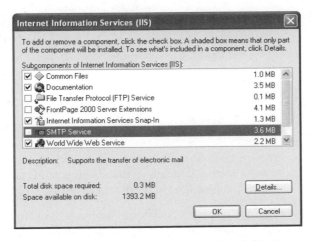

5 To remove default IIS applications and virtual directories, select World Wide Web Service (but don't select its check box), and then click the Details button. This figure shows that only the World Wide Web Service has been enabled.

Update IIS immediately and often Install the newest Windows XP service pack (if not already installed) as well as all current IIS security hotfixes immediately after installing IIS. Additionally, enable automatic notification with Windows Update to remain notified of new IIS vulnerabilities and hotfixes. It's also wise to subscribe to Microsoft's security notification e-mail lists to learn about those security hotfixes that are not released via Windows Update.

Remove all virtual directories that are not absolutely required by your Web site
IIS often installs sample virtual directories, such as the Printers and Scripts directories
already mentioned. These virtual directories contain script code and other features that
are common to many IIS installations, and they are often relied upon by attackers who
want to compromise IIS installations. Removing these virtual directories therefore
reduces the ability of IIS to be hacked.

Disable parent paths for all virtual directories   *Parent paths* allow remote users
who connect to a virtual directory, such as http://www.tailspintoys.com/data/, to specify
a parent file or directory on the Web server's file system using standard Windows
directory syntax. For example, if the virtual directory was located on the Web server
in C:\Inetsrv\Data, a remote user could request http://www.tailspintoys.com/data/.. to
display the contents of the directory C:\Inetsrv. Allowing the hacker to traverse directories in such a fashion leaves the computer very vulnerable.

Run the IIS Lockdown Tool   The IIS Lockdown Tool uses templates for various
types of Web server configurations and modifies the IIS configuration of your computer according to the template chosen to provide only the minimum required permissions that accomplish the tasks at hand. The IIS Lockdown Tool is available from
www.microsoft.com/security. If you have trouble finding it, search for **IIS Lockdown
Tool** on the site.

---

tip   **Using the IIS Lockdown Tool Effectively**

The IIS Lockdown Tool should be run after IIS has been installed and updated. It will
automatically perform some of the other recommended procedures for securing IIS, and
it might also undo others, or even restrict some features so much that they won't work
at all. Running the Lockdown Tool first allows you to review the changes it makes,
implement additional changes it hasn't made, and undo changes you don't like.

Avoid using FTP, if at all possible   FTP passes unencrypted data, including user
names and passwords, across the network. If you must provide FTP services, avoid
using anonymous FTP. Anonymous FTP will allow anyone to access your FTP server,
giving them whatever rights the IIS Anonymous account has on your Windows XP
installation. To disable anonymous access, right-click Default FTP Site in the Internet
Information Services snap-in (located in the Administrative Tools folder). Choose
Properties, select the Security Accounts tab, and clear the Allow Anonymous Connections check box. A warning message will appear informing you that FTP logons are
unencrypted. Click Yes, and then click OK.

Configure IIS logging properly   To identify attacks and track successful security
violations, it is critical to properly log all attempted and successful accesses to IIS. To
do this, follow these steps:

1 Open the Internet Information Services snap-in located in the Administrative Tools folder. Expand Web Sites in the left pane of the console, and click Default Web Site, as shown here.

2 Right-click Default Web Site and choose Properties from the shortcut menu.

3 On the Web Site tab of the Default Web Site Properties dialog box, select Enable Logging. Select W3 Extended Log File Format in the Active Log Format list, and then click the Properties button.

4 In the Extended Logging Properties dialog box, shown on the next page, select the Extended Properties tab. Click to place a check mark next to Extended Properties, and then select the following extended properties: Client IP Address, User Name, Server IP Address, Server Port, Method, URI Stem, Protocol Status, Win32 Status, and User Agent. Click OK.

5   If you're providing FTP services, repeat the process, but this time start with the FTP Sites folder.

InsideOut

Examining Log Files

The W3C Extended Log File Format is extremely common. It is used by IIS to log accesses made to its FTP, HTTP, and SMTP servers, as well as by ICF to log inbound network accesses. Understanding this log file format is key for debugging problems with applications and for detecting both attempted and successful network attacks.

Figure 20-1 shows an IIS log file opened with Notepad that shows HTTP accesses to an IIS server that has been configured with the extended logging properties previously recommended.

On smaller screens, the individual rows of the log file might wrap. The log file begins with comments showing the name and version of the application that created the log as well as the date and time it was created. Each row of the example log file corresponds with one HTTP request made to the server. Empty fields are indicated with a hyphen. In order, the fields show:

- The time of the request (in GMT format)
- The IP address of the remote client (in this example, the client was running on the same computer, so the client address is localhost)
- The user name supplied by the browser client
- The IP address of the server that the browser client connected to
- The IP port on the server that the browser client connected to

- The HTTP method request (such as GET or POST) made by the client
- The Uniform Resource Identifier (URI) stem of the requested document
- The status message returned by the server to the browser client, such as 200 ("OK") or 404 ("File not found")
- The Win32 status message generated when IIS attempted to carry out the browser client's request
- The identification string passed to the server by the browser client

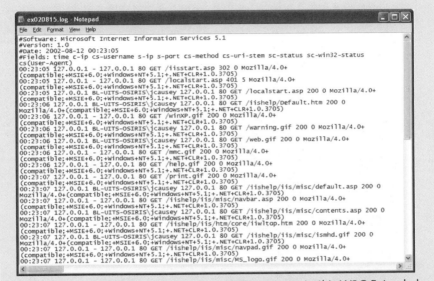

Figure 20-1. Notepad is used to view HTTP accesses in this W3C Extended Log File Format log file.

These log files can be found in the %SystemRoot%\System32\Logfiles directory. IIS HTTP logs can be found in the W3SVC1 subfolder in Windows XP Professional, and FTP logs can be found in the MSFTPSVC1 subfolder. By default, one log file will be created each day that each service is accessed.

Examining these log files is a key troubleshooting step when trying to determine why IIS (or another application using this log file format) is behaving unexpectedly. Examining them regularly is also important for detecting attempted security violations as well as successful attacks. It's also valuable for performing forensic analysis after a break-in has taken place.

Paging through tons of log file entries can be extremely tedious. Rather than reading them manually with Notepad, there are utilities available that can automatically generate reports from W3C log files, such as AWStats (available at their Web site, *http://awstats.sourceforge.net*).

Using Netstat to Observe IP Connections

One important skill when attempting to determine if an attack is under way involves viewing TCP/IP connections established between Windows XP and remote hosts. The Netstat command-line tool included with Windows XP is a powerful tool for viewing these connections.

The best way to view current TCP and UDP connections, as well as determine which Windows XP application maintains each connection, is to open a command prompt and type **netstat –ao**. The –a option displays all connections and listening ports, and the –o option displays the process ID that owns each TCP/IP connection, as shown in Figure 20-2. You can use Windows Task Manager to determine which application has each process ID listed by Netstat. To do this, open Windows Task Manager (Ctrl+Alt+Del) and select the Processes tab. If you don't see a column labeled PID, choose View, Select Columns. Select the PID column (and any others you'd like to view) and click OK.

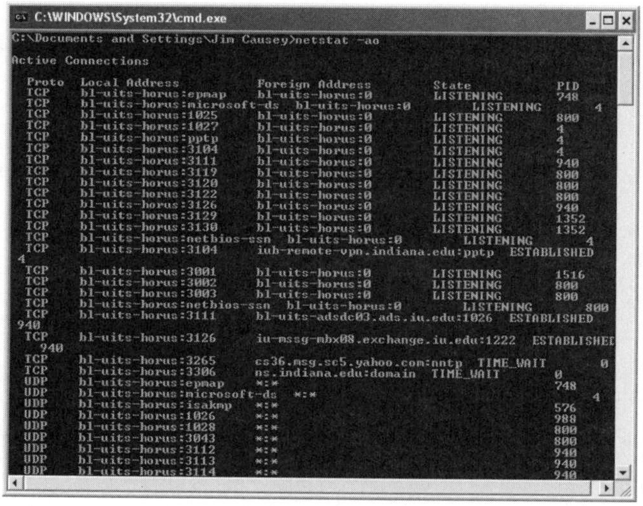

Figure 20-2. Netstat is a powerful tool for viewing active TCP and UDP connections.

The first column displayed by this netstat command shows whether the connection has been made via TCP or UDP. The second column shows the local address or host name and port for the connection, and the third shows the remote host and port for the connection. The fourth column shows the state of the connection, and the last column shows which local Windows XP process ID is responsible for the connection.

The most effective use for Netstat is to view the output in search of remote addresses that are unfamiliar to you. Once suspect addresses are located, you can determine whether the applications they are connected to are legitimate (for instance, perhaps the connection is accessing your Web server or maintaining a Windows Messenger conversation with your computer) or whether they are a Trojan horse application installed on your computer. You can also determine if a DoS attack is being attempted on your computer by looking for large numbers of connections in the CLOSE_WAIT or SYN_RECEIVED states.

Configuring Network Shares

Improperly configured network file and printer shares can pose significant security vulnerabilities. By default, Windows XP grants the Everyone group Full Control on a newly created share (except for printer shares, where Everyone is granted Print rights). On a system using the FAT32 file system, this allows anyone to write, change, or delete any files found within the share. On a system using the NTFS file system, unless rights are specifically removed at the file system level, the same conditions will exist. Additionally, with printer shares, allowing anyone to submit documents grants anyone the ability to consume printer resources or even cause the printer or the Print Spooler service to crash by sending a malformed document.

These conditions leave Windows computers (and the networks on which they reside) dangerously vulnerable to worms such as the famous Nimda worm, which scanned the network for available Windows systems and saved copies of itself to any share that provided Everyone access. This simple process served as a DoS attack, filling hard disks and bringing networks across the Internet to their knees with SMB traffic.

For maximum safety, the Everyone group should never be used on a file share.

---

tip **Evaluating Simple File Sharing**

Simple File Sharing was added as a feature to Windows XP to simplify the process of sharing resources with friends, colleagues, and family members. Simple File Sharing uses the Everyone group extensively and does not distinguish between network users. For this reason, to provide security, Simple File Sharing should be disabled on any computer connected to the Internet. In fact, because worms such as Nimda are often triggered via macros in e-mail or document files, the use of Simple File Sharing is an unacceptable vulnerability on any computer that participates in a network that connects in any way via e-mail or otherwise with the outside world. To remove Simple File Sharing, see "Removing Simple File Sharing," page 426.

Securing Printers

In addition to removing access to printer shares via the Everyone group, it's important to understand the security risks posed by printers connected directly to the network.

These printers, which typically offer TCP/IP, AppleTalk, IPX/SPX, and DLC among other network printing protocols, are normally configured out of the box to allow anyone to remotely administer them (either by not requiring remote logon authentication or by using a standard user name and password) and to use insecure SNMP for management.

It's important to lock down these features immediately when bringing a printer online. Disable all protocols that will not be used to print directly to the printer, change the administrative password (and user name, if possible), disable SNMP (if possible, and if SNMP is not needed), and update the printer's firmware to the latest available revision.

In fact, it's often wise to configure a network-connected printer to allow incoming connections only from the computer that will share the printer itself (as well as any other specified computers that might need to remotely manage the printer). This will cause any attempts to hack into the printer to be dropped. This allows the network printer to receive documents from the computer that manages its print queues, as well as allowing system administrators to control the printer remotely, without exposing it to attack from the network as a whole.

Why all this concern for a networked printer? At best, an insecure printer can be used to print unauthorized documents; at worst, it can become the target of a DoS attack, rendering it unable to print when needed and consuming paper and ink supplies needlessly. In fact, a network firmware upgrade or buffer overrun exploit could allow a remote attacker to take control of the printer and use it as a local packet sniffer or as part of a DDoS network.

Securing Remote Access Connections

Chapter 17, "Remote Access and Virtual Private Networking," covers the process of establishing both inbound and outbound remote access and VPN connections, and briefly mentions the use of security options. What are the best security options to use when configuring your own remote access connections?

The basic security options on the Security tab for a connection allow identities to be established using either a password or a smart card, or to automatically pass Windows logon names and passwords (and domains, if applicable) to the remote access server, and/or to connect only if data encryption is available on both the client and the server, as shown in Figure 20-3.

For more security options, select Advanced (Custom Settings) instead of Typical (Recommended Settings), and click the Settings button to open the Advanced Security Settings dialog box shown in Figure 20-4.

Chapter 20: Maintaining Network Security

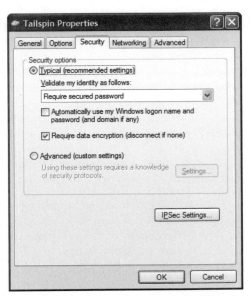

Figure 20-3. Remote access and VPN connections enforce basic security through the Typical setting.

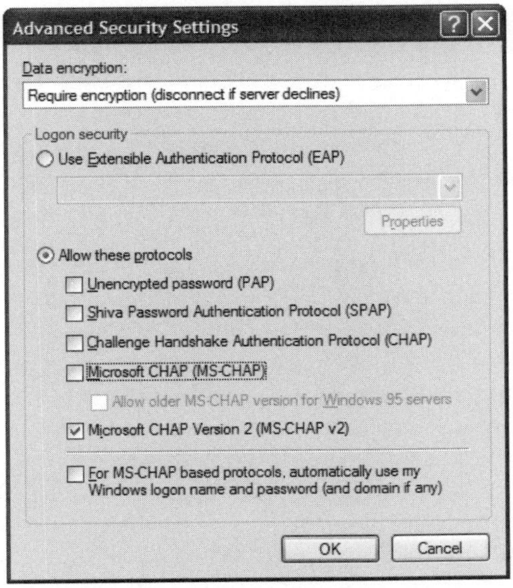

Figure 20-4. More advanced remote access and VPN security settings can be configured in the Advanced Security Settings dialog box.

The Data Encryption box lets you select from four options: to not allow encryption, to attempt to use it, to require it, or require maximum strength encryption. This dialog box also lets you select Use Extensible Authentication Protocol (EAP) to use a smart card or other authentication mechanism, or to use an Internet- or Microsoft-standard remote access authentication protocol (selected from the Allow These Protocols section). The protocols are listed in order of security, from lowest to highest. Password Authentication Protocol (PAP) passes authentication information in clear text, Shiva Password Authentication Protocol (SPAP) is designed for use with Shiva remote access servers, Challenge Handshake Authentication Protocol (CHAP) encrypts passwords, and the Microsoft CHAP (MS-CHAP) protocols include Microsoft-specific logon information including domain-related data.

When configuring connections, use the settings recommended by your network administrator for outbound remote access or VPN connections. If you are configuring a remote access or VPN connection server, select the most secure options that will allow your entire range of clients to connect. For instance, if you intend to only allow hosts running releases of Microsoft Windows 95 or later to connect to your Windows XP computer, you should use MS-CHAP v2.

Securing Network Protocols

One of the most common techniques for violating security and privacy on networks involves intercepting transmissions sent via unencrypted protocols. It's critical to avoid sending personal information, such as credit card numbers, across the network in the clear. It's also important to avoid sending user names and passwords across the network in clear text because a hacker that intercepts them can use the user names and passwords to log on to systems and initiate local attacks or even take complete control. The following practices will help to minimize this threat.

Encrypt wireless network traffic whenever possible   When using wireless communications, use Wireless Encryption Protocol (WEP) with as large a key length as possible. WEP is hardly perfect because fundamental flaws in WEP's key design allow it to be penetrated by a dedicated hacker with sufficient computing resources. Additionally, it only encrypts communication between wireless network adapters and wireless access points (or between adapters when configured in ad hoc mode). As soon as traffic is bridged to a wired medium, it travels without encryption. However, using WEP definitely reduces the chances that your wireless communications will be easily intercepted and deciphered. See Chapter 19, "Wireless Networking," for more information about WEP and wireless network configurations.

Encrypt all TCP/IP traffic whenever possible   The Internet Protocol Security (IPSec) standard provides a uniform process for securely encrypting TCP/IP traffic, including authentication, key negotiation, and packet encryption. Windows XP supports IPSec for both VPN tunneling (via the IPSec/L2TP standard discussed in

Chapter 17, "Remote Access and Virtual Private Networking") and for normal TCP/IP communications. IPSec configuration for standard TCP/IP traffic is done by setting a system policy, which allows IPSec to be configured for all computers within a domain or organizational unit as well as on a per-computer basis.

To configure IPSec policies on a Windows XP computer, open Local Security Policy from the Administrative Tools folder. Select IP Security Policies On Local Computer in the left pane to view the default IPSec policies that come with Windows XP, as shown in Figure 20-5.

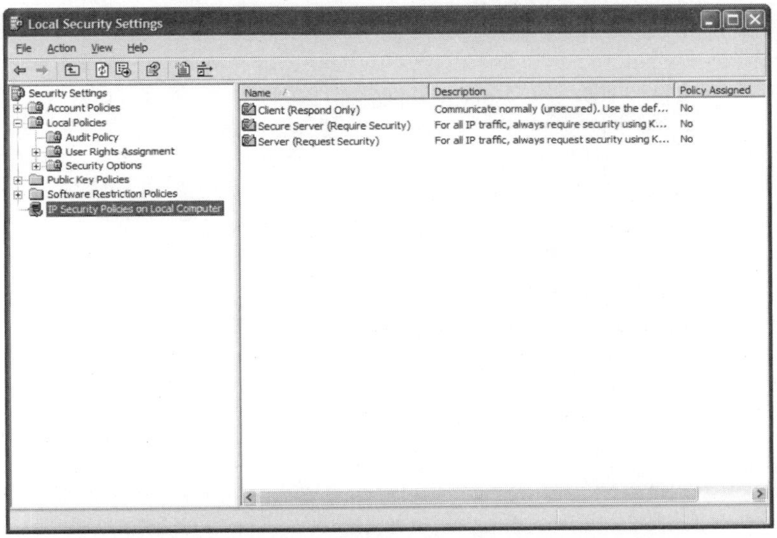

Figure 20-5. IPSec policies are defined in Local Security Policy.

The simplest way to activate IPSec is to use one of the predefined policies. The first policy, Client (Respond Only), communicates normally with remote TCP/IP hosts using unsecured traffic unless a particular server requests IPSec encryption. At that point, communication with that specific server over the specific requested port will be encrypted; all other traffic will remain unencrypted. The second policy, Secure Server (Require Security), requires all inbound and outbound TCP/IP traffic to be secured using Kerberos authentication (against an Active Directory domain or other authentication system that uses Kerberos). *Kerberos* is an authentication mechanism originally developed at MIT. All unencrypted traffic, or traffic to or from hosts that cannot be authenticated using Kerberos, will be dropped. The third policy, Server (Request Security), is a compromise between the others. If this policy is in place, Windows XP will always ask remote communication partners to use encryption via Kerberos trust, but will communicate without encryption if it is not available.

> **tip**   **Accelerate Your IPSec Traffic**
>
> Because IPSec traffic is encrypted, it requires significant CPU resources to process each IP packet. If you intend to use IPSec, it is wise to invest in a high-end network adapter that includes an onboard processor that automatically handles IPSec encryption and decryption tasks at the hardware level, leaving the system's CPU free to perform other tasks.

To activate one of these policies, simply right-click it and choose Assign.

If you want to have finer control over IPSec policies, including selecting specific encryption algorithms, using a different authentication technique (such as a shared key or assigned certificates), or defining specific ports and servers that require IPSec communications, you can develop a custom IPSec policy. For more information on the details of IPSec communication, consult the Windows XP Help and Support Center (choose Start, Help And Support).

> **note**   You might find many references, even in the Windows XP Help and Support Center, that claim that IPSec cannot be used with NAT. This is no longer strictly the case. Most modern residential gateways and NAT devices support IPSec communications, either out of the box or via a firmware upgrade. Some devices, however, will only support traffic with one IPSec-enabled computer behind the NAT gateway at one time.

Avoid applications that use clear text when transmitting sensitive data. If at all possible, avoid using the Telnet protocol to communicate with your Windows XP host or to a UNIX-based server because it passes user names and passwords in clear text. Never e-mail credit card numbers, passwords, or any other sensitive data. If you intend to use your credit card online, make certain that you only submit such sensitive data over an SSL-encrypted HTTP connection to a Web host that has a valid security certificate.

Protecting Windows XP from Viruses

Viruses are one of the most common, and insidious, threats to system security. They can be transmitted via e-mail, via removable media, or can even be deposited on unsecured network shares by Internet worms.

Using quality antivirus software with Windows XP is critical to maintaining the security and integrity of your system. The most effective antivirus programs are designed to automatically scan all files as they are created, read, or otherwise accessed, allowing them to be *quarantined* before any harmful acts can take place. Quality antivirus software should be able to handle macro viruses as well as executable viruses and should also include the ability to integrate with your e-mail application to scan attachments and e-mail messages before they are opened.

When using antivirus software, you must keep the antivirus pattern files updated! *Pattern files* tell the antivirus scanning engines how to detect the latest viruses, and out-of-date pattern files leave Windows XP nearly as vulnerable as if you were using no antivirus software at all. Many antivirus applications include the ability to automatically download pattern updates from the manufacturer on a regular basis.

When choosing an antivirus package, be sure to select a recent version that is certified to work with Windows XP. There are a number of vendors of quality antivirus tools on the market.

Coping with E-mail Security Threats

Many of the most publicized security attacks of recent memory have come from self-propagating worms that use e-mail as their delivery mechanism. More traditional viruses can also use e-mail to deliver their payloads by exploiting the scripting functionality built into recent e-mail applications such as Outlook and Outlook Express. Follow these practices to protect yourself from these threats:

- Use the most recent version of your e-mail application. Microsoft has updated Outlook and Outlook Express to reduce their vulnerability to virus and worm attacks via e-mail, and patches continue to be released as new vulnerabilities are detected.

- Never open an attachment from an address you don't recognize. Never open an attachment without first scanning it with up-to-date antivirus software.

- Always configure Outlook Express to use the Restricted Sites zone for incoming e-mail. For more information on how to do this, see "Security Tab," page 199.

- Always configure Outlook Express to warn you when other applications attempt to send e-mail using your identity. See "Security Tab," page 199, for more information.

Detecting Trojan Horse Applications

Trojan horse programs can be extremely difficult to ferret out, particularly because they are not commonly detected by antivirus applications and are normally concealed within innocuous applications. To avoid these programs, never download and install applications unless you are extremely confident that they were developed by a reputable vendor. However, even some reputable vendors install spyware.

How can you detect these applications? An application such as ZoneAlarm will warn you of suspicious outbound Internet connections and notify you of which application is making them. See "Inbound vs. Outbound Firewalls," page 568, for more information on ZoneAlarm.

Part 5: Advanced Networking

You can also use Netstat to view all current TCP/IP connections and track down suspicious process IDs. See "Using Netstat to Observe IP Connections," page 584, to learn more about Netstat.

Additionally, you can use a Trojan-detection tool to scan your computer for Trojan horses, much like antivirus software scans for viruses. One of the most popular tools for detecting and removing Trojan horses and spyware is Ad-aware by Lavasoft. You can learn more about Ad-aware and download the tool from the company's Web site at *www.lavasoft.de*. Figure 20-6 shows Lavasoft's Ad-aware in action.

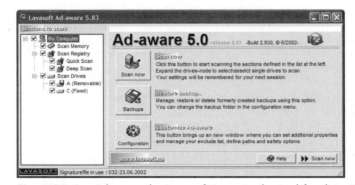

Figure 20-6. Ad-aware by Lavasoft is a popular tool for detecting Trojan horses and spyware.

Using Internet Explorer Safely

Browsing Web sites poses another potential avenue for violating the security of your computer and the data stored on it. Internet Explorer includes a number of features designed to improve the look and feel of the Internet; however, these features also increase the risk of surfing the Web.

Proper use of the Internet Zones feature, as described in "Security Zones," page 144, can help protect Windows XP from exploits that can be delivered via client-side scripting technologies such as JavaScript as well as illicit Web-hosted applications using Java or ActiveX controls. It is also crucial to remain up-to-date on the latest patches for Internet Explorer to eliminate any newly detected security threats.

Cookies are used by many Web sites to track user preferences, but they can also be used to spy on your viewing habits. Trojan horse and spyware detection utilities can often detect and remove such cookies, and Internet Explorer 6.0 includes advanced cookie management features that allow you to select which types of cookies, if any, that you want to have automatically downloaded to your computer. You can learn more about these settings in "Understanding Privacy and Content Settings," page 148. If you are concerned about cookies but want to retain the ability to use them for convenience on some Web sites, consider using the High privacy setting. This setting will prevent sites that do not provide privacy statements from generating cookies and will require your explicit consent before generating any personally identifiable cookies.

Using Administrative Privileges

It is common practice for Windows XP users to log on using an account that has administrative privileges. This practice eases the process of performing system configuration and software installation. However, being logged on as an administrator leaves the system vulnerable to attack because any Trojan horse or virus that is accidentally launched using the logged on user's credentials will have full control over the computer.

For maximum safety, it's best to log on as a Power User (or other type of User) for performing most day-to-day functions and only switch to an administrative account when you need to perform system maintenance or configuration. Once those tasks are done, you should log back out and rely on one of the user level accounts. Being logged on as a Power User or User allows Windows XP to protect itself from malicious applications (or accidental damage) using NTFS permissions and system policy.

> **note** Many Windows applications have traditionally required administrative privileges in order to properly install; however, this is changing because the Windows logo requirements now specify that normal user applications must not require administrative rights in order to be installed successfully.

Protecting Files Using NTFS

Chapter 13, "Selecting a File System," discusses the differences between FAT32 and NTFS, and discusses the strengths and weaknesses of each. To maximize system security, however, it is best to only use NTFS on any partition that will be made accessible via the network. In fact, due to its ability to audit file access (useful when performing forensic analysis of a security violation) and its ability to protect files from unauthorized local access, NTFS should be used on all system and boot partitions as well to prevent damage to the operating system or important personal data.

Auditing Logon Events

Tracking user logons is crucial for being able to detect undesired logon attempts to your Windows XP computer as well as for diagnosing problems with desired account accesses.

Auditing must first be enabled at the system level before it becomes effective. To enable system auditing, launch Local Security Settings by opening Local Security Policy from the Administrative Tools folder. Double-click Local Policies, and then select Audit Policy. From here, you can audit either successful or failed (or both) account logon events, account management events (such as password changes), directory service access, logon events, object access, policy changes, privilege uses, process tracking, and system events. For basic security purposes, enable auditing for Audit Account Logon Events and Audit Logon Events. Right-click the first of these audit policies, choose Properties, and select both the Success and Failure options. Then repeat the steps for the other policy.

Once auditing is enabled, you can review the logon successes and failures in the Security Event Log by opening Event Viewer in the Administrative Tools folder and clicking Security in the left pane, as shown in Figure 20-7.

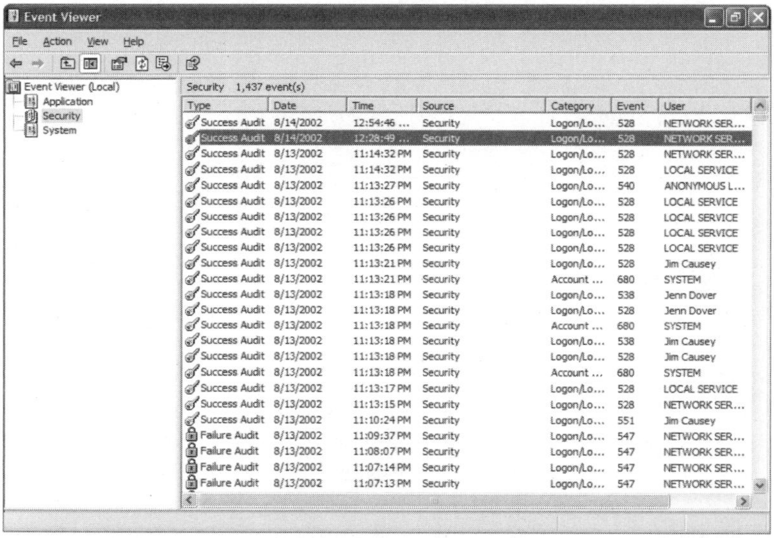

Figure 20-7. The Security Event Log shows system, file, and directory auditing messages.

Auditing File System Access

NTFS volumes enable the tracking of all access to particular files using the auditing features built into NTFS. Auditing can be useful when trying to diagnose security problems as well as for detecting and tracking undesired access to files on the computer.

To enable auditing on a file or directory, right-click the file or directory and choose Properties. On the Security tab, click the Advanced button, and then select the Auditing tab, which is shown in Figure 20-8.

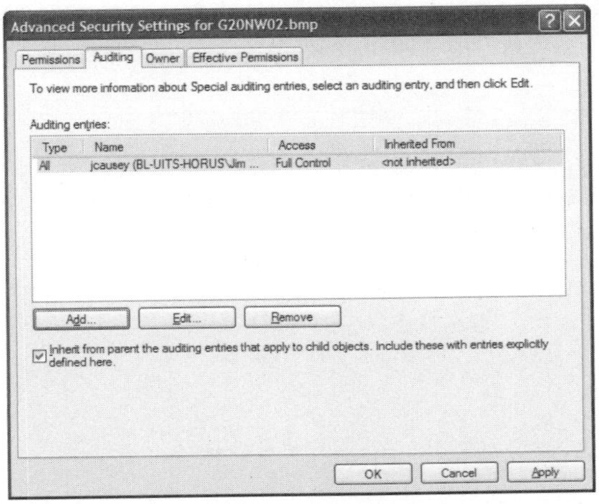

Figure 20-8. NTFS allows file and directory accesses to be audited.

Click the Add button to add an auditing entry. Auditing entries work much like advanced NTFS permissions. You can select the users whose attempted access will be audited, the types of access that will be audited, and whether success, failure, or both success and failure of those attempted accesses will be audited. As with NTFS permissions, auditing entries can be inherited from parent directories.

Once auditing is enabled, auditing messages will appear in the Event Log's Security node when the specified files or directories are accessed in the fashion specified by the auditing entries.

Managing EFS

Encrypting File System (EFS) is a powerful tool for preventing files from being read by others, even those with administrative access or those who are able to physically access your Windows XP computer. However, its use can be potentially disastrous without the creation and management of security keys.

EFS allows Windows XP users with administrative privileges to designate users as *file recovery agents*, or users that can provide keys that can be used to decrypt a file should the user account that originally encrypted the file be damaged or lost. The administrator must create a self-signed security certificate (or use a third-party certificate) to generate recovery keys that can then be stored in case files need to be recovered.

> **caution**   It is essential to designate file recovery agents *before* EFS is used to encrypt files; otherwise, the file recovery agents will be unable to decrypt any file that was encrypted before they were designated.

For more information on managing file recovery certificates and keys for EFS, search for these topics in the Windows XP Help and Support Center: **Best Practices: File encryption, Managing Certificates,** and **Recovering Data.**

Monitoring Windows XP Network Performance

Microsoft Windows XP was designed from the ground up to provide high levels of network performance. Many factors, however, can contribute to the speed and reliability of a network, and detecting and resolving network performance issues can be difficult. The good news is that Windows XP provides a wide range of tools that can be used to troubleshoot network performance.

The process of monitoring network performance involves examining different parts of the network, including various operating system and network hardware components, to look for patterns that could contribute to network difficulties. Once you isolate those potential problems, you can then take steps to resolve them. Finding those patterns can be difficult in some cases, and in order to solve networking performance problems, you'll need to become a detective of sorts.

Monitoring Network Performance

Network performance monitoring uses a variety of tools and techniques to detect issues with network speed and throughput. Performance monitoring can be performed diagnostically when performance issues have already been noted, or preventatively, by periodically sampling performance to detect trends and aid in planning.

> **tip** Keep in mind that performance monitoring is not the same as troubleshooting network connectivity between hosts on your network or on the Internet. You can learn more about troubleshooting connectivity in Chapter 12, "Solving Connectivity Problems."

Understanding Bottlenecks

A *bottleneck* is a process, device, or other entity that is responsible for reducing performance. For example, if a computer's network adapter has a hardware fault that causes it to process data slowly, and that computer receives hundreds of requests from network clients every minute, that network adapter will act as a bottleneck on the computer's ability to serve data because the computer will have to wait for the adapter to service requests. Any computer component, service, or network component can become a bottleneck. In small networks, locating bottlenecks is often easy. In large networks, detection often becomes far more complex.

InsideOut

The Computer as a Network Bottleneck

When monitoring network performance to detect bottlenecks, don't forget to consider the computer itself as a potential factor. For example, your Windows XP computer might have 128 MB of RAM and an older, slow CPU. Perhaps a printer is attached to the computer and shared over your network. Several folders containing important data are also shared over the network from the computer. You might start receiving reports from network users complaining about slow access to the computer. Most likely, they have to wait to open files, and printing documents on the shared printer is slow. Clearly, in this case, the bottleneck for opening these files and printing to this particular printer is that the computer is simply not powerful enough to serve large numbers of network requests.

If networking to a certain computer or service seems slow, always examine the computer providing the service. The computer's hardware must be able keep up with the demands placed on it, and if demands exceed its power, the problem will appear to users as though the network is in slow motion. In fact, it is not the network at large,

> but the computer providing the data that is slow. Performance monitoring can include many factors, so always make sure you are looking at all parts of the picture when you are trying to determine the cause of a problem.

Detecting Bottlenecks with Windows XP Command-line Tools

Windows XP includes a number of command-line tools to diagnose local and remote network issues. These tools are covered in detail in "Using Command-line Tools Included in Windows XP," page 345. Not only are these tools useful for determining whether computers or networks are functioning, but also for detecting network performance issues.

When a networking problem is first detected, it's often wise to use Ping and PathPing to begin your troubleshooting process. By pinging a remote computer, you can determine the amount of time required for traffic to travel between the two computers. If this value seems large, you can isolate where the slowdown is taking place by using PathPing, which will ping every host that routes traffic between your computer and the remote target. If all hosts take a long time to respond, the problem most likely lies with your computer, your local network, or with your connection to the Internet. If, however, some hosts respond quickly and others do not, you can determine which are acting as bottlenecks on the particular connection you are trying to troubleshoot.

Netstat is also a powerful tool for network troubleshooting on individual computers. If networking in general on a particular system seems slow, or one network server application such as Internet Information Services (IIS) on a particular computer seems slow, Netstat can determine if that computer is being flooded with connections and requests, and can show which applications are serving each of those requests.

Using Windows Task Manager

Windows Task Manager is a Windows XP tool that enables you to start and stop tasks and processes. You can also get information about logged on users as well as gather some system and network performance statistics.

To launch Windows Task Manager, press Ctrl+Alt+Del. If Use The Welcome Screen is enabled in User Accounts in Control Panel, Windows Task Manager will appear. If it's not enabled (or if you're connected to a domain), the Windows Security dialog box will appear, and you'll need to click its Task Manager button to open Windows Task Manager.

Chapter 21

In Windows Task Manager, the Networking tab, shown in Figure 21-1, provides you with a real-time graph of network utilization. This allows you to view each network adapter and the percentage of network bandwidth it is consuming. You also see the link speed and its current state, such as operational or disconnected.

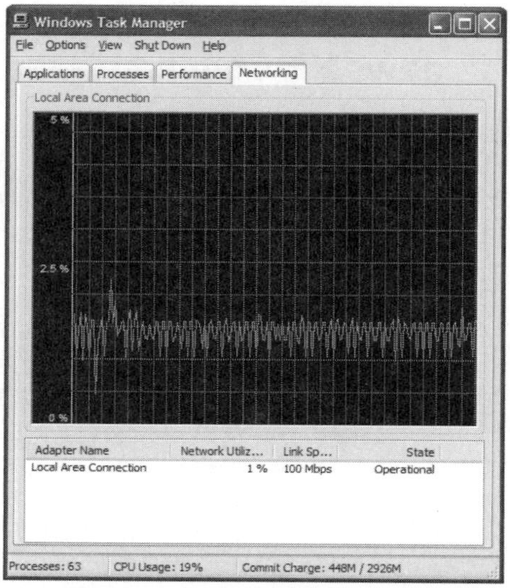

Figure 21-1. The Networking tab gives you real-time information about the bandwidth utilization of your network connections.

Normally, network utilization will fluctuate depending on the traffic on your network. If there is little network activity, the utilization will be low. If users are downloading large files from your computer, or you are using an application on another computer, the network utilization can be high. If utilization is consistently above 80 percent, you might have a bottleneck on your computer or on the network.

> **note** The network utilization graphs only display network utilization used by adapters on your computer. They do not monitor the network as a whole and provide an independent view of total network bandwidth in use.

Aside from LAN connections, the Networking tab also displays Internet connections, VPN connections, and any other active connections found in the Network Connections folder. If several connections are active, the Networking tab divides into several graphical panes so that you can view the network utilization of all connections, This is shown in Figure 21-2.

Chapter 21: Monitoring Windows XP Network Performance

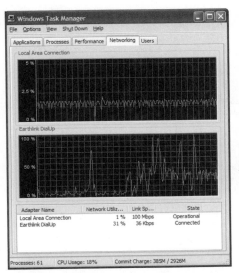

Figure 21-2. If several network connections are active, the Networking tab displays them all.

Aside from gathering basic information, some additional settings that you can use on the Networking tab are provided in the following list.

- If you choose View, Update Speed, you can change the speed of data refresh on the graph. The default speed is Normal, but if you want information to be updated more frequently on the graph, choose the High option.

- If you choose View, Network Adapter History, you can choose to see the network utilization in terms of traffic sent and received (in different colors) as well as the total traffic. By default, only the total is displayed. However, you might be able to gather more insight into network performance by comparing the incoming and outgoing traffic.

- If you choose View, Select Columns, shown in Figure 21-3 on the next page, you can select the data that is displayed on the Network tab. By default, you see the network adapter name, network utilization, link speed, and state. However, there are a number of additional columns that you can display including bytes sent and received. If you want to use any of the additional columns, select the desired columns and click OK.

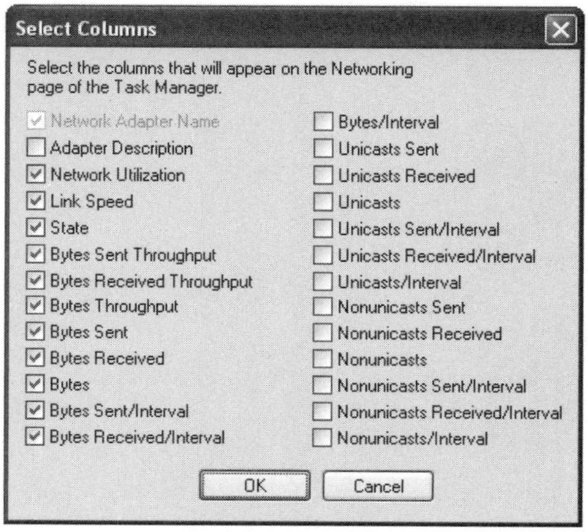

Figure 21-3. You can display additional information by selecting the columns you want to view.

The Windows Task Manager Performance tab gives you information about CPU and page file use as well as current memory utilization, as shown in Figure 21-4. If you are having general performance problems on your computer, or you believe that the computer is too busy to properly service network requests, examine the Performance tab. Consistently high readings indicate that the CPU or memory is unable to meet the demands placed on it, or some program or process is consuming CPU cycles and memory. In the latter case, you can also look on the Application and Processes tabs for more information about any programs or processes that are consuming too many resources.

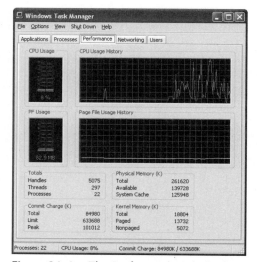

Figure 21-4. The Performance tab displays statistics about CPU usage and page file usage history as well as memory use.

Using the Performance Tool

Windows XP includes a more advanced performance monitoring tool simply called Performance. The Performance tool has been around since the days of Microsoft Windows NT, but the full version of the product is included in both Microsoft Windows XP Professional and Microsoft Windows XP Home Edition. The Performance tool provides you with real-time information about different performance objects, such as the system paging file, the CPU, network interfaces, physical disks, and other system objects.

A *performance object* is a category of performance monitoring. Under each performance object, *performance counters* are available to monitor different portions of the performance object. For example, the performance object Memory includes performance counters such as page reads per second, page writes per second, and available bytes. To monitor a counter, select the counter and the objects you want to monitor, and then collect data about those counters. Once that data has been collected, you can analyze the data to make a decision about what action, if any, needs to be taken to increase performance.

Starting Performance

The Performance tool is a Microsoft Management Console (MMC) snap-in located in the Administrative Tools folder in Control Panel. When you start Performance, you see a two-paned view. The snap-in contains the console root in the left pane. The right pane displays a chart view and the counters that are currently being monitored, as shown in Figure 21-5.

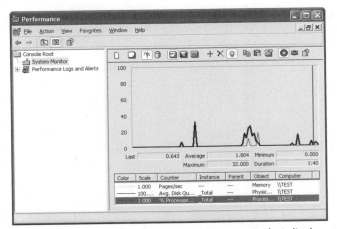

Figure 21-5.   Performance is an MMC snap-in that displays a chart view by default.

Along the top of the chart window, you see a toolbar that contains buttons for the following items:

Button	Name	Function
	New Counter Set	This option clears any counters that are currently being monitored. You can then add new counters.
	Clear Display	This option clears the existing display so that monitoring begins again.
	View Current Activity	This option, enabled by default, views current activity.
	View Log Data	You can record a log file of any counter sessions and then open it to view past performance.
	View Graph	This option, enabled by default, shows a graphical view of all current performance counters.
	View Histogram	You can view the counter data in a histogram format rather than a chart format.
	View Report	You can view counter data in a report format rather than a chart format.
	Add	This option adds counters to the chart/histogram/report.
	Delete	You can select a counter in the counter list and delete the counter from the current counter set.
	Highlight	You can select a counter and then highlight it in the graph by clicking this button.
	Copy Properties	You can copy the properties of a selected counter list for pasting into a different counter set.
	Paste Counter List	You can paste any copied counter properties from one counter set to another.
	Properties	Opens the System Monitor Properties dialog box, which lets you set general properties for the Performance snap-in.
	Freeze Display	This option freezes all activity so that you can analyze the current view.
	Update Data	This option becomes enabled if you have frozen the data. Click the button to start recording data again.
	Help	Get help with Performance topics.

Creating a Counter Set

To create a counter set, you must first identify what you want to monitor. For example, suppose that your computer becomes congested with network requests. Users complain that accessing shared information on your computer is slow, and you notice that access to shared resources from your computer is also slow. Once you have identified the problem, follow these steps to create a new counter set containing the objects and counters that you want to monitor:

1 In Performance, ensure that System Monitor is selected in the left pane of the console.

2 In the right pane, click the New Counter Set button, and then click the Add button.

3 The Add Counters dialog box appears, as shown here. Notice at the top of the dialog box that you can monitor the local computer or another computer on your network by entering the UNC path. Choose a performance object category from the Performance Object list. The available counters for the object appear in the Select Counters From List box. If the performance object you chose has more than one instance, choose an instance from the list in the right portion of the Add Counters dialog box. For example, the Network Interface object will have an instance for each network adapter you have installed.

4 Select All Counters if you want to monitor all counters in a performance object. Each performance object can include many counters, so you'll probably want to click Select Counters From List instead and select specific counters from the list. You can click Add after each counter you select, or you can press

Part 5: Advanced Networking

Ctrl, click multiple counters, and then click Add. Each time you click Add, the counters are immediately activated and monitoring begins in Performance. You can keep the Add Counters dialog box open and add additional counters.

> **tip** If you are not sure what a counter does, click the Explain button and a message box with an explanation will appear.

> **note** You're not limited to adding counters from a single performance object. At any time, you can select a new performance object from the Performance Object list and then select counters for that object. When you click Add, they will be displayed in addition to any counters you've selected from other performance objects.

5 When you have added all the necessary counters, click the Close button.

> **tip** **Limiting the Counters to Monitor**
>
> It is important that you only use those counters that you think will help you examine possible performance problems. Adding nonessential counters to the chart, histogram, or report is often more confusing than helpful. Try monitoring a few counters at a time and eliminate the counters that are not giving you any useful data so that you can locate issues that might be causing network performance problems.

In Figure 21-6, several counters from the Network Interface performance object are being monitored. You can switch between chart, histogram, and report view as you examine the data.

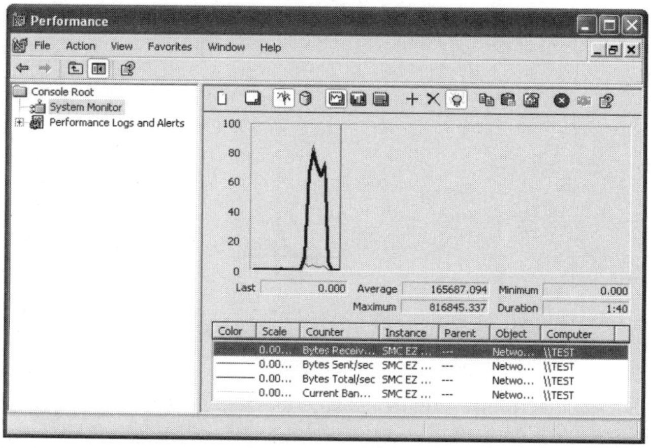

Figure 21-6. The counters you selected now appear in the chart area.

Chapter 21: Monitoring Windows XP Network Performance

> **tip** **Customize the Performance Display**
>
> As you are using System Monitor in Performance, remember that you can click the Properties button and adjust the appearance of charts and histograms as well as the colors that are used to represent the counters. The properties dialog box options are self-explanatory and customizing them might make your chart and histogram easier to interpret.

Logging Data

One difficulty when using the Performance tool is that its usefulness depends on the quality and quantity of data you gather. Monitoring counters for a few minutes will likely not give you a true picture of any performance issues and problems being experienced on your network. If you need to gather data over a certain period of time, such as several hours or even a day, you can log the data, and then open the log file in Performance at a later time. The following steps show you how to create a log file.

1 Select Performance Logs And Alerts in the left pane of the console. Right-click Counter Logs in the right pane and choose New Log Settings.

2 In the New Log Settings dialog box that appears, enter a name for the log and click OK.

3 The properties dialog box for the new log file appears, as shown next. On the General tab, you see the current name and location of the log file, which is stored in C:\Perflogs in a default Windows XP installation. Use the Add Objects and Add Counters buttons to add the counters and objects you want to log. By default, data is sampled every 15 minutes, but you can increase or decrease this value as desired. You can also set an administrative password to prevent access to the log files.

Chapter 21

4 On the Log Files tab, shown next, you can choose to create a text file, binary file, binary circular file, or SQL Database file. Unless you have experience with log files, the easiest file type to work with is the Text File (Comma Delimited) option.

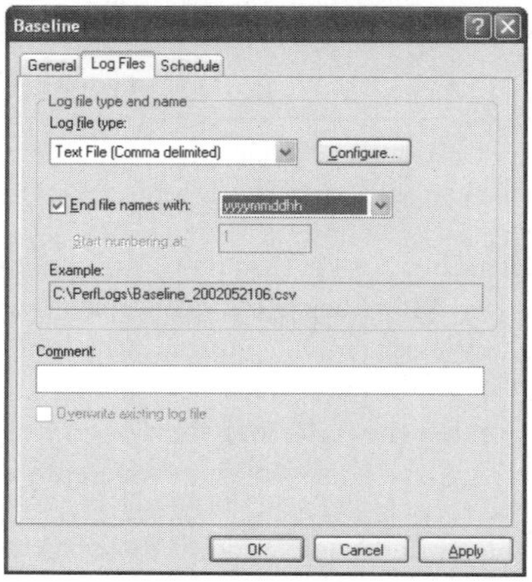

5 Once you've selected the kind of log file you want to create, click the Configure button. In the Configure Log Files dialog box, shown next, you can change the location of the log file and its name, and you can configure a maximum size. By default, log files can grow in size to 1 MB, but you might consider lowering this value so that the files are easier to manage and read. Make any desired selections and click OK.

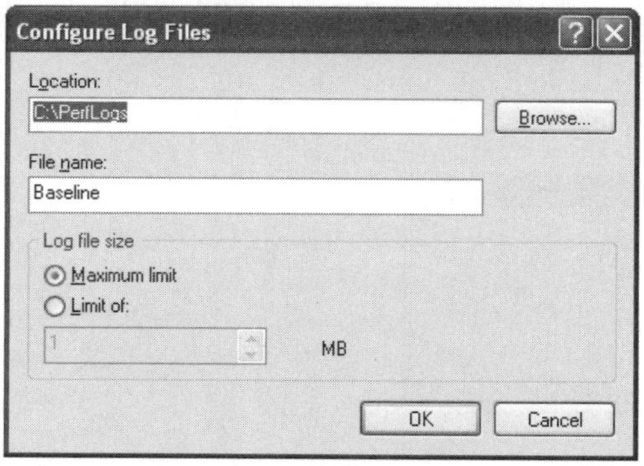

6 Select the Schedule tab, shown next, and configure when the log should start and stop, or you can choose to manually start and stop the log.

7 When you are done, click OK. The log file now appears in the right pane when Counter Logs is selected in the left pane. If you chose to manually start the log file on the Schedule tab, right-click the log file and choose Start from the shortcut menu. To stop logging to the file, right-click the file again and choose Stop.

8 Once the log file is created, you can then open and review the log file.

Configuring Performance Alerts

As with other log files, you can create an administrative alert in Performance. An *administrative alert* is a notification issued when a specified value falls below a certain baseline value. To configure an alert, follow these steps:

1 Expand Performance Logs And Alerts in the left console pane.

2 Right-click Alerts and choose New Alert Settings. In the New Alert Settings dialog box, enter a name for the alert and click OK.

3 The properties dialog box for the alert appears. On the General tab, shown on the next page, click the Add button to select the counters that should trigger an alert. Enter the desired trigger values for the alert in the Alert When The Value Is box and the Limit box. These values determine the baseline for the counter so that an alert is triggered when the value crosses the baseline (up or down, depending on your choice). Select an interval for sampling the data and set a password if necessary.

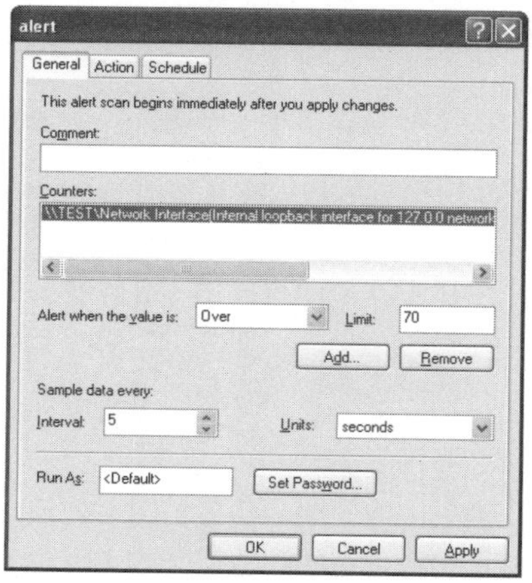

4 On the Action tab, shown next, select the action that you want to occur when the alert is triggered. You can log an entry to the application event log, send a network message, start logging to a log file, or run a program.

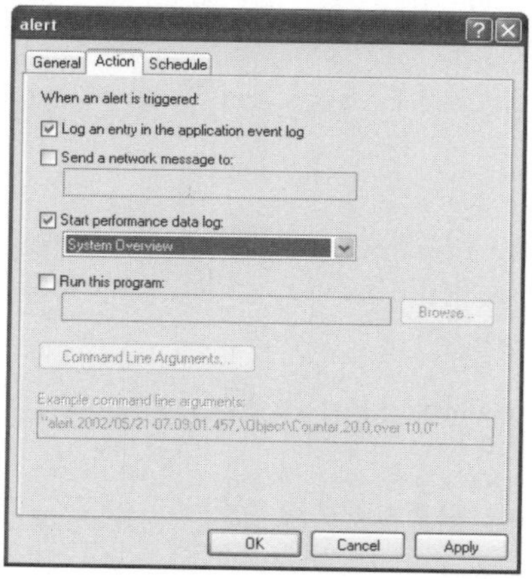

5 The Schedule tab allows you to schedule a start and stop time for the scan, or you can start and stop the scan manually. Make any desired changes and click OK.

6 The alert now appears in the Alerts window. Right-click the alert and choose Start if you chose to manually start the alert on the Schedule tab.

note Remember that using Performance Monitor adds additional overhead to the system on which it's running and can slow that system down, thus reducing system performance and also possibly skewing the data being collected. Therefore, it's best to use it only when trying to gather specific data, and its potential effect on the computer's performance must be remembered when analyzing the data.

Part 6

Appendix

Windows XP Service Pack 1

Microsoft has traditionally released update packages for Windows NT and Windows 2000 called *service packs*. These service packs combine fixes for bugs and security flaws as well as new features and functionality. Microsoft continues this tradition with Windows XP Service Pack 1 (SP1).

Windows XP SP1 includes more of the fruits of Microsoft's Trustworthy Computing Initiative (see Chapter 20, "Maintaining Network Security," for more details). SP1 includes fixes for security vulnerabilities found throughout both Microsoft Windows XP and the applications (such as Windows Messenger) included with Windows XP. Many of these fixes were made available as hotfixes before the release of SP1. However, SP1 also includes additional patches and refinements.

In addition, Windows XP SP1 includes enhancements to system reliability, built-in support for a wider range of hardware, and the Microsoft .NET Framework, a software component that is key to applications developed in Microsoft's new .NET component environment.

Default Applications

The most important network-related change in Windows XP SP1 affects how Windows XP manages default applications for common Internet-related tasks.

By default, Windows XP includes Microsoft Internet Explorer for Web browsing, Microsoft Outlook Express for e-mail and newsgroup browsing, Microsoft Windows Media Player, and

Microsoft's Java virtual machine. Third-party applications can be installed to perform these tasks, but often Windows opens Microsoft tools by default to perform these tasks even after third-party tools are installed.

Windows XP SP1 includes a new component in Add Or Remove Programs in Control Panel. It appears in the left pane of the Add Or Remove Programs dialog box and is named Set Program Access And Defaults. To access it, open Add Or Remove Programs in Control Panel, and click Set Program Access And Defaults, as shown in Figure A-1.

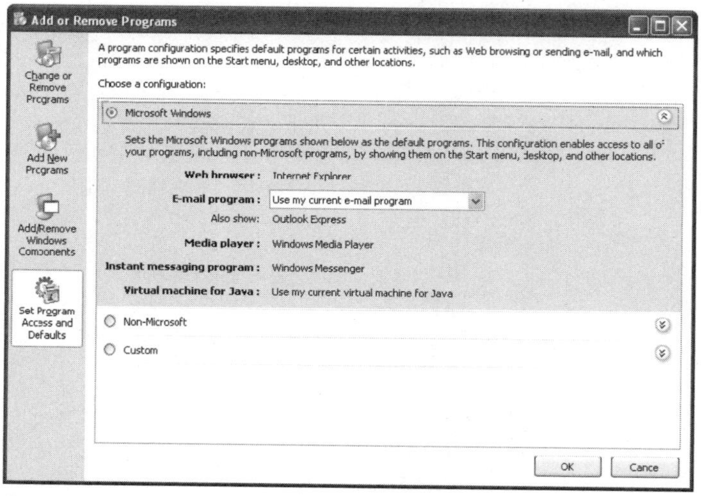

Figure A-1. Set Program Access And Defaults is available in Add Or Remove Programs in Control Panel in Windows XP SP1.

Set Program Access And Defaults manages which applications are used by default by the operating system for Web browsing, e-mail, multimedia, instant messaging, and Java applications.

Three main configuration choices are available:

- **Microsoft Windows.** This option preserves access to non-Microsoft applications via their normal desktop and Start menu shortcuts, and uses Microsoft's applications as the system's defaults.

- **Non-Microsoft.** This option uses non-Microsoft applications whenever available and actually hides Microsoft's tools.

- **Custom.** This option allows you to individually choose whether to use a Microsoft application or a third-party application for each category, and if a third-party application is chosen, whether to also enable or hide the Microsoft-equivalent application for the category.

The settings for each main option can be accessed by clicking the arrow on the right side of the dialog box next to the button for each entry. Selecting an option also expands that option's settings.

With the introduction of Windows XP SP1, many new Windows computers might be delivered from their manufacturers with some or all of the Microsoft applications replaced or even hidden in favor of third-party tools.

Glossary

1000Base-T   Also referred to as Gigabit Ethernet, an Ethernet standard capable of 1 gigabit per second (Gbps), or 1,000 Mbps, over twisted-pair wiring.

100Base-T   Also called Fast Ethernet, an Ethernet standard that has a capacity of 100 Mbps over twisted-pair wiring.

10Base-T   An Ethernet standard with a capacity of 10 Mbps over twisted-pair wiring.

A

access control list (ACL)   A list associated with a file or other resource that contains information about which users or groups have permission to access the resource.

access method   The way in which a computer accesses a network at the physical layer of the OSI reference model. CSMA/CD is considered an access method used in Ethernet networks. *See also* Carrier Sense Multiple Access with Collision Detection.

Active Directory   The directory service used by modern Windows domains. Active Directory holds all user and group accounts as well as information about network resources, policies, and other objects.

Active Server Pages (ASP)   A server-side scripting language used by Web content developers that provides much of the interactive content on the Internet. ASP applications can be used to create dynamic Web content. ASP is supported by Internet Information Server (IIS) in Windows XP Professional. *See also* Internet Information Server.

Address Resolution Protocol (ARP)   A protocol used by computers to resolve IP addresses to physical (or MAC) network addresses, so that traffic can be forwarded appropriately on a network. A transmitting computer begins the process of transmitting IP address data by sending an ARP broadcast to all network devices on the local subnet, asking which maintains the specified IP address. If a computer replies, communications between the two can be established. If the ARP broadcast fails to determine the physical address of the target computer's network adapter, an error message is generated. *See also* MAC address.

Advanced Digest Authentication

Advanced Digest Authentication is a lightweight process that permits secure authentication of users across network security devices (such as firewalls). It does not require client-side software and does not send user credentials in a clear-text format over public networks. IIS supports Advanced Digest Authentication.

AppleTalk AppleTalk is a networking protocol developed by Apple Computer, Inc. for communication between Apple Macintosh computers.

authentication The process of verifying the identity of a user or computer to grant access to the local computer or network resources. Authentication is typically performed by checking a user name and password, often in conjunction with other security protocols, such as EAP and MS-CHAP.

Automatic Private IP Addressing

(APIPA) A service that automatically assigns IP addresses to network clients when no DHCP server is available. When a Windows 2000 or Windows XP computer starts up, it makes a DHCP query in an attempt to get a network address. If the DHCP server fails to answer, APIPA is used by the client to assign an IP address in the range of 169.254.0.1 to 169.254.255.254. This particular range of addresses was set aside for use by the Internet Assigned Numbers Authority (IANA) for use only on private, internal networks.

B

bandwidth The speed of transmission of a digital communications system as measured in bits per second.

bridge A hardware device (or piece of software) that connects two physically dissimilar networks, such as an Ethernet network and a Token Ring network, or an Ethernet network and a wireless network. Windows XP includes a feature known as Network Bridge that can function as a software bridge.

C

cable modem A device that connects a computer or local area network to a broadband network that shares the same cable used to deliver cable television. Cable modems are used primarily to deliver broadband Internet access. Some cable companies use a shared access method, where bandwidth is shared among users in certain areas or neighborhoods. In many new cable implementations, there is so much bandwidth available that performance is usually not a problem.

Carrier Sense Multiple Access with Collision Detection (CSMA/CD)

A contention-based network media access method. Using CSMA/CD, network hosts listen for traffic on the network and attempt to transmit data as soon as no traffic is heard. If multiple hosts transmit at once, a *collision* occurs, and all transmitting hosts retry their communications. *See also* token passing.

Challenge Handshake Authentication Protocol (CHAP)

An encrypted authentication mechanism that does not transmit the password in clear text across the initial connection. Instead, a handshake process allows the client to prove its identity. A revision of CHAP, MS-CHAP revises the authentication process to supply specific information needed to authenticate to Windows networks.

client A computer that connects to another remote computer (often called a server) to request resources such as files or remote printers. *See also* server.

cluster The smallest amount of disk space that can be allocated to hold a file (or a portion of a file) on a disk. Smaller clusters allow disk space to be more efficiently utilized, but increase the amount of disk activity (and therefore time) required to open large files.

compression The process of shrinking files and folders by removing redundant data. *Lossless* compression is fully reversible in that the original data is perfectly restored when the file is subsequently decompressed and accessed. NTFS supports lossless compression of files, folders, and drives in Windows XP.

cookie A small text file that Web servers place on a user's computer to later identify the individual on subsequent Web site visits; often used to customize the browser's return experience. Although cookies facilitate personalized settings for each Web site, they are also a potential source of personal information theft, unsolicited e-mail (or spam), and undesired tracking of Internet use. Internet Explorer 6 contains cookie management features that can help control cookie usage and protect privacy.

crossover cable A cable that directly connects two computers for networking purposes without an intervening hub or other network device. The crossover cable looks like a Category 5 cable, but the wires are reversed so that direct communication can take place.

D

denial of service attack (DoS) A network attack intended to make its target, either local or remote users, unable to function properly. DoS attacks normally work by crashing a computer or network service, or by overloading it so heavily that it becomes unresponsive.

dial-up connection Any connection that uses a device called a *modem* to communicate over a telephone line. Dial-up connections are often used to access the Internet as well as RAS servers on corporate networks. *See also* modem.

Digital Subscriber Line (DSL) A broadband Internet access method that runs over standard copper telephone wiring using different channels to transmit and receive data at much higher speeds than a traditional analog dial-up modem. DSL circuits must be supported by the user's phone company, and the user must live within a certain distance of the telephone company's switching office to use DSL. Most data services use asymmetric DSL (ADSL), which divides the phone line into three channels. One channel is used for voice, whereas the other two channels are used for data transmission and reception. Symmetric DSL (SDSL) is a variant that provides equal upload and download speeds.

direct cable connection (DCC) A direct computer-to-computer connection that uses a crossover cable, a parallel cable, or a null modem cable to connect two computers for networking purposes. When only two computers need to network, DCC is an inexpensive option. DCC can also be used when two computers need to temporarily network with each other.

DNS server A DNS server resolves Domain Name System requests sent by remote clients. DNS servers maintain databases of local host-name-to-IP address mappings and can also communicate with remote DNS servers to resolve remote addresses. *See also* Domain Name System.

domain controller A special server computer in a Windows domain that authenticates users on the network and provides security and other network resources. Microsoft Windows domain controllers run server versions of the Windows operating system, such as Windows NT, Windows 2000, and later releases.

Domain Name System (DNS) A hierarchical, distributed database that maps host names to IP addresses. These DNS mappings enable the user to find a computer by supplying the destination's user-friendly domain

619

name (such as www.microsoft.com or detroit.support.tailspintoys.com) and letting a DNS server resolve (*look up*) the fully qualified domain name (FQDN) into its associated IP address (such as 192.168.3.42), which is the address format actually used to route traffic over TCP/IP networks. TCP/IP networks include Windows networks as well as the Internet.

domain   A Microsoft network that uses one or more Windows servers designed to manage the network and provide network services for Windows clients. A domain contains one or more domain controllers that hold the user account database as well as other information about network services. Additional servers can be used to provide other administrative services for the domain or to serve files to users on the network.

Dynamic Host Configuration Protocol (DHCP)   A protocol used to automatically configure client IP address information for computers when they join a network. DHCP specifies the manner in which the DHCP client and server negotiate an address for the client's use. The process of assigning addresses involves a DHCP server and a DHCP client. The DHCP server holds information about the address range in use, the remaining addresses available, the network gateway, the DNS server addresses, the WINS server addresses, and other administratively configurable options. A particularly important function of the DHCP server is to administer the lease period. The lease period is the amount of time that any DHCP client is allowed to keep its address without checking in with the server. At the end of the lease, the client must query the server to see if the address is still valid.

E

Encrypting File System (EFS)   A feature of NTFS that encrypts files so that hackers and even system administrators cannot view them.

It can be enabled for single files or entire folders (and subfolders). EFS also includes features to decrypt files in case an original user's encryption keys are lost. *See also* encryption.

encryption   The process of scrambling data in a complex and reversible way to provide security to data residing on a computer or traversing a network. A key is required to decrypt and read the data. *See also* Encrypting File System.

Ethernet   A network protocol that specifies the interface design (how the cable jacks and adapter receptacles should be built) and signaling process for LAN communications. Ethernet uses a signaling scheme known as CSMA/CD and operates at a capacity of 10 Mbps or greater. *See also* Carrier Sense Multiple Access with Collision Detection.

Extensible Authentication Protocol (EAP)   An authentication method that provides security extensions so that administrators can employ alternative security technologies, such as smart cards or biometric devices, for users logging on to the network.

F

FAT32 file system   The most recent version of Microsoft's FAT file system. FAT32 can be used as an optional file system for Windows XP and is also accessible by many other operating systems including Windows 95 OSR2, Windows 98, and Windows Millennium Edition (Me). FAT32 lacks many of the advanced features offered by NTFS. *See also* file allocation table; NTFS file system.

Fiber Distributed Data Interface (FDDI)   A fiber-optic LAN/WAN networking technology that is capable of 100 Mbps transfer. FDDI works much like a Token Ring network, but two rings are used, providing redundancy should the primary ring fail.

Glossary

file allocation table (FAT)   A file system developed by Microsoft for its MS-DOS operating system and later used by Windows. FAT file systems rely on an allocation table that specifies where clusters containing files are located. *See also* FAT32 file system; NTFS file system.

File Transfer Protocol (FTP)   A protocol used to move files from one computer to another. In addition to moving files from one place to another, FTP can be used to perform basic file management tasks such as creating directories, deleting files and directories, and renaming the contents of directories.

firewall   A solution provided by software or a hardware device that protects a LAN or WAN from attacks that originate from hosts outside the protected network. Firewalls can employ a number of methods to protect an internal network, including table access, port filtering, and network address translation (NAT). Windows XP includes a software firewall called Internet Connection Firewall (ICF). *See also* Internet Connection Firewall; network address translation.

Fortezza   A security standard outlined by the United States government to ensure that software systems meet the requirements of the Defense Message System architecture. This architectural specification encompasses cryptography, confidentiality, data integrity, authentication, and access control requirements. Fortezza is supported by Internet Information Server in Windows XP Professional.

G

gateway   The device or computer that maintains a network's connection to other networks or to the Internet. Without a default gateway, TCP/IP traffic cannot be routed to other networks.

Group Policy   A management tool that enables network administrators to control computer configurations as well as user accounts and applications. With Group Policy, network administrators can control desktop settings, Internet Explorer settings, applications, security settings, and many other settings on desktop computers in a Windows domain environment. Local Group Policy can be implemented on stand-alone computers or those in a workgroup setting; however, in a domain environment, it can be overridden by policies specified at the OU or domain level.

H

HomePNA   A networking technology that uses a home or small office's existing telephone lines as the network infrastructure. HomePNA adapters use RJ-11 phone jacks and plug directly into the existing telephone cabling. The HomePNA network is capable of 10 Mbps transfer and does not interfere with standard voice conversations.

hub   A device that connects networked computers to one shared network segment. All devices connected to the hub share the same bandwidth. By definition, hubs contain no intelligence and simply connect multiple computers to a network electrically. *See also* switch; router.

Hypertext Transfer Protocol (HTTP)   The protocol used to transfer Web pages from one location to another. HTTP specifies the way that a client and server interact when transferring content such as Hypertext Markup Language (HTML) code for the purpose of displaying a Web page in a user's browser software.

I

Identities   A feature in Microsoft Outlook Express 6 in which multiple identities can be created so that different users can have different mail folders. By specifying a different identity, each user can access their personal mail. However, in Windows XP, if different user accounts are created for each user, identities are not necessary because each user has his or her own Outlook Express mail folder. User accounts also provide greater privacy than using multiple identities in Outlook Express.

IEEE 802.11b   At the time of this writing, the most common wireless network standard. 802.11b networks operate with a maximum speed of 11 Mbps using radio waves.

IEEE 802.1x   A standard for providing port-based authentication for wired and wireless Ethernet networks.

infrared   A method of performing wireless network communications using infrared light. Infrared networks typically adhere to the Infrared Data Association (IrDA) standards.

Institute of Electrical and Electronics Engineers (IEEE)   An organization of engineering professionals who develop standards for hardware and software. *See also* IEEE 802.11b; IEEE 802.1x.

Integrated Services Digital Network (ISDN)   An older network dial-up technology that uses existing phone lines (without the distance limitations of DSL) to provide digital speeds of typically 64 Kbps up to 128 Kbps. ISDN is not as popular today because consumers are favoring faster, cheaper, and always-on connections such as DSL and cable.

Internet Connection Firewall (ICF)   A software firewall solution included in Windows XP. ICF is designed to protect Windows XP (as well as any other computer sharing the same Internet connection) from unwanted outside network access or attacks.

Internet Connection Sharing (ICS)   A feature provided in Windows XP that allows one computer to share its connection to the Internet with other computers on the local network. *See also* network address translation.

Internet Control Message Protocol (ICMP)   A diagnostic and maintenance protocol used on TCP/IP networks. Applications using ICMP include Ping, Tracert, and PathPing.

Internet Information Server (IIS)   A full-featured software suite that enables the creation and hosting of Web, FTP, and SMTP services. The version included in Windows XP Professional allows up to 10 concurrent connections and is designed for developing Web sites or hosting small intranet sites.

Internet Protocol (IP)   A routable networking protocol for addressing and routing network traffic; part of the TCP/IP suite of Internet networking protocols.

Internet Protocol Security (IPSec)   A standard for securing TCP/IP communications. IPSec includes facilities for authentication, key exchange, and traffic encryption. *See also* Layer Two Tunneling Protocol; virtual private network; Kerberos authentication.

Internet service provider (ISP)   A company that provides Internet access to users for a fee.

Internet   The world's largest public network, containing millions of hosts and Web sites.

Internetwork Packet Exchange (IPX)   A routable protocol used by Novell for its NetWare operating system; an optional protocol that can be installed in Windows XP.

K

Kerberos authentication   An open-standard authentication mechanism used to securely authenticate users, typically over a public medium such as the Internet. Kerberos allows computers as well as users to be uniquely identified without transmitting identification data in clear text (which could be intercepted). *See also* Internet Protocol Security.

L

latency   The time required for data to travel from one point to another on a network.

Layer Two Tunneling Protocol (L2TP)   A standard for establishing virtual private network (VPN) communications across the Internet. *See also* Internet Protocol Security.

local area network (LAN)   A network situated in one geographical location, often in one building. A LAN can be a workgroup consisting of only a few computers, or it can be a large domain consisting of thousands of computers. *See also* wide area network.

M

Media Access Control (MAC) address   An addressing scheme that uniquely identifies individual physical network adapters on a network whether those adapters are connected to a computer or a network management device.

metabase   A repository of configuration information for IIS as well as any sites being served from a particular IIS installation.

N

NetBIOS Extended User Interface (NetBEUI)   A network protocol created by IBM and supported in Windows XP for routing network traffic. It has been largely supplanted in Windows XP by TCP/IP.

NetBIOS   The default application programming interface used for networking in earlier versions of Windows. Originally combined with NetBEUI (which is still supported), it can be paired with other networking protocols such as IP and IPX. NetBIOS uses 15-character names to identify individual computers.

network adapter   A device that enables a computer to be connected to a network; sometimes referred to as a network interface card (NIC).

network address translation (NAT)   A process of converting IP addresses; most often used to allow one public IP address to be shared by multiple systems, each of which has only a private IP address. NAT features are often included for address management and security purposes in residential gateway devices.

Network File System (NFS)   A file system designed to allow diskless workstations to mount file systems from other computers. These mounted file systems appear to be local to the user and all of the applications running on the workstation. NFS uses a collection of remote procedure calls (RPCs) operating over UDP and TCP to affect connectivity. NFS is widely used as the protocol for sharing and connecting to files and folders on UNIX-based networks.

network share   A resource, such as a directory or a printer, provided by a Windows computer for access by other network users.

network   A collection of computers organized to share resources and data without manually transferring them via removable media.

NIC   *See* network adapter.

NTFS file system   The file system of choice for Windows XP computers. NTFS provides file-level security as well as additional features, such as compression and encryption. *See also* FAT32 file system; compression; Encrypting File System.

null modem cable   A cable used to connect two computers using their serial ports. The computers then communicate over the cable directly rather than through a network hub. The null modem cable provides a good temporary network solution, but it is too slow for permanent networking needs and is limited to connecting only two computers.

O

Offline Files   A Windows XP Professional feature that provides local access to remote files when the local computer is disconnected from the network. This situation might occur during an outage or when a portable computer is removed from the network for mobile use. The user can continue to work with the cached copies of the offline files. Windows XP synchronizes the local and network copies when the computer is reconnected to the network.

organizational unit (OU)   An object used in Active Directory domains for management and organizational purposes. An OU can be delegated to different administrators who can then manage its contents. OUs can contain network resources such as users, groups, printers, shared folders, and other data.

P

Password Authentication Protocol (PAP)   A clear-text authentication scheme in which a server asks for a user name and password from a client computer that is attempting to log on. PAP submits the data in clear-text format, which makes this type of authentication insecure.

performance counter   Measures the activity of a certain portion of a performance object when using the Performance tool in Windows XP. The Performance administrative tool is useful for monitoring and troubleshooting network performance on a computer-by-computer basis.

performance object   A grouping of related computer activities in the Windows XP Performance tool from which specific performance counters can be selected to monitor and troubleshoot Windows networks.

Point-to-Point Protocol (PPP)   A remote access protocol that provides features such as authentication, encryption, and protocol encapsulation that allow remote users to connect to a network via dial-up or other methods. PPP is the basis for the PPTP and L2TP protocols. *See also* Layer Two Tunneling Protocol.

Point-to-Point Protocol over Ethernet (PPPoE)   A type of broadband Internet connection that is not always connected, but instead requires a user name and password to connect. To conserve IP addresses, many ISPs offering broadband services now use PPPoE so that the user is logged out when the connection is not in use.

Point-to-Point Tunneling Protocol (PPTP)   A Microsoft protocol for establishing virtual private network (VPN) connections over networks such as the Internet. *See also* virtual private network.

Powerline networking   A networking technology that uses a home or small office's electrical lines for networking purposes. Powerline adapters plug directly into a wall receptacle, and the building's existing electrical cabling is used for networking.

private folder   In Windows XP, a private folder prevents all users of the particular computer, including any computer administrators, from viewing the contents of the folder. The private folder is an additional Windows XP method for securing information locally when Simple File Sharing is in use.

protocol   A standard for network communication. A protocol defines the ways in which network data is transmitted, routed, and processed.

R

remote access   The dial-up process of connecting to a remote server and being authenticated by that server so access to a remote network is possible. Windows 2000 networks use remote access servers so that dial-in clients can access the network.

Remote Assistance   A new feature in Windows XP that allows another networked computer (local or Internet) to use Terminal Services to see the desktop of a computer user who needs assistance (known as a *novice*). The novice sends an invitation for help to a user designated as the *expert*. The expert can connect to the novice's computer, see the novice's desktop, and even take control of the computer to fix the problem, if the novice grants permission.

Remote Desktop   A new Terminal Services feature of Windows XP Professional. Using Remote Desktop, a user can access an enabled remote computer and control the remote computer through a terminal window as if logged on locally.

residential gateway   A device used on home or small office networks that manages traffic between the Internet and the LAN. Many residential gateways include additional features and functions, such as DHCP leasing of IP addresses and firewall functions including NAT.

RJ-11   The connector type used to connect telephones to phone jacks. Some home networking options, such as HomePNA, use RJ-11 connectors to connect computers to a home's existing telephone wiring and use that wiring to create a local area network without disrupting telephone usage.

RJ-45   The connector type used to connect twisted-pair Ethernet cabling to Ethernet jacks.

router   A device that directs traffic between networks. A router examines the destination address for data and determines which of its remote network ports is best suited to receive that data. *See also* hub; switch.

S

satellite Internet   An Internet access system that includes a special modem, satellite equipment, and a satellite dish to provide broadband Internet access. Upload speeds are significantly slower than other broadband technologies, but satellite Internet is usually available where no other broadband solutions exist. The only requirement is that the dish have a clear line-of-sight to the area of the sky in which the satellite is located.

Secure Sockets Layer (SSL)   An encryption algorithm used to secure network traffic; commonly used by secure Web servers.

Server Message Block (SMB)   A file-sharing protocol that enables a network computer to access files located on other network computers. Windows XP supports the SMB protocol.

server   A network computer that performs an administrative function for the network. Some servers are responsible for authenticating the credentials of users who attempt to log on to the network, while others might hold applications and data and *serve* them to authenticated network users on demand.

Simple File Sharing   A new feature included in Windows XP that offers an easy way to configure the sharing of certain resources over the local area network so that other users can either read or have full access to shared resources. Simple File Sharing is enabled by default, but in Windows XP Professional, it can be disabled in favor of using more sophisticated NTFS permissions. It cannot be disabled in Windows XP Home Edition.

Glossary

Simple Mail Transfer Protocol (SMTP)   The current protocol standard for host-to-host mail transport. SMTP specifies how communication works between a mail server and its end users. Its main function is to facilitate the delivery of e-mail from one server to another.

Simple Network Management Protocol (SNMP)   A protocol that was developed to provide a standard method of assessing information about the health of a network device as well as remotely configuring the device.

switch   A device that connects multiple networked devices together, providing each device connected to the switch with full dedicated connections to the other connected devices. *See also* hub; router.

T

Telnet   An insecure protocol designed to provide remote access to a computer by performing terminal emulation, thus allowing a user to communicate with a computer as though he or she were typing directly at a local console. Telnet is a text-only protocol and is used primarily by UNIX-based systems. Telnet sends all data, including user names and passwords, in clear text; its use should be avoided for security reasons.

token passing   A technique for controlling network access. With token passing, only one computer at a time possesses the *token*, which gives it the right to transmit data on the network. Once transmission has successfully occurred, the token is passed to the next computer. The token always moves around the network sequentially, ensuring that all computers have an opportunity to transmit. *See also* Carrier Sense Multiple Access with Collision Detection.

Token Ring   A type of network that uses token passing techniques to control network access. *See also* token passing.

topology   Term used in networking to describe the physical placement of computers, cables, hubs, routers, and so forth.

Transmission Control Protocol (TCP)   A connection-oriented networking protocol; part of the TCP/IP suite of network protocols.

Transmission Control Protocol/Internet Protocol (TCP/IP)   A suite of protocols for communicating across large routed networks like the Internet; originally developed by the United States Defense Advanced Research Projects Agency (DARPA).

U

User Datagram Protocol (UDP)   A sister protocol to TCP. Whereas TCP was developed to provide connection-oriented service and a means of error detection and compensation, UDP was designed for maximum throughput. UDP depends on the physical component of the network to be reliable or for other protocols to compensate for any data loss. As a result of this simplicity, UDP has very little communications overhead and is particularly useful when it is more important for data to arrive quickly than reliably, such as in delivering streaming media.

V

virtual private network (VPN)   A network that encapsulates data securely and transmits it over a public network, thus providing access to a secured remote private network without exposing important data to interception. *See also* Point-to-Point Tunneling Protocol; Layer Two Tunneling Protocol; Internet Protocol Security.

W

wide area network (WAN)   A network that is dispersed over several geographic locations, often worldwide in scope.

Wi-Fi   Popular name for wireless network technologies using radio waves for communication. *See also* IEEE 802.1b.

Windows Internet Naming Service (WINS)   A protocol developed to provide a standard for resolving NetBIOS names to their associated IP addresses.

Windows Messenger   The instant messaging program included with Windows XP. Windows Messenger can be used to conduct instant messaging, voice messaging, and even video sessions with Whiteboard collaboration or application sharing.

Wired Equivalent Privacy (WEP) A security standard that uses an encryption key as a means for securing wireless network traffic.

wireless access point   A wireless networking device used to create and manage wireless networks in infrastructure mode and to bridge wireless and wired networks.

wireless local area network (WLAN)   A local area network built using wireless networking technologies.

wireless metropolitan area networks (WMAN)   A wireless network that enables communication between different locations within a single metropolitan area.

wireless personal area networks (WPAN)   A network that resides in one small (personal) space, such as a single room. WPANs are used for networking devices in individual rooms or small homes as well as connecting individual electronic components (such as digital cameras and computers) for data transfer purposes.

wireless wide area network (WWAN)   Wide area networks that are connected by wireless means. Global System for Mobile Communications (GSM), Cellular Digital Packet Data (CDPD), and Code Division Multiple Access (CDMA) are examples of common wireless technologies that can be used by WWANs.

workgroup   A small collection of computers that are networked together to share resources. Workgroups generally reside in homes and small offices and generally contain fewer than 20 computers. Each computer is administered individually, and there is no centralized security or management between the computers. However, workgroups are highly effective ways to share resources. One example of such sharing involves using Internet Connection Sharing (ICS) to share a single connection to the Internet.

Index to Troubleshooting Topics

Index

About the Authors

Curt Simmons is a popular technology author who has written or coauthored more than 20 books about the Windows operating system, Microsoft networking technologies, and the Internet. Curt has a master's degree in education and is a Microsoft Certified Systems Engineer (MCSE) and Microsoft Certified Trainer (MCT).

James Causey is a senior software engineer and the author of numerous books on Windows, TCP/IP, and advanced networking topics. He holds MCSE and Microsoft Certified Professional+Internet (MCP+I) certifications and has experience with everything from front-line technical support to software development.

The manuscript for this book was prepared and galleyed using Microsoft Word 2002. Pages were composed by Microsoft Press using Adobe PageMaker 6.52 for Windows, with text in Minion and display type in Syntax. Composed pages were delivered to the printer as electronic prepress files.

coverdesigner
GIRVIN/Strategic Branding & Design

coverillustrator
Todd Daman

interiorgraphicdesigner
James D. Kramer

productionservices
Publishing.com

technicaleditor
Curtis Philips

copyeditor
Anne Marie Walker

interiorartist
JordanaGlenn

compositors
Lisa Bellomo and Jordana Glenn

proofreader
Andrea Fox

indexer
Rebecca Plunkett

Work smarter—
conquer your software from the inside out!

Hey, you know your way around a desktop. Now dig into Office XP applications and the Windows XP operating system and *really* put your PC to work! These supremely organized software reference titles pack hundreds of timesaving solutions, troubleshooting tips and tricks, and handy workarounds in a concise, fast-answer format. They're all muscle and no fluff. All this comprehensive information goes deep into the nooks and crannies of each Office application and Windows XP feature. INSIDE OUT titles also include a CD-ROM full of handy tools and utilities, sample files, an eBook links to related sites, and other help. Discover the best and fastest ways to perform everyday tasks, and challenge yourself to new levels of software mastery!

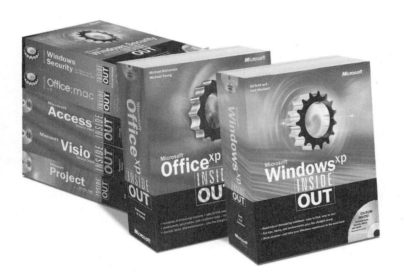

MICROSOFT® WINDOWS® XP INSIDE OUT
ISBN 0-7356-1382-6

MICROSOFT WINDOWS SECURITY INSIDE OUT FOR WINDOWS XP AND WINDOWS 2000
ISBN 0-7356-1632-9

MICROSOFT OFFICE XP INSIDE OUT
ISBN 0-7356-1277-3

MICROSOFT OFFICE V. X FOR MAC INSIDE OUT
ISBN 0-7356-1628-0

MICROSOFT WORD VERSION 2002 INSIDE OUT
ISBN 0-7356-1278-1

MICROSOFT EXCEL VERSION 2002 INSIDE OUT
ISBN 0-7356-1281-1

MICROSOFT OUTLOOK® VERSION 2002 INSIDE OUT
ISBN 0-7356-1282-X

MICROSOFT ACCESS VERSION 2002 INSIDE OUT
ISBN 0-7356-1283-8

MICROSOFT FRONTPAGE® VERSION 2002 INSIDE OUT
ISBN 0-7356-1284-6

MICROSOFT VISIO® VERSION 2002 INSIDE OUT
ISBN 0-7356-1285-4

MICROSOFT PROJECT VERSION 2002 INSIDE OUT
ISBN 0-7356-1124-6

Microsoft Press® products are available worldwide wherever quality computer books are sold. For more information, contact your book or computer retailer, software reseller, or local Microsoft® Sales Office, or visit our Web site at microsoft.com/mspress. To locate your nearest source for Microsoft Press products, or to order directly, call 1-800-MSPRESS in the United States (in Canada, call 1-800-268-2222).

Prices and availability dates are subject to change.

Microsoft
microsoft.com/mspress

Comprehensive information and tools—
straight from the
Windows 2000 Server team!

Deploy, manage, and optimize Microsoft's next-generation operating system with expertise from those who know the technology best—the Microsoft Windows 2000 Server development team. This RESOURCE KIT gives you seven comprehensive guides—thousands of pages packed full of technical details—plus hundreds of tools and utilities on CD. It's the complete kit you need to help maximize system performance and reduce ownership and support costs. Get seven volumes of authoritative Windows 2000 Server drill down, straight from the source!

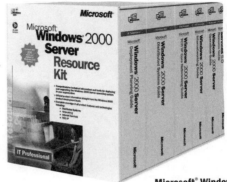

Microsoft® Windows® 2000 Server Resource Kit
ISBN: 1-57231-805-8

Also available in separate volumes!

These powerhouse guides—available separately and distilled from the MICROSOFT WINDOWS 2000 SERVER RESOURCE KIT—make it easy to find the exact technical information you need to optimize system performance and reduce costs.

Microsoft® Windows® 2000 Server Deployment Planning Guide
ISBN: 0-7356-1794-5

Microsoft Windows 2000 Server Distributed Systems Guide
ISBN: 0-7356-1795-3

Microsoft Windows 2000 Server Operations Guide
ISBN: 0-7356-1796-1

Microsoft Windows 2000 Server Internetworking Guide
ISBN: 0-7356-1797-X

Microsoft Windows 2000 Server TCP/IP Core Networking Guide
ISBN: 0-7356-1798-8

Microsoft Press® products are available worldwide wherever quality computer books are sold. For more information, contact your book or computer retailer, software reseller, or local Microsoft® Sales Office, or visit our Web site at microsoft.com/mspress. To locate your nearest source for Microsoft Press products, or to order directly, call 1-800-MSPRESS in the United States (in Canada, call 1-800-268-2222).

Prices and availability dates are subject to change.

Microsoft®
microsoft.com/mspress

Target your problem and
fix it yourself—
fast!

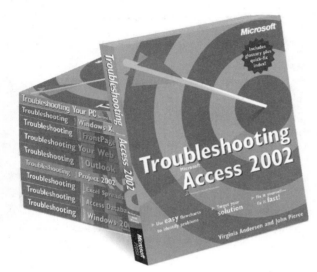

When you're stuck with a computer problem, you need answers right now. TROUBLESHOOTING books can help. They'll guide you to the source of the problem and show you how to solve it right away. Get ready solutions with clear, step-by-step instructions. Go to quick-access charts with *Top 20 Problems* and *Prevention Tips*. Find even more solutions with *Quick Fixes* and handy *Tips.* Walk through the remedy with plenty of screen shots. Find what you need with the extensive, easy-reference index. Get the answers you need to get back to business fast with TROUBLESHOOTING books.

Troubleshooting Microsoft® Office XP
ISBN 0-7356-1491-1

Troubleshooting Microsoft Access Databases
(Covers Access 97 and Access 2000)
ISBN 0-7356-1160-2

Troubleshooting Microsoft Access 2002
ISBN 0-7356-1488-1

Troubleshooting Microsoft Excel Spreadsheets
(Covers Excel 97 and Excel 2000)
ISBN 0-7356-1161-0

Troubleshooting Microsoft Excel 2002
ISBN 0-7356-1493-8

Troubleshooting Microsoft Outlook®
(Covers Microsoft Outlook 2000 and Outlook Express)
ISBN 0-7356-1162-9

Troubleshooting Microsoft Outlook 2002
(Covers Microsoft Outlook 2002 and Outlook Express)
ISBN 0-7356-1487-3

Troubleshooting Your Web Page
(Covers Microsoft FrontPage® 2000)
ISBN 0-7356-1164-5

Troubleshooting Microsoft FrontPage® 2002
ISBN 0-7356-1489-X

Troubleshooting Microsoft Project 2002
ISBN 0-7356-1503-9

Troubleshooting Microsoft Windows®
(Covers Windows Me, Windows 98, and Windows 95)
ISBN 0-7356-1166-1

Troubleshooting Microsoft Windows 2000 Professional
ISBN 0-7356-1165-3

Troubleshooting Microsoft Windows XP
ISBN 0-7356-1492-X

Troubleshooting Your PC, Second Edition
ISBN 0-7356-1490-3

Microsoft Press® products are available worldwide wherever quality computer books are sold. For more information, contact your book or computer retailer, software reseller, or local Microsoft Sales Office, or visit our Web site at microsoft.com/mspress. To locate your nearest source for Microsoft Press products, or to order directly, call 1-800-MSPRESS in the U.S. (in Canada, call 1-800-268-2222).

Prices and availability dates are subject to change.

microsoft.com/mspress

Self-paced
training that works
as hard as you do!

Information-packed STEP BY STEP courses are the most effective way to teach yourself how to complete tasks with the Microsoft Windows operating system and Microsoft Office applications. Numbered steps and scenario-based lessons with practice files on CD-ROM make it easy to find your way while learning tasks and procedures. Work through every lesson or choose your own starting point—with STEP BY STEP'S modular design and straightforward writing style, *you* drive the instruction. And the books are constructed with lay-flat binding so you can follow the text with both hands at the keyboard. Select STEP BY STEP titles also prepare you for the Microsoft Office User Specialist (MOUS) credential. It's an excellent way for you or your organization to take a giant step toward workplace productivity.

- **Home Networking with Microsoft® Windows® XP Step by Step**
  ISBN 0-7356-1435-0

- **Microsoft Windows XP Step by Step**
  ISBN 0-7356-1383-4

- **Microsoft Office XP Step by Step**
  ISBN 0-7356-1294-3

- **Microsoft Word Version 2002 Step by Step**
  ISBN 0-7356-1295-1

- **Microsoft Project Version 2002 Step by Step**
  ISBN 0-7356-1301-X

- **Microsoft Excel Version 2002 Step by Step**
  ISBN 0-7356-1296-X

- **Microsoft PowerPoint® Version 2002 Step by Step**
  ISBN 0-7356-1297-8

- **Microsoft Outlook® Version 2002 Step by Step**
  ISBN 0-7356-1298-6

- **Microsoft FrontPage® Version 2002 Step by Step**
  ISBN 0-7356-1300-1

- **Microsoft Access Version 2002 Step by Step**
  ISBN 0-7356-1299-4

- **Microsoft Visio® Version 2002 Step by Step**
  ISBN 0-7356-1302-8

Microsoft Press also has STEP BY STEP titles to help you use earlier versions of Microsoft software.

Microsoft Press® products are available worldwide wherever quality computer books are sold. For more information, contact your book or computer retailer, software reseller, or local Microsoft Sales Office, or visit our Web site at microsoft.com/mspress. To locate your nearest source for Microsoft Press products, or to order directly, call 1-800-MSPRESS in the United States. (in Canada, call 1-800-268-2222).

Prices and availability dates are subject to change.

microsoft.com/mspress

Get a **Free**
e-mail newsletter, updates,
special offers, links to related books,
and more when you

register on line!

Register your Microsoft Press® title on our Web site and you'll get a FREE subscription to our e-mail newsletter, *Microsoft Press Book Connections.* You'll find out about newly released and upcoming books and learning tools, online events, software downloads, special offers and coupons for Microsoft Press customers, and information about major Microsoft® product releases. You can also read useful additional information about all the titles we publish, such as detailed book descriptions, tables of contents and indexes, sample chapters, links to related books and book series, author biographies, and reviews by other customers.

Registration is easy. Just visit this Web page and fill in your information:

http://www.microsoft.com/mspress/register

Microsoft®

- -

Proof of Purchase

Use this page as proof of purchase if participating in a promotion or rebate offer on this title. Proof of purchase must be used in conjunction with other proof(s) of payment such as your dated sales receipt—see offer details.

Microsoft® Windows® XP Networking Inside Out
0-7356-1652-3

CUSTOMER NAME

Microsoft Press, PO Box 97017, Redmond, WA 98073-9830